Intensive Interventions with High-Risk Youths

Intensive Interventions with High-Risk Youths: Promising Approaches in Juvenile Probation and Parole

edited by
Troy L. Armstrong

CRIMINAL JUSTICE PRESS
a division of Willow Tree Press, Inc.
Monsey, New York
1991

Library of Congress Cataloging-in-Publication Data

Intensive interventions with high-risk youths: promising approaches in juvenile probation and parole/edited by Troy L. Armstrong.

p. cm.

ISBN 0-9606960-7-5 : $25.00

1. Social work with juvenile delinquents. 2. Social work with juvenile delinquents—United States. 3. Juvenile probation—United States. 4. Juvenile parole—United States. I. Armstrong, Troy.

HV9069.I66 1990

364-3'6'0973—dc20 90-24254

CIP

Table of Contents

ABOUT THE CONTRIBUTORS

Troy L. Armstrong is Associate Professor of Criminal Justice, California State University, Sacramento, California.

David M. Altschuler is Research Scientist, Institute for Policy Studies, Johns Hopkins University, Baltimore, Maryland.

Naya Arbiter is Director of Programs, Amity, Inc., Tucson, Arizona.

S. Christopher Baird is Senior Vice President, National Council on Crime and Delinquency, Madison, Wisconsin.

William H. Barton is Senior Research Associate, Center for the Study of Youth Policy, University of Michigan, Ann Arbor, Michigan.

Gordon Bazemore is Senior Research Associate, Pacific Institute for Research and Evaluation, Walnut Creek, California.

Jeffrey A. Butts is a Doctoral Candidate and Research Assistant, University of Michigan, Ann Arbor, Michigan.

Todd R. Clear is Professor, School of Criminal Justice, Rutgers University, Newark, New Jersey.

Jeffrey A. Fagan is Associate Professor, School of Criminal Justice, Rutgers University, Newark, New Jersey.

Norma Feinberg is Associate Professor, Sociology Department, Duquesne University, Pittsburgh, Pennsylvania.

Peggy Glider is Director, Research and Evaluation, Amity, Inc., Tucson, Arizona.

Donna M. Hamparian is Senior Research Associate, Federation for Community Planning, Cleveland, Ohio.

Andrew R. Klein is Chief Probation Officer, Quincy Court, Quincy, Massachusetts.

Wesley A. Krause is Supervising Probation Officer, Staff Development, San Bernardino County Probation Department, San Bernardino, California.

Rod Mullen is Executive Director, Amity, Inc., Tucson, Arizona.

Ted B. Palmer is Research Manager, California Youth Authority, Sacramento, California.

Craig Reinarman is Assistant Professor of Sociology, University of California, Santa Cruz, California.

Norman Skonovd is Research Manager, Institutions and Camps Research, California Youth Authority, Sacramento, California.

J. Fred Springer is Associate Professor of Political Science and Public Policy Administration, University of Missouri, St. Louis, Missouri.

Joseph B. Vaughn is Associate Professor of Criminal Justice, Central Missouri State University, Warrensburg, Missouri.

Richard G. Wiebush is Senior Research Associate, National Council on Crime and Delinquency, Madison, Wisconsin.

For Judy,
Jessica and Zachary.

Introduction

by
Troy L. Armstrong

The history and main features of intensive intervention programs in juvenile community corrections are described. Current intensive intervention programs for high-risk youths are driven by the same concerns that have fostered intensive supervision in adult probation and parole: prison overcrowding, the public outcry for protection from dangerous offenders, demands for increased accountability in corrections, and the goal of reducing recidivism. However, unlike adult programs, which are predominantly surveillance/supervision-oriented, juvenile programs also emphasize intensive treatment/service provision. Notable in the current generation of intensive intervention projects have been Project New Pride, the Violent Juvenile Offender Research and Development initiative, the Skillman Aftercare Experiment, the Paint Creek Youth Center, and two pilot projects in Philadelphia Family Court. Salient current issues include: philosophy and goals; caseload size and frequency of contact; classification procedures and client targeting; and evaluation.

OVERVIEW

Community-based strategies for managing juvenile offenders, especially those classified as chronic and/or violent, have undergone significant changes in the U.S. over the past few years. Crime patterns, public fear and demands, legislative mandates, and professional innovation in the correctional field have forced a reevaluation of how probation and parole services can better intervene with delinquent youths. The dramatic increase during the 1960s and early 1970s in arrests of juveniles committing serious crimes against persons and property, public uneasiness and fear over media claims of a rising national epidemic of youth crime, the widespread perception of the failure of existing probation and parole methods, as well as the often repeated announcement of the death of rehabilitation, have all highlighted the need for major reform in correctional philosophy and practice.

Much of the recent shift in community corrections has focused upon that segment of the delinquent population commonly referred to as the high-risk, hard-core, dangerous, violent and serious juvenile offender. A striking divergence in intervention strategies characterized efforts during the 1980s to reduce the criminal behavior of this group. On the one hand, steps have been taken to lower the age of jurisdiction of juvenile courts, to facilitate the waiver of larger numbers of juveniles to adult criminal court, and to enact harsher determinate sentencing laws for repeat juvenile offenders. On the other hand, there has been considerable experimentation with programs and supervision strategies designed to maintain a subset of the serious juvenile offender population—defined in various ways in different jurisdictions—in the community either as an alternative to incarceration or after early release from secure correctional facilities. Ironically, this latter development—the community-based supervision of serious juvenile offenders—has been driven by the nationwide push to "get tough" with youth crime. The massive crowding of juvenile institutions that has recently resulted, in part, from high conviction rates and determinate sentencing statutes has forced the creation of safety valve mechanisms intended to guarantee acceptable levels of community protection.

In response to pressure to handle a more difficult population of juvenile offenders in the community and to the need for transforming probation and parole into a more highly accountable and tangible sanctioning system, a number of more intensive, highly structured programs have emerged. Generally, these efforts have stressed: (1) the use of various surveillance techniques, such as team supervision, saturation surveillance (i.e., monitoring for 24 hours per day, 7 days per week), and high-tech interventions (e.g., electronic monitoring, random drug testing); (2) objective schemes to determine risk levels; and (3) more specialized treatment and intensified service provision.

The appearance of these apparently novel programs does not, however, constitute a unique revolution in community corrections for several reasons. First, these programs are only part of a much larger intensive supervision movement currently occurring in American corrections and can, in fact, be shown to be largely derivative from developments in adult corrections. Second, the past quarter-century has witnessed a number of intermittent experiments to develop more intensified supervision for juvenile probationers and parolees. However, the current wave of intensive supervision programs for juvenile offenders can be readily distinguished from both current initiatives in the adult arena and prior experiments in the juvenile system.

INTENSIVE SUPERVISION FOR ADULT OFFENDERS

Most of the recent emphasis in the emerging intensive supervision movement has focused upon the specialized management of adult offenders in the community. The increasing reliance on a non-secure approach reflects a largely pragmatic response to certain escalating problems in managing felony offenders in adult corrections, as opposed to the influence of any theoretically driven impetus to test new or innovative ideas in crime control or rehabilitation of serious offenders. However, as is the case with juvenile intensive supervision, these recent developments have been preceded by a number of earlier experiments.

Earlier intensive supervision programs for adult offenders had, with rare exception, targeted probationers. Intensive aftercare or parole experiments have always been relatively rare in comparison to "front-end" interventions. According to Clear and Hardyman (1990), the earlier wave of adult intensive probation supervision (IPS) programs in the 1960s focused almost exclusively on determining the optimal number of clients amenable to supervision on individual caseloads. These experiments have been characterized as the "search for the magic number" (Carter and Wilkens, 1984). The widely-shared assumption at that time was that once the caseload size was reduced, the supervising officer would be freed to conduct case management activities and to provide required services in a more intensive, responsive and traditional manner (Latessa, 1987).

Assessment has revealed that reduced caseload responsibilities do not always translate into increased attention paid by the supervising officer to client problems and needs (Latessa, 1979; Latessa et al., 1979). In fact, Clear and Hardyman (1990) suggest that the three major lessons of these earlier experimental projects were:

1. Intensive supervision is difficult to achieve, i.e., intensity of supervision does not simply equate with smaller caseloads.
2. Close contact, when achieved, does not necessarily guarantee greater success in crime control.
3. Intensive supervision produces an "interaction effect," i.e., close monitoring helps some types of offenders but lessens others' chances of success.

In summarizing the effects of reduced caseload size on supervision performance, Latessa (1989) observes that IPS produced increased contacts and services, but the expected reduction in criminal behavior did not materialize.

In contrast to these initiatives in the 1960s, the current wave of adult IPS programs is driven by two primary factors, the prison crowding problem and the present emphasis on a surveillance-orientation image of community corrections (Byrne, 1990). Today's adult programs tend to be characterized by a heavy reliance on intrusive elements adopted for surveillance and social control, including stringent curfew hours, house arrest, electronic monitoring, team supervision, drug and/or alcohol testing and monitoring, and the assignment of restitution and community service orders. Philosophically, these procedures are clearly consistent with the principles of punishment and deterrence that continue to dominate the adult justice system. Of course, the litmus test of this strategy will be whether the enhanced surveillance techniques truly provide greater public safety.

Some observers have questioned the ability of these programs to deliver positive results across a wide array of identified promises. For example, Clear and Hardyman (1990) list five stated goals of the new intensive supervision movement—reduced prison crowding, increased public protection, rehabilitation of offenders, demonstrating the potential of community corrections, and cost saving—and note that if this multitude of goals are achievable under one program approach, intensive supervision would have to be considered the wonder child of the criminal justice system.

EARLIER INTENSIVE SUPERVISION PROJECTS FOR JUVENILE OFFENDERS

At roughly the same time that these specialized, community-based interventions with adult offenders were again being tried, similar experiments were beginning to appear in the early 1980s in the juvenile justice system (Armstrong, 1988; Krisberg et al., 1989; Steenson, 1987). While both adult and juvenile intensive supervision movements are premised on the imposition of higher levels of offender accountability and social control, are driven by very similar problems, and exhibit many common design characteristics, a very fundamental difference exists in their philosophical underpinnings and stated goals. While the adult model and its major variants operate almost exclusively as a punitive, social-control approach to community-based supervision, the juvenile model usually maintains a continuing adherence to treatment/rehabilitation as a fundamental part of intensive supervision. The resulting approach appears to combine elements of broadened social control, enhanced surveillance, and highly intrusive monitoring of behavior with more specialized and diversified treatment, as well as substantially increased levels of service provision. Thus, in spite of major inroads over the past 15 years by proponents of a get-tough philosophy, a very strong resistance persists within the field against totally renouncing the tenets of the traditional juvenile court movement—especially beliefs affirming the essential role of the rehabilitative ideal (Armstrong et al., 1990; Armstrong and Altschuler, 1982; Maloney et al., 1988).

As was true of experiments in the 1960s in the adult system, the primary focus of the earlier intensive programs for juvenile offenders was on whether decreased caseload size had a positive effect on performance levels (Banks et al., 1977; Carter and Wilkins, 1984; Neithercutt and Gottfredson, 1973). Perhaps the best documented set of experiments were the demonstration programs designed, operated and evaluated by the California Youth Authority (CYA) during the 1960s and early 1970s. These projects were exclusively concerned with the maintenance of aftercare populations in the community. The CYA's Parole Research Project (Johnson, 1962) began in Alameda County in the summer of 1959, creating 10 experimental caseloads of 36 parolees each. These were compared with 5 control caseloads of twice that size, using a random assignment research design. No significant differences in recidivism rates were found between standard and reduced caseloads.

Subsequently, a number of other experiments with reduced caseload sizes were conducted by CYA. Probably best known was the Community Treatment Project (CTP), which began operations in 1961 and continued through 1974 (Palmer, 1971, 1973, 1974a). The CTP matched experimental subjects on the basis of an interpersonal maturity scale and placed these juvenile parolees in the community under intensive supervision (i.e., 12 youths per caseload). In addition to closer monitoring, a wide array of special services and treatment strategies were made available to the experimental cases. Although the degree of success achieved in the project has been widely disputed, some findings were clearly promising. The experimental group showed a significantly lower arrest rate than the control group; on 24-month parole follow-up, the experimentals also performed significantly better on the measure of reduced recidivism. On the other hand, the control group demonstrated lower rates of recidivism after four years of follow-up (Palmer, 1974b).

Another CYA-sponsored experimental project, the Narcotic Control Program (NCP), was conducted from 1962 through 1967. The majority of participants were older adolescent, male parolees who were targeted for a variety of special program services including: drug testing (e.g., nalline testing, urinalysis, skin search for needle marks), caseload sizes ranging from 15 to 30 wards, intensive supervision, short-term reconfinement, and individual and group counseling. It was concluded, however, that NCP had not shown "any superior or unique effectiveness in reducing general recidivism, or specific drug-involved recidivism, among wards admitted to the program" (Roberts, 1970).

In 1966, CYA launched a three-year experimental project, the Los Angeles Community Delinquency Control Project (CDCP), targeting juvenile parolees for participation in an intensive rehabilitation program in lieu of the regular CYA parole program. The average caseload per CDCP agent was 25 wards in comparison to the average caseload of 72 wards for a regular parole agent. The principal intervention techniques were increased individual counseling, group counseling, family counseling, increased use of foster and contract group home placement, short-term custody for limit setting and protection, social and recreational activities, remedial academic instruction, and educational backup for the public school system. No statistically significant differences were found between the experimental and regular parole subjects on any of the identified parole performance measures—parole revocation, reason for revocation, time to revocation, and severity of revocation offense (Pond, 1970).

The group of program experiments just described is somewhat unusual or atypical in being directed exclusively at juvenile parolees, but some important insights can be gained from these examples about the nature and direction of the overall intensive supervision movement over the past three decades. First, much of what is currently being touted as new and innovative had already been considered and put into practice as much as 25 to 30 years ago. Second, all of these programs combined elements of social control and surveillance with various treatment strategies. None was devoted exclusively to the goal of risk management, a characteristic commonly shared by the current wave of programming. Third, experimental programs that focused primarily upon reduced caseload sizes ceased to be funded by the mid-1970s as interest in specialized treatment began to wane nationwide. Only over the past decade, as new problems threatened to overwhelm much of the juvenile justice system, has renewed interest been sparked in intensive supervision techniques for handling juvenile probation and parole populations.

CURRENT JUVENILE INTENSIVE SUPERVISION PROGRAMS

The recent reemergence of intensive supervision experiments for juvenile offenders was driven by a very similar set of problems and crises as catalyzed developments in the adult movement. Notable among those factors were mounting juvenile institutional overcrowding, the persistent public outcry for greater community protection, the demand for a tougher and more accountable type of community-based intervention (including both probation and parole), the inability to reduce recidivism rates among chronic serious juvenile offenders, and the staggering costs of secure, institutional confinement. Although juvenile training schools nationwide showed slight declines in total population between 1974 and 1979, largely as a result of the effects of the deinstitutionalization movement, these trends have been reversed since 1979 (Krisberg et al., 1986). Moreover, in fiscal year 1986, the 50 states spent a total of $1.46 billion to operate secure juvenile facilities, with annual per capital costs ranging from $23,000 in the western states to $45,300 in the northeastern states (Allen-Hagen, 1988). These costs are greatly escalated if crowding requires new construction since building new beds costs from $50,000 to $200,000 each.

An equally powerful argument for correctional reform has been the body of research findings that point to the continuing, disproportionate criminality of a small number of chronic, serious juvenile offenders who recidivate at extremely high rates when placed in the community. Longitudinal studies (Wolfgang et al., 1972; Farrington and West, 1977; Hamparian et al., 1978; Shannon, 1978; McCord, 1979) have shown that a small subset of delinquents are responsible for the vast majority of serious youth crime. Further, research on program effectiveness suggests that this group is highly resistant to conventional intervention strategies (Coates, 1984; Gadow and McKibbon, 1984; Agee, 1979; Bleich, 1978).

Collectively, these concerns have generated a powerful argument for rethinking much of what constitutes philosophy and practice for managing adjudicated delinquents. Part of this rethinking centers on the increased use of community-based options, but these options are structured to operate quite differently from existing forms of juvenile probation and parole. The current juvenile intensive supervision movement is part of this new response. It represents a direct reaction to widespread calls for substantially higher levels of accountability, responsibility, and control in managing juvenile offenders in the community. These recent experiments continue to place some emphasis on assigning juvenile offenders to smaller caseloads, but the motivation appears to be somewhat different than in the 1960s and early 1970s. This shift toward more of a get-tough stance is exemplified in the far more extensive usage of intensive surveillance and monitoring techniques. At the same time, however, concern does continue for the provision of treatment and services.

The basic approach to juvenile intensive supervision can be most accurately described as "intermediate intervention" as opposed to "intermediate punishment," a term used to describe intensive supervision in the adult system (McCarthy, 1987). With rare exceptions, juvenile programs are blends of enhanced supervision/surveillance and treatment/service provision. This basic characteristic was substantiated in a national survey conducted by Armstrong (1988) of juvenile court jurisdictions reporting intensive probation supervision programs. Not surprisingly, the vast majority (78%) of the responding probation agencies/departments stated that the primary goal of the program was to provide more intensive surveillance of clients than in standard probation. Yet, the overwhelming majority of responding jurisdictions (92%) also noted that the provision of services to these youths was essential. The best way to conceptualize the variation in goals and practice among these programs is to envision a continuum of intervention goals ranging from extremely high levels of surveillance (i.e., a pure enforcement model) to the goal of achieving long-term behavioral change in clients (i.e., a pure rehabilitation model). The survey revealed that no more than three or four of the 60 programs occupied either extreme of this continuum. Between the two poles stretched a number of program permutations representing hybrid versions of the two basic models, incorporating various mixes of surveillance and treatment techniques and components.

Another critical and widely shared program feature identified in the survey included a stated policy of trying to exclusively target high-risk juvenile probationers (defined in terms of offense history, severity of current criminal charge, and/or personal needs and problems) who required levels of supervision exceeding those offered by standard probation. Further, some form of objective classification/assessment procedure was usually employed to determine the precise level of risk and/or need. Romig and Lick (1988) state that the following are critical: specific goals and activities, objective selection criteria, well-structured components geared to high-risk youth, small caseload sizes, and a variety of consequences available for violations. Yet, in spite of efforts to bring clarity to this rapidly expanding movement, considerable conceptual and definitional confusion continues to persist over exactly what these programs look like, what they share in common, and what they are trying to accomplish.

Still another important dimension of the recent juvenile intensive supervision movement has been the effort to selectively include a number of different social control and treatment features within the broader framework of these programs, depending on the particular characteristics of the client population. Several chapters in this volume explore how and why such specialized approaches have been incorporated into the design and operation of intensive intervention programs. Bazemore argues that engaging serious juvenile offenders in employment training and work experience represents a far more proactive approach to normalizing behavior than traditional modes of supervision and treatment. Similarly, Klein provides a compelling case for the efficacy of restitution and community service as required features in intensive supervision programs. The chapter by Mullen et al. asserts that drug and alcohol treatment, especially as based upon a therapeutic community model, should be an integral part of intensive supervision programming for youths known to have significant substance abuse problems. And Vaughn shows how electronic monitoring is being used in programs for youths known to pose special problems in community supervision.

MAJOR PROGRAM INITIATIVES WITH JUVENILE INTENSIVE SUPERVISION

A number of research-based programs experimenting with various forms of intensive supervision for juvenile offenders have emerged during the past decade. The pace of these developments has escalated markedly since the mid-1980s. These efforts have addressed a wide range of issues in the design, implementation and evaluation of programs attempting to maintain serious juvenile offenders both on probation and parole in the community. Although these programs are far too numerous to discuss individually, it is important to provide a brief description of some, especially those that resulted from careful planning, have been well documented, and have been formally evaluated with experimental or quasi-experimental designs.

In this introductory overview, the review of both older and current juvenile intensive *probation* supervision programs will be addressed more briefly than intensive *aftercare* since the former are detailed in chapters by Barton and Butts, Fagan, Feinberg, Klein, and Wiebush and Hamparian.

The current, widespread movement toward intensive supervision for "high-risk" juvenile probationers has been appearing since the early to mid-1980s in a somewhat piecemeal fashion, and has not been marked by any centralized or national planning and development effort. In Armstrong's survey (1988) of juvenile intensive probation supervision, approximately 35% of juvenile court jurisdictions nationally were experimenting with some form of intensive supervision. Although programs were found to exhibit a wide diversity in design and goals, the one characteristic shared across all programs was the fact of increased level of face-to-face contacts with the probationer in contrast to the lower frequency of contact with youths on standard probation.

One program that merits special mention since it led to the only federally funded national replication of an intensive supervision approach for juvenile probation is Project New Pride. Designed as an alternative to institutionalization in state correctional facilities, the program, which is based in Denver and is a highly structured non-residential option for chronic delinquents, teaches vocational skills through coupling on-the-job training with classroom instruction (James and Granville, 1984). Differential opportunity theory is the most appropriate conceptual framework for understanding the design and goals of New Pride. The major components of the New Pride model are focused upon better equipping clients to compete in the legitimate opportunity structures of society. The strategy utilized in this program in preparing youths for employment is based upon a series of assessment procedures: 1) identifying the youth's vocational interests; 2) identifying the youth's strengths and liabilities in relation to his/her interests; and 3) helping the youth to develop realistic goals and identifying the steps necessary to achieve those goals. Once these procedures are completed, the following activities are initiated with clients: 1) remedying academic deficiencies; 2) providing intensive supervision and counseling; and 3) offering vocational training and job placement.

In Project New Pride considerable emphasis has always been placed on community protection, since youths participating in this program have, on the average, been arrested six or more times and have frequently been adjudicated delinquent more than once. As chronic offenders, they are perceived as a high-risk group in need of close supervision. New Pride's assertion that this population can be worked with safely and effectively in the community is supported by the fact that over 90% of its clients do not have any subsequent contact with the juvenile justice system, and more than 70% return to public schools on a regular basis (James and Granville, 1984). Further, the cost of maintaining a juvenile probationer in New Pride is only $4,500 per year in comparison to the cost of $28,000 per year for incarcerating a youth in a Colorado juvenile corrections facility.

These impressive statistics, combined with the continuing search for promising alternatives to incarceration, in 1979 resulted in replication and evaluation of New Pride in 10 cities nationwide. The Pacific Institute of Research and Evaluation (PIRE) conducted the national evaluation of the New Pride Replication Program (Gruenewald et al., 1985) between 1980 and 1984. The results of this evaluation are discussed in considerable detail in Palmer's chapter in this volume.

The current wave of programs in juvenile probation generally predate the emergence of most juvenile intensive parole experiments by several years. Commonly, the approaches being implemented in parole have borrowed heavily from ideas and strategies already being applied in juvenile probation, but undergo varying degrees of alteration as adaptation to specific circumstances and needs occur.

Notable among experiments with intensive parole or aftercare programming was the Violent Juvenile Offender Research and Development Program (VJO). Funded in 1980 by the U.S. Office of Juvenile Justice and Delinquency Prevention (OJJDP), the project was an ambitious and carefully designed attempt to develop community-based programs to normalize the behavior of an important subset of the serious juvenile offender population, namely, the chronically violent adolescent. The proposed model of intervention simultaneously emphasized community protection, accountability and rehabilitation, and represented the integration of control, strain and social learning theories (Fagan et al., 1984). In this integrated framework were identified four theoretical principles which underlay the model: social networking, provision for youth opportunities, social learning, and goal-oriented interventions. To translate these principles into structural components for service provision, emphasis was placed on continuous case management, diagnostic assessment, job training skills and placement, and individual and family counseling.

Five test sites were selected to participate in this initiative: Boston, Denver, Memphis, Newark and Phoenix. The experimental design featured a multi-phased program with at least four stages: diagnostic assessment, secure care, community-based residence and community living. The desired intensity of community supervision was achieved by maintaining caseloads of only six to eight youths per officer. Through the use of a "transition house" and intensive supervision upon return to the community, it was hoped that these youth would experience a smooth and gradual reentry process. Unfortunately, only three of the five program sites were operational for a sufficient length of time to generate the necessary outcome data with which to measure long-term effectiveness. A discussion of the findings from the various test sites can be found in Palmer's chapter in this volume.

Other recent aftercare efforts that warrant examination are the two program sites for the Skillman Intensive Aftercare Experiment, which involved experimental intensive aftercare programs for delinquents released from secure confinement to their homes in Detroit and Pittsburgh (Deschenes, 1989). The two sites were chosen to represent differing organizational and community contexts. Each program operates under the auspices of a private-sector, community-based agency, and is designed to manage the activities of approximately 50 youths for six months at the point of community transition. Both programs exhibit the following essential elements: (1) Highly motivated and energetic caseworker/trackers who have been properly trained to carry out their responsibilities. (2) Pre-release assessment and planning involving visits by the aftercare caseworker to the youth and his or her family. (3) Continuity of programming between residential and aftercare components. (4) High frequency of face-to-face contacts (daily) and low caseloads for aftercare workers. (5) Special efforts to mobilize supportive community services, particularly in the areas of education, employment and family counseling. (6) Specific efforts to reduce drug and alcohol abuse or dependency. (7) Recreational activities that develop prosocial skills.

The theoretical orientation of both programs is grounded in the concepts of social learning (Bandura, 1977; Bandura and Schunk, 1981) and relapse prevention (Marlatt and Gordon, 1985). The assumptions of this dual approach are that behavior is learned through processes of instruction, modeling, reinforcement and shaping, and that the avoidance of future negative behavior can be achieved through learning new behavior patterns.

The Detroit program has placed considerable emphasis on having the transitional workers make early contact in the correctional facility with those youths who will be participating in intensive aftercare. Supervision of caseloads that are restricted to 8 to 10 clients each is handled by a team comprised of a caseworker and a family social worker; the client's family is visited at least once per week. Face-to-face contact between team members and the juvenile parolee occurs at least twice per day for the six months of program participation. The Pittsburgh program, operated by VisionQuest, has a multistaged reentry process in which youths first go to a group home for one month following institutional release. This stage is followed by return to the parental home. Home placement is characterized by very intensive tracking and counseling. Aftercare workers meet with their clients at least three times per day for the first 60 days and twice a day for the duration of the program.

The evaluation design of both programs entails random assignment of clients to experimental and control groups, and, for purposes of analysis, the development of a number of baseline and outcome measures. At this point, the evaluation is incomplete and preliminary results have not been released.

Another intensive juvenile corrections program is the Paint Creek Youth

Center (PCYC), which is currently being evaluated by the Rand Corporation. Located in Bainbridge, OH, and operated by New Life Youth Services of Cincinnati, this program is one of several being assessed as part of the OJJDP-funded Private Sector Corrections Initiative (OJJDP, 1988). This initiative was designed to determine whether any of several well-known, private correctional programs for committed juvenile offenders were more effective in reducing recidivism than traditional training schools. PCYC is a 33-bed, staff-secure facility offering a 12-month residential program and employing a variety of treatment techniques, including Positive Peer Culture, Reality Therapy, daily group therapy sessions, and a problem-oriented record system for tracking misconduct. As a condition of the experimental evaluation design, it was required that at least 75 serious delinquents be targeted for participation and that they be selected from training school candidates by random assignment. Other design requirements were: a phased program involving a mix of settings, ranging from residential to supervised community reintegration; individualized treatment plans; continuous case management; and a low staff-to-client ratio.

The aftercare component of the Paint Creek Program has considerable relevance to the present discussion. Designed to closely resemble the intensive aftercare program currently operating in the juvenile probation department in Delaware County, OH (see the Wiebush and Hamparian chapter in this volume, and Altschuler and Armstrong, 1990, for a more detailed description of this aftercare model), the intensive aftercare component of PCYC is structured to have four sequenced levels of reintegrative activity, each with an increasing degree of individual responsibility and freedom of mobility for the client. Upon leaving the residential program at Paint Creek, youths are moved into various community placements: their parental homes, group homes, or independent-living settings. They are put on house arrest status for the first two weeks following community reentry, and are only allowed outside freedom-of-movement to attend school, to go to work, or to participate in specialized treatment. Supervision is very intensive, with caseloads restricted to six to eight youths per aftercare worker. Two face-to-face contacts must be scheduled each day between workers and these youths. Graduation can only occur after six months of participation in intensive aftercare; clients must either be working or attending school regularly to qualify for graduation. As is the case with the two Skillman programs, findings on the relative effectiveness of PCYC have yet to be published by the Rand Corporation, although preliminary results from the evaluation concerning reduced rates of recidivism appear promising (Greenwood et al., forthcoming).

Other carefully designed intensive aftercare programs currently in operation and undergoing rigorous evaluation include two pilot efforts based in the Philadelphia Family Court (Altschuler and Armstrong, 1990). Both are targeting high-risk juvenile offenders being released from state training schools, and are utilizing greatly reduced caseload sizes to facilitate a much higher level of contact between workers and clients. Although outcome data are not yet available from either evaluation, both programs are representative of the current wave of community-based experiments to impose higher levels of control on selected juvenile parolees and to simultaneously provide a broader range of needed services and valuable resources.

The Philadelphia Intensive Aftercare Program is designed so that aftercare workers supervise caseloads of no more than 12 "high-risk, habitual offenders." Once a youth is assigned to participate in this program, the aftercare worker is expected to visit the juvenile and the appropriate facility staff at the correctional institution once every month until the time of release. Once released, these youths are maintained on intensive aftercare caseloads for approximately six months. The first six weeks of supervision require at least three face-to-face contacts per week, with a third of the contacts expected to occur during "non-traditional" hours (i.e., evenings and weekends). For the remainder of post-release supervision, one face-to-face or telephone contact with school, employer or other service provider is required every two weeks, and the parents or guardians must be contacted (in person or phone) at least once per week. Contact with the youth can be reduced to two face-to-face contacts per week after six weeks of satisfactory adjustment, and to one per week after 12 weeks of satisfactory adjustment.

The second Philadelphia aftercare program, the Habitual Offender Unit, differs largely on the basis of applying more stringent criteria for referral into the program (all participants having at least three prior adjudications). All aftercare workers maintain caseloads of 25 youths, only half of whom are on the street at any one time. This design feature is intended to promote a much closer working relationship between the worker and institutional staff as well as the confined youths. Further, very strict rules regarding violation of parole are enforced for youths in this program. Rearrest or even technical violations tend to result in certification to the adult court.

NATIONAL ASSESSMENTS OF JUVENILE INTENSIVE SUPERVISION

Several attempts have been made within the past decade to assess the national experience with juvenile intensive aftercare and intensive probation supervision. The first was an exploratory study of community-based programs—both residential and nonresidential—for serious juvenile offenders who were either on probation or parole status. Funded by OJJDP, this national survey was conducted by the National Center for the Assessment of Alternatives to Juvenile Justice Processing at the University of Chicago, between 1980 and 1982 (Armstrong and Altschuler, 1982). The study design generated an initial purposive sample of 25 promising programs, from which

11 were chosen for in-depth site visits. The selected programs had all been designed to provide clients with intensive treatment and service delivery, while imposing high levels of social control and supervision. These goals were achieved in various ways but tended to reflect a common approach entailing the use of certain key categories of program organization: 1) case management, 2) reintegration, 3) involvement and achievement, 4) control and security, 5) education, and 6) counseling (Altschuler and Armstrong, 1984).

Though not explicitly defined as a survey of juvenile intensive supervision, the study clearly qualified as such since, without exception, the identified programs imposed greater degrees of structure and more frequent staff-client contact than would have been the case if these youths had been placed on standard probation or parole caseloads. For example, a number of the programs, especially those offering day treatment, utilized community tracking where individual staff members or contracted teams of surveillance officers followed the activities of clients on a 7 day-a-week, 24 hour-per-day basis. Analysis of programs in the sample revealed that three required dimensions of organizational design appeared to underlie all models of operation: intervention strategies, educational approaches, and reintegrative techniques (Altschuler and Armstrong, 1983). All programs in the sample had identified these functional areas as critical in achieving positive results with serious juvenile offenders being supervised in the community. Another dimension of programming that received almost constant attention was the need to deploy more sophisticated and elaborated methods of control to ensure acceptable levels of community protection. However, the assessment found little in the way of valid outcome data about effectiveness since the vast majority of programs had not been formally evaluated.

More recently, OJJDP funded two projects in 1988 to assess current trends and innovations nationwide in the intensive supervision of juvenile probationers and parolees. These two projects are required not only to document the current state-of- the-art in intensive supervision programming, but also to develop a recommended program prototype model for testing and evaluation in selected jurisdictions. To date, information is available only from the assessment phases of these two studies, but a number of interesting findings have already emerged.

The project examining intensive probation supervision, "Post-Adjudication Non-Residential Intensive Supervision Program," is being conducted by the National Council on Crime and Delinquency (NCCD). Much of the assessment process has focused on identifying programs nationwide and coordinating site visits to a small set of these programs. By definition, programs were included in the broader sample on the basis of serving as post-adjudication, nonresidential alternatives to out-of-home placement (including correctional confinement) for high-risk juvenile probationers. Programs were only considered if they stated that services were being delivered to delinquents who met some definition of "high risk." Each program's own definition of high risk as well as its procedures for assessment of risk was accepted.

Based upon its initial survey, NCCD has been able to draw a number of preliminary conclusions about the current status of intensive supervision for juvenile probationers (Krisberg et al., 1989). Most programs directed considerable attention to providing some level of risk control in their stated goals and in their daily operations. This stance required these programs to conduct some form of risk assessment for making a determination of the level of control and surveillance to be imposed on individual clients. Further, in all of these programs the degree of supervision and the level of services were substantially greater than those provided to youth on traditional probation supervision. Generally, the programs were characterized by high levels of contact by the probation or surveillance officer, small caseloads, strict conditions of compliance, and, sometimes, the use of electronic monitoring and/or periodic drug testing. The sample was also found to contain a number of programs with mixed client populations, i.e., providing services simultaneously to both high-risk probationers and parolees.

Most of the visited jurisdictions stated that they developed intensive supervision on the philosophical premise that the needs and problems of high-risk probationers could best be met in a non-institutional setting if sufficient levels of control could be exercised over the behavior of these youths in the community. The provision of treatment and services was an underlying goal of all of these programs. However, the actual mix of rehabilitative and control strategies was guided by prevailing community values. Further, in some programs treatment was not identified as an immediate goal and was consequently described as a byproduct of intensive supervision. Programs that were included in the site visits were operated both by public probation departments and by private vendors under contract with state and county agencies. Despite the emphasis on frequent contacts, there was no commonly agreed-upon standard to determine how much contact constituted "intensive." Nevertheless, all visited programs had reasonably high contact standards when compared to traditional probation. Another widely shared feature was a marked decrease in the number of contacts as clients entered the final stages of intensive supervision. Further, these programs were characterized by a wide range of variation in "length of stay"; this varied from a relatively brief period of 90 days to as much as 12 to 14 months of participation.

For the purpose of site visits, NCCD sought to identify programs that had a delinquency causation theory/theories reflected in program goals, policies, and operational procedures. In fact, the majority of programs did not exhibit a clearly articulated theoretical base, but the array of services and controls being utilized, in most instances, suggested the sense of a model based on the idea of integrated theory. For example, most programs emphasized educational or vocational components reflecting themes grounded in strain theory (providing opportunities for law-abiding behavior). Likewise, the programs as a group sought to reinforce pro-social behavior by identifying and rewarding the successful completion of tasks and responsibilities that are legal and socially acceptable, a principle regularly sounded in social learning theory.

Analysis of programs in the site visit sample has revealed two basic models of operation: day treatment and direct supervision. Together, they represent a broad array of treatment philosophies and operational strategies. The former approach tends to be utilized when resources must be mustered to respond to an identified area such as basic education or development of a vocational skill. The latter approach is found more often in juvenile justice systems where a substantial range of supportive, community resources are already available. Here, primary emphasis is placed on structuring and monitoring the clients' behavior through intensified supervision and surveillance activities. NCCD found, with little surprise, that systematic, formal outcome data for either of these two approaches were virtually nonexistent.

The other OJJDP-funded assessment project, "Intensive Community-Based Aftercare Program," is being conducted by the Institute for Policy Studies at Johns Hopkins University in collaboration with the Division of Criminal Justice at California State University, Sacramento. A detailed description of the project can be found in this volume's chapter by Altschuler and Armstrong. The intensive aftercare project closely resembles the multi-staged research and development design employed in the NCCD assessment effort. It differs largely in targeting interventions for juvenile offenders released from secure correctional confinement and who have been identified as at especially high risk for reoffending or as belonging to specialized subpopulations in need of intensified services. The project also examines a wider range of placement options, including both residential and non-residential settings.

As appears to be the case with the juvenile intensive probation supervision movement, intensive aftercare with juvenile parolees is grounded in some notion of enhanced surveillance and heightened social control, but, programmatically, it has assumed a number of forms, combining various mixes of intensified surveillance and monitoring with highly specialized treatment modalities and supportive service provision. Further, most of the programs that were identified as innovative and promising were largely concentrated within a small number of jurisdictions, where for a variety of circumstances and reasons the momentum for change in juvenile parole practice had led to a significant level of experimentation and reform. A final observation about the findings of the intensive aftercare assessment project to date is that, similar to the NCCD project, few of the surveyed programs had been even haphazardly evaluated, and it is impossible to say with any precision whether the programs were, in fact, successful.

CRITICAL ISSUES

Philosophy and Goals

Whether in the adult or juvenile justice system, a wide array of philosophical principles and desired goals have been identified as appropriate to the design and operation of intensive supervision programs. For example, Byrne (1990), in discussing the future of intensive supervision for adult probationers, states that program designers and administrators nationwide have typically identified multiple goals including punishment, diversion, cost effectiveness and recidivism reduction. He notes that two of these goals are most often articulated by these programs as playing a central role: diversion from incarceration to reduce prison crowding and enhanced social control to increase public safety.

Clear and Hardyman (1990) also list an imposing set of purported goals of the new intensive supervision movement for adult offenders. They state these identified goals to be:

- reduced prison crowding
- increased public protection
- rehabilitation of offenders
- proof of the overall value of probation, and
- cost savings.

These two authors voice considerable skepticism about the ability of current programs to deliver on such bold promises, and they even suggest that not only is it unrealistic for a single program to target all of these goals simultaneously, but also it is contradictory in some respects.

Goals and philosophical tenets identified in the juvenile versions of intensive supervision tend to display the same wide range of expression with respect to operating assumptions, desired effects, and anticipated results as is found in adult programs. The one notable shift in focus is, of course, the much more explicit and substantive emphasis on merging treatment/service provision and rehabilitation with the enhanced level of surveillance. This formulation assumes that only through the stabilization of high-risk behavior effected by the imposition of greater control and more structure can the longer term goal of successful rehabilitation occur.

As a final observation about the major philosophical orientation of both adult and juvenile intensive supervision, it is imminently clear that central and common to all programming efforts in this movement is the presence of supervision and surveillance methods designed explicitly to ensure an increased level of social control. As Byrne (1990) notes, intensive supervision from the perspective of crime control and reduction entails transferring the technology of control from the institution to the community, thereby continuing a reliance on the philosophy of incapacitation as offenders are diverted from secure correctional placement. In the same vein, Harland and

Rosen (1987:43) identify (a) the fundamental commitment to an increased level of social control and (b) a focus on risk management as the two principal philosophical characteristics of this surveillance-oriented approach:

> First, is a relatively short-term focus on in-program crime control and compliance with other release conditions. Second, is primary reliance upon incapacitative and specific determent techniques to stimulate as closely as possible in the community the more completely controlling effects of a custodial sanction.

Yet, exactly what this primary emphasis on a community-based incapacitative effect means with respect to the whole range of program goals and actual operational procedures can vary markedly. Surveillance and high level of intensive monitoring can, in some instances, be ends in themselves (i.e., ensuing immediate risk control over specific offenders) and, in other instances, can be used as a means to achieve quite difficult effects (i.e., stabilizing immediate problems to address the longer-term normalization of behavior).

In this volume, a number of chapters touch upon the particular goals and philosophical principles that have driven the design and implementation of intensive supervision programs. Clear explores the significance and implications of a number of rationales for the surging interest and fascination with this programming approach. His analysis focuses upon two identified goals that are largely responsible for the current popularity of intensive supervision, namely, the desire to get tough with serious youth crime and the need to develop a logical and relatively inexpensive response to system overcrowding. In their review of the emergence of intensive aftercare, Altschuler and Armstrong also examine the major philosophical precepts and operational goals characterizing this development in community-based corrections. Special attention is paid to assessing the extent to which programs have attempted to balance the goals of social control and rehabilitation.

Caseload Size and Frequency of Contact

Much of the continuing debate about the efficacy of intensive supervision for managing the behavior of high-risk offender populations still focuses on the potential value of reduced caseloads and increased frequency of contact for improving performance levels. Ultimately, inquiry into the effectiveness of these strategies must be linked since a reduced caseload, with rare exception, presupposes greater frequency of contact between staff and clients. The logic of these procedures is that offender performance in the community will improve and rearrest rates will be reduced. This follows from the assumption that overly large caseloads are an obstacle to the successful supervision of high-risk offenders, and that greater intensity of supervision will increase the likelihood of satisfactory community adjustment.

Research results on these issues in adult corrections have not been particularly positive or promising. Clear and Hardyman (1990) have concluded in their appraisal of the impact of reduced caseloads in the 1960s that: (1) improved offender performance was not necessarily achieved; and (2) reduction in caseload size often did not ensure greater frequency of contact. Noonan and Latessa (1989) have further noted that even when increased frequency of contact does occur, there is no guarantee that recidivism rates will be reduced. Much the same has proven to be the case with juvenile offenders (Johnson, 1982; Pond, 1970; Baird, 1983; Neithercutt and Gottfredson, 1973).

Without exception, the chapters in this volume providing program descriptions as well as their operational and procedural guidelines (Mullin et al., Barton and Butts, Fagan and Reinarman, Feinberg, Klein, Skonovd and Krause, Wiebush and Hamparian) indicate that intensive supervision is defined, in part, by a marked reduction in the number of clients per caseload. At the same time, the frequency of contact was far higher in these intensive supervision units than was the case with standard caseloads. For example, Wiebush and Hamparian cite instances in the Delaware County, OH program where face-to-face contacts occur as often as twice per day. Fagan and Reinarman mention the requirement of contact once per week in the Contra Costa County program; Feinberg states that a minimum of two face-to-face contacts was mandatory in the Allegheny County program. Based upon these studies, it appears the policy of reduced caseload size was effective in systematically promoting higher frequency of contact, a feature not always present in the earlier generations of intensive supervision programs.

Classification Procedures and Client Targeting

In much the same way that reduced caseload size and frequency of contact are linked issues, there is a need to simultaneously consider classification/assessment procedures and the targeting of appropriate client populations. If the decision is made to reduce caseload size and increase frequency of contact with certain specified offenders, then it is crucial to accurately select cases appropriate for higher levels of supervision (Noonan and Latessa, 1989). However, some offenders appear to experience greater difficulty in making a successful community adjustment if placed under conditions of intensive supervision, a problem of inappropriate targeting referred to by Clear and Hardyman (1990) as the "interaction effect." The implications of this kind of inappropriate decision making are explored in the Altschuler and Armstrong chapter, where they argue that intensification of control with relatively low-risk offenders will only exacerbate the potential for recidivism.

If a major underlying principle of intensive supervision programs is the selection of that population of clients who will benefit the most from their involvement, a central objective must be the use of procedures providing the most objective and accurate predictions of both future conduct (risk) and the nature/extent of present problems and deficits (need). Individualized assessment that is capable of generating highly reliable predictions is key to this process. The juvenile intensive supervision movement has been characterized during the 1980s by widespread efforts to develop and deploy formal classification and assessment schemes. Over the past decade, quantitative assessment instruments have, in fact, demonstrated an increasing ability to accurately estimate risk levels for aggregated juvenile offender populations, thereby aiding efforts to assign offenders to the proper level of supervision.

The most effective scales for assessing risk generally contain some combination of factors related to prior delinquent history, emotional stability, substance abuse, and employment or school performance (Baird, 1984). Baird's chapter sounds a cautionary note about the danger of applying the label of "high risk" on the basis of severity of the presenting offense since a growing body of research continues to demonstrate that offense severity is only weakly or even inversely related to subsequent arrests and adjudications. Assessment of need should also be closely linked to the determination of risk level since intervention for the purpose of effecting long-term behavioral change must somehow consider the youth's underlying problems. Further, if such problems are not addressed, they will result in increased opportunities for recidivism to occur. Current approaches in the assessment of need are characterized by efforts, based largely on technical advances in diagnostic and evaluative procedures, to further subdivide juvenile offenders into carefully defined subpopulations.

Among the high-risk youths most often targeted for referral to intensive supervision programs, an important subpopulation comprises dangerous or violent offenders. An additional targeted subpopulation—which sometimes overlaps with the chronic and/or violent offender categories—comprises multi-problem youths who are excellent candidates for reoffending based on the nature and severity of their needs.

In the present volume, a number of the authors devote attention to various aspects of the assessment/classification process that are linked to decision making for program referral. Klein notes that youths are identified as suitable for participation in the Quincy Court Intensive Supervision Program on the basis of obtaining high scores on a risk/need scale developed by the Office of the Massachusetts Commissioner of Probation. Likewise, Wiebush and Hamparian's discussion of four intensive supervision programs currently operating in Ohio describes formal instruments and means used to determine risk and need levels. Similarly, Skonovd and Krause note that prospective clients for California's Regional Youth Education Facility are chosen after obtaining a high score on a client risk assessment scale.

A wide range of factors is mentioned in various chapters as constituting criteria for referring and excluding youths from participating in intensive supervision programs. Usually, these acts are defined as either chronic and/or serious offenses. For example, the "cutting edge" for eligibility in the program described by Fagan and Reinarman was violence: A juvenile probationer was judged to be appropriate if he posed a physical threat to others (i.e., defined either as a record of documented violence or a potential for violence). Feinberg and Klein discuss programs that are targeting serious, repeat offenders. In contrast, the three in-home, intensive supervision programs in Detroit described by Barton and Butts exclude youths charged with violent offenses, having serious psychiatric problems, or having no viable home to which to return. The Lucas County, OH program in Wiebush and Hamparian's chapter also excludes offenders whose offenses involve a weapon, victim injury, or drug trafficking. Wiebush and Hamparian observe that where program goals focus on recidivism reduction, eligibility is open to high-risk offenders who achieve certain scores on risk assessment instruments. In contrast, risk scores are not the primary determining factors in programs that focus explicitly on serving as alternatives to incarceration and where the nature of the presenting offense largely determines who will be placed on intensive supervision.

Evaluation

In a recent overview of developments in adult intensive supervision, Byrne (1990) notes the common complaint of researchers about the poor quality of existing program evaluations, especially those providing "hard" data about effectiveness. In a similar way, juvenile intensive supervision programs have produced few scientifically acceptable program evaluations. Both of the current OJJDP-funded national assessments of juvenile intensive supervision (Krisberg et al., 1989; Altschuler and Armstrong, 1990), as well as Armstrong's national survey of juvenile intensive probation (1988), indicate a notable lack of well-designed evaluations. However, as has been well documented, this history of limited evaluation plagues the entirety of the American corrections field and should not be viewed as a problem confined to the study of juvenile intensive supervision.

A major question is whether decreased caseload size and more frequent contact between the client and supervising agent will result in more favorable outcomes. To the extent this question has been addressed, the anticipated reduction in criminal behavior has not materialized. Further, some question persists about the extent to which reductions in caseload size have actually resulted in a greater intensification of contact, suggesting that this whole issue perhaps needs to be explored again in a more rigorous fashion.

Another concern in evaluation is the possible overreliance on recidivism as the primary if not the sole measure of effectiveness. Arriving at a reasonable understanding of why offenders lapse back into illegal behavior requires a basic perception of social conduct as a process rather than a single event (Glaser, 1973). Too often, success in correctional intervention is measured as though it were an all-or-nothing matter, i.e., measured as a dichotomous variable. Although recidivism, whether defined as rearrest, reconviction, or reimprisonment, will always have a bottom-line significance for the justice system, since it represents a straightforward, easily measurable index of failure, its value for explaining exactly why or how an offender has reassumed a negative pattern of behavior is extremely limited. This suggests the value of having multiple outcome measures, including both psychological and behavioral indicators of positive change.

The present volume attempts to rectify to some extent the continuing absence of formal, high-quality evaluations of juvenile intensive supervision by including a number of such studies that collectively examine a wide array of process and outcome measures of program design, performance and effectiveness. Baird's chapter carefully delineates issues that are critical to any comprehensive evaluation of intensive supervision programs. Barton and Butts explore whether recidivism is lowered, whether the quality of family relationships is improved, whether performance levels in jobs and schools are raised, and whether intensive supervision programs are more cost-effective than state training schools. Skonovd and Krause analyze whether intensive supervision has a positive impact on recidivism rates, with particular emphasis on understanding how the intensive, individualized treatment orientation of the Regional Youth Educational Facility serves to aid the community adjustment and rehabilitative process. While exploring program effectiveness in reducing recidivism and stimulating behavioral change (both short- and long-term), Fagan and Reinarman also address the fascinating question of whether variation in supervisory style and approach within a single program might play a role in shaping differential outcomes. The Feinberg chapter is notable in providing a longitudinal analysis of program effectiveness. Among the key factors addressed in this study as potentially having impact upon program outcomes are age, race, and prior offense histories.

CONCLUSION

The current wave of juvenile intensive supervision programs that began in the 1980s suffers in large measure from a lack of conceptual, operational and philosophical clarity. Identifying their essential nature and central operating procedures is difficult since they are marked by a wide diversity in design and goal. Other than the commonly shared features of reduced caseload size and an emphasis on imposing higher levels of social control over clients, these programs vary along a number of structural dimensions and have resultingly incorporated a vast array of components, procedures and techniques to achieve a number of different goals.

Some programs utilize extensive drug and alcohol testing; others focus primary attention upon restitution and community service; some deploy high-tech monitoring systems that rely heavily upon electronic monitoring and other intrusive surveillance techniques; most combine bits and pieces of these various specialized components and approaches. The result is that some look basically like drug and alcohol treatment programs, while others resemble versions of community tracking services, and others focus primarily upon job training and placement and reparative sanctioning. Perhaps as program development and professional communication continue into the 1990s, a higher level of agreement will emerge about the essential ingredients or components of these programs and what they can and should try to achieve with particular offender groups within the broader set of philosophical principles and justice goals.

On a more positive note, a considerable degree of consensus appears to exist over the need to target so-called high-risk offenders for participation in these programs. Yet, the way in which this population is defined varies substantially from jurisdiction to jurisdiction. In part, these differences are a matter of variation in the stated goals and objectives of programs. However, there are clear indications that substantial efforts are underway to bring greater objectivity and precision to the screening and decision-making process for selecting appropriate participants. The use of more formal and more quantitative assessment techniques will ensure a growing ability to target those youths who require more structured interventions and/or services and resource provision.

As enthusiasm continues to mount nationally for this programming approach, several cautionary notes need to be sounded. The often-stated aim of better managing juvenile offenders in the community may, in fact, backfire and cause excessive institutional crowding unless innovative sanctioning procedures are devised in lieu of revocation. The imposition of extremely high levels of social control based upon the use of quite intrusive techniques for monitoring behavior may generate a substantial increase in the number of observed minor law violations and technical violations of probation and parole conditions. Unless this circumstance is taken into consideration when deciding upon the most appropriate responses to detected misconduct, problems such as overclogged court calendars and overcrowded correctional facilities will only be exacerbated. A second caution involves the possibility of a "net-widening" effect. Scarce resources will be wasted and cost effectiveness lost if many less serious offenders are swept into the programs, and if low-risk offenders are supervised with unnecessary intensity. The latter may perform more poorly than if they had been placed on standard caseloads.

Another observation worthy of reiteration concerns the fact of a persisting commitment to the traditional juvenile court value of child-saving in the design and operation of these programs. Regardless of how get-tough or surveillance-oriented these programs appear to be, the theme of treatment and service provision as means to achieve the ends of rehabilitation is voiced somewhere in the statement of goals and philosophy, although often not asserted as primary. This characteristic clearly distinguishes the broader intent of the current juvenile intensive supervision movement from developments in the adult area, where the principles of enforcement and control often assume the status of being the singular purpose. It is unlikely that program planners and administrators in the juvenile justice field will lose sight of this dual commitment to treatment and deterrence in the implementation of such programs in the foreseeable future.

In sum, the current wave of juvenile intensive interventions appears to be gaining every-increasing popularity and momentum. The well documented organizational and definitional confusion about essential design features, as well as ambiguity in central goals and mission, have not slowed the growing interest in these programs among correctional authorities. Given this trend, the major challenge is to ensure the use of procedures that: explicitly state the goals of the intervention; objectively classify youths for possible participation; precisely match supervision and service types and levels to the appropriate clients; and, produce "hard" outcome data about effectiveness.

REFERENCES

Agee, V.L. (1979). *Treatment of the Violent Incorrigible Adolescent*. Lexington, MA: D.C. Heath and Company.

Allen-Hagen, B. (1988). "Public Juvenile Facilities: Children in Custody." *Juvenile Justice Bulletin* (October). Washington, DC: U.S. Office of Juvenile Justice and Delinquency Prevention.

Altschuler, David and Troy Armstrong (1990). "Intensive Community-Based Aftercare Programs: Assessment Report." Washington, DC: U.S. Office of Juvenile Justice and Delinquency Prevention.

—— (1983). "Four Models of Community-Based Interventions with the Serious Juvenile Offender: Therapeutic Orientations, Educational Strategies, and Reintegrative Techniques." *Corrective and Social Psychiatry and Journal of Behavior Technology Methods and Therapy* 29(4):116-130.

Armstrong, Troy (1988). "National Survey of Juvenile Intensive Probation Supervision, Parts I and II." *Criminal Justice Abstracts* 2(2,3):342-348, 497-523.

—— and David Altschuler (1982). *Community-Based Program Interventions for the Serious Juvenile Offender: Targeting, Strategies and Issues*. Chicago, IL: School of Social Service Administration, University of Chicago, National Center for the Assessment of Alternatives to Juvenile Justice Processing.

—— D. Maloney and D. Romig (1990). "The Balanced Approach In Juvenile Probation: Principles, Issues and Application." APPA *Perspectives* 14(1) 8-13.

Baird, S. Christopher (1984). *Classification of Juveniles: A Model Systems Approach*. San Francisco, CA: National Council on Crime and Delinquency.

—— (1983). *Report on Intensive Supervision Programs in Probation and Parole*. Washington, DC: U.S. National Institute of Corrections.

Bandura, Albert (1977). "Self-Efficacy: Toward a Unifying Theory of Behavioral Change." *Psychological Review* 84:191-215.

—— and Dale H. Schunk (1981). "Cultivating Competence, Self-Efficacy, and Intrinsic Interest Through Proximal Self-Motivation." *Journal of Personality and Social Psychology* 41(3):586-598.

Banks, J., A.L. Porter, R.L. Rardin, R.R. Sider and V.E. Unger (1977). *Summary: Phase*

1 Evaluation of Intensive Special Probation Projects. Washington, DC: U.S. National Institution of Law Enforcement and Criminal Justice.

Bleich, Jeffrey (1987). "Toward an Effective Policy for Handling Dangerous Juvenile Offenders." In *From Children to Citizens, Vol. II, The Role of the Juvenile Court,* edited by Francis S. Hartman. New York, NY: Springer-Verlag.

Byrne, James M. (1990). "The Future of Intensive Probation Supervision and the New Intermediate Sanctions." *Crime & Delinquency* 36(1):6-41.

Carter, Robert M. and L.T. Wilkins (1984). "Caseloads: Some Conceptual Models." In *Probation, Parole and Community Corrections,* 2nd ed., edited by R. Carter and L. Wilkins. New York, NY: Wiley and Sons.

Clear, Todd R. and Patricia L. Hardyman (1990). "The New Intensive Supervision Movement." *Crime & Delinquency* 36(1):42-60.

Coates, Robert B. (1984). "Appropriate Alternatives for the Violent Juvenile Offender." In *Violent Juvenile Offenders: An Anthology,* edited by R. Mathias et al. San Francisco, CA: National Council on Crime and Delinquency.

Deschenes, L. (1989). "The Skillman Intensive Aftercare Project." Paper presented at the American Society of Criminology Annual Meeting, Reno, NV.

Fagan, Jeffrey, M. Forst, and T. Vivona (1988). "Treatment and Reintegration of Violent Juvenile Offenders: Experimental Results." San Francisco, CA: URSA Institute.

Farrington, David and D. J. West (1977). "The Cambridge Study in Delinquency Development." Cambridge, UK: Institute of Criminology, Cambridge University.

Gadow, D. and J. McKibbon (1984). "Discipline and the Institutionalized Violent Delinquent." In *Violent Juvenile Offenders: An Anthology,* edited by R. Mathias et al. San Francisco, CA: National Council on Crime and Delinquency.

Glaser, Daniel (1973). *Routinizing Evaluation: Getting Feedback on Effectiveness of Crime and Delinquency Programs.* Rockville, MD: U.S. National Institute of Mental Health, Center for Studies of Crime and Delinquency.

Greenwood, Peter, S. Turner, and K. Rosenblatt (forthcoming). *Implementing and Managing Innovative Correctional Programs: Lessons from OJJDP's Private Sector Initiative.* Santa Monica, CA: Rand.

Gruenewald, Paul, S. Lawrence, and B. West (1985). "National Evaluation of the New Pride Replication Program: Executive Summary." Walnut Creek, CA: Pacific Institute for Research and Evaluation.

Hamparian, Donna, R. Schuster, S. Dinitz, and J. Conrad (1978). *The Violent Few: A Study of the Dangerous Juvenile Offender.* Lexington, MA: Lexington Books.

Harland, Alan T. and C.J. Rosen (1987). "Sentencing Theory and Intensive Supervision Probation." *Federal Probation* (4):33-42.

Johnson, B.M. (1962). "Parole Performance of the First Year's Releases—Parole Research Project: Evaluation of Reduced Caseloads." Research Report No. 27. Sacramento, CA: California Youth Authority.

James, Thomas and J. Granville (1984). "Practical Issues in Vocational Education for Serious Juvenile Offenders." In *Violent Juvenile Offenders: An Anthology,* edited by R. Mathias et al. San Francisco, CA: National Council on Crime and Delinquency.

Krisberg, Barry, O. Rodriguez, A. Bakke, D. Neuenfeldt, and P. Steele (1989). "Demonstration of Post Adjudication Non- Residential Intensive Supervision Programs: Assessment Report." San Francisco, CA: National Council on Crime and Delinquency.

—— I.M. Schwartz, P. Litsky, and J. Austin (1986). "The Watershed of Juvenile Justice Reform." *Crime & Delinquency* 32(1):5-38.

Latessa, Edward J. (1987). "The Effectiveness of Intensive Supervision with High Risk Probationers." In *Intermediate Punishments: Intensive Supervision, Home Confinement and Electronic Surveillance*, edited by Belinda McCarthy. Monsey, NY: Criminal Justice Press.

—— (1979). "Intensive Supervision: An Evaluation of the Effectiveness of an Intensive Diversion Unit." Unpublished doctoral dissertation, Ohio State University, Columbus, OH.

—— E. Parks, H. Allen, and Eric Carlson (1979). "Specialized Supervision in Probation." *Prison Journal* 59:27-35.

Maloney, Dennis, D. Romig, and T. Armstrong (1988). "Juvenile Probation: The Balanced Approach." *Juvenile & Family Court Journal* 39(3):1-62.

Marlatt, G. Allen and J. R. Gordon (eds.) (1985). *Relapse Prevention: Maintenance Strategies in the Treatment of Addictive Behaviors*. New York, NY: Guilford Press.

McCarthy, Belinda (ed.) (1987). *Intermediate Punishments: Intensive Supervision, Home Confinement and Electronic Surveillance*. Monsey, NY: Criminal Justice Press.

McCord, Joan (1979). "Some Child-Rearing Antecedents of Criminal Behavior in Adult Men." *Journal of Personality and Social Psychology* 37:1477-1486.

Neithercutt, M.G. and D.M. Gottfredson (1973). *Caseload Size Variation and Difference in Probation/Parole Performance*. Pittsburgh, PA: National Center for Juvenile Justice.

Noonan, Susan and E.J. Latessa (1989). "Intensive Probation: An Examination of Recidivism and Social Adjustment." In *Correctional Counseling and Treatment*, 2nd ed., edited by P.C. Kratcoski. Prospect Heights, IL: Waveland Press.

Palmer, Theodore B. (1974a). "The Youth Authority's Community Treatment Project." *Federal Probation* 38(1):3-14.

—— (1974b). "The Community Treatment Project: A Review of Accumulate Research in the California Youth Authority." Sacramento, CA: California Youth Authority.

—— (1973). "The Community Treatment Project in Perspective: 1961-1973." *Youth Authority Quarterly* 26(3):29-43

—— (1971). "California's Community Treatment Program for Delinquent Adolescents." *Journal of Research in Crime and Delinquency* 8(1):74-92.

Pond, E.M. (1970). "The Los Angeles Community Delinquency Control Project: An Experiment in the Rehabilitation of Delinquents in an Urban Community." Research Report No. 60. Sacramento, CA: California Youth Authority.

Roberts, C.F. (1970). "A Final Evaluation of the Narcotic Control Program." Research Report No. 58. Sacramento, CA: California Youth Authority.

Shannon, Lyle (1978). "A Longitudinal Study of Delinquency and Crime." In *Quantitative Studies in Criminology*, edited by Charles Wellford. Beverly Hills, CA: Sage Publications.

Steenson, David (ed.) (1986). "A Symposium on Juvenile Intensive Probation Supervision: The JIPS Proceedings." Minneapolis, MN: Hennepin County Bureau of Community Corrections, Juvenile Division.

Wolfgang, Marvin, R. Figlio, and T. Sellin (1972). *Delinquency in a Birth Cohort*. Chicago, IL: University of Chicago Press.

Part I

Conceptual Issues in Juvenile Intensive Interventions

Juvenile Intensive Probation Supervision: Theory and Rationale

by
Todd R. Clear

A review examines the rationale for juvenile intensive probation supervision (JIPS) and its implications for program operations. The proper role of JIPS is to control risk, but only serious delinquent behavior warrants the stringent measures imposed in this type of supervision. If not limited to the most serious cases, the current wave of JIPS programs may end as ignominiously as its predecessor did two decades ago. Now, as then, the promises of JIPS seem to outstrip the means available, and activities surpass available knowledge.

The rationale for intensive supervision of juveniles seems straightforward enough: probation supervision is a good thing, more should be even better. But 15 years of correctional self-aggrandizement despite our pitifully inconsistent ability to affect the behavior of delinquents in more than marginal ways leads most of us to view this rationale for intensive supervision with some skepticism. After all, probation supervision is *not* uniformly a good thing, and more is not necessarily better.

If juvenile intensive probation supervision (JIPS) is to be a useful part of a system of juvenile justice strategies, the program must meet a particular need by filling a gap in the array of juvenile justice methods. A rational planner would approach this problem in a logical fashion—by assessing the range of juveniles handled by current methods, identifying a cohort for which current methods are inadequate and justifying JIPS as precisely the right modality for that cohort because of the unique compatibility of the JIPS approach with the cohort's needs.

In urban environments, JIPS has been promoted as a relevant approach for chronic, high-risk juvenile offenders. This belief has been strengthened by the increasing involvement of juveniles in drug delivery systems, especially those distributing crack. Even though there are considerable difficulties in reliably identifying juvenile offenders who are truly "chronic" or "high risk," the idea of JIPS has been advanced as necessary for managing them. To some extent, this argument is bolstered by reports indicating the success of intensive supervision with adult offenders carrying the same labels.

Instead of starting with a careful assessment of juvenile offenders' needs, too many contemporary JIPS programs have resulted instead from an inverted process. The juvenile justice agency first decides to have a JIPS program, then it defines a subpopulation of juveniles "appropriate" for the program. Creating a JIPS component comes first; fitting JIPS into the array of available services comes second.

Informed observers might debate which approach is better, but all would agree that when developing a particular program becomes an end in itself, rather than a means to achieve some larger goal, the possibility of goal displacement occurs. The program then becomes more important than the need it is purported to serve.

Indeed, it is not irrefutably clear that some segment of our juvenile population is poorly served by current methods or that perceived gaps in service can be remedied by JIPS. Yet the JIPS movement is currently a ubiquitous national phenomenon. It is therefore important to step away from this nearly uniform move to embrace JIPS and to ask two key questions: "Why is JIPS so popular?" and "What can JIPS do that needs to be done and is not already being done?" In responding to these two questions, a theory and a rationale for JIPS can emerge.

TWO REASONS FOR THE CURRENT POPULARITY OF JIPS

Most observers would agree that there are two main reasons why JIPS is such a popular concept in the mid-1980s: (1) the generalized desire to get tough with offenders, and (2) the specific desire to deal with overcrowded facilities. Note that neither reason stems from a careful assessment of gaps in services to juvenile justice clients.

Desire to Get Tough

After years of relative poverty, the community corrections movement is now finding it easier to get money if the correct lingo is used. Los Angeles, Philadelphia, Georgia, New Jersey, Texas, and New York have all appropriated large sums of money (from $500,000 to millions of dollars) to support "intensive" programs. In many of these jurisdictions, government funding of other services was exceedingly tight, yet expensive new "intensive probation" programs were funded. Having been virtually ignored by these funding agencies for over a decade, probation agencies cannot be blamed for moving quickly to capture a fiscal windfall through the promise of intensive measures.

The cynics among us are reminded of the heyday of the U.S. Law Enforcement Assistance Administration (LEAA), when obtaining funds for special programs seemed simple. In those days, the catch-words were "service delivery," "individualized treatment," and "rehabilitation." Today the monetary faucets are turned on by different phraseology, such as "control," "surveillance," and "enforcement." When we were unable to deliver on the results we promised in the days of LEAA, our credibility with those who funded us suffered. Should we fail to deliver on the current "toughness" rhetoric, will our credibility suffer even more?

Whether we succeed in our newly adopted stance of toughness depends in part on our commitment to those values. This is at least a little troubling (Harris, 1984). If we could peer into the soul of most juvenile justice administrators who are charging after the JIPS idea, would we really find a resolve to "get tough, controlling and firm," or would we find instead a desperate seeker of funds for a depleted operation—an individual who is willing to embrace the rhetoric of the times to get the money? Is it really possible for probation to "out-tough" the institutions? And if it is possible, do we really want to do it?

If intensive supervision probation (ISP) in adult corrections provides any gauge, probation administrators can make ISP pretty tough when they put their minds to it. By stacking a long list of conditions and enforcing them with impunity, several ISPs have gained such a stern reputation that many offenders request prison in its stead, and those who dare to participate in the program may experience significantly higher chances of revocation than had they received traditional supervision (Petersilia and Turner, 1989).

System Overcrowding

In the adult system, a correctional resource crisis has given impetus to the intensive movement. With jails and prisons packed beyond legal capacity, community corrections administrators have leaped into the breach with a "solution": tough new probation programs to deal with persons who should be incarcerated but for whom there is no room. This aspect of the new intensive probation programs is based on desperation—something has to be done. Indeed, system overcrowding is *not* an affirmative argument for the new intensive methods; most advocates are not saying that intensive probation is good, right, or even appropriate. Instead, the argument is on the negative side, that nothing else can be done. This leaves the distinct impression that if prison capacity in the U.S. were doubled, the heart would be removed from the adult intensive probation movement.

To a lesser extent, a similar motivation is operating in the juvenile justice system. Facilities and institutional programs are full; intake pressure on these operations needs to be reduced. Given the recent surge in birth rates, and in the number of youth reaching age-at-risk of delinquency, the overcrowding problem may get worse before it gets better. In all probability, the rationale for JIPS will be tied increasingly to population control in juvenile institutional facilities.

Selling JIPS as an alternative to an institutional program appears to have three potentially negative consequences. First, the ability of intensive programs to identify and select true diversion cases is at best uneven and at worst dismal (Krisberg and Austin, 1980). Most so-called "alternatives" are used instead as "add-ons" to what would otherwise be regular probation sentences. Second, many of these programs target the "least serious" of the institution-bound population (Erwin, 1984; Administrative Office of the Courts of New Jersey, 1984). The result is a flip-flop of correctional resources, which places the least serious offenders under the strictest supervision available within the system, while more dangerous offenders emerge from a period of incarceration to regular aftercare, where supervision is puny by comparison with most JIPS programs. Third, because of their enhanced strictness, JIPS programs often produce a failure rate equal to or higher than that of regular probation (Bennett, 1986; Petersilia, 1987). When JIPS cases fail, the youths frequently receive a more severe punishment than they would have received had they failed on regular probation.

For these three reasons, intensive program may actually *exacerbate* the system resource problems that they were designed to solve.

Promises, Promises

Underlying these two justifications of JIPS—getting tough and reducing crowding—is a chronic pattern in our justice system that is bound to leave many of us uneasy. We make promises that we have no intention of keeping and no ability to keep.

Indeed, in adult corrections there is now very little relationship between what the judge says at sentencing and what the sentenced individual will actually experience. A five-year sentence, after deductions for parole, clemency, good time, time served and so forth, may actually amount to only two years or even less. In Oregon, a nine-month jail sentence often results in more time served than a two-year prison sentence.

Some critics of the system have observed that when the judge says "five years" the person ought to serve *five full years* (Van den Haag, 1976). These critics have it backwards, for judges have no business saying "five years" when the system lacks the ability to deliver on that promise.

When JIPS programming takes the form of "enhanced, tough probation," it confronts the same dilemma—making promises that the system has no intention of, or capacity for, keeping. The special conditions of an intensive program commonly involve curfews, urine checks, fines, supervision fees, restitution, community service, treatment program attendance, restrictions on associations, employment, and living situation constraints, and all of these special conditions must be fully enforced over a two- to five-year period. Certainly these conditions are not unreasonable to impose on people who have committed crimes. Yet do we really mean each of these conditions as a threat? What if the person misses curfews? What if probation fees are not paid (as happens about half of the time, nationally)? Are we willing to allocate scarce institutional resources to enforce each of these requirements when the person is otherwise doing well? Generally, the answer is no. Our promises are therefore hollow.

Two statements are really implicit in these "get-tough" versions of probation. The first statement is to the general public: "We are no longer the 97-pound weaklings of the criminal justice system—look how tough we are!" The second is to the JIPS client: "Here is a long list of things we are telling you to do. If you don't do some of them all of the time (or all of them some of the time), probably nothing is going to happen. Still, it would be nice if you would do them."

What would a JIPS program be like if it made only those promises that it was willing (and committed) to keep? Conversely, what is the likely future of JIPS programs that continue to promise unreasonable or impossible conditions? The answer to the first question is that the program might not look so tough (because it would be much more circumspect in the conditions imposed, which would be individualized), but it would actually be tougher because it would enforce what is promised. The answer to the second question is that making too many promises leads inevitably to a lack of credibility.

The Recent History of JIPS

The 1980s are not the first time that there has been an "intensive" movement in correctional field services. Much of the research on intensive programs is based on the first wave of projects, which originated in the late 1970s under the financial wing of LEAA. An experiential base thus exists from which to evaluate the potential usefulness of JIPS as a control method.

Every comprehensive review of studies of intensive programs has produced the same general commentary: The success rates of the more intensive programs generally are no better—and often are *even worse*—than those of regular probation (Neithercutt and Gottfredson, 1973; Banks et al., 1981; Byrne, Lurigio and Baird, 1989). The few programs that produced positive results seemed to take advantage of specialized services targeted for a specially designated group (Gendreau and Ross, 1980; Romig, 1986). To specialize, however, does not always guarantee success.

Those who argue for JIPS because it is more effective than regular probation have a difficult time marshaling evidence to support their view. Why, then, do so many argue the need for JIPS programming because it is "more effective"? The lack of success in the history of JIPS does not mean that it cannot work today. There is some emerging evidence that JIPS programming can be more effective than regular probation (Gendreau and Ross, 1987). However, if promising toughness is a trap, promising effectiveness may also be one. At best, the jury is still out.

SORTING OUT THE BASIS FOR JIPS

Thus far, this summary has been pretty grim. It seems that JIPS has no strong heritage of effectiveness, makes too many promises of toughness, and has a problematic relationship with system crowding. Its popularity is at the least puzzling in light of these facts. Indeed, a very real possibility exists that the JIPS movement will prove to be a fad that will fade under careful review by those who would hold JIPS accountable for at least improving something.

If JIPS is to survive the inevitable critical appraisal that follows any innovation, it will do so because it has found a legitimate place in the juvenile justice arsenal. The ultimate place of JIPS in the juvenile justice system will be a product of its *philosophical* orientation, *programmatic* consistency with that orientation, and *technical* delivery on programmatic promises.

Philosophy

The purposes of JIPS are similar to the legitimate purposes of any correctional program. These are punishment (often called "desert" or retribution), and risk control.

Punishment embodies the age-old idea that a person who does something wrong ought to receive some response that demonstrates, at least symbolically, social disapproval of the wrongful act. There are many theories of punishment, but all have in common a few consistent themes, which are summarized in Figure 1.

The concept of punishment flows from a fairly simple formula: Those who do wrong should suffer painful consequences for their wrongful choices. This is a basic notion represented by such phrases as "no wrong unpunished," "an eye for an eye," and "don't do the crime if you can't do the time."

The government is interested in punishment precisely because of the forbidden act. No further justification is needed. The government is not, however, given *carte blanche* to inflict punishment. A forbidden act of minor harmfulness does not justify a severely painful punishment (for example, five years in prison for shoplifting is repugnant). Likewise, a seriously harmful act calls for more than minor pain or loss (for example, forcible rape should not lead to unsupervised probation). A requirement thus exists that the degree of pain, loss or suffering imposed by government to punish an unlawful act ought somehow to be commensurate with the act's seriousness.

Figure 1. The Concept of Punishment (Desert)

Theorem: Use of government power against an individual is justified when he or she has committed a forbidden act that is worthy of condemnation or blame.

Purpose: Purpose of government action is to impart some measure of harm, loss or pain as an intentional (visible) symbol of the reprehensibleness of the citizen's forbidden conduct.

Limitations:
1. Amount of harm, loss or pain should be proportional to the reprehensibleness of the conduct so that different levels of irresponsible behavior may be recognized.
2. Unintentional or collateral loss over and above that due to the citizen because of the reprehensibleness of the act must be avoided.
3. The government is obligated to inflict, harm, loss or pain as punishment but only to the extent justified by the reprehensibleness of the act.

The juvenile justice system has long been criticized for paying inadequate attention to the need for proportional punishment. Some argue that those youths who commit very serious crimes are too often treated with undue leniency (Feld, 1981), while others point out that fairly minor misbehaviors can result in responses of a severity far out of proportion with the act itself (Krisberg and Schwartz, 1983). The requirement that corrections should punish offenders sets both lower and upper limits on what can be done to a given juvenile delinquent.

There are two additional considerations in punishment. First, the collateral effects of the punishment must be limited as much as possible. That is why in this culture we do not cut off the hands of thieves—we realize that to do so would impose unintentional harm far beyond the appropriateness of the symbolic retribution. For this reason, our prisons are declared unconstitutional when they impose pain or suffering in excess of that punishment which results from loss of freedom due to incarceration. Second, the state must demonstrate why an act is sufficiently reprehensible to justify the pain, loss or suffering imposed in response. The mere fact of a crime does not require punishment; the act must be of a willful nature to justify punishment.

Risk control as a rationale is entirely different from punishment. The conceptual basis for risk control is presented in Figure 2.

Risk control is purely utilitarian in its interest. Government may not use power against a citizen unless that power is necessary to advance the greater good. In the area of juvenile justice, this means that the use of power may be necessary to avoid some greater, future harmful act, and the government is able to alleviate that risk through purposeful intervention.

Certainly, some risk always exists. But risk control does not give the government *carte blanche* to intervene in the lives of all citizens to alleviate all

Figure 2. The Concept of Risk Control

Theorem: Use of government power against a citizen is justified when use of the power will contribute to the greater good for all citizens.

Purpose: The purpose of government action is to reduce or eliminate the probability of some harmful act occurring among the general citizenry. Use of government power may be adjusted depending on both probability of occurrence and seriousness of a harmful act.

Limitations:
1. The government is obligated to use the least intrusive or least painful method available to reduce or eliminate the probability of a harmful act.
2. The government's desire to alter an act's probability may not be used as an excuse to impose gratuitous pain or suffering of a citizen.
3. Burden of proof falls on the government that (a) real probability of commission of harmful act exists, and (b) intervention is necessary to reduce or eliminate that probability.

risk. Intervention must be based on both the seriousness and the probability of commission of a new harmful act. Nobody would condone a five-year prison sentence for a person likely to repeat shoplifting, nor would we condone life imprisonment of a person who has a negligible chance of committing rape. The potential harm must be severe and the probability of its commission high. Most people would have no problem with incarceration of a person who is very likely to commit a serious assault.

Because risk control imposes intrusions on the individual for the benefit of the whole, certain limitations apply to its use. First, the least intrusive method available to control the risk must always be chosen. Use of a significantly painful control cannot be justified when a lesser control would work just as well. This is one way of saying that a risk control measure cannot be used as a proxy for retributive punishments. It is thus improper to incarcerate someone because of risk-control interests while saying, "If the risk isn't there, the incarceration is acceptable anyway because this person deserves the punishment." The test of risk control is separate from the requirement to punish.

Finally, the burden of proof that risk is present falls on the government, as does the need to show that a particular approach is necessary to control risk. Any paranoiac can find risk to be present when, in fact, it is not, and all manner of inhumane gestures can be advanced as necessary to benefit the larger society. The government must show that the finding of risk is grounded in fact and that a lesser intervention would be ineffective.

Other than punishment or risk control, no other reasons exist to justify government intrusion into the lives of juveniles for reasons of delinquent conduct. To some degree, these two philosophies of punishment and risk control are mutually exclusive. Punishments may be imposed regardless of risk, and risk may be controlled without concern for the reprehensibleness of a given act. However, a juvenile justice system that seeks to perform only one function and not the other will suffer grievously from external pressures. To ignore risk is to threaten openly the community's desire for security. To ignore punishment is to ridicule the community's behavioral values. The fact that a given intervention helps to control risk does not justify it as deserved. Conversely, the existence of risk says nothing about the amount of punishment deserved. The punitive and risk-control dimensions are thus separate concerns of the juvenile justice system. Because an act is forbidden, society seeks to punish. Because a wrongful actor has harmed society, the community seeks to avoid further harms. One rationale is not tied to the other.

A problem arises when one tries to put the two together. Which is ascendant—punishment or risk control? Which should control our actions? The answers to these questions are neither easy nor obvious, and researchers have reached no consensus.

In the area of juvenile justice, the tradition of guarding the child's "best interest" suggests a solution: No intrusion may be allowed that inflicts greater harm than the pain, loss or suffering justified by the delinquent behavior, but within this limitation *any* action taken must be justifiable in terms of risk control. Punishment (desert) thus sets the upper limit of what may be done to a juvenile found delinquent, whiile risk control defines actions that *must* be taken, as long as they do not exceed in intrusiveness what may be done as punishment.

Program

Keeping this philosophical orientation in mind, let us now consider how well JIPS programs fit into the system. What does this philosophy of punishment and risk control suggest that a JIPS program should be?

Inspection of the elements common to JIPS programs sheds some light on their philosophical orientation. The specifics of any given program will be unique, but JIPS programs have many components in common, as summarized in Figure 3. Aside from intensified contact and specialized assessments, all of these common elements are also used in many regular supervision programs. Indeed, use of these components in JIPS is similar to their usage in regular supervision. The main difference—in many settings, the only difference—is the intensity with which a collection of the components can be applied to a specific client. This is why many JIPS workers refer to their jobs as "real probation, the way it always should have been."

Most of the strategies relate to risk control because JIPS is, appropriately, a program designed exclusively for offenders who represent a serious risk to the community. In fact, the most basic JIPS strategy—frequency of contact—is almost purely a risk-oriented approach. This becomes clear when one recalls that the purpose of punishment is to inflict pain, loss or suffering intentionally. It would be senseless to say to a juvenile: "You have committed a serious act, and the painful consequence will be talking to a probation officer many

Figure 3. Common Components of JIPS Programs

Basic Strategy
- Frequent contact (at least twice monthly, often weekly or more)
- Specialized assessment for service delivery
- Emphasis on both surveillance and treatment

Common Risk-Control Strategies
- Random or surprise home visits
- Electronic surveillance
- Home detention
- Curfew requirements
- Search and seizure
- Residential treatment
- Big-brother/volunteer
- Referrals to treatment agencies

Common Punishment Strategies
- Work crews
- Community service
- Restitution
- Victim-offender conferences
- Fines

times over the next few months." The requirement of talking to a probation officer is not the imposition of pain, loss or suffering. Rather, the requirement is imposed because we believe that more frequent contact is necessary to lead the juvenile to practice more law-abiding behavior. The goal of the penalty intensity is always to control risk, never merely to punish. We are comfortable imposing intensity only when the juvenile's act is serious enough to warrant intensive intrusion, but the intrusion is designed to control risk.

The proper role of JIPS is thus to control risk, but only in the case of those juveniles whose delinquent behavior was serious enough to warrant the relatively extreme measures imposed by JIPS. Moreover, only those clients who represent a substantial risk should be included in a JIPS program with its frequent contact, surveillance, intensive treatment and concentrated services. Otherwise, the JIPS get-tough measures are being used as a proxy for painful interventions, and this is inappropriate.

This is not to say that JIPS programs should ignore the need to impose punishment. Indeed, a tradition of community service, restitution and other punitive requirements is a part of most JIPS programs. Often, people are confused about the philosophical intentions of these requirements, for we recognize that the attitudes of many juveniles are changed for the better by involvement in community service. A simple conceptual test shows that these interventions, while *potentially* rehabilitative, are used *because they are punitive*. For example, even if we knew beforehand that restitution (or community service, for that matter) would not change a particular juvenile's attitude, we would still impose the intervention. The reasoning would be something like this: "Just because the kid's attitude is bad doesn't mean that he can avoid paying back the victim or the community. He has to pay that price because his actions deserve it." The underlying rationale is clearly punitive, although we are pleased that in many instances the imposition of such punishment seems to have a remarkably ameliorative effect on juvenile attitudes. Yet even without the ameliorative effect, we would feel justified in imposing these sanctions because they demonstrate the unacceptableness of the behavior.

The same logic does not apply to the risk control components of JIPS. If we knew beforehand that family therapy, routine urinalysis or curfews were destined to fail, we would not say "Do it anyway, because the delinquent actions warranted it." Instead, we would search for some alternative mode of risk control that might be more likely to work. If that search left us with unusually intrusive risk-control measures as the only option (i.e., a training school or residential placement), we would consider first whether the juvenile's past behavior and the current risk to society combine to justify such a severe intrusion. If they did not, we would not impose excessive risk control, regardless of the likely failure of less excessive methods.

In the search for programmatic risk controls, one has only two general options. The first is *incapacitative* and seeks to place controls on the juvenile such that he or she is unable (or less able) to commit undesirable acts. Curfews, urinalysis and electronic surveillance are commonly used for this purpose. The second risk-control strategy is *treatment*, which attempts to achieve a permanent change in the thinking, feeling, or behaving patterns of the juvenile such that the youth no longer (or less frequently) makes delinquent choices.

It should be emphasized that treatment is as legitimate a risk-control approach, at least in theory, as incapacitation. However, contemporary risk-control proposals are currently dominated by calls for incapacitative controls (partly because of the mistaken belief that treatment controls have failed). Nevertheless, the appropriate test concerning imposition of a specific risk-control measure is to ask which measure best satisfies the dual criteria of managing the risk while being least intrusive. Given these criteria, treatment-oriented controls are often preferable to the more popular incapacitation strategies.

What JIPS does uniquely, therefore, is enhance the risk-control potential of community supervision by providing more intensive incapacitative and treatment interventions. It is this enhanced intensity that makes the controlling interventions of JIPS so attractive and promising. This is not true of the punitive aspects of JIPS; supervision intensity does not necessarily improve the success of punitive interventions to such an extent that JIPS is required for successful punishment to occur. The important role of JIPS involves better risk control, not administration of better punishment.

Technology

The unfortunate reality is that many JIPS programs fail to deliver technically on the call for greater risk control. One reason for this failure is selection of the wrong clients.

For example, many JIPS programs claim to be designed for the "serious juvenile offender." The claim leads to good public relations (as in "we're getting tough with the serious offender"), but in fact programs are often confused about what qualifies a juvenile offender as "serious." Certainly most people would agree that a juvenile who is adjudicated delinquent because of an act that would be a serious felony for an adult is a "serious offender." Remarkably, studies show that such juveniles do not always represent a high risk of future criminal acts, or even a risk of serious future criminal acts (Wolfgang et al., 1972). Thus, JIPS program admission criteria that focus on the so-called serious offender may tend to select persons who have committed universally abhorrent acts, but who may not represent a significant future risk to society. While these juveniles may require enhanced punishment to demonstrate the repugnance with which we regard their acts, they may require no enhanced risk control. In fact, to require that expensive risk-control programs, such as JIPS, serve this group of juveniles is a misallocation of scarce resources that are sorely needed to deal with the true risks.

An equivalent technical problem confronts those who try to use either clinical or statistical devices to screen for the so-called "high-risk" juvenile who qualifies for JIPS assignment. The track record of clinical judgments as to who constitutes a high risk is uniformly miserable. As a matter of fact, subjective judgments are poor as to who even constitutes a "risky" case. Many of the high risks are missed while numerous low-risk individuals are falsely suspected of being "dangerous." Indeed, the error rates of clinical judgment systems that deal with juveniles are so indefensibly high that many experts advocate abandoning the clinical model for predicting (Meehl, 1954).

Recently, it has become popular in the adult justice system to use "objective" instruments to assess offender risk levels. The efficiency and usefulness of these approaches as applied to adults has been increasingly well-documented. Application of these same approaches to juveniles is, however, relatively new. There have been a few notable successes in designing statistical instruments for juveniles (Baird et al., 1984), but the more common experience has been frustratingly bad. The main reason for this may be that the best variables for predicting future criminal behavior are prior record measures (Gottfredson and Gottfredson, 1985), and most juveniles have simply not had time to develop the kind of prior record that demonstrates risk. It is not only difficult to develop an instrument that satisfactorily assesses risk in juveniles, but it also appears that instruments which work well in one jurisdiction do not necessarily transfer successfully to other jurisdictions (Clear and Gallagher, 1985).

This is not good news for JIPS. If a program is designed especially for the highest risks in the juvenile system, then an inability to locate those cases reliably is at the least disquieting. Many professionals are outraged when they read or hear such a statement. They believe they "know a dangerous juvenile when they see one," and they cling to this claim despite an overwhelming literature documenting the erroneous nature of such predictions. This false confidence is based on self-fulfilling prophesies. When professionals apply the JIPS program to the so-called "risky" juvenile, and when the juvenile then completes the program successfully, they reason that without JIPS this high-risk delinquent would never have made it. Should the juvenile fail, they reason, "of course the kid failed, he was a high risk." The person who classifies a case as high risk can thus escape any admission of erroneous judgment.

For many—if not most—JIPS programs, however, the reality is starker. Many juveniles who are wrongly labeled "high risk" and in need of close supervision are given a version of "toughened-up" probation or aftercare. The possibility exists that a tough JIPS program increases the stress on the mislabeled low-risk juveniles and therefore *increases* their chance of failure. This may be occurring in adult intensive programs (Erwin, 1984).

At the very least, there is a labeling effect for failures. A juvenile who technically violates JIPS is perceived in a different way, and is treated more harshly, than a juvenile who technically violates regular probation. If the juvenile was classified wrongly as a high risk in need of JIPS, this harsh reaction can be an injustice of major proportions. What appears to the decision maker as a "serious, high-risk juvenile offender who failed intensive probation," and is treated according to that label, may in reality be simply a moderate- to low-risk juvenile who reacted poorly to the pressures of surveillance.

There are other types of technical problems such as the ones that follow.

(1) The actual rate of reinvolvement in delinquency by juvenile offenders is quite low, on the order of 15% to 25% (Wolfgang et al., 1972). This is one of the reasons why accurate prediction is so difficult. Even when using valid assessment instruments, it is unusual to identify a group of juvenile offenders who have a greater than 50% chance of committing new, felonious behavior. To call a target group high risk when its true probability of harmful future conduct is less than 50% is to stretch the credibility of the term "high risk."

(2) Our incapacitative measures are fraught with problems, the greatest of which may be that application of an incapacitative measure is seldom neutral in its impact on a juvenile. Indeed, the more extreme versions of a measure may actually exacerbate the probability of harmful conduct. The short-term gain of incapacitation may be cancelled out by the long-term increases in

offending behavior owing to damage caused by intrusive, incapacitative interventions (Petersilia et al., 1986).

(3) The track record of treatment-based risk controls is meager, to say the least. Many of the most cherished programs in juvenile justice have been proven ineffective or even damaging when evaluated carefully (Finckenauer, 1984). When these treatment programs fail, the outcome is not simply neutral; it may be negative in its effect on the behavior of the juvenile (Adams, 1961; Warren, 1973).

(4) What we know about delinquent careers suggests that for the most active offender it is not realistic to expect to eradicate delinquency (Vachss and Bakal, 1979). Instead, intensive methods may be effective in hastening termination of the criminal career, but desistance from crime may not occur for five to ten years. In short, the effects of intensive methods may not be immediately evident, even if they are present for the high-risk juvenile.

In summary, despite a seemingly uniform desire to develop JIPS programming, the technical base for doing so is exceedingly weak. Unfortunately, this weak base underlies all aspects of programming, including research on prior programs, current techniques for treatment and incapacitation, and selection of those assigned to the program.

Being Realistic About The New JIPS Movement

This review is purposely pessimistic in response to an unprecedented—and largely unwarranted—optimism in the mid-1980s about the concept of JIPS. Frankly, the current JIPS wave sweeping the nation may end as ignominiously as its predecessor did two decades ago. Now, as then, our promises seem to outstrip our means, and our activities surpass our knowledge.

The possibility exists, of course, that we are on the verge of a whole new era of community supervision for both adult and juvenile offenders. If it occurs, unquestionably JIPS would have a role to play in such a shift. For too long we have conveniently ignored the valuable role that a range of community-based sanctions can play in a fully articulated correctional system.

The role of JIPS is not automatic; to simply "have" an intensive program is not enough. Assessment of the theory behind JIPS and examination of its rationale suggests a more careful definition of its use.

- JIPS is the most elaborate and powerful risk-control method that a community can apply, without incarceration, to juveniles.
- Success of JIPS is dependent upon successful identification of appropriate clients who represent the highest risks managed in the probation system.
- The technical base on which JIPS bases offender assessment to incapacitation and treatment is admittedly weak.
- The philosophical underpinning of JIPS is linked subtly to efficiency in formulating promises and careful delivery on these promises.

One final comment: In juvenile justice, the relationship between risk control and punishment is complicated. As most observers investigate the overall intrusiveness of an effective risk-control system, they will find its magnitude to be such that punishment interests in the case are diminished. In other words, once the risk posed by high-risk offenders is effectively controlled, there may be little or no need to add pain, harm or suffering as punishment. With JIPS, enough is enough.

REFERENCES

Adams, Stuart (1961). "Interaction between Individual Interview Therapy and Treatment Amenability in Older Youth Authority Wards." In *Inquiries Concerning Kinds of Treatments for Kinds of Delinquents*. Sacramento, CA: California Board of Corrections.

Administrative Office of the Courts of New Jersey (1984). *Manual for the Intensive Supervision Program*. Trenton, NJ.

Baird, Christopher S., G.M. Storrs and H. Connelly (1984). *Classification and Case Management for Juvenile Offenders: A Model Systems Approach*. Washington, DC: A.D. Little.

Banks, J., A.L. Porter, R.L. Rardin, T.R. Silver and V.E. Unger (1981). *Phase I Evaluation of Intensive Special Probation Projects*. Washington, DC: U.S. Department of Justice.

Bennett, Lawrence (1986). "How Effective Is Intensive Supervision?" Unpublished manuscript.

Byrne, James, Arthur Lurigio and Christopher S. Baird (1989). "The Effectiveness of Intensive Supervision in Probation." *Research in Corrections* 2 (2):1-75.

Clear, Todd R. and Kenneth W. Gallagher (1985). "Probation and Parole Supervision: A Review of Current Practices." *Crime & Delinquency* 31(3):423-443.

Erwin, Billie S. (1984). *Evaluation of Intensive Probation Supervision in Georgia*. Atlanta, GA: Department of Offender Rehabilitation (mimeo).

Feld, Barry C. (1981). "Juvenile Court Legislative Reform and the Serious Young Offender: Dismantling the 'Rehabilitative Ideal'." *Minnesota Law Review* 65(2):167-242.

Finckenauer, James O. (1984). *Juvenile Delinquency and Corrections: The Gap Between Theory and Practice*. Orlando, FL: Academic Press.

Gendreau, Paul and Robert Ross (1987). "Revivification of Rehabilitation: Evidence from the 1980's." *Justice Quarterly* 4(3):349-408.

—— (1980). *Effective Correctional Treatment*. Toronto: Butterworths.

Gottfredson, Stephen D. and Don M. Gottfredson (1985). "Prediction Techniques: An Assessment of Current Research." Paper prepared for the National Academy of Sciences Panel on Criminal Careers, Washington, DC.

Harris, M. Kay (1984). "Strategies, Values and the Emerging Generation of Alternatives to Incarceration." *Review of Law and Social Change* 7(1):141-170.

Krisberg, Barry and James Austin (1980). *The Unmet Promise of Alternatives to Incarceration*. San Francisco, CA: National Council on Crime and Delinquency (mimeo).

—— and Ira Schwartz (1983). "Rethinking Juvenile Justice." *Crime & Delinquency* 29 (3):333-364.

Meehl, Paul E. (1954). *Clinical vs Statistical Prediction*. Minneapolis, MN: University of Minnesota Press.

Neithercutt, M. and D.M. Gottfredson (1973). *Caseload Size Variation and Difference in Probation/Parole Performance*. Washington, DC: U.S. National Institute of Juvenile Justice.

Petersilia, Joan (1987). *Expanding Options for Criminal Sentencing*. Santa Monica, CA: Rand.

—— and Susan Turner (1989). "Expanding Effectiveness of Intensive Supervision: Six Month Follow-up of the BJA Experiments." Unpublished paper. Santa Monica, CA: Rand.

—— Susan Turner, and Joyce E. Peterson (1986). *Prison vs Probation in California: Implications for Crime and Offender Recidivism*. Santa Monica, CA: Rand.

Romig, Dennis (1986). "Juvenile Intensive Probation Supervision: The Defensible Basis." Paper presented at a symposium on Juvenile Intensive Probation Supervision, Minneapolis, MN.

Vachss, A.H. and Y. Bakal (1979). *The Life-Style Violent Juvenile*. Lexington, MA: Lexington.

Van den Haag, Ernest (1976). *Preventing Crime: On an Old and Painful Question*. New York, NY: Basic Books.

Warren, Marguerite Q. (1973). "All Things Being Equal..." *Criminal Law Bulletin* 9(2):483-502.

Wolfgang, Marvin E., Robert M. Figlio, and Thorsten Sellin. (1972). *Delinquency in a Birth Cohort*. Chicago, IL: University of Chicago Press.

Intensive Aftercare for the High-Risk Juvenile Parolee: Issues and Approaches in Reintegration and Community Supervision

by
David M. Altschuler
Troy L. Armstrong

Intensive, community-based parole for high-risk juvenile offenders released from secure correctional confinement is the focus of an ongoing research and development project sponsored by the U.S. Office of Juvenile Justice and Delinquency Prevention. Based on a comprehensive literature review, a national mail survey of juvenile corrections and parole officials, telephone interviews with the directors of recommended programs, and on-site fact-finding at 23 programs in 6 states, a framework has been developed to guide the design and implementation of intensive, community-based program models. The framework includes: (1) five underlying principles of programmatic action; (2) three program elements essential to the translation from theory and principles to actual implementation; and (3) 10 areas of concrete service provision. The principles embody the framework's assumptions, which were derived from an integrated theory addressing the multiple causes of, and behavior-change strategies associated with, recidivism. The three program elements include: (1) "enabling" organizational characteristics; (2) continuous case management (assessment and classification, individual case planning, incentives and graduated consequences, surveillance-service mix, and brokerage and community linkages); and (3) management information and program evaluation. Establishing realistic conditions of parole, and responding swiftly but proportionately to rule infractions and technical parole violations, are additional key considerations.

It is both unfortunate and ironic that the one area of juvenile corrections that should receive the greatest emphasis and attention frequently ends up being short-shrifted at best and ignored or entirely forgotten at worst. The community-based aftercare or parole phase of corrections represents one of the most critical points in justice system processing. This is when the supposedly beneficial cumulative effects of the institutional experience should be transferred to community settings, reinforced, monitored and assessed. Particularly in the case of the chronic/serious juvenile offender who has been released from secure confinement and may be at high risk for reoffending, the intensification of community-based aftercare may well increase the likelihood of a youth remaining crime-free. The problem, however, is that for a variety of reasons juvenile aftercare is largely a wasteland within the larger juvenile justice system.

The neglect of juvenile aftercare has, in part, been fueled by strong pressures from many quarters—the public-at-large, legislatures and state executives, and segments of the correctional community itself—to direct primary attention and the limited available resources to other aspects of the overall correctional process. The outcry for harsher sanctions and punishment over the past ten years has led to a variety of changes in the way the juvenile justice system operates. These changes include: (1) reduced judicial discretion; (2) determinate sentencing involving mandatory correctional confinement for certain prescribed offenses (e.g., drug trafficking, violent crimes involving a firearm) and offenders (e.g., chronic); (3) automatic waiver of juveniles charged with certain crimes to criminal court jurisdiction; and (4) lowering the age at which all young offenders come under the jurisdiction of criminal courts. The overall result in many states has been a tendency to lock up more and more juveniles for longer periods.

Eventually, however, these securely confined juvenile offenders are released. When this happens, they enter an already overburdened juvenile aftercare system that has historically been assigned low priority in the competition for scarce resources. The fact of the matter is that recidivism rates of released youths are alarmingly high. Further, recent changes in commitment policies have exacerbated the serious overcrowding problem already present in many juvenile correctional institutions, thereby greatly reducing the possibility of meaningful treatment in these settings. Moreover, the costs of institutionalization are prohibitively expensive.

Responding to these concerns, the U.S. Office of Juvenile Justice and Delinquency Prevention (OJJDP) in the Department of Justice issued a request for proposals entitled "Intensive Community-Based Aftercare Programs" in

July 1987. The research and development initiative was designed to assess, develop, test and disseminate information on intensive community-based aftercare prototypes/models for chronic serious juvenile offenders released from secure confinement. The project is viewed by OJJDP as one means to assist public and private correction agencies in developing, implementing and evaluating innovative and promising programs. OJJDP has been explicit in stating its intended goals:

> Effective aftercare programs focused on serious offenders which provide intensive supervision to ensure public safety, and services designed to facilitate the reintegration process may allow some offenders to be released earlier, as well as reduce recidivism among offenders released from residential facilities. This should relieve institutional overcrowding, reduce the costs of supervising juvenile offenders, and ultimately decrease the number of juveniles who develop lengthy delinquent careers and often become the core of the adult criminal population [*Federal Register* 52(133):26238-26239, 1987].

The Johns Hopkins University's Institute for Policy Studies, in collaboration with the Division of Criminal Justice, California State University at Sacramento, was funded to conduct the multistaged project. Thus far, the researchers have completed: (1) a comprehensive literature review focused on research, theory and programs; (2) a national mail survey of juvenile corrections and parole officials intended to identify innovative or promising programs and approaches; (3) telephone interviews with the directors of 36 recommended programs; and (4) on-site fact-finding at 23 different programs spread across six states, including three statewide systems. Based on this completed work, the researchers have been developing an empirically based, theory-driven framework to guide the development, design and implementation of intensive community-based aftercare program models.

The chapter, a summary of work completed to date, examines the following concerns:

(1) Identification and review of key topics and issues in juvenile intensive aftercare, including definitional considerations, target populations, assessment and classification for risk and need, and theory-driven program interventions; and,

(2) Development of an intervention model for juvenile intensive aftercare encompassing the following features: the integration of social control, strain, and social learning theories; five underlying principles for programmatic action; three program elements and five sub-elements; and ten service areas.

OVERVIEW

A dismal record has been compiled by the correctional field in its effort to reduce the recidivism rate of juvenile offenders released from secure, correctional confinement. This failure appears to occur disproportionately with a subgroup of institutionalized juvenile offenders who have established a long record of criminal misconduct that began at an early age. This subpopulation has been identified and tracked repeatedly over the past 15 years in a series of youth cohort studies (Wolfgang et al., 1972; Farrington and West, 1977; Hamparian et al., 1978; Shannon, 1978; McCord, 1979), revealing a persistent pattern of intense and serious delinquent activity. Not surprisingly, substantial numbers of this high-risk group are plagued by a multitude of problems. They have not only engaged in frequent criminal acts against persons and property, but also experience a variety of emotional and interpersonal problems, some accompanied by physical health problems. Most come from family settings characterized by high levels of violence, chaos and dysfunction; many are engaged in excessive alcohol and drug consumption and abuse; and a substantial proportion have become chronically truant or have dropped out of school altogether.

It appears that any effort to lower rates of recidivism with serious and chronic juvenile offenders must entail a substantial intensification of intervention strategies focusing upon these problem areas. It follows logically that strategies for intervention should concentrate on the development of specially-designed programs and procedures that: systematically target high-risk parolees for participation; provide highly structured supervision and control; carefully monitor performance in the community; and ensure the delivery of a wide variety of essential services.

While aftercare services to date have not generally been influenced by major innovation, important new insights about youth crime have emerged over the last decade. For example, the recognition of the existence of a small, criminally active subpopulation of chronic serious delinquents has provided a new way of looking at the overall problems of youth crime and its impact on American society (Wolfgang et al., 1972; Mann, 1976; Hamparian et al., 1978; Zimring, 1978, 1979; Smith et al., 1979; McDermott and Joppich, 1980; Vachss, 1981; Altschuler and Armstrong, 1984, 1982a; Fagan and Hartstone, 1984; Fagan and Jones, 1984). The need to identify and respond appropriately to this category of youthful offenders has, in turn, led to a major rethinking of how the juvenile justice system should be structured and operated, both in terms of philosophy and practice. Among researchers and practitioners alike, this realization has created a sense of urgency to develop and implement specially-designed intensive programs whose goals include the closely supervised reentry of this population into the community, accompanied by sufficient service and support to ensure a reasonable level of community protection and public safety.

One of the common problems besetting the aftercare practitioner has been the difficulty of supervising the offender's transitional experience, which entails moving from the closely monitored and highly regimented life in a secure correctional facility to the relatively unstructured and often confusing life in the community. The inability of correctional personnel (institutional and aftercare workers) to coordinate activities and provide continuity of service and supervision from institutional confinement to community living has long plagued efforts to achieve successful community adjustment for offenders. Further, recognizing the multifaceted needs and problems of youth in correctional programs leads to the realization that aftercare field staff and community social institutions must be directly involved with correctional facility staff. The key challenge is determining how to create and bolster the partnership, as well as how to maintain and institutionalize it.

Recommendations for improved communication, shared decision making, coordinated planning and clear lines of authority are certainly not new and have been made numerous times. Unfortunately, however, these recommendations have met with only a modicum of success (Nelson et al., 1978). Part of the problem is that because of numerous difficulties—such as funding limitations, bureaucratic and professional intransigence and turf battling, understaffing and inefficient deployment of existing staff, community fears and resistance, inadequate or nonexistent community resources—juvenile parole agencies, correctional facilities and community-based social institutions have been unable and/or unwilling to enter into an actively functioning, working partnership. A new commitment toward jointly planned and funded aftercare that includes a high level of quality control and monitoring is clearly needed.

DEFINITIONAL ISSUES

The recent rapid spread of a nationwide juvenile intensive probation supervision movement (JIPS) has important implications for the design and operation of juvenile intensive aftercare programs (see chapters in this volume by Armstrong, Clear, Wiebush and Hamparian; also, Steenson, 1986). Although grounded largely in notions of enhanced surveillance and heightened social control over offenders being maintained in the community, JIPS has taken a variety of forms incorporating combinations of intensified surveillance and monitoring coupled with highly specialized treatment modalities and supportive service provision.

Broadly speaking, intensive aftercare can be conceived as operating in two major ways. First, it can be defined in the context of decision making and planning for the *early release* of juveniles from secure confinement. Generally, this strategy is generated either by a desire to reduce an institution's total population (downsizing) or by the need to make room for other offenders for whom secure correctional confinement is deemed appropriate. In either case, the strategy entails selectively targeting certain categories of youth within the institutional population that, based upon some judgment or form of risk scaling, are determined to pose the least threat to the community (Bakal and Krisberg, 1987).

If the decision is made to utilize intensive supervision with this population, enhanced risk management in the community ends up being employed with a population that may not, in fact, constitute the "highest risk" group. Further, the intensification of control with this group, as will be discussed below, holds the possibility of exacerbating the potential for recidivism. Consequently, rather than relying on intensive aftercare supervision, this population might be more effectively managed by placement on regular juvenile parole caseloads.

In contrast, the second form of intensive aftercare derives from the idea of imposing higher levels of supervision on youth being released after serving a *full institutional term*. The central purpose underlying this strategy is to aid in a smoother transition into the community and thereby lower the probability of recidivism. Two significant variations in this form of intensive aftercare can be found. The first variation arises when a decision is made to initially place *all youth* reentering the community on a special intensive supervision status. This is a reflection of the belief that the first few months of release pose the greatest hazard for recurrence of criminal misconduct for all parolees. The second variation occurs when a decision is made to *target selectively* certain youth for inclusion in specially-designed intensive aftercare programs. This selection process is usually based on some form of risk- and/or need-assessment scaling that identifies these individuals as members of particular subgroups posing the greatest likelihood of reoffending once returned to the community.

It is important to note that certain groups of youth may be classified or identified during their correctional confinement as exhibiting some major problem (e.g., attention deficit disorder), or as having been committed for some particularly serious offense (e.g., a sex crime) requiring a specialized intervention strategy. Here, logic dictates that if a specialized institution-based program or approach is to have relevance for intensive aftercare, then intensive aftercare should represent either the introduction or the intensification of specialized service provision, which may or may not be accompanied by intensive surveillance.

Depending upon the way in which intensive aftercare is conceptualized, three very different populations can be targeted: medium- to low-risk parolees, all parolees, and high-risk parolees. This range of options on who participates can have significant implications for the design and operation of the program with regard to risk management and other provided services. If there were unlimited resources, or if very few juvenile offenders were held in secure correctional facilities, corrections and parole officials might be tempted to "go for broke" and include all confined juveniles in an intensive aftercare program. Even under these circumstances, however, research and experience elsewhere (Clear, 1988a; Jackson, 1982; Petersilia et al., 1977; Zimring and Hawkins, 1973) strongly suggest that those securely confined offenders who would not ordinarily be expected to engage in further criminal activity may end up doing worse when subjected to intensive supervision. Though it is not clear exactly how this occurs, a number of possibilities have been raised.

Overloading an individual with a long list of conditions, requirements and restrictions accompanied by stringent and frequent surveillance may increase the likelihood of future misconduct and detection, particularly for technical violations of parole. Or, low-risk parolees (i.e., those predicted to have subsequent low rates of recidivism) may react negatively to what they perceive as excessively harsh and unwarranted levels of supervision. Given these possibilities, intensive aftercare status could be a disincentive to the development of responsible, law-abiding behavior. Therefore, great care should be exercised in determining which offenders to target and what the possible repercussions may be.

A case in point is the use of electronic monitoring, where the tendency for overreliance and abuse of the technology is always present (Clear, 1988b; Armstrong et al., 1987; Vaughn, this volume). One of the substantial dangers is that sustained use may result in an extraordinarily high level of technical violations of parole and subsequent revocations. This could obviously have the unintended consequence of aggravating the institutional overcrowding problem rather than helping to solve it. Thus, it may well be advisable to regard technical infractions of parole conditions as early warning signals rather than grounds for revocation. Moreover, this also suggests the virtue of structuring the entry point in an intensive aftercare program at a mid-range of restrictiveness and intrusiveness, initially relying on the imposition of only several *enforceable* conditions to which the offender will be held accountable.

Relying on several carefully chosen parole conditions that bear some relation to what the offender specifically needs and that can be realistically enforced holds the potential for being taken far more seriously by offenders than does a laundry list of conditions. Simply stated, assigning offenders large numbers of conditions and restrictions, many of which are virtually meaningless to both the parolee and supervising officer, is of questionable value and may be counterproductive. Since many of the conditions are simply not enforceable, the result is that the conditions are frequently not taken seriously and the credibility of the entire parole system is thereby undermined.

TARGET POPULATION

The development and implementation of an intensive juvenile aftercare program requires a decision about which youth in secure confinement should be eligible for intensive aftercare. A prime target for special, more intensive handling throughout their contact with the juvenile justice system is the "serious" juvenile offender. Over the past two decades, increasing attention has been directed toward the growing problem posed by this category of adolescent offenders, defined in terms of both the chronicity and the severity of their behavior. This troubling trend in American delinquency is graphically illustrated by the fact that between 1960 and 1975 juvenile arrests for violent crime rose more than 290% (Strasburg, 1978:13). By the mid-1980s, official crime statistics (U.S. Federal Bureau of Investigation, 1984, 1985, 1986) revealed that juveniles under the age of 18 were responsible for slightly more than 25% of all arrests for violent crime (i.e., murder, rape, aggravated assault, robbery and arson), although this age group represented less than 15% of the total U.S. population.

From the perspective of crime control and reduction, this population of serious juvenile offenders is a source of great concern for both the justice system and the larger society, not so much because of its chronic violence but because of the persistence and pervasiveness of its illegal acts across a broad range of crime, violent *and* nonviolent. Research (Wolfgang et al., 1972; Hamparian et al., 1978; Shannon, 1978; McCord, 1979) has clearly demonstrated the existence and impact of chronically violent juvenile offenders, who represent a very small percentage of the juvenile offender population. More important, however, is the insight that juvenile criminal violence should most accurately be viewed not as the central problem facing the juvenile justice system but as an indicator of a more pervasive problem—a serious antisocial orientation that is manifested in a wide spectrum of continued criminal behavior (Bleich, 1987).

The key point is that those juvenile offenders who may have been disposed to commit a number of violent acts appear to be even more inclined to commit a multiplicity of other nonviolent antisocial and criminal acts. In addition, research on the effectiveness of programs for chronic juvenile offenders has shown that these high-rate offenders often exhibit a qualitatively different response to "traditional" treatment and are uniquely resistant to "conventional" rehabilitation programs (Coates, 1984; Gadow and McKibbon, 1984; Agee, 1979). Regardless of intervention strategy, substantial numbers within this serious offender population display subsequent behavior marked by frequent criminal offenses, often occurring at a faster rate once they have experienced secure confinement. Based upon such findings, many professionals in the field are calling for new approaches that stress higher levels of supervision, surveillance and treatment.

Another population of juvenile offenders that may be an excellent candidate for special, more intensive intervention is the group of delinquents that exhibit particular problems and needs requiring highly specialized treatment. This categorization tends to include a number of emotional, cognitive and other developmental problem areas that hinder normal psychological, social, intellectual and career development. The central issue is that these youths have a poor prognosis for successful community reintegration and adjustment, unless their special problems are responded to in the appropriate fashion through specialized programming and service provision. Very often, these youths are multiproblem individuals who are plagued by the presence of numerous disabling factors. Further, these deficits can coincide with violent and chronic delinquent behaviors, thereby posing a more complex problem.

The set of special-needs subpopulations currently receiving increased attention in the juvenile correctional system includes youth who are emotionally disturbed/mentally disordered, learning disabled, developmentally disabled, and drug and alcohol-dependent.

ASSESSMENT AND CLASSIFICATION FOR RISK AND NEED

One common source of confusion in conducting risk assessment is the lack of clarity in distinguishing between crime seriousness and the risk of future criminal activity. Prediction research has repeatedly shown (Clear, 1988a; Jackson, 1982; Petersilia et al., 1977; Zimring and Hawkins, 1973) that the relationship between the seriousness of the current offense and the likelihood of committing future offenses is extremely weak if not inverse. Consequently, the inclusion of a youth who has only committed one serious offense into a risk-based aftercare program may well be regarded as a misuse of risk-based aftercare. Inclusion of such offenders also may mean that intensive aftercare is being used to maintain punishment and control for the purposes of satisfying the public. This, of course, can undermine the risk-minimization goal. The reason is that if intensive aftercare takes on more and more of a punishment orientation, it may dilute the reintegrative and normalizing efforts designed primarily to impact high-risk offenders.

Accumulating evidence, as noted, suggests that subjecting low-risk offenders to intensive supervision practices may increase the chances of failure. Should this occur, the effect may well be to make the very problem that intensive aftercare was in part intended to solve—overcrowding—even worse. It should also be emphasized that to the extent that the seriousness of the current offense is part of a larger pattern of misconduct, particularly prior violent behavior, then including such offenders into a risk-based aftercare program does not violate the assumptions about risk that underlie risk-based aftercare approaches.

In short, widespread interest across the country in standardized formal risk assessment can be viewed as a positive step that may help to determine: (1) which offenders should receive aftercare supervision priority; (2) how many levels of supervision are needed; (3) what the contact standards should entail; (4) which cut-off scores should be used to designate how many cases can be realistically handled by parole officers; (5) and how aftercare resources—including field staff—can be allocated and deployed in the most effective and efficient fashion. A more formalized assessment and classification process could also help in developing consistency and equity in aftercare decision making.

In structuring decision making about which individuals to release from secure confinement, at what times, at what levels of restrictiveness, with which forms of supervision to impose upon their movement in the community, and with what kinds of service provision and other conditions of parole, it is incumbent upon correctional officials to determine which factors, or clusters of factors, characterize those offenders who are most prone toward reoffending. This determination has long been a major concern for correctional administrators, researchers and planners. Whether consciously acknowledged or not, juvenile parole officers are in one way or another making decisions about which youths on their caseload will be dealt with to a greater and lesser degree. The principal issue, then, is not really whether some form of classification is being performed, but how it's being performed: whether classification is part of a structured and systematically planned process; how grounded it is in agency practices, local laws, confinement policies and community conditions; and to what extent the offenders who are most likely to recidivate are in fact being correctly identified. The central task in bringing a reasonable level of precision and logic to this decision-making process is to identify those features and characteristics of offenders that allow us to predict, with an acceptable degree of confidence, what kinds of behaviors to expect once they are released into the community.

The identification of risk factors and the assessment of their predictive power must be carefully placed within a context of what kinds of future behaviors are being examined. This variation in targeted behavior can range from the risk of committing violent acts or other types of new offense, to the risk of a designated violation of probation or parole conditions. The accuracy with which these different kinds of behavior can be predicted varies tremendously. Obviously, specific predictions of particular kinds of serious crimes (violence) are much more difficult to make than are more general predictions (recidivism). For example, the prediction of future violence is notoriously difficult to achieve without generating a high rate of accompanying "false positives." A number of studies have identified accurate predictors of chronic juvenile violence (Polk and Schaefer, 1972; Wolfgang et al., 1972; Hamparian et al., 1978; Strasburg, 1978; Lefkowitz, 1980; Shannon, 1980). However, when the results of these studies are compared, conflicting claims remain about the nature and predictive power of specific variables.

A major development in the application of predictive schemes with juvenile offender populations has been the emergence of formal assessment scales and instruments to aid in decision making related to caseload management and supervision, as well as to guide decisions about institutional release and community placement. As the public demand for greater offender accountability and higher levels of community protection increased during the 1980s, there was a substantial rise in the use of classification to assign offenders to the proper level of supervision.

Quantitative assessment instruments have demonstrated a reasonable degree of accuracy in estimating risk levels for aggregated juvenile offender populations. In contrast to adult offenders, devising valid scales for juveniles is certainly complicated by the fact that, in maturational terms, youth are more often volatile and impulsive, more often experience rapidly changing personal circumstances and needs, and are less likely to develop long-standing patterns of behavior and habits on which to predict future misconduct. However, there is considerable similarity among the more successful scales regardless of where they were designed and tested (Baird et al., 1984). The better scales generally contain some combination of features related to prior delinquent history, emotional stability, substance abuse and employment or school performance. Studies conducted in a number of states show that prior delinquency history indices that include such items as age at first adjudication, number of prior adjudications, and number of prior commitments are the best predictors of future delinquent behavior (Baird, 1973, 1990; Baird et al., 1979; Wenk, 1975; Wenk and Emrich, 1972). These same studies indicate that drug usage and emotional stability variables increased the overall predictive efficiency of the scales.

In a review summarizing the results of a large body of prior research efforts in the development of risk-assessment instruments with juvenile parolees, Baird et al. (1984:16) stated that the following variables appear to be universally predictive of continued criminal involvement for juveniles:

1) age of first adjudication,
2) prior delinquent behavior (combined measure of number and severity of priors),
3) number of prior commitments to juvenile facilities,
4) drug/chemical abuse,
5) alcohol abuse,
6) family relationships (parental control),
7) school problems, and
8) peer relationships.

In bringing closure to the discussion of risk factors and their ability to provide greater understanding of the proneness of certain delinquent youth to reoffend, it is crucial to suggest how this information can best be linked to the design and implementation of intervention strategies. As Catalano et al., (n.d.:28) have insightfully observed, "The factors which increase risk of a return to...delinquency provide a catalog of factors to address, but do not provide an approach which links these factors together in a way that has implications for intervention." As suggested above, key assumptions must be identified and delineated in such a way as to show how particular risk factors, or risk-factor clusters, are associated with the causal antecedents and correlates of delinquent behavior. These critical intersections of theoretical formulation and risk must then be combined into an integrative framework that provides the most powerful explanation of how risk in various forms and under different circumstances lends itself to reoffending behavior. In this way, it will be possible to begin specifying the most promising theory-driven components, procedures and processes for intervention that address the identified risk factors.

PROGRAMMING IMPLICATIONS AND THEORY-DRIVEN INTERVENTION

Significant in the discussion of definitional issues and implications for goals and objectives is the question of what it takes programmatically to achieve the required level of supervision and service provision for high-risk juvenile parolees. The answer, it can be argued, is grounded in the research and program experiences that occurred with the philosophical shift toward community-based corrections and reintegrative approaches. Much of the current insight about reintegration and aftercare is drawn from the movement to expand and improve upon non-custodial correctional alternatives that were most prevalent during the 1960s and 1970s. Some of the approaches and techniques that proved useful in diverting offenders from secure confinement are, in fact, prime candidates for transferability to aftercare settings. For example, the introduction of innovations into the institutional system and the community-based alternatives network in earlier years had been characterized by such developments as:

1) the involvement of private agencies and citizens, as well as non-correctional public agencies in the community corrections process through the use of both volunteers and paraprofessionals and through purchase-of-service agreements;

2) a concomitant adoption of a new stance by the community corrections agency, which stresses resource brokerage and advocacy rather than direct delivery of all services to offenders;

3) the development of specific techniques, such as team supervision and drug/alcohol testing, to assure higher levels of surveillance and control over high-risk parolees; and

4) the development of classification procedures to gauge likeliness to commit crime in the future and to assess service needs as a way both of matching individual offenders with appropriate correctional responses and of optimizing the use of scarce correctional resources.

What seems eminently clear is that aftercare directly addresses two of the widely acknowledged deficiencies of the current system's focus on punishment and incapacitation: (1) that institutional confinement does not adequately prepare youth for return to the community and (2) that those lessons and skills learned while in secure confinement are not reinforced outside the institution. These difficulties are regularly discussed in the correctional field as primarily relating to that brief, initial period of community readjustment (three to six months following release) when a disproportionate amount of failure occurs (Irvin, 1970; MacArthur, 1974; Jackson, 1982). It therefore seems obvious that a key to aftercare success (i.e., a lowered rate of recidivism) is the discovery of ways to create supports and reinforcement in the community setting, as well as to monitor early signs of deterioration in behavior and overall community adjustment.

An exploration of ways to increase the chances of aftercare success, however, must go beyond the identification of new and innovative procedures for more intensely structuring supervision and surveillance. Advances in the technology of control will, unquestionably, be a vital part in the design of any intensive aftercare program, but will not likely by themselves provide the answers. Since it is generally agreed that large numbers of delinquents processed through the system to the stage of institutional confinement have experienced high levels of social, emotional and environmental deprivation and, in fact, demonstrate maturationally arrested development at early stages in their psychosocial development (Strasburg, 1978; Taylor, 1980; Altschuler and Armstrong, 1983), aftercare for chronic juvenile offenders is likely to entail a wide array of services.

The common kinds of problems and deprivations faced by many of these youths draw attention to the importance of working on those areas and life skills that can provide youths with an opportunity to develop those competencies necessary for survival in the community. Thus, beyond dealing with psychosocial difficulties, family and peer group pressures, and problems involving substance abuse, some of these other elements might include: a focus on job search skills and vocational training, the development of social and educational competency, the opportunity to access meaningful employment, and the development of supports within existing or newly developed social networks.

In the face of the obstacles and demands currently confronting the aftercare system, there is no doubt that an accelerated search must be launched for acceptable and effective approaches to community reintegration that address the set of disparate goals characterizing the contemporary correctional field. These goals must then be operationalized and integrated into a coherent intensive program model that can contribute to a safe, well-run, fair and cost-effective juvenile aftercare system. In general terms, successful intensive aftercare programs must be driven by four primary goals: (1) increased community protection, (2) enhanced offender accountability, (3) improved service provision/competency development, and (4) reinforcement of positive community linkages or establishment of positive linkages where none exist.

Theory-Driven Interventions and Integrated Perspectives

Efforts to develop more refined theory-driven programming approaches involving the integration of existing theories have largely taken place over the past ten years. "Integrated" theories combine formerly free-standing theories into a number of new intervention paradigms. The integrated reformulations are an extremely important development because of the increasingly recognized fact that a contributing source of past failures of correctional programs has been the reliance on narrow, unicausal theories of delinquency (Fagan and Jones, 1984; Greenwood and Zimring, 1985; Meier, 1985; Ferdinand, 1987).

Even more problematic is the fact that major deficiencies and misdirections in both past and present intervention strategies are, in part, the result of the relative lack of connection between theory and practice.

To a considerable extent, theory and practice have developed and evolved independently of each other. As a consequence of this insularity, theory has in many cases not benefited from the innovation and creativity spawned by practice. Conversely, practice has not been driven by a clear, logical and consistent explanation that makes explicit why and how particular delinquency- and recidivism-reduction strategies should be pursued at all. Theoretically grounded practice, however, can provide an essential framework and referent for helping practitioners, researchers, and policymakers alike to interpret and understand how the fundamental aspects of intervention strategies contribute to successful programs. These concerns focus upon:

1) a program's basic value assumptions about the nature of delinquent behavior;
2) the view of delinquency causation and change that underlies the model or strategy embraced by a program and its implications for why we expect a particular approach to work;
3) major principles and tenets on which the intervention rests;
4) degree of client change sought and the range of client attributes targeted for attention; and
5) specific program components, features, and processes that characterize the day-to-day program experience for participants and staff.

One problem that has hindered the linkage of theory and practice has been the inability of any of the individual theoretical paradigms to adequately explain the complex, multifaceted nature of delinquency and recidivism. In turn, it has been impossible to rely entirely upon the set of linked propositions contained in any one theory to develop fully satisfactory intervention principles and implementable program elements. The long-standing search for causes of crime and delinquency (and thus suggestions for appropriate strategies for their reduction) has led to the formulation of a number of wide-ranging frameworks, including those related to personality, learning processes, social class, poverty and economic inequality, anomie, social bonding, cultural deviance, biology, and social structure and opportunity.

Among theories most applicable to chronic and serious delinquency, the most prominently discussed include control, strain, social learning, cultural deviance, differential association, labeling, and various integrations that combine a number of these. Rather than being in irreconcilable conflict, a number of the classic theories may be essentially addressing different aspects of a complex and multifaceted problem. Moreover, some of these theories have undergone revision as new thinking has spurred various reformulations. In addition, some of the theories may well be more or less applicable to unique or special-needs populations.

Attempts to integrate theoretical frameworks have largely centered on various combinations of social control, strain and social learning theories. The integrated models can be viewed as an important advance since, as noted above, the previous tendency to rely on narrow, unicausal theories of delinquency is considered by many to be a major contributing factor to the past failure of numerous delinquency programs.

As early proponents of integrated theory, Weis and Hawkins (1981) argued that such a step was crucial in developing explanatory models since collectively these theories can compensate for major deficiencies in the individual formulations, thereby generating more comprehensive and valid explanations of delinquent behavior. Other efforts to develop integrated theory approaches have been made by Elliott and Voss (1974), Conger (1976), Elliott et al., (1979, 1985), and U.S. Office of Juvenile Justice and Delinquency Prevention (1981). These integrated approaches can be likened to a grafting process whereby multiple theories are carefully connected together to more fully explain delinquency than is possible through the use of any single theory. For example, the criticism that a motivational element is absent in control theory is addressed when the motivational element integral to strain and social learning theory is introduced.

The integration of strain, control and social learning theories is particularly appealing since recent research suggests that the explanatory power of this integrated model is quite high and that the relationships between theoretical variables in the model are relatively stable. The initial attempt to combine these three theories was undertaken by Elliott et al. (1979). This particular integration was also used to formulate the community reintegration model used in the OJJDP Violent Juvenile Offender Initiative. In short, based on the various risk factors associated with recidivism and the comprehensive nature of what is needed in a system of intensive community-based aftercare, a strong case can be made for combining these same three theories into an integrated model guiding the development of intensive community-based aftercare for chronic and serious juvenile offenders.

INTEGRATED THEORY AND ITS IMPLICATION FOR INTENSIVE AFTERCARE

A more all-encompassing conceptual framework that takes into account both psychological and sociological explanations of delinquency, as well as individual and environmental factors, is established when strain, control and social learning theories are combined into a single integrated model. The strength of such a formulation is that each of the theories contributes a particular perspective and mode of reasoning, thereby deepening our understanding of the various causal and behavior-change processes involved.

Efforts to integrate the strands from various theoretical traditions often generate opposition and criticism. Theory integration is not equivalent to taking one free-standing theory in its totality and simply tacking it on to others; rather, modification must be achieved through selectively choosing certain propositions from the appropriate theories and then recombining them to produce more powerful explanatory frameworks. The key is to logically graft together those aspects of theories that take into account and—in theory, at least—best explain the causes, correlates and change relevant to chronic, serious delinquency in general and recidivism in particular.

Control Theory and Intensive Aftercare. Control theory has biological, psychodynamic and psychosocial formulations, but in its most widely cited version (Hirschi, 1969) the theory suggests that a failure in socialization and bonding to prosocial values and activities is the chief causal factor in delinquency. While control theory generally asserts that all youngsters have frustrated wants and unfulfilled needs (i.e., constant strain), the critical element is the strength of social controls that serve to regulate behavior and restrain the impulse toward delinquent behavior. These controls involve rewards and punishments that result from one's behavior; such controls may be either personal (internal and invoked by the individual), or social (external controls provided by others). Control theory places particular importance on the role of socialization units in determining delinquent behavior. This focus on socialization units and on elements that bond an individual to society—attachment, affection, and sensitivity to others; commitment to conformity and conventional society; involvement in conventional activities; and belief in the legitimacy and moral validity of the law—justifies the inclusion of control theory into an integrated model of intensive, community-based aftercare.

A major criticism is that pure control theory lacks a motivational dimension. In short, the theory assumes that youths will become delinquent unless social bonds prevent this from occurring. The problem is the postulate that delinquency is naturally motivated and that there are essentially no external pressures generating this deviant behavior (Vold and Bernard, 1986). Just because youth who are not tied by social bonds could become delinquent does not explain why they would do so; there is a difference between a conducive factor, which permits behavior, and a generative factor, which pushes people towards a particular act (Box, 1987). The key point is that *many weakly bonded youngsters do not become delinquent.*

Strain Theory and Intensive Aftercare. This formulation was first set forth in the work of Albert Cohen (1955) and later adapted in a modified form by Cloward and Ohlin (1960). It asserts that delinquency, notably the subcultural variety found in lower-class adolescent males, largely results from blocked opportunities for conformity. From this perspective, delinquency is a response to actual or anticipated failure to fulfill societally induced needs and to meet societally accepted goals and aspirations through conventional channels. Elliott and Voss (1974) expanded the premise to postulate that the goal/opportunity disjunction, which provided the motivation for delinquency, could also be found in middle-class youth, who were just as likely to aspire beyond their means as were lower-class youth. As a result, delinquency can be seen as a youth's reprisal against the perceived causes of the frustration, or it can provide the means to achieve goals through antisocial and illegal conduct. Viewed in this way, strain theory can be used to explain how youth become alienated from societally sanctioned conventional modes of conduct and why such youth may rebel. Among strain theory's implications for intervention are the need for social reforms directed at education, employment, community empowerment, discrimination, and poverty.

Social Learning Theory and Intensive Aftercare. Social learning theory explicitly recognizes the influence that both conventional *and* deviant socializing groups—particularly peers—and activities can have upon behavior. In addition to emphasizing the importance of the delinquent adolescent peer group in the initiation and reinforcement of delinquent behavior, social learning theory also focuses directly on the process whereby youths are socialized into delinquency. Since delinquency is learned and maintained in much the same way as is conforming behavior, it is logical to assume that efforts focused to develop and positively reinforce bonds to conventional groups and activities are critical. Social learning theory suggests that reinforcement contingencies operate within the web of social relationships (Akers et al., 1979). It is such contingencies that determine whether a youth learns conforming or delinquent behavior. Differential involvement with others who are reinforcing either conventional or delinquent behavior can substantially affect whether or not a youngster will be delinquent and whether he or she will persist in this behavior.

Figure 1: Integrated Control–Strain–Social Learning Model

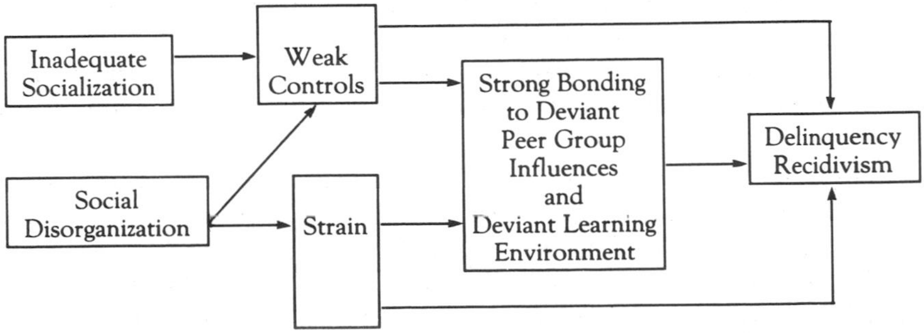

Inadequate Socialization
Weak Controls
Strong Bonding to Deviant Peer Group Influences and Deviant Learning Environment
Delinquency Recidivism
Social Disorganization
Strain

Theoretically Derived Principles of Programmatic Action

The proposed integrated model postulates that serious, chronic delinquency in general, and recidivism of juvenile parolees in particular, are substantially related to: (1) weak controls produced by inadequate socialization, social disorganization and strain; (2) strain, which can have a direct effect on delinquency quite independent of weak controls and which is also produced by social disorganization; and (3) peer group influences, which serve as an intervening social force between a youth with weak bonds and/or strain on the one hand, and delinquent behavior on the other (see Figure 1).

The pathways by which these social forces and circumstances produce delinquency or recidivism are multiple. That is, while in some cases the effect of strain on delinquency may be mediated by weak controls as well as by the normative orientation of the groups to which a youth is bonded, in other cases strain or bonding to delinquent groups may have a direct and independent effect on delinquency. What is most important about the integrated model is its presupposition that the joint occurrence of strain, weak controls by conventional groups, and strong bonds to delinquent groups produces a greater probability of delinquency or recidivism than does any of the three theories alone.

The integrated model as outlined above thus provided an empirically informed theoretical base that guided the selection of five underlying principles of programmatic action for successful intensive aftercare. These principles are:

1. preparing youth for progressively increased responsibility and freedom in the community;
2. facilitating youth-community interaction and involvement;
3. working with both the offender and targeted community support systems (e.g, families, peers, schools, employers) on qualities needed for constructive interaction and the youths' successful community adjustment;
4. developing new resources and supports where needed; and
5. monitoring and testing the youths and the community on their ability to deal with each other productively.

These principles, in turn, lead directly to the specification of three major program elements, five sub-elements, and ten types of service (see Figure 2).

The five principles are derived directly from the integration of the three key theories, and they specify a set of goals through which program elements and specific services can be identified. As such, the principles set the stage for the delineation of particular models of operation, which may include a variety of different program components, features and processes. The principles are described below, with specific reference to their derivations from the integrated model.

Figure 2: Intervention Model for Juvenile Intensive Aftercare

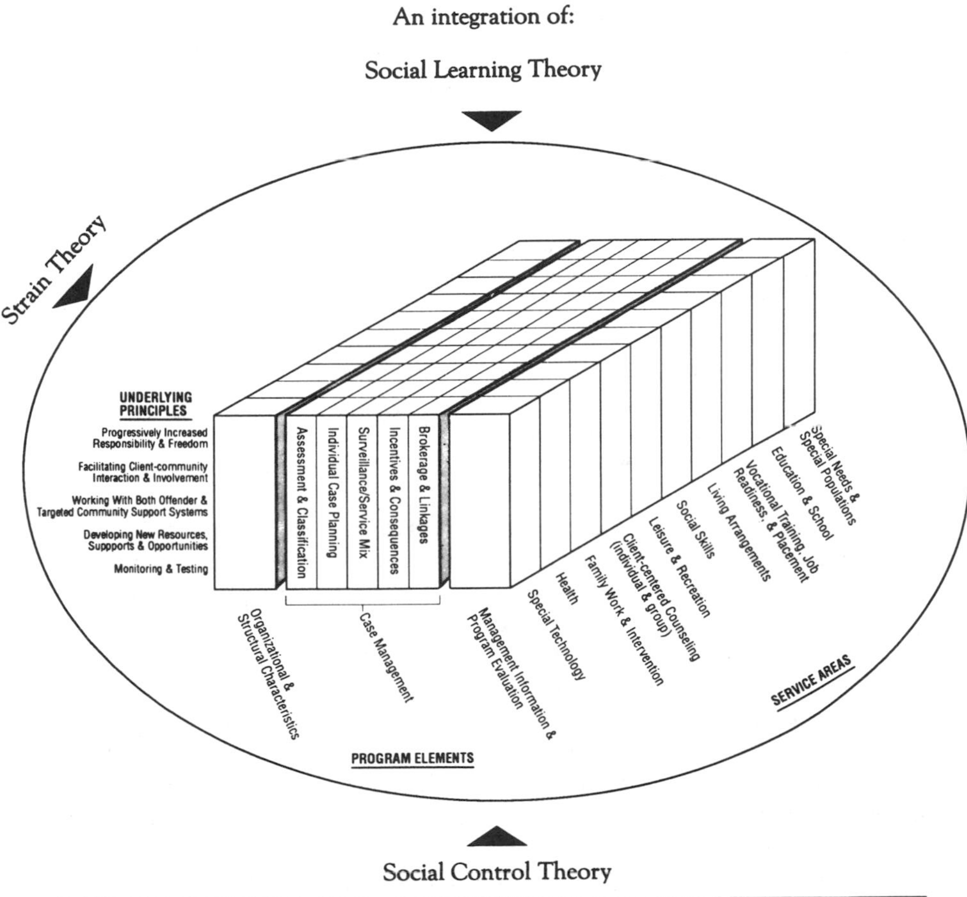

1. *Preparing Youth for Progressively Increased Responsibility and Freedom in the Community.*

Almost all youth in secure correctional facilities will eventually return to the community. Moreover, by the time a youth has been committed to a secure facility, a variety of problems, needs and deficits are likely to be evident. These include: family difficulties; peer relationships; social and living skills; education, training and job readiness; emotional and psychological well-being; behavior control, self-discipline and maturity; and substance abuse.

As described, the integrated model suggests: (1) that a variety of circumstances govern a person's socialization, bonding and expectations for achievement; and (2) when conducive and generative factors related to weak controls, strain and social reinforcements for deviant behavior occur conjointly, this generates a higher probability of delinquent or recidivist behavior than would any of the factors alone. This means that assessment and classification for risk and need are essential to determine the full range of services that each youth will require in order to maximize the chances of a successful outcome. The development of needed skills and competencies (e.g, behavioral, emotional, cognitive) is requisite if attachment and commitment to conventional others and pathways of action are to be accomplished. Those youth most at risk and in greatest need can then be objectively identified so that an appropriately intensive, individualized service plan can be developed. The assessment process and resulting service plan would be used to establish an initial judgment on the level and type of parole/aftercare that will be considered. Ideally, the intensive service plan should inform the planning of activities during the secure confinement period and also serve as a guide for decision period. Essential considerations across this continuum are consistency, continuity and gradual transitioning.

A planned and gradual transitioning process focuses attention on preparing youth for progressively increased responsibility and freedom in the community. This means that the services provided and a youth's progression in a program must be designed to provide a clear basis by which youths know at all times how they can advance their standing in the facility, what is expected of them, and, most significantly, how their accomplishments in the facility will be linked to the parole portion of their service plan. There is no real substitute for a close working relationship among the youth, facility staff, and parole staff; it is essential. In some fashion, therefore, parole needs to be "backed-in" to the operation of the secure facility in order to build this genuine continuum of care and supervision.

Providing youth with a comprehensible and predictable pathway for movement or progression from disposition and confinement to parole termination, and having a rating or reporting system to measure advancement, are critical aspects of facility/parole operation and practice. These two features can help to establish structure, consistency and routine feedback. It is important to frequently emphasize youths' achievements, deficiencies and expectations because these can affect the youths' perceptions of fairness, increase the chances that accomplishments will give youths a greater investment in the facility/parole process, and hold the youth accountable.

A number of different systems have been used by various programs and facilities to monitor progress, reward responsible behavior and/or sanction misbehavior, and guide advancement. These can range from relatively simple mechanisms involving periodic case reviews to elaborately structured token economies in which particular privileges are tied to the attainment of specific levels or stages. Behavioral, contingency or social contracting has also been used as a way to individualize intervention so that broad strategies are tailored to the specific needs of each youth.

Whatever kind of system is used, it is important to provide the youth with frequent assessments, positive reinforcements, immediate accountability and consequences for misconduct, and clarity as to what is expected and how it relates to the parole plan. Together, these characteristics of a facility/parole master plan take the youth along a pathway upon which each step toward unsupervised community living can build. Providing increasingly greater autonomy and responsibility with parole functioning as one of the "landings" on a staircase places youths in a position where they have more at stake in their own accomplishments and, conversely, more to lose if they "act out." As a result of such a process, an incentive to do well can be engendered, with the ultimate goal being "redirection." In short, the movement toward unsupervised community living needs to be somehow linked to new opportunities for reward. In this manner, the move from a secure facility to parole status to making about placement and service provision during the post-confinement unsupervised community living becomes more of a transitional and planned experience, not an abrupt and unprepared plunge.

2. *Facilitating Youth-Community Interaction and Involvement.*

In combination, social control and social learning theory highlight the critical role that family, schooling, peers and significant others play in the initiation and maintenance of a lifestyle. Strain theory adds to this the importance of having opportunities available so that youth can have a realistic chance to experience some form of success and to accomplish reasonable goals. If attachment and commitment to conventional others and activities are to develop, then it is incumbent on facility and parole staff to see that opportunities to interact and be involved with conventional others are, in fact, promoted, initiated and reinforced. In this way, the chances are increased that positive role models from the community can be identified and tapped.

The integrated model makes clear that it is vital to identify sources of external support among a youth's personal social network (e.g., family, close friends, peers in general) and important community subsystems (e.g., schools, workplaces, churches, training programs, community organizations, youth groups). Requiring that staff become involved in this kind of endeavor is an essential step toward obtaining for the youth a stable and constructive attachment. Whether the locus of contact is initially inside or outside a program facility, the involvement of community resources is conceived as a way for the planned and selective use of normalizing contacts to maximize reintegrative potential and to begin building an external system of support for each youth. This kind of social networking is also one way to help youth to develop their own interpersonal skills in the furtherance of fostering and practicing improved social and communication skills. This strategy highlights both the need and value of beginning to decrease the level of dependence upon staff that inherently develops during any period of extended secure confinement.

It is important to acknowledge that facilitating youth-community interaction and involvement also frequently involves having the youth come into contact with deviant forces and influences in the community. Strictly speaking, this is not regarded as negative; in fact, dealing successfully with temptations, judging risks, making mistakes and accepting consequences, and learning resistance skills are all part of this second principle of intensive aftercare. In short, making available experiences and contacts with external support systems can provide learning opportunities and social skill development that can help youths better cope with the full range of community forces and influences likely to be encountered.

3. *Working with both the Offender and Targeted Community Support Systems for Constructive Interaction and Successful Community Adjustment.*

Hawkins and Weis (1985) make the case that formation of a social bond to conforming others can be complicated by the presence of impediments such as uncaring or inconsistent parents, poor school performance, unfair teachers or other circumstances which make conventional involvement unrewarding. Youth who face these situations are more likely to engage in delinquency as well as to associate with peers sharing similar experiences. To the extent that such youths provide each other with social and psychological supports, rewards and reinforcements that do not emerge from conventional groups and activities, there is an increased likelihood of delinquency or recidivism.

It is therefore essential that families, schools, peer groups and employers—as well as significant others who can serve as role models and mentors—become both *targets of intervention and partners in service provision.* To create an environment conducive to the development of social bonding may mean that as much, if not more attention has to be focused on the units of socialization as on the youth. Whether the focus is on schools, training programs, recreation centers, employers or family, there may well be resistance to getting involved with a "bad seed" or risky kid. This suggests that special, intensive contact with potential external sources of bonding may be needed.

Too often it is assumed, for example, that linking up a youth with a school or job, or getting the child back into the home, is accomplishing the goal of reintegration. The problem, of course, is that many times the external sources of social control have already become thoroughly alienated from this youth and simply do not want to expend any more time or energy on him or her. This all-too-common circumstance underscores the need for parole workers to establish some form of quid pro quo with the community resource. From the parole side of any such agreement, it is incumbent upon the aftercare worker that a commitment be made and rigorously adhered to regarding the provision of regular backup and physical presence, as well as the offering of special expertise to these community resources, be they family, schools, employers or other community agencies. For example, if an incarcerated offender is to return home, then it is the clear responsibility of the parole system to see that someone works with the family members, prepares them to deal with the youth, and clarifies with them the nature of the youth's situation as it relates to family strengths and weaknesses. Even when independent living is planned, it is unlikely that family ties with the youth will cease totally. There will probably be some sort of role for the family to play, and this relationship needs to be identified and agreed upon.

It is generally unrealistic to expect schools to welcome juvenile parolees with open arms. In many cases, schools enroll these youth because of legal requirements, but this does not mean that they are willing or able to work proactively with the youth, to look for warning signals, and to provide specialized teaching methods that may be necessary for their educational mainstreaming. Therefore, it may be important, for example, to reach an agreement with the school that parole workers will be available to help in various ways: to monitor attendance, to provide back-up assistance in the event of behavioral problems, and, importantly, to train school staff in techniques for handling recalcitrant students. Similarly, parole staff may be able to provide services to potential employers willing to hire parolees. Such services might include screening the youths for interest and aptitude, providing transportation, assisting in monitoring and supervision, and helping in obtaining or providing job training.

In sum, the thrust toward maximum offender involvement with community resources requires that actions be taken by staff to establish and maintain pathways conducive to the development of external bonds. This means that potential support systems and individuals in the community may require various kinds of concrete services, assistance and encouragement themselves; in these instances, potential units of socialization can be viewed as recipients or beneficiaries of service provided by parole workers. Ultimately, there is a complementary relationship in which community resources become both providers of services and targets of intervention. If properly managed by aftercare staff, this linkage can further benefit the overall effort to utilize community resources in the reintegration of youth into the community.

4. Developing New Resources and Supports Where Needed.

The next principle is providing youth with convenient and accessible work, education and training, and recreational opportunities, as well as other services geared to special-needs populations (e.g., emotional disturbance, repeat sex offenders, severely learning disabled, developmentally disabled, arsonists, drug or alcohol addiction, suicidal youth, and severely acting-out and violent youth). Strain theory makes explicit that the discrepancy between personal goals and conventional opportunities for meeting personal goals can produce a delinquent response. Elliott et al. (1985) specifically note that, according to strain theory, individuals who are unable to revise or adjust their goals in the face of actual or anticipated failure to achieve societally induced needs or goals (e.g., status, power, acceptance, money, material possessions) end up being forced to consider unconventional alternative means (often referred to as alternative opportunity structures) either to satisfy these needs or to retaliate.

The strain portion of integrated theory certainly directs attention to creating opportunities where none exist. Moreover, creation of a context for social bonding to occur in certain situations would necessitate the creation and maintenance of opportunities. Consequently, advocacy—whether it focuses on meeting the special needs of individual youths, families and neighborhoods, or on broader questions involving types of programs and services (e.g., vocational training, job development and placement, basic literacy training)—is clearly an important part of any broad-based intensive aftercare intervention strategy. To the extent that communities offer few or no conventional activities because of economic deprivation or social disorganization, it is clear that these root problems must be addressed.

One point should be made in connection with the issue of adjusting or revising personal goals because it links the aspiration-opportunity disjunction with the earlier principles. An element alluded to by strain theory (in its warning about youth who are unable to adjust or revise goals), and directly addressed by the combination of control and social learning theories (in focusing on the need to develop the requisite skills and competencies for meaningful involvement and interaction with different support systems), is the importance of conducting assessments to determine what kinds of specific goals and aspirations are realistic and potentially achievable by different youth. While learning to deal positively with failure, anxiety and disappointment is a matter of developing new skills, part of appropriate coping may also involve a youth's learning to adopt conventional goals. Understanding the distinction between handling failure/disappointment positively and optimizing the opportunity for success can be quite important. While being able to deal with failure positively is one skill to learn, another is pursuing a conventional path that minimizes future failure. The point is that pursued opportunities must be realistic.

Finally, it should be noted that some of the roles and responsibilities highlighted by this fourth principle, as well as other roles and responsibilities discussed above, are likely to involve more than one person, division, agency, organization and even service delivery system. This suggests that attention to planning, coordination and implementation is critical if the principles are to have any chance of being successfully implemented. It is at the level of specific program elements and services that the integrated model specifically addresses these important requirements. Developing new resources and supports is likely to produce a situation in which a number of traditional barriers—professional and institutional—will have to be overcome and new alliances developed. This is no small task for the transition process (from disposition and secure confinement to aftercare), in which courts, correctional institutions, parole authorities, private service providers, and different "units of socialization" have traditionally had different ideas about what to do with offenders, how to handle the sanctioning process, who should be making the various decisions about length of stay, etc.

Some of the conflicts are attributable to differences regarding goals, attitudes, overall philosophy, and professional backgrounds, while statutory and environmental constraints, bureaucratic and organizational turf issues, funding priorities, and competition for funds and control also play a big role. Whether the issue is shared resources, jointly run programs, jurisdictional authority, etc., it is clearly at this level of planning and action that advocacy takes on special meaning. For example, developing new resources may mean new uses for already existing resources. Similarly, developing new external supports may involve getting two traditionally rival groups to work together. However conceived, it is on this front that the advocacy battle may have to be waged the hardest and also the most diplomatically.

5. *Monitoring and Testing the Youths and the Community on their Ability to Deal with Each Other Productively.*

The last principle is largely derived from what social learning theory says about the process of socialization. Encouraging the formation and reinforcement of bonds to conventional groups and activities, while at the same time providing consistent, clear, swift, and graduated sanctions for misconduct and rule violations, requires close monitoring and supervision of youths. Despite the considerable effort expended on positive reinforcement, incentives, and instilling in youths a sense of involvement in the post-confinement program, there is an explicit assumption that for some youth there may be misconduct and difficulties. The monitoring and testing is designed first and foremost to identify and detect early warning signals that indicate a potential for trouble and, failing to do this, to detect immediately any violations.

Graduated sanctions that are proportional to the violation are essential. Often the impact of sanctions is diluted when they are overused or maintained for too long. By the same token, piling on parolees an endless list of conditions—some of which bear little relation to the problem, and others which are either unenforceable or commonly ignored—makes little sense since they undermine the credibility of the entire sanctioning system. This designation of graduated, community-based sanctions may well extend to electronic monitoring, which may prove very effective on a selective, short-term basis, but may quickly lose its deterrent value. There is a danger that long-term use of electronic monitoring will simply result in a greater number of parole revocations and subsequent reincarcerations on grounds that may be rather insignificant given the previous delinquency of this population. Therefore, electronic monitoring may hold the greatest promise when used as a short-term strategy that imposes immediate consequences for rule violations or when used to provide greater structure for a limited period at the very beginning of parole. This principle of selective application of particular sanctions may also be true in a number of other techniques such as home detention, drug and alcohol testing, etc.

Just as it is critical to monitor and test every youth, it is equally important to determine in a systematic fashion the extent to which conforming behavior is being appropriately reinforced by the designated sources of external support. This may mean that aftercare workers will need to work with family, instructors, employers and others in the youth's social environment about how best to provide concrete and social rewards for accomplishments. The ultimate goal is that the control eventually becomes internalized by the youth and maintained through external supports in the environment.

Program Elements

The five principles are general in the sense that they allow for a reasonable degree of flexibility in exactly what components, features, and processes will be utilized programmatically to respond to the problems and needs of these youth. While it is important to give planners and practitioners sufficient latitude to consider a range of components, features and processes that best suit the needs of both their own communities and confined youth, three major program elements and five sub-elements have been identified as central to the translation from theory and principles to actual implementation:

1.0. Organizational and Structural Characteristics
2.0. Case Management
2.1. Assessment, Classification and Selection Criteria
2.2. Individual Case Planning
2.3. A Balance of Incentives and Graduated Consequences Coupled with Realistic, Enforceable Conditions
2.4. Surveillance/Service Mix
2.5. Brokerage and Linkage to Community Resources
3.0. Management Information and Program Evaluation

Organizational Factors and the External Environment. The prospects that an intensive aftercare initiative can be implemented as designed are affected by the authority, influence and credibility that the administering aftercare agency/unit has in the larger juvenile justice system, the level of resources committed to aftercare, and the support or opposition the aftercare agency/unit has within the larger governmental and external environment in which it operates. A complicating factor is that by its nature, intensive aftercare must cut across traditional agency boundaries and professional interests. Moreover, juvenile parole functions and responsibilities assume a number of different forms from jurisdiction to jurisdiction because of variations in state laws, legislative guidelines, institutional arrangements and administrative rules. This means that the specific strategy adopted to create an atmosphere receptive to an intensive aftercare initiative must be highly sensitive to political, bureaucratic and service delivery system dynamics.

There is little question that the integrity of the aftercare program is in jeopardy unless key decision makers in each segment of the juvenile justice system (e.g., police, probation, judiciary), and in other involved agencies (e.g., mental health, child welfare, education, labor), have a clear understanding and acceptance of the overall approach, division of labor, lines of authority, system of service delivery and program accountability. This understanding and the accompanying policies and procedures must be communicated "down the line" to all involved staff.

Developing a strategy to gain support can be complicated since juvenile aftercare is structured and administered differently across—and even within—states. There may well be the need to neutralize in some way those potentially opposing or resistant forces and interests that can hamper the effort. It is advisable to involve representatives from as many of the "centers of power" as possible (e.g., state and local officials, union representatives, members of the judiciary and legislature, community organizers, and others) in the planning and oversight of the intensive aftercare program.

Case Management. One of the most serious problems that has historically confronted aftercare is the lack of meaningful involvement of the primary aftercare worker until the final phase of confinement, if at all, prior to release. Typically, incarcerated youngsters have already been shunted from the police to detention, court intake, adjudication, disposition, institution and aftercare. At each of these junctures, a variety of independent decisions are usually made by different individuals regarding the youth's problems and needs (legal and personal), what should be done, how to proceed and when, and who should be involved. Frequently, since much pertinent information can be lost or distorted in the process of interagency communication, little continuity characterizes the handling of these youngsters. The result is a highly destructive process marked by no single locus of accountability, which leaves both the youth and staff enormous leeway to shirk responsibility.

In the proposed framework, five broad areas of responsibility are identified as central to intensive aftercare case management: (1) a disposition/confinement/parole process that is composed of steps that are closely coordinated, consistent, mutually reinforcing and continuous; (2) some form of behavioral, contingency or social contracting; (3) a comprehensible and predictable pathway for client progression or movement; (4) the direction of each step or phase of post-confinement toward the next step and to all successive steps; and (5) a rating or reporting system to monitor a youth's behavior and measure progress. In short, these broad responsibilities establish the basis for developing an unambiguous, goal-oriented set of expectations for clients concerning: the "individualized facility-parole master plan" (e.g., goals and objectives for each aspect of the process), and the relationship of achievements to overall aftercare movement and progression.

The case management element is composed of five sub-elements providing explicit guidance on the design and utilization of the individualized facility-parole master plan with respect to what should happen before, during and after institutionalization. The first sub-element consists of *assessment, classification, and selection criteria*, which are the mechanisms used to identify intensive aftercare participants and to develop an appropriate service/surveillance mix. Ultimately, the provision of more intensive, highly specialized and individualized services must reflect a correctional system's ability to assess and clarify much more precisely the risks, problems and needs presented by different juvenile offenders. This is extremely important because evidence suggests that low- or moderate-risk offenders may do worse under intensive supervision. Certainly one of the dangers is that high levels of surveillance are more likely to uncover technical violations of parole, a circumstance that can lead to revocations and reincarceration for questionable reasons.

The second sub-element is *individualized case planning*. Once high-risk institutionalized youth are selected for specialized intensive aftercare, individual case planning is required in order to determine: (1) how identified risk factors will be addressed through a combination of aftercare programming and supervision; (2) what additional need factors are present in the youth and which of these are linked to the offender's social network (e.g., family, close friends, peers in general) and community (e.g., schools, workplace, church, training programs, specialized treatment programs); and (3) how the risks, needs and associated circumstances of each youth will be approached programmatically.

The third sub-element incorporates *incentives and graduated sanctions* as part of aftercare. This is a recognition of the fact that traditional aftercare/parole has long been burdened with unrealistic and unenforceable conditions, has been mostly a system for negatively sanctioning misconduct and violations, and has been largely devoid of positive reinforcements and inducements. The result has been that little use is made of graduated sanctions, that too many questionable and unrealistic conditions are placed on juvenile parolees, and that recognition (tangible and symbolic) of achievement is scarce. Unless a system of graduated sanctions is made available as a response to infractions, parole officers have little recourse except either to do nothing—entirely undermining the aftercare process—or to impose sanctions that are disproportionate to the misconduct, thereby further alienating the youth and serving no useful purpose. Stated simply, juvenile parole must begin to give equal attention to positive reinforcements and incentives on the one hand, and graduated sanctions and accountability on the other.

The fourth sub-element consists of aftercare *programming and surveillance*. Both are required if intensive aftercare stands any chance of reducing recidivism. Given the high levels of social, emotional and environmental deprivation exhibited by large numbers of delinquent youth reaching the stage of secure correctional confinement, it is difficult to imagine achieving any meaningful, long-term success in normalizing the behavior of this population in the community without providing or accessing the wide array of services specified in the framework. At the same time, however, the problem this population poses for achieving community protection necessitates a simultaneous focus on an enhanced level of surveillance and control.

The fifth sub-element is *brokerage and linkage to community resources*. Working with both the offender and community support systems (e.g., families, schools, peer groups, employers, and significant others) emphasizes the critical role that the surrounding external environment plays in the future life chances of parolees. Reinforcement and support from conventional groups may well be one key to ensuring that readjustment to the post-confinement community is successful and that gains achieved both in the institution and in an aftercare program persist. Therefore, the basis must be set early for involvement of various community resources. This can only occur if aftercare staff work in the community directly with schools, employers, training programs, specialized service providers, etc. By using such resources to maximize service provision, more conventional modes of interaction and involvement can be achieved; other segments of the community not typically involved in corrections can be tapped; and behaviors appropriate to community living can be presented and tested. In addition, use of other individuals and resources can be a valuable backup in the event of specialized problems such as serious emotional turmoil or developmental disability. The demands that such programming impose on staff are exceedingly high. Working with both juvenile offenders and support systems may require that different staff members specialize and that a team approach be utilized.

Management Information and Program Evaluation. The final program element in the model emerges from all the other elements, as well as from the underlying principles. It is imperative to maintain close oversight over implementation and quality control and to determine the overall effectiveness of the program. With regard to process evaluation, an ongoing management information system is required to ensure the operational integrity of the program. This entails the collection of appropriate data to assess day-to-day operations and performance. To the extent that implementation diverges from design principles and elements, no test of the model is possible. The availability of timely information enables needed adjustment and changes to be made before the program has veered substantially off course. In addition to collecting basic information on who is served and in what ways, it is also important to assess and document staffing patterns and selection, job responsibilities, staff turnover and job performance.

Assessing outcome is quite complex and is discussed in later chapters. Suffice it to say that some of the common problems which must be addressed include: the absence, or inappropriateness of, comparison groups; simplistic and narrow measures of outcome (including an overreliance on recidivism to the exclusion of behavioral, social, emotional, and cognitive functioning); inadequate time frames associated with outcome follow up; small sample sizes; and attrition or loss of subjects (particularly problematic in a longer follow-up period). Since the methodological requirements for sound outcome evaluation are quite technical, this responsibility should be assigned only to well-qualified individuals.

Service Areas

Ten different service areas have been identified as central to comprehensive provision of service for intensive aftercare. While it is highly unlikely that any one program would or even could provide this range of services, a strong argument can be made that a comprehensive system of aftercare providing an adequate continuum of interventions must be equipped in some fashion to deliver this array of services. Though these ten service areas will only be summarily described here, a quite detailed discussion of each area can be found in Altschuler and Armstrong (1990).

Special-Needs Subpopulations. Among those juvenile offenders who may be targeted for intensive aftercare are so-called "special-needs" offenders. These commonly include juvenile offenders who exhibit drug and alcohol dependence, developmental disabilities, learning disabilities, mental disorders and emotional disturbance, or a history of sex offenses. It is not uncommon for some juvenile offenders to exhibit several of these kinds of problems simultaneously.

In spite of the repeated call over the past decade for harsher sanctioning of serious and chronic juvenile offenders, rehabilitation and provision of supportive services has managed to maintain a foothold, precarious as it may be in some places, within the correctional arena. Certainly one manifestation of this philosophical commitment is the continuing attention paid to classifying delinquent youths on the basis of treatment-relevant characteristics, and then matching rehabilitative modalities with the differentially defined groups. In support of this movement to employ differential treatment, there has for some time been an emphasis on identifying or targeting particular special-need subpopulations and providing them with some form of specialized treatment and handling. The diagnostic categories, based on special problems and needs, are often utilized with youths who have compiled juvenile court careers characterized by a history of chronic and severe delinquent behavior, i.e., they are often among the most serious offenders within the system. Consequently, they have frequently penetrated deeply into the juvenile justice system and are having their special problems and needs identified and responded to at the institutional and post-release stages of processing.

Education. Basic education—as well as vocational training, job readiness, job development and job placement— represent two other broad service areas requiring close attention and care. The reintegration of juvenile parolees into acceptable educational settings is a complex problem marked by a long history of failure (Polk, 1984; Sametz and Hamparian, 1987). The depth of educational deficits exhibited by substantial numbers of these returning youth requires careful planning for matching educational opportunities with client abilities and circumstances. Further, the return to various educational settings is complicated by the presence of negative learning labels assigned to these youth prior to their institutional commitment.

Some educators even take the position that the regular public school system should not be responsible for handling the educational needs of these youth when they reenter the community. This stance arises from their perception that such youth have already been given every possible chance during earlier periods of enrollment. The effort to move youth from secure confinement to community-based educational settings requires addressing at least two major conceptual and programmatic issues: (1) pedagogical concerns such as innovative teaching methods and specialized curriculum design, and (2) structural and managerial concerns such as the coordination and flow of information and services across organizational boundaries, as well as public versus private sector sponsorship.

Vocational Training and Jobs. Beyond the need for basic or remedial education, prior experience with seriously delinquent juvenile populations suggests that often, regardless of the chronicity or severity of this antisocial behavior, most youths who reach the point of correctional confinement have unrealistic job expectations and have no knowledge of the work ethic or experience with actual work situations (Armstrong, 1985; Bazemore, this volume; James and Granville, 1984). Given these characteristics, reintegrative strategies that stress skill development, vocational training, job readiness and placement appear to be quite appropriate and promising.

Living Arrangement. The need to select an appropriate living environment, especially for high-risk subpopulations, raises several issues that need to be addressed. It has been documented (Armstrong and Altschuler, 1982a;

Hartstone and Hansen, 1984; Bleich, 1987) that a substantial percentage of chronically delinquent youth returning from secure confinement cannot be placed with their own families for various reasons (e.g., long history of domestic conflict and violence, high level of family fragmentation and dysfunction, and the absence of any identifiable family). This circumstance requires the presence of placement options such as halfway houses, group homes, foster care and independent living. The problem of residential placement of high-risk parolees may constitute sufficient reason for the gradual transitioning of these groups through the staged use of alternative living arrangements and ultimately into permanent, independent living situations.

Social Skills. Social skills training is another component in the available arsenal of intervention techniques being used with delinquent youths, many of whom are regarded as marginally socialized. As Weathers and Liberman (1975) have observed, this is a very commonly used approach since many juvenile offenders are the products of home environments where there was inadequate parenting. This kind of training is generally intended to teach socially acceptable behavior and to provide basic living skills.

Recreation and Leisure. Providing structured recreational and leisure activities as part of the reentry service package for high-risk juvenile offenders is supported by both logic and expertise. In many instances, this population is plagued by a lack of skills and/or dearth of interest in avocational areas from which most youngsters derive considerable personal satisfaction as well as an enhancement in self-esteem and self-confidence. Equally important is the value of many recreational activities for developing a sense of cooperation and teamwork that readily translates into other kinds of collective activities requisite for success in the workplace and in various social arenas.

A number of community-based programs that work with severely delinquent youth contain components designed to offer their clients the opportunity to participate in various sporting activities, to become familiar with and engage in individual hobbies, and/or to develop physical skills in areas such as dance, boxing and gymnastics. For example, the Violent Juvenile Offender (VJO) project was based on a community reintegration model that identified recreation and leisure-time activities as one of seven key treatment approaches necessary to strengthen social bonds and to address individual problems and needs (Fagan and Jones, 1984). The individual program sites in the VJO initiative included organized sports, physical activities and solitary pursuits under this category. Likewise, a national survey of community-based interventions for serious juvenile offenders (Armstrong and Altschuler, 1982b) discussed a number of innovative and promising programs that placed a great deal of emphasis on a variety of recreational and leisure-time activities. The authors noted the importance of these activities in advancing rehabilitation:

> . . .sport and recreational pursuits represent an acceptable and meaningful way to channel energy, vent frustration, provide excitement and exhilaration,

> enhance self-esteem, establish close personal rapport with one's peers and leaders, motivate and reward appropriate behaviors, discourage disruptive and uncooperative actions, and acquire skills and hobbies which may spark vocational interests and/or educational pursuits [1982b:187].

Client-Centered Counseling. Client-centered counseling, whether administered on an individual or group basis, has always been one of the mainstays in the arsenal of treatment interventions for the remediation of delinquent behavior. Within the counseling approaches can be found a wide variety of specialized treatment modalities. Mann's pioneering work (1976) on the treatment of serious juvenile offenders notes that no single treatment modality appears to be equally effective with this entire population. Others (Glasser, 1965; Whittaker, 1974; Haley, 1980; Taylor, 1980) have also argued for the need to differentially define the serious juvenile offender population for purposes of psychodynamic and psychotherapeutic intervention.

Research has shown that some offenders benefit more from the exclusive application of various forms of individual counseling, while others may benefit more from group counseling or a mix of both individual and group techniques. In a discussion of matching counseling approaches to the differing profiles of serious juvenile offenders, Strasburg (1978) observes that one promising strategy for dividing this population into distinctive treatment groups involves assigning these youths to one of three categories: (1) psychotic delinquents (numerically the smallest of the three groups); (2) disturbed delinquents (still a relatively small group and composed largely of antisocial psychopathic personality types); and (3) non-seriously disturbed delinquents (easily the largest group, defined as having a neurotic impulsive nature). Treatment strategies (whether individual, group, or a mix) would diverge widely depending on the category in which a youth was placed.

Family Work. The research literature is filled with accounts of efforts to determine the link between delinquent behavior and family variables. Sociological studies have focused primarily on structural variables such as family size, birth order, broken homes, social class and employment status of parents (Andrew, 1976; Cohen, 1955; Glueck and Glueck, 1950; Hirschi, 1969; Slocum and Stone, 1963). Psychological and psychiatric studies have extensively examined factors related to intra- and interpersonal dynamics drawn from clinical experience (Andry, 1971; Johnson, 1979; Loeber and Stouthamer-Loeber, 1986; McCord and McCord, 1984; Patterson and Stouthamer-Loeber, 1984; Rutter and Madge, 1976; West and Farrington, 1973). Factors targeted in these inquiries are often referred to as family functioning variables, and include parental affection/acceptance, family relationships, parental supervision/discipline, and family deviance/disorganization. Another avenue of research has entailed attempts to integrate sociological and psychological factors into an empirically defensible framework (Bahr, 1979; Johnson, 1979). The search for family-linked, structural variables as correlates of delinquency has yielded positive and reasonably consistent findings with low explanatory power (Geismar and Wood, 1988). This general finding suggests that a more promising route to pursue is the testing of family-linked variables, not defined in structural terms, but defined in terms of psychosocial behavior and functioning that captures the underlying dynamics of family life.

Health. The presence of physical health problems among serious juvenile offenders, sometimes chronic in nature, is not uncommon. Physical and dental examinations, as well as a full range of health services, must certainly be made available to this population. As Fagan et al. (1984:222) suggested in their conceptualization of a community reintegration model for violent juvenile offenders, behavioral contracting, "...should include goals oriented toward self-maintenance which include general hygiene, nutrition, physical fitness, and other personal needs." Further, these kinds of juvenile offenders, who are by definition at high risk for sexual activity and substance abuse, should be provided with public health education about birth control and teen parenting, as well as the dangers of AIDS and sexually transmitted diseases.

Special Technology. Within the emerging array of known juvenile intensive supervision practices, considerable emphasis is being placed on various kinds of specialized technology, including two-way radios, computerized answering machines, electronic monitoring devices and drug and alcohol testing equipment. A recent national survey of juvenile intensive probation supervision programs (Armstrong, 1988) has shown that the use of such items is already widespread and is becoming increasingly popular. Evidence suggests that these specialized technologies are beginning to be incorporated into juvenile aftercare programs and will eventually play a substantial role in the intensified control function for juvenile parolees.

CONCLUSION

Concern over institutional overcrowding, high rates of recidivism and escalating costs of confinement have fueled a renewed effort to bring reform and innovation to current juvenile aftercare/parole practices. As a result, there is currently a great deal of interest in intensified aftercare/parole, whether it be for purposes of greater surveillance, monitoring and accountability; service provision, competency development and advocacy; or some combination of the two.

In a historical and philosophical sense, intensive juvenile aftercare is being driven by many of the same issues and forces that have led to the development of intensive supervision efforts in both adult and juvenile probation. Techniques and innovations that are being used in intensive probation—such as classification for risk and/or need, electronic monitoring and saturation surveillance—are now being incorporated into intensive juvenile aftercare.

Intensive aftercare for juveniles can best be conceptualized as consisting of two basic forms: (1) early release, and (2) regular parole subsequent to serving a full institutional term. Generally, the early-release strategy is based on the desire to reduce either the size of an institution's population or the length of stay, thereby making room for other offenders being committed. By contrast, the central purpose of the regular parole strategy is to aid in a smoother transition into the community of designated high-risk offenders, thereby reducing the chances of reoffending. Depending on which form of aftercare is chosen, three different populations can be targeted: low- to medium-risk parolees, all parolees or high-risk parolees. The decision of appropriate target population has significant implications for the design and operation of these programs, especially with regard to risk management and the type of service provision.

One of the potential dangers associated with intensive aftercare is that it may result in an extraordinarily high level of detected technical violations and rule infractions. To the extent that this increases parole revocation, the unintended consequence may be the exacerbation of the institutional overcrowding problem. It, therefore, may be advisable to regard technical violations of parole conditions as early warning signals rather than as grounds for revocation. This possibility underscores the advisability of structuring the entry point into an intensive aftercare program at a middle level of restrictiveness and intrusiveness. Approached in this way, intensive aftercare provides a graduated set of surveillance sanctions that can be used as a series of progressively stringent responses to technical misconduct and rule violation.

Among institutionalized and paroled juvenile offenders most at risk of reoffending, the specific risk factors most commonly identified in the literature include three offense/justice/-system-related items and four need-related items. The justice system factors include the amount and severity of prior delinquency (i.e., justice system contact), the early onset of adjudication or justice system involvement, and the number of previous commitments. The need items most commonly connected to recidivism relate to experiences with—and the nature of—family, school, peer group, and drug and/or alcohol involvement. In addition, many of these youngsters have a variety of other needs and problems (e.g., behavioral, emotional, cognitive), all of which must ultimately be addressed in any comprehensive approach to confront the dynamics of delinquency.

As was made abundantly clear in considering how the integrated theoretical framework addresses common risk factors and problem areas, there can be little doubt that attention must be addressed to basic education tied to job preparedness and living/social skills (including the development of legitimate opportunities and avenues associated with the use of such skills), peer relationships and involvement with other potential role models, and the family. Drug and alcohol problems, as well as other special needs (e.g., learning disabilities), that at the very least make it more difficult to remain crime-free, must also remain at the center of attention. Close monitoring and supervision are also clearly an essential part of the reintegrative picture, in terms of basic surveillance, evaluating parole performance, diverting potential problems, and responding appropriately and proportionately to mistakes, failure, relapse and misconduct.

In the final analysis, the provision of more intensive, highly specialized, and individualized services can and should reflect the correctional system's increased ability to assess and identify much more precisely the problems and needs of different juvenile offenders. The offenders should be identified as subpopulations that are defined in relation to aggregated sets of risk and/or need factors. The correctional systems in a number of jurisdictions have begun to formalize and standardize the process within institutional settings, at the point of reentry into the community, and during the aftercare experience. Decision making can be, and is increasingly guided by the use of various risk- and need-assessment instruments, scales and protocols. Linked to these enhanced diagnostic and classification tools is the effort to identify specific service areas as logically and theoretically responsive to the causes and correlates of delinquent behavior among high-risk juvenile offender populations and to the dynamics of behavior change, rehabilitation and treatment. By engaging the identified risk factors and utilizing the integrated theoretical framework to formulate: (1) a set of overall principles; (2) program implementation elements that are central to translating theory and principles to action; and (3) specific program services that give form and meaning to an intervention plan, the intensive aftercare movement can hope to begin moving toward the development of carefully designed, reintegrative program approaches.

REFERENCES

Agee, V.L. (1979). *Treatment of the Violent Incorrigible Adolescent.* Lexington, MA: D.C. Heath and Company.

Akers, A.K., M.D. Krohn, L. Lanza-Kaduce and M. Radosevich (1979). "Social Learning and Deviant Behavior: A Specific Test of a General Theory." *American Sociological Review* 44:636-655.

Altschuler, David and Troy Armstrong (1990). "Intensive Community-Based Aftercare Programs: Assessment Report." Washington, DC: U.S. Office of Juvenile Justice and Delinquency Prevention.

—— (1984). "Intervening with Serious Juvenile Offenders: A Summary of a Study on Community-Based Programs." In *Violent Juvenile Offenders: An Anthology,* edited by Robert A. Mathias et al. San Francisco, CA: National Council on Crime and Delinquency.

—— (1983). "Four Models of Community-Based Interventions with the Serious Juvenile Offender: Therapeutic Orientations, Educational Strategies and Reintegrative Techniques." *Corrective and Social Psychiatry and Journal of Behavior Technology Methods and Therapy* 29(4):116-130.

Andrew, J.M. (1976). "Delinquency, Sex, and Family Variables." *Social Biology* 23:168-171.

Andry, R.G. (1971). *Delinquency and Parental Pathology*. London: Staples Press.

Armstrong, Troy (1988). "National Survey of Juvenile Intensive Probation Supervision, Parts I and II." *Criminal Justice Abstracts* 20(2,3):342-348, 497-523.

—— (1985). "Teaching the Toughies: Mainstreaming Delinquent Youths in Custody Back into Community-Based Educational Settings." Paper presented at the Annual Meeting of the Academy of Criminal Justice Sciences, Las Vegas, NV.

—— and David Altschuler (1982a). "Conflicting Trends in Juvenile Justice Sanctioning: Divergent Strategies in the Handling of the Serious Juvenile Offender." *Juvenile and Family Courts Journal* 33(4):15-30.

—— and David Altschuler (1982b). *Community-Based Program Interventions for the Serious Juvenile Offender: Targeting, Strategies and Issues*. Chicago, IL: School of Social Service Administration, University of Chicago, National Center for the Assessment of Alternatives to Juvenile Justice Processing.

—— Gary Reiner and Joel Phillips (1987). *Electronic Monitoring: An Overview*. Washington, DC: U.S. Bureau of Justice Assistance.

Bahr, S.J. (1979). "Family Determinants and Effects of Deviance." In *Contemporary Theories About the Family*, edited by W.R. Burr et al. New York, NY: Free Press.

Baird, S. Christopher (1983). *Report on Intensive Supervision Programs in Probation and Parole*. Washington, DC: U.S. National Institute of Corrections.

—— (1973). "Juvenile Parole Prediction Studies." Joliet, IL: Illinois Department of Corrections, Division of Research and Long Range Planning.

—— R.C. Heinz and B.J. Bemus (1979). "The Wisconsin Case Classification/Staff Deployment Project." (Report No. 14.) Madison, WI: Department of Health and Social Services, Division of Corrections.

—— G.M. Storrs and H. Connelly (1984). *Classification of Juveniles in Corrections: A Model Systems Approach*. Washington, DC: Arthur D. Little.

Bakal, Yitzhak and Barry Krisberg (1987). *Placement Needs Assessment for Youth Committed to Oregon Training Schools*. San Francisco, CA: National Council on Crime and Delinquency.

Bleich, Jeffrey (1987). "Toward an Effective Policy for Handling Dangerous Juvenile Offenders." In *From Children to Citizens, Vol. II, The Role of the Juvenile Court*, edited by Francis S. Hartman. New York, NY: Springer-Verlag.

Box, S. (1987). *Recession, Crime and Punishment*. Totowa, NJ: Barnes and Noble Books.

Catalano, R.F., E.A. Wells, J.M. Jenson and J.D. Hawkins (n.d.). "Transition and Aftercare Services for Adjudicated Youth." Seattle, WA: University of Washington School of Social Work.

Clear, Todd R. (1988a). "Statistical Prediction in Corrections." *Research in Corrections* 1(1):1-52.

—— (1988b). "A Critical Assessment of Electronic Monitoring in Corrections." *Policy Studies Review* 7(3):671-681.

Cloward, R.A. and L.E. Ohlin (1960). *Delinquency and Opportunity: A Theory of Delinquent Gangs*. New York, NY: Free Press.

Coates, R.B. (1984). "Appropriate Alternatives for the Violent Juvenile Offender." In *Violent Juvenile Offenders: An Anthology*, edited by R. Mathias et al. San Francisco, CA: National Council on Crime and Delinquency.

Cohen, A.K. (1955). *Delinquent Boys: The Culture of the Gang*. New York, NY: Free Press.

Conger, R.D. (1976). "Social Control and Social Learning Models of Delinquent Behavior: A Synthesis." *Criminology* 14:17-40.

Elliott, D.S. and H. Voss (1974). *Delinquency and Dropout.* Lexington, MA: D.C. Heath.

—— S. Ageton and R. Cantor (1979). "An Integrated Perspective on Delinquent Behavior." *Journal of Research in Crime and Delinquency* 16(1):3-27.

—— D. Huizinga and S.S. Ageton (1985). *Explaining Delinquency and Drug Use.* Beverly Hills, CA: Sage.

Fagan, Jeffrey and Eliot Hartstone (1984). "Strategic Planning in Juvenile Justice—Defining the Toughest Kids." In *Violent Juvenile Offenders: An Anthology,* edited by R. Mathias et al. San Francisco, CA: National Council on Crime and Delinquency.

—— and Sally Jo Jones (1984). "Toward a Theoretical Model for Intervention with Violent Juvenile Offenders." In *Violent Juvenile Offenders: An Anthology,* edited by R. Mathias et al. San Francisco, CA: National Council on Crime and Delinquency.

—— C.J. Rudman and E. Hartstone (1984). "Intervening with Violent Juvenile Offenders: A Community Reintegration Model." In *Violent Juvenile Offenders: An Anthology,* edited by R. Mathias et al. San Francisco, CA: National Council on Crime and Delinquency.

Farrington, David and D.J. West (1977). "The Cambridge Study in Delinquency Development." Cambridge, UK: Institute of Criminology, Cambridge University.

Ferdinand, Theodore (1987). "The Methods of Delinquency Theory." *Criminology* 25(4):841-862.

Gadow, D. and J. McKibbon (1984). "Discipline and the Institutionalized Violent Delinquent." In *Violent Juvenile Offenders: An Anthology,* edited by R. Mathias et al. San Francisco, CA: National Council on Crime and Delinquency.

Geismar, L. L. and K. M. Wood (1986). *Family and Delinquency: Resocializing the Young Offender.* New York, NY: Human Sciences Press.

Glasser, W. (1965). *Reality Therapy: A New Approach to Psychiatry.* New York, NY: Harper and Row.

Glueck, S. and E. Glueck (1950).*Unraveling Juvenile Delinquency.* Cambridge, MA: Harvard University Press.

Greenwood, Peter and Franklin Zimring (1985). *One More Chance: The Pursuit of Promising Intervention Strategies for Chronic Juvenile Offenders.* Santa Monica, CA: Rand.

Haley, J. (1980). *Leaving Home: The Therapy of Disturbed Young People.* New York, NY: McGraw-Hill.

Hamparian, Donna, Richard Schuster, Simon Dinitz and John Conrad (1978). *The Violent Few: A Study of the Dangerous Juvenile Offender.* Lexington, MA: Lexington Books.

Hartstone, Eliot and Karen Hansen (1984). "The Violent Juvenile Offender: An Empirical Portrait." In *Violent Juvenile Offenders: An Anthology,* edited by R. Mathias et al. San Francisco, CA: National Council on Crime and Delinquency.

Hawkins, J.D. and J.G. Weiss (1985). "The Social Development Model: An Integrated Approach to Delinquency Prevention." *Journal of Primary Prevention* 6:73-97.

Hirschi, T. (1969). *Causes of Delinquency.* Berkeley, CA: University of California Press.

Irvin, John (1970). *The Felon.* Englewood Cliffs, NJ: Prentice-Hall.

Jackson, Patrick (1982). *The Paradox of Control.* New York, NY: Praeger.

James, Thomas and Jeanne Granville (1984). "Practical Issues in Vocational Education for Serious Juvenile Offenders." In *Violent Juvenile Offenders: An Anthology,* edited by R. Mathias et al. San Francisco, CA: National Council on Crime and Delinquency.

Johnson, R.E. (1979). *Juvenile Delinquency and Its Origins*. Cambridge, UK: Cambridge University Press.

Lefkowitz, M.M., L.D. Eron, L.O. Walder and L.R. Huesmann (1977). *Growing Up to Be Violent: A Longitudinal Study of the Development of Aggression*. New York, NY: Pergamon Press.

Loeber, R. and M. Stouthamer-Loeber (1986). "Family Factors as Correlates and Predictors of Juvenile Conduct Problems and Delinquency." In *Crime and Justice: An Annual Review of Research, Vol. 7*, edited by M. Tonry and N. Morris, Chicago, IL: University of Chicago Press.

MacArthur, Verne (1974). *Coming Out Cold*. Lexington, MA: Lexington Books.

Mann, Dale (1976). *Intervening with the Convicted Serious Juvenile Offender*. Washington, DC: U.S. National Institute for Juvenile Justice and Delinquency Prevention.

McCord, J. and W. McCord (1964). "The Effects of Parental Role Model on Criminality." In *Readings in Juvenile Delinquency*, edited by R.S. Cavan. Philadelphia, PA: J.B. Lippincott.

McCord, Joan (1979). "Some Child-Rearing Antecedents of Criminal Behavior in Adult Men." *Journal of Personality and Social Psychology* 37:1477-1486.

McDermott, Joan and Gisela Joppich (1980). *The Serious Juvenile Offender*. Hackensack, NJ: National Council on Crime and Delinquency, National Assessment Center for Integrated Data Analysis.

Meier, Robert (1985). *Theoretical Methods in Criminology*. Beverly Hills, CA: Sage.

Nelson, Kim, Howard Ohmart and Nora Harlow (1978). *Promising Strategies in Probation and Parole*. Washington, DC: Office of Development, Testing and Dissemination, U.S. National Institute of Law Enforcement and Criminal Justice.

Patterson, G. and M. Loeber-Stouthamer (1984). "The Correlation of Family Management Practices and Delinquency." *Child Development* 55:1299-1307.

Petersilia, Joan, Peter Greenwood and Marvin Lavin (1977). *Criminal Careers of Habitual Felons*. Santa Monica, CA: Rand Corporation.

Polk, Kenneth (1984). "The New Marginal Youth." *Crime & Delinquency* 30(3):462-480.

Polk, K. and W.E. Schaefer (1972). *School and Delinquency*. Englewood Cliffs, NJ: Prentice-Hall.

Rutter, M. and N. Madge (1976). *Cycles of Disadvantage: A Review of Research*. London, UK: Heineman.

Sametz, Lynn and Donna Hamparian (1987). "Reintegrating Incarcerated Youth into the Public School System." *Juvenile and Family Court Journal* 38(3):27-37.

Shannon, Lyle (1980). "Assessing the Relationship of Adult Careers to Juvenile Careers: The Transitional Years (16-24)." Paper presented at the Annual Meeting of the American Society of Criminology, San Francisco, CA.

—— (1978). "A Longitudinal Study of Delinquency and Crime." In *Quantitative Studies in Criminology*, edited by Charles Wellford. Beverly Hills, CA: Sage Publications.

Slocum, W.L. and C.L. Stone (1963). "Family Culture Patterns and Delinquent-Type Behavior." *Marriage and Family Living* 25:202-208.

Smith, Charles, Paul Alexander, Thomas Halatyn and Chester Roberts (1979). *A National Assessment of Serious Juvenile Crime and the Juvenile Justice System: The Need for a Rational Response, Vol. II*. Sacramento, CA: American Justice Institute, National Juvenile Justice System Assessment Center.

Steenson, David (1986). "A Symposium on Juvenile Intensive Probation Supervision: The JIPS Proceedings." Minneapolis, MN: Hennepin County Bureau of Community Corrections, Juvenile Division.

Strasburg, Paul (1978). *Violent Delinquents: A Report to the Ford Foundation from the Vera Institute of Justice.* New York, NY: Monarch.

Taylor, Leah (1980). "The Serious Juvenile Offender: Identification and Suggested Treatment Responses." *Juvenile and Family Court Journal* 31(2):23-34.

U.S. Federal Bureau of Investigation (1986). *Uniform Crime Reports.* Washington, DC: U.S. Government Printing Office.

—— (1985). *Uniform Crime Reports.* Washington, DC: U.S. Government Printing Office.

—— (1984). *Uniform Crime Reports.* Washington, DC: U.S. Government Printing Office.

U.S. Office of Juvenile Justice and Delinquency Prevention (1981). *Violent Juvenile Offender Program, Part I.* Washington, DC.

Vachss, Andrew and Yitzhak Bakal (1979). *The Life-Style Violent Juvenile: the Secure Treatment Approach.* Lexington, MA: Lexington Books.

Vold, G.B. and T.J. Bernard (1986). *Theoretical Criminology,* 2nd ed. New York, NY: Oxford University Press.

Weathers, L. and R. Liberman (1975). "Contingency Contracting With Families of Delinquent Adolescents." *Behavior Therapy* 6:356-366.

Weis, J.G. and J.D. Hawkins (1981). *Reports of the National Juvenile Justice Assessment Centers: Preventing Delinquency.* Washington, DC: U.S. National Institute for Juvenile Justice and Delinquency Prevention.

Wenk, E.A. (1975). "Juvenile Justice and the Public Schools: Mutual Benefit through Educational Reform." *Juvenile Justice* 26(3):7-14.

—— and R.L. Emrich (1972). "The Assaultive Youth: An Exploratory Study of the Assaultive Experience and Assaultive Potential of California Youth Authority Wards." *Journal of Research in Crime and Delinquency* 9(2):171-196.

West, D.J. and D.P. Farrington (1973). *Who Becomes Delinquent?* London, UK: Heineman.

Whittaker, J.K. (1974). *Social Treatment: An Approach to Interpersonal Helping.* New York, NY: Aldine.

Wolfgang, Marvin, Robert Figlio and Thorsten Sellin (1972). *Delinquency in a Birth Cohort.* Chicago, IL: University of Chicago Press.

Zimring, Franklin (1979) "American Youth Violence: Issues and Trends." In *Crime and Justice: An Annual Review of Research, Volume I,* edited by Norval Morris and Michael Tonry. Chicago, IL: University of Chicago Press.

—— (1978). "Background Paper." In *Confronting Youth Crime, Report of the Twentieth Century Fund Task Force on Sentencing Policy Toward Young Offenders.* New York, NY: Holmes and Meier.

—— and Gordon Hawkins (1973). *Deterrence: The Legal Threat in Crime Control.* Chicago, IL: University of Chicago Press.

Intervention With Juvenile Offenders: Recent And Long-Term Changes

by
Ted B. Palmer

From the early 1960s to early 1970s there was a broad surge of confidence in intervention's ability to change and control offenders on both a short- and long-term basis. This high optimism was largely replaced by widespread pessimism during 1975-1981. However, by 1983-84 evidence for the "relatively-little-works" view and *for a "several-things-sometimes-work" view became increasingly known. As a result, a mixed and unsettled atmosphere emerged regarding effectiveness. During the rest of the '80s, intervention regained strength in terms of focus, direction and "legitimacy." In effect, it bounced back from the artificially created, "near-illegitimacy" previous years and from its partial banishment as well. This re-legitimization is a major development in American corrections, one with sizable implications. As the 1990s begin, intervention has a recognized and generally accepted role with serious and multiple offenders. This role can doubtlessly extend beyond such offenders, and it pertains to high-and middle-risk youths and adults alike. Intervention's role can be played via skill-development methods, control/surveillance techniques, psychologically oriented programs, and combinations of all three. Intensive supervision often emphasizes one or more of these approaches. Clearly, intervention's responsibilities can be numerous and broad.*

INTRODUCTION

As in other areas of life, the tide provides apt metaphors for correctional intervention's changes over the past three decades. Starting with a rising tide of hope and major experimental studies that reported on the relative success and failure of various efforts in the 1960s and early 1970s, intervention with juvenile offenders swiftly receded to a low tide of widespread pessimism, and few comprehensive studies examined new program initiatives in the period extending from 1975 to 1981. During the 1980s, however, new, swifter, and somewhat different tides began to appear. Involved were crosscurrents or mixed views as to whether correctional intervention could or even should change offenders on other than a short-term, behavior-control basis. Essentially, a mix of skepticism and conditional (albeit slowly growing) optimism existed with respect to the possible effectiveness of correctional intervention. And above all, pragmatism and concern for public protection prevailed.

Beside its long-term ebbs and flows, correctional intervention has undergone significant content changes in the past half-decade, including a substantially increased use of intensive intervention approaches and formal risk/needs classification procedures. This has occurred both within and especially outside institutional settings, and has been utilized with a wide range of offenders. Another development involves the increased use of alternatives to incarceration; and still another is a widened *range* of treatment and supervision techniques. Before discussing these changes and long-term trends in corrections, it would be useful to ask, "What broad, common, and/or long-standing themes are found in today's intervention approaches with juvenile offenders, and what combinations of themes characterize approaches being used with these individuals?"

One long-established theme is that of improving the offender's self-concept, increasing his or her self-understanding, and changing his attitudes toward others—thus, *personal or interpersonal change*. Individual, group, and/or family counseling often play major roles in this effort. Further, some degree of external control or surveillance (a second theme mentioned below) is also regularly employed, certainly in community settings. Together, these two themes—referred to as an approach when occurring in combination—generally resemble many 1960s-to-mid-1970s interventions: i.e., programs sharing the assumption that rehabilitation and habilitation are achievable and appropriate goals. Until about 1975, the theme of personal/interpersonal change was emphasized; since the late '70s or early '80s, the theme of external controls has dominated.

The second theme, already suggested above, centers on issues of *external controls/surveillance*. During much of the 1980s, this was often combined with techniques for life-skills development. Much less emphasis was placed on combining this theme of external controls with self-concept/self-understanding than had been the case before 1975. Approaches that emphasize external controls do not necessarily require the assumption that rehabilitation should be a principal goal of corrections. Nor do they assume that considerable interpersonal/psychological intervention must occur in order to reduce illegal behavior, even in the short run. At any rate, the theme of external controls/surveillance has played an increasingly major role in corrections since the mid-1970s. In fact, historically it has perhaps played the largest single role in the design and implementation of intervention approaches (community-based strategies included), and has utilized the most resources for the preponderance of offenders (juveniles and adults alike).

The third theme centers on *life-skills development*, e.g., vocational or educational development. Occasionally, "cognitive" and/or social/interpersonal skills training is also included. Outside institutional settings, these techniques are often combined with considerable emphasis on external controls. Beginning in the early 1980s, life-skills development has often been supplemented by community service and/or restitution.

Current approaches reflect some merging of these themes. For instance, together with the presumed importance of skills-development, it is often assumed that substantial internal/psychological change, as well as changed attitudes toward others and increased acceptance of responsibility, may be important to achieving longer-term recidivism reduction. Therefore, it is assumed that rehabilitation—whether acknowledged as such—must play a relevant role, even if this role is downplayed and varies somewhat from its pre-1975 emphasis on changes in self-concept, self-understanding, and attitudes toward others. Though community service and restitution were used prior to 1975, they first became major program components in the later 1970s. Their widespread use since that time reflects, in part, the increased concern of the 1980s with both victims and offender accountability.

In a fourth theme, special emphasis is given to certain types of *commitment offense or recurring behavior problems*, such as sexual offending or substance abuse, as a basis for designing intervention strategies. Specifically, it involves techniques that focus on the goal of resolving those particular conditions and behaviors. In specific programs this is often combined with the second and third themes: external controls and/or skills development.

Today's intensive probation or intensive aftercare programs for juvenile offenders often combine a number of these themes into one, more comprehensive approach. Intensive programs existed in the 1960s and early-1970s, but in somewhat different form. For instance, they gave more emphasis to theme one (personal or interpersonal change) and less to theme two (external controls/surveillance). This shift in the nature of intensive intervention is discussed later and is closely related to the following factors and issues of the 1980s: increased institutional crowding, special offender populations, and, more broadly, maintenance of serious offenders in the community.

Though issues of institutional crowding and an interest in specially defined and/or serious juvenile offenders occurred prior to the 1980s, existing needs and concerns in these areas are probably more intense, widespread, and explicit than before. Insofar as these issues and interests are *not* new or unique, they have largely continued to move correctional intervention along paths it has travelled in one way or another for over 30 years.

Continuity notwithstanding, corrections has followed varied and often diverging paths with respect to philosophy and practice over the past three decades. Though crowding and concern with serious offenders are not unique to the 1980s, what *has* perhaps been unique are the sheer intensity and complexity of recent correctional pressures and demands, and the increased fiscal and other social constraints, tensions and needs. Beginning in the early-1970s, these forces helped generate a wider range of correctional techniques and strategies than existed before. Recent approaches, many of which are innovative and some of which show promise, are especially reflected in themes three and four, i.e., life-skills development and emphasis on special offender populations. Variants of both are often combined, and, together with theme two (external controls/surveillance), they have appeared as part of the intensive intervention movement of the 1980s. As mentioned below, research findings and increased practical experience with various approaches have helped support and direct some of these interventions for adult and juvenile offenders, particularly in the last several years.

Today, some of the sharp distinctions traditionally drawn between treatment and control have somewhat softened. Through continued practical experience accompanied by careful documentation and—when feasible—serious experimentation, it should be possible to eventually develop effective programs that combine various themes discussed above. In the long-run, it is crucial to discover those combinations of principles, processes and procedures which help produce and support effective interventions for specified offender categories.

To better understand how more effective programs might be developed, it is important to review the state of correctional intervention, tracing major developments from the early 1980s to the present. As part of this review we will emphasize interventions with serious, usually multiple-offense juvenile delinquents. First, however, the following should be noted regarding treatment and effectiveness.

GOALS AND NATURE OF TREATMENT

Within the justice system, increased protection of society is the primary or *socially centered* goal of treatment. At the individual offender level, this goal is achieved when the youth's or adult's behavior is modified so that it conforms to the law. It is promoted, but not in itself achieved, by modifying his attitudes, by strengthening him as a person, by reducing various external pressures and increasing supports or opportunities, and/or by helping him become more satisfied and self-fulfilled within the context of society's values (Palmer, 1983, 1984).

Attitude change, increased coping ability, etc. comprise the secondary or *offender-centered* goal of treatment. Though this goal has absolute value in itself, it is—given the justice system's main role in society—chiefly a "means" to the socially centered "end" of public protection. Treatment methods that focus directly or predominantly on illegal behavior mainly emphasize this socially centered goal. This type of emphasis is observed, for example, in some forms of "behavior modification." Methods which focus on attitude change, coping ability, etc., operate indirectly on behavior, yet may or may not emphasize the offender-centered goal. Though most treatments, such as counseling and vocational training, mainly rely on this indirect approach, they often deal directly with illegal and unacceptable behavior. In any event, they, like all other approaches, are ultimately concerned with public protection.

Increased public protection, i.e., reduced illegal behavior, is shared as a primary goal by approaches that rely on *punishment* and *incapacitation.* However, what distinguishes treatment from these social-protection strategies is its manner of focusing, not so much on illegal behavior per se, but on the following: (a) factors which have presumably generated or helped maintain the individual's illegal behavior; and/or (b) factors which may help offset or eliminate those causal, triggering, or sustaining conditions. In addition, treatment is more concerned than either punishment or incapacitation with offender-centered goals. It is this emphasis which places treatment into a rehabilitative or habilitative context.

As a vehicle of change, treatment usually tries to reach its socially-centered and offender-centered goals by focusing on such factors and conditions as the offender's *adjustment techniques, interests, skills, personal limitations, and/or life-circumstances*. It does so in order to affect the offender's future behavior and adjustment. These efforts may be referred to as *programs* or *approaches* insofar as they (a) involve specific components or inputs (e.g., counseling or skill-development) that are organized, interrelated, and otherwise planned so as to (b) generate changes in the above factors and conditions, e.g., in the offender's skills or life-circumstances. These changes, in turn, may (c) help generate the desired future events, e.g., reduced illegal behavior.

Treatment efforts may include external controls, e.g., surveillance or restrictions on physical movement; in fact, they almost always do. In this chapter the primary focus is on interventions that *utilize, develop, or redirect the powers and mechanisms of the individual's mind and body* (as opposed to reducing, physically traumatizing, disorganizing or devastating them, by whatever means). These may be called positive treatment programs, in contrast to drastic or traumatic approaches such as electroshock, psychosurgery, mutilation/dismemberment, sterilization/castration, physical stigmatization, and public humiliation, e.g., via stock and pillory. Thus, in this chapter intervention is defined as a combination of treatment and external control (Palmer, 1983; 1984).

Effectiveness

The main index or indices of a program's effectiveness should closely reflect the fact that intervention's primary goal is increased public protection agaainst illegal behavior. Such protection is directly reflected in "recidivism," defined as any form of repeat offending. Recidivism, as measured by arrests, parole revocation, incarceration, etc., has long been used to assess the impact of rehabilitation, punishment, and incapacitation alike. Despite its complexities and the differing ways it is measured, this index is widely accepted by researchers, practitioners, policymakers, and the public itself, and is usually considered a key element in any outcome evaluation.

When evaluating rehabilitation, in particular, additional measures are nevertheless common; sometimes, in fact, they substitute for recidivism. These measures generally reflect intervention's secondary or offender-centered goal, and thus involve attitude change, personality change, skill development, etc. Such indices often—yet often do not—correlate with recidivism itself. Beyond that, they are generally recognized as meaningful in their own right. However, since intervention's primary goal, increased public protection, is socially-centered rather than offender-centered, we will in this chapter consider the main index of program effectiveness to be the *reduction of recidivism*, especially as measured by arrests, convictions, and similar actions that largely reflect offender misbehavior.

Status of Correctional Intervention as of the Early- to Mid-1980s

Effectiveness of Intervention. As of 1983-84, a mixed and generally unsettled atmosphere prevailed regarding the effectiveness of correctional intervention. Neither the general pessimism of 1975-1981 nor the global optimism of the 1960s seemed justified, or in fact existed. More moderate views or camps—the "skeptic" and "sanguine"—had replaced them (Palmer, 1983, 1984). General pessimism, of course, had been triggered by Martinson's "What Works?..." article (Martinson, 1974).

Some "skeptics" believed it was clear that relatively few rehabilitation programs worked, i.e., reduced recidivism. This view was based on what they considered to be enough adequately conducted research over at least two decades. These individuals, who might be called "relatively settled skeptics," also suggested that rehabilitation programs—when they occasionally worked—reduced recidivism by inconsequential amounts. Given these views, they concluded that rehabilitation held little promise and merited only a minor role. Chief among these proponents were followers of early-Martinson, such as Greenberg (1977) and, in some respects, Conrad (1982).[1]

The remaining "skeptics" believed very little was settled regarding effectiveness. This reflected the view that adequate information about effectiveness was lacking and that many programs had been inadequately implemented. They believed that, from a rigorous scientific standpoint, it was not known if any of the major intervention approaches were effective. They believed that flawed research design and/or inadequate implementation called into question and, in a sense, neutralized or undermined, the many positive outcomes that had been reported during the prior 25 years. Among this group of skeptics were Sechrest et al. (1979), Empey (1978), and Martin et al. (1981).

Nevertheless, these less settled "skeptics" found acceptable evidence that some individual programs may have worked, imperfect/inadequate program implementation and flawed research design notwithstanding. Accordingly, they suggested that a few approaches merited further study and might be appropriate for certain offenders. Still, they felt the overall picture regarding the effectiveness of most existing approaches was not only unclear but could not be considered positive.

The more "sanguine" camp itself had reservations. For instance, this group believed most programs that had been studied had not demonstrated lower recidivism, certainly not for their overall sample. "Sanguines" also felt that research designs were, on average, mediocre. Nevertheless, persons in this camp pointed out that of the few hundred programs which had been evaluated and reviewed, some 35 to 45% were associated with reduced recidivism (positive outcome) either for their overall sample or for specified, not insubstantial, portions thereof. Regarding these positive outcomes, they believed that many studies—35% or more—had been at least adequately researched, and that most reductions in recidivism were statistically significant for reasons other than large sample-size or various artifacts. Thus, "sanguines" believed that although *most* studies had not demonstrated reduced recidivism with reasonable scientific assurance, *many* had done so; they had followed widely accepted, long-standing research methods and standards. Again, this aspect of assessment was independent of how well or poorly the program—the intervention itself—had been implemented.

Though "sanguines" recognized that the design and analysis of almost no study was absolutely ironclad and incontrovertible, they believed that excellent—not just adequate or passable—studies were far from rare and were sometimes associated with clear reductions in recidivism. Presumably, if more programs had been adequately implemented/operationalized and were at all relevant to the problems and needs of offenders, more studies might have shown positive results, and/or the results from some individual studies might have been stronger. In any event, it seemed unlikely that *fewer* outcomes would have been positive, and/or that outcomes would have been weaker on average, if programs had been better implemented than they were.

One substantial group of "sanguines" believed that certain offenders, called "treatment amenables" in the 1960s and early-1970s, responded positively to several types of programs under various conditions. Likewise, many of the remaining offenders responded positively to few interventions. Their position—called the Basic Treatment Amenability (BTA) view—implied that, for amenables, of whom there were presumably many, the exact nature of intervention was perhaps not crucial. This, in turn, reflected the assumption that many such offenders were already rather motivated and perhaps otherwise prepared—e.g., via academic, vocational, or other skills—to curtail their illegal behavior. Under these conditions, any of several programs might presumably have offered them a sufficient springboard to do so, i.e., offered a few basic resources or possibly an appropriate opportunity. Another group of amenables were perceived as less actively seeking change, but still somewhat open to it. This was presumably because—whether skilled or not—they were not fully committed to, or at least were conflicted about, illegal behavior.[2]

BTA proponents felt that the positive results reported for many studies reflected the presence of many such amenables—one or both types—within the study sample. Most such "amenables," particularly the former, might today be called lower-risks (i.e., good-risks), based on formal classification procedures. However, the latter group of individuals might be classified as middle-risk, depending on the particular population from which they were drawn and with which they were compared. Among BTA proponents were Adams (1974), Glaser (1975), Wiederanders (1983), and, by 1980, Wilson (1980), who has remained, however, partially committed to the skeptic camp.

The second group of "sanguines" has been described as proponents of the Differential Intervention [DI] point of view. These individuals partly accepted the Basic Treatment Amenability premise that some offenders are substantially better prepared than others to respond positively to a wide range of interventions. However, they felt that almost all offenders—including BTA-amenables and resistive or very troubled individuals—would respond positively, neutrally, or negatively depending to a considerable degree on the specific intervention used. Even though given offenders might be relatively open (or somewhat open) to change, particular interventions might produce negative reactions or simply be irrelevant. Among the principal DI proponents were Palmer (1975, 1978), Warren (1966, 1971), Gendreau and Ross (1979), Jesness and Wedge (1983), Hunt (1971), Quay and Parsons (1970), Romig (1978), Andrews and Kiessling (1980), and Megargee et al. (1979).

In short, DI proponents believed there was a substantial relationship between the offenders' personal characteristics and the type of program to which they responded. They also believed: (a) the type of setting, e.g., its degree of physical structure and security, affected some offenders more than others; and (b) programs had to be well-implemented, particularly when used with more resistant or troubled offenders. Many DI proponents felt that some offenders probably required more than the standard rehabilitative approaches of the 1960s and 1970s; instead, this group might have needed as much or more by way of external controls, high levels of structure, and considerable surveillance. Finally, DI proponents believed that positive results for one or more groups of offenders were sometimes counterbalanced and thereby "masked" by negative results for others. In such cases, studies would show no *overall* difference between experimentals (Es) and controls or comparisons (Cs).

Sanguines believed that certain aspects of intervention had already demonstrated considerable promise for some offender groups. Programs incorporating these components, features or techniques often reduced recidivism by as much as 15% to 35%. This position was based on studies that not only had positive outcomes, but that usually met traditional standards of scientific evidence and which were sometimes partially replicated. Together, these studies involved a range of methods, conditions, and settings. For instance:

1. In institutional settings, reduced recidivism for "higher maturity" and/or "middle-risk" individuals is associated with offender-staff or offender-offender interactions that are relatively stable, extensive and possibly intensive.[3] In community settings, success is generally associated with smaller caseloads and/or relatively comprehensive, pragmatically-oriented use of resources. Reduced recidivism is also related to offender-staff matching (Lipton et al., 1975; Palmer, 1984).

2. Vocationally-oriented training programs for youthful offenders who are over the age of 16—both in institutions and in the community— are associated with lower rates of recidivism than standard institutional care or standard parole. These programs seem most successful when they provide the offender with a marketable skill (Lipton et al., 1975; Palmer, 1984).

3. Individual therapy or counseling can be effective with institutionalized males "when it has a pragmatic orientation and is enthusiastically administered by interested and concerned therapists to older (16-20) amenable offenders" (Lipton et al., 1975:211; Palmer, 1984).

4. Middle-risk offenders and/or those with relatively strong personal controls generally perform better in open or minimum security settings than in high security settings. In contrast, higher-risk individuals seem to respond better to closed or high security settings than to open or minimum security settings. The latter offenders are often described as "lower or middle maturity," power oriented," and/or "aggressive" (Palmer, 1984).

As will be seen, the factors of smaller caseloads and increased contact, mentioned in item one above, are relevant to the design and operation of intensive supervision programs.

Common Ground. Despite important differences, many "sanguines" and some "skeptics" (particularly the less settled) shared common ground. In particular, many sanguines and some skeptics seemed to largely agree on at least three points regarding serious or multiple offenders—individuals who have received increasing attention since 1975:[4]

1. To be effective with these individuals, intervention must be more broadly based than in the past. Specifically, it would usually have to involve a multiple modality approach, e.g., simultaneous or successive combinations of such program components as vocational or academic training, individual or group counseling, recreation, cultural enrichment, or other services/activities. Given the often complex, long-standing, and interrelated problems of most such offenders, single-modality approaches seemed unlikely to work (Palmer, 1983, 1984).

2. To achieve other than minimal impact, intervention would often have to be more intensive than before, e.g., regarding frequency of contacts (Palmer, 1983, 1984).

3. To adequately work with these offenders, selective matching with given

intervention strategies was important. For example, a program's full range of resources, such as its entire set of components, would not automatically be applied to each participant. Instead, only certain components or combinations would be used, at least at any one time, with particular subgroups of offenders. The specific intervention strategies would be selected, adapted, and timed, for example, according to the needs and interests of the respective subgroups. As a result, differing subgroups would usually receive different combinations and/or amounts of the given components. If only one component was present, differing amounts might be used with different subgroups. Supporting this view was long-standing evidence that most program populations contained at least two or three sizable subgroups, even if most participants had similar committing offenses or offense histories (Palmer, 1983, 1984).

Collectively, this core of general agreement suggested that, for future programs to substantially affect other than minor offenders, their major features should probably be better focused than in the past on the life-circumstances and personal/interpersonal characteristics of these individuals.

Developments Since 1984-85

The existence and possible implications of a core of similar views among representatives of the two principal camps became apparent to many correctional practitioners and researchers by 1985. This growing awareness helped initiate and sustain a quiet, osmotic-like process which, by the later 1980s, resulted in a tacit, de facto consensus among many practitioners, researchers, policymakers and academics regarding certain aspects of correctional intervention. Basically, this consensus involved the following views:

(a) In contrast to the clearly pessimistic outlook that prevailed between 1975 and 1981, some forms of intervention *could* probably reduce the recidivism of many individuals, including certain serious, multiple offenders.

(b) Rehabilitation/habilitation might be both a possible and useful correctional goal after all.

(c) Most standard forms and typical variants of treatment-oriented intervention—e.g., variants of individual or group counseling—were no longer considered intrinsically demeaning or necessarily onerous to offenders.

(d) When viewed as a package that combined explicit external controls and elements that ensured accountability, some forms of community-based intervention were now considered less risky to the public than before.

This consensus has been quite significant. For instance, in light of views (a) and (b), programs and research relating to rehabilitation or treatment were, by the later 1980s, less often considered either anachronisms or exercises in naivete and futility. Nor was rehabilitation as likely to be considered antithetical to various justice system reforms. In addition, rehabilitation programs were less often described as the tool of a broad, presumed conspiracy by a middle- and upper-class "establishment" which allegedly used various interventions (and incarceration per se) not just to curb crime but to help control socially disadvantaged groups (American Friends Service Committee, 1971; Brenner et al., 1971; Lerman, 1975; Mitford, 1971; Platt, 1969; Quinney, 1974; Rothman, 1971; Schur, 1973; Stapleton and Teitelbaum, 1972).

In short, some sharp edges of various correctional debates of the 1970s and early 1980s had softened, and the consensus had helped reduce various scientific, philosophical, and even political impediments to program development and research. Though increased institutional crowding and society-wide fiscal constraints had been very influential in generating a reexamination of community-based interventions, the core elements, supported by the consensus, provided a substantive framework for guiding the *general direction and emphasis* of many new research and development efforts with a wide range of juvenile offenders (Cullen and Gendreau, 1988; Cullen and Gilbert, 1982; McCarthy, 1987; O'Leary and Clear, 1984).

For instance, when supported by aspects (a) and (b) of the consensus, agreement on the value of core elements such as increased contact and multiple modality programming has helped shape numerous intensive interventions throughout the U.S. Especially notable have been intensive probation programs, often used in lieu of incarceration for a range of juvenile offenders, as well as a number of intensive parolee programs for adults. As discussed later, however, the core elements were by no means the sole stimuli and supports for such programs.

In any event, as various impediments to intervention decreased during the mid-1980s, momentum for program development and research increased. By 1987, specific core elements such as multiple modality programming and greater attention to offender needs gave increasing direction, context, and support to the development of, and a role for, *needs assessment*, an area which had previously evolved relatively slowly. However, most support and direction for needs assessment probably came from the continuing focus on risk assessment (Baird, 1982; Clear, 1988; Gottfredson and Tonry, 1987; Gottfredson and Gottfredson, 1986).

By the late-1980s, the level of program development efforts again resembled what had been occurring during the 1965-1975 period: i.e., many planners, practitioners, and researchers were proceeding in a relatively business-like and systematic manner with the task of testing, developing, implementing and evaluating promising methods and strategies. Based on the consensus achieved somewhat earlier, individuals from the skeptic and sanguine camps were moving in similar directions. Perhaps most important, the search for effective interventions for a wide range of offenders, including serious, multiple offenders, had been re-legitimized.

Despite these developments, an unsettled atmosphere still characterizes corrections with regard to the long-term effectiveness and utility of such intervention. The issues that remain in question are scientific, philosophical, and practical; and some are quite basic (Byrne, 1990; Byrne et al., 1989; Clear and Hardyman, 1990; Cullen and Gendreau, 1988; Cullen and Gilbert, 1982; Harris, 1987; O'Leary and Clear, 1984; Petersilia, 1990; Sechrest et al., 1979; Van Voorhis, 1987; von Hirsch, 1976). They focus not only on what constitutes acceptable evidence of a given program's effectiveness and on how much recidivism reduction is actually occurring, but also on which offenders should receive which interventions.

To many practitioners and others involved with multimodal interventions that require major resources, the typical answer to the "who" question has been: "The more troubled individuals, particularly multiple offenders."[5] This set of offenders, who may or may not have histories of violence, are generally easy to identify either on the basis of official records or interview and testing procedures. However, some of these individuals are difficult to distinguish from other subsets of offenders, such as moderately-motivated individuals whose skill levels and motivation to change are difficult to determine. Given this difficulty, the ability to assign various offenders to appropriate interventions remains open to genuine question. Though this situation does not diminish the overall legitimacy of intervention, it contributes to today's unsettled atmosphere and will probably do so for several years.

As will be seen, another source of today's unsettled atmosphere is the continuing difference of opinion over how well or poorly certain approaches work. Open to question are not only group therapy/counseling, individual therapy/counseling, physical challenge, and confrontation (deterrence/shock), but family intervention and vocational training as well.[6] Various meta-analyses and literature reviews conducted since the mid-1980s have left a fairly strong cumulative impression that several programs or approaches *have* very likely affected recidivism, at least under certain conditions and not just for BTA-amenables and/or low-risk offenders.[7] At present, this impression is more widely and perhaps strongly held than at any time during the 1980s. Moreover, largely because most meta-analyses have reached agreement that many programs are associated with positive outcomes, this impression is being challenged less often on empirical grounds. Interventions (including community-based ones) that address the issues of long-term crime control and behavioral change have assumed a widely recognized and accepted role with many offenders, including serious and multiple offenders. Moreover, this role applies across a broad range of intervention strategies, including complex "psychological" and/or skill-development approaches, as well as control/surveillance-centered approaches.

Despite these findings, neither meta-analyses nor reviews of the literature indicate that particular methods have been found whose outcomes are fairly consistently (e.g., three-fourths of the time) marked by *major* reductions in recidivism, specifically those characterized by reductions of 25% or more. Instead, reductions have generally been about equally distributed over a range extending from low, to moderate, and then to high. This applies to the full set of reported studies, not just those examining serious and multiple offenders.

The absence of even a few clearly powerful yet widely applicable types of programs further contributes to the continuing unsettled atmosphere surrounding intervention, including community-based intervention.[8] It may reflect the impact of several factors, such as the following: (a) Even effective programs may demonstrate only moderately positive outcomes when success is gauged on the basis of all participating offenders, i.e., all subgroups combined. (b) Programs that may be potentially powerful are sometimes poorly implemented and therefore may hardly reduce recidivism. (c) Many programs that are grouped together and considered a single approach may actually be dissimilar, and some of the subgroups of programs may not be powerful. (d) In many programs that were grouped together and analyzed as a single approach, particular methods that may have been applied across-the-board to all participating offenders may only have been relevant to, and therefore effective with, some participants.[9]

Today, several methods seem promising, but none has been shown to consistently produce major reductions while also applying widely. Yet, these and other efforts have received increased empirical support and are being given direction by the previously-mentioned core elements. Further, recent meta-analyses and reviews of published research from the 1980s have helped to change or at least modify the views of many critics within corrections regarding the actual/potential effectiveness of intervention. In retrospect, it appears that (a) the sheer weight of numbers (the volume of positive outcome studies, especially across differing analyses/reviews), combined with (b) the apparent convergence of evidence from such studies—several of them good to excellent in quality of research—has partly offset many individuals' questions about research adequacy.

INTENSIVE INTERVENTION

As shown in the meta-analyses and reviews of published literature covering studies conducted between 1960 and 1988, intensive supervision programs existed well before the onset of the current wave of such interventions in 1981-1982. At approximately that point, a new generation of *intensive supervision* programs began to emerge. It did so in response to three rapidly emerging issues: (a) institutional crowding; (b) cost-escalation, e.g., for constructing and operating secure facilities; and, (c) society's growing desire to prevent, reduce, and control the troublesome and sometimes dangerous behavior of its serious as well as less-serious offenders, whose numbers were perceived as rapidly increasing. These issues were linked to several widely accepted views, such as the perspective that standard probation and parole practice often provided inadequate control over many offenders, including serious and multiple offenders. These beliefs included:

- probationers and parolees *should* be carefully controlled, especially by being held "strictly accountable" for their misbehavior;
- many presently incarcerated individuals probably *could* have been safely worked with in community settings if appropriately designed interventions had been used; and,
- for various philosophical and practical reasons, community supervision is often *preferable* to incarceration, even when institutional crowding and cost issues are minimal.

At any rate, it has been in the context of crowding, costs, peace-of-mind and public safety that both intensive probation and intensive parole supervision have acquired their recent salient features or emphases. This intensive supervision movement has increasingly emphasized the quantity of staff-client interaction, especially surveillance-centered contacts. Before 1980, "intensive supervision" generally meant no more than two or three contacts per month rather than the standard *one*; this situation existed in operations other than experimental programs or in other special circumstances.[10] However, by 1983-1984 the number of contacts in intensive supervision programs had often become as many as two-to-four per week. As late as 1980, this quantity might have been criticized by various reformers and academicians as "overly intrusive social control." But, by the last half of the 1980s, this level of contact was common, was widely accepted, and was almost unquestioned (Harris, 1987; Lerman, 1975; Petersilia, 1990; Rothman, 1971; Schur, 1973).

As intensive supervision programs took shape in the early 1980s, the relative priority or emphasis placed on rehabilitation as a goal changed significantly. Specifically, its role was reduced in comparison to strategies focusing on short-term behavior control. Given the growing concerns and discontent regarding probation and parole practice, and given rehabilitation's overall decline since Martinson and others began attacking it around 1975, this shift occurred fairly easily and quickly.

The priority given to short-term, behavior-control goals as opposed to longer-term, rehabilitative/habilitative goals reflected the influence of at least three interrelated views and assumptions. First, it reflected the rather global view of many policymakers, academicians and practitioners that rehabilitation as a means of crime control and reduction was probably not achievable. Second, it represented the assumption shared by many professionals that rehabilitative efforts would neither change nor control the behavior of the more serious and/or multiple offenders, who are presumably the main clientele of intensified supervision. (This included juveniles and adults alike.) Third, it reflected the assumption that standard probation approaches, which were usually recognized as combining a modest level of control with a very modest amount of service, would simply not work with this difficult population. Therefore, what was thought to be needed was a sizable expansion of both control and service features. In particular, this involved a number of *external controls*. The external controls included unannounced spot checks, closely monitored curfew, house arrest, electronic monitoring, employment or education, and other elements such as restitution and community service, and substance abuse testing. These intensive supervision programs might be called the *control/surveillance-centered programs of the 1980s (CSPs)*. To the extent that satisfactory evaluations have been conducted and are available, their effectiveness will be reviewed below.

The increased use of intensive intervention strategies with emphasis on quantity of contacts was a major program development of the 1980s. This approach was designed not only as an alternative to institutionalization but as an alternative to community residential placement, i.e., an option to 24-hour, out-of-home, secure or non-secure, settings. Since this community-based strategy was characterized by such features as more frequent contacts, being administered by probation, and an emphasis on external controls/surveillance, it was called *intensive probation supervision (IPS)*. Within any given agency, IPS, by definition, differed from the standard caseload approach. Differences in design and operations were felt to be sufficient for the approach not to be considered simply a "probation enhancement."

Whereas IPS was initially designed for use in lieu of secure placement, a second intensive approach used increasingly in the 1980s focused on the post-placement phase and is called *intensive aftercare supervision (IAS)*. Though remaining less widespread than IPS, this approach is usually implemented following some period of institutionalization in secure, state-level facilities, e.g., training schools. As a result, it is likely that IAS targets youths and adults who generally have more serious offense histories than those for whom *IPS* is used. Several states, such as Utah and Colorado, sometimes use intensive aftercare supervision subsequent to 24-hour residential placement in the community—a placement which, itself, may have been used in lieu of state-level confinement in a training school.

Some state correctional systems experimented with one form of IAS—the halfway houses—as early as the late 1950s, and relied on it heavily during the mid-1960s.[11] These residential placements, which were transitions from secure confinement, involved more contacts with authority figures and more actual or potential social control than occurred with standard parole. Yet, at the same time, halfway houses were a multi-modal approach since they simultaneously involved control *and* service (Allen, 1978; Keller and Alper, 1970). In fact, external control was rarely considered the primary goal in the operation of these halfway houses.

Whether used with adults or older adolescents, halfway houses were largely designed, like many of today's IAS's, to help their residents handle the often difficult transition from institution to community. They also helped facilitate early release, whether or not a difficult transition seemed likely. As with intensive *probation* supervision, halfway houses have been largely reserved for non-violent individuals who seem unlikely to engender community opposition or media attention.

The most current national evaluation of halfway houses found that "the evidence is about equally divided between lower recidivism rates for halfway house residents or no difference in recidivism rates when compared to a control or comparison group." More specifically, "experimental design studies [N = 2] found no significant differences in recidivism rates between the sample of former halfway house residents and a control group. The quasi-experimental design studies [N = 17] indicated in 11 studies that former residents exhibited a lower rate of recidivism comparatively (primarily in comparison with institutional parolees). Five studies indicated no difference in recidivism rates. One study found a higher rate of recidivism for the halfway house sample" (Seiter et al., 1977:26).

Together with the continuing, relatively routine use of halfway houses, other kinds of intensive aftercare supervision have been increasingly used in recent years. Particularly with juveniles, IAS is being used in a wider range of ways than before and more often with a broad age-range.

Despite the increased use of IAS and IPS, comprehensive reviews suggest that few methodologically sound results are available regarding the effectiveness of such programs. For instance, with respect to *intensive probation supervision for juveniles (JIPS)*, the National Council on Crime and Delinquency (NCCD) conducted a national survey, funded by the U.S. Office of Juvenile Justice and Delinquency Prevention (OJJDP), of 41 currently operating programs designed mainly as alternatives to out-of-home placement, i.e., to residential or institutional placement for adjudicated youths. All programs were operated by local probation, either directly or through contracts with private service providers. Twenty of the 41 programs were selected for further study after meeting additional criteria, e.g., having operated more than 12 months, either statewide or in a large county, and having "some degree of data available on clients, outcome information, and/or program policies/procedures" (Krisberg et al., 1989:38).

Based on all available information about representative programs, NCCD concluded (Krisberg et al., 1989:40, 70):

> Systematic, formal outcome evaluation at the program level was generally nonexistent... Formal information after program completion was rare...Even the most comprehensive programs we visited generally lacked formal evaluations to measure their effectiveness as an alternative to out-of-home placement."

In short, it was virtually impossible to reach any definite conclusion about the effectiveness of these programs, particularly since their impact on the recidivism rates of program participants was essentially unknown.

A similar conclusion was reached by Armstrong, based on his 1986 national survey of intensive probation programs. Among the 31 juvenile intensive supervision (JIPS) agencies (out of a total reporting-sample of 60) that had attempted "some form of evaluation,...few had developed a methodologically sound design for data collection and analysis." Furthermore, although 19 of those agencies provided "recidivism rates" (usually revocation-of-probation-status rates) for both their JIPS and standard probation wards, there was no reason to believe that, in any given agency, these two groups of youths had comparable characteristics or risk-levels prior to their respective assignments, or that either random assignments or necessary statistical adjustments in recidivism rates had occurred. Moreover, "minimal information was provided" regarding *post*-supervision contacts with the justice system. Thus, as in the NCCD survey, little could be said about comparative effectiveness (Armstrong, 1988a, 1988b).

Regarding the programs and youths themselves, both the Armstrong and the NCCD surveys left little doubt that considerable emphasis was being placed on increased contacts, i.e., more than in standard probation. Most programs used this technique in order to achieve behavior control, and, among other things, to thereby avoid out-of-home placement or institutionalization; in fact, this was considered one of their principal goalss. Nevertheless, IPSs were typically characterized by a *dual* or multi-modal strategy, one that combined increased level of contacts and surveillance with some rehabilitative components. The presence of vocational/educational training, counseling, etc., suggested to both NCCD and Armstrong that rehabilitation, or at least a concern with service provision, had far from disappeared. This feature was present despite the shift away from treatment that began in the mid-1970s and soon made it easy to place a social control orientation on many intervention approaches. This finding regarding the presence of treatment/service provision as a major design feature in juvenile intensive supervision programs contradicts frequent assertions, mostly voiced from 1980 to 1985, that rehabilitation was "dead" (Armstrong, 1988a, 1988b; Krisberg et al., 1989).

These surveys indicate that different jurisdictions vary considerably in their eligibility criteria—specifically, in their lower-limit of offense seriousness—not just for inclusion in JIPS, but for out-of-home placement in general. Despite these differences, however, most jurisdictions identified in the two surveys would probably agree that youths in yet another national study—the New Pride Replication Program—*were* valid candidates for 24-hour residential placement or institutionalization, as well as for JIPS if an alternative were sought. In New Pride, program participants had to be 14 to 17 years old at intake and had to have at least three convictions within the previous 24 months for serious misdemeanors or felonies (the average being seven), any or all of which could have been violent. The evaluation of this project was conducted during 1980-1984 by the Pacific Institute for Research and

Evaluation (PIRE) for the U.S. National Institute of Juvenile Justice and Delinquency Prevention, the federal funding agency. PIRE examined 10 newly established programs in medium-to-large cities (Gruenewald et al., 1985; National Institute of Justice Reports, 1985).

Each program was modeled after Denver's New Pride project, which had operated since 1973. The basic design required an initial six-month intensive phase involving daily or near-daily contact with each youth. This was followed by six months of decreasing involvement with staff. Each program site was run by a private, non-profit, community-based agency. The primary focus was on concentrated service provision, including a combination of alternative schooling, vocational training, and job placement. The activities emphasized skill-building and self-reliance (thus, "New Pride") far more than surveillance and external control. Peer group influence was also addressed and counseling was mainly used on an as-needed basis. This set of program components was designed to address and overcome presumed causal factors in the individual's delinquency, and multiple causation was assumed. The major findings for the seven sites that remained in operation for at least three years were: Essentially no significant ($p < .05$) differences in recidivism, e.g., new petitions and readjudications, were found between New Pride youths and their controls after an average of 2.6 years follow-up from program entry.

In addition to programs described elsewhere in this volume, other studies of intensive supervision for serious or chronic juvenile offenders have recently been completed or are currently in progress (Byrne, 1990; Byrne et al., 1989; Clear et al., 1987; Petersilia and Turner, 1990). Included, for example, are the Michigan and Pennsylvania Skillman operations, and Ohio's Paint Creek (Deschenes, 1989; Turner, 1989; U.S. Department of Justice, 1988).

The finding that few valid outcome studies exist regarding the effectiveness of intensive probation supervision for juveniles (and adults) also applies to *intensive aftercare supervision*. For instance, based on their recent, OJJDP-funded, national survey of—and interviews with—over 80 current, IAS programs that were recommended by state officials, practitioners, and others as "innovative, commendable, or promising," Altschuler and Armstrong drew the following conclusion: "Since few of the programs were even haphazardly evaluated, it is impossible to know with any precision whether the programs were in fact successful." This observation also applies to the 26 programs from the larger sample of 80 that were site-visited and found to have the same problem, namely, an almost total lack of "process and outcome data with methodologically sound research findings" (Altschuler and Armstrong, 1990).

After reviewing IAS programs other than those included in their recent national survey, Altschuler and Armstrong indicated that a "dearth of evaluations [that] focused on juvenile aftercare programs has been noted in a number of recent reports and publications containing literature reviews." Moreover, based on their extensive review of the literature that mainly focused on 1970 to 1988, these authors drew the following conclusions: (a) Aftercare studies "tended to be more descriptive and impressionistic than empirical and evaluative"; and, regarding the latter, (b) "Only a small number of the aftercare evaluations used an experimental or a quasi-experimental design." In any event, few scientific studies of *intensive* aftercare have been conducted (Altschuler and Armstrong, 1990).

Despite this fact, Altschuler and Armstrong found that reduced recidivism was associated with two aspects of aftercare: pre-release or furlough, and post-institutional financial-and-employment assistance. Though the studies in question focused almost entirely on older adolescent and adult populations, many may have been relevant to somewhat younger offenders as well. Moreover, it was unclear whether the individual program components focused on in these studies were part of more *comprehensive, quantitatively intensive* interventions. Also unknown is the nature of the populations (e.g., high-, medium- or low-risk) targeted for participation in these programs, although all had been institutionalized or otherwise confined (Altschuler and Armstrong, 1990).

One large-scale, national evaluation of comprehensive, intensive aftercare supervision for serious, high-risk individuals does exist. In 1981-1985, OJJDP implemented the Violent Juvenile Offender Research and Development Program to test the feasibility and effectiveness of IAS with male, adolescent offenders who not only had a presenting violent offense, but one or more prior adjudications for a serious felony. In each of the four test sites that met the minimum participation standards—Boston, Memphis, Newark, and Detroit—program clients (Es) were first placed, for an average of six months, in "small secure facilities." After that, they were "reintegrated to the community through transitional facilities," via a community-based residence. This stage was followed by "intensive supervision," e.g., frequent contacts in small caseloads, "upon return to their neighborhoods." Control youths (Cs) were placed in "standard juvenile correctional programs," i.e., institutionalized for an average of eight months, then put on standard parole in regular-sized caseloads. Mean age at release from secure confinement was 17.1 for Es and 17.5 for Cs. For Es, the average time in the community-based residence and on intensive supervision was 2.2 and 1.3 months, respectively; for Cs, the comparable phases were 0.5 and 1.0 months, respectively (Fagan et al., 1988; Fagan and Hartstone, 1986).

Based on a blend of delinquency-causation theories, the intensive aftercare programs tried to emphasize "the development of social bonds and 'unlearning' delinquent behavior while developing social competence and skills" (Elliott et al., 1979; Hawkins and Weiss, 1985). To achieve these goals, most sites focused on: (a) job training, and especially job placement, (b) education, and/or (c) assistance with family and peer issues. A continuous case-management approach was used, based on initial diagnostic procedures and treatment planning for each youth.

On an approximately two-year follow-up after release from secure confinement, Es outperformed Cs ($p < .05$) on rearrest-rate in one site, Cs outperformed Es in another, and no significant differences were found in the rest and when all four sites were combined. However, the validity of these findings is unclear because: (a) Es and Cs in most sites were not well-matched on crucial variables such as number of prior petitions and prior adjudications, and no statistical adjustments for this deficiency were indicated; and (b) possible matching on *other* important variables relevant to the treatment intervention and to the outcome measures (except age) was not reported. Still, the study demonstrated that, under specified organizational conditions, e.g., administrative commitment and particular external/societal circumstances, one can establish and operate, for a number of years, complexly designed IAS programs for serious and violent juvenile offenders. In addition, it may be possible to implement such programs generally in accordance with theory-based principles. Finally, the authors of this evaluation seemed to imply that the 2.2 and 1.3 month periods of residential care and follow-up supervision in the community may have been too short for adequate social bonding and other theoretically-important goals to be achieved—intensity of intervention notwithstanding (Fagan et al., 1988).

ISSUES AND PROSPECTS

Though interventions based on rehabilitative/habilitative strategies, i.e., personal growth-centered themes, declined in status and usage from the mid-1970s through the early 1980s, they regained considerable strength in the past several years as knowledge-building resumed. Yet, as corrections enters the 1990s, the continued development of these approaches at other than a snail's pace is far from assured. One question is whether these growth-centered interventions will be little more than (a) mere appendages to management and control-centered or punishment/just desert-centered strategies, and (b) convenient vehicles for providing merely a modest level of services, except to persons who actively seek them or are in obvious need.

Within the American correctional system, surveillance/control, incapacitation, and risk-classification seem likely to continue for at least several years at about their present level of intensity, breadth and degree of public and professional acceptance. Under these circumstances, the relative status and specific role of growth-centered interventions are not likely to change radically during most of the 1990s. However, their status and role will probably increase substantially during that time, and important knowledge-building can certainly occur. If these changes take place, treatment-oriented interventions would not be implemented as mere appendages.

However, with regard to *knowledge-building* about effective programs, progress in the 1990s *could* be minimal if fewer than two of the following goals are achieved:

1. A higher percentage of the evaluations of intervention should be *well-designed* than in the past, and many fewer should be questionable as to quality. For instance, random assignment should be utilized more often, and, when employed, E/C matching on a number of crucial variables should be assured rather than simply assumed to invariably accompany this procedure.[12] Though evaluation designs thus far have ranged from mediocre to good, far too many are located at the mediocre end of the research continuum. The percentage of good-to-excellent evaluations is much too low.

2. A much higher percentage of programs than was the case from 1960 to 1988 should be purposely designed as *replications or partial replications*. Replicated (cross-validated) results could increase practitioners' and policy-makers' confidence about implementing particular programs or approaches. The initial replications might focus on seemingly promising, feasible, and relevant approaches, e.g., those associated with sizable reductions in recidivism, fairly representative settings and offender populations, and adequately implemented designs.[13]

3. *Purposive variations (PVs)* of earlier studies should be conducted more often than in the past. These could be especially useful if (a) the previous studies had yielded significant and sizable positive results, and (b) those same studies had been at least partly replicated. For instance, a PV study could test the results from a previously reported-upon promising program that dealt with 'X' (rural males, aged 13-16) in setting and population 'Y' (urban males, aged 17-20).

To maximize the value of PVs and planned replications, one should carefully describe not only the general nature and key features of the setting and sample, but as many of the following characteristics as possible: (a) *program* goals, philosophy, atmosphere, staff, staff roles, resources, relations with community and outside agencies, and general operating procedures; and (b) *organizational or agency* structure, relationships between components, and key policies/procedures.

4. Wherever possible, studies should describe the main *offender subgroups* that comprise the overall target populations. Separate outcome analyses should be conducted for each subgroup whose size is not too small for determining statistical significance. These "differentiated analyses" could be valuable whether or not differing interventions have been used with these subgroups. This procedure could help to accurately identify one or more techniques that may be particularly successful or unsuccessful with some, but not other offenders. Of course, a meaningful offender classification is needed in order to delineate the respective subgroups.[14]

5. *Intervention processes*—e.g., specific techniques, strategies and program features—should be identified and described more often and fully than before.

When this procedure occurs as part of well-designed research studies in which positive outcomes ($p < .05$) are found, researchers may obtain clues or even stronger leads regarding which factors substantially contribute to the success of growth-centered interventions. Though many techniques, strategies and features may contribute to positive outcomes, only a few of these factors probably account for *most* of the success.

Achievement of this goal is especially important for advancing correctional knowledge and practice, and some progress has already been made in this regard. For instance, several possibly important techniques, strategies and features were identified as early as 1968, and others have subsequently been added to this list[15] (Andrews and Kiessling, 1980; Palmer, 1968).

Intensive Intervention in the 1990s

During much of the 1990s, intensive intervention, especially intensive probation supervision (IPS), will probably address many of the same issues as in the 1980s. Issues likely to remain pressing include: (a) avoidance or reduction of institutional crowding and residential placement; (b) high construction costs; (c) the public's desire for protection against certain categories of offenders under community supervision. In addressing these issues, the 1980s-style "control/surveillance-centered programs" (CSPs), which seemed to satisfy most policymakers and others, will probably receive heavy use.

Given these circumstances, CSPs may not substantially change in the next few years, particularly in their focus and approach. However, operational fine-tuning will probably occur; e.g., not only using risk-assessment instruments to help determine participation and rate of contact, but—partly as an economy move—reducing or eliminating presumably non-essential program features. The specifics of this fine-tuning will reflect each jurisdiction's particular philosophy, situation, and resources, and program changes will apply to additions, reductions, and substitutions alike. For example, in some jurisdictions advanced technology and equipment will be added to increase control and efficiency; in others, such features may be reduced or phased out. Across many jurisdictions the sheer number of high-contact caseloads will probably increase. Often, these caseloads will be characterized by either increased or decreased service-provision; they may also be used mainly to control a broader range of offenders, including "special-populations" such as substance abusers and sex offenders.

To address issues of institutional overcrowding, reduced residential placement, high construction costs, and public protection, relatively complex programs and services are not absolutely essential, particularly if achieving low or reduced recidivism rates is not a principal goal. For instance, if a given jurisdiction's chief purpose in using intensive intervention is short-term *public protection*, it could address that goal by combining heavy surveillance, relatively little service provision, and rapid program-removal (i.e., probation or parole revocation) following even minor offenses and second- or third-time technical violations. In this context, program structure and operations could be relatively simple; moreover, fairly high recidivism and/or reincarceration rates might be considered evidence of success (short-term community protection). Eventually, of course, such rates could substantially increase crowding and thus become counterproductive in terms of reducing this condition.

Similarly, if short-term reduction of *crowding* is a given jurisdiction's principal concern or objective, not only are complex programs and services unnecessary, but it is not even necessary to include serious, chronic, or high-risk offenders in the target population. This is because, for population purposes, one body equals another, regardless of its circumstances or problems; as a result, non-serious, medium-risk or, conceivably, low-risk individuals could suffice. The key constraining condition is that these offenders would not have been institutionalized had intensive intervention been unavailable.

Finally, it might be added that if short-term protection is the central concern, long-term change in individuals could obviously be considered irrelevant, even with chronic or high-risk offenders. This applies regardless of a program's possible complexity. Nevertheless, it seems likely that *long-term* change, including long-term recidivism reduction, would often require relatively complex programs or substantial services. Moreover, these efforts would not just be limited to serious and/or high-risk offenders.

Addressing the issues identified above may therefore be more an organizational than a program-development challenge in the 1990's. However, one major challenge would be the development of demonstrably effective, community-based, intensive intervention programs for seriously troubled offenders. This would apply especially to those considered most likely to recidivate (high risks). Such a challenge would exist not only because of (a) the public's continued concern about these individuals' illegal behavior, but because (b) there is a paucity/absence of clear evidence about the ability of relatively integrated, complex, multi-modal programs of the 1980s to substantially reduce the recidivism rates (E/C, $p < .05$) of serious offenders, particularly those defined as high risk.

Clear evidence of recidivism reduction was not even found in the premier intensive intervention experiments of the 1980s: the New Pride study of intensive probation supervision and (except for one setting) the Violent Juvenile Offender study of phased community reintegration (aftercare). Certainly, evidence existed that the post-program recidivism rates were less than the pre-; this finding, itself, bore on public protection. Yet, similar pre/post reductions also probably occurred in comparison programs. In addition, the percentage of recidivists in both the E and C groups was generally high.

This lack of conclusive results does not mean intensive programs lacked utility or were less valuable than comparison programs. For example, the research literature clearly shows that E/C recidivism rates are often comparable (Gendreau and Ross, 1979, Gensheimer et al., 1986; Palmer, 1975; Panizzon et al., forthcoming; Van Voorhis, 1987; Whitehead and Lab, 1989). Moreover, insofar as E programs help avoid extreme or unacceptable institutional conditions they may comprise a generally more humane approach—as long as they do not involve equally extreme conditions themselves. Nevertheless, results from 1980s research suggest that several years may pass before E programs that *outperform* Cs on recidivism, particularly on longer-term recidivism, are developed and documented. This applies not just to overall target offender samples but to various offender-subgroups (Fagan et al., 1988; Gruenewald et al., 1985).

Yet, even without programs that have been shown to be more effective, intensive intervention could focus heavily on the following offenders: (a) less serious or less severely troubled offenders, and/or (b) middle-risk individuals who would otherwise be institutionalized. Many such youths and adults may be at critical stages and can still "tilt either way" regarding illegal behavior. With these individuals, integrated, intensive intervention programs can perhaps tip the balance away from illegal behavior more often than traditional program. Many such programs might be modifications of some which were assessed in the 1980s.

In sum, intensive programming in the 1990s will probably continue along the two main paths travelled thus far. "Path 1" 's main goal will focus on reducing or avoiding not only institutionalization/placement, particularly in connection with crowding, but related construction costs as well. Achievement of this goal will often be possible via control/surveillance accompanied by relatively little service, e.g., skill development. This approach will often require less-than-complex-or-highly-integrated programs, particularly with non-serious offenders. To achieve different or additional goals, especially long-term recidivism reduction (E/C) with these or other individuals, carefully conceived blends of various approaches may be needed (Clear and Hardyman, 1990; McCarthy, 1987; O'Leary and Clear, 1984).

"Path 2" will probably emphasize rehabilitation/habilitation's long-standing goal of helping offenders overcome problems, conflicts, and/or deficits, and grow or change as individuals. While often containing considerable control/surveillance, this path will place more emphasis than Path 1 on various combinations of (a) *counseling* directed at personal/interpersonal problem-solving and conflict-resolution, and (b) *life- and social- skills development* focused on personal competence-building, especially via vocational and educational training. Within Path 2, some programs will emphasize control/surveillance over rehabilitation/habilitation while others will do the opposite. In both cases, emphasis will partly depend on the proponents' theoretical leanings and possibly on the socio-political setting, as well as the nature of the offender sample (Altschuler and Armstrong, 1990; Cullen and Gendreau, 1982, 1988; O'Leary and Clear, 1984).

Whatever the emphasis, these programs will probably be more complex and costly than most Path 1s. Their main targets should probably be the more troubled and troublesome offenders, and/or those scoring fairly high on recidivism-prediction scales. This approach would apply to intensive probation supervision and intensive aftercare alike. As with Path 1 programs, careful research will be needed to adequately assess Path 2's impact and cost-effectiveness as compared to traditional programs. Given Path 2's goals, long-term follow-ups may be particularly relevant. This will at least be true more than with Path 1 programs, which are directed mainly at solving immediate problems such as crowding. If skills-development receives heavy emphasis while problem-solving via counseling receives little, the skills approach might be considered a separate path rather than a "branch": i.e., it would be outside rather than within the 1960s-1970s rehabilitation frame work, at least if rehabilitation is narrowly defined.

Development of successful programs would be accelerated if various principles, features, and preconditions of effective intervention were identified and, where possible, included. This approach would apply to programs for all offenders, not just the more troubled and/or high-risk. In this regard, some factors that were singled-out between the late-1960s and early 1980s might provide useful leads. The former were believed to play major roles in certain pre-1980 programs associated with substantially reduced arrests and/or convictions for many serious, multiple offenders [16] (Barkwell, 1980; Lee and Haynes, 1980; Palmer, 1969, 1974, 1975; Persons, 1967; Ross and Gendreau, 1980).

In working with very difficult and/or high-risk offenders, it may often be insufficient to develop intervention plans based largely or exclusively on the needs-classification checklists increasingly used since the mid-1980s. Instead, much more careful and integrated diagnosis and planning may be needed in order to determine, not just the main focus or foci of intervention, but each of the following: major initial decisions, e.g., type of placement; particular environmental pressures/resources and how to address or access them; sources of offender motivation-and-interest; specific intervention methods/ techniques to which the individual offender might respond positively or negatively; the priority and timing of program components; and, staff roles for effective intervention. This far more complex assessment might be particularly appropriate if the goal is other than short-term behavior-control. It might also be appropriate if an offender is considered unusually volatile, crisis-prone, or resistive. In short, checklists, by themselves, may be useful in specifying some areas that need attention, and approximately how much attention is needed. However, they are quite limited in indicating *how* to proceed. Careful individualized assessment is a precondition for the latter, more complex task (Benoit and Clear, 1981; Palmer, n.d., 1984).

Also emphasized in the 1990s will be work on special populations, e.g., substance abusers and sex offenders. This will proceed along Paths 1 as well as 2, with possible increasing emphasis on the latter (rehabilitation/habilitation). Regarding Path 2 in particular, the "resolve-personal-problems" and the "develop-or-increase-skill/capacities" perspectives will *both* be considered relevant, since it will be difficult to maintain the position that many substance abusers or sex offenders do not need interventions involving aspects of both approaches. Though recent literature reviews (Gendreau and Ross, 1987; Panizzon et al., forthcoming) suggest that promising programs are being developed for some such individuals, more research is needed to test their comparative effectiveness and especially their long-term impact. It is encouraging to see that special-population offenders are usually not viewed as undifferentiated entities, i.e., all essentially alike, even though their respective offense categories are identical. Partly for this reason, it is generally not assumed that any one approach will succeed with all members of the respective categories or even subcategories, e.g., all "substance" or "drug" abusers. In turn, however, these added distinctions among offenders call for further highly detailed studies and/or for well differentiated analyses.

The following problem has existed for at least the past three decades and should be kept in mind when planning programs for serious offenders: Many or most policymakers, as well as numerous practitioners, find it hard to recognize or accept the extent and interrelatedness of most such individuals' difficulties. This applies not just to personal problems/conflicts, but to life- and social-skills deficits and to offenders' ambivalence about changing their lives.[17] As a result, planners often substantially underestimate (a) the strength and extent of programming, support, and sometimes pressures that are needed to motivate and help such individuals confront, unravel, or overcome those difficulties/deficits, and (b) the amount of time needed to readjust and stabilize their lives. This error is made independently of the equally important *recognized* fact that most such offenders also have various strengths and skills, both actual and potential.[18]

Though the strength of offenders' "will power" or motivation is generally recognized, what is often overlooked or minimized is, therefore, the difficulty of harnessing and *redirecting* these powers/forces. To do this one must first detach or partly detach the individuals from activities, interests, desires, and loyalties that sometimes lead to illegal behavior, and must then redirect those offenders along less troubled paths. In short, one must not overlook the fact that offenders' current interests, commitments, feelings, self-images, ambivalences, psychological defenses, and/or unexpressed fears often actively block or divert the socially-more-acceptable use of actual or potential strengths and skills.[19] It is perhaps overly optimistic to expect short-term programs to help most such individuals redirect their strengths and skills, even if those individuals are motivated.

Although circumstances described above affect offenders at all socioeconomic levels and across all ethnic and social groupings, *social, economic, and historical disadvantages* appear to complicate the achievement of such redirection. For instance, when the fact of their social and economic disadvantages is recognized by many such offenders during adolescence or early adulthood, this awareness may further affect an already troubled self-image. The individuals' resulting bitterness and possible alienation may make positive, long-term change even more difficult to achieve.

Troubled, multi-problem offenders are not ipso facto "sick" and are not necessarily examples of deep-seated pathology. Nevertheless, when developing intervention plans it remains important not to overlook or minimize the extent of these individuals' need.[20] Thus, e.g., most serious and high-risk offenders, and even many middle-risk offenders, may be usefully viewed as having a combination of the following: (a) various developmental problems to address, frequently including life- and social-skills deficits; (b) personal commitments, ambivalence, and long-standing or situational feelings to relinquish, resolve, or control; and, (c) major environmental pressures, social disadvantages, and/or limited supports to deal with. It is often the convergence of these factors that makes intervention difficult. If some of these factors are only minimally addressed, a shift toward prosocial behavior may be only temporarily and/or moderately achieved. This may occur even if other limiting or negative factors—such as (a) and (c)—are adequately addressed (Elliott et al., 1979; Hawkins and Weiss, 1985). Limited shifts in a prosocial direction will not just reflect the offenders' perceived available alternatives; they will also express their ambivalence regarding change and will reflect the nature of their current loyalties and motivations.

For individual offenders, certainly the more serious or troubled, intervention should involve habilitative efforts or personal and social growth/development. This should occur whether or not crowding and cost-containment are simultaneously present as broader correctional issues or even principal goals. Though a habilitation/developmental framework may be easier to visualize and accept with *youths*, it is relevant to adults as well and may be useful in the 1990s as an integrating concept. Moreover, though the following partly involves semantics, "habilitation," if defined developmentally, is relatively free of certain stereotypes that accompany "rehabilitation." As a result, there may be a near-term tactical advantage in emphasizing habilitation. For instance, *unlike* habilitation, stereotypes of *rehabilitation* sometimes connote a fairly thorough overhauling or reconstituting of once-developed but subsequently 'fallen,' 'partly broken,' 'failed,' or even 'sick' individuals—generally *adults*. Moreover, it is often erroneously assumed that such individuals may have been left with few internal strengths on which to draw. A developmental or habilitation framework may also be useful in at least the early-1990s because rehabilitation's "name" has not been completely "cleared" following its quasi-banishment from American corrections during 1975-1985, and despite its re-legitimization in recent years.

As implied, a habilitation framework does not suggest that offenders are never manipulative, hurtful, highly resistive, seriously troubled, or disturbed, and that none of their actions or predicaments may be considered partly the result of personal failures. Nor does it suggest that offenders may never require substantial controls while developmental issues are being addressed. However, it does suggest that corrections, in the 1990s and beyond, should carefully examine the subject of *engaging and redirecting motivations*. Though engaging/redirecting may be a very individualized matter relative to the condition and circumstances of any given youth or adult, correctional research, assisted if necessary by other fields, could perhaps identify general principles, essential preconditions, and important specific strategies of intervention. At any rate, if individuals' strengths and skills are to be *used*, and if reintegration is to occur and last, motivation must somehow play a leading role.

Given intervention's bumpy and somewhat twisting road over the past 15 years, it might be useful to close on a mundane note that combines both the "skeptics'" and "sanguines'" concerns, experiences, and hopes: Without scientifically sound research to independently determine if and with whom programs have worked, interventions that have received even strong testimonials and high acclaim will probably fade after several years. This has occurred repeatedly in recent decades, even with programs deemed exemplary but whose evaluation research proved mediocre. In the long-run, sound evaluation is both an appropriate basis, and perhaps among the *surest* bases, for legitimacy, confidence, and deserved survival. And over the decades, despite its shortcomings, evaluation has contributed greatly to intervention's progress.

APPENDIX A

Whitehead and Lab (W&L) analyzed 50 studies of juvenile offenders conducted during 1975-1974 in institutional and community settings. Using fairly stringent success criteria, they found that 24 to 32% of the studies evidenced what they called "program effectiveness" (success). More specifically, to be considered effective, W&L required phi coefficients (.20+ or .30+) that reflected large or major reductions in recidivism—not just (a) statistically significant E/C differences, or even (b) *any* reduction, however small. Of the four categories of studies analyzed, those most often successful were "system diversion" (40% of those programs) and "community corrections-oriented approaches," i.e., probation or parole (35%). Least often successful were "non-system diversion," i.e., absence of intervention—no programming or contact (17%), and institutional residential programs (14%). Using a more common but less stringent criterion—$p < .05$, chi square—44% of the 50 programs that comprised the entire meta-analysis had positive outcomes. Nevertheless, by using only the stricter criteria, the .20+ or .30+ phis, Whitehead and Lab concluded that the present results, collectively, provide "little encouragement for advocates of correctional intervention. No single *type* of intervention displays overwhelmingly positive results on recidivism" (emphasis added). Yet, since several *individual* programs within given types evidenced substantial gains for Es vs. Cs, W&L acknowledged that some (individual) programs—e.g., system diversion programs—are able to reduce recidivism, among experimental clients significantly.

Whitehead and Lab's is the meta-analysis currently cited by individuals who believe intervention does not, in general, work. This conclusion could be defended relative to W&L's study if one not only adhered to (a), but also required (b), and could satisfy (c) in the following three points: (a) Focus exclusively on generic approaches (*types* or categories of intervention), which are analyzed as undifferentiated entities; therefore, omit results from the *individual* studies which comprise those approaches; (b) require "overwhelmingly positive results" for most such approaches or for each approach, as W&L apparently did; and (c) generalize from a set of studies that represent the main range of intervention approaches. However, regarding this last point the following observation should be made: Of the 50 studies in the meta-analysis, 30 involved juvenile diversion alone; W&L primarily generalized from this one approach to intervention as a whole. Moreover, prior reviews, including a 44-study meta-analysis, had largely shown that "juvenile diversion," viewed collectively—i.e., not distinguishing between system- and non-system diversion—was among the approaches least often successful when Es and Cs were compared on behavioral measures, regardless of the success standard being used. Related to these findings is the fact that, understandably, few such diversion programs had focused on relatively serious offenders. It is often recognized that E/C differences are relatively difficult to demonstrate with individuals who are non-serious, or, more specifically, low-risk offenders, and for whom quantitatively less improvement on recidivism can occur. Consequently, on average, diverted individuals are presumably among the low risks, i.e., good risks.

NOTES

1. In 1979, Martinson changed his earlier views and suggested that many programs had produced positive rehabilitative effects (Allinson, 1978; Martinson, 1979).

2. This set of amenables, as well as certain specified subgroupings, resembled one or more "personality types" described by some DI proponents. Based on "I-level" classification, the following types resembled the amenables in question: Immature Conformist; Neurotic, Acting-out; Neurotic, Anxious (Warren, 1971). These were

later termed Passive-Conformist, Assertive-Denier, and Anxious-Confused, respectively (Palmer, 1978, n.d.).

3. *Maturity level*-for instance, higher, middle, or lower maturity—is based on the Interpersonal Maturity Level System, also known as I-level, i.e., Integration Level (Warren, 1971). Each level contains a number of subgroups, or "subtypes." *Risk*, when identified at the middle or higher level, was usually derived from base expectancy scores and is neither theoretically derived from nor closely related to Maturity level (Baird, 1982; Clear, 1988; Gottfredson and Tonry, 1987).

4. These offenders were not uncommon among correctional, especially incarcerated populations. Some had lengthy histories of crime, some of which was violent or otherwise serious. Yet, many appeared to be provisionally open to change and only moderately committed to illegal behavior.

5. In this context, efforts that "require major resources" are those involving relatively complex treatment programs, e.g., intensive counseling combined with other components. Not included, however, are programs that mainly rely on external controls or do not use other major components.

6. Meta-analyses and other published reviews of research suggest the latter two are among the most effective.

7. Chief among the meta-analyses are those conducted by Garrett (1985), Lipsey (1989, forthcoming), Davidson et al., (1984), Whitehead and Lab (1989) and Gensheimer et al., (1986). Whitehead and Lab's analysis produced atypical conclusions and is discussed in Appendix A. Major literature reviews were conducted by Gendreau and Ross (1981, 1987), Van Voorhis (1987), Whitehead and Lab (1989) and, most recently, Panizzon et al. (forthcoming). In most meta-analyses and reviews of published research, multi-modal programs were routinely analyzed and reported in terms of their seemingly dominant component.

8. Any collection of individual programs will be said to comprise a "type" if those programs resemble each other in terms of specified, salient or dominant factors, e.g., components such as family counseling or variants therapy.

9. Here, we exclude the few recent programs in which offenders with different risk (and perhaps need) levels received substantially different interventions (Baird, 1982; Byrne et al., 1989; Clear, 1988).

10. For instance, additional contacts were common with indisputably disturbed individuals for whom incarceration nevertheless seemed inappropriate.

11. Today's halfway houses are often called transitional living arrangements.

12. This applies to whichever Es and Cs—groups or subgroups—are being compared: (a) everyone who entered the respective programs; and (b) everyone who completed them. Two other points should be noted: (1) Es and Cs should not be poorly matched on any crucial variables; and (2) the value of increasing the percentage of well-designed studies is independent of the fact, indicated by some meta-analysts, that program implementation may have been better in well-designed studies than in mediocre studies.

13. Since 1965, many unplanned or, at best, minimally planned partial replications have occurred. Collectively, evaluations of these programs often produced converging or mutually-reinforcing evidence regarding the effectiveness of the given interventions; yet, they produced some opposing evidence as well. If these studies had been

specifically designed as replications, their contributions to knowledge-building would have been greater.

14. Differentiated analyses are a key analytic tool in various approaches, particularly the differential intervention approach. Results from such analyses can provide practitioners and policymakers with important information about the organization and operation of particular programs, and about the types of offenders for whom those programs or parts thereof are most and least effective.

15. For instance, based on the careful observation and analysis of a large, multi-year, well-implemented-and-matched, random assignment study of juvenile multiple offenders in an intensive, personal-growth-centered, in-lieu-of-institutionalization program that operated in three California cities, Palmer et al. (1968) described the following as "significant contributors" to the success of that program: "a. matching of specific types of clients (offenders) with certain types of workers (agents); b. level of ability and perceptiveness of worker; c. intensive and/or extensive intervention by workers with regard to several areas of the client's life—made possible by low caseload assignments; d. emphasis upon the working through of the worker/ward relationship as a major vehicle of treatment;...."

16. Included, e.g., was California's Community Treatment Project (CTP) (Palmer, 1978, 1975, 1974), and other studies of juveniles, such as those by Persons (1967), Barkwell (1980) and Lee and Haynes (Project CREST) (1980). Excluded are studies that mainly involve less serious and/or non-serious offenders, e.g., Massimo and Shore (1963), Shore and Massimo (1979), and the Andrews and Kiessling (1980) study of the Canadian Volunteers in Corrections (CaVIC) program. It might be noted that the arrest and/or conviction measures which were used in studying these programs obviate the still occasionally encountered criticism that the success of such programs, e.g., CTP, reflects little more than program staffs' and/or other agency staffs' recommendations/decisions to revoke or restore parole/probation—and is therefore illusory. In general, however, the critics in question persistently avoid mentioning the fact that arrests and convictions, not revocations and restorals, are the outcome measures in question, and that these events obviously occurred prior to any staffs'/officials' recommendations/decisions to revoke/restore in response to those events (Empey, 1978; Lerman, 1975, 1968; Wilson, 1980). The criticism is further obviated by the also unacknowledged fact that—e.g., in CTP—arrests and convictions were also significantly and substantially reduced not just during parole (i.e., while under program/agency jurisdiction), but separately for a 4-year follow-up starting with discharge from all state jurisdiction/control (Palmer, 1978, 1975, 1974). Following such discharge, program staff and other agency officials no longer interacted with clients at all, let alone made decisions about their possible arrests and convictions.

17. This problem applies somewhat less in the case of special populations. In general, it also applies whether or not offenders are considered different from each other in intervention-relevant ways.

18. Even this, however, is far from universally accepted.

19. Stated differently, it is mainly the coexistence and interaction of the following which often makes those strengths and skills unavailable or which limit their usage in socially acceptable contexts: (a) particular motivations, defenses, attitudes, feelings, and conflicts, on the one hand; and, (b) the above-mentioned deficits plus (c) major external pressures and/or an insufficiency of reliable supports, on the other. In this connection it is sometimes assumed that by substantially reducing factor (b), by also

addressing and relieving (c), and by providing legitimate social opportunities, many or most serious, multiple offenders can be fairly quickly and perhaps permanently "turned around," possibly within six or so months (Elliott et al., 1979; Hawkins and Weiss, 1985). Sometimes, such change may in fact occur. Nevertheless, though strategy (b) + (c) + opportunity may be valuable or even vital as far as it goes, it can overlook or obscure the major interfering/limiting power of factor (a); and this factor has considerable relative importance for a high percentage of offenders.

20. The medical model characterized in the text has seldom been invoked since the early- or mid-1970s, at least not as a major or primary factor. Thus, when currently used to criticize or characterize various psychologically or social/psychologically weighted accounts of offenders and/or delinquency-causation (whether or not for serious/chronic offenders), it comprises a largely obsolete argument. Moreover, since almost no current psychological explanations of delinquency rest substantially on 'diseased-entity' and/or 'deep-personality deviation' premises, the criticism/characterization in question is essentially a straw man argument or an exaggeration at best. Many psychological or social-psychological explanations, e.g., draw heavily on social learning theory, not, e.g., on certain varieties of psychoanalysis.

REFERENCES

Adams, S. (1974). "Evaluative Research In Corrections: Status And Prospects." *Federal Probation* 38(1):14-21.

Allen, H. et al. (1978). *Halfway Houses*. Washington, DC: U.S. National Institutes of Law Enforcement and Criminal Justice.

Allinson, R. (1978). "Martinson Attacks His Own Earlier Work." *Criminal Justice Newsletter* (December) 9:4.

Altschuler, D. and T. Armstrong (1990). "Intensive Community-Based Aftercare Programs: Assessment Report." Baltimore, MA: Johns Hopkins University, Institute for Policy Studies.

American Friends Service Committee. (1971). *Struggle for Justice: A Report On Crime And Punishment In America*. New York, NY: Hill and Wang.

Andrews, D.A. and J. Kiessling (1980). "Program Structure And Effective Correctional Practices: A Summary Of The CaVIC Research." In *Effective Correctional Treatment*, edited by R. Ross and P. Gendreau. Toronto, CAN: Butterworths.

Armstrong, T. (1988a). "National Survey Of Juvenile Intensive Probation Supervision (Part I)." *Criminal Justice Abstracts* 20(1):342-348.

—— (1988b). "National Survey Of Juvenile Intensive Probation Supervision (Part II)." *Criminal Justice Abstracts* 20(2):497-523.

Baird, C. (1982). "The Wisconsin Workload Determination Project—Two Year Follow Up." Washington, DC: U.S. National Institute of Corrections.

Barkwell, L. (1980). "Differential Probation Treatment Of Delinquency." In *Effective Correctional Treatment*, edited by R. Ross and P. Gendreau. Toronto, CAN: Butterworths.

Barton, W. and J. Butts (1990). "Viable Options: Intensive Supervision Programs For Juvenile Delinquents." *Crime & Delinquency* 36(2):238-256.

Benoit, K. and T. Clear (1981). "Case Management Systems in Probation." Washington, DC: U.S. Department of Justice.

Brenner, R. et al. (1971). *Children and Youth in America: A Documentary History*. (2 Vols.) Cambridge, MA: Harvard University Press.

Byrne, J. (1990). "The Future Of Intensive Probation Supervision And The New Intermediate Sanctions." *Crime & Delinquency* 36(1):6-41.

—— A. Lurigio and C. Baird (1989) "The Effectiveness Of The New Intensive Supervision Programs." *Research in Corrections* 2(2):1-75.

Clear, T. (1988). "Statistical Prediction In Corrections." *Research in Corrections* 1(1):1-52.

—— S. Flynn and C. Shapiro (1987). "Intensive Supervision In Probation: A Comparison Of Three Projects." In *Intermediate Punishments: Intensive Supervision, Home Confinement, and Electronic Surveillance*, edited by B. McCarthy. Monsey, NY: Criminal Justice Press.

—— and P. Hardyman (1990). "The New Intensive Supervision Movement." *Crime & Delinquency* 36(1):42-60.

Conrad, J. (1982). "Research And Developments In Corrections: A Thought Experiment." *Federal Probation* 46(2):66-69.

Cullen, F. and P. Gendreau (1988). "The Effectiveness Of Correctional Rehabilitation." In *The American Prison: Issues in Research Policy*. New York, NY: Plenum.

—— and K. Gilbert (1982). *Reaffirming Rehabilitation*. Cincinnati, OH: Anderson.

Davidson, W. et al. (1987). "Diversion of Juvenile Offenders: An Experimental Comparison." *Journal of Consulting And Clinical Psychology* 55:68-75.

—— (1984). "Interventions With Juvenile Offenders: A Meta-analysis Of Treatment Efficiency." Washington, DC: U.S National Institute of Juvenile Justice and Delinquency Prevention.

Deschenes, L. (1989). "The Skillman Intensive Aftercare Project." Paper presented at the American Society of Criminology Annual Meeting, Reno, NV.

Elliott, D., S. Ageton and R. Canter (1979). "An Integrated Theoretical Perspective On Delinquent Behavior." *Journal of Research in Crime and Delinquency* 16(1):3-27.

Empey, L. (1978). *American Delinquency: Its Meaning and Construction*. Homewood, IL: Dorsey.

Fagan, J., M. Forst and T. Vivona (1988). "Treatment And Reintegration Of Violent Juvenile Offenders: Experimental Results." San Francisco, CA: URSA Institute.

—— and E. Hartstone (1986). "Innovation And Experimentation In Juvenile Corrections: Implementing A Community Reintegration Model For Violent Juvenile Offenders." San Francisco, CA: URSA Institute.

Garrett, C. (1985) "Effects Of Residential Treatment On Adjudicated Delinquents: A Meta-Analysis." *Journal of Research in Crime and Delinquency* 22:287-308.

Gendreau, P. and R. Ross (1987). "Revivification Of Rehabilitation: Evidence From The 1980's." *Justice Quarterly* 4(3):349-407.

—— (1979). "Effective Correctional Treatment: Bibliotherapy For Cynics." *Crime & Delinquency* 25:463-489.

Gensheimer, L. et al. (1986). "Diverting Youth From The Juvenile Justice System: A Meta-analysis Of Intervention Efficacy." In *Youth Violence: Programs and Prospects*, edited by S. Apter and A. Goldstein. New York, NY: Pergamon.

Glaser, D. (1975). "Achieving Better Questions: A Half-Century's Progress In Correctional Research." *Federal Probation* 39:3-9.

Gottfredson, D. and M. Tonry (eds.) (1987). *Prediction and Classification*. Chicago, IL: University of Chicago Press.

Gottfredson, S. and D. Gottfredson (1986). "Accuracy Of Prediction Models." In *Criminal Careers and Career Criminals* (Vol. I), edited by A. Blumstein. Washington, DC: National Academy Press.

Greenberg, D. (1977). "The Correctional Effects Of Corrections: A Survey Of Evaluations." In *Corrections and Punishment*, edited by D. Greenberg. Beverly Hills, CA: Sage Publications.

Gruenewald, P., S. Laurence and B. West (1985). "National Evaluation of the New Pride Replication Program. Executive Summary." Walnut Creek, CA: Pacific Institute for Research and Evaluation.

Harris, M. (1987). "Observations Of A 'Friend Of The Court' On The Future Of Probation And Parole." *Federal Probation* 51(4):12-22.

Hawkins, J. and J. Weiss (1985). "The Prevention Of Delinquency Through Social Development." *Journal of Primary Prevention* 6:73-97.

Hunt, D. (1971). *Matching Models in Education*. Toronto, CAN: Ontario Institute for Studies in Education.

Jesness, C. and R. Wedge (1983). "Classifying Offenders: The Jesness Inventory Classification System Technical Manual." Sacramento, CA: California Youth Authority.

Keller, O. and B. Alper (1970). *Halfway Houses: Community-Centered Correction and Treatment*. Lexington, MA: Lexington Books.

Krisberg, B. et al. (1989). "Demonstration of post-adjudication and non-residential intensive supervision programs: assessment report." San Francisco, CA: National Council on Crime and Delinquency.

—— (1989). "Demonstration of Post-Adjudication Non-Residential Intensive Supervision Programs: Selected Program Summaries." San Francisco, CA: National Council on Crime and Delinquency.

Lee, R. and N. Haynes (1980). "Project CREST And The Dual-Treatment Approach To Delinquency: Methods And Research Summarized." In *Effective Correctional Treatment*, edited by R. Ross and P. Gendreau. Toronto, CAN: Butterworths.

Lerman, P. (1975). *Community Treatment And Social Control: A Critical Analysis Of Juvenile Correctional Policy*. Chicago, IL: University of Chicago Press.

—— (1968). "Evaluative Studies Of Institutions For Delinquents: Implications For Research And Social Policy." *Social Work* 13(3):55-64.

Lipsey, M. (forthcoming). *Juvenile Delinquency Treatment: A Meta-Analytic Inquiry Into The Viability Of Effect*. New York, NY: Russell Sage Foundation.

—— (1989). "The Efficacy Of Interventions For Juvenile Delinquency." Paper presented at the American Society of Criminology annual meeting, Reno, NV.

Lipton, D., R. Martinson and J. Wilks (1975). *The Effectiveness of Correctional Treatment: A Survey of Treatment Evaluation Studies*. New York, NY: Praeger.

Martin, S., L. Sechrest and R. Redner (1981). *New Directions in the Rehabilitation of Criminal Offenders*. Washington, DC: National Academy Press.

Martinson, R. (1979). "Symposium On Sentencing: Part II." *Hofstra Law Review* 7(2):243-258.

—— (1974). "What Works?—Questions And Answers About Prison Reform." *Public Interest* 35:22-54.

Massimo, J. and M. Shore (1963). "The Effectiveness Of A Comprehensive Vocationally Oriented Psychotherapeutic Program For Adolescent Delinquent Boys." *American Journal of Orthopsychiatry* 33(4):634-642.

McCarthy, B. (ed.) (1987). *Intermediate Punishments: Intensive Supervision, Home Confinement, and Electronic Surveillance*. Monsey, NY: Criminal Justice Press.

Megargee, E., M. Bohn, Jr. and F. Sink (1979). *Classifying Criminal Offenders: A New System Based On The MMPI*. Beverly Hills, CA: Sage.

Mitford, J. (1971) "Kind And Usual Punishment In California." *Atlantic Monthly* 227:45-52.

National Institute of Justice Reports (1985). "Introducing New Pride." September:9-12.

O'Leary, V. and T. Clear (1984). *Directions For Community Corrections In The 1990s.* Washington, DC: U.S. National Institute of Corrections.

—— (n.d.). "Individualized Intervention With Young Multiple Offenders." (Unpublished manuscript.)

—— (1975). "Martinson Revisited." *Journal of Research in Crime and Delinquency* 12:133-152.

—— (1974). "The Youth Authority's Community Treatment Project." *Federal Probation* 38(1):3-14.

—— (1984). "Treatment And The Role Of Classification: A Review Of Basics." *Crime & Delinquency* 30(2):245-267.

—— (1983). "The 'Effectiveness' Issue Today: An Overview." *Federal Probation* 47(2):3-10.

—— (1978). *Correctional Intervention and Research: Current Issues And Future Prospects.* Lexington, MA: Lexington Books.

—— et al. (1968). "Recent Findings And Long-Range Developments At The Community Treatment Project. Report No. 9, Part I." Sacramento, CA: California Youth Authority.

Panizzon, A., G. Olson-Raymer and N. Guerra (forthcoming). "Delinquency Prevention: What Works/What Doesn't." Sacramento, CA: Office of Criminal Justice Planning.

Persons, R. (1967). "Relationship Between Psychotherapy With Institutionalized Boys And Subsequent Community Adjustment." *Journal of Consulting Psychology* 31(2):137-141.

Petersilia, J. (1990). "When Probation Becomes More Dreaded Than Prison." *Federal Probation* 54(1):23-27.

—— and S. Turner (1990). "Comparing Intensive And Regular Supervision For High-Risk Probationers: Early Results From An Experiment In California." *Crime & Delinquency* 36(1):87-111.

Platt, A. (1969). *The Child Savers: The Invention of Delinquency.* Chicago, IL: University of Chicago Press.

Quay, H. and L. Parsons (1970). *The Differential Behavior Classification Of The Juvenile Offender.* Morgantown, WV: Robert F. Kennedy Center.

Quinney, R. (ed.) (1974). *Criminal Justice in America.* Boston, MA: Little, Brown and Company.

Romig, D. (1978). *Justice for Our Children.* Lexington, MA: Lexington Books.

Ross, R. and P. Gendreau (1980). *Effective Correctional Treatment.* Toronto, CAN: Butterworths.

Rothman, D. (1971). *The Discovery of the Asylum: Social Order and Disorder in the New Republic.* Boston, MA: Little, Brown and Company.

Schur, E. (1973). *Radical Non-intervention: Rethinking the Delinquency Problem.* Englewood Cliffs, NJ: Prentice-Hall.

Sechrest, L., S. White and E. Brown (1979). *The Rehabilitation Of Criminal Offenders: Problems And Prospects.* Washington, DC: National Academy of Sciences.

Seiter, R. et al. (1977). *Halfway Houses. National Evaluation Program. Phase I Summary Report.* Washington, DC: U.S. National Institute of Law Enforcement and Criminal Justice.

Shore, M. and J. Massimo (1979). "Fifteen Years After Treatment: A Follow-up Study Of Comprehensive Vocationally Oriented Psychotherapy." *American Journal of Orthopsychiatry* 49:240-245.

Stapleton, W. and L. Teitelbaum (1972). *In Defense of Youth*. New York, NY: Russell Sage Foundation.

Turner, S. (1989). "Preliminary Results On The Paint Creek Youth Center." Paper presented at the American Society of Criminology Annual Meeting, Reno, NV.

U.S. Department of Justice (1988). "A Private-Sector Corrections Program For Juveniles. Paint Creek Youth Center." Washington, DC: U.S. Office of Juvenile Justice and Delinquency Prevention.

Van Voorhis, P. (1987). "Correctional Effectiveness: The High Cost Of Ignoring Success." *Federal Probation* 51(1):56-62.

Von Hirsch, A. (1976). *Doing Justice: The Choice of Punishments*. New York, NY: Hill and Wang.

Warren, M. (1971). "Classification Of Offenders As An Aid To Efficient Management And Effective Treatment." *Journal of Crime, Law, Criminology, and Police Science* 62:239-258.

—— et al. (1966). "Interpersonal Maturity Level Classification: Juvenile. Diagnosis and Treatment of Low, Middle, and High Maturity Delinquents." Sacramento, CA: California Youth Authority.

Whitehead, J. and S. Lab (1989). "A Meta-analysis Of Juvenile Correctional Treatment." *Journal of Research in Crime and Delinquency* 26(3):276-295.

Wiederanders, M. (1983). "Success on Parole: Final Report." Sacramento, CA: California Youth Authority.

Wilson, J. (1980). "'What Works?' Revisited: New Findings On Criminal Rehabilitation." *Public Interest* 61:3-17.

Part II

Programming Issues and Specialized Approaches in Juvenile Intensive Supervision

Work Experience and Employment Programming for Serious Juvenile Offenders: Prospects for a "Productive Engagement" Model of Intensive Supervision

by
Gordon Bazemore

The "productive engagement" approach to intensive supervision of juvenile offenders is described. Important features of this new approach include the systematic use of offender work and employment to achieve public protection, and an emphasis on providing restitution to victims and the community at-large. Advantages of the new model, compared to the more passive surveillance and treatment/services approaches to intensive supervision, are outlined.

INTRODUCTION

The majority of intensive supervision programs (ISPs) for juvenile offenders in operation today are best characterized along a continuum that gives major priority to surveillance at one end and treatment or services at the other (Armstrong, 1988). Modeled primarily after ISPs in adult probation, a pure "surveillance" approach would place exclusive focus on monitoring offenders through curfews, home visits, electronic surveillance and the like to ensure that risk to the public from reoffending is minimized. Conversely, the ideal type "treatment/services" approach would target serious offenders for intensive therapeutic interventions as well as for services such as remedial education. This approach to ISP appears to be derived from programs such as those funded in the early 1980s under the U.S. Office of Juvenile Justice and Delinquency Prevention's (OJJDP) Serious Juvenile Offender initiative (Fagan, Rudman and Hartstone, 1984) and the New Pride replication programs of the late 1970s (Gruenewald, Laurence and West, 1985). The latter approach is focused on rehabilitative as well as incapacitative objectives, emphasizing the assumed relationship of services to decreases in reoffending.

The concern with surveillance and treatment overlap in many programs, and the strengths, weaknesses and different emphases of both approaches are discussed in detail in other chapters in this volume. What both approaches seem to share, however, is a passive orientation toward the offender, who is seen as the target of monitoring and surveillance on the one hand, or a recipient of services on the other. *Avoidance* of certain behaviors (e.g., new offenses, drinking alcohol) and/or submission to treatment (e.g., attending counseling or remedial classes) are generally the primary indicators of program success. Neither the surveillance nor the treatment/services emphasis demands an active, behavioral commitment. In this regard, most intensive supervision programs are not unlike other community supervision approaches that have been similarly criticized for responding to offenders as passive recipients of services or punishment (Maloney, Romig and Armstrong, 1988; Schneider, 1985; Harris, 1984).

This chapter describes an evolving "third approach" to intensive supervision that relies heavily on employment and work experience. Focused on engagement of the offender in productive activity, the most important feature of this approach is the systematic use of work and employment as tools to accomplish the primary goal of intensive supervision—public protection through "incapacitation in the community." While also interested in competency enhancement and other assumed benefits of work experience, proponents of this fusion of intensive supervision and work experience, or employment programs, emphasize the increase in control possible through "programming" blocks of offenders' time in productive activity (cf., Klein, 1988a:95-97). Unlike surveillance approaches that place juvenile justice workers in the role of waiting for new offenses or violations of conditions of supervision to occur, or treatment/services approaches that require practitioners to deliver therapy or remedial services to passive recipients, the "productive engagement" model makes offender completion of positive requirements major indicators of program success. In addition to successful job and work experience performance, first among these requirements is restitution to victims and community service. The emphasis on reparative justice and victim accountability is thus a major feature of this approach.[1]

For the most part, the few recent attempts in the criminological literature to describe "promising approaches" to community supervision of juvenile offenders have had little to say about programs and practices emphasizing work experience and employment (e.g., Greenwood and Zimring, 1985). Compared with some of the more glamorous and well-publicized juvenile offender experiments of the 1980s, including wilderness programs and special projects such as "Scared Straight," these work-related programs also seem to have garnered less "media appeal.[2] Thus, it is necessary to describe these new work experience/employment efforts—which characterize the productive engagement approach—in some detail and also place them in the context of previous programs. The following section considers the theoretical basis for employment/work experience in the community response to delinquency, and provides a brief review of available empirical and experiential evidence on the viability and impact of such efforts.

Because many employment programs for offenders and "at-risk" youth have had difficulty in achieving community acceptance and long-term stability, the bulk of this chapter considers "themes," assumptions and working principles that appear critical to the successful "marketing" of these new offender employment approaches in local communities. These qualitative features are important in distinguishing the emerging model of intensive supervision from other approaches and from previous offender employment efforts. As such, they may offer a guideline for future development of prototypical programs.

JUVENILE OFFENDERS IN WORK EXPERIENCE AND EMPLOYMENT PROGRAMS

Although work-related education and remedial training have been occasionally emphasized in some community programs and correctional agencies (Knox, 1981), employment and work experience has generally taken a back seat to casework or treatment priorities in juvenile justice. In recent years, however, the field of juvenile corrections and community supervision has seen a renewal of interest in such efforts for delinquent and at-risk youth (James and Granville, 1984; Jenkins, 1988a). At the federal level, at least two recent special initiatives appear intended to focus directly on strategies to improve and expand employment options and job skills for delinquent offenders (U.S. Office of Juvenile Justice and Delinquency Prevention, 1987).

Among policymakers generally, and a growing spectrum of the justice and lay community in particular, there is increasing consensus about the need for greater opportunities for offender employment as part of a coherent correctional or delinquency prevention strategy. Several practical reasons for this increased interest include:

- Providing a legitimate income to permit prompt, efficient payment of the maximum amount of restitution to victims.
- Offsetting some of the costs of correctional programs through contract arrangements for offender labor and deductions from paychecks for fees and fines.
- Providing exposure to conventional peers and role models, and to norms that support employment and a "work ethic."
- Reinforcing to youthful offenders through work requirements the message of the cost of crime.
- Creating public and private benefits of work projects in local communities.
- Offering the opportunity to learn responsible money management, and to develop offender competencies.

One of the strongest rationales in recent years for supporting employment and work experience programs grows out of the need for cost-effective community supervision options for chronic and serious offenders. As both crowded facilities and concerns with public protection have led many probation departments to experiment with intensive probation supervision, some have looked for approaches that require less staff commitment. Relying heavily on existing community organizations and employer resources, and generally involving group supervision of offenders, effective use of employment offers the potential for a more cost-effective means of achieving "community incapacitation."

Although policy initiatives in juvenile justice are often not closely tied to any theoretical base (National Council on Crime and Delinquency, 1981; Hackler, 1978), a focus on the role of employment and work experience in the prevention and correction of delinquency and crime is firmly grounded in the implications of several schools of thought in academic criminology. From the perspective of "strain theory" (Cloward and Ohlin, 1960; Cohen, 1955), for example, income and/or status derived from employment might be expected to mitigate the disjunction between cultural goals and legitimate means of achieving these goals, thus reducing the motivation for continued delinquency. In Greenberg's (1977) more recent statement of strain theory, access to income provided from jobs is postulated to reduce juvenile property crimes by lessening frustration resulting from the inability to purchase consumer goods (e.g., clothes, cars) vital to status and popularity in the adolescent world.

Differential association theory and some of its variants such as social learning theory (Elliott, Ageton and Canter, 1979; Akers, 1977) might also argue for a possible linkage between employment and reductions in delinquency. Such reductions would be expected as a result of increased interaction with positive role models and exposure to values supportive of conventional behavior and antithetical to deviance (Sutherland, 1939).

Generally, a range of social-psychological theories focusing on self-concept (e.g., Kaplan, 1980; Reckless and Dinitz, 1972) would suggest that productive work might engender feelings of success and self-esteem. Societal reaction perspectives (Schur, 1973; Becker, 1963) might imply that "positive labeling" and a less negative self-image would result from treating young offenders as resources for useful work rather than as recipients of supervision or services. From these perspectives, improvements in self-esteem would thus be expected to remove the need to achieve positive regard through deviance.

Finally, the theoretical approach most pertinent to the connection between work and delinquency is control theory (Hirschi, 1969; Briar and Piliavin, 1965). Drawing on this perspective, one might expect employment to decrease delinquency in a correctional program if it strengthens bonding to legitimate institutions or provides a "stake in conformity" that gives the offender something to lose by further violations (Toby, 1957).

Empirical research on the hypothesized relationship between employment and delinquency/crime—especially the impact of work on recidivism—is in its infancy. Although several empirical studies suggest decreases in reoffending as a result of employment (Thornberry and Christiansen, 1984; Berk, Lenihan and Rossi, 1980), the bulk of research investigations suggest no relationship or even a positive correlation between working and delinquency (Greenberger, Steinberg and Ruggiero, 1982; Shannon, 1976; Hirschi, 1969). These findings have typically been based on simplistic comparisons between employed and unemployed juveniles, however, and have not taken account of such critical variables as school status, hours worked per week, pay, job status and numerous other factors pertaining to the type of job (Agnew, 1986). A recent more sophisticated study by Agnew (1986), which controls for these variables, indicates lower delinquency among young workers whose jobs have certain characteristics (e.g., shorter hours, higher pay), and points researchers in the direction of more productive modes of inquiry sensitive to type of job. While much can be learned from existing studies and even more from the record of special programs, complex questions remain about the role of the work experience in reducing delinquency—especially with regard to examining the implications of popular theories.

Unfortunately, testing and refinement of propositions derived from any of these theories about the relationship between employment and delinquency (and subsequent application of this knowledge to policy) has been severely limited by two factors. First, youth access to jobs and work experience has been increasingly restricted in the past two decades by a widening of the gap between youth and adult employment, and especially between employment of minority and non-minority youth (Wetzel, 1987; Williams and Kornblum, 1985). Shifts in the national economy have dramatically reduced the number of entry-level jobs that used to provide footholds into the world of work, while relocation of these jobs to suburban areas and advanced schooling and credential requirements for applicants have exacerbated the access problem for many youth (Blake, 1988; Duster, 1987). Although employment prospects are generally bleak for all young people, additional obstacles are faced by disadvantaged, at-risk and delinquent youth seeking work. Employers are often concerned about added liability, whether youths can be trusted and how they will interact with fellow employees. When social workers and juvenile justice practitioners have attempted to encourage employers to hire young offenders, a common response has been that offering jobs to delinquents may be viewed as rewarding law-breaking behavior while depriving "straight" kids in the community of employment (Smith, Walker and Baker, 1987; Ball et al., 1981).

Second, the nature of those jobs and work experiences available to at least some young people may be of equal concern to those who view work as a potentially positive socialization experience. In the job market as it currently exists, opportunities may be rare for the associations and interactions suggested by major delinquency theories to be the basis for a possible reduction in offending. Postulated linkages between reductions in delinquency and employment that might be derived from these theories seem to rely on an idealized work experience often bearing little resemblance to conditions in jobs actually occupied by working adolescents. According to Agnew (1986:22), "Most juvenile jobs are characterized by low pay, low prestige, and poor working conditions. Such jobs probably do little to reduce strain or increase social control. In fact, [some research] suggests that the typical adolescent job may do much to *increase strain* and *reduce social control.*" [emphasis in original]

Further, "segregation" of young people in jobs such as those in the fast-food industry allows for little adult interaction and hardly seems conducive to the development of "conventional bonds" (William T. Grant Foundation, 1988; Waldinger and Bailey, 1985). There is little in the nature of such work experiences that would necessarily increase associations with nondeviant role models, and if reducing delinquency is the primary goal, some of these jobs may do more harm than good (Greenberger and Steinberg, 1986). It is not surprising, therefore, that some studies have found little positive impact on delinquency resulting from employment in typical "youth jobs" (Greenberger, Steinberg and Ruggiero, 1982; Shannon, 1976; Hackler and Hagan, 1975).

To address the problem of naturally occurring barriers to job access and job retention, since the late 1960s there has been increasing recognition that special programs are needed for delinquents or at-risk youth (Smith, Walker and Baker, 1987; Butler and Mangum, 1982; Brickell, 1980). Often supported with federal funds, such efforts as job preparation, job-seeking skills and work orientation training have been designed to facilitate access to the job market, and to instill work attitudes and discipline needed to improve retention.[3] More ambitious job development and "supported work" programs in the 1970s provided ongoing assistance to young workers and sought to further increase access by engaging employers in the youth employment process, often through subsidies and other incentives (Ball et. al, 1981). These and other efforts to improve access and retention have experienced at least mixed success with offender and other at-risk populations (Zimmerman, 1980; Mangum and Walsh, 1978). Overall, a fair reading of the literature suggests that despite a few highly publicized negative examples and persistent theoretical and design problems, there have been many well-conceived, high-quality youth employment programs (Levin and Ferman, 1985; Taggart, 1981).

Although more research is needed on the long-term effects of employment and work experience programs on recidivism and long-term adjustment, several follow-up studies indicate positive, though varied, impact on recidivism (Lab, 1988; Willman and Snortum, 1982; Knox, 1981). In addition, recurring problems that have weakened both state and federal employment efforts for at-risk youth typically do not appear to be attributable to the performance of clients in these programs. It is encouraging to note that even serious and chronic juvenile and adult offenders seem to have done as well or better than other clients in employment and work efforts (Klein, 1987; James and Granville, 1984). Summarizing the performance of the most difficult clients in a number of supported work programs (50% of whom had prior contacts with the criminal justice system, and 30% of whom were on probation at the time), Mangum and Walsh (1978:69), for example, note that:

> Large numbers of youths who have been viewed traditionally as unemployable or unwilling to work are, in fact, anxious to work and capable of working...Individuals who have been written off as unemployable can work productively and customers are prepared to pay for the goods and services they produce. This finding has policy implications beyond the fact that such individuals have untapped potential. It means that supported work and its progeny might reduce the net public subsidy for government funded training and employment programs by charging a reasonable amount for the goods and services produced by participants while in the program.

Even more hopeful have been programmatic efforts to address the problem of negative characteristics in existing youth jobs and to improve the "readiness" of many at-risk youths for future employment through structured work experience. Some programs have gone beyond job preparation and placement activities in an attempt to "design" employment opportunities and paid work experiences more tailored to achieve educational and other socialization objectives, as well as improve later job retention and achieve production outcomes (Blake, 1988; Grice, 1988; National Commission on Resources for Youth, 1974). Typically publicly funded and intended as transitional steps to occupational ladders and/or additional schooling, these programs often combine educational credit and instruction with strict discipline and adult supervision. Participants may be engaged in one of a variety of community improvement or public works projects.

Compared with many "naturally occurring" jobs available to youths, these structured work efforts seem more capable of providing the conditions of positive socialization that popular theories of delinquency suggest lead to reductions in offending. Drawing at least indirectly on the more organizational and policy-focused expressions of control or containment theories, recent innovative youth work programs focused on conservation projects and/or service efforts (Blake, 1986; Rosenberry, 1986) emphasize "bonding" through attachment to positive adult role models and the development of "commitments" or "stakes in conformity" by participation in useful work (Polk and Kobrin, 1972; Briar and Piliavin, 1965). Programs with this "positive youth development" focus (Jenkins, 1988a; Polk and Kobrin, 1972) also include a concern with changing the public image of delinquents and at-risk youth from being regarded as "problem" clients of social service agencies to being viewed as potential community resources.

Unfortunately, such programs have generally been small and underfunded with few resources for collection of even descriptive data. As a result, with the exception of positive evaluations of some Youth Conservation Corps programs (Wolf, Leiderman and Voith, 1987; Marans, Driver and Scott, 1972), there has been little empirical examination of their impact or of theoretical propositions about work and delinquency supported by these approaches. Further, while they have generally served delinquent as well as nondelinquent youth, such programs have never been well-integrated into local juvenile systems. A hopeful sign for the future, however, is the gradual adoption of key principles of these theoretically-grounded approaches in many of the incipient juvenile-justice-sponsored work and employment programs to be described in subsequent sections of this chapter.

GAINING SUPPORT IN LOCAL COMMUNITIES: "MARKETING" OFFENDER EMPLOYMENT

The preceding review suggests that there has been no shortage of sound program concepts. However, a close reading of accounts of previous efforts to develop employment and work experience options for young offenders and other at-risk youth reveals common problems in the ability to obtain local support and maintain commitment—to "sell" communities and employers on the need for youthful offender employment (e.g., Levin and Ferman, 1985; Ball et al., 1981). Jobs programs for young offenders often begin with an "image problem" in many communities and may quickly become easy targets for local politicians and other detractors wishing to play on the themes of "make work" or "commit a crime, get a job" to attack vulnerable public programs. Even the most theoretically coherent and well-managed efforts may suffer from failure to develop support and symbiotic ties to employers, policymakers and local organizations; in the case of serious offender programs, such support would seem even more critical to stability and longevity.

Because social workers frequently find the idea of "marketing" distasteful, they typically do little to counter these images of their programs. When they do engage in community "outreach," the appeal often plays on humanitarian sentiments to "help" offenders, as opposed to emphasizing the mutual benefits to employers and the value of youth work to the community as a whole. Underlying this failure in marketing and ability to garner community support for youth employment has been a set of negative assumptions about the interests and abilities of offenders or other adolescents to perform even menial work tasks successfully. Still heavily influenced by the traditional therapeutic or social work model, job training and placement programs have often been inclined toward highlighting deficits rather than potential competencies of youthful clients, and emphasizing remedial counseling-focused intervention and assistance rather than more active job experience approaches.

In this context, the most urgent current focus for those interested in the potential of offender employment as a correctional tool should be on issues of program implementation, local acceptance and survival (Betsey, Hollister and Papageorgiou, 1985). Until the process of implementing and institutionalizing coherent programs is better understood, theoretical questions of impact of employment on future delinquency cannot be clearly examined. Toward this end, this chapter examines a group of program efforts that have achieved some success and stability, and have even expanded in spite of the reduced funding environment of the 1980s by building a base of local community support—apparently based on mutual benefits to employers, neighborhood organizations, youths, victims and the juvenile justice system. Unlike most previous youth employment efforts, these programs share a capacity for effectively marketing offender employment and work experience in their local communities.

For the most part, the programs described have been spin-offs of juvenile restitution programs.[4] Not initially concerned with employment per se, project directors sought strategies to ensure that young offenders had legitimate means to pay restitution. Many gradually developed more comprehensive employment components that could essentially guarantee a paid work opportunity to offenders who did not have a job or who could not be easily placed in a private-sector position (Bazemore, 1987).

Drawn from interviews with some 30 project directors, review of program descriptions and other documentation, and occasional site visits,[5] this discussion is not based on completed empirical research. Rather, these observations are presented as a descriptive account of common themes and working principles that seem to distinguish these offender employment efforts from past programs that were less successful in building a strong base of community support. It is hoped that the discussion will generate debate about effective models and "design principles" for future serious offender programs, as well as raise a number of research questions for more systematic empirical examination. Many impact questions remain, and much more intensive observational investigation is needed to understand program process.

EMPLOYMENT MODELS FOR SERIOUS OFFENDERS: THE RESTITUTION PROGRAM EXPERIENCE

With no prescribed national model and employment as a secondary goal, what has most characterized employment components in restitution programs has been their local diversity. A range of approaches and combinations of approaches have been developed and continue to evolve. Among the most common are:

- Subsidized individual placements, which use public funds, fees or fines to pay salaries or stipends to offenders—who then pay restitution or have it deducted from their paychecks—for work in public or private nonprofit agencies (Rubin, 1988).
- Private-sector job banks, which are based on agreements with local small businesses to reserve job slots for restitution clients (Klein, 1980).
- Project-supervised work crews, which use groups of offenders who are generally paid through contracts with government agencies and/or subsidy funds to complete socially beneficial projects (Jenkins, 1988c; Bazemore, 1987).

A less utilized "Youth Enterprise" approach involves forming a "youth business" in which offenders may produce goods or deliver services to earn monies for restitution and the ongoing support of the enterprise (McAtee, 1988; James and Granville, 1984).

Generally, because program managers seem to prefer not to refer more serious offenders to private- or public-sector employers without at least initially observing them in such a structured setting, restitution work programs that have served more chronic and higher risk delinquents have emphasized program-supervised projects. In this way, the work program serves a screening function that allows offenders to demonstrate a capacity to work with others, and aids project staff in more effectively matching offenders and work projects. Such work may also provide training and the work orientation necessary for adjustment to private-sector jobs (Jenkins, 1988b; Butler and Mangum, 1982). Finally, project-supervised work allows program professionals more discretion in the selection of type of work and a supervision approach designed to address general educational, socialization and community improvement objectives.

Not including residential work efforts that permit other variations (Rubin, 1988), such program-supervised work has generally relied on the "work crew" format, with small groups of young offenders (generally six to ten) working with a trained supervisor paid by the program or juvenile court. Funding sources for payments in the programs vary from one locale to another, as does type of work preferred, expertise of supervisors, percentage of wages allocated to restitution, staffing and use of volunteers, etc. Often begun as spin-offs of widely adopted community service work crews in which funds are found to pay youths (who then pay a portion of wages to victims as restitution) from contracts and other sources, most crew-based programs continue to allow for and require a certain amount of unpaid work services in addition to paid work (Maloney, 1987).

If there is an emerging "prototype" for the serious offender work crew, it is undoubtedly the Youth Conservation Corps (YCC) approach (Rosenberry-Hood, 1986). Modeled after the depression-era California Conservation Corps, modern YCCs emphasize environmental, community improvement and work projects, with a general focus on "high-demand" social service projects. This work is generally supported by contracts with county, state and other government agencies as well as private and non-profit organizations. While most conservation corps have not yet been formally linked with juvenile departments, the YCC model has been successfully replicated as part of probation departments in several Oregon counties (Maloney, Romig and Armstrong, 1988; Mosier, 1988), and, as noted earlier, some programs have been positively evaluated (Wolf, Leiderman and Voith, 1987). Other crew-type and related group work efforts for serious offenders have been institutionalized in local juvenile justice systems in Toledo, OH and Erie, PA (Rubin, 1988).

Although more systematic evaluation of these still relatively new employment efforts will be necessary to determine any long-term impact on recidivism and other outcome measures, what has been clear thus far is the capacity of these programs to find jobs for large numbers of young offenders and to convince employers and the community of the benefits of offender employment (Bazemore, 1987; Klein, 1980). Unlike the popular wilderness programs that remove offenders from the community for recreation-focused "challenge" experiences and that gained wide media attention in the 1980s (Greenwood and Zimring, 1985), these programs also feature a very practical emphasis on reintegrating offenders into their local communities and emphasize concrete skill-focused, as well as behavioral, objectives. Further, although many other work programs for at-risk youths have accepted juvenile offenders, restitution programs have an impressive track record with some of the most serious offenders (Schneider, 1982; Schneider et al., 1982), and are gradually becoming part of the mainstream of many local juvenile justice systems. Restitution programs also appear to be bringing new dimensions to youth employment not seen in typical remedial approaches. Many appear to be integrating competency development and other employment objectives with reparative justice principles and, as such, provide the most complete illustration of critical principles of the emerging productive engagement model of intensive supervision.

What has been most unique about these programs compared with previous employment efforts, however, has been their capacity to develop a strong base of support by selling the concept of offender work in local communities. Three "marketing" themes appear to be primarily responsible for this success in achieving local commitment and in turn influencing the practical approach of these programs to offender employment and work experience. These include:

- Highlighting traditional or "conservative" values in youth employment.
- Emphasizing the public value and economic benefits of offender work.
- Prioritizing strict, consistent supervision to ensure public safety, quality of project work and a more positive outlook toward offender capabilities.

THE APPEAL TO TRADITIONAL VALUES

Especially when there are few positive local precedents for youth employment efforts, developing a public image that does not conflict with local attitudes appears to be especially important. In addition to the perceived risk associated with employing serious offenders in the community, managers of work programs often confront the objection that many "good kids" cannot get jobs. Thus, in the experience of programs successful in "selling" the public on offender employment, appeals to mainstream or "conservative" values have generally been more effective than arguments emphasizing the need to expand opportunities for deprived youth or to support remedial training.[6]

First, local communities generally need to be convinced that delinquents are not being "rewarded" for their crimes by receiving a job placement. The careful selection of placements and work projects that do not compete with others for livelihoods has helped to demonstrate that offenders are generally not competing with other youths for scarce jobs. Some projects now solve the competition problem by making their work slots available to nondelinquent as well as delinquent youths (Jenkins, 1988b). Overall, the goal has been to emphasize a public view of offender work as a community asset and sentencing requirement rather than a benefit or treatment for delinquents.

The appeal to "hold offenders accountable" to victims by requiring restitution payments has been one of the most powerful arguments used in support of employing offenders. Emphasizing that paid work options are required to provide a source of income for offenders to pay back victims, successful program managers have given precedence to the need for victim restitution over any presumed benefits to the young offender. It is also argued that working hard and having a proportion of wages deducted to repay victims gives offenders a sense of the value of property or other damages resulting from their offenses.

Other conservative themes in marketing offender employment focus on the work ethic and the need for youth to contribute to the community and their own support. By pointing out that many offenders have never had an opportunity or been required to work and should be taught basic work values, program advocates have managed to build upon community concern about a future of untrained workers or non-workers who must rely on public support or illegitimate activities.

Business executives and employers have responded well to these same appeals for accountability and promotion of the work ethic but have also supported offender employment for a variety of other reasons. While the interest of small business in access to a ready source of minimum-wage labor cannot be discounted, the restitution employment experience suggests that an assumption of interest in only the "bottom line" is often a distortion of the range of motives behind employer willingness to hire delinquents. In past programs, such assumptions have led to rather misguided efforts to offer extensive (and often unnecessary) subsidies to private businesses in exchange for their participation without addressing the real concerns behind their unwillingness to hire young people or support work projects (Ball et al., 1981). In the restitution program experience with youth employment, sensitivity to complaints that young people lack a basic job orientation and exhibit very low retention rates has been the primary basis for gaining the support of employers. Promising motivated workers who have had real work experience in a project crew or community service placement, these practitioners often persuade employers and/or their organizations to provide financial and other in-kind support for public work projects when they cannot themselves offer a job. Employers have been effectively "sold" on supervised public work crew projects as training vehicles that can instill job discipline. By supporting such programs, employers can also help to enhance the quality of life in the community and improve their own public relations.

The fiscal wisdom of investing in public works or of providing jobs that will enable the repayment of victims—especially when these costs are contrasted with those of incarceration—has also been a strong source of support. Cost-effectiveness as a selling point has been enhanced in juvenile restitution employment programs by the demonstrated capacity of many of these efforts to build on the resources of other community-based organizations. While reliance on local resources should in no way be seen as an argument against the need for federal support of offender employment efforts—and many programs owe their initial existence to federal funding—the difference between these programs and those of the past appears to be primary use of outside support to build a strong local funding and resource base in the community.

Because such effective collaboration with community organizations takes time and is often contingent on establishing a reputation or "track record," some restitution programs have introduced employment components by executing well-planned, highly visible work projects. Often of short duration—for example, a weekend—and performed without pay, these efforts then become part of what is essentially a "portfolio" of program accomplishments and credibility. The typical pattern has been to start small, do a superior job, and capitalize on the public relations value of the effort (Klein, 1980). In several small towns in Oregon, for example, juvenile courts—hoping to gain public support for restitution and employment projects—assigned weekend work crews to community beautification projects such as clearing brush piles and other eyesores near the town limits and refurbishing welcoming signs. In Quincy, MA, favorable press coverage for such efforts as the restoration of an island park by a project crew contributed greatly to the "Earn-It" program's positive community image. Other projects such as those in which offenders assist the elderly, fight forest fires or restore dilapidated housing have also created public good will (Herb, 1988; Blake, 1986).

Once credibility and competence have been established through well-planned efforts, public and private community agencies have been more willing to provide financial as well as "in-kind" support for program activities. For example, the Chamber of Commerce in Quincy, MA became the key sponsor and coordinator of Earn-It's job bank. Projects in eastern Oregon and Idaho received major support from local Private Industry Councils, as well as from such "character building" organizations as Boys' Clubs and 4-H (Mosier, 1988). Other community organizations, as well as businesses, labor unions and civic groups, have sometimes taken responsibility for specific program tasks such as job preparation classes and crew supervision or have provided a steady source of volunteers. In some areas work programs are exploring the possibility of partnerships and referral agreements with comprehensive, established youth work agencies such as Youth Conservation Corps (Jenkins, 1988a).

As important as building organizational allies is not making enemies unnecessarily. In any discussion of youth employment strategies, for example, concerns about competition with the livelihoods of others or threats to organized labor are inevitably raised. While restitution employment programs are not always protected from potential conflicts with unions, many of the more comprehensive programs have gained strong support from local labor leaders by including them on boards and consulting them before taking on work projects (Burkhardt, 1987; YBarra, 1987). In Riverside, California's "Jobs Against Crime" program, the director has been able to negotiate apprenticeship agreements with building trade locals to accept referrals who successfully complete his program (YBarra, 1987).

Overall, whether approaching business leaders, labor, funding agencies or civic groups, what appears to be unique among these project directors is an entrepreneurial stance in efforts to expand offender employment. By offering the community a strong track record of completed public work projects and disciplined, motivated youths prepared for entry level positions in local businesses and other agencies, program managers have been able to present both offenders and the justice system in a new positive light. Rather than appeal strictly on the basis of social work or philanthropic values, these practitioners have been able to "sell" employers and the community what is essentially a "product" and ask organizations to work with them in a partnership for community improvement.

PUBLIC AND PARTICIPANT VALUE OF YOUTHFUL OFFENDER WORK

In selecting work projects and job placements, program managers must be sensitive to a number of practical considerations, such as ease of implementation, visibility and public relations value, safety, cost, and funding potential. In addition, while remunerating victims remains a primary motivation behind employment components in these restitution programs, many are becoming increasingly concerned with dimensions of employment other than its potential as a source of income. The value of work performed by young offenders to employers and the community has been a primary emphasis when selecting and seeking support for work projects.

While attention to both community needs and the needs of young people to learn and benefit from the job experience are important in successful employment or work experience programs (Michel, 1980:3-4), assumptions about the general incompetence of young offenders in many of these efforts have often led to an overemphasis on molding the work to fit the needs of the worker. Unfortunately, this has sometimes resulted in inadequate attention to the value and quality of the work itself, and to predictable charges of "make work."

Managers of restitution work components have generally argued that the needs of young offenders and the public need not conflict, and have insisted that the value of a work project *to the community* is, in fact, often the major criterion in determining whether work will also be meaningful to youth. No matter how sensitive a program is to client needs, "make work" offers few benefits to participants. In addition, the underlying objective of changing the image of the youthful offender to one of a potential "resource" or "asset" in the community has appeared to require primary concern with the public value of project work.

Impact on the Community

Increasingly, when jobs in private businesses have been scarce or inappropriate for a young, high-risk offender, restitution project managers have relied on work projects suggested or sponsored by governmental agencies responsible for social services, public works or conservation. Because much needed work of this kind never gets done in most communities, finding projects that are viewed as useful and valuable has not been difficult. Examples of representative projects in rural areas include mosquito abatement, stream or river bank clean-up, building ski shelters, restoring county fairgrounds, and building or painting recreational access signs. In cities, projects like building and repairing park play structures, putting in community gardens, restoring and landscaping senior citizens centers, and weatherization projects have been popular. Service-oriented tasks can include working with the retarded, children in day-care activities, or the elderly in shopping and nutritional assistance programs (see, for example, Blake, 1986).

Because work projects that are needed and valued in one community may be different from those considered useful in another, some managers take additional steps to avoid the make-work charge and ensure that work will be valued. To establish employer "buy-in," economic advisory committees composed of local business leaders have been established and asked for advice on projects. Civic leaders and groups such as tourism councils have been asked for recommendations for projects that would improve the local quality of public life in the community.

By tying projects to private business growth, the theme of enhancing "economic development" has helped to deflect standard attacks on public work, and has opened doors to public/private partnerships and important support from local business organizations (Maloney, 1988; Jenkins, 1988b). Projects designed to improve the local business climate have ranged from graffiti clean-up in business districts to landscaping and other improvements in industrial parks. Restoring riverfront areas has resulted in small economic boons in some cities by making abandoned spaces attractive for recreational purposes, and useable for small businesses such as restaurants and other establishments (Klein, 1980). "Transition team jobs," in which program youths perform "adjunct" tasks for private companies under project supervision, are in operation in Oregon and other areas (Jenkins, 1988b). While receiving additional training, youths are paid by these companies to perform work that typically is not of interest to regular employees.

Impact on Youth

How does this very pragmatic focus on community needs effect the needs of youthful offenders for a positive work experience? Because few young persons in their first jobs enter anything resembling a "career track," the term "real jobs" (usually private sector) is often a misleading and inappropriate one in youth employment programs (cf., Duster, 1987; Auletta, 1983). Especially for relatively short-term placements, the debate about whether jobs "might lead to a career" is not a realistic concern of most programs, whether focused on public work or private placements. More important is the nature of the work experience itself.

Although it is generally assumed that for socially marginal, high-risk offenders any job is better than no work experience at all, program managers are often concerned with offering a positive image of legitimate employment to youth who may never have worked before. Thus, while their key selling point has been the public and private value of offender work, many seek out projects or placements that also teach good employment habits, civic values and a basic appreciation for work. Some also appear to be sensitive to recent cautions about adverse effects on adolescents of certain kinds of work (Greenberger and Steinberg, 1986) and are concerned that, at minimum, the experience not foster negative reactions to legitimate employment.

Unlike the "youth ghetto" isolation so common in many adolescent jobs, restitution project work crews often offer an opportunity for significant adult-juvenile interaction (Waldinger and Bailey, 1985). In addition, such jobs demand an ability to get along with fellow workers and accentuate the need for interdependence in the work setting. Practitioners have also exhibited concern with positive impact of the work experience of young offenders by trying to develop projects or placements that:

- Have a clear beginning and end, resulting in a tangible finished "product."
- Teach a variety of employment skills and values in relation to a real work experience.
- Minimize overly complex procedures but require youth to perform a diversity of tasks.
- Build in educational content about the world of work and careers and attempt to provide academic credits for participation.

Although sometimes monotonous and physically tiring, many of these jobs are given added meaning and dignity by their larger public value to the community. Programs appear to be growing increasingly sensitive to communicating the broader environmental and/or "quality-of-life" implications of this public work to young people. This message may make the difference between the offender's perception of the work activity as "hanging sheet rock" versus "historical preservation," shoveling gravel" versus "restoring a trout stream," and "clearing brush" versus "building a firebreak."

SUPERVISION: THE FOCUS ON QUALITY WORK, PUBLIC PROTECTION, AND A NEW OUTLOOK TOWARD THE OFFENDER

A unique approach to supervision has been a third common element distinguishing successful offender work programs from past efforts to employ delinquents and other youth. Unlike other work programs that have relied primarily on referral to outside employers following periods of job counseling or training, many of the most effective of the programs discussed here offer at least some period of project-supervised work. They have thus often been able to structure the work experience to meet special needs of offenders, as well as respond to public need. Three features of supervision in restitution work crews critical in selling offender employment projects to the community and ensuring their success include: an insistence on quality work, a concern with minimizing risk to the community, and the promotion of positive assumptions about the capacity of young offenders to perform effectively in work assignments.

The quality of work emphasis is an important guarantee to community agencies who may contract for project labor, as well as to future employers who may be asked to hire young people after they have completed the program. Like the emphasis on the public value of project work, the quality theme is a major guard against community perception of projects as "make work." While many recognize the importance of flexibility in accommodating youths who may never have been confronted with the discipline of work, an increasing number of project managers argue that it is better to live with a relatively high attrition rate than to sacrifice the integrity of the work program for a few unmotivated youths (cf. Rosenberry, 1986). Thus, rules such as program termination for three late arrivals or two "no-shows," regardless of excuses, are not uncommon and are seen as vital to ensuring quality performance. Strictly enforced regulations also facilitate prompt payment of restitution and reinforce to youth the importance of regular attendance and good behavior on the job.

Practically, many program managers have adopted sequential stages of punitive response or "graduated sanctions" for inadequate performance. That is, prior to responding with the most serious sanction, program managers try to "get the offender's attention" by such responses as adding community service hours, restricting earnings from the job, and instituting curfews and/or house arrest (Klein, 1988). Some projects are also able to allow offenders a second chance that follows a "cooling-off" period of a week or more, often accompanied by some punitive sanction.

Positive incentives, as well as an attempt to instill pride in the task, appear to be at least as important as punitive sanctions in ensuring youth commitment to performance standards. In addition to possible early release from supervision, praise and various types of recognition, wages are also used as a positive incentive. While victims receive first priority, most programs allow offenders to keep some proportion of their earnings as an incentive for good work performance and/or for prompt payment of restitution (Bazemore, 1987). Some programs also "stagger" the use of wage incentives, requiring a week of successful job performance, for example, before any earnings can be kept—or even withholding any payment to the wage earner until the victim is completely paid back. In either case, most would agree that allowing offenders to keep some of their earnings is a strong motivating factor for good work performance, increases the projects' control or "leverage" over offender behavior, and reinforces the value attached to the work itself. From a practical standpoint, as some project directors point out, wages may be needed to make working possible for some youths: Some need earnings to purchase gloves or special clothing for outdoor work; others need money for transportation, lunches, etc. (Frush, 1987).

The consistent discipline and strict enforcement approach to supervision is vital to ensuring control and "community incapacitation" of offenders, and an important reassurance to citizens concerned with potential risk posed by these youths in community work settings. The often physically demanding nature of the work and hours—particularly in the conservation crew format—is believed to be an added factor in incapacitation, minimizing the likelihood of reoffending for the duration of an offender's program supervision. Following the general emphasis on maximizing the amount of offender time that is "programmed" through supervised activities, some managers also build group recreational activities around work activities (McAtee, 1988).

Another factor reinforcing the promise of public protection is the emphasis on careful screening and placement. Unlike most other youth employment programs, many of these work-focused ISP efforts are able to provide employers and the community with evidence of a young offender's ability to work with others in a tightly structured and closely supervised crew setting prior to regular employment or return to less supervised community living. Client interviewing and assessment of interest and motivation also facilitates an effective "match" between the youth and type of work (some projects are also able to place youths according to interest and aptitude).

Careful selection of project supervisors is also vital to maintaining consistency and control. While programs seem to vary in the characteristics preferred for work supervisors, a few common themes are evident in discussions with managers. Often project managers attempt to select supervisors who, in addition to their maturity and affinity for working with groups of young offenders, have special sets of practical skills (e.g., contracting). In most cases, however, specific skills are considered less important than an ability to make decisions and plan projects—while allowing youth maximum opportunity to participate in all stages of the process—and a willingness to work hard at often physically demanding jobs (Bazemore, 1987). If not actually discouraged, the counselor or social work orientation is given much less importance in this context than the capacity to organize work and function as a role model (Maloney, 1988). On many crews, supervisors labor alongside youths, often setting the work pace. The sensitivity of supervisors relaying the message of the value inherent in even menial work (e.g., environmental impact) may also provide added meaning for youth and increase young offenders' commitment to the task itself.

Even more important than the particular type of supervisor is an outlook toward young offenders and their productive capabilities that has been uncommon in most remediation-based employment training or job readiness programs. In such programs, youth are assumed to require extensive counseling and classroom preparation prior to actually beginning work. The problem with such approaches is best summed up in a question asked by Judge Anthony Kline, one of the founders of the California Conservation Corps: "How can we expect dropouts to drop-in to another school?" Many at-risk youth who have probably done poorly in the classroom may feel further demeaned, if not bored, by additional remedial instructional requirements or job counseling.

Compared with earlier remedial education programs, these new efforts appear to rely much more on an active, immediate approach which assumes that young people "learn by doing." Though many have never held a job or even been required to work in family settings, offenders in restitution work programs are generally assumed to be capable of productive, quality work performance given the right task and supervision. This approach appears consistent with critiques of the more passive job training approaches based primarily on classroom instruction and counseling, which have shown generally poor results for offenders (Center for Study of Social Policy, 1986; Goldman et al., 1972). Noting that job *retention* is typically a larger problem than placement, employers and their organizations now also seem to be insisting on a more experiential emphasis in training programs and have been generally supportive of "hands-on" approaches that allow young people to learn job discipline and employer expectations in a real work setting (Newell, 1987).

IMPLICATIONS FOR A NEW ISP AND JUVENILE JUSTICE MISSION

This chapter has focused on "themes" or principles common to new offender employment programs that appear to be overcoming a primary obstacle to past efforts: resistance in local communities. These programs share an affirmative, entrepreneurial approach that has helped to "market" offender employment based on an emphasis on conservative or traditional values, the public value of youth work and a unique approach to supervision. However, more consideration is needed of prospects for and challenges involved in promoting this approach in contrast to the more dominant models of intensive supervision. A work experience/employment emphasis in community supervision is also likely to conflict with both the traditional treatment/casework model still dominant in juvenile justice, as well as with punitive and surveillance approaches frequently promoted in the 1980s.

In the larger context of juvenile justice, the productive engagement approach implies a "new mission" for community supervision of juveniles. Like the restitution movement (Schneider, 1985), the focus on employment has grown out of dissatisfaction with traditional casework probation and is viewed as part of an effort to "revitalize" juvenile court supervision (Maloney, Romig and Armstrong, 1988). Where traditional juvenile justice approaches fall back on the "best interests of the child" and an individual treatment agenda, the new employment and reparative justice programs are more compatible philosophically with an "accountability" rationale. Neither punitive nor paternalistic, accountability goes beyond concern with the individual delinquent to include the interests of victims and the community. Juvenile justice in this view should require that offenders act responsibly to restore damages and devote appropriate resources to help facilitate this action (Klein, 1988; Schneider, 1985).

Work experience and the accountability emphasis is not, however, inconsistent with surveillance and control requirements in intensive supervision. Rather, the approach attempts to lessen the amount of staff time devoted to surveillance by programming offender time, while also offering the benefit of productive work and reparations to victims. A productive engagement focus in intensive supervision would also not preclude treatment when required, and may even support diagnostic and monitoring concerns. For example, the work crew regimen described earlier is especially conducive to identifying offenders who continue to abuse drugs and alcohol (Klein, 1987); few crew workers would be able to survive the long hours and physical labor without showing signs of immediate fatigue due to heavy use.

Overall, however, a productive engagement approach would place much less emphasis on therapeutic treatment (e.g., counseling, family therapy). More attention would instead be focused on ensuring accountability to victims and providing opportunities for work and competency development. To avoid inevitable deficits in resources allocated to such tasks as developing work sites, collecting and monitoring restitution payments, and supervising work projects, juvenile departments that have been successful with the new approach ultimately seem to move away from allegiance to "treatment ethic" priorities and the assumption that most offenders need such services.

While the accountability orientation does not *prohibit* various forms of treatment for offenders who need services (e.g., drug and alcohol abusers, the mentally ill), the difference, as expressed by the former director of juvenile offender programs in Kansas, is that treatment is used "prescriptively" rather than "programmatically." The assumption that most offenders will need little or no treatment in the therapeutic sense makes possible a shift in priorities toward ensuring that offenders fulfill reparative obligations and develop practical competencies; treatment is provided as needed, generally on a referral basis (Coates, 1988). Further, the treatment of the individual delinquent as someone who is "sick," disturbed" or "incompetent" is replaced by a view of the offender as someone who "did wrong" but is capable of acting responsibly to repair damages. According to one advocate of this approach, the concern of practitioners becomes less with the "mental health of the convicted armed robber who now feels good about himself" than with efforts to "make it right" with victims and channel the offenders into an appropriate work setting (Klein, 1988).

The productive engagement approach also appears consistent with some of the recent critiques of intensive supervision for adults, which have emphasized the tendency to place an excess of conditions on offenders unrelated to the offense itself or level of risk to the community, thus almost guaranteeing violations (e.g., Clear, 1987; Clear, Flynn and Shapiro, 1987). By designating active, behavioral requirements that give supervisors objective indicators of successful adjustment, the new model may also place limits on what can be expected of offenders in community supervision and provide needed clarity to what have become overly complex requirements. For the offender, an active commitment is required, but the generally fewer conditions of supervision seem likely to be viewed as less arbitrary and perhaps more just.

If reparative sanctions and work requirements are viewed as sufficient sanctions for achieving control and punishment, the model also seems capable of reducing the amount of time supervisors must devote to surveillance. By clearly designating successful completion of requirements and allowing more structured time in active work settings, required time under supervision may also be reduced. Treating these sanctions as add-ons to other requirements, however, could actually increase time on supervision and increase the chance of violating conditions, thus defeating the purpose of the program as an alternative to incarceration (Clear, 1987). Fortunately, research examining the efficacy of using restitution for juvenile offenders as a "sole sanction" (without probation or other requirements) is strongly supportive of the idea that restitution and community service are potent sanctions in themselves (Schneider and Schneider, 1984).

This restructuring of offender time suggests a different role and a new agenda for supervisors in ISP programs. The nature of staffing patterns and assignments in a productive engagement approach might also be expected to differ from those more typical of a treatment model or its punitive and surveillance analogues. Monitoring and facilitating completion of restitution and work requirements, work project development and supervision, and community outreach may replace surveillance activities and/or other staples of traditional casework. To formalize this new role and agenda for supervisors, what has often occurred is a restatement of organizational mission that includes a shift in staff titles and functions as well as offender requirements to accommodate the new priorities. Part of the revised mission statement of the Deschutes County, OR Juvenile Department exemplifies this change:

> Traditionally, juvenile courts have depended upon casework probation as a means to control and improve juvenile offender behavior. The Deschutes County Juvenile Department will demonstrate that employment and training can be a more effective disposition than casework counselling. Time-ended periods of probation will be centered around successful completion of community service hours, successful completion of job training and placement, and payment of Court ordered restitution" [Maloney, 1987:3].

While courts have for many years made referrals to community agencies for various job-related services as part of the normal casework function, what has been unique in the new work-oriented programs is an increased assumption of "ownership" by juvenile justice professionals of the employment and competency development problems of their clients. Refusing to simply abdicate these concerns to schools and other agencies, chief probation officers, judges and other professionals in these juvenile probation departments have shown aggressive leadership in mobilizing community resources to employ youthful offenders.

SUMMARY, POLICY CONCERNS, AND ISSUES FOR RESEARCH

The work experience focus in juvenile justice, and the themes that distinguish it, appear to offer the basis for a new paradigm for community supervision of serious juvenile offenders. Combined with the emphasis on reparative sanctions such as restitution and community service, a "productive engagement" model may have several advantages over the more passive surveillance and treatment/services approaches to intensive supervision. Positive benefits claimed by proponents of these approaches include:

- Accomplishing productive work that can improve communities and the business climate.
- Providing restitution to victims, including service to community organizations.
- Rewarding youth with a legitimate income for positive performance in a productive work experience.
- Providing a closely supervised means of incapacitating offenders through programmed activities that build heavily on community resources.
- Offering a new public image for serious offenders and at-risk youth as potential resources for community improvement rather than liabilities and threats to community safety.

Because of this, very positive potential offender work requirements are increasingly viewed as "right and just," regardless of their other impacts on juvenile justice and offenders. However, before launching into an attempt to initiate or replicate programs, questions about feasibility, options and strategies, and the broader implications of these approaches, deserve careful consideration.

First, like any other community effort that claims to be an alternative to incarceration for serious offenders, even the most effective employment and work experience programs must answer the charge that they have simply become part of the "widened net" of social control that has coopted many other alternatives (Austin and Krisberg, 1981). Research on these programs must examine the recruitment process to see if the most serious offenders are, in fact, being referred. In addition, empirical studies should take note of whether work requirements and reparative sanctions are utilized as alternatives to other conditions of supervision or treated as add-ons to other requirements; are offenders more likely to fail for rule violations in these programs and are their terms of supervision longer or shorter? Whether this approach can also be expected to reduce recidivism or offer other positive benefits for offenders after program termination is an empirical question that has yet to be well-explored in the limited empirical research on other ISP approaches as well (McCarthy, 1987). The issue of recidivism should be examined in the context of hypotheses that might be generated by various theories of delinquency. To what extent do variations in supervision, type of work and job setting effect reoffending?

To be avoided in policy and program development is the view of jobs for offenders—even when the work experience and employment options are carefully designed and supported—as a panacea for the problems of delinquency and crime. As the discussion of job characteristics has emphasized, the nature of the work, supervision and assumptionns about young offenders may be more critical than the fact of employment itself. Acknowledging that even the best jobs provided in any youth employment program are unlikely to lead directly to careers or permanent occupations, the learning and socialization features of work projects should take on primary importance.

While productive work as an active learning experience is a growing emphasis in many of the best youth work programs, one important concern that has yet to be addressed in most is the need for linkage between these efforts and the formal education process. In a highly credentialed society, failing to establish educational credit for good performance in public work efforts may leave work program advocates open to charges of cynicism. Although changing the public image of marginal youth as potential resources through completing useful public work is an important first step, a more long-term objective should be to promote new ways for young people to work and complete schooling requirements (Blake, 1986; Pearl, 1972).

The connection between work experience for offenders and access as well as commitment to schooling is itself the basis for an entire research agenda in the context of some of the theoretical perspectives discussed earlier. The employment/schooling relationship is of major concern given the warnings of some researchers that the impact of some types of work experiences on educational performance may be generally negative (Steinberg et al., 1982).

Other sources of tension remain between and within these evolving programs over the relative amount of emphasis on discipline and the conception of work as punitive or productive rather than educational. The question of whether separate programs for serious delinquents can be expected to have any positive "socializing" impact should also be of primary interest to both researchers and policymakers (Polk and Kobrin, 1972). Others may questions whether any mandated program can or should be expected to benefit youthful offenders beyond temporary incapacitation during the period of supervision.

This descriptive report should be considered a first step, which in emphasizing broad philosophical "themes" that distinguish these new approaches raises many questions about actual program implementation and long-term impact. More research of a qualitative or ethnographic nature is needed to describe (1) day-to-day program operations, (2) interactions between supervisors and young offenders, and (3) perception of youths themselves about the program (Higgins, 1988).

NOTES

1. Although restitution and/or community service requirements are fundamental to the "productive engagement" model of ISP, this chapter deals only indirectly with these topics. Other chapters in this volume address philosophical and practical concerns surrounding reparation and victim accountability in serious offender programs.

2. Sharing an emphasis on challenging offenders in situations that require working with others, work experience and employment programs offer a number of additional benefits not present in the primarily recreational wilderness programs. Unlike the wilderness approaches, which generally involve removing offenders to remote locations, the work programs' emphasis on keeping the offender in the community gives priority to reconciliation and reintegration, thus sending a very different message about the responsibility of local communities for their own delinquency problems.

3. For summaries of the characteristics and impact of many of these programs in the 1970s, see Taggart, 1981 and Zimmerman, 1980. Descriptive accounts of more recent, smaller-scale efforts may be found in some of the publications of Public/Private Ventures, a foundation-supported agency providing education, technical assistance and research in youth employment and training.

4. Originally funded in 1976 as part of an OJJDP initiative, most of the 85 demonstration restitution programs survived the termination of federal support by developing state and local sources of funding. An estimated 400 new projects have been initiated since the early 1980s. Funded initially as an alternative to incarceration, restitution programs were designed to serve more serious offenders. One of the most interesting findings of the evaluation—which compared recidivism among restitution participants and others receiving alternative dispositions (Schneider, 1986)—was that the most serious offenders performed equally well in completing restitution requirements and did not present additional risk to the community (Schneider, 1982). Some practitioners (e.g., Klein, 1988) have also reported good adjustment in project-initiated employment for these "high-risk" youth. (For summaries of research and descriptive materials on juvenile restitution programs, see Bazemore and Seljan, 1985; Schneider, 1985).

5. Much of this work was accomplished during 1986 as part of the Restitution Education Specialized Training and Technical Assistance program, while providing technical assistance and support on restitution to juvenile justice agencies. In this effort, exemplary projects were often used as models for program development in other jurisdictions, and their staff were utilized in training and technical assistance.

6. This new focus is, of course, not unrelated to the generally more conservative national political climate of the 1980s. However, program managers represent a wide range of political perspectives and juvenile justice philosophies, and by no means do

they necessarily endorse more general trends in this conservative direction. Rather, this appeal has been, in part, a means of countering the less positive public image of many juvenile justice programs of the 1960s and 1970s, which were characterized by some as "liberal" or excessively lenient responses to juvenile crime (see, for example, Maloney, Romig and Armstrong, 1988; Klein 1980).

REFERENCES

Agnew, Robert (1986). "Work and Delinquency Among Juveniles Attending School." *Journal of Crime & Justice* 9:19-41.

Akers, R. L. (1977). *Deviant Behavior: A Social Learning Approach*. 2nd ed. Belmont, CA: Wadsworth.

Armstrong, Troy (1988). "National Survey of Juvenile Intensive Probation Supervision (Part I and Part II)." *Criminal Justice Abstracts* 20(2-3):342-348, 497-523.

Auletta, Ken (1983). *The Underclass*. New York, NY: Vintage.

Austin, James and Barry Krisberg (1981). "Wider, Stronger, and Different Nets: The Dialects of Criminal Justice Reform." *Journal of Research in Crime and Delinquency* 18(1):165-196.

Ball, Joseph, Carl Wolfhagen, David Gerould and Loren Solnick (1981). *The Participation of Private Businesses as Work Sponsors in Youth Entitlement Demonstration*. Washington, DC: Manpower Demonstration Research Corporation.

Bazemore, S. Gordon (1987). *Jobs Components in Juvenile Restitution Programs*. Washington, DC: U.S. Office of Juvenile Justice and Delinquency Prevention.

—— and Barbara J. Seljan (1985). "Selected Summaries of Research Reports and Documents from the Evaluation of the National Juvenile Restitution Initiative." Walnut Creek, CA: Pacific Institute for Research and Evaluation.

Becker, Howard (1963). *Studies in the Sociology of Deviance*. New York, NY: Free Press.

Berk, R. A., K. J. Lenihan and P. H. Rossi (1980). "Crime and Poverty: Some Experimental Evidence from Ex-offenders." *American Sociological Review* 45:766-786.

Betsey, Charles L., R. G. Hollister and M. R. Papageorgiou (eds.) (1985). *Youth Employment and Training Programs: The YEDPA Years*. Washington, DC: National Academy Press.

Blake, Gerald (1988). "Education and the Employability of Youth." *Youth Policy* 10(12):26-28.

—— (1986). "Project Main: Classwork in the Community Benefits Senior Citizens." *Children Today* 8(July-August):15-25.

Briar, S. and I. Piliavin (1965). "Delinquency, Situational Inducements, and Commitments to Conformity." *Social Problems* 13(1):35-45.

Brickell, Henry M. (1980) "Practitioners' Perspectives on Youth Programs." In *The Vice President's Task Force on Youth Employment: A Review of Youth Employment Problems, Programs, and Policies*, Volume 3, edited by Brian Linder and Robert Taggart. Washington, DC: U.S. Department of Labor and Training Administration.

Burkhardt, Robert (1987). Personal communication with the director of the San Francisco Conservation Corps, San Francisco, CA.

Butler, Eric and Garth Mangum (1982). *Lessons from Youth Programs: Volume One*. Salt Lake City, UT: Olympus Publishing.

Center for the Study of Social Policy (1986). *Youth Unemployment: A Literature Review*. Washington, DC.

Clear, Todd R. (1987). "The New Intensive Supervision Movement." Draft paper, Rutgers University, Newark, NJ.

—— Suzanne Flynn and Carol Shapiro (1987). "Intensive Supervision in Probation: A Comparison of Three Projects." In *Intermediate Punishments: Intensive Supervision, Home Confinement and Electronic Surveillance*, edited by Belinda McCarthy. Monsey, NY: Criminal Justice Press.

Cloward, Richard A. and Lloyd E. Ohlin (1960). *Delinquency and Opportunity: A Theory of Delinquent Gangs*. New York, NY: Free Press.

Coates, Benjamin (1988). Paper presented at the Restitution Education Specialized Training and Technical Assistance Regional Workshop on Restitution in Juvenile Correctional and Residential Settings, Seattle, WA.

Cohen A. K. (1955). *Delinquent Boys: The Culture of the Gang*. New York, NY: Free Press.

Duster, Troy (1987). "Crime, Youth Unemployment, and the Black Urban Underclass." *Crime & Delinquency* 33(2):300-316.

Elliott, Delbert S., Suzanne S. Ageton and R. J. Canter (1979). "An Integrated Theoretical Perspective on Delinquent Behavior." *Journal of Research in Crime and Delinquency* 16:3-17.

Fagan, Jeffrey A., Cary J. Rudman and Eliot Hartstone (1984). "Intervening with Violent Juvenile Offenders: A Community Reintegration Model." In *Violent Juvenile Offenders: An Anthology*, edited by Robert A. Mathias et al. San Francisco, CA: National Council on Crime and Delinquency.

Frush, Ruth (1987). Personal communication with the director of the Restitution and Community Services Work Program of Blackhawk County Juvenile Court Services, Waterloo, IA.

Goldman, I. J., M. Kohn, J. Epstein, I. Geiler and R. G. McDonald (1972). *Youth and Work Training Programs: An Evaluative Study*. Albany, NY: New York State Division for Youth, Youth Research Inc.

Greenberg, D. (1977). "Delinquency and the Age Structure of Society." *Contemporary Crises* 1:66-86.

Greenberger, Ellen and Laurence Steinberg (1986). *When Teenagers Work: The Psychological and Social Costs of Adolescent Employment*. New York, NY: Basic Books.

—— Laurence D. Steinberg and Mary Ruggiero (1982). "A Job Is a Job Is a Job ... or Is It?: Behavioral Observations in the Adolescent Workplace." *Work and Occupations* 9(1):79-96.

Greenwood, Peter W. and Franklin E. Zimring (1985). *One More Chance. The Pursuit of Promising Intervention Strategies for Chronic Juvenile Offenders*. Santa Monica, CA: Rand.

Grice, Michael (1988). "Youth Entrepreneurship: Empowerment Through Innovation." *Youth Policy* 10(12):28-30.

Gruenewald, Paul, Susan Laurence and Barbara R. West (1985). "National Evaluation of the New Pride Replication Program Final Report." Walnut Creek, CA: Pacific Institute for Research and Evaluation.

Hackler, James C. (1978). *The Great Stumble Forward*. Ontario, CAN: Mathuer.

—— and John L. Hagan (1975). "Work and Teaching Machines as Delinquency Prevention Tools: A Four-Year Follow-Up." *Social Service Review* 49(1):92-106.

Harris, M. Kay (1984). "Rethinking Probation in the Context of the Justice Model." In *Probation and Justice: Reconsideration of Mission*, edited by Patrick D. McAnany et al. Cambridge, MA: Oelgeschlager, Gunn and Hain.

Herb, John A. (1988). "Creative Funding for Restitution Programs." In *Restitution Improvement Curriculum: A Guidebook for Juvenile Restitution Workshop Planners*, edited by H. Ted Rubin and Marlene Thornton. Washington, DC: U.S. Office of Juvenile Justice and Delinquency Prevention.

Higgins, Catherine (1988). *Youth Motivation: At-Risk Youth Talk to Program Planners*. Philadelphia, PA: Public/Private Ventures.

Hirschi, Travis (1969). *Causes of Delinquency*. Berkeley, CA: University of California Press.

James, Thomas S. and Jeanne M. Granville (1984). "Practical Issues in Vocational Education for Serious Juvenile Offenders." In *Violent Juvenile Offenders: An Anthology*, edited by Robert A. Mathias et al. San Francisco, CA: National Council on Crime and Delinquency.

Jenkins, Ron (1988a). "Oregon's Innovative Approach to Juvenile Justice: 1983-Present: An Overview." *Youth Policy* 10(12):16-18.

——(1988b). Personal communication with the director of the Juvenile Justice Alliance of Portland, OR.

——(1988c). "Structured Work Crews." *Youth Policy* 10(12):33.

Kaplan, Howard B. (1980). *Deviant Behavior in Defense of Self*. New York, NY: Academic Press.

Klein, Andrew R. (1980). *Earn It: The Story So Far*. Quincy, MA: Citizens for Better Community Courts, Inc.

—— (1987). *Restitution for High Risk, Chronic and Violent Juvenile Offenders*. Quincy, MA: Quincy District Court.

—— (1988). *Alternative Sentencing: A Practitioner's Guide*. Cincinnati, OH: Anderson.

Knox, G. W. (1981). "Vocational and Educational Upgrading for Juvenile Delinquents: Community-Based Programs and the Current 'State of the Art.'" Chicago, IL: National Center for the Assessment of Alternatives to Juvenile Justice Processing, University of Chicago.

Lab, Steven P. (1988). *Crime Prevention: Approaches, Practices and Evaluations*. Cincinnati, OH: Anderson.

Levin, Martin and B. Ferman (1985). *The Political Hand: Policy Implementation and Youth Employment Programs*. New York, NY: Pergamon Press.

Maloney, Dennis (1987). "Mission Statement for Deschutes County Juvenile Department." Bend, OR: Juvenile Department.

—— (1988). "The Balanced Approach for Juvenile Justice." Paper presented at the Second Annual Conference on Juvenile Restitution, San Diego, CA.

—— Dennis Romig and Troy Armstrong (1988). "Juvenile Probation: The Balanced Approach." *Juvenile and Family Court Journal* 39(3):1-63.

Mangum, Garth and John Walsh (1978). *Employment and Training Programs for Youth: What Works Best for Whom?* Washington, DC: U.S. Department of Labor, Office of Youth Programs.

Marans, Robert, B. L. Driver and J. C. Scott (1972). *Youth and the Environment: An Evaluation of the 1971 Youth Conservation Corps*. Ann Arbor, MI: Institute for Social Research, University of Michigan.

McAtee, Frank (1988). Personal communication with the director of Sonoma County Probation Camp, Forestville, CA.

McCarthy, Belinda R. (ed.) (1987). *Intermediate Punishments: Intensive Supervision, Home Confinement and Electronic Surveillance*. Monsey, NY: Willow Tree Press.

Michel, Ann (1980). "Public Sector Job Creation—A Means to an End." In *The Vice President's Task Force on Youth Employment: A Review of Youth Employment Problems, Programs, and Policies*, Vol. 3, edited by Brian Linder and Robert Taggart. Washington, DC: U.S. Department of Labor and Training Administration.

Mosier, James (1988). "Partnerships for Juvenile Justice." *Youth Policy* 10(12):31-33.

National Commission on Resources for Youth (1974). *New Roles for Youth in the School and the Community*. New York, NY: Citation Press.

National Council on Crime and Delinquency (1981). "The National Evaluation of Delinquency Prevention. Final Report to the Office of Juvenile Justice and Delinquency Prevention." San Francisco, CA.

Newell, Dennis (1987). Personal communication with the director of the Eastern Oregon Private Industry Council.

Pearl, Arthur (1972). *The Atrocity of Education*. St. Louis, MO: New Critics Press.

Polk, Ken and Solomon Kobrin (1972). *Delinquency Prevention Through Youth Development*. Washington, DC: U.S. Department of Health, Education, and Welfare.

Reckless, W. C. and S. Dinitz (1972). *The Prevention of Juvenile Delinquency: An Experiment*. Columbus, OH: Ohio University Press.

Rosenberry-Hood, Margaret (1986a). "Urban Conservation and Service Corps Programs. Report †3: Program Design and Implementation Issues." Washington, DC: Human Environment Center.

—— (1986b). *A Conservation and Service Corps Workbook*. Washington, DC: Human Environment Center.

Rubin, H. Ted (1988). "Fulfilling Juvenile Restitution Requirements in Community Correctional Programs." *Federal Probation* 53(3):32-42.

Schneider, Anne L. (1986). "Restitution and Recidivism Rates of Juvenile Offenders: Results from Four Experimental Studies." *Criminology* 24(3): 533-552.

—— (1985). *Guide to Juvenile Restitution*. Washington, DC: U.S. Office of Juvenile Justice and Delinquency Prevention.

—— and Peter R. Schneider (1984). *The Effectiveness of Restitution as a Sole Sanction and As a Condition of Probation: Results from an Experiment in Oklahoma County*. Eugene, OR: Institute for Policy Analysis.

Schneider, Peter, R. (1982). "Restitution as an Alternative Disposition for Serious Juvenile Offenders." Eugene, OR: Institute for Policy Analysis.

—— Anne. L. Schneider, William Griffith and Michael J. Wilson (1982). "Two-Year Report on the National Evaluation of Juvenile Restitution Initiative: An Overview of Program Performance." Eugene, OR: Institute of Policy Analysis.

Schur, Edwin M. (1973). *Radical Non-Intervention: Rethinking the Delinquency Problem*. Englewood Cliffs, NJ: Prentice-Hall.

Shannon, Lyle (1976). "Predicting Adult Careers from Juvenile Careers." Paper presented at a meeting of the Pacific Sociological Association, San Diego, CA.

Smith, Thomas J., Gary Walker and Rachel A. Baker (1987). *Youth and the Workplace: Second-Chance Programs and the Hard-to-Employ: A Report Commissioned by the William T. Grant Foundation*. Philadelphia, PA: Public/Private Ventures.

Steinberg, Laurence D., Ellen Greenberger, L. Garduque, Mary Ruggiero and A. Vaux (1982). "Effects of Working on Adolescent Development." *Developmental Psychology* 18:385-395.

Sutherland, Edwin (1939). *Principles of Criminology*. Third edition. Philadelphia, PA: J.B. Lippincott.

Taggart, Robert (1981). *A Fisherman's Guide: An Assessment of Training and Remediation Strategies*. Kalamazoo, MI: W. E. Upjohn Institute for Employment Research.

Thornberry T. P. and R. L. Christiansen (1984). "Unemployment and Criminal Involvement: An Investigation of Reciprocal Causal Structures." *American Sociological Review* 49:398-411.

Toby, Jackson (1957). "Social Disorganization and Stake in Conformity: Complementary Factors in the Predatory Behavior of Hoodlums." *Journal of Criminal Law, Criminology and Police Science* 48:12-17.

U.S. Office of Juvenile Justice and Delinquency Prevention (1987). "Fiscal Year 1987 Program Plan." Washington, DC.

Waldinger, Roger and T. Bailey (1985). "The Youth Employment Problem in the World City." *Social Policy* 16:1.

Wetzel, James R. (1987). *American Youth: A Statistical Snapshot*. Washington, DC: William T. Grant Foundation Commission on Work, Family and Citizenship.

William T. Grant Foundation (1988). "Youth and America's Future: William T. Grant Foundation Commission on Work, Family and Citizenship." *Youth Policy* 10(12):5.

Williams, Terry and W. Kornblum (1985). *Growing Up Poor*. Lexington, MA: Lexington Books.

Willman, M. T. and J. R. Snortum (1982). "A Police Program for Employment of Youth Gang Members." *International Journal of Offender Therapy and Comparative Criminology* 26:207-214.

Wolf, Wendy C., Sally Leiderman and Richard P. Voith (1987). *The California Conservation Corps: An Analysis of Short-term Impacts on Participants*. Philadelphia, PA: Public/Private Ventures.

YBarra, Manuel (1987). Personal communication with the director of the Jobs Against Crime program, Riverside County Probation, Riverside, CA.

Zimmerman, David R. (1980). "Public Sector Job Creation for Youth: Some Observations on Its Role and Effectiveness." In *The Vice President's Task Force on Youth Employment: A Review of Youth Employment Problems, Programs, and Policies*, Vol. 3, edited by Brian Linder and Robert Taggart. Washington, DC: U.S. Department of Labor and Training Administration.

Variations in "Doing" Juvenile Intensive Supervision: Programmatic Issues in Four Ohio Jurisdictions

by
Richard G. Wiebush
Donna M. Hamparian

The similarities and differences between four juvenile intensive supervision programs in Ohio communities are described. Issues that confronted each agency in the development process are highlighted, as are local factors that helped shape each program. All programs were characterized by reduced caseload size, increased frequency of officer-client contact, use of team supervision, and the balanced use of control and treatment. Variations were noted in program purpose and client selection criteria, the size of the eligible client pool, the extent of "in-house" programming, and the composition of the supervision teams.

INTRODUCTION

The recent widespread development of intensive supervision programs (ISPs) in Ohio's juvenile corrections agencies has mirrored national trends. Since the mid-1980s, both interest and implementation have grown dramatically. This interest has recently culminated in the consideration to mandate legislatively the use of intensive supervision in all Ohio juvenile courts.

Intensive supervision has a strong intuitive appeal for policymakers and practitioners alike. The use of small caseloads, tightly structured programming and program components designed to facilitate offender control (e.g., surveillance) all "make good sense." Yet there is also a degree of faddishness involved in the intensive supervision movement. This has frequently resulted in hasty implementation and/or the "borrowing" of ISP models developed in, and for, other jurisdictions. Clear, Flynn and Shapiro's (1987:43) warning regarding this tendency in adult corrections is also applicable to the juvenile system: "This thinking is a bit naive—programs work because they fit their specific contexts, not because they are sure fire ways to solve the overall problem. The evaluation literature is full of examples of programs that were effective in one setting, but failed in others."

The importance of this caveat is highlighted by the findings of several national surveys of adult and juvenile ISPs (Baird, 1983; Byrne, 1986; Armstrong, 1988a, 1988b). As these studies indicate, intensive supervision is not "a" program. Rather, ISPs are characterized by a high degree of variation in goals, client selection criteria and processes, and the extent to which several different control and treatment services are utilized.

These findings, as well as the present authors' involvement in the development of several Ohio ISPs, suggest that program planners will be faced with a myriad of issues in developing an ISP. Further, it is our belief that resolution of these issues must be informed by careful attention to local factors such as the political environment, agency philosophy and tradition, and resource availability. While we believe that ISP "models" and selected program components are to a certain extent transferable, the ultimate determination of ISP purpose, structure and functioning must emerge from—and fit—the local context.

The purpose of this chapter is to illustrate and substantiate the preceding statements. To do so, we will explore in some detail the similarities and variations in the design of ISPs currently operating in four very different Ohio juvenile jurisdictions. In addition, we will highlight the issues that confronted each agency in the developmental process and identify the local factors that helped shape the unique nature of the respective programs.

The first section is a description of the ISPs in the four agencies. These include county-administered probation departments in: (1) a major metropolitan area (Cleveland/Cuyahoga County); (2) a medium-sized city (Toledo/Lucas County); and (3) a predominantly rural county (Delaware). The fourth agency—the Ohio Department of Youth Services (ODYS)—has statewide responsibility for the institutional care of felony offenders committed by the 88 county juvenile courts, and for the supervision of those youth when they are released on parole. This range of agency types allows for a comparison of intensive programming across organizations of varying size and with different jurisdictional responsibilities, i.e., state vs. county, and probation vs. parole.

The program descriptions provide the background for the second section of the chapter. This section examines several critical ISP design issues, with particular attention to the way the agencies addressed each.

DELAWARE COUNTY JUVENILE COURT

The Delaware County Court is the smallest of the four agencies represented. One judge, a court administrator and a probation staff of five counselors handle approximately 650 complaints per year and have fewer than 220 youth under supervision at any one time. With respect to agency size and the characteristics of the youth under supervision,[1] the court is typical of most of the county juvenile courts in Ohio.

Beginning in the fall of 1984, the court began a process of change that resulted in a total restructuring of traditional court services and processes. This change was highlighted by the use of a four-tiered classification system based on risk and the development of a wide range of programming options.

The desire to identify and serve high-risk and serious offenders more effectively was a major impetus for the changes that were instituted in the system, and the use of intensive supervision for probationers was one of the first changes made by the court. Initiated in October 1984, the Delaware ISP is one of the oldest intensive programs in Ohio. It is also a relatively small program, with an average of 17 youth on the caseload at any time.

The program targets two types of probationers for intensive supervision. First are those who are assessed as having the greatest likelihood of recidivism (regardless of the nature of the presenting offense), as indicated by a high score on the court's risk prediction instrument. The second, much smaller, group is comprised of youth who are repeat felony offenders and for whom the ISP serves as an alternative to incarceration. This dual target group makes Delaware County unique among the four jurisdictions represented because the others target either one subset of the offender population (high-risk) or the other (incarceration-bound).

Also setting Delaware's ISP apart is its emphasis on rehabilitation. Although the ISP stresses public safety by incorporating several offender control elements, the court's primary agenda is the effective treatment of youth. This is partially reflected in the variety of "in-house" treatment services developed in recent years and in the court's extensive networking with community resources. It is also reflected in the tenor and spirit (aggressive intervention) that provide the context for service delivery. Court staff recognize this strong rehabilitation orientation and refer to their "treat 'em till they drop" philosophy.

This basic philosophical stance has implications for client selection. Unlike the other probation agencies, Delaware County serves high-risk status offenders in its ISP—a position that has been rejected by those agencies that believe status offenders do not constitute a significant public safety issue. Further, Delaware is the only county to routinely override risk scores and place youth into intensive supervision based on what are essentially "needs" issues.[2]

The program operates 16 hours per day, 7 days per week to provide "saturation" coverage. It incorporates random and unannounced surveillance, along with scheduled probation officer contacts. Contact standards are high. During the initial phases of the program, ISP youth are seen at least twice a day. (This is in contrast to "regular" probationers, who are seen an average of once each week.) Throughout most of the program, contact continues on a daily basis but eventually diminishes to about once per week (see Table 3).

In spite of the rehabilitation ethic, the Delaware County ISP requires accountability and is quite demanding. Most ISP youth have an initial five-day stay in detention. This is followed by a two-week minimum period of house arrest, and then ten days of needing "prior permission" from the probation officer before moving from place to place. Strict curfews, mandatory school attendance and random urinalysis provide additional control measures throughout a youth's stay on intensive supervision.

Violations are responded to with immediate and graduated consequences. These may involve the loss of "good days" (i.e., extending the amount of time under intensive supervision), the reimposition of house arrest and/or short-term stays in detention. Most ISP youth will have three or more technical violations filed against them during their 10-to-12 month stay. It is rare, however, for probation to be revoked for such violations or for minor new offenses.

A central assumption underlying the ISP intervention strategy is that staff must assume total control over the offender until responsible behavior is displayed. As evidence of self-discipline progressively emerges, external control by the probation officer gradually diminishes. This is the basis for the highly-structured "phase system" that governs frequency of contact and determines youth movement through the program.[3]

For Delaware County, the high degree of structure afforded by the program is seen as meeting a critical need of most ISP youth, who typically come from families that are characterized by a lack of structure and consistency.[4] In this sense, the several control measures and frequent disciplinary actions are seen as tools for rehabilitation.

Treatment programming is informed by a comprehensive assessment of needs. (The presentence investigation report takes approximately four hours to complete.) This is frequently supplemented by specialized evaluations such as psychological or substance abuse assessments. Individual treatment plans, which are incorporated in a behavioral contract, consist of offender- specific elements as well as some that are common for all ISP youth. Mandated services include involvement in either individual or family counseling, and participation in a structured group that addresses life-skills issues. Further, most youth (87%) are involved in some form of substance abuse treatment. This level of involvement does as much to define the nature of intensive supervision as do the several control elements and the high frequency of contact.

The ISP is staffed by a team of individuals whose activities are supervised and coordinated by the court administrator. Case management, service referral and the delivery of some direct services are the responsibility of the full-time ISP probation counselor. The surveillance function is performed by two part- time "monitors" who work primarily evenings and weekends. These core staff are supplemented by student interns who perform various functions—some administrative and some direct service—depending on program needs and student capabilities. And because more than three-fourths of all ISP clients and families receive in-home counseling services through the court's family advocate program, these staff are also considered part of the ISP team. Finally, because of the court's small size the judge is able to play a highly active role on a day-to-day basis, and routinely participates in client selection and programming decisions.

In spite of some of the constraints associated with attempts to provide innovative programming in smaller jurisdictions (e.g., limited internal and community-based resources), the Delaware County ISP has achieved a consistently high degree of intensity and delivered a remarkable range of services during its first four years of operation. The program has attracted considerable attention and has developed an experiential base that has strongly influenced subsequently developed Ohio ISPs.

Results from a recent program assessment (Wiebush, 1989) indicate that the agency's investment in intensive supervision has had important benefits. During 1985—the first full year of operations—the ISP served 30 youth, 18 (60%) of whom were not adjudicated for a new offense as either juveniles or adults during an 18-month follow-up. The 40% recidivism rate is somewhat higher than the overall recidivism rate for the court (29%) but is much lower than the projected recidivism (75%) for this group of offenders. Further, commitments to state institutions were reduced from 16 in 1984 to just four in 1985. Much of this reduction is attributed by court staff to the existence of the ISP.

LUCAS COUNTY JUVENILE COURT

The Lucas County (Toledo) ISP serves a medium-sized (population 450,000) urban county court. The court refers approximately 1,000 youth for probation services each year and has about 500 under supervision at any one time.[5] The probation staff consists of 19 line probation counselors.

The Lucas County Intensive Supervision Unit (ISU) is the only one of the four programs that is designed to serve specifically and solely as an alternative to incarceration. Although the program was developed in conjunction with an agencywide classification system, and was programmatically influenced by the Delaware and Cuyahoga County programs, the agency faced local issues that resulted in its rejection of the risk-based ISP models used in the other Ohio sites.[6]

A paramount issue was the court's high rate of commitments to state institutions. Although Lucas County is only the fifth largest of the six major metropolitan counties in Ohio, it has had the highest rate of commitments among these counties for several years. In the mid-1980s, between 225 and 250 youth were incarcerated each year. Although these commitments represented no costs for the county, they were a major source of concern for county and state officials. The use of intensive supervision as an alternative for selected institution-bound offenders was seen as a way of reducing commitments by approximately 20% to 30%.

To ensure that the program serves as an alternative to incarceration, client selection is conducted on a post-commitment basis rather than on the basis of risk/need scores.[7] If a committed youth is evaluated by ISU staff and considered appropriate for the program, the presiding judge is petitioned by the ISU for a change in the commitment order.[8] During the first 14 months of the ISU (October 1987 through November 1988), 106 youth were formally evaluated, and 58 (55%) were placed into intensive supervision.

The ISU team is housed as a separate unit within the probation department. Staff consist of four intensive probation counselors, two full-time surveillance officers and a unit supervisor. Additional team members include staff from the community service program, who supervise ISU youth in community service work and serve as part-time surveillance staff.

Staff roles and contact standards are similar to those found in the other Ohio sites. The unit supervisor serves as liaison to the court, coordinates all staff activities, and also provides direct services to ISU clients in the form of family counseling. The probation counselors have a maximum caseload of 15 and blend the case manager/broker role with that of direct service provider. They see youth a minimum of twice per week during the first four to five months of the program. (Youth on regular probation are seen an average of twice each month.) This frequency declines in later program stages to a minimum of twice per month. Surveillance staff function primarily as monitors and see youth at least twice each day, seven days per week, for the first several months of the program (see Table 3 for frequency of contact by program phase).

Program components are much like those found in Delaware County, reflecting a balance of treatment and control approaches. Individual, group and family counseling are mandatory for all youth, in addition to those services to which they are referred for their particular needs. In addition to surveillance, youth are subjected to several other control elements including urinalysis, house arrest, and hourly monitoring of school attendance and behavior.[9]

Lucas County has a number of program components that are unique among the Ohio jurisdictions. Some of the differences are tied to the nature of the program. That is, because the ISU is an alternative to incarceration, the program tends to be more punitive than the other ISPs reviewed here. For example, all youth are mandated to perform community service (for as many as 100 hours). Youth spend six to eight hours on Saturdays, usually for about two months, engaged in work activities with other ISU clients. Further, although the other jurisdictions tend to curtail surveillance activities in later phases, the ISU maintains almost daily surveillance throughout a youth's program stay.[10]

The ISU has also incorporated several treatment components not found in the other sites. These include: (1) required participation in an intensive therapeutic group; (2) bimonthly formal youth and family conferences to assess progress with the case plan; and (3) the use of a coupon system that allows for positive and concrete reinforcement of gains made by youth through the awarding of various prizes and privileges (e.g., concert tickets, relaxed curfew).

The Lucas County ISP model has critical implications for the juvenile justice system in Ohio and warrants careful attention and evaluation. Its attempt to provide highly structured community-based supervision to youth who previously would have been incarcerated is particularly welcomed in a state (and county) that has traditionally placed a strong reliance on institutional methods. Moreover, its post-commitment selection criterion reveals an attention to the issue of net-widening that is often missed in programs that bill themselves as alternatives to incarceration. Yet, as is the case with many adult ISPs, questions remain regarding the nature of the selection process and the characteristics of the clients included in the ISU. For example, to what extent are jurists committing marginally appropriate youth to a state institution under the assumption that the ISU will intervene? These and related issues are discussed more fully in the second section of this chapter.

Preliminary data suggest that the ISU is reducing the total number of commitments. From January through November 1988, 254 youth were committed to ODYS by Lucas County, and the ISU diverted 46 (18%) of these commitments. The 209 youth who were actually sent to a state institution represent a reduction of approximately 10% compared to the commitments for a similar period in 1986 and 1987. These data, albeit not fully controlled, seem to indicate that the program has not widened the net of social control and has in fact begun to meet program objectives.

CUYAHOGA COUNTY JUVENILE COURT

The Cuyahoga County (Cleveland) Juvenile Court was one of the first major metropolitan jurisdictions in the U.S. to implement an ISP using a locally developed and empirically based risk assessment process. The county is the largest in Ohio, with a population of 1.5 million. The court has six judges and approximately 1,500 youth under probation supervision at any one time.[11] The probation staff consists of 72 officers located in five district offices.

The impetus for the development of the intensive program was the desire of the administrative judge to identify earlier and intervene more effectively with that small percentage of the court's population who become chronic delinquent offenders. In addition to enhancing public safety, the court also viewed intensive supervision as a way of interrupting the development of delinquent careers and thereby avoiding eventual out-of-home placement or commitment.

An intensive research and planning effort was initiated in January 1986 to develop: (1) a risk assessment instrument; (2) a classification and workload deployment system; and (3) an ISP. Led by a full-time project coordinator, the developmental process lasted approximately nine months and eventually involved over 30 different court staff members, representing all levels of the organizational hierarchy.

The resulting ISP design heavily influenced the structure and activities of subsequently developed Ohio programs (i.e., Lucas, ODYS). This influence is revealed in the similarities of the programs along several broad dimensions, including:

- the development of the ISP as part of an agencywide classification system and the use of quantified risk instruments to determine client selection;
- a basic philosophical position that blends control and treatment approaches;
- the use of team supervision and the bifurcation of service and surveillance roles;
- daily contact with intensive youth and extended hours/days of coverage; and
- the use of behavioral contracts and the phase system.

The ISP target population is high-risk offenders.[12] While the majority of youth in ISP are identified as intensive through an initial risk assessment, about one in five are clients who committed a new felony offense while under "regular" supervision.[13] Stemming from an emphasis on public safety and a desire not to use ISP resources for what is viewed as essentially a chronically unruly population, the ISP excludes high-risk status offenders from participation.

The size of the Cuyahoga ISP—in absolute numbers and the proportion of the total caseload represented—is the most striking feature that distinguishes it from the other county probation programs. As originally designed, the Cuyahoga County ISP had the capacity for 180 youth, representing approximately 12% of the probation caseload. However, because of the court's belief in ISP, in 1989 the program was being expanded to serve almost one in four youth under supervision. This expansion was to be accomplished primarily through the lowering of the risk-score cut-off point to include youth previously supervised in a "high" supervision category. When the expansion is completed, more than 40% of the probation staff will be involved in intensive supervision. In these respects, the size of the Cuyahoga County ISP is more like that of ODYS, the state agency described in the next section, than the other county probation departments, in which less than 10% of the supervision population is handled intensively. In spite of the size of the ISP, the structure and content of service delivery in Cuyahoga County is similar to that found in the other probation ISPs.

The program elements that focus on offender control are virtually identical. In addition to multiple daily surveillance contacts, all youth: (1) undergo a 30-day period of house arrest; (2) are required to abide by strict curfews; (3) have hourly school reports on attendance and behavior; and (4) must comply with all program rules on a daily basis in order to earn "good days" (see Table 4 for a full list of control elements).

There are some differences with respect to the kinds of treatment services delivered. For example, no treatment components (apart from individual counseling) are mandatory for all ISP youth. Further, because the county has a rich variety of community resources, ISP youth tend to receive fewer direct services from probation counselors and are not as involved in court-operated programming. Rather, the basic service delivery model is service brokerage.[14] As in the other counties, youth in Cuyahoga are typically involved in multiple forms of programming.

Cuyahoga County's caseload size and contact standards also differ from those of the other sites. ISP caseloads, with 30 youth per counselor, are twice as high as in the other agencies. Consequently, face-to-face contact standards are lower (once per week versus two to five times per week). This lower minimum standard for probation counselor/youth contact is partially a function of resource availability, but is also influenced by the service-broker role. Because youth are extensively involved with other agencies, there is less need for multiple weekly contacts between officers and youth. Nonetheless, current contact standards represent a fourfold increase over past supervision practices. Previously, with caseloads as high as 60 to 75 youth, all youth would be seen just once per month.

The team structure in Cuyahoga County is also currently in transition. Under the original design each of six teams was responsible for 30 youth and consisted of two surveillance staff, a probation counselor and a team leader (supervisor/coordinator). This approach had several benefits but also represented a degree of overstaffing, particularly in relation to the supervisory role and, to a lesser extent, the surveillance function. As program expansion continues, the team structure is being modified to produce a slightly broader span of supervisory control and some reduction in the surveillance staff-youth ratio. The new staffing configuration will consist of six teams, each of which will serve 60 ISP youth. Each team will consist of a team leader, two probation counselors and three surveillance staff.

An evaluation of the Cuyahoga County ISP is currently being conducted, and a final report is expected in the fall of 1989. An interim assessment (Hamparian and Sametz, 1989) followed 127 youth who were placed on intensive probation during the program's first year. As with the other sites, the preliminary nature of the data requires caution, though results appear quite positive. Fewer than one-third of the youth (30.7%) were adjudicated for a new offense during the nine months following their placement into intensive supervision. Results from the full 18-month follow-up will provide a better gauge of the program's long-term success, when the recidivism of ISP participants can be compared (using similar time frames) to the 74% recidivism of the high-risk youth in the risk instrument construction sample.

THE OHIO DEPARTMENT OF YOUTH SERVICES (ODYS)

The ODYS is the state agency responsible for the institutional treatment and parole supervision of felony offenders committed to it by the 88 Ohio county juvenile courts.[15] Some 3,000 youth are released each year from the nine institutions of the ODYS to aftercare status. The juveniles are then supervised in the community by 93 youth counselors (state employees) who operate from seven ODYS regional offices.

In early 1986, the department began a two-year planning process to develop comprehensive classification systems designed to govern institutional placement and programming, and the intensity of community supervision. The impetus for the project emerged from two factors. First, the ODYS was subject to increasing public and legislative scrutiny regarding its effectiveness with violent and chronic offenders. Second, annual budget increases were far below those required to keep pace with a burgeoning committed population. (For example, the average daily ODYS institutional population increased from 1,662 in 1984 to 1,704 in 1985, and again to 1,776 in 1986.) Consequently, there was a need to enhance the agency's ability to identify its "worst" offenders and to reallocate existing resources in such a way that they would be disproportionately concentrated on the chronic offender subpopulation.

The parole supervision strategy resulting from the planning and development process featured the use of an empirically based risk assessment instrument to determine placement in one of three levels of community supervision. Those youth at the highest end of the risk spectrum—with an aggregate predicted recidivism of 75%—are placed into intensive supervision. Moderate-risk youth (48% recidivism) and low-risk youth (23% recidivism) are placed into "regular" and "low" supervision, respectively.

The selection of risk of recidivism as the primary criterion for determining intensity of supervision reflected a gradual evolution in the department's mission toward a greater emphasis on public safety. While assessment of need continues to be an integral part of individual case planning, and efforts at rehabilitation have not been abandoned by staff, issues of offender control and accountability have moved closer to the forefront of the department's perceived and expressed responsibilities. This is particularly true with respect to the agency's high-risk population, which can be seen as constituting the "deepest-end" juvenile offenders in the state.

The intensity of supervision maintained over ODYS high-risk youth represents a dramatic departure from past supervision practices. The caseloads of intensive counselors have been reduced from 25-30 "street" cases to about 13. ISP standards specify a minimum of 20 contacts during the first 90 days of supervision, or an average of more than six contacts per month. Even with a good adjustment during the course of supervision, most intensive supervision youth continue to be seen once per week throughout the parole period. This is in contrast to prior standards that specified an average of two contacts per month. Moreover, the addition of a surveillance component has meant that most ISP youth are seen an additional six to eight times per month, and that supervision coverage extends to evenings and weekends.

Several other changes in supervision practices have been instituted in conjunction with greater supervision intensity. First, individualized, formal contracts are developed with each high-risk youth and his or her family. These contracts specify supervision conditions and treatment objectives, and help insure that a comprehensive needs assessment is conducted for each youth.

Second, a strong emphasis has been placed on the need to immediately sanction all violations of ISP/aftercare conditions. In conjunction with this, each ODYS region has developed a schedule of sanctioning options that ties the severity of the agency's response to that of the youth's infraction.[16] This system serves to reinforce youth accountability and also serves as a disincentive to reliance upon parole revocation for minor or technical violations.

The third significant change in supervision practice involves the use of a team approach to supervising the intensive caseloads. Like the county probation ISPs, the team notion is based on the splitting of service and surveillance functions. However, ODYS has added a new dimension to the team concept. Each team consists of three intensive counselors and two surveillance staff. While parole officers have primary case responsibility for their own caseload of 13 intensive youth, they share responsibility for the caseloads of the other team members. Consequently, the ISP officers must have a basic knowledge of the circumstances of as many as 26 additional intensive youth. The benefits of this approach are that any staff member can provide "coverage" for other ISP staff and that a built-in support system for ISP staff is provided.

The fundamental components of the ODYS ISP are quite similar to those of the county programs. Reduced caseloads, high contact standards, the use of surveillance staff, extended coverage and strict program requirements are among the similarities. By virtue of its statewide responsibility, however, the organization and structure of the ODYS program varies from those in the counties in a number of important ways. For example, not all ODYS high-risk youth are supervised in intensive caseloads. Since most of the regions contain a large number of counties (as many as 23), logistical considerations required restricting the ISP target population to those high-risk youth residing in the major metropolitan areas of each region (e.g., Cleveland, Akron, Cincinnati, Toledo, Columbus). Youth from these areas constitute the majority of the state's high-risk youth—about 82%. However, this restriction means that a substantial proportion (18%) of the high-risk group is served in mixed caseloads. And, although these youth receive the higher number of youth counselor contacts, they are not subject to surveillance.

There are in effect seven ISPs in ODYS—one for each administrative region. The ISPs are similar in that all are governed by the same basic policies and procedures. Yet each region has been given the latitude to develop its own style of intensive supervision, and this has resulted in some programmatic variations. Further, the proportion of youth identified as high-risk—and the number of staff consequently involved in intensive supervision—varies considerably by region. For example, although the Akron and Cincinnati regions supervise a comparable number of parolees, the proportion of high-risk youth in Akron requires the allocation of just three staff to the ISP, while the higher intensive supervision caseload in Cincinnati results in the assignment of nine staff members.

The ODYS classification system and intensive supervision programs began in the Akron region in February 1988, and have been phased in on a regional basis over an 18-month period. Consequently there are no statewide data available to assess their impact. However, preliminary data from the first year of program operation in Akron indicate substantial decreases in parole revocations and recommitments. A comparison of data for the first year of program operation (March 1988 through February 1989) and the year prior to implementation (March 1987 through February 1988) reveals a 39% reduction in revocations—from 75 to 46—and a 34% reduction in recommitments—from 89 to 59—even though total caseload size was similar for the two periods. While the extent to which these reductions are attributable to the ISP is not yet known, both the direction and the magnitude of change in these important measures are considered encouraging.[17]

Table 1: Basic Parameters of the Ohio Programs: Models, Goals and Client Selection

	Jurisdiction			
Characteristic	*Delaware*	*Lucas*	*Cuyahoga*	*ODYS*
Agency type	County probation	County probation	County probation	State parole
Program model	Probation enhancement and alternative to to incarceration	Alternative to incarceration	Probation enhancement	Parole enhancement
Program goals	Reduced recidivism Reduced commitments Reduced out-of-home placement	Reduced commitments	Reduced recidivism Reduced commitments Reduced out-of-home placement	Reduced recidivism Reduced re-commitments
Primary client selection criterion	High risk score	Post-commitment status	High risk score	High risk score
Additional criteria	Chronic felony offenders; high needs	Excluded offenses = use of weapon, victim injury, drug trafficking	Status offenders excluded	Metro area resident; 2+ violent offenders Auto. Included
Philosophy, supervision emphasis	All stress "balanced" approach – relatively equal emphasis on public safety and rehabilitation.			

Table 2: ISP Program Size and Staffing Patterns

	Jurisdiction			
Characteristic	*Delaware*	*Lucas*	*Cuyahoga*	*ODYS*
Total agency caseload*	225	500	1,500	1,500
ISP caseload	17	60	360**	525
ISP staff/youth ratio (P/P officers)	1:17	1:15	1:30	1:13
Surveillance staff/youth ratio	2:17	2.5:60	3:60	2:39
Team configuration	Court Administrator 1 ISP Probation officer 2 Surveillance staff (p/t) Student interns Family advocates	1 Unit supervisor 4 ISP Probation officers 2 Surveillance staff (f/t) 2 Surveillance staff (p/t) 3 Community service staff (p/t)	1 Team leader 2 ISP Probation officers 3 Surveillance staff (f/t)	3 ISP Probation officers 2 Surveillance staff (p/t)
Number of teams	1	1	6	1-3 per region 14 total
Coverage	7 days; 14 hrs/day	7 days; 14 hrs/day	7 days; 24 hrs/day	7 days; 14 hrs/day

* Caseload = cases under supervision at any one time.
** Projected figure for Summer 1989.

Table 3: Contact Standards by Type and Phase*

Type Contact	Jurisdiction Delaware	Lucas	Cuyahoga	ODYS
Phase I				
Probation/parole officers direct with youths	5/week	2/wk	1/wk	6.5/month
family, direct	(n.s.)	4/month	n.s.	2/month
surveillance**	11/wk	14/wk	17/wk	4/wk
Duration (minimum)	21 days	30 days	30 days	90 days
Phase II				
Probation/parole officers direct with youths	5/wk	2/wk	1/wk	4–6/month
family, direct	(n.s.)	2/month	n.s.	2/month
surveillance**	11/wk	10/wk	8/wk	4/wk
Duration (minimum)	28 days	50 days	75 days	60 days
Phase III				
Probation/parole officers direct with youths	3/wk	1/wk	1/wk	2–6/month
family, direct	(n.s.)	2/month	n.s.	1/month
surveillance**	0–11/wk	7/wk	5/wk	2–4/wk
Duration (minimum)	70 days	50 days	75 days	60 days
Phase IV				
Probation/parole officers direct with youths	1–3/wk	2/month	as needed	2–6/month
family, direct	(n.s.)	1/month	n.s.	1/month
surveillance**	none	5/wk	3/wk	2–4/wk
Duration (minimum)	By contract	26 days	75 days	60 days

n.s.: not specified.

* ODYS does not use the phase system to govern youth movement through the program. Youth are reclassified at three, five and seven months, based on reassessment of risk.

** Includes direct and telephone contacts.

Table 4: Program Components—Control Elements*

	Jurisdiction			
Components	*Delaware*	*Lucas*	*Cuyahoga*	*ODYS*
Surveillance	X	X	X	X
Curfew	X	X	X	X
Front–end detention	X	–*	–	–
House arrest	X	X	X	0
Prior permission	X	–	–	–
Electronic surveillance	–	–	0	–
Urinalysis	0	X	0	0
Daily sanctioning (phase system)	X	X	X	–
Hourly school reports	X	X	X	–
Formal, graduated sanction schedule	–	X	–	X

Note: Most Lucas ISP youth do have front–end detention, but it is not mandated.
X = Mandatory component
– = Component not available
0 = Component optional, varies by youth

PROGRAMMATIC ISSUES

In this section, we intend to delineate some of the most critical questions that confronted the Ohio agencies and that will need to be addressed by any organization developing an ISP. An additional purpose is to demonstrate the influence of local circumstances in producing ISP design variations. The topical areas discussed include client eligibility and selection, program services, and staffing. However, prior to this discussion, it will be useful to note several characteristics, primarily related to philosophy and goals, that are shared by the four sites. These factors helped shape the context within which ISP design and implementation took place, and are important to understanding the thrust of the programs.

Table 5: Program Components—Treatment Elements

Component	Delaware	Lucas	Cuyahoga	ODYS
	Jurisdiction			
Individualized contracts	X	X	X	X
Individual counseling (non-probation/parole officer)	0	0	0	0
Family counseling or family conferences	0	X	0	0
Group counseling	X	X	0	0
In-home family services	X	-	X	-
Community sponsors, advocates	-	-	-	-
Alternative education	0	0	0	0
Job training	0	0	0	0
Substance abuse counseling	0	0	0	0

X = Mandatory component
- = Component not available
0 = Component optional, varies by youth

First, all the agencies were motivated to adopt ISPs because they recognized the shortcomings of traditional responses to serious or chronic offenders. There was a need to fill the service gap that existed between traditional probation/parole and out-of-home placement or incarceration.

Second, all the agencies faced resource constraints and believed that this service gap could best be bridged by reallocating existing resources. In order to target a disproportionate share of those resources to their most problematic youth, all undertook ISP development within the larger context of developing classification and attendant workload deployment systems.

The third similarity is that each program hopes to use ISP as a vehicle for reducing the incidence of incarceration. Although Lucas County's program is the only one designed exclusively as an alternative to incarceration, the Delaware County ISP also expressly accommodates this goal. The other sites attempt to prevent the need for institutionalization through earlier intervention (Cuyahoga County), or by reducing the likelihood of recommitment (ODYS). There is a generally shared belief among the organizations that the effects of institutionalization are deleterious and that intensive community supervision can provide a positive alternative for most youth, while also serving the interests of the larger community.

Fourth, all the programs were implemented in a nationally prevailing "get-tough" atmosphere. This resulted in an intensive approach that differed substantially from the reduced caseload experiments popular in the early 1970s. In particular, the ISPs all incorporated a number of aggressive control elements (e.g., surveillance) that were not previously used by the agencies, and that appeared to give an entirely new cast to probation and parole services. The new emphasis on public safety and offender accountability was also publicly emphasized by several of the agencies.

The fifth and perhaps most striking similarity among the programs is that the infusion of public safety language and the addition of control elements to offender programming has not significantly affected the basic philosophical approach to working with delinquent youth. None of the agencies has abandoned a youth-centered, service-delivery, rehabilitation-oriented approach in favor of one that would emphasize control, surveillance and deterrence. While there are some variations in emphasis across sites, each agency appears to have: (1) broadened its perspective to include responsibility for community safety as well as "the best interest of the juvenile"; (2) consequently taken a more balanced approach to supervision; and (3) largely transformed in practice what are perceived as control elements into additional tools for rehabilitation. With respect to the last of these developments, for example, surveillance activities are frequently seen as generating the possibility for enhanced family interaction, more quickly identifying offender "games," and providing immediate responses to positive and negative behaviors.

Client Eligibility and Selection

There are several variations across the Ohio jurisdictions with respect to ISP client eligibility and selection. These variations derive from differences in program purpose, resource availability, the relative importance attached to offender "needs" issues, and the use of overrides.

Program Purpose

The broadest distinction in client eligibility flows from the different purposes inherent in the two basic ISP models used in Ohio. In the probation/parole enhancement model (Cuyahoga, Delaware, ODYS), the intent is to reduce the likelihood of recidivism among high-risk offenders who have been placed under community supervision. Selection for ISP is controlled by the administrative agency (i.e., it is a case management decision), and is primarily determined by quantified risk measures. Youth with a high likelihood of recidivism, regardless of the nature of their presenting offense, are automatically included in the ISP.[18]

In contrast, Lucas County's focus on reducing institutional commitments results in ISP selection (subject to judicial approval) of youth from among those who have been committed to a state institution by the court. Because youth are committed due to the nature of the offense (i.e., a felony) and not because of their statistical likelihood of recidivism, risk scores are irrelevant in defining the target population.

This raises a key issue in relation to goals and client selection. High-risk youth are not necessarily "serious" offenders in terms of the type of offenses committed. Two factors contribute to the distinction between the groups. First, empirically-based risk scores are only partially influenced by the nature of the current offense.[19] In addition, total risk scores are often inversely related to offense seriousness. At the county probation level, it is not atypical for a chronic status offender or misdemeanant to score much higher on risk than a youth charged with more serious felony offenses. Second, in Ohio only felony offenders are considered by law "serious" enough to warrant eligibility for commitment to a state institution. Consequently, youth who are most likely to recidivate may not be eligible for commitment, while those who are actually committed may not be the highest risks. In practice, this distinction means that were Lucas County to have used risk score criteria for ISU inclusion (instead of post-commitment status), the ISU would have significantly reduced its chances of accessing the target population of institution-bound offenders.

Directly related to the need to link selection strategies carefully with target group characteristics is the need for goal clarification and prioritization. If program goals are unclear, neither the target group(s) nor selection criteria can be precisely identified. Further, there is a tendency for agencies to want a program to achieve multiple ends, i.e., to reduce recidivism, commitments, and other forms of out-of-home placements. Given the potential differences in target group characteristics, a lack of specificity with respect to the relative priority of program goals has the potential to result in incomplete or inappropriate selection criteria. For example, in those jurisdictions where there are multiple program goals, the use of "high-risk" as the sole criterion for ISP selection may not be sufficient to ensure that the program will also capture those youth most likely to be committed or placed out of the home.

This is not to suggest that the pursuit of multiple goals is impossible or that a focus on one goal cannot have impact on the others. In Delaware County, although high-risk youth are targeted by the ISP, the unit is also designed to serve felony offenders who otherwise would be committed. Consequently, there are two distinct goals and two separate selection criteria. There are also early indications that ODYS's primary goal of recidivism reduction among high-risk parolees has had some impact on a secondary goal of reduced commitments by effecting reductions in the number of youth who are revoked or recommitted.

"High" Risk and Resource Availability

In those jurisdictions using risk assessment instruments to determine ISP client selection, an important issue is determination of what likelihood of recidivism constitutes "high" risk. Is it youth with a 50% or greater likelihood, or those with 70% or 85%? The answer to this question results in the selection of a "cut-off" score on the risk instrument, the score above which a youth will be included in ISP and below which will result in other types of supervision. The selection of cut-off scores is solely a function of agency policy decisions and is not inherent in the results of the research used to develop the instrument. That is, there is no "right" recidivism probability for ISP inclusion. Rather, decision makers must balance their "sense" of what constitutes high risk with philosophical and resource considerations in identifying the high-risk group. For example, the view could be taken that anyone with a greater than 50% chance of recidivism should be considered high-risk. However, if half the agency's population has such a likelihood, the attempt to provide intensive services to that number of youth would stretch agency resources to the point where the meaning of "intensive" would be substantially altered. An additional question is whether a 50% likelihood of recidivism (and, conversely, of success) warrants or justifies the intrusiveness associated with the kind of intensive supervision used by the Ohio programs.

In the Ohio sites, the aggregate recidivism associated with the high-risk cut-off scores falls into a fairly narrow range: 70% to 80%. However, the percentage of each agency's population identified as high risk varies considerably. In Delaware, just 10% to 12% of youth score high, while in ODYS (21%) and in Cuyahoga (29%), the percentage of youth identified as high risk is much greater. Again, these differences in the size of the eligible population are not a function of some objective measure of who should be in ISP, but are tied instead to the local agency's balancing of what is desirable and what is possible.

Definition of who constitutes high-risk can also vary with an agency's jurisdictional responsibilities. Because ODYS has statewide jurisdiction and receives youth from the 88 counties, the universe of offenders that it assesses for risk is substantially different from that assessed on the local level. Because the identification of high-risk youth is conducted in relation to the rest of the agency's population, it is quite possible that a youth measured as high risk in Delaware or Cuyahoga will not score as intensive if committed to ODYS. This presents unique problems for the state agency, especially with judges from predominantly rural counties who send their "worst" youth to ODYS, only to have them frequently released on parole under "low" supervision.

High-Need Youth

Nationally, needs assessments are frequently used in conjunction with risk assessments to identify ISP clients. The former are used not only because they help identify which clients may need the most attention (a workload issue), but also because high-need youth may be more likely to recidivate.

Among the Ohio sites, only Delaware County routinely uses assessment of need to determine ISP eligibility. While risk score is a primary selection criterion, a moderate risk, high-need youth will frequently be placed into ISP. This practice emerges from Delaware County's strong rehabilitation orientation and the agency's belief that important risk-related need factors are not incorporated in its risk instrument.

Several considerations influence the extent to which need factors inform ISP decisions in the other jurisdictions. First, these agencies tend to have a somewhat greater emphasis on public safety issues. Combined with resource constraints, this emphasis led to explicit decisions by Cuyahoga County and ODYS to exclude need as an ISP selection criterion, and to focus exclusively on risk measures. (By virtue of its "commitment" criterion, neither risk nor need measures are primary determinants of eligibility for the Lucas County ISP.) However, all three jurisdictions pay careful attention to need issues once youth have been selected for ISP, and use the results of assessments to shape individual program and service decisions.

A second factor influencing decisions not to use separate needs assessments to determine ISP eligibility is the nature of juvenile risk assessment instruments. Juvenile "risk" instruments, unlike adult scales, are heavily influenced by what are usually considered "need" items (e.g., family dysfunction, school attendance, etc.). On the ODYS instrument for example, half the items and more than half the points are accounted for by need-related issues. This indicates the influence of youth needs on risk of recidivism, but it also partially obviates the need for a separate needs assessment tool as a method for client selection.

Status Offenders

Related to the needs issue is the appropriateness of including status offenders in an ISP.[20] As a group, status offenders tend to be a high-need (and time-consuming) population, and could be seen as likely candidates for the intensive attention and structure afforded by an ISP. In addition, a large number of status offenders score high on the risk instruments used in Ohio.

However, although they may tend to be chronic offenders, status offenders typically engage in behavior that does not constitute a significant threat to public safety. Consequently, the decision to include or exclude high-risk youth from this subgroup in an ISP is largely determined by agency philosophy and program goals.

The opposing positions taken by Delaware and Cuyahoga counties on this issue are illustrative. Faced with the prospect of a large number of status offenders in its program, the Cuyahoga court decided to exclude this group from ISP eligibility regardless of risk score. In contrast, Delaware County routinely places status offenders into its ISP. In 1985, almost half of all intensive youth were status offenders. As with the "needs" issue, Delaware's position is primarily informed by its philosophical orientation toward the rehabilitation of all offenders— regardless of the threat they may or may not pose to public safety.

Overrides

An override allows for the placement of an offender into an ISP where case circumstances warrant intensive supervision in spite of a moderate- or low-risk score. Consequently, this mechanism expands the selection criteria for ISP. Overrides are used in the three Ohio jurisdictions where risk score is the primary selection criterion. However, the jurisdictions vary widely with respect to the types of overrides employed and the frequency with which they are used. These variations reflect different positions taken by the agencies on several key issues.

Delaware and Cuyahoga counties utilize discretionary overrides, whereby an officer can request placement into an ISP because of significant problems not captured by the risk instrument. This approach provides staff with greater flexibility and the opportunity for input in the case decision-making process. As indicated earlier, Delaware frequently uses this mechanism to serve high-need youth.

However, unless discretionary overrides are closely monitored, there is the danger that the practice could become routinized or abused, and thereby: (1) erode selection criteria; (2) subvert the entire risk assessment rationale; and (3) swell the ISP population with marginally appropriate youth. Although Cuyahoga County has provisions for discretionary overrides, the granting of override requests is severely restricted in order to avoid these possible negative consequences.

The ODYS override provisions are unique among the Ohio jurisdictions in that youth with selected offense histories (two or more violent felony offenses) are automatically included in the ISP. This decision was influenced by research findings regarding this subset of offenders and also by "political" considerations.[21] ODYS recognized that to ignore community and judicial concerns regarding certain types of offenders (regardless of risk score) could cripple the acceptance of the intensive approach and the classification system in general. Yet unless the range of offender types who are mandatorily placed into ISP is narrowly defined, this practice has the same potential to overburden an ISP as do uncontrolled discretionary overrides. For example, if all youth sent to ODYS for aggravated burglary were overridden into ISP, almost half the agency's aftercare population would be intensive.

A particularly sensitive issue concerns "judicial overrides," i.e., direct sentencing to ISP regardless of risk/need scores. In those jurisdictions where control of the ISP rests with the probation/parole agency, some conflict over this issue is certain to arise. In fact, in one of the Ohio sites, early attempts by the agency to block direct sentencing led to threats from the bench to cite for contempt of court. This type of conflict has been diminished over time by repeated efforts to ensure judicial understanding of the need to maintain the integrity of the selection process, and of the negative impact of overrides on limited ISP resources.

Client Selection and Net Widening

The potential for widening the net of social control is inherent in both of the basic ISP models. With respect to ISP as an alternative to incarceration, Barton and Butts (1988) have recently documented how one metropolitan county's ISP was used as a supplement to incarceration rather than as an alternative. In Lucas County, although ODYS commitments were reduced during the first 18 months of program operation, the danger of similar effects still exists. While the program anticipated potential net-widening and structured its selection process to guard against such a development, two factors have the potential to subvert program goals. First, because of the program's existence, jurists may be more likely to commit a marginal youth, making the assumption that ISP will intervene. Clear, Flynn and Shapiro (1987) have noted that judges in one adult jurisdiction have sentenced offenders to incarceration while "welcoming an application for intensive supervision." Second, the absence of formalized and detailed selection criteria, beyond that of having been committed, may induce the ISP to select first those youth who are "borderline" commitments and who otherwise may have been handled on regular probation.[22]

The probation enhancement model of ISP also results in a level of intensified control for certain offenders who normally would be dealt with under less restrictive conditions. This is a function of the use of the risk predictor for determining ISP selection. Because these instruments for juveniles generate scores that are only marginally related to offense seriousness, the second-time shoplifter may be as likely to be subjected to ISP as the second-time felony offender. Absent a risk-driven ISP, the former offender would likely be handled with minor supervision requirements.

Some of these effects may be unavoidable, given broader program goals (i.e. early intervention) and the realities of system functioning. However, identification and anticipation of these potential effects, and steps to control them, are necessary to minimize unintended net-widening consequences.

PROGRAM COMPONENTS AND SERVICES

Defining "Intensive"

In their surveys of adult and juvenile jurisdictions using the ISP, Baird (1983), Byrne (1986) and Armstrong (1988a, 1988b) all found substantial variation in what constituted "intensive" supervision. An increase from one face-to-face contact per month to two such contacts resulted in some programs identifying themselves as intensive. In other sites, multiple daily contacts were the standard for definition as intensive.

In spite of the differences in the nature of the Ohio sites, there is a marked similarity in the intensiveness of the programs. Each agency established caseload size at approximately half that of regular supervision, and the number of face-to-face contacts by the intensive officer is at least twice that provided to regular clients. ODYS, for example, has one of the lowest ISP contact standards among the four agencies. Yet during the first six months of aftercare, an ISP youth will have a minimum of 32 face-to-face contacts, while a regular youth will have just 14.

Each of the agencies has also provided sufficient resources to the ISP to ensure that intensity is defined not only in comparison to regular clients, but also in relation to a broader standard of an "appropriate" level of supervision. The simple doubling of an initially low contact standard (e.g., from once to twice per month) was not seen as constituting an intensity that had substantial legitimacy. Instead, each of the agencies determined that multiple contacts per week, and in some cases daily contacts, were necessary to provide the desired level of control and service.

However, to define intensity of service in terms of caseload size or number of contacts alone is problematic for several reasons. First, there are obviously a number of additional dimensions of community supervision in relation to which intensity of supervision might be defined. These include the hours during which services are made available to clients (i.e., are "banker's hours" appropriate for intensive supervision?), and the range and mix of treatment services provided to youth and their families.

A second concern with a focus on contacts and caseloads is that it reflects a deeply ingrained assumption that reduced caseloads lead to increased contacts, and that this in turn translates into greater effectiveness. The first part of this equation has been borne out by some research (Banks et al., 1977), but has been contradicted by others.[23] It has also been found that specifying higher contact standards for high-risk (adult) probationers does not automatically mean that those standards will be met (Latessa, 1987; Bennett, 1987). Finally, an increase in contacts alone does not lead to lower recidivism (Banks et.al., 1977). Consequently, whether contact or surveillance standards are set at two, five or 20 times per week may be irrelevant in relation to youth outcomes. While frequency of contact may be considered critical to community acceptance of ISPs, the quality of services provided and the way in which they are tailored to offender risk and needs appears to be the more central issue in relation to offender success (Baird, 1986; Romig, 1986).

Further, given that high contact levels are an integral part of the definition of ISP, the nature of staff-client interactions also requires attention. If it is assumed that increased officer interaction with youth will have potential benefits, it becomes important to: (1) specify what is supposed to occur during these frequent contacts; and (2) ensure that ISP officers have the requisite knowledge and skills to conduct those activities. This issue has been raised by several authors (Baird, 1983; Clear and Shapiro, 1986) in relation to adult programs, and it is an issue for juvenile ISPs as well. The potential problem of staff inability to use an increased level of interaction productively with high-risk youth was illustrated by one Ohio officer's comment that "there are only so many times a week you can tell a kid to act right." This is a staff selection and training issue that bears directly on whether "frequency of contact" is to have any meaningful relationship to "intensity of service."

Variations in Operationalizing Intensity

As is evident from the program descriptions and the preceding section, the Ohio sites tend to define their ISPs in similar ways and offer comparable programs and services. However, several different avenues were taken in order to achieve the desired levels of intensity, and these help shape the particular identity of each program.

In Delaware County, where resource considerations were paramount, the high frequency of contact was partially achieved by altering the way in which some contacts were made, and through the use of a wider range of staff. Specifically, the requirement that ISP youth report on a daily basis to the probation office substantially increased the number of contacts that could be made without a demand for additional resources. In addition, the use of family advocates (in-home family counselors) and student interns meant that auxiliary staff could contribute to levels of supervision as well as provide additional treatment resources.

The use of existing resources to enhance supervision is a characteristic of other Ohio sites as well. Lucas County, for example, was able to achieve 16-hour-per-day, seven-day-per week surveillance by using two previously underutilized resources. First, community service "crew leaders" (probation staff) were on duty during daytime hours but did not have significant responsibilities until after 3 p.m., when community service work actually began. Consequently, several of these staff were assigned the additional responsibility of providing surveillance activities in the schools. Second, detention center desk staff were enlisted to make telephone calls to ISP youth on Sundays, a traditionally slow day for those staff.

Finally, ODYS provides an example of in-program variations in the way in which intensity is defined through its differential handling of urban and nonurban high-risk youth. Because the nonurban high-risk youth were geographically dispersed, the use of pure caseloads and surveillance was effectively precluded. Consequently, in spite of similar risk scores, two very different forms of intensive supervision are provided.

Tailoring Services To Youth Needs

All the Ohio programs stress the need for individualized interventions within the context of ISP programming. This emphasis is highlighted by the common use of individualized contracting to establish the parameters and conditions of supervision. Implicit in this approach is the recognition that effective treatment requires careful assessment of need, and the matching of youth and families with appropriate services.

Yet there is also an apparent contradiction to this approach built into several of the ISPs, by virtue of the program components that are mandatory for all youth. Typically, for example, youth will not only be subject to the same levels of control, but will also be required to participate in individual counseling, family counseling and various group educational formats. In some sites all ISP youth are subject to random urinalysis. Consequently, while the ISPs tend to be guided by an individualized approach, there is also an undercurrent of a "throw everything at them and hope something sticks" methodology. This type of programming overload may make a program appear rigorous and uncompromising to the public, but it also raises questions of effectiveness and efficiency with respect to service delivery.

Services Unique to Juvenile ISPs

ISPs for juveniles are largely modeled after those developed for adult jurisdictions. Use of the team approach, surveillance, restrictive curfews and periodic urinalysis are a few examples of program elements common to both types of jurisdictions (see Byrne, 1986; Goldstein, 1986; Pearson and Bibel, 1986; and Erwin, 1987, for examples of adult program components). However, as Goldstein (1986) has pointed out, the transferability of ISP from adult to juvenile is limited by the need to attend to issues that are unique to juveniles. Predominant among these are educational and family issues.

For each of the Ohio ISPs, programming in these areas forms a critical piece in the service delivery package. In the three county probation departments, school attendance is mandatory for all youth. The importance of the requirement is stressed through the use of the "school verification report," which teachers use to make hourly notations regarding class attendance, behavior and participation. Further, a youth's progress toward program completion is heavily contingent upon successful performance in these areas, in that the granting of a "good day" is denied if any of the reports are negative.

Because many ISP youth have a history of school underachievement and dysfunctioning, all the programs have had to access and develop close working relationships with alternative education programs, including GED and special education providers. Particular attention has been devoted to youth in need of special education services because in three of the four jurisdictions special education status has been found to be strongly associated with risk.

School issues for ODYS are particularly problematic. First, school reintegration is often hampered by a youth's previous reputation and the labeling resulting from the training school commitment. Perhaps more importantly, the majority of ODYS youth are age 17 or older when released to aftercare. For many, continuation in the traditional school setting is often an unrealistic option. As a result, programming relating to alternative education, vocational training and job-preparedness skills have assumed central importance for the agency's ISP units.

All the agencies have also placed particular emphasis on family-related issues. Efforts in this area are viewed as inseparable from attempts to effect changes in youths' behavior. Consequently, all families are required to participate in development of the youths' contract and to specify their own responsibilities in its execution. In Lucas County, a youth is considered ineligible for ISP participation if the family is seen as "unworkable." In several sites, family members are required to participate in parents' groups and/or family counseling, and there has been some success in mandating parental involvement in treatment for their own problems (e.g., substance abuse).

Table 6: Multi-Purpose Components

	Jurisdiction			
Components	*Delaware*	*Lucas*	*Cuyahoga*	*ODYS*
School attendance	X	X	X	X (or work)
Community service	0	X	0	0
Restitution	0	0	0	0

X = Mandatory component
0 = Component optional, varies by youth

Sanctioning Program Violations

Intensified levels of supervision and surveillance are likely to result in the discovery of violations that previously would have gone undetected. The question of how to respond to such infractions presents several difficulties. Failure to respond to violations may threaten the integrity of the ISP with respect to both client and public perception. In some adult ISPs (e.g., New Jersey), strict enforcement has resulted in the return of a large percentage of ISP clients to prison (Pearson and Bibel, 1986). However, it has also reinforced the notion of the program as strictly public safety-oriented. This approach, particularly if taken in relation to behaviors that would not ordinarily be considered crimes (e.g. curfew violations, failure to attend

treatment), has the potential to undermine the attainment of other program objectives. That is, such policies could result in artificially inflated "recidivism" rates or, in the case of ISPs that are designed as alternatives to incarceration, merely serve to delay that incarceration.

In response to these issues, some of the Ohio programs have developed formalized sanctioning "schedules" that tie a range of permissible responses to the seriousness of the infraction. This continuum of sanctions involves the use of a number of alternatives (e.g. house arrest, more restrictive curfew, increased length of stay) that can provide meaningful yet proportional responses. Further, the agencies have all stressed the need to provide immediate consequences for all infractions. This reflects a treatment approach that emphasizes constant reinforcement, but it also discourages the practice of ignoring minor violations until their cumulative number "justifies" the use of revocation proceedings.

Staffing Patterns and Issues

Caseload Composition

Should ISP youth be supervised on caseloads consisting only of intensive youth, or should they represent a portion of each staff member's caseload? Discussion of this question in the Ohio sites focused on: (1) the potential for staff burnout; and (2) the viability of having an intensive "program" without specialized caseloads. For most of the agencies, the latter consideration far outweighed the former. While recognizing the potential for staff burnout resulting from continuous work with only the most difficult youth, the agencies felt that adequate support for staff could be achieved via the use of a team approach. Further, the distribution of intensive youth across a large number of (mixed) caseloads was envisioned as having the potential for significant variations in the intensity and quality of service delivery, as well as building in communication problems between surveillance and service staff. Several other considerations supported the use of specialized caseloads, including the desire to enhance program visibility and create an opportunity to utilize the "best" staff for work with the agency's "worst" youth.

Team Composition

Each jurisdiction uses some variation of a team approach for service delivery. The degree of effort and the variety of staff required to deliver intended ISP services required an approach that would allow for the most efficient integration and coordination of roles.

For each jurisdiction, the core of the team is composed of the ISP officers and the surveillance staff. The incorporation of other staff into the team is largely determined by the extent to which related staff are integral to service delivery, and the relationship of agency supervisors to ISP line staff.

In Lucas County, the inclusion of the mandatory community service component in the ISU means that the work supervisors spend a considerable amount of time interacting with ISP youth. Were these staff not included as part of the team, the opportunity to share information routinely regarding youth performance and attitudes would be lost. The inclusion of these staff also helps to ensure that treatment strategies can be both comprehensive and uniform in application. This rationale also underlies Delaware County's inclusion of family advocates and student interns in the team.[24]

The desired relationship of supervisory staff to the ISP unit may also inform choices regarding team composition. Should supervisors responsible for ISP staff have exclusive responsibility for those staff, or should they have responsibility for non-ISP staff as well?

At one level this is a question of the size of the agency and the ISP. In Delaware County, with a total probation staff of five and just one intensive counselor, a separate supervisor for the ISP "unit" is a moot point. However, where teams consist of multiple line staff, surveillance officers and other staff, alternative approaches are possible. On the one hand, the involvement of multiple staff and the specialized nature of the program may be seen as requiring a separate coordination and supervision role. Where this has been done (Cuyahoga and Lucas), the supervisor may also provide additional direct services for youth that serve to enhance the overall model. On the other hand, the value of this approach may be called into question by the extremely narrow span of supervisory control. In one ODYS region, for example, the utilization of one supervisor solely for the ISP team would have resulted in that person having responsibility for a total of five staff (three probation/parole officers and two surveillance officers), while the remaining supervisor would have had responsibility for 12 "regular" parole officers. From a supervisory workload perspective, this would have represented a gross imbalance and one that would not have been offset (in ODYS's view) by any gains accruing to the ISP.

Staff Roles

There are several dimensions along which staff roles are differentiated, including service brokerage and delivery, surveillance, auxiliary service (e.g., student interns) and staff supervision. Just as these roles are incorporated into the team structure in various ways, so too are they conceived and executed somewhat differently across sites. (Because the ISP line officer and surveillance roles are common to all sites, they are the focus of this discussion.)

Among the ISP probation/parole officers, roles extend along a continuum from case manager/service broker to direct service provider. None of the agencies has specified a narrowly defined role for officers at either end of this continuum. Consequently, the differences in probation/parole officer roles across sites tend to be ones of relative emphasis.

In the larger agencies, ISP staff function predominantly as service brokers.

With some exceptions, ODYS and Cuyahoga County staff limit attempts at direct service provision beyond that of individual counseling. In Lucas and Delaware Counties, officers tend to assume more direct service responsibilities. In addition, both these agencies have developed a number of "in-house" services (e.g., family and group counseling) that provide ISP with a greater direct service capability.

In all the sites, the use of behavioral contracting and/or the phase system has altered substantially the practice of traditional casework and counseling. These approaches have provided sharply defined foci for counseling activities. That is, much counseling is now done in relation to the attainment of contract objectives and around the specific daily behaviors that have resulted in the awarding or withholding of credit for a "good day."

Ultimately however, the ISP staff role definition and execution will hinge on the particular style and qualifications of individual staff. As with "regular" probation officers, if an ISP officer has skills in a particular area, he or she is likely to use them, regardless of role definitions. Variations in role definition are therefore as likely within sites as across them.

The concept of the surveillance officer role is virtually uniform among the Ohio agencies. The view of ISP as much more than an attempt to suppress delinquent behavior led to a rejection of the notion that surveillance staff should have a "cop mentality." However, the role is defined in a fairly narrow fashion and is generally limited to monitoring a youth's whereabouts, reporting back to staff on violations and intervening only to defuse crisis situations. Although there are alternative role conceptualizations (e.g. youth advocate, mentor), these are seen as more appropriately included in the role of the probation/parole officer.

Several influences have served to shift the way in which the surveillance role has been executed. First, as has been reported regarding the adult ISP experience (Erwin, 1987), the frequency of contact between surveillance staff and youth has frequently resulted in the development of close and supportive relationships. Second, the type of staff attracted to youth service positions tend to see themselves as "helpers." Again, regardless of role definition, these staff will likely attempt to provide some basic forms of counseling.

Where surveillance staff have had the skills to perform this additional counseling role, ISP staff have welcomed the additional resource. However, the assumption of counseling activities by surveillance staff carries with it a number of potential problems, including youth manipulation of staff, mixed messages given to youth, and potential conflict over treatment goals and strategies. These problems began to emerge in one ODYS region, necessitating a reclarification of team member roles and a precise delineation of the acceptable parameters for counseling and related activities by the surveillance staff.

SUMMARY AND CONCLUSION

We have reviewed the goals, organization and programmatic features of ISPs currently operating in four Ohio juvenile agencies. These agencies range from a small, predominantly rural court to large metropolitan probation and statewide parole organizations. Although the agencies are very different from each other, each has developed an ISP that must be considered highly intensive, whether measured in terms of extent of supervision and control, or the range of services provided to clients.

The several approaches to intensive supervision have a number of characteristics in common, including the use of system-wide classification as a method for focusing resources on those youth identified as needing intensive supervision. Broad programmatic similarities include significantly reduced caseload size, a high frequency of contact, the use of team supervision and a balanced use of control and treatment elements. That the programs exhibit comparable levels of intensity, and share several basic features, suggests that comprehensive ISP programming is not restricted by agency size or jurisdictional responsibility, and that some degree of replication can occur. Yet, each of the programs was strongly influenced by local considerations. This is reflected in the variations that occur across the sites along several important dimensions. These include program purposes and client selection criteria, the proportion of each agency's population that is served in intensive supervision, the extent to which "in-house" programming is utilized, and the composition of the supervision teams. On these and other issues, it was the philosophical, operational, and political realities of each local system that guided decision making and ultimately provided each ISP with its unique configuration.

In conclusion, we want to summarize a number of questions that require careful attention by juvenile agencies that are developing, or reviewing currently operational, ISPs. First, are program goals clear and realistic? Imprecise goals, or those that address a multitude of problems, are often suitable for public consumption, but may result in "programmatic indigestion." Without clear and focused goals, client selection and program components may be inappropriately suited to achieving intended results.

A second and related question is whether the client selection criteria and process will ensure that the intended target population is actually the one served. Will the use of risk/need instruments, for example, best identify "serious offenders" or those most likely to be placed out of home? Further, are there subsets of the eligible population that need to be excluded from program participation (e.g., high-risk status offenders, violent offenders)? Finally, what steps need to be taken to ensure that, regardless of the criteria used, the selection process will not be eroded by influences such as direct/indirect sentencing or the widespread use of overrides?

Third, assuming that additional funding for the ISP is not available, how can current resources be reallocated, and what mechanisms and criteria will be used to effect redistribution?

A fourth set of questions concerns the nature of intensive services. Is intensity of supervision to be defined solely in terms of increased contacts, or will it include other dimensions of service delivery? If a variety of treatment and control components are to be utilized, to what extent should they be individualized, and which should be mandated for all clients? In addition, given the increased likelihood of discovering violations of supervision conditions through more frequent monitoring, what will be the nature of the agencies' response? How can the need for strict enforcement of program requirements be reconciled with the need to avoid potential subversion of program goals and the need to respond to violations in a proportionate fashion?

Finally, how are staff roles to be defined, differentiated and coordinated? Particularly key issues in this area include the expected nature of counselor-client interaction, the "fit" between counselor skills and role expectations, and specification of the respective roles of service and surveillance staff.

NOTES

1. Three-fourths of court-supervised youth are males, less than 5% are minorities, and about 7% are from families receiving public assistance. A relatively small percentage of the cases are felony offenders (11%) or violent offenders (8%). However, approximately one in five youth have three or more adjudications in their history, and a substantial proportion can be considered a "high-need" group. Forty percent of the youth have two or more of the following characteristics: a history of family violence, parental substance abuse, sibling court involvement, special education status or a first adjudication at age 13 or younger.

2. For example, a youth with a "moderate" risk score would normally be placed on "regular" probation. However, if that youth had significant family or school problems, staff might determine that placement into intensive supervision was warranted, in spite of a risk score that did not indicate a high likelihood of recidivism.

3. There are four phases, which vary in duration, generally lasting between one and three months. Actual time spent in each is determined by the speed with which youth accumulate "good days." Each subsequent phase is characterized by progressively diminishing contacts and fewer restrictions on youth movement (see Table 3). This system is used by all three probation agencies described and is an adaptation of the Calhoun County (MI) model (see Burton, n.d.).

4. For example, in 1985 50% of ISP youth came from families characterized as having "major" disorganization, and 23% of the youth were victims of physical or sexual abuse. In half the cases, alcohol abuse was a problem for the youth's father. Forty

percent of the families had been referred to a court or welfare agency for abuse, neglect or dependency (Wiebush, 1989).

5. Two-thirds of the youth referred to probation are male, one third are minorities and 43% of the families receive public assistance. More than one in five youth (23.4%) has a record of three or more adjudications, and 18% of those placed on probation have committed felony offenses. Problems such as family violence, parental and youth substance abuse, physical or sexual abuse of the youth, and involvement in special education occur in roughly one-fourth to one-third of the cases (Wiebush and Hamparian, 1988).

6. The county does use risk and need instruments to determine placement in one of four supervision levels for all other probationers.

7. Two screening processes are used by the ISU. The first excludes offenses involving a weapon, victim injury or drug trafficking. A second, more in-depth, process attempts to identify those youth considered most amenable to the methods of the intensive program. Considerable weight is given at this stage to the anticipated cooperation of family members in treatment and supervision.

8. Because most delinquency cases in Lucas County are heard by referees, the ISU selection process is comparable to a review of all referee commitments by ISU staff and an "appeal" of selected commitments to the judge.

9. During the first 30 days of the program, youth are subject to complete house arrest. They are not allowed out of their homes, even with parents, except for school or ISU activities. This is followed by the imposition of curfews. Urinalysis, randomly required of all ISU youth, is conducted weekly during the first month and then on an "as needed" basis. School performance is monitored through the use of "school verification reports." All youth carry a form that is signed daily by the teacher of each class. Teachers also provide an evaluation of youth's behavior, participation and preparedness in class.

10. Many of these program components are in fact viewed as serving several correctional purposes. They are clearly intended to be retributive, and are designed to impress youth with the seriousness with which the court and the community take the offending behavior. They also serve incapacitation (house arrest, Saturday work) and/or risk-control purposes (urinalysis, surveillance). Finally, controls such as house arrest are seen as contributing to a rehabilitative "stabilization" period, and elements such as community service are believed to provide the opportunity to develop good work habits and increase vocational skills.

11. Almost half (48%) of the youth under supervision are black or in other minority groups. Forty-one percent are placed on probation for a felony offense. These two characteristics sharply differentiate Cuyahoga County youth from those supervised in Delaware and Lucas Counties. The extent to which identified youth and family problems exist among probationers is more similar in the three counties. In Cuyahoga County, between one-fourth and one-third of the youth have substance abuse problems and a history of family violence, are in special or alternative education, and/or have parents with substance abuse problems. In addition, almost half the Cuyahoga County youth have "major" truancy problems or have dropped out of school (Wiebush and Hamparian, 1986a).

12. Those who score 23 points or more (of a maximum possible 31 points) are placed

into intensive supervision. These youth have an aggregate 74% likelihood of recidivism.

13. The reassessment instrument is designed to virtually ensure that any moderate-risk youth who commits a felony while on regular supervision will get sufficient points to qualify for intensive supervision.

14. There are several notable exceptions to the general approach. First, ISP probation counselors are involved in weekly individual counseling with clients. Second, the use of the phase system (and surveillance) means that ISP staff are much more aware of, and responsive to, the daily behavior of youth than they would be under the traditional service brokerage model. Third, several ISP counselors have been trained to conduct formal group treatment for ISP clients.

15. Ohio law restricts those eligible for ODYS commitment to youth who have been adjudicated for a felony offense. In practice, approximately half (49%) of all committed youth have three or more felony adjudications in their history, and 38% of the youth have seven or more total adjudications (any type). One in four committed youth has a prior ODYS commitment. As would be expected, committed youth come from highly problematic family situations. There is a history of parent criminality in 19% of the cases, a record of parental substance abuse in 38% of the cases, and recorded family violence or abuse/neglect/dependency charges in 51% of the cases (Wiebush and Hamparian, 1986b).

16. Potential violations have been organized into three categories of seriousness. Category I violations are considered least serious (e.g., "negative attitude," occasional curfew violations) and cannot lead to parole revocation. Increased reporting or imposition of short-term house arrest might be alternative sanctions. Category II violations (e.g., failure to attend a court-ordered program) may result in revocation if the behavior is chronic. A new adjudication for multiple misdemeanor offenses or a felony offense constitutes Category III violations, which likely result in revocation.

17. It may be that reductions have occurred proportionately among all three supervision categories. Further, if significant reductions have taken place among ISP youth, it is possible that such reductions are a result of an aggressive departmental effort to reduce revocations generally (because of institutional overcrowding) and not of program effects. A planned evaluation of the Akron ISP should shed light on these issues.

18. In some sites nationally, certain serious offenses are grounds for automatic exclusion from ISP. That is not the case in the three Ohio agencies using the risk-based model.

19. For example, on the Cuyahoga County risk instrument, commission of a felony offense will account for just three points, although the total possible score is 31 and the high-risk cut-off is 23.

20. Status offenders in Ohio are under the jurisdiction of the county juvenile courts, and are subject to the same processing and dispositions as delinquent offenders. However, they may not be held for longer than five days for pretrial detention, and they may not be committed to ODYS. Court practices vary widely with respect to the handling of status offenders. Some courts routinely attempt to divert or handle them informally, while others will process them formally.

21. In the research used to develop the risk instrument, those with two or more violent

offenses who scored "low" and "moderate" risk were much more likely to recidivate than other youth in those score groups.

22. Lucas County staff are attuned to these issues and tend to be militant regarding efforts at indirect sentencing to the ISP. Further, Lucas County data suggest that a substantial number of ISP youth are serious/chronic offenders. Nonetheless, the general tendency of the court to overcommit, and the absence of a specifically targeted subset of the committed population, lays the groundwork for net-widening effects.

23. For example, the Wisconsin Bureau of Community Corrections time study, reported in Baird (1983).

24. Where agencies use volunteers in the delivery of key services to ISP youth, these staff might also constitute part of the team. Note that the Ohio sites have resisted using volunteers for work with ISP youth. The problem of generally unsophisticated staff working with often very sophisticated youth has been cited as a major issue, as has difficulty in coordinating and retaining volunteers. In Lucas County, volunteers have been used to serve the ISP indirectly. The extensive use of volunteers with the agency's lowest risk youth played a critical role in freeing up sufficient resources to staff the ISP.

REFERENCES

Armstrong, Troy L. (1988a). "National Survey of Juvenile Intensive Supervision (Part I)." *Criminal Justice Abstracts* 20(2):342-348.

—— (1988b). "National Survey of Juvenile Intensive Supervision (Part II)." *Criminal Justice Abstracts* 20(3):497-523.

Baird, Christopher (1986). "Juvenile Intensive Probation Supervision : A Discussion of Evaluation Issues." Paper presented at the Symposium on Juvenile Intensive Probation Supervision, Minneapolis, MN.

—— (1983). *Report on Intensive Supervision Programs in Probation and Parole*. Washington, DC: U.S. National Institute of Corrections.

Banks, J., A. Porter, R. Rardin, T. Silver and V. Unger (1977). *Phase I Evaluation of Intensive Special Probation Projects*. Washington, DC: U.S. Department of Justice.

Barton, William H. and J. Butts (1988). "The Ever Widening Net: System Adaptations to the Introduction of New Programs in a Juvenile Court." Paper presented to the American Society of Criminology, Chicago, IL.

Bennett, Lawrence A. (1987). "A Reassessment of Intensive Service Probation." In *Intermediate Punishments: Intensive Supervision, Home Confinement and Electronic Surveillance*, edited by Belinda McCarthy. Monsey, NY: Willow Tree Press.

Burton, William A. (no date). *Calhoun County Juvenile Court Intensive Probation*. (Monograph.) Marshall, MI: Calhoun County Juvenile Court.

Byrne, James M. (1986). "The Control Controversy: A Preliminary Examination of Intensive Probation Supervision Programs in the United States." *Federal Probation* 50(2):4-16.

Clear, Todd R. and C. Shapiro (1986). "Identifying High-Risk Probationers for Supervision in the Community: The Oregon Model." *Federal Probation* 50(2):42-49.

—— S. Flynn and C. Shapiro (1987). "Intensive Supervision in Probation: A

Comparison of Three Projects." In *Intermediate Punishments: Intensive Supervision, Home Confinement and Electronic Surveillance*, edited by Belinda McCarthy. Monsey, NY: Willow Tree Press.

Erwin, Billie (1987). "New Dimensions in Probation: Georgia's Experience with Intensive Probation Supervision." *Research in Brief*. Washington, DC: U.S. National Institute of Justice.

Goldstein, Harvey (1986). "Adult IPS and JIPS: Is There A Relationship?" Paper presented at the Symposium on Juvenile Intensive Probation Supervision, Minneapolis, MN.

Hamparian, Donna M. and L. Sametz (1989). "Cuyahoga County Juvenile Court Intensive Probation Supervision: Interim Report." Cleveland, OH: Federation for Community Planning.

Latessa, Edward J. (1987). "The Effectiveness of Intensive Supervision with High-Risk Probationers." In *Intermediate Punishments: Intensive Supervision, Home Confinement and Electronic Surveillance*, edited by Belinda McCarthy. Monsey, NY: Willow Tree Press.

Pearson, Frank S. and D. Bibel (1986). "New Jersey's Intensive Supervision Program: What Is It Like? How Is It Working?" *Federal Probation* 50(2):25-31.

Romig, Dennis (1986). "JIPS: The Defensible Basis." Paper presented at the Symposium on Juvenile Intensive Probation Supervision, Minneapolis, MN.

Wiebush, Richard G. (1989). *An Assessment of the Delaware County Intensive Supervision Program*. Columbus, OH: Ohio Governor's Office of Criminal Justice Services.

—— and D. Hamparian (1988). *Risk Assessment, Classification and Intensive Supervision in the Lucas County Juvenile Court*. Cleveland, OH: Federation for Community Planning.

—— (1986a). *Probation Classification: Design and Development of the Cuyahoga County Juvenile Court Model*. Cleveland, OH: Federation for Community Planning.

—— (1986b). *Risk Assessment for ODYS Aftercare Supervision: Summary Report of Research Process and Results*. Columbus, OH: Ohio Department of Youth Services.

Use of Electronic Monitoring with Juvenile Intensive Supervision Programs

by
Joseph B. Vaughn

Use of electronic monitoring in juvenile intensive supervision programs is a relatively new phenomenon, dating from 1986. The technology is described, and experience in adult programs is summarized. A survey of nine juvenile programs yields data on objectives, eligibility criteria, participant profiles, monitoring and supervision procedures, costs, problems and benefits. Many of the anticipated problems have not occurred, though few programs have yet alleviated institutional overcrowding. Electronic monitoring and home detention have shown promise, but they require clear objectives and careful planning.

Public attention to the juvenile justice system and its dispositional practices was brought to the forefront over 20 years ago when the U.S. Supreme Court decided *In Re Gault* (1967). The debate has continued with the courts, criminal justice system and public often at odds. Seemingly, we are unable to reach a consensus or develop workable alternatives. To some extent, this is attributable to the shifting of objectives from rehabilitation to crime control precipitated by rising crime rates and a perceived crisis in the adult correctional system. Even though the adult system typically receives more public attention, problems of the juvenile and adult systems seem to parallel each other.

In 1985 there were 1,040 publicly operated juvenile detention, correctional and shelter facilities in the U.S., housing over 51,000 youths (Bureau of Justice Statistics, 1986). These institutions have been criticized for several reasons. They are viewed as expensive and archaic operations that merely allow youth gangs to flourish. Treatment programs are ineffective because they are overcrowded. In a review of one state's system, it was found there were too many youths being inappropriately confined. Almost half of the juveniles incarcerated had no history of a serious offense (Commonweal Research Institute, 1989).

Juvenile probation practices were also being subjected to public scrutiny and criticism. In a review of the literature, Armstrong (1988) identified reasons for the growing disenchantment with probation. Officials are assigned the seemingly incompatible roles of social control and rehabilitation. There is a growing demand from the public for more effective crime control and a corresponding decline in its willingness to accept the rehabilitative ideal. Administration of the system has been questioned, with charges ranging from inadequate standards and training, to poor management, to inadequate funding, to a lack of measurable objectives.

Similar problems were being experienced in the adult system. From 1972 to 1982 the population in federal and state prisons more than doubled. By 1984 more than 430,000 men and women were incarcerated in these institutions (Thompson, 1984). The ripple effects of overcrowding precipitated a correctional case-law revolution that raised a variety of challenges to the constitutionality of the nation's correctional system. Solutions to crowding were mandated by the courts in some 39 states, the District of Columbia, Puerto Rico and the Virgin Islands (Reid, 1985). Construction of new facilities was expensive, with the cost of a single cell estimated to range from $25,000 to $75,000 (Funke, 1985). Prompted by leegal pressures, alternatives to incarceration (including increased use of probation and parole) were explored. By the end of 1982 seven out of ten convicted offenders were being supervised in the community (Bureau of Justice Statistics, 1983).

Other alternatives were explored, including restitution, community service, prerelease programs, early parole and intensive supervision programs. Corrections struggled to find a way to reduce overcrowding and at the same time maintain a reasonable degree of public safety. Advances in technology made possible the use of electronic monitoring and home confinement as one possible solution. Programs were first developed for use with adult offenders, and, as experience grew, applications were developed for juveniles. Use of the technology has given rise to a number of questions and issues that remain unanswered. Because electronic surveillance is relatively new, little research has been conducted. Most of the existing literature is descriptive in nature (Schmidt and Curtis, 1987). Even so, electronic monitoring and home confinement are gaining acceptance as viable social control strategies.

This chapter describes the technology that has made possible the inclusion of larger numbers of offenders in home detention programs. Use by the adult system is briefly reviewed as it spawned use of the technology by juvenile programs. In November 1988 a survey of the existing juvenile programs was conducted (Vaughn, 1989). Results of that survey are presented, along with an examination of the concerns voiced over use of the technology as an adjunct to juvenile intensive supervision programs.

THE TECHNOLOGY

One of the earliest references to the use of an electronic monitoring device was reported in the literature over 20 years ago. A portable device was utilized to track the location of parolees, mental patients and research volunteers in Massachusetts (Gable, 1986). The first formalized use of the technology by a criminal justice agency occurred during 1983 in Albuquerque, NM. District Court Judge Jack Love was inspired by a "Spiderman" comic strip to experiment with the concept of enforcing home detention with the aid of an electronic monitoring device (Niederberger, 1984). Favorable marketing conditions created by overcrowding and fiscal constraints led to commercialization of the technology, and its introduction into the corrections field.

The primary purpose of the equipment is to monitor an offender's compliance with curfew restrictions mandated in the terms of their release. Existing technology can be placed in one of two broad categories: continuously signaling/monitoring (referred to in the early literature as an active system), and programmed contact (referred to in the early literature as a passive system). A continuously signaling system is composed of a transmitter, home receiver unit and central computer. The transmitter, which is worn by the offender, broadcasts an encoded signal. When subjects are within range of the receiver (normally within 150 feet) the transmitter's signal is received, indicating that they are at home. When they leave the residence reception of the signal is interrupted, and a message is sent to the computer indicating their absence. Upon their return, signal reception is resumed, and notification is made of their arrival. If an offender leaves home during an unauthorized period, a violation report is generated. However, if the offender leaves home at a time when he or she is authorized to do so, the times of arrival and departure are noted but no violation report is generated.

There are a number of variations in how the programmed contact systems operate. In one system the offender is required to wear an encoder device, and the central office computer generates random calls to his or her home. When the telephone call is received, the offender is required to insert the encoder device into a verifier box to confirm his or her presence. The system will generate reports that indicate if the telephone is not answered, a busy signal is received or the offender fails to properly insert the encoder device into the verifier box. Other programmed contact systems rely on the use of video telephones or voice verification techniques. When the random calls are made to an offender, he or she is required to transmit a photograph or provide a voice sample that is then compared to information stored in the computer. Drive-by systems have been developed that require the offender to wear a transmitter. A receiver is then placed in the car of a probation officer, who makes random checks by driving past the residence or other locations at which the offender is supposed to be.

The primary difference between the continuous signaling and programmed contact systems is that one provides more information on compliance with the curfew. The continuous signaling systems record when the offender enters and leaves the residence. The programmed contact system can only confirm the presence of the offender in the residence at the time the random phone call is made.

Recently, hybrid systems that combine the features of continuous signaling and programmed contact systems have been developed. Other products are currently undergoing research and development. A number of options can be added to basic systems, such as remote alcohol testing or tamper-resistant features. The remote alcohol testing feature allows the supervising officer to have the offender transmit the results of an examination taken in their home over the system to the probation office. Tamper-resistant features provide notification when the offender attempts to manipulate the monitoring devices. It is anticipated that the number of vendors and types of available equipment will increase as use of the technology becomes more common.

ADULT PROGRAM EXPERIENCE

Electronic monitoring was believed to offer a number of benefits to correctional agencies. Initially its expected benefits included a reduction of personnel costs associated with supervising offenders, a reduction in institutional populations, and delayed or reduced need for construction of additional facilities. While it is too early to pass judgment, serious questions can be raised as to whether these benefits will be achieved. As more experience has been gained, administrators have begun to look toward the humanistic benefits that might be achieved through its use. Programs could be designed to focus on rehabilitation in the home rather than the artificial environment of an institution. Adverse effects on the family might be reduced by using alternatives to incarceration. Staff time could be used more efficiently, allowing additional time to be spent with those offenders who need it. While cost reduction remains the primary selling point of the technology, agencies are beginning to focus more on program aspects and the societal benefits to be achieved.

As previously mentioned, there is little experience to draw from and evaluations are almost nonexistent. In March 1986 there were only ten programs in the U.S., two of which were not operational (Vaughn, 1986). The type of offender eligible for the programs varied from agency to agency. As might be expected, the states developed applications directed toward felony offenders, while the county programs initially focused on low- risk offenders, primarily misdemeanants. Offenders were placed under electronic supervision for varying periods of time, generally ranging from one to four months. Most of the programs monitored a limited number of persons—from four to 20—at any one time. The program failure rate was approximately 10%.

By February 1987, less than one year after the original study began, use of the technology had expanded to more than 50 programs in 21 states, monitoring over 800 offenders (Schmidt, 1987). The trend at that time was toward larger programs and the inclusion of higher-risk offenders. The program failure rate remained relatively stable. One year later, 33 states had implemented monitoring programs involving nearly 2,300 offenders (Schmidt, 1988). Programs had been developed by a broad range of state and local criminal justice agencies including departments of correction, probation and parole as well as courts, sheriff's offices and police departments. A majority of the programs monitored only a small number of offenders, generally less than 30, though some were quite large. The people being monitored were predominantly male, and over half were under age 30. They had been convicted of a wide range of crimes: Slightly over one-fourth had been charged with a traffic offense, 20.1% with a property offense and 9.7% with a crime against a person.

Even with the apparent success of many adult programs, there were a number of concerns expressed over use of the technology with juveniles. No one knew whether juveniles were mature or stable enough to handle responsibilities imposed by an electronic monitoring program, and concern was expressed that the rate of lost or tampered-with equipment would be significantly higher than in the adult programs. It was also feared that juveniles might have less impulse control than adults and would simply "run away," resulting in a high failure rate. Any monitoring program is intrusive by its very nature, and questions were raised about whether it would interfere with the life of all family members and effectively result in their confinement as well. In the event of a dysfunctional family unit, forcing the child to remain in the home might subject him or her to physical or mental abuse. Nationwide there was some fairly strong emotional and philosophical opposition to use of the technology with juveniles. It was feared children might be stigmatized by having to wear a monitoring device.

Some staff members were concerned that programs would replace them, result in their being reassigned to less desirable positions or decrease their numbers. Some police and prosecutors were skeptical about whether the program could adequately ensure public safety. As limited program experience was gained with juveniles, officers began to suspect that undetected violations were occurring that were assisted and condoned by family members. The first two juvenile programs operated in rural North Carolina and midwestern Indiana. It was questioned whether the program would work as well with high-risk urban youth. Given these concerns, it is understandable why many agencies have been slow to adopt the technology for use with juveniles.

JUVENILE PROGRAM EXPERIENCE

In November 1988 a survey was conducted of the known juvenile programs in the U.S. (Vaughn, 1989). From information supplied by equipment manufacturers, 11 programs were identified, nine of which participated in the telephone survey. Two of the respondents were private companies that provide monitoring services on a contract basis, and seven were government agencies. One of the private contractors provided monitoring services for two of the government agencies. The following agencies participated in the survey: (1) Pulaski County, AK Juvenile Court; (2) Orange County, CA Probation Department; (3) Riverside County, CA Probation Department; (4) Opportunity House, West Palm Beach, FL; (5) Marion County, IN Juvenile Court; (6) North Carolina Office of Court Administration's Juvenile Court Counselor Service; (7) Dallas County, TX Juvenile Court; (8) Program Monitors, Inc. (PMI), Dallas, TX; and (9) Texas Youth Commission.

Use of electronic monitoring in juvenile programs is a relatively new phenomenon. The oldest known program was instituted by the North Carolina Office of Court Administration's Juvenile Court Counselor Service in May of 1986. At the time of the survey, the programs in existence ranged in age from five to 31 months. Three of the programs were adapted from existing adult programs in their jurisdiction. After starting as adjuncts to the adult programs, and using their equipment, they later separated from the adult system and began operating their own programs.

Program Objectives

The most common reason for use of the technology was a lack of adequate detention facilities. Some agencies cited a need to enhance existing home confinement programs. The Dallas County, TX Juvenile Court began its program in response to a proposal from a private contractor, while Opportunity House in West Palm Beach, FL offers the program to government agencies on a contract basis.

Five of the eight programs had more than one application for the technology, which was used most commonly as an alternative to pre-hearing detention. Four agencies used it as a supplement to probation, three used it for early release from an institution. One program applied the technology as an alternative sanction for parole violations. The objectives to be achieved by the programs, other than to reduce overcrowding, were not clearly documented by many of the agencies. Some, however, did set forth goals prior to program implementation. Among these were:

- Increase the number of minors safely released into existing home confinement programs.
- Reduce the number of minors returned to juvenile detention for violating home confinement restrictions.
- Reduce the number of field contacts required of home confinement officers in order to free them for other tasks.
- Provide a reasonably safe alternative to custody for relatively low-risk offenders.

- Provide for early reunification with the family.
- Provide reentry into the community.
- Allow for return to school.
- Increase the number of persons using the equipment in existing adult programs to increase the cost-effectiveness of those programs.

Eligibility Criteria

Screening of applicants for participation in the program is conducted primarily by the agency responsible for providing supervision. In two programs—those in Marion County, IN and Dallas County, TX—participants are assigned directly by the court and no screening is done by the agency. In Riverside County, CA potential participants are first identified and screened by the detention hall staff and then referred to the probation department. The private contractor, Opportunity House, identifies potential participants, conducts a screening interview, and then applies to the court for the person's release. The court has on occasion referred clients to Opportunity House without prior screening. Although the private contractor may refuse to accept these individuals, this has not yet occurred. Many of the program directors identified the screening process as the critical stage in the program. During the interview the family and child must be made aware of both the nature of the program and their responsibilities. The process used by the agencies ranged from use of a formal assessment instrument designed specifically for the program to reliance on the "gut feelings" of the interviewer as to the probable success of the participant. During the interview the agency is guided by its established eligibility and exclusion criteria.

All of the programs surveyed required that, to be eligible, a person would have otherwise been detained. Some required that the juvenile serve a minimum amount of time in detention prior to release. Other criteria identified by the agencies included ownership of a telephone for operation of the monitoring equipment, existence of a suitable home, agreement that home visits be allowed, a cooperative attitude of both parents and child, and parents' willingness to assume liability for equipment.

There were a number of automatic exclusion criteria established by programs. While some were quite restrictive, four of the programs had no such criteria. Typically, exclusion criteria established at a program's inception were modified as experience was gained. In one case, the criteria remain in place but were not followed by the court when making release decisions. Among the criteria used were:

- A residence that is incompatible with equipment operation. One program specifically excludes those living in house trailers because they interfere with operation of the transmitting device.
- No telephone or one that has certain features, such as call waiting or call forwarding, that interfere with the equipment's operation.

- Violent offenders.
- Lack of a suitable home environment or an uncooperative attitude on the part of the parents.
- Unwillingness of the juvenile to participate in the program.
- Those who pose a risk of escape or have a prior history of escape.
- Juveniles with mental problems.
- Alcohol or drug abusers.
- Those who have committed a "serious" felony. This is normally defined according to the grade of offense under a particular state's laws.
- Residential burglars.
- The crime victim resides in the home.

The choice of exclusion criteria has been guided by a number of factors. The technical requirements for operation of the equipment are the primary concern for some programs. Others give consideration to the political aspects of including certain categories of offenders. Past history and behavior patterns play a role in every program's decision to exclude an individual from participation; this holds true regardless of whether the agency's decision is made using a formal assessment instrument or is based on the interviewer's personal perception. It is worth noting that some programs began with very strict exclusion criteria based on type of offense. However, experience indicated that offense type, by itself, is a poor indicator of the potential for success or failure.

There was little documentation available for the release decisions. A notable exception is the Riverside County, CA Probation Department's pilot project. Of the 183 juveniles meeting the eligibility requirement—the program was restricted to those required to serve a minimum sentence in the detention hall as a condition of probation—108 (59%) were rejected by the staff as ineligible. Seventy-five percent of those rejected were refused admission to the program because they had less than ten days left to serve, lived out of the county, were to be released to someone other than a parent or relative, were released to other placements, or were released to the border patrol. Under the program restrictions, participants must have a minimum of ten days left to serve in confinement, live in the county and be released to a parent or relative. Twelve of the juveniles (11%) were rejected because they did not have a telephone; one, because of lack of a suitable home environment; and 13 (12%), because either the parent or the juvenile was unwilling to participate. Only two minors (2%) were rejected because they represented an escape risk.

An examination of these statistics reveals that the vast majority (86%) were excluded from the program for administrative reasons. Either they did not have a telephone, lived outside of the county, or had too little time remaining to make participation practical, or alternative methods of release were to be used. Of those who were eligible, 12% percent were unwilling to participate. Only 2% were excluded because they were felt to pose a risk of escape. Only one was denied access to the program because he did not have a suitable home environment.

Profile of Participants

A profile of those accepted into the programs is difficult to establish because statistics were not available at the time of the study. Three agencies did provide profiles, based on pilot projects they had conducted or on a limited sample of offenders. In Orange County, CA the average participant was 15 years old and considered to be in the medium- to high-risk category. A breakdown of the type of offense shows that 42% had committed crimes against property, 11% had committed crimes against persons, 29% were probation violators, with unspecified "other" offenses accounting for the rest of the participants. There were more pretrial detainees (65%) than post-adjudication (35%) participants.

In Riverside County, CA the average participant was a 17-year-old Caucasian or Hispanic male who had one prior arrest or adjudication for theft. A majority of the juveniles (80.5%) had been placed in the program for technical violations of probation or violations of the motor vehicle code. Only 18.5% had been adjudicated for serious crimes involving assault, weapons or drugs. With only one exception, all of the minors had been adjudicated prior to their placement.

The North Carolina program consists predominantly of black males who are between ages 14 and 17. No other demographic information was provided by the agency.

Monitoring and Supervision Procedures

Once in the program, monitoring of the equipment and supervision of the client is accomplished in one of several ways. The two private contractors offer different services. Opportunity House monitors the equipment and provides supervision during participation in vocational or treatment programs, but does not make home visits. PMI monitors the equipment and makes home visits twice a week to verify that it has not been tampered with. Three of the seven public agencies surveyed use the services of a private contractor to monitor the equipment. Reports are submitted to them by the private contractors, and arrangements can be made for immediate notification of violations if necessary. One agency has equipment monitored for it by another criminal justice agency. Only three of the seven public agencies surveyed actually monitor their own equipment.

All seven of the public agencies provide field supervision for their clients. Five provide the sole supervision, though one of these relied on officers from the adult probation department to provide field supervision at the inception of the program. The other two public agencies provide field supervision of the juveniles and also rely on the private contractor to contact them twice a week to verify the equipment has not been tampered with. Only Opportunity House, a private contractor, does not conduct home visits or field contacts with the participants. Two of the agencies have no set minimum number of contacts, the number varying with perceived need and staff availability. The amount of contact provided by the remaining five agencies varies from twice a day to once a month.

All of the participants are placed under a curfew and some programs are more restrictive than others. While one may require a 24-hour-a-day curfew, another may establish a particular time, 7:00 p.m. for example. Depending on the program, exceptions to the curfew may or may not be granted. All agencies allow or require the juvenile to attend school, work, or participate in treatment and vocational programs. In the event of a medical or other emergency the juvenile is permitted to leave the house. The agency must be notified prior to leaving or as soon as possible afterward. Some programs view the relaxing of curfew restrictions as a reward for acceptable behavior. As the child makes satisfactory progress through the program, more freedom is allowed. Other agencies view the program as an extension of the detention facility and grant exceptions only in rare circumstances.

In the event a curfew violation is reported by the computer, the agency has a number of options. Staff can respond immediately or wait until the next day to confront the juvenile. Five of the programs first telephone the residence to ascertain if the report was caused by an equipment problem or a momentary absence from the range of the receiver, or if an actual violation has occurred. Three of the programs immediately respond to the residence (two of these telephone first) to verify the violation. The programs in Texas determine their response policy based on the perceived threat the individual poses. With some clients they respond immediately, and with others they wait until the next business day. Three of the programs have a policy of waiting until the next day to confront the child, although one of them attempts to telephone the residence when the report is received.

There are problems and benefits with any policy adopted. Immediate responses and telephoning the residence allow the agency to confirm the violation physically. Such confirmation is believed to be a prerequisite to successful termination if a court hearing is required. If false alarms occur frequently, valuable staff time is consumed unnecessarily. If the situation continues the staff will become disillusioned with the equipment. Participants may lose confidence in the equipment's ability to monitor them accurately and may begin violating the program's restrictions. Some would argue that if an immediate response is necessary due to the perceived threat the child poses, the wrong individuals are being placed in the program.

Adopting a policy of not responding until the next day conserves staff time, particularly in large geographic areas. This policy, however, can create problems when the number of false alarms is high. Both participants and staff will become wary of the equipment's reliability. Having to confront the juvenile a number of times when they did not violate the curfew makes it more difficult to obtain an admission when they do. Verification of the violation is not possible, absent a confession, unless an immediate response is made. To date no court has been willing to accept the computer printout as prima facia evidence of a violation. It is technologically possible in those programs using both continuously signaling and programmed contact devices to mitigate this problem. If the continuously signaling equipment detects a violation, the programmed contact device can then be used confirm the violation. This of course assumes the participant is being monitored simultaneously by both types of equipment.

Program Statistics

It is still too early to evaluate the effectiveness of these programs. Some agencies have not yet compiled adequate statistics and were able to provide only estimates. The information presented here is based on the available statistics and estimates from eight of the responding programs (see Table 1).

From May 1986 through November 1988, approximately 845 juveniles were under electronic monitoring and home detention. The average length of monitoring ranged from 16 to 90 days. All of these programs were relatively small, monitoring from two to 20 children on the day the survey was administered. The failure rate in the program ranged from 4.5% to 30%. Programs reported that a majority of the unsuccessful terminations resulted from commission of technical violations rather than new offenses. Although the data are incomplete, there were only five known new offenses committed during the program. From the available data, the number of absconders is believed to be low, with only 18 having been reported. Although recidivism figures are not yet available, one program reported only two revocations after completion of the program: one for a technical violation and one for commission of a new offense. The reader is again cautioned that these figures are based on incomplete and in some cases estimated data.

Only ten pieces of equipment were lost or damaged by program participants. Of the five that were lost, four were intentionally removed by the participant, and one was lost through carelessness when the strap broke. One piece of equipment was intentionally lost by the juvenile because he believed it could track his whereabouts. The other five pieces were damaged but recovered.

Two respondents compared adult and juvenile programs—PMI and the Orange County, CA Probation Department. The juveniles show less judgment and often act against their own best interests. The "cabin fever" syndrome occurs more quickly with juveniles than adults, generally within one month. To avoid this problem, exceptions to curfews or some alteration of their routine must occur. The most critical time for preventing failures in the

Table 1: Program Comparison

Agency	*Date Began*	*Current Application*	*Average Length of Monitoring*	*Number Currently Monitored*	*Number Completed Program*	*Number Failed Program*	*Failure Rate*
Pulaski County, AR Juvenile Court	April 1988	Pre-hearing detention. Probation violation.	3 weeks	2	30	2	6.6%
Orange County, CA Probation Dept.	August 1987	Pre-hearing detention. Probation. Furlough release from juvenile facility.	16 days	20	350 (approx.)	n/a	25.0% (approx.)
Riverside County, CA Probation Dept.	July 1988	Early release from shock probation detention in juvenile hall.	17 days	8	67	3	4.5%
Opportunity House, West Palm Beach, FL	June 1987	Pre-hearing detention. Post adjudication probation.	n/a	2	49	6	12.2%
Marion County, IN Juvenile Court	July 1986	Pre-hearing detention.	6 weeks	n/a	144	14	9.7%
North Carolina Office of Court Administration	May 1986	Pre-hearing detention. Early release from training school.	20 days	10	110	33	30.0%
Dallas County, TX Juvenile Court	January 1988	Pre-hearing detention.	45 days	14	64	14	21.9%
Texas Youth Commision	December 1987	Early release from institution. Parole violation sanction.	90 days	4	31	n/a	30.0% (approx.)

Note: Program statistics are based on incomplete reporting. In some cases they have been estimated by program director. See text for explanation.

juvenile program is during the first six to eight days. In the experience of PMI, approximately half of those who fail do so during the first week on the program. It is speculated that this occurs for two reasons: The initial shock of detention has worn off for pretrial detainees, and family problems are intensified by the increased amount of time spent in the home. For both juveniles and adults, parolees tend to take the program more seriously and have a better compliance record. Pretrial detainees have far more violations and remain absent for longer periods of time. The company believes this occurs because the technology is being used as a reward for good behavior for parolees and as a punishment for inappropriate behavior by the pretrial detainees.

The Orange County Probation Department's juvenile program has a higher failure rate (approximately 25%) than the adult program (5%). However, the department states that this should not be interpreted to mean the program is less successful with juveniles than adults. The juvenile program is directed at medium- to high-risk offenders, while the adult program is used predominantly with low-risk offenders. The department also finds that juveniles on electronic monitoring have a higher success rate than the target population of the three home detention programs that do not use electronic monitoring.

Program Costs

Equipment acquisition costs are most commonly paid for by the agency. Three departments do not own the equipment and are charged a user fee by the private contractor who provides the monitoring service. Marion County, IN obtained part of its equipment through a grant, with the remainder paid for by the prosecutor's office. North Carolina received a grant from a private foundation to fund program costs. Perhaps the most unusual acquisition process occurred in Riverside County, CA, where a local court found the adult facilities were overcrowded and ordered the county to fund an electronic monitoring and home detention program for adults. The juvenile program was then allowed to use equipment funded under this court order. In December 1988, the funding order for the adult program was rescinded when a new jail was completed. A moratorium was then placed on the juvenile program. The department plans to implement another program in the future.

Because there is no common method used to compute program costs, comparison between programs is not possible. The cost of equipment alone ranged from $3.17 to $11 per day, depending on whether it was leased or purchased and the amortization schedule used. Others provided a yearly program cost ranging from $46,317 to $77,000. The cost of alternative programs ranged from $42 to $500 per day. Some programs estimated a cost savings of $98,420 to $113,400 per year. Determining cost benefit is difficult. If the cost of alternative programs is compared to equipment acquisition, there is an obvious cost savings. Prior to accepting claimed savings at face value, it is necessary to compute the actual costs to society. It may well be that the detention center's budget is decreased but that the supervising agency's budget must be increased. Unless real reductions are achieved by detention centers and institutions, the cost of monitoring is an additional expense. It is also necessary to calculate personnel and other fixed costs prior to claiming a savings. It may be necessary, as one progrram found, to add additional personnel. No agency has to date been able to reduce the number of personnel employed by adding a monitoring program.

To help offset expenses, two programs charge participants a user's fee. One agency charges $2 per day but will waive the fee if the family is indigent. The other charges $10 per day and will reduce it to $6 per day if it creates a financial hardship. The remaining programs do not charge a fee. In one program, participation is actually a financial benefit to the family. In Riverside County, CA, participants are selected from a group of offenders who must serve time in the detention hall as a condition of probation. The parents of these children must pay the agency $25 per day while the child is incarcerated. If the child is placed in the monitoring program, the fees no longer apply.

Monitoring Equipment

For some agencies, selection of equipment is determined by the existing adult program or by the contract service provider. Of those selecting their own equipment, the reasons given for their choice ranged from their impression of the manufacturer's capability to the desirability of a particular feature. Three agencies use continuously signaling equipment exclusively, one uses programmed contact units exclusively, and four have the option of using either continuously signaling or programmed contact systems.

Three agencies contract with a service provider for equipment. Pulaski County, AK is provided only continuously signaling equipment. Dallas County, TX, and the Texas Youth Authority have the option to use either continuously signaling or programmed contact equipment. Dallas County starts the juvenile on a programmed contact system, and then uses the continuously signaling equipment if behavioral problems develop because the programmed contact equipment is less expensive. The Texas Youth Authority begins with continuously signaling equipment and then places the child on a programmed contact system if they perform well in the program. The authority starts with the continuous signaling units because its participants are considered to be higher risk and are more closely supervised. The programmed contact units used by both Dallas County and the Texas Youth Authority operate with a video-telephone and do not require the offender to wear a monitoring device, which for some participants is preferable.

Riverside County, CA, and West Palm Beach, FL's Opportunity House use only continuously signaling equipment. Orange County, CA uses only programmed contact units but officials want to experiment with a hybrid system that combines the capabilities of both continuously signaling and programmed contact to add more flexibility to the program. Marion County, IN and the North Carolina Office of Court Administration use both continuously signaling and programmed contact systems. Offenders are sometimes placed on both types of equipment simultaneously. When a violation report is received from one, the other is used as a check. In some programs the removal of one type of equipment is used as a reward for appropriate behavior.

The equipment generally functions as the manufacturers claim it will, and most programs report few problems. Of the problems that have occurred, many will be resolved as the manufacturers continue to improve on the equipment. Equipment that has a tamper-resistant feature has been found to cause a number of false tamper reports. The device is sensitive and will produce an alert signal if the transmitter is accidentally hit on a piece of furniture. This problem can become particularly acute with young offenders. Compatibility problems with telephone and electrical systems in some houses cause false violation reports or preclude use of the equipment. The construction of some homes will interfere with transmitters used in the continuously signaling systems. Low battery power has caused false violation reports to be transmitted.

Some concern has been expressed over the use of programmed contact systems because they are more disruptive to the family. Agencies are reluctant to have the offenders called during the night, fearing that excessive calls will induce fatigue in the child by disturbing their sleep, as well as disrupting the entire family. In at least one program, however, the use of a programmed contact system is viewed as desirable because it requires a juvenile to participate, or "do something to facilitate the monitoring process." Although the device is capable of having the computer generate random calls, that feature is not used by PMI. Instead, staff members make the calls. They find that contact with a human who can be empathic, rather than a computer, reduces the irritation factor created by random calling.

Program Problems

A number of program difficulties have arisen because the concept was new and the agencies had little or no experience to draw upon. The problems encountered thus far can be categorized into three basic areas: administrative problems, problems with the family, and problems with the participants. Agencies have quickly realized the program is more labor intensive than they had anticipated. Many of the participants are in the program for a relatively short period of time, and continual turnover in clients creates a heavy workload for data entry and system maintenance personnel. The amount of time spent screening applicants, installing equipment and retrieving it is significantly increased if participants are in the program for a short period of time. While the equipment may free up more time for supervision officers because they can reduce the number of nightly checks, administrative time may be increased. Some agencies have found it necessary to add additional staff to maintain the program; none have been able to decrease the number of personnel. There were a number of hidden costs involved in program implementation. Prices quoted to agencies typically cover only the cost of equipment and do not take into consideration administrative and personnel expenses. The cost of telephone service is but one example. The equipment requires installation of dedicated telephone lines. One agency soon discovered their monthly telephone service charges were exceeding $300 per month.

Although it has not yet become a prevalent problem, the lack of a telephone in an offender's home has caused some difficulties. Sometimes, the family cannot afford the installation charge or owes past-due bills, and the phone company will not provide service. In some instances, a juvenile has been placed on the program only to have the family default on their telephone bill and have service disconnected. Occasionally a juvenile will be ordered into a program by the court without the judge first ascertaining whether they have a suitable residence or a telephone. It has been possible in some cases for the agency to make arrangements for limited service with the telephone company. When this is not possible, the child is denied access to the program by those agencies who do not have funds to pay for telephone services. Not all juveniles want to participate in the program, and in a few cases juveniles or their families have lied about whether they had a telephone to avoid being placed on the equipment. This is more common if an agency operates another home confinement program without electronic monitoring.

Collection of user fees is difficult when the client is a juvenile. If the parents do not pay, the child is punished through revocation. In most instances there is no way to collect fees from the juvenile. It is particularly difficult for private contractors charging a user's fee directly to the client. The private contractor is dependent on payment to remain in business. As one stated, "What do I do, repossess the kid's tennis shoes if they don't pay?"

Family problems are more acute when the person being monitored is not the head of the household. Home detention and electronic monitoring programs, in effect, place the whole family on community detention. A child does not have the control or influence necessary to require adjustments to family routine or the ability to move to another residence if necessary to make participation possible. Some families want the child placed in detention, not in the home. If returned to the home, he or she becomes an inconvenience for the family. There are several known instances of parents sabotaging the child's progress. They have taken the juvenile out of the house in violation of the curfew, or called the department and falsely accused the child of violating the program's restrictions. Parents may rely too much on the equipment to supervise the child. In effect, the technology becomes an "electronic babysitter." Concern has also been expressed, and in some cases found warranted, that the child is being returned to an abusive environment. These difficulties further underscore the need to address the problems of the family as a whole and not assume monitoring by itself is sufficient.

Other than the normal difficulties of supervision, program directors identified three problems unique to juvenile programs. First, among many of their clients, the perception of the juvenile justice system is that it is too lenient. As one director noted, it is hard for them to take the system seriously when they receive a 90-day sentence in a halfway house for the same crime that would lead to a five-year prison sentence for an adult. Escapes from the adult and juvenile programs in some areas are viewed differently. An adult who absconds is charged with felony offense of escape, while the juvenile sanction for the same activity is at worst a return to detention.

Second, the summer months cause unique problems with juveniles under electronic monitoring and home detention. Adults would be leaving their home for work. Children are out of school in the summer and, absent any employment, are restricted to the house 24 hours a day. The situation is problematic in two ways: There may be no adults home to supervise the child during the day, and boredom quickly sets in. This leads to an increase in behavioral problems. Programs operating during the summer have found it necessary to relax curfew restrictions and allow the child to go outdoors under parental supervision.

Third, some pretrial detainees who believe they are going to be committed to an institution see little reason to abide by program restrictions. One agency found the problem particularly acute the night before the dispositional hearing: The child assumes he or she is going to be committed and therefore stays out all night. No one has yet devised a solution to this problem.

Program Benefits

The benefits are felt to outweigh the problems encountered in program operation. Although it has not yet been empirically demonstrated, most agencies feel the programs are successful in reducing the number of days spent in detention and are having a positive impact on institutional population. The programs allow the child who would otherwise be detained to remain in the home and participate in counseling, educational or vocational activities, while at the same time providing a reasonable amount of security for the community. The equipment allows for closer supervision than the staff could provide and prevents them from having to work 24 hours a day. They are now able to maintain closer supervision over larger numbers of clients without having to increase home visits.

By returning the child to the home, agencies are given an opportunity to work with the family and address problem areas. Some find there is an unexpected rehabilitative aspect. Parents report increased communication and dialogue between themselves and the child. Before, when a disagreement arose, the child would merely leave the house. Under the program, however, he or she is required to remain in the house, forcing the parents and child to discuss and deal with the problem.

One of the primary benefits for pretrial detention programs is that the department can place the child back in a natural environment with supervision. This provides the court with a much clearer picture of how the child would perform on probation, allowing it to make a more informed sentencing decision.

From the juvenile's standpoint, many have commented that "there is light at the end of the tunnel." With most programs there is a certain completion date. If the child complies with the restrictions until that date, he or she is removed from the program, unlike many other programs that either do not have an established completion date or have one that extends over a long period. The programs provide a second chance for juveniles who are released to other programs and violate the condition of their release. The additional level of supervision afforded by electronic monitoring allows the child to be given an opportunity to remain in the community. Departments believe the increased control represents a real consequence for violation of program restrictions, a necessary condition if they are to be viable.

Some departments find they are able to improve their relationship with the community and other criminal justice agencies, which now view the department as an agency that is enforcing court orders and enhancing public safety.

CONCLUSION

Many of the anticipated problems were never realized by the juvenile programs. In most programs the failure rate for those under electronic monitoring is believed to be less than the normal rate for the target populations. Some programs have a higher success rate with juveniles than adult offenders. While the rate of equipment damage is greater in some programs for juveniles than in those for adults, it is still considered to be at a tolerable level and less than what was expected. There is no evidence that children were stigmatized by wearing the equipment. They reported no adverse effects and, in some instances, the monitoring device actually became a status symbol. Some problems did develop with family members, but this varied among the different programs. While some reported family members attempting to sabotage the child's participation, others reported that family members were supportive of the program. The philosophical and emotional issue of whether children should be subjected to monitoring will be resolved as more departments begin using the technology. Fears of staff reductions or reassignment were unwarranted.

One lesson learned from the adult programs is that an agency should carefully consider *why* they want to use the technology *before* the program is implemented. Juvenile applications, for the most part, have begun in much the same way adult programs did. The primary consideration has been reducing populations in crowded facilities. In some instances the programs were offshoots of an existing adult program. While the technical issues were resolved during implementation of the adult program, the philosophical question has in many instances remained unanswered.

Clearly stated objectives are important to a program's success for a number of reasons. Simply defined, an objective is nothing more than a statement of desired future conditions. To formulate an objective one must assess the current status of the organization, develop alternative courses of action and determine the direction the agency should take. Reduction of institutional populations is a laudable goal, but experience from the adult programs indicates it is perhaps unachievable. The pressures on the system are too great to be relieved by the establishment of any one program. Perhaps the best that can be achieved is to allow an agency to use its limited bed space more efficiently by being more selective. Reduction of institutional populations may never be achieved, but a change in the types of individuals placed there may be possible.

If the "why" is addressed during the planning stage, as has been done by some agencies, other objectives for use of the technology may become apparent. In addition to the administrative concerns of reducing institutional populations and the efficient use of staff time, there are humanistic goals that should be explored. Some of the objectives that have been suggested by existing juvenile programs include: early reunification with the family; reentry into the community; continuation in school; and creation of an intermediate sanction between unsupervised probation and commitment to a youth facility. It is neither humanistically nor economically beneficial to place people in detention who do not need to be there (Nagel, Wice and Neef, 1977).

Notably absent from the stated program objectives was the issue of providing treatment programs and family counseling in the home environment rather than in the artificial setting of an institution. While many programs ultimately do so, this is not one of the reasons given for their implementation. Experience from the adult program indicates the potential for modification of the peer group relationship, creation of better family relationships and institution of self-discipline (Friel, Vaughn and del Carmen, 1987). While none of these benefits have been empirically validated, they have been observed in some offenders. The duration of these changes remains unknown. Even with this uncertainty, it would seem worthwhile to pursue these objectives actively.

If the only stated objective is to reduce institutional populations, a majority—if not all—of the programs will ultimately be evaluated as failures. By searching for and identifying other reasons for its use, the technology's worth as an adjunct to a program can be determined more accurately. Continual evaluation of innovative programs is critical. It is only through evaluation that one is able to determine what is beneficial and should be continued. Equally important is to determine those aspects that are not working and need to be abandoned or modified. Program directors should engage in both short- and long-term evaluations. The format of a short-term evaluation should provide the information necessary to manage the program on a day-to-day basis. For example, knowledge of a short-term change in the program's failure rate would allow the director to modify the eligibility criteria to include a wider range of clients or exclude those who do not perform well. The adjustment, indicated by an increasing rate of failure, may be as simple as limiting the number of participants to allow for increased staff contacts. Without adequate statistics and a continuing process of evaluation, the problems are not identified or corrected until it is too late to benefit the program's participants.

Long-term evaluations are designed to discover what, if any, sustained benefits are derived from the program. Properly designed, they allow for the tracking of individuals to monitor success or recidivism. It may then be possible to identify the differences in those who succeed versus those who fail. This information may then be used to modify the existing programs. As experience is gained, comparison between programs should be facilitated by extended evaluations, allowing for a transfer of knowledge that will benefit every agency and ultimately society as a whole.

There is a growing belief that alternatives to detention should be used as a means to alleviate overcrowding, and as a more humane and effective form of offender treatment. Electronic monitoring and home detention programs have shown promise as a viable tool. It is premature to attempt an assessment of the impact these programs will have on the juvenile justice system. However, the technology, by itself, cannot solve the problems currently faced by the system. It should not become a substitute for sound decision making by corrections officials. Although it is gaining acceptance as a national crime control strategy, there is no empirical support of its viability. Therefore, care must be taken that electronic monitoring, like other community control programs advanced in the 1960s and 1970s, not be embraced too quickly (Blomberg, Waldo and Burcroff, 1987).

REFERENCES

Armstrong, T. (1988). "National Survey of Juvenile Intensive Probation Supervision." *Criminal Justice Abstracts* 20 (June):342-348.

Blomberg, T., G. Waldo and L. Burcroff (1987). "Home Confinement and Electronic Surveillance." In *Intermediate Punishments: Intensive Supervision, Home Confinement and Electronic Surveillance*, edited by Belinda McCarthy. Monsey, NY: Willow Tree Press.

Bureau of Justice Statistics (1986). *Children In Custody: Public Juvenile Facilities, 1985*. Washington, DC: U.S. Department of Justice.

——— (1983). *Probation and Parole, 1982*. Washington, DC: U.S. Government Printing Office.

Commonweal Research Institute (1989). *Reforming the California Youth Authority: How To End Crowding, Diversify Treatment, and Protect the Public Without Spending More Money*. Bolinas, CA.

Friel, C., J. Vaughn and R. del Carmen (1987). *Electronic Monitoring and Correctional Policy: The Technology and Its Application*. Washington, DC: National Institute of Justice.

Funke, G. (1985) "Economics of Prison Crowding." *The Annals* 478 (March):86-99.

Gable, R. (1986). "Application of Personal Telemonitoring to Current Problems in Corrections." *Journal of Criminal Justice* 14:167-176.

In Re Gault, 387 U.S. 1 (1967).

Nagel, S., P. Wice and M. Neef (1977). *Too Much or Too Little Police: The Example of Pretrial Release*. Beverly Hills, CA: Sage.

Niederberger, W. (1984). "Can Science Save Us Revisited." Paper presented at the annual meeting of the American Society of Criminology, Cincinnati, OH.

Reid, S. (1985). *Crime and Criminology*, 4th Ed. New York, NY: Holt, Rinehart and Winston.

Rowan, J. R. and C. J. Kehoe (1985). "Let's Deinstitutionalize Group Homes." *Juvenile and Family Court Journal* 14:1-4.

Schmidt, A. (1988). *The Use of Electronic Monitoring by Criminal Justice Agencies*. (Discussion Paper). Washington, DC: U.S. National Institute of Justice.

——— (1987). *The Use of Electronic Monitoring by Criminal Justice Agencies*. (Discussion Paper). Washington, DC: U.S. National Institute of Justice.

——— and C. Curtis. (1987). "Electronic Monitors." In *Intermediate Punishments: Intensive Supervision, Home Confinement and Electronic Surveillance*, edited by Belinda McCarthy. Monsey, NY: Willow Tree Press.

Thompson, J. (ed.) (1984). "Prison Crowding: A Symposium." *University of Illinois Law Review* 78(5):203-421.

U.S. National Advisory Commission on Criminal Justice Standards and Goals (1973). *Corrections*. Washington, DC: U.S. Government Printing Office.

Vaughn J. (1989). *A Survey of Juvenile Electronic Monitoring and Home Confinement Programs*. Warrensburg, MO: Center for Criminal Justice Research.

——— (1986). *Electronic Monitoring of Offenders*. Austin, TX: Criminal Justice Policy Council.

A Comprehensive Therapeutic Community Approach for Chronic Substance-Abusing Juvenile Offenders: The Amity Model

by
Rod Mullen
Naya Arbiter
Peggy Glider

The development of a joint public/private cooperative program involving Amity, an Arizona nonprofit agency specializing in substance abuse services, and the Arizona Department of Corrections, is described. The Amity model addresses the multiple risk factors of chronic adolescent substance abusers who have committed crimes. The traditional adult-oriented therapeutic community modality has been modified for work with adolescent delinquents. The principles and operational components of the model are summarized.

INTRODUCTION

In March 1989 Frederick Goodwin, M.D., Director of the U.S. Alcohol, Drug Abuse, and Mental Health Administration, said that, while the total number of young people abusing drugs seems to be falling, "the social pathology induced by drugs and alcohol is getting worse, and users are getting younger in this highly vulnerable population." While a number of surveys show a national decline in the use of illicit drugs by youth, those youngsters who enter the juvenile justice system appear to be more chemically dependent than ever before. Frequently, they have been born into families that neglected or abused them, or that have failed to provide conditions for normal development. Without successful intervention, many of these youth will become increasingly involved in substance abuse, pursue adult criminal careers, and be at high risk for HIV/AIDS infection and transmission.

With the widespread availability of "crack" and other powerful drugs at relatively low prices per dose and easily administered through smoking, adolescent substance abusers can now become rapidly addicted and enmeshed in a life of drug use, drug dealing, other criminal activities, violence, sexual abuse and prostitution. Intervention for such youth cannot be a half-measure; it must be intense and long term to meet their multiple needs. Many cannot be *rehabilitated* because they have not yet been *habilitated* by family, school and other social institutions. Cooperative efforts between criminal justice agencies and private treatment providers offer one method of providing the extensive services needed to help these youngsters adjust successfully to living in society and avoid further involvement with the justice system. This chapter describes the development of a joint public/private cooperative effort between Amity, an Arizona non-profit agency specializing in substance abuse services, and the Arizona Department of Corrections (ADC). The Amity model addresses the multiple risk factors of chronic adolescent substance abusers with criminal involvement. It has modified the traditional adult-oriented therapeutic community modality to work with adolescents, specifically those who have: (1) been incarcerated in ADC juvenile institutions; (2) been identified by ADC as "dependent" and/or "abusive" in regard to their use of drugs and alcohol, and (3) have histories of violence, gang involvement and prostitution.

RESEARCH FINDINGS

Etiology

Research evidence over the past few years clearly establishes that serious, persistent delinquency and chronic use of illicit drugs by adolescents have common etiological roots. Frequently identified factors are:

- a family history of alcoholism or drug abuse;
- family management problems (poorly defined rules; disorganization; inconsistence, negative communications; and ineffectiveness);
- early antisocial behavior;
- favorable family attitudes toward drug or alcohol use;

- early use of drugs;
- academic failure;
- adolescent antisocial behavior;
- association with drug-using peers; and
- favorable attitudes towards drug use (Hawkins et al., 1987; Brunswick and Boyle, 1979; Kandel, Simcha-Fagan and Davies, 1986; Donovan and Jessor, 1984; Elliott, Huizinga and Ageton, 1985; Jessor and Jessor, 1987).

Dembo and associates (1987, 1988, 1989) studied several groups of male and female detainees entering a Florida juvenile detention center. These studies showed that among both males and females there was a high percentage of physical and sexual abuse. A total of 51% of those interviewed claimed to have been seriously physically abused by an adult in more than three ways; 46% were sexually victimized one or more times, and for 83% of these youths the victimization first occurred at age 13 or younger. This abuse was significantly correlated with lifetime frequency of use of illicit drugs and other deviant behavior. Dembo poses a "development damage" view of the effects of child physical and sexual maltreatment that views these experiences as important factors in leading adolescents to become disengaged from conventional norms and behavior, and to initiate various patterns of deviant behaviors, particularly when the youth come from high-risk environments that include poverty and poor parenting.

High rates of physical and sexual victimization among adolescents referred to the juvenile justice system constitute risk factors that have not been given adequate consideration in the etiology of adolescent drug addiction (Dembo et al., 1987, 1988, 1989). Because clinical experience reveals that often youth (or adults) will not reveal details of physical or sexual victimization to an interviewer, it is quite likely that Dembo's data significantly underreport this phenomenon.[1]

Alice Miller, a Swiss psychoanalyst who has written a number of books exploring the relationship between child-rearing practices and later adult behavior, has made a convincing argument that the anger that abused children cannot direct toward their abusers is stored in the unconscious. This leads to uncontrolled discharge of anger through self-destructive behavior (such as drug addiction, abusive relationships and suicide), as well as through outbursts (violence, cruelty and child abuse) directed toward others as they become older (Miller, 1983). Her paradigm is consistent with the clinical experience of many practitioners working today with adolescents.

The Drug/Crime Connection

In asking the "chicken-or-egg" question about drugs and crime, Speckart and Anglin's 1985 review of the research literature concluded that addiction is a significant criminogenic agent responsible for elevated levels of crime.

In 1986, the U.S. National Institute of Justice set up the Drug Use Forecasting (DUF) program, taking voluntary and anonymous urine samples from and conducting interviews with arrestees in the central booking facilities of the largest cities across the U.S. and making it possible to determine the prevalence of drug use among criminal justice populations. DUF data demonstrate that drug use and criminal behavior by adults were completely intertwined. In 21 major cities, 50% to 85% of all arrestees have tested positive for illicit drugs at the time of arrest. DUF has also found that 74% and 45% of all arrestees charged with violent or income-generating crimes tested positive for a drug (U.S. National Institute of Justice, 1989).

While the DUF system has not yet included data from teenage arrestees, there is sufficient evidence to conclude that drug use and criminality are similarly coexistent for this population. Elliott and Huizinga (1984) discovered that almost half of serious juvenile offenders also used multiple illicit drugs. Another study showed that half of the juveniles adjudicated for violent crimes used alcohol or drugs prior to their violent behaviors, and 40% reported using drugs immediately prior to their offense (Hartstone and Hansen, 1984). In the past few years, crack cocaine has become widespread, changing the face of drug abuse nationwide. While few studies have focused on the criminality of adolescent crack users, recent work by Inciardi on 600 Miami youths who were "seriously delinquent" showed that most were habituated to marijuana by age 11 and to crack before age 13. These adolescent drug users confessed to an average of 702 crimes per individual in the previous year, with their first crimes beginning at a mean age of 11. Ninety percent had been arrested, almost half had been incarcerated, but only 13.4% reported any drug treatment (Inciardi and Pottieger, in press). In addition, 88.4 % of the sample reported carrying weapons most or all of the time, with more than half carrying handguns. Those who were both dealers and users of crack were the most violent, committing 50% more major felonies per offender than nonusing crack dealers. In addition, this group committed 500% more felonies than youthful drug users with no participation in crack dealing (Inciardi, 1989). Because many studies have demonstrated that controlling addiction significantly reduces crime, the question for policymakers in regard to these young but extremely active drug-using criminals is no longer "What does it cost to treat them?" but rather "What does it cost not to treat them?" (Wexler, Lipton and Johnson, 1988; Anglin and McGlothlin, 1984).

Because research has substantiated that adolescents who come into contact with the criminal justice system are at high risk of becoming antisocial, drug-abusing, criminal adults, (Dembo et al., 1987), it is particularly important to intervene with these youngsters in an intense and effective manner in order to maximize their opportunity to overcome dysfunctional patterns of behavior, adjust successfully to living in society, and develop social networks in the community that support their newly acquired positive values and behavior. As Hawkins (1984) has said, "A comprehensive system of interventions holds the greatest promise...treatment and control approaches of increasing intensity are needed to deal with youth already experiencing serious multiple problems."

THERAPEUTIC COMMUNITIES

The self-help therapeutic community (TC) is one of the most substantial intervention mechanisms developed in the past three decades for changing the behavior of drug abusers. It takes a holistic approach to the problem of drug abuse, seeing it as a symptom of a disorder of the entire person, with a need for a global change in lifestyle, including sobriety, elimination of antisocial activity, employability, and adoption of prosocial attitudes and values. "The TC views drug abuse as deviant behavior reflecting impeded personality development and/or chronic deficits in social, educational and economic skills. Its antecedents lie in socioeconomic disadvantage, poor family effectiveness, and in psychological factors" (DeLeon, 1981).

History of TCs

TCs for drug addiction (in contrast to Maxwell Jones's programs that democratized mental hospitals) were born out of Alcoholics Anonymous (AA), just as AA was itself inadvertently conceived from Dr. Frank Buchman's Oxford Groups of the 1920s. In 1958 Charles Dederich, former alcoholic and AA zealot, discovered in conducting his own brand of extremely confrontative encounter groups that some heroin addicts attending the groups stopped using drugs (Rom-Rymer, 1981).

While keeping the self-help orientation of AA, Dederich moved away from its religious overtones and instead emphasized self-reliance in a highly structured community where residents lived and worked 24 hours a day. His Synanon approach specified an autocratically controlled "family" that promoted positive peer pressure for an anti-drug lifestyle based on hard work, caring for other members of the "family," confrontation of bad behavior and brutal honesty in encounter groups. Because other treatments of opiate addicts had been failures and addicts were widely regarded as hopeless, Dederich's Synanon[2] drew national attention for its success, grew rapidly, and inspired the formation of Daytop Village, Phoenix House, Odyssey House and other similar programs in New York City to combat the heroin crisis of the 1960s.

By the early 1970s over 2,000 drug treatment programs could be traced to Synanon (DeLeon and Beschner, 1976). The original Synanon/Daytop/Phoenix House model was characterized by its: (1) focus on adult, mostly male, opiate addicts; (2) rigidity in structure and procedures; (3) harsh discipline for serious program violations; (4) separation of residents from family and community; (5) ex-addict staff (trained "on the job" in the TC); (6) hierarchical structure, usually male-dominated, that equated progress in the program with moving up the "ladder" of program responsibilities; (7) an implicit acceptance of a very high dropout rate in the initial stages of treatment; and (8) an anti-psychological, anti-medical (disease model) orientation toward drug addiction (groups were called "games" to distinguish them from group therapy).

By the mid-1970s, however, mutation had begun. Many TCs were larger, better established and reaching out to adolescent substance abusers, polydrug abusers, women with children, criminal justice clients who came to the TC as an alternative to incarceration and school-aged children through prevention programs. The autocratic leader, thought to be an absolute prerequisite, produced some embarrassing abuses, and TCs began to move toward a less authoritarian style of management. Many TCs began to involve the family or other relatives of the client from the moment of entry into the program, while others recognized the need to work with codependence issues, and offered family therapy in addition to supportive orientations and family meetings. TCs began to recruit academically trained professionals to work alongside their ex-addict staff as demands for special services increased, and to meet the requirements of funding sources who were frequently skeptical about the competency of ex-addicts. The heavy confrontation and rigid discipline that had worked for males clients who were in their thirties and forties were not accepted by younger clients, females and adolescents, and many programs became more plastic. Some conducted outcome research and discovered that increased time in treatment invariably resulted in a greater likelihood of post-treatment success (DeLeon, Wexler and Jainchill, 1982; Coombs, 1981; DeLeon, 1988).

There was also an increasing recognition that the TC needed to devote more effort to preparing clients for successful reintegration into the community. Sophisticated vocational training programs began to augment the normal chores of maintaining program facilities, and reentry programming became common to reduce the number of post-treatment relapses. Some of the larger TC programs became human service conglomerates that provided: prevention programs for school aged youth; intervention services; out-client programs; employee assistance programs; programs for special populations; methadone maintenance programs; and programs designed especially for criminal justice clients, in addition to traditional TC programs (DeLeon and Beschner, 1976).

In the past 15 years, the TC model has spread worldwide and flourished in South America, Europe, and Asia. Recent innovations include treatment of dual-diagnosed clients, application of TC methods to methadone clients, AIDS prevention and treatment of HIV-infected drug abusers (Nebelkopf, 1989; Yablonsky, 1989; Sugarman, 1987).

Adaptations for Corrections

Stay'N Out

Because drug abusers are by definition criminals, and because various studies have shown that addicts engage in four to 20 times more crime when addicted than not, it was to be expected that TCs would eventually be adapted to work specifically with the criminal justice system (Speckart and Anglin, 1985). A particularly successful model that developed in the late 1970s is Stay'N Out, which provides a 9-12 month intensive program, staffed by ex-addicts and ex-offenders, that works hand in hand with correctional officials within a medium-security New York State prison. Outcome research sponsored by the U.S. National Institute on Drug Abuse has shown significant reductions in post-treatment drug abuse, criminality and recidivism, while simultaneously demonstrating improved parole outcomes, employment and other prosocial behavior (Wexler, Lipton and Foster, 1985; Wexler, Falkin, Lipton, Rosenblum and Goodloe, 1988). This disproved the declaration that "nothing works" in correctional drug treatment (Lipton, Martinson and Wilks, 1975; Wexler and Williams, 1986). Many so-called prison TCs were indeed failures, but, on examination, it is clear that many never followed the basics of the model and were poorly implemented (Camp and Camp, 1989).

Amity/Pima County Jail Project

As part of comprehensive drug abuse legislation passed by Congress in 1986, the Bureau of Justice Assistance of the U.S. Department of Justice issued a call for proposals for "national models" for drug abuse treatment in jails. Amity had been providing limited services in the Pima County Jail in Tucson, AZ for over five years and submitted a joint proposal with the Pima County Sheriff's Department to modify the Stay'N Out model for the jail setting.

The Amity/Pima County Jail Project created a strong, positive, anti-drug environment within an isolated unit of the direct supervision jail for sentenced offenders who were serving a minimum of 45 days. All inmates are informed about the drug treatment program at the time of intake, and are selected on the basis of a history of substance abuse and a voluntary commitment to abide by program norms. The program uses standard TC techniques, structure and activities, but because few inmates stay longer than four months, the program gears much of its efforts to preparing program participants to continue their drug treatment after leaving the jail. Over 50% of participants go on to community-based drug treatment after completion of their sentence, with approximately 25% transferring voluntarily to Amity's long-term residential TC. The jail program is staffed by a team of treatment professionals (most of whom are ex-addicts trained by Amity) that works closely with corrections officers in the unit; the program is managed by two coordinators—one a corrections officer and the other an experienced Amity treatment director. This demonstration of partnership sets a standard for cooperation within the program, now over two years old (Arbiter, 1988).

While Amity had worked with both adult and juvenile probation and parole for many years, the jail project was the first opportunity for the program to take responsibility for providing seven-day-a-week treatment within a correctional institution, meeting the needs of the offenders *and* addressing the concerns of security officers and jail administrators. The success of the program has given Amity valuable information now being used in developing institutional programs in ADC juvenile institutions.

Amity/IPS Program

In addition to the jail program, Amity has been involved with intensive probation supervision (IPS) for four years. The Pima County Superior Court, in cooperation with the Pima County Adult Probation Department, has sent over 70 men and women to Amity as an alternative to prison. Recent studies from the Rand Corporation indicate that many IPS programs are experiencing violation rates as great or greater than regular probation (Turner, 1989), thus failing to relieve prison overcrowding. However, the length of stay among Amity IPS clients surpasses that of other Amity residents. Because length of stay has been the most important predictor of post-treatment success in all major outcome studies, it is not surprising that of the 40 residents who have remained in the program for longer than 180 days, only four were rearrested from 1985 through 1988. This project indicates the effectiveness of using criminal justice sanctions to hold probationers in treatment, and the effectiveness of TC treatment in altering behavior.

Currently, two IPS officers handle the Amity caseload, working closely with counselors so that expectations are congruent and post-treatment follow-up is compatible with treatment plans developed by clients, IPS and Amity. Officers and counselors credit this cooperation as the key ingredient for the success of the program. The lessons learned from this project—specifically regarding the necessity for communication, cooperation, shared methods, and expectations between juvenile parole officers, corrections administrators, and Amity treatment staff—have been valuable in the design of the adolescent treatment model, and are expected to be invaluable in the implementation of the project.

Adaptations for Adolescents

While several existing TCs mix adults with adolescents, and report good success with adolescent clients during and after treatment, none of these programs accept younger adolescents (aged 15 and under). With most state licensing authorities insisting that adults in treatment be separated from adolescents, the more common practice among current TC programs is to provide separate facilities for juveniles, as well as separate staff and program activities designed particularly for adolescents.

Phoenix House

Phoenix House is a traditional TC, one of the two largest in the U.S. It has several separate adolescent facilities, the largest a 250-bed facility in New York City. A recent study by DeLeon shows that adolescent Phoenix House residents achieved positive post-treatment outcome results similar to those for adult residents even though these adolescents have much more serious criminal histories than adolescents referred to outpatient settings (DeLeon and Deitch, 1985). DeLeon also found that adolescent early dropouts did not achieve the same degree of success as early adult dropouts; he concluded that adolescent clients needed a minimum of a year in residential treatment for post-treatment success.

Phoenix House adolescent facilities use the same treatment methods with adolescents and adults, facilitating "self-help" change though sequenced stages of learning, characterized as "growing up" or "maturation." Its social organization is a family surrogate model, vertically stratified (DeLeon and Deitch, 1985). Phoenix House: moves its clients through progressive phases; features a highly structured daily regimen; relies on residents to manage the community under staff supervision; has a hierarchical job-responsibility system; centers its therapeutic activities around peer encounter groups; and uses ex-addict staff as the primary clinical staff. In the latter stages of the program, youth may hold jobs outside the community, attend public school and make visits home. The "cardinal rules" of "no use of drugs or alcohol," and "no violence or threats of violence" are the same as for adult residents, but to this is added "no sex." Violation of cardinal rules is serious and can be cause for expulsion. The feeling of safety in the TC environment depends upon the no violence/no threats norm.

DeLeon and Deitch note that adolescent residents are different in some ways from adults (earlier use of drugs, higher incidence of family deviance, shorter criminal histories, greater responsivenesss to extrinsic—usually legal—pressures, and beset by the normal turbulence of adolescence) and go on to list some adaptations Phoenix House has made to accommodate them in the TC:

- more attention to breaking down "images" associated with negative social functioning;
- greater focus on the need to confess guilt feelings about negative behavior, thus interrupting negative peer processes and providing the basis for new social learning;
- minimization of sexual activity, both didactic and therapeutic

approaches to clarify sexual issues, and resolutions of feelings about aberrant sexual histories;
- increased supervision to prevent absconding and antisocial behavior, and to reduce negative peer activities;
- more recreational opportunities to promote leisure skill-building and to prevent boredom;
- greater family involvement while the adolescent is in treatment, and family training to support behavioral and value changes;
- five hours daily of academic classes until high school diploma or GED is earned; and
- enhanced aftercare to promote continued family participation and placement of those youngsters who cannot return home, but need further support (DeLeon and Deitch, 1985).

Abraxas

In the early 1970s, the Abraxas program in Pennsylvania began providing adult TC services. It gradually abandoned its adult TC activities and modified itself to serve adolescent clients only. Abraxas now has several adolescent programs following the same modified TC model, and is particularly interesting because it operates almost exclusively as an alternative to incarceration for adolescent male drug and alcohol abusers involved in the juvenile justice system. Almost all Abraxas clients are under court order to receive treatment. Abraxas recruitment staff, many of them former juvenile probation officers, are known as "court liaisons"; they work closely with probation officers and judges, and regularly facilitate intensive training experiences at the Abraxas campus to help court personnel understand the program.

Abraxas operates a three-phase program. The first phase is at a remote rural facility, where new clients participate in various forms of structured therapy, advance in a job privilege hierarchy and complete their secondary education within a nine-month time period. They then transfer for three to six months of transition in a smaller urban facility, followed by several weeks of support in the community.

Pompi and Resnick (1987) found that client retention was significantly higher for Abraxas clients than for a comparison group of clients from nine other TC programs whose population of adults had significantly fewer court referrals. Pompi and Resnick attribute the high retention of Abraxas clients to court pressure. This is consistent with the findings of other researchers (Leukefeld and Tims, 1988; Condelli, 1987). Abraxas administrators also state that dramatically increasing the number of program staff, removing female clients,[3] and designing the physical environment of the program specifically for the needs of adolescents has improved retention and post-treatment success (Pompi, 1989).

THE AMITY ADOLESCENT THERAPEUTIC COMMUNITY

History

Responding to the pleas of local probation officers, Amity[4] began accepting a few older (all close to their 18th birthday) male adolescents into its adult TC in the early 1980s. When program evaluation showed that these adolescents had a considerably lower length of stay than adult residents,[5] separate program activities and living quarters were arranged in the adult facility, although many activities were still shared. Retention for adolescents improved strikingly as a result of these changes. In 1983, Amity responded to a request for proposal from the ADC to provide residential services for youngsters aged 12 to 18 incarcerated in juvenile institutions and determined to have substance abuse difficulties. For several months, Amity took ADC youth directly from institutions to the adult program site. While youth and adults slept in separate quarters and participated in many different program activities, the youth often worked with adult clients on projects, ate with them and were in encounter groups together. The response by youth to this arrangement was immensely positive. Closeness to adults who were involved in the process of change and who were honest about their mistakes gave the youth credible role models and reduced their dependence upon negative peer role models. As the program grew and the ages of referrals became younger, it was determined that a separate facility was needed for the adolescent program. Additionally, accepting referrals from agencies other than ADC required a license that could only be obtained if adolescents and adults were completely separated.[6]

In the spring of 1985, the adult and adolescent programs were separated when a new facility—a former private school on 60 acres in direct proximity to the adult facility—was secured. Amity then began accepting referrals from Arizona juvenile courts, several Arizona Native American tribes, the Department of Economic Security and private sources. For several months after the separation from the adult program, the adolescent program struggled. The absent-without-leave rate jumped dramatically as adolescents "voted with their feet" regarding their disappointment at being separated from the adult residents and shared activities. Eventually, the program stabilized, and it has served between 30 and 45 adolescent residents continuously for the past four years. Some of the programmatic observations made during that period were:

- It was essential for youth to "buy in" to the program before they entered. (This was particularly important for ADC-referred youth, who not only often knew each other from the "streets" but formed negative institutional bonds; frequently those who made the most earnest pleas for entrance had arranged "split contracts" with other ADC-referred youth and left within days of entry.)

- ADC-referred youth did not respond well to academically trained counselors or to counselors who did not share similar backgrounds. While "recovering role models" have been the foundation of adult therapeutic communities, concern by Arizona state licensing authorities about having ex-felons in contact with children has brought severe restrictions.[7] However, particularly at the beginning of treatment, these youth only accepted as credible those counselors who shared similar family, ethnic, and social backgrounds and who had experienced "life on the street" as they had. Because these recovering role models had obviously made the journey from the streets to mainstream social values and lifestyles, they demonstrated that it was possible. They also were not awed by the drug culture and street sophistication of the youth.
- Transition and aftercare services were essential (most of the youth served went back into the same environment that they came from before treatment, with no supportive services).
- An increased staff-to-youth ratio was needed to replicate the sense of "family" and community that had occurred when the youth were living at the adult facility. Continuity of staff was crucial; rapid staff changes triggered insecurity, absconding and antisocial activity.
- Families needed to be met and assessed much earlier in treatment. Because many families refused to attend orientations or see their youngsters while in treatment, counselors often left family assessment until late in the program, discovering too late that their information on families was not accurate and that post-treatment plans often had to be dramatically altered. In many cases, families were too abusive or criminogenic for youth to return home.)
- Stable funding was important to ensure that the program did not take wild economic plunges when funding sources changed their priorities or failed to be funded adequately by the state legislature.
- Separation of boys and girls, except for occasional program activities, increased retention for the girls significantly (the boys' retention declined moderately).
- Some homosexual activity (especially among female juveniles) appeared to be based on institutional learned behavior designed to upset the supervising adults; ignoring it caused almost immediate cessation. Excessive "sexual posturing" on the part of boys or girls usually indicated a history of sexual victimization.
- Having more than 45 youngsters living together produced negative peer effects almost immediately and made the program much harder to manage. These effects included more antisocial behavior, attempts to abscond, and influence of negative peer models in the program, and less respect for staff members).

The Amity/ADC Model

ADC officials commissioned an evaluation of all their "purchase-of-care" contracts, which was completed in the spring of 1988. The report confirmed conclusions already reached by ADC Juvenile Services/Purchase of Care: (1) Many programs had such a high runaway rate that ADC was operating a "revolving door" between ADC institutions and community placements. (2) Many programs did not effectively meet the social/psychological needs of their clients. (3) ADC needed to design its request for proposal (RFP) and contracting process to develop services for its youth, not merely to accept the services that already existed (EMT Associates, 1988).

ADC had also conducted its own substance abuse survey of incarcerated youth, which confirmed by self-report that not only were 25% currently addicted or serious abusers, but another 25% were "marginally dependent, abusive," and 49% of the most severe substance abusers received no treatment services at all (Baumgardner, 1988). ADC officials frankly admitted that the services that *were* provided were completely inadequate. ADC had met officially and unofficially with community providers for over two years to redesign its approach to community services. In the spring of 1988, it issued two RFPs: one for comprehensive services for adolescent substance abusers, and another for sex offenders. The contracts would be to one agency (or a consortium of agencies under unified management) to provide all of the services throughout Arizona for ADC wards. Substance abuse services were to begin within juvenile institutions, move to residential care, then to transitional homes in Tucson and Phoenix, and finally through an aftercare component that would provide supervision and support in the community to ensure that those who had completed the program did not relapse.

Amity was already looked upon favorably by ADC because of its relatively low runaway rate and reasonable per diem cost, focus on severe substance abusers, willingness to work closely with ADC, and ability to work with the most seriously impaired youth in the juvenile system. In September 1988 the contract for comprehensive substance abuse services was awarded to Amity, but because of ADC administrative difficulties almost a year passed before program implementation could begin. The residential program, which Amity has been providing for over five years, is continuing and expanding. The first institutional program began in October 1989, and the planned completion of implementation is November 1990. Thus, what is described here is very much a "work in progress," with many implementation issues yet to be resolved.

Principles and Characteristics of the Model

- The target population for this program represents an immediate high risk to society through its delinquent/criminal activity in the community, and a long-term risk if not resocialized to function appropriately. If these juvenile offenders are not positively changed by their contact with ADC, its mission of "protecting the public" will not be fulfilled. Beginning the program in a secure institutional setting takes advantage of incarceration time for starting the treatment process, protects the public, and provides meaningful consequences for antisocial behavior.

- The target population suffers from multiple disabilities and needs services that are holistic, intensive, and long term to be successfully habilitated. Episodic interest by the system based only on antisocial behavior is not adequate. The program must address chemical dependency, as well as family, social, vocational and educational needs. It must also address sexual behavior and reduction of HIV/AIDS risk.
- The program acknowledges a developmental model of behavior (Kohlberg et al., 1987), which presumes that needs not fulfilled in childhood must be met and that childhood trauma must be resolved before psychological, social, and moral growth[8] can occur. Because most offenders come from dysfunctional families, the program must act as a strong alternate family, with positive values to which program participants can bond.
- Treatment must be both phased and flexible. Movement through the program is based on increased freedom of action tied to increased responsibility and internalization of program goals. Progress through the program is expected to be inconsistent. Expulsion from the program is not desirable except under extreme circumstances; participants who are unable to meet expectations in one phase of the program will be returned to a more restrictive phase until they have developed the skills and attitudes that allow them to move forward.
- Continuity in philosophy and in day-to-day operations is crucial. Treatment and correctional staff must work closely together throughout the program to ensure that expectations are congruent.
- Positive relationship-building skills are crucial to normal functioning in all aspects of living; learning these skills is a crucial factor for post-treatment success in the community.
- Most important, the youngsters in the program represent an important social asset. They can be changed from social burdens to productive citizens.

Goals of the Program

- Resolution of underlying problems/dynamics fueling dysfunctional behavior so that return to antisocial, drug-abusing and criminal behavior after treatment is minimized or eliminated.
- Bonding to positive adult role models, positive peers, and positive and conventional social values.

Table 1: AMITY, Inc. Age Group 12–18 years
Amity/Catalina Mountain Project*

N = 28
33% Hispanic
45% Caucasian
3% Black
19% Native American

- Divorced parents: 42%
- Parents that have been incarcerated: 39%
- Physical abuse: 585
- Average age first alcohol use: 9.3
- Average age first drug use: 9.5
- Average age first offense: 7
- Average age first arrest: 11.5
- Average age first incarceration: 12
- Chronic substance use prior to present arrest: 52%
- Drug distributor: 53%
- Chronic 'crack' use: 45%
- Average number of reported misdemeanor offenses 12 months prior to present incarceration: 550
- Average number of reported felony offenses 12 months prior to present incarceration: 191

*Catalina Mountain Project is the Amity drug treatment project within the Catalina Mountain Juvenile Institution. All data in Table 1 were collected in November 1989. The data were reported by the incarcerated adolescents themselves. While it is too early to make representations about accuracy, it is interesting to note that these data are consistent with Inciardi's findings in Miami (Inciardi and Pottieger, in press).

- Acquisition of needed skills: education (schooling); impulse control; vocational training; recreation and leisure skills; positive relationship-building skills; problem-solving skills; relapse prevention and coping; consequential thinking; and drug-refusal skills.
- Control of program participants to prevent drug use or criminal activity while in the program (protection of the community).
- Successful reintegration into society with a strong support network involving family (if available), significant others, employers and positive peers.
- Follow-up evaluation to demonstrate that the program has altered the course of offender behavior in a way that provides a significant benefit to society by reducing criminal activity and drug abuse, and improving employment skills, educational achievement, and overall functioning.

- Establishment of a superior working relationship between Amity treatment staff and ADC staff at the administrative level, within the institutions and with parole to improve case management of offenders and enhance positive parole outcomes. Regular cross-training of ADC staff by Amity and Amity staff by ADC is required (40 hours per year minimum, additional training as needed).

Developmental Needs

The observations underlying the entire Amity model are that most, if not all, of the youngsters referred to the program come from very dysfunctional homes. Many have been physically or sexually abused; others were simply not wanted or were victims of a chaotic family life in which their normal developmental needs were not met. While these youngsters are usually quite "streetwise" and sophisticated beyond their years, they are still developmentally arrested. It is our observation that they cannot grow psychologically, socially or morally until their developmental needs are met. Further, the Miller (1983) hypothesis assumes that the repressed rage and pain experienced in childhood must be expressed now, as it was experienced as a child, in an irrational, emotional manner. Although the behavior modification aspects of the program will probably be effective in changing behavior while in the program, if repressed emotions are not expressed and directed to the source, the individual will continue out of control and will act self-destructively and/or compulsively to hurt others. Skill building is important, but no amount of skills can substitute for uncovering the underlying psychogenetic material in order to resolve compulsive, out-of-control behavior.

Staffing

The quality, enthusiasm, dedication and continuity of the staff are the most important ingredients of the Amity program. While the TC model often talks about programs being "peer-run," with mature adolescents (many of whom are at the developmental level of small children), affectionate staff who relate to youth without psychological mumbo-jumbo are a respite from peers who are often inconsistent, angry and out of control. When peers act out, the emotional ties to staff keep the entire peer group from being negatively affected. Staff are instructed to forget "professional distance." The Amity motto is, "If you are not close enough to the youngsters to get your feelings hurt, you are not close enough to do any good." Condelli (1987) found that a significant factor for retention in treatment by adolescents was their perception of staff "wanting them to stay" for the full duration of the program. Amity staff members are expected to have positive and high, but realistic, expectations for all the youth they work with;[9] other requirements follow.

- Staff are expected to understand the psychodramatic aspects of their work. Youngsters who have never been able to express their feelings of hurt and rage to their own parents will, as part of their growth, express those feelings to the staff member who bonds with them most closely.

- Training emphasizes that relationships formed with youth must go beyond the confines of working hours or adolescents' formal participation in the program. The relationships formed must be "real" and perceived as such by residents.
- Staff are selected on the basis of their previous experience with youngsters, or on the basis of their enthusiasm and willingness to be trained. Staff are academically trained professionals, workers from other human service agencies or former addicts who have completed an internship program and who have received their certification as professional counselors from the Therapeutic Communities of America Credentials Committee or as Certified Addictions Counselors.
- Staff are balanced to reflect the ethnic, cultural and racial makeup of the residents.
- Staff members must, as a condition of employment, participate in two week-long training sessions per year in addition to other regular staff training programs held on and off the facility. The intense workshops focus on family dynamics. Amity's experience is that many staff (not only recovering addicts and alcoholics) who are motivated to work with youth are themselves from dysfunctional families and often inadvertently begin to recreate dysfunctional dynamics with the youth in the TC.
- Staff members are expected to work closely together, to communicate well, and to share the values of the TC, no matter what their background. All members of the staff— administrative, custodial and secretarial—are considered part of the therapeutic environment, and must participate in meetings and trainings. Training emphasizes that they are the "surrogate family" and mini-community for the juvenile residents, and that in order to play that role they must form strong bonds among themselves.
- Staff participate regularly in encounter groups with each other to resolve differences, get to know one other better and demonstrate to the residents that the encounter group is a powerful learning tool used by role models, not just a technique imposed on youngsters because they are "sick." Most TC programs emphasize positive peer culture and the establishment of strong bonds between positive peers. However, few stress strong bonds to staff though it is unlikely that peers, no matter how positive, can fulfill the developmental need for a "parental" bond to a strong, affirming adult.
- Low staff turnover is crucial for the Amity program. Youth come from chaotic homes and neighborhoods where there is no consistency, adults are not stable and expectations are constantly changing. Staff turnover or staff movement can precipitate anxiety and the feeling that Amity is just

another in the long line of institutional placements to which these youth have been referred. A primary task of the adolescent program director is to meet the needs of the staff and weld them into a strong "family/community," with shared values and consistent expectations for themselves as a group and individually so that youth have access to them as adult models and surrogate family members to meet their developmental needs. While regular encounter groups, social activities and good staff benefits have counteracted moderate salaries to keep Amity staff turnover lower than many youth programs,[10] the coming year will be a challenge as the program moves to several different sites and as many new staff members are added.

Physical Environment

If the staff and the daily routine of the program (including daily and weekly ceremonies) are two legs of a tripod, the third is the physical environment. Few programs give physical environment much emphasis, and many programs for adolescents look, smell, and feel like institutions. Because many of the youth came from home environments that did not "feel" like home, it is particularly important that all program components have a home-like ambiance. Ideally, facilities should be designed and built from the ground up to reflect the needs of the program and its residents, but, in actuality, cost constraints dictate that existing facilities must be modified for program activities. With the exception of the institutional components of the program, which are governed by ADC rules and standards, Amity has refused to acquire facilities that cannot be modified to feel more like homes than institutions. The current adolescent facility is an old Arizona guest ranch with many small rooms that include private bathrooms. For many of the youngsters, fresh from dormitory living in a juvenile institution, these are the most pleasant living arrangements they have ever had. The facility also has many large community rooms for meetings and community activities. Further, program staff arrange the environment to reflect all of the many cultural backgrounds of residents. Individual rooms are made to reflect the culture and the interests of the occupants, with no two looking alike except for neatness. The residential facility has a nondenominational outdoor pavilion decorated with ornaments from a variety of cultures.

Work

Many sociologists have pointed out that in our attempts to protect the young, we have completely excluded them from the adult world, which is to a great extent the world of work. Unlike earlier times, when children not only had necessary chores within the family but were able to see their parents and other adults involved in the work roles they would soon assume, today's youth are as mystified about what adults do as their elders are about youth interests.

One of the greatest socializing influences on youth—the adult workplace—is no longer available. Adolescence, a social condition that did not exist two centuries ago, is prolonged, and physically mature youngsters have an extended childhood in which irresponsibility is culturally sanctioned (Coleman, 1972). Particularly for the juveniles who come to Amity from the ADC, the notion of work is foreign. In some cases, their parents or adult role models were on welfare or engaged in criminal activities to support themselves. These antisocial youngsters have often modeled themselves after dysfunctional adults or older peers, and have learned how to support themselves by dealing drugs, stealing, or prostitution—productive work is considered "square" and a sign of acculturation to despised conventional values.

One of the most important jobs of the TC is to integrate delinquents into functional community roles that move them toward adulthood (Missakian and Mullen, 1974). This is achieved in the following ways:

- At all Amity components, everyone has "chores" to help in the maintenance of the facilities.
- Many staff members have skills and are not only "counselors." They assume responsibility for physical areas of the facility and teach youngsters how to work.
- Prevocational skills are emphasized. While there is a strong vocational program, not all juveniles at Amity will learn a marketable skill while a resident. But if they learn discipline by working with others on common tasks and learn the attitudes necessary at the workplace, they will be much more likely be able to find a job, hold it and be an attractive trainee than if their skills were significant but their ability to follow directions, cooperate, and work hard was minimal.
- Whenever possible, residents are involved in the work of building, maintaining and operating the facility. This gives them a feeling of ownership and takes them out of the passive "child/dependent" role.
- Work offers juveniles an opportunity to socialize with adults and learn how adults work, how they think, and what their standards and expectations are. "Bonding" often occurs at work.

Groups, Retreats, Workshops and Psychodrama

While the peer encounter group has been and remains the center of therapeutic activity for the TC, it is important for adolescents that the group not be left entirely to peers, who are capable of using the notion of "anything goes in group" to perform psychological attacks on the weakest members, or who completely subvert the purposes of encounter groups by avoiding the kind of emotional honesty that leads to out-of-group behavioral change. For the group to be effective, it has to be safe for its participants to talk about painful or embarrassing things, as well as to use the group for peer confrontations. While many juveniles become sophisticated group facilitators after many months in the program, it is not uncommon for other youngsters to have a difficult time accepting the advice or authority of a peer and to become subversive. Much more than adult TCs, encounter groups must be carefully structured, seeded with adolescents who have good group facilitation skills, and usually attended by staff members who have extensive encounter group experience and understanding of adolescent needs. Mature and understanding leadership is particularly important for making the encounter group "safe" for adolescents to talk about "family secrets," embarrassing sexual encounters and other sensitive personal matters.

"Retreats" lasting two or three days are scheduled several times a year. The events involve encounter groups, teaching sessions, art activities, field trips and other workshop activities. The activities always involve the senior staff of the adolescent program and put them in direct contact with the residents in a very personal manner. Frequently, these groups, with their concentrated time together, are the settings in which youth feel safest to talk about their most difficult and painful experiences. These experiences are commonly enjoyed by youngsters and looked forward to with anticipation as an emotional adventure—the equivalent of an emotional wilderness challenge experience.

Psychodrama has long been used in the TC. In fact, the first book written about the TC was by Yablonsky, a student of Moreno, the inventor of psychodrama. Moreno called the TC "residential psychodrama—an opportunity for all in the community to role play for each other" (Yablonsky, 1989). Frequently, in intense encounter groups psychodramatic incidents occur spontaneously; staff are trained to know how to take advantage of these opportunities in order for residents to express deeply buried feelings and then to "de-role" the participants and help explain the content of the psychodrama. In the 1950s, Corsini (1951, 1958) wrote a series of articles describing adaptations of Moreno's psychodramatic techniques in prisons and with incarcerated adolescents. His observation that both adult and adolescent populations were trapped in roles and interactions that were completely misunderstood by them has lost little potency in 30 years.

Psychodrama is effective because it takes the real life events of each student and integrates behavioral, cognitive, and effective methods of teaching social skills and resolving problems. Psychodrama can be as profound as dealing with an incestuous relationship, and as ordinary as dealing with conflict among peers or a counselor by role playing. Most importantly, psychodrama emphasizes spontaneity and the "teachable moment"—no classroom is required, and the opportunity exists in the moment to develop new, healthy social relationships based on new responses to old situations.

The popularity of retreats among adolescent residents emphasizes the need for ritual and ceremony—absent in their lives and in the lives of most in modern society. Such simple rituals as morning wake-ups, the standard TC "morning meeting," formal dining, and an end-of-day ceremony or bedtime stories, give a sense of wholeness and substance to lives that have been devoid of such formality and repetitiveness. One of the appeals of youth cults and gangs is the meaning and stability provided by ceremony and ritual.

Education

Amity provides its own on-site school at the residential facility. The school is staffed by credentialed teachers (Amity employees) and features small individualized classes, special education—classes for the learning disabled and emotionally handicapped—and GED preparation. Most students have a learning disability and almost all are considerably below their grade level (see Table 2).

ADC provides teachers and regular classes for all students while in ADC juvenile institutions. Amity staff support the institutional academic program, and prepare both the student and residential program to continue academic instruction when the adolescent transfers to the residential phase of the program.

Small classes, adult and peer support, and sanctions for nonattendance or indifferent performance all help to make significant academic progress the rule, not the exception. Additionally, teachers participate in encounter groups with students where issues of resistance, "learning is not hip" images, and other blocks to academic progress can be addressed and discussed by teachers,

Table 2: AMITY, Inc. Age Group 12–18 years
Educational Achievement Levels at Entry

Average age: 15.5*
Average years formal education: 8.1
Percent students with handicapping conditions:
(documented or suspected)
- Learning disabled: 39%
- Emotional handicap: 26.8%
- Educable mentally handicapped: 0.4%

Average grade equivalents based on achievement test scores:
- Reading: 8.6
- Language: 7.7
- Math: 7.4

Percent of students below grade level at entry:
- Reading: 61%
- Language: 85.4%
- Math: 78.1%

Average increase of grade equivalents in achievement test scores from entry to 7–12 months in treatment:
- Reading: 1.9
- Math: 1.8

*Data compiled on 41 students who attended school at AMITY January-November 1988

peers, and other staff members. While most youngsters cannot completely reach their age-appropriate grade levels while at Amity, many have taken their GED and gone on to junior college. The most important lesson learned is that they *can* function adequately in a classroom environment.

Active Leisure and Physical Competence

All program components have an exercise program that not only improves attitudes but prepares juveniles for participation in sports and other active leisure activities. Frequently, residents have "written off" physical exercise and physical activities as inconsistent with their self-image. In other cases, physical activity has become limited to ritualized weight lifting or a form of basketball called "institutional ball" that recreates many aspects of running the gauntlet. In Amity, most find regular exercise—another ritual—enjoyable and stabilizing. Program staff find that youth who rise early and exercise hard are less likely to get into trouble during the day and more likely to sleep well at night; this alone has made the exercise program popular with staff.

In general, discipline and teamwork are best taught through physical activities because attention spans for cognitive tasks are often short, particularly at the beginning of the program. In the institutional segment of the program, ADC instructors teach youth to march and regularly participate in competitions.

Research literature (Beschner, 1986; Schneider, 1989) has repeatedly shown a correlation between adolescents who score high on risk-taking behavior and adolescent substance abuse. For this reason, there has recently been a resurgence of interest in challenging outdoor activities and wilderness experiences. Amity staff are currently developing an outdoor wilderness experience as a regular part of the curriculum's residential component. All youth are taught a variety of recreational and leisure activities, including horseback riding, swimming, hiking, baseball, basketball and football. Because Arizona weather provides opportunities for year-round outdoor activity, these skills become important in designing post-treatment recreational outlets.

Involvement of Family, Significant Others

Beschner (1986) cites several studies that urge family participation from the beginning of drug abuse treatment in order to improve the post-treatment success of adolescents. This is echoed by Kumpher and DeMarsh (1986). Condelli (1987) shows that perceived pressure by family or significant others is a salient factor in legal constraints as well as retention in treatment programs for adolescent substance abusers. The Amity program makes phone contacts with parents and in-home visits when juveniles are first assigned to the institutional program. In many cases, the family of origin may not have a functioning, positive parent who can be involved and supportive of behavioral change on the part of the adolescent. Occasionally, a relative, sibling, foster parent or even an involved neighbor may be the "significant other" who can become involved in orientations, trainings, family support groups, workshops and family therapy.

With the target population that Amity has served ("high-risk adolescents" with chronic patterns of substance abuse, dysfunctional families, childhood physical and sexual victimization, and significant criminal histories), however, it is often the youth receiving treatment who extends himself or herself to a sibling or a parent. Not infrequently an adolescent's example of accepting help inspires the parent. To the extent that it is financially possible, Amity has offered its services to family members of adult or adolescent residents. As a result of such outreach, several parents or older siblings have entered the adult TC, and some younger siblings have attended activities through Amity's prevention program, Matrix Community Services. When family support is available, efforts are made by program staff in the Enrollment and Family Services Department to encourage the supportive individual(s) to become immediately involved. Often, the immediate effort is to have the family member be involved in training activities with other supportive family members, and not with the adolescent in treatment. This gives the adolescent the opportunity to break negative ties and to reveal "family secrets," if there are any, and gives the parent the opportunity to identify with other parents who have had similar experiences.

For those juveniles who are to be reunited with their families, the period of transition is one more intense training for family members so that they can become completely supportive of the goals of treatment. Family members go through the relapse prevention strategy with the Amity staff, the parole officer and the juvenile so that they understand the relapse triggers and can identify "high-risk" situations. For those who do not have families to return to, the emphasis is on developing supportive relationships in the community. Significant others, often adult Amity graduates, play a surrogate parent role and go through the same training as parents.

Transition Aftercare and Relapse Prevention

Most of the current research literature on adolescent treatment emphasizes the need for well-developed transition services. While there is good evidence that juvenile offenders can perform well while in treatment programs under close supervision, there is considerably less evidence showing that they are able to maintain the gains they have made without support. After residential treatment, Amity program participants will go to small (six to ten youth) transition homes in urban settings where they will: (1) perform community service and restitution activities; (2) begin to reintegrate with family or to develop a support network of peers and adults consistent with their new behavior and attitudes; (3) begin employment or full-time education; and (4) engage in a very intensive program of relapse prevention similar to that outlined in the Haggerty monograph on Project ADAPT for reintegration of adolescent offenders into the community (Haggerty et al., 1989).

Parole officers will work with family or significant others, Amity treatment staff and the adolescent to develop a post-treatment plan that all agree on. This will include identifying high-risk situations, support groups (12-Step or other programs), key relationships, frequency of involvement with Amity staff and the parole officer, frequency of groups, and "emergency procedures" for episodes when the adolescent is losing control.

After transition is completed, the participant will move to supervised aftercare. Contact with parole and treatment staff will be frequent for the first weeks (or months) until it is clear that plans developed at transition are being adhered to. Gradually, the parolee will be supervised less and less. Whenever possible, those leaving transition and not moving home will be encouraged to live together in groups of two or three to support each other's recovery and fill the need for positive peer relationships. Frequent visits by or to "bonded" staff members will help to ensure maintenance of treatment gains.

For those adolescents who at transition are too young to live independently and who do not have an intact home to return to, Amity will develop a stable, long-term living arrangement (therapeutic foster care) that will allow them to continue their progress until they are old enough to live on their own.

Special Needs

Adolescent programs are frequently designed and implemented by the dominant culture for the dominant culture. Ethnic minorities often find that the staff, physical environment, and program activities do not reflect their own background and further derogate their own experiences. Amity hires and trains staff who are culturally sensitive, and arranges the environment to reflect the variety of cultures of the residents. In many cases minority youth are ignorant of their own culture. Amity makes an effort to teach the cultural heritage of each of the cultures of the residents. Celebrations include black, Native American, Jewish, Hispanic, and civic and religious holidays; each celebration is taken as an opportunity to teach all of the youth the contribution of each culture and ethnic group. This approach was particularly successful with Native American youth, most of whom had no acquaintance with their culture. A medicine man came to the program and taught both staff and youth several simple ceremonies that *all* youth in the program participated in; the pride that Native American adolescents felt was reflected in their very high retention rates in the program.

Both the criminal justice system and treatment programs tend to be first adult driven, then male driven. The needs of women are repeatedly neglected or relegated to secondary importance. However, there is evidence that when the needs of female clients are met, not only are their outcomes favorably influenced but male program participants are helped too (Stevens, Arbiter and Glider, 1989). The adolescent females referred to Amity by ADC have very distinctive needs (see Appendix A).

- They are disproportionately victims of early childhood sexual abuse. Many have had experience as prostitutes, have been raped, and need female counselors and role models who can help them talk about their sexual victimization. They also need to understand that they can get affection and affirmation from the opposite sex without exercising their sexuality.
- Many of these adolescent females have had abortions; for most this is a traumatic and usually a shameful experience.
- Increasing numbers of girls referred to the program have young children. Interestingly, they appear to be much more highly motivated to be good parents than adult female residents in Amity's adult therapeutic community. Arrangements are made for children to visit frequently, and parenting classes are provided.
- Sex education for these young women is *critical*. Most have regularly engaged in high-risk behaviors for HIV infection or transmission. While to date there have been no known instances of HIV-infected adolescent residents, this is a short-lived phenomenon.

SUMMARY

Amity, working with ADC, has helped to design and is currently implementing a program which targets juvenile offenders incarcerated in ADC institutions and identified by ADC as being chemically dependent. Both the research literature and many years of program experience dictate a response to these juveniles that is intensive, long-term, and comprehensive and that addresses the many deficiencies that they have. While these young offenders pose a significant threat to the communities they live in because of their active criminality, it is important to recognize that they are disproportionately victims of dysfunctional, maladaptive, and often physically or sexually abusive families. One of the unique aspects of this comprehensive approach is that it draws on the TC model, one of the most powerful interventions developed for chronic adult addicts, and adapts it for an adolescent population. Further, the model expects to uncover and help to alleviate the root causes of antisocial and self-destructive behavior. The program will serve over 250 youth simultaneously at several program components when program implementation is completed.

APPENDIX A

Belinda: A Case Study

The most confusing aspect of working with criminally involved, substance-abusing adolescents is that they may be at different developmental levels simultaneously. Thus, a 15-year old Hispanic girl, Belinda, may be developmentally arrested at the point where her prostitute mother allowed a "trick" to sexually molest her, so that the mother could get a "fix," and did not protect Belinda (who was unable to express her hurt because of her age, her mother's lack of interest or sympathy, and her fear of losing her mother's affection).

Belinda has prostituted for two years. Further, she has a child of her own, and has both strong maternal feelings and rage/hatred toward the child, who demands of her what she never received from her own mother and forces her further away from her own developmentally necessary period of individual role experimentation. At Amity, Belinda is involved in the following activities:

- She plays baseball on the Amity team. Belinda is an enthusiastic player, practicing every day. She has never had an opportunity to play before. She began to learn while in the Amity program in the juvenile institution, where she was incarcerated for four months; this was her fourth ADC incarceration.
- Belinda has two friends made while in the institutional program. One of the staff members she was fond of moved from the institutional program to the residential program shortly after Belinda was transferred.
- She spends time with a 23-year old female, Hispanic staff member who grew up in the barrio near her neighborhood. The staff member was a prostitute and an addict, has been drug-free for three years and is now getting married. Belinda relates to the older woman partly as "mom," partly as "sister," partly as "best friend." Belinda finds that she can sometimes talk about painful and degrading experiences with the staff member; and then, feeling "safe" because of the acceptance and understanding, share those experiences and feelings with other girls in the program.
- Belinda is spending time on the weekend with her daughter, who is brought to the program by her grandmother. Grandmother is caring for the baby and is impatient for Belinda to leave the program to relieve her of the responsibility. Mom is in jail for prostitution, and Belinda's grandmother is attending parent/significant-other orientations every month. Since she has been attending, she has put less pressure on Belinda to leave. Belinda is also involved once a week in a class on parenting skills; she seems proud of what she has learned and feels that she will be a better parent.
- She looks forward to bedtime stories every night, read by one of the staff

members who lives at the facility. She never had that kind of experience when she was at home.

- Belinda is going to school consistently for the first time in five years. She is learning how to read and write. Classes are very small and individualized so that she is not overly embarrassed by her lack of ability. She works with another girl in her dorm who is at the same level.
- Her job assignment is in the kitchen. Her grandmother taught her to cook, and she is somewhat egotistic about her abilities. Several times Belinda was put in charge of the kitchen and supervised a crew of her peers in preparing a special meal for the facility. Everyone praised her, and she felt she was making an adult contribution to the community. Belinda thinks that she may become a cook when she completes the program. The Amity cook has offered to teach her menu planning and food ordering as well as to expand her repertoire beyond Mexican cuisine. She knows that she must be able to read and calculate in order to organize menus, and that has helped to motivate her at school.
- Belinda sometimes attends mixed encounter groups with boys. She is fond of Alex, and has occasionally talked with him outside of the group. Although she was a prostitute for two years, and used heroin and cocaine intravenously before smoking crack, she is very shy around Alex and finds it difficult to communicate. She has never tried to talk to someone of the opposite sex without being high or without sex being the ultimate object of the encounter.
- Belinda is just learning about AIDS. Since she has been at Amity, she learned that four friends from her neighborhood in Phoenix are infected and that one has already died. The nurse is talking to all the young people about AIDS. Belinda is frightened. She realizes that she may be infected. She is ambivalent about being tested, but all the staff were tested a year ago (to reduce the residents' fears of testing), and it is now easier for her to consider being tested.
- Belinda has an uncontrollable hatred directed toward the program director; she does not know why. When he observed her one day drawing a "jail-house" tattoo on her thigh with pen, ink, and matches—and confronted her in a loud voice—she lost control of herself, threw herself at him, bit him and kicked him. She never knew her father, but was molested by a series of men brought by her mother to the apartments they lived in while the mother was prostituting. The program director is working with program staff to set up a "retreat" for a dozen of the girls in the program. He is working with the clinical director to arrange a psychodrama to see if Belinda can express and direct her rage toward her molesters—and toward her mother.
- Belinda and other girls have been attending seminars regularly to talk about family dynamics and how they affect behavior. The girls are seeing videotapes by Claudia Black about how children of alcoholics or drug

> abusers develop shame and feel that they are defective. After seeing the videotapes and talking with the staff and her peers, Belinda has started to remember details about her childhood. When she came to Amity she could not remember anything before the age of nine—the age at which she went to live with her grandmother.

This one example illustrates some of the different developmental needs of a typical Amity resident.

NOTES

1. Our clinical observation has been that for a majority of clients with histories of physical or sexual victimization it often takes months or even years for the client to reveal the incidents. Often there is an unwillingness to attribute anything "bad" to an idealized parent. Even more frequently, the client has completely submerged the memory of victimization. Since these incidents are shameful, there is further reason to be unwilling to reveal them casually; for a child whose only physical affection from a father was incest, there is often the feeling as an adult that one "caused" and promoted the incestuous relationship.

2. While Synanon was the original TC, it never accepted government support (remaining true to its AA roots) and, by the late 1960s, considered itself a "social movement" that cured drug addicts as a by-product of engaging in a healthy lifestyle. Synanon was involved for many years in a variety of program experiments to improve treatment of drug addicts. However, none of the data were ever published, and little is known except by Synanon administrators and program participants. By the end of the 1970s Synanon had turned away from drug treatment, and became embroiled in a criminal case and several civil cases concerning illegal activities by Dederich and his associates. At the time of this writing, Synanon is not involved in drug rehabilitation.

3. Abraxas does have females in transitional facilities, but not in the main facilities. Mixing males and females was found to be too disruptive.

4. Amity, Inc. provides a variety of substance-abuse related services: (1) An adult TC for 175 residents. (2) A prevention/intervention program that contacts 25,000 high-risk youth per year. (3) A National Institute on Drug Abuse-funded AIDS outreach/research program, intervening with intravenous drug abusers and their sexual partners. (4) The Amity/Pima County Jail Project, serving approximately 70 men and women incarcerated in the Pima County Medium Security Addition. (5) The adolescent TC described in this chapter.

5. Average length of stay for the Amity adult TC between 1981 and 1987 was 297 days for men and 279 days for women. For TCs nationally, the average is between 90 to 120 days (DeLeon, 1989). Because length of stay is the most important predictor of post-treatment success, this appears to indicate significant improvement in an area (retention) that is receiving increasing attention by both researchers and practitioners.

6. While licensing considerations and governmental funding preclude any real consideration of mixing adult and adolescent populations for most programs, this remains an important and unresolved issue. Stratification into age-peer groups is a significant problem—a legacy of our recent transition from agrarian to industrial to post-industrial society. When the peer group is further condensed into adolescents who all share dysfunctional family relationships, negative peer associations, low

impulse control, inability to delay gratification and criminal histories, the possibility of orienting them toward positive societal values becomes a task worthy of Hercules. Haggerty et al.'s (1989) Adapt program points out that delinquent youth need opportunities for involvement in conventional activities and interactions with conventional others. Being restricted to an entire population of juvenile deviants makes that a very difficult task to accomplish, hence the criminogenic properties of both adult and adolescent correctional institutions. TCs have specialized in converting social deviants to conventional values, which, like new converts, they preach with a zeal unmatched by those who have been born to normalcy. However, with youngsters, who are in the perplexing period of adolescence (not to mention accompanying substance abuse problems), it is more difficult to "convert" to adult values—indeed part of normal adolescent behavior is rebellion against adult values. While there are some difficulties and dangers in treating adults and adolescents together, the benefits of having adult role models may, in a carefully managed TC that can provide separate programming specifically for adolescent needs, outweigh the difficulties. Recovering adults espousing conventional values with a very strong antidrug, anticrime orientation may be the only credible and available adult role models available for these youngsters during their own recovery (Haggerty et al., 1989).

7. In 1987, the Arizona State Legislature passed a law forbidding anyone ever convicted of one of 16 listed felonies (including robbery, burglary and sales of drugs) to ever work with youngsters in facilities licensed by the state. Amity, being the only organization in the state that explicitly used ex-addicts as role models with youngsters, found itself with many of its key clinicians sidelined. For example, a decorated Vietnam veteran was convicted of possession of cocaine in the 1970s. He served a short sentence and soon thereafter began working with youth. His record was expunged. Over the next ten years, he managed several successful youth programs. However, when he was fingerprinted in Arizona, his old conviction came up, and he was forbidden to work at the adolescent facility. Amity worked with state legislators for two years to change this law. It was changed in 1989 so that "exceptions for good cause" can be made.

8. Kohlberg's work on moral development provides a useful paradigm for adolescent or adult substance abusers and criminals. Based on a solid foundation of developmental research, Kohlberg sees maturation as moving from preconventional norms, which are excessively self-centered, to conventional norms centered on supporting society and the status quo, to postconventional morality—the recognition of a "higher authority." Put in these terms, the job of socializing institutions is no more or less than moving clients from preconventional morality to conventional morality. Kohlberg suggests that the key ingredients for moral development are: credible role models demonstrating moral levels slightly above the participant; moral conflict that reveals the flaws in current moral reasoning and practice; opportunities to play many social roles; and sustained responsibility for others. At Amity, Kohlberg's work is presented regularly in staff training, and both staff and residents are encouraged to view the program as "a school for moral development."

9. Over the years we have found that a cynical attitude is corrosive for adolescent and adult clients, probably because it echoes early childhood messages of self-derogation and negativity. Counselors and other staff who work with adolescent clients must be emotionally tough. They cannot fall apart when they are tested or deceived by youth, but they also must have a positive outlook—a "romantic" view of the possibilities for improvement by each adolescent. More than any other factor, youth respond to *expectations* to "become their best" by adult role models to whom they are emotionally bonded.

10. This is based upon the observation of the authors in visiting youth programs across the country. At many programs, a 50% staff turnover rate is not infrequent during the course of a single calendar year.

REFERENCES

Anglin, M. and W. McGlothlin (1984). "Outcome of Narcotic Addict Treatment in California." In *Drug Abuse Treatment Evaluation: Strategies, Progress and Prospects (NIDA Research Monograph 51)*, edited by F. Tims and J. Ludford. Washington, DC: U.S. National Institute on Drug Abuse.

Arbiter, N. (1988). "Drug Treatment in a Direct Supervision Jail: Pima County's Amity Jail Project." *American Jails* 2(2):35-40.

Baumgardner, T. (1988). "Substance Abuse Survey of Juvenile Institutional Population." Unpublished report prepared for the Arizona Department of Corrections.

Beschner, G. (1986). "Treatment for Childhood Chemical Abuse." In *Childhood and Chemical Abuse: Prevention and Intervention*, edited by S. Griswold-Ezekoye, K. Kumpfer and W. Bukoski. New York, NY: Haworth.

Brunswick, A. and J. Boyle (1979). "Patterns of Drug Involvement: Developmental and Secular Influences on Age at Initiation." *Youth and Society* 11(2):139-162.

Camp, G.M. and C.C. Camp (1989). *Building on Prior Experiences: Therapeutic Communities in Prisons*. (Report prepared for Narcotic and Drug Research, Inc.) New York, NY: Criminal Justice Institute.

Coleman, J. (1972). "The Children Have Outgrown the Schools." *Psychology Today* 5(9):72-75, 82.

Condelli, W. S. (1987). "Client Evaluations of Therapeutic Communities and Retention." In *Therapeutic Communities for Addictions*, edited by G. DeLeon and J.T. Ziegenfuss. Springfield, IL: Charles C Thomas.

Coombs, R. (1981). "Back on the Streets: Therapeutic Communities' Impact Upon Drug Users." *American Journal of Drug and Alcohol Abuse* 8(2):185-201.

Corsini, R. J. (1951). "Psychodramatic Treatment of a Pedophile: The Case of Manuel." *Group Psychotherapy* 4:166-171.

—— (1958). "Psychodrama with a Psychopath." *Group Psychotherapy* 11(1):33-39.

DeLeon, G. (1989). Personal communication with the Research Director, Therapeutic Communities of America.

—— (1988). "Legal Pressure in Therapeutic Communities." In *Compulsory Treatment of Drug Abuse: Research and Clinical Practice* (NIDA Research Monograph 86), edited by C. Leukefeld and F. Tims. Washington DC: U.S. National Institute on Drug Abuse.

—— (1981). "The Role of Rehabilitation." In *Drug Abuse in the Modern World: A Perspective for the Eighties*, edited by G.G. Nahas and H.C. Frick. New York, NY: Pergamon.

—— and G. Beschner (1976). "The Therapeutic Community." In *Proceedings of the Therapeutic Communities of America Planning Conference*, edited by George DeLeon and George M. Beschner. Washington, DC: U.S. National Institute on Drug Abuse.

—— and D. Deitch (1985). "Treatment of the Adolescent Substance Abuser in a Therapeutic Community." In *Treatment Services for Adolescent Substance Abusers*, edited by A.S. Friedman and G.M. Beschner. Washington, DC: U.S. National Institute on Drug Abuse.

—— H. Wexler and N. Jainchill (1982). "The Therapeutic Community: Success and Improvement Rates Five Years After Treatment." *International Journal of the Addictions* 17(4):703-747.

Dembo, R., M. Dertke, L. LaVoie, S. Borders, M. Washburn and J. Schmeidler. (1987). "Physical Abuse, Sexual Victimization and Illicit Drug Use: "A Structural Analysis Among High-Risk Adolescents." *Journal of Adolescence* 10:13-33.

—— L. Williams, E. LaVoie, E. Berry, A. Getreau, E. Wish, J. Schmeidler and M. Washburn (1989). "Physical Abuse, Sexual Victimization, and Illicit Drug Use: Replication of a Structural Analysis Among a New Sample of High-Risk Youths." *Violence and Victims* 4(2):131-138.

—— E. Wish, M. Dertke, E. Berry, A. Getreau, M. Washburn and J. Schmeidler (1988). "The Relationship Between Physical and Sexual Abuse and Illicit Drug Use: A Replication Among a New Sample of Youths Entering A Juvenile Detention Center." *International Journal of the Addictions* 23(11):1102-1123.

Donovan, J. and R. Jessor (1984). *The Structure of Problem Behavior in Adolescence and Young Adulthood, Research Report No. 10—Young Adult Follow-up Study*. Boulder, CO: Institute of Behavioral Science, University of Colorado.

Elliott, D. and D. Huizinga (1984). "The Relationship Between Delinquent Behavior and ADM Problems." Paper presented at the ADAMHA/OJJDP State of the Art Research Conference on Juvenile Offenders with Serious Drug, Alcohol and Mental Health Problems.

—— S. Ageton (1985). *Explaining Delinquency and Drug Use*. Beverly Hills, CA: Sage.

EMT Associates, Inc. (1988). *Final Report for the Evaluation of Juvenile Residential Group House and Day Support Contract Services, Report Submitted to Arizona Department of Corrections Purchase of Care Unit, May 1988*. Sacramento, CA.

Haggerty, K. P., E. A. Wells, J. M. Jenson, R. F. Catalano, and J. D. Hawkins (1989). "Delinquents and Drug Use: A Model Program for Community Reintegration." *Adolescence* 24(94):439-456.

Hartstone, E. and K. Hansen (1984). "The Violent Juvenile Offender: An Empirical Portrait." In *Violent Juvenile Offenders: An Anthology*, edited by R.A. Mathias et al. San Francisco, CA: National Council on Crime and Delinquency.

Hawkins, J. (1984). *Drug Abuse, Mental Health, and Delinquency: Summary of Proceedings of Practitioners' Conference on Juvenile Offenders with Serious Drug, Alcohol and Mental Health Problems*, Washington, DC: Office of Juvenile Justice and Delinquency Prevention, U.S. Department of Justice.

—— D. M. Lishner, J. M. Jenson and R. F. Catalano (1987). "Delinquents and Drugs: What the Evidence Suggests About Prevention and Treatment Programming." In *Youth at Risk for Substance Abuse*, edited by D. M. Lishner et al. Washington, DC: U.S. National Institute on Drug Abuse.

—— (1989). *The Crack/Violence Connection Within a Population of Hard-Core Adolescent Offenders, National Institute on Drug Abuse Technical Review on Drugs and Violence*. Rockville, MD: National Institute on Drug Abuse.

Inciardi, J.A. and A. Pottieger (in press). "Kids, Crack and Crime." *Journal of Drug Issues*.

Jessor, R. and S. Jessor (1977). *Problem Behavior and Psychosocial Development: A Longitudinal Study of Youth*. New York, NY: Academic Press.

Kandel, D., O. Simcha-Fagan and M. Davies (1986). "Risk Factors for Delinquency and Illicit Drug Use From Adolescence to Young Adulthood." *Journal of Drug Issues* 60(1):67-90.

Kohlberg, L., R. DeVries, G. Fein, D. Hart, R. Mayer, G. Noam, J. Snarey and J. Wertsch (1987). *Child Psychology and Childhood Education: A Cognitive-Developmental View*: New York, NY: Longman.

Kumpher, K. and J. DeMarsh (1986). "Family Environmental and Genetic Influences on Children's Future Chemical Dependency." *Journal of Children in Contemporary Society* (1/2):49-83.

Lipton, D., R. Martinson and J. Wilks (1975). *The Effectiveness of Correctional Treatment*. New York, NY: Praeger.

Leukefeld, C. and F. Tims (1988). "Compulsory Treatment: A Review of the Findings." In *Compulsory Treatment of Drug Abuse: Research and Clinical Practice, NIDA Research Monograph* 86, edited by C. Leukefeld and F. Tims. Washington DC: National Institute on Drug Abuse.

Miller, A. (1983). *For Your Own Good: Hidden Cruelty in Child-Rearing and the Roots of Violence*. New York, NY: Farrar, Straus, Giroux.

Missakian, E. and R. Mullen, (1974). "The Productive High School." Paper submitted to the Career Education Program of the U.S. National Institute of Education.

Nebelkopf, E. (1989). "Innovations in Drug Treatment and the Therapeutic Community." *International Journal of Therapeutic Communities* 10(1):39-52.

Pompi, K. (1989). Personal communication.

—— and J. Resnick (1987). "Retention of Court-Referred Adolescents and Young Adults in the Therapeutic Community." *American Journal of Drug and Alcohol Abuse* 13(3):309-325.

Rom-Rymer, J. R. (1981). "An Empirical Assessment of Mowrer's Theory of Psychopathology Applied to a Therapeutic Community." Doctoral dissertation, Florida State University. Ann Arbor, MI: University Microfilms International.

Schneider, P. (1989). *Promising Approaches for the Prevention, Intervention and Treatment of Illegal Drug and Alcohol Use Among Juveniles: Assessment Report*. (Research Report #1, prepared for the U.S. Office of Juvenile Justice and Delinquency Prevention.) Bethesda, MD: Pacific Institute for Research and Evaluation.

Speckart, G. and M. Anglin (1985). "Narcotics and Crime: An Analysis of Existing Evidence for a Casual Relationship." *Behavioral Sciences and the Law* 3(3):259-282.

Stevens, S., N. Arbiter and P. Glider. (1989) "Women Residents: Expanding Their Role to Increase Treatment Effectiveness in Substance Abuse Programs." *International Journal of the Addictions* 24(5):425-434.

Sugarman, B. (1987). "Structure, Variations and Context: A Sociological View of the Therapeutic Community." In *Therapeutic Communities for Addictions*, edited by G. DeLeon and J. T. Ziegenfuss. Springfield, IL: Charles C Thomas.

Turner, S. (1989). Personal communication at the "What Works" Conference, sponsored by the Narcotic and Drug Research Institutes, New York, NY.

Wexler, H., G. Falkin, D. Lipton, A. Rosenblum and L. Goodloe (1988). "A Model Prison Rehabilitation Program: An Evaluation of the 'Stay 'N Out' Therapeutic Community." (Unpublished report prepared for the U.S. National Institute on Drug Abuse) . New York, NY: Narcotic and Drug Research, Inc.

—— D. Lipton and K. Foster (1985). "Outcome Evaluation of a Prison Therapeutic Community for Substance Abuse Treatment: Preliminary Results." Paper presented at the American Society of Criminology Annual Meeting, San Diego, CA.

—— and B. Johnson (1988). *A System Strategy for Treating Cocaine/Heroin-Abusing Offenders in Custody*. Washington, DC: U.S. National Institute of Justice. (Issues and Practices in Criminal Justice series.)

—— and R. Williams (1986). "The Stay'N Out Therapeutic Community: Prison Treatment for Substance Abusers." *Journal of Psychoactive Drugs* 3:221-229.

U.S. National Institute of Justice (1989). "Drug Use Forecasting: January to March, 1989 Data." Washington, DC.

Yablonsky, L. (1989). *The Therapeutic Community: A Successful Approach for Treating Substance Abusers*. New York NY: Gardner.

Restitution and Community Work Service: Promising Core Ingredients for Effective Intensive Supervision Programming

by
Andrew R. Klein

The assumption that restitution and community service work are not appropriate sanctions for higher-risk offenders is totally unfounded. Restitution and community service make intensive supervision programs truly "intensive." The experience of Quincy, MA and other communities suggests that restitution and community service can help reduce recidivism and commitment rates, and allow even high-risk juvenile offenders to become contributors to the community.

INTRODUCTION

It has long been assumed within the field of juvenile justice, as well as by experts outside it, that monetary restitution and/or unpaid community work service programs—indeed any alternative to institutionalization—should be confined to less serious, nonviolent delinquents who commit less serious offenses. This belief is rooted in two assumptions. First, more serious, chronic or violent offenders must be confined in order to protect the public and are therefore unavailable for such programs. Second, even if available, such delinquents would surely fail at first opportunity.

Many restitution/community work service programs reinforce this maxim by carefully screening out any but first-time or less serious offenders. Once these programs have established themselves and have developed positive reputations based on high completion rates, they are reluctant to jeopardize this success by admitting hard-core delinquents who are much more prone to failure.

Like many commonly shared beliefs in the juvenile justice system, the assumption that participation in restitution and/or community work service programs is not appropriate for higher risk delinquents is totally unfounded. In fact, these programs form an excellent component for community-based supervision of high-risk defendants. Restitution/community work service make intensive supervision programs truly "intensive." Whether the delinquent be put to work in an unpaid job to perform community service or in a paid job to earn money to pay his victim restitution, both activities provide an invaluable tool for supervising offenders in the community. Both provide work, which constitutes a constructive, productive and cheap means to incapacitate the juvenile without institutionalizing him or her. Free time is drastically reduced, and offender control is correspondingly increased. Further, restitution and community work service programs help break down offender rationalization and develop basic job/work skills, which are essential if the offender's risk of recidivism is to be reduced. These programs, in effect, create "community cells" for high-risk delinquents (see, for example, Kramer, 1986). Unlike more costly detention cells, however, these cells allow young offenders to become more competent at becoming citizens, not more proficient miscreants.

As Armstrong (1980) has so eloquently written, restitution and community work service are "sanctions for all seasons," for repeat as well as first-time offenders, for violent as well as property offenders. Tightly administered restitution/community work service programs can minimize recidivism during the course of the program and after it is completed. Finally, high-risk, chronic and violent juveniles will successfully complete such programs when systematically enforced by the referring court in concert with program staff (Schneider, 1982).

For the same reasons, many programs calling themselves "intensive supervision" that are not built around restitution/community work service operate at a distinct disadvantage. Many without these components, in fact, are only "intensive" compared to traditional probation supervision, which may be quite minimal. For example, the standard for "maximum" supervision of highest risk juveniles in the Massachusetts probation service is one contact every two weeks.

Of course, given their poor-to-nonexistent work skills and job histories—coupled with short attention spans, an inability to accept authority, and possibly a penchant for violence—high-risk delinquents cannot simply be placed into traditional restitution/community work service programs. Nor can existing restitution/community work service programs expect such offenders to perform like other offenders. Special work sites must be selected. School dropouts with no appreciable work skills and no experience in the work arena require elementary work assignments. One strategy to achieve this goal is to organize them into small, tightly supervised work crews. In this context, large doses of organized community work service should be performed before offenders are allowed to work in individual community placements, much less let loose in the private sector.

Another factor of considerable importance is the need for programs to expect that many high-risk offenders will fail in the first several attempts. Strategies must be developed for dealing promptly and effectively with these initial failures, before they are allowed to escalate. If failures are identified and dealt with quickly, eventual success can be achieved. Progress with this population is incremental in nature. Successful programs must incorporate a system of rewards and punishments for good and bad performance. As the high-risk juvenile's performance improves, controls can be loosened and vice versa. By responding incrementally and progressively to both bad and good behavior, programs can avoid the ultimate sanction of institutionalization while insuring an eventual, acceptable completion rate.

National studies have revealed that completion rates for competently administered juvenile restitution/community work service programs across the U.S. run about 80% (Schneider et al., 1982). This holds consistently true for juveniles in rural as well as urban areas, for whites as well as minorities, and for first offenders as well as chronic offenders with an average of six prior felony convictions (that is, "felonies" if they had been tried as adults). The range among all the varying groups is markedly narrow. The rate of successful completion, for example, varies from a high of 90% for youths with no prior offenses to a low of 70% for youths with five or more priors.

There are alternative means to create "community cells," which many intensive supervision programs employ. These range from programs that make juveniles spend prolonged periods under house arrest, called home confinement, to programs that fill up their days with assorted group and individual counseling, and even group cooking/dining experiences (crime control through culinary arts?). As researchers have suggested, the intensity of the supervision, as opposed to its content, is probably more important in reducing recidivism. According to Wilson, studies have found that "how strictly the youths were supervised, rather than what therapeutic programs were available, had the greatest effect on the recidivism rate..." (1981:13). He went on to note that "if one measures offense *frequency*, some kinds of programs involving fairly high degrees of restrictiveness and supervision may make some difference" (Wilson, 1981:16). However, restitution/community work service programs have distinct advantages over other types of programs in respect to occupying high-risk juveniles' time. They address certain basic requirements of the justice system that are often missing in many other programs.

First, such programs enable victims to receive restitution. Victims of crime deserve to be reimbursed for their damages, losses and injuries. The costs to the little old lady who is mugged is the same whether the mugger is a first offender or a tenth. The community in which the crime occurs deserves to be paid back literally through fines or cost assessments, or figuratively through community work service. Crime costs everyone, whether committed by a shoplifter or a rapist.

The act of paying back also confronts the juvenile offender with his or her offense. It helps bring home the results of the act, the fact that another person or persons may have suffered as a result. The juvenile may not realize, for example, the value of a stolen or damaged item until he or she has to go to work and pay the costs of replacing or repairing it. The victim is personalized, making it more difficult for the juvenile to dismiss him or her as irrelevant. Some programs encourage victims to meet with their offenders to ensure the fullest effects of this aspect of restitution programs.

Second, restitution/community work service programs hold offenders accountable for their behavior in the community. It is no less important to hold a repeat offender accountable than a first offender, a violent offender or a property offender. Ironically, juvenile corrections commits much time and resources to insure that trivial and less serious offenders are held accountable through restitution/community service programs. It is equally compelling to hold more serious juvenile offenders similarly accountable. Unlike institutionalization, usually reserved for these more serious offenders, restitution/ community service programs do not do something "to" or "for" defendants, but make them do something for themselves and others.

Third, programs teach juveniles skills, ranging from reading and writing to learning how to secure and hold a job. Correctional programs that allow delinquents to leave supervision with as many deficits as when they took them in are, at best, postponing the delinquent's criminal career. As a number of experts have argued, in addition to "accountability," competency development" should be an underlying aim of the juvenile justice system (see, for example, Maloney, Armstrong and Romig, 1987). Some programs have developed special educational and training components to augment skill development, ranging from general equivalency diploma (GED) tutoring to job apprenticeships.

Fourth, "restitution works"—as proclaimed by the Charleston, SC juvenile program in its poster depicting a youngster stooped in labor. Extensive research indicates that compared to their peers who are not required to pay restitution and/or perform community work service, offenders so ordered recidivate at the same rate or, more frequently, at a lower rate. This includes juveniles given counseling, placed on probation or even sentenced to detention for short periods of time. Unlike findings about most criminal justice programs and their effectiveness, the research concluding that restitution works has employed experimental designs that randomly assigned matched delinquents into the different correctional programs (see Schneider, 1986).

The results are not difficult to understand. It stands to reason that offenders who learn essential work skills and discipline, break down rationalization of their criminal behavior, and come to have empathy for their victims will fare better than offenders who simply see a counselor periodically, are policed by probation officers to avoid negative acts, or are locked up with peers in secure detention.

In 1985 the Quincy (MA) District Court probation department developed a juvenile intensive supervision program that built upon its highly acclaimed restitution/community work service program named Earn-It (Klein, 1982), begun a decade earlier by the author and the court's First Justice, Albert L. Kramer. The court serves an urban area of approximately 300,000, contiguous to the south side of Boston. While the court has jurisdiction over both adults and juveniles, the program took only defendants sentenced in the juvenile session. All were between ages 15½ and 17. The program was initially funded by a small state block grant that provided the probation department with two additional probation aides. Both served alternately as work crew supervisors and surveillance officers. Between them, they worked seven days a week, 24 hours a day. The staff-to-client ratio was 7.5 to 1. The program was designed to handle 15 high-risk delinquents at any one time. That figure represented about one-fifth of the court's juvenile probation caseload, including every juvenile probationer who scored in the top half of those judged to represent "maximum" risk for recidivism on the validated state risk predictor scale. The predicted rate of recidivism for offenders who scored similarly was almost 90% (Brown et al., 1984). Over the course of the first two and a half years of the program, seven juveniles were admitted to the program who had previously been committed to the state juvenile correctional department until age 18. (The court had revised and revoked their commitments on condition that they participate and complete the program. Several other juveniles were offered this sentence revision but refused it, preferring to wait until they could be released outright on home parole.) Another dozen were admitted after the court had found them in violation of their probation and permitted them to enter the program in lieu of commitment.

The Quincy program shares, perhaps, many typical aspects of an intensive supervision program for high-risk juveniles that revolves around restitution/community work service programming. However, all programs must adapt to local environments and are, therefore, unique in detail. For this reason, although the Quincy program is used as a generic model for the following discussion, it should be understood that it will be discussed in broad terms.

DEFINING HIGH RISK

As any honest practitioner will admit, there are two sure ways to guarantee that any intensive supervision program succeeds. The first is to define success loosely, i.e., the juvenile is not transferred to adult court for a new crime while under supervision. The second is to "cream," i.e., admit into the program only the most manageable cases. These may include juveniles who have committed a serious act but have no history of delinquent behavior and are unlikely to commit any new offenses.

If a program is, however, truly targeting high-risk offenders, there are a number of risk prediction scales available to project a defendant's likelihood for reoffending. These scales tend to be less accurate for younger juveniles who obviously have shorter track records to measure. These kinds of scales are useful because they will guard against programs expending great amounts of time and money on juveniles who probably will not reoffend anyway. Commonly used risk scales are generally based on regression analysis of defendants already determined to be recidivists. Researchers determine retrospectively what distinct factors separated recidivists from their non-recidivating peers. It has been shown that individual factors found to correlate with but not cause recidivism may vary from one jurisdiction to another. For example, in some communities, gang membership may be a predictive factor for reoffending. In others, this factor may not be relevant because gang activity is minimal. However, a substantial number of risk factors have been discovered to predict high rates of recidivism among juvenile offenders across the country (see, for example, Klein, 1988).

The Quincy program used the twice-validated state prediction scale developed by the Massachusetts Commissioner of Probation, substantially borrowed from the Wisconsin scale developed almost a decade earlier (Cochran et al., 1981). Any juvenile who scored below ten was rated as highest risk, with an expected recidivism rate of almost 90%, contrasted with an average rate of 30% for all juveniles placed on probation in Massachusetts. The same data also revealed that those juveniles who do recidivate do so quickly. Almost one-third do so within 30 days of being placed on probation, and almost all do so within six months (Brown et al., 1984).

PROGRAM THEORY AND PRINCIPLES

Not only do risk classification scales help insure that intensive programs are admitting appropriate juveniles, but they help to define program content. Program activities that mitigate individual risk factors will mitigate recidivism. For example, programs that stop abusive drinking or keep juveniles away from poor peer influences will be more successful than programs that don't. Mitigating risk factors should be the guiding principle of any intensive supervision program. While programs cannot change history, they can alter the defendant's environment and change his or her routine so as to reduce risk of future criminal involvement.

Simply increasing juvenile/probation officer contact does not necessarily accomplish this goal. Mandatory restitution/community service work, however, can dramatically alter the high-risk offender's daily environment, change his associations, cut down his access to drugs and alcohol, and more. By putting the defendant to work—either in a paid or unpaid job—coupled with nightly curfews and mandatory school attendance during the day, the level of supervision becomes almost total. School, work and home become the "community cell" that keeps the offender off street comers and out of other people's cars and houses. Unlike high-priced institutional cells, these community cells are cheap, available and not overcrowded.

Creating the community cells is only the first step. Recidivism data reveal that those who reoffend do so quickly upon being placed on probation. This finding argues for tight monitoring, especially during the initial phases of intensive supervision programs. In short, the programs should be highly structured and intense, especially in their initial phases. This can be contrasted to traditional probation supervision routines, in which it often takes several weeks for the probation officer to even be assigned his probationer. For this reason, intensive programs should be sequential, beginning at maximum intensity and then loosening as the defendant's behavior warrants.

Unlike institutional cells, there are no locks on community cells. The need for active, even proactive, supervision is imperative. A strategy must be developed to monitor each component of the community cell. In the school component, the program must establish a liaison with the school truant officer, guidance department, or teachers to ensure that a juvenile is attending each and every day. The program must know as soon as a youth skips school, or is suspended or expelled. In the community work service component, the program must be organized with work crews under the direct supervision of program personnel to ensure that the juvenile reports on time and remains on the job. While individual juveniles may subsequently be placed individually at different work sites or be helped to obtain paid private jobs, they must initially be directly monitored by the program. Work crew supervisors can also perform random tests for alcohol and/or drug use that other sponsors or employers cannot or would not do. The program should ensure that its crew leaders are trained in administering such tests. Program staff must also enforce home curfews, working cooperatively with parents when appropriate. There are many means to enforcing curfews, ranging from random phone calls and periodic home visits to periodic police patrol pass-through and electronic monitoring.

Unlike traditional probation supervision that occurs Monday through Fridays, 9 a.m. to 5 p.m., community cells must be supervised 24 hours a day, seven days a week. Many crimes, after all, are committed after dark and during weekends, after regular probation office hours. Ironically, juveniles also commit a large number of daytime home burglaries when they are supposed to be in school.

Most high-risk juveniles have been through the system repeatedly. They have been counseled to death, yelled at, warned, and threatened again and again. They have learned how to look contrite before the judge and feign remorse for their behavior. These offenders have not, however, learned how to change their behavior. Intensive supervision programs must ignore the juveniles' attitudes and concentrate on their behavior. Objectively measuring the response to counseling is problematic; attitude improvement does not necessarily translate into improvement of behavior in the community. Therefore, most intensive supervision programs must rely on enforcing other elements, such as school attendance and home curfew, that can be measured objectively. Unlike other intensive programs, the core aspects of a restitution/community work service program are also measurable. The defendant either does or does not work and pay restitution. The beauty of restitution/community work service is that it can be based totally on behavior and performance that is easily measured.

When the juvenile's behavior does not meet expectations, the program must respond appropriately and quickly. Judge Kramer has likened the response to a tourniquet that is tightened to discourage noncompliance and loosened to reward compliance (see, for example, Kramer, 1986). Sanctioning is progressive and incremental. Others have described Kramer's "tourniquet sentencing" as "progressive discomfiture." As high-risk offenders can be expected to have a higher probability of failure, programs should be designed to respond at the first act of noncompliance—the first no-show on the job, the first curfew violation, etc. The sanction must be real, but proportional. This strategy may keep the offender so busy making up for technical violations that he or she has neither the time nor the energy to commit new crimes. The sanction—whether it be increased hours of community work service, lowered curfews, house arrest on weekends or short-term detention—also has a traditional deterrent effect.

Research conducted by the Massachusetts Commissioner of Probation has documented an absolute correlation between technical probation violations and subsequent recidivism (Brown et al., 1984). In other words, probationers who fail to report as ordered, pay their restitution, or perform their work service are publicly declaring their intent to commit a new offense shortly. If programs fail to respond to the technical violation, they are saying, in effect, "go ahead."

Two possible mistakes are commonly made by intensive supervision programs in the area of enforcement of conditions. They tend to rush too quickly to use their ultimate sanction, institutionalization, or wait too long to sanction negative behavior. Both extremes set high-risk offenders up for failure: The former sets them up for almost immediate commitments; the latter, for eventual commitment by inadvertently encouraging bad behavior. Programs must develop a range of increasingly severe sanctions allowing them to deal with negative behavior immediately; institutionalization is always available as a last resort.

Unlike programs that rely on counseling or increased probation office visits, restitution/community work service projects have built in a whole range of such intermediate sanctions. While the former must resort to punitive measures such as curfew restrictions or home confinement, the latter can impose more constructive sanctions that build onto the juvenile's core program. Hours of community work service, for example, can be added to a noncomplying defendant's sentence. Interest on unpaid restitution can be tacked onto the initial restitution order.

Finally, as much as possible, programs should utilize existing restitution/community work service resources. This obviously reduces costs considerably. If a work-site already accepts community work service referrals, for example, it might accept an entire work crew of high-risk juveniles, especially if the crew comes with its own supervisor. If the court already has a bookkeeping system to account for and disperse restitution payments, the additional accounts of high-risk juveniles will probably not be noticed.

These were the guiding principles adopted by the Quincy program. It sought to incapacitate offenders in the community through restitution/community work service obligations, coupled with school attendance and nightly curfews. Second, the program was organized sequentially, with the initial sequence being very highly structured, and later stages gradually loosened as offender's performance warranted. Third, all phases were tightly monitored, based on the delinquents' behavior, not attitude. Sanctions were imposed immediately for any program violations, utilizing the concept of tourniquet sentencing. Finally, wherever possible, the program used existing court restitution/community work service resources.

QUINCY PROGRAM DESCRIPTION

Upon being placed on probation or released to probation from a state juvenile facility, defendants are screened for high risk. As a condition of their probation or release, they are ordered to perform a minimum of 250 hours of community work service and pay any restitution determined. The maximum number of hours ordered was 1,000. Average restitution orders come to $350. In addition, the probationers are ordered to attend school and abide by curfews set by the program. If suspended, expelled or caught skipping school, they are required to report for community work service until re-enrolled. Abstinence from alcohol and drugs is required, as is submission to periodic urine and saliva testing programs to enforce same.

The program is organized into four phases. In the first phase, which lasts approximately three weeks, youths' community work service schedules vary depending upon their individual schedules and whether they are in school or working. Most perform community work service after school, initially from 2:30 p.m. to 6:30 p.m. during the week and from 8:30 a.m. to 4:30 p.m. on Saturdays. Initially, curfews begin at 7 p.m. On Sundays, the juveniles are confined to their homes. The second phase lasts from one to two months. It proceeds like the first, except the juveniles are given a little more freedom.

They are excused from two afternoons per week of community work service, and curfews are relaxed several hours. Appropriate juveniles are transferred from the work crews to individual placements in the community at nonprofit or government agencies. This procedure allows slots to open for the next group of high-risk delinquents who need to be placed on work crews. In addition, juveniles are given community work service credit for attending various counseling/skill development or self-help programs. For example, depending upon their individual needs, they might be allowed to attend Alcoholics Anonymous (AA) meetings, a counseling program, and job training and GED classes for credit. This gives juveniles a positive reward for complying with court-ordered treatment.

The third phase lasts one month. Community work service is further reduced. Juveniles who are not already employed obtain help in locating salaried jobs after school. If not attending school, full-time work is secured. If unemployable due to age, penchant for violence, instability or complete absence of work skills, juveniles receive stipends for additional community work service. As a result, even these youth are able to begin earning the money necessary to satisfy court-ordered restitution or other monetary assessments. Payment plans are negotiated based on earnings. Curfews are eliminated, and juveniles are assigned regular (i.e., nonprogram staff) probation officers who see them weekly.

The final phase consists of the juvenile performing only one day a week of community work service until the original court order is completed. Unless employed on that day, the youth usually perform their service on Saturdays. Payments of restitution are required until the victims are fully reimbursed in accordance with the court order. Monitoring of both payments and community work service is taken over by the juveniles' regular probation officers. This phase lasts as long as necessary depending upon the amount of restitution still owed, but the community work service obligation usually ends after the first month.

If the juvenile performs perfectly, the entire program can be completed in less than five months. However, almost all violate their conditions at some point, requiring them to be held back in whatever phase of the program they are then in. Due to the seriousness of their violations, some are demoted to a previous phase. As a result, many defendants remain on curfews for several months and may not advance from the second to the third phase. Many juveniles end up completing substantially more than the 250 hours of community work service originally ordered. They are ordered to do more hours as a result of sanctions imposed for various program violations. For example, if a juvenile in phase two commits a new but minor offense, such as minor in possession of alcohol, he may be ordered to begin the first phase again. The average high-risk juvenile takes more than six months to complete all four phases, but not all participants complete the program.

Program Components

Community Work Service

Community work service—also known as community service, community restitution, symbolic restitution, and community service orders—is not a new concept. Historians document town drunks in colonial Massachusetts being sentenced to chop wood on the Boston Commons so that they may be of "good aberrance" (Weston, 1957). Community work service did not, however, gain widespread acceptance in this country until the early 1970s, when the U.S. Supreme Court outlawed the practice of sentencing indigent defendants to jail for nonpayments of fines. In *Tate v. Short* (U.S. Supreme Court, 1971), the high court held that offenders could not be imprisoned for nonpayment unless the court found the nonpayment to be willful.

As there has been much written on the topic, the following discussion will focus primarily on community work service as it relates to intensive supervision of high-risk juveniles. Supplementary references, however, are widely available (see, for example, Klein, 1988; Schneider, 1985).

Community work service programs pursue two basic strategies in putting offenders to work in the community. They place offenders in nonprofit agencies either singly or in groups. Generally, individual offenders are referred for supervision by the receiving agency. Groups of offenders are organized into work crews, usually supervised by program staff but doing work for a community agency. Some agencies may agree to supervise these crews themselves. In either case, the work is usually basic, depending upon the skills of the offenders assigned.

For high-risk offenders, particularly those who resist authority and have a penchant for physical expression (not to mention oral profanity), placement on work crews would appear to be preferable. Once a juvenile has shown requisite self-control, he can be moved from the highly structured crew to more loosely supervised individual placements in agencies. Agencies that may be reluctant to supervise high-risk juveniles may be willing to accept them if they come with their own supervisor. In addition, work crews can tackle more ambitious work assignments than individual volunteers. In Hennepin County, MN, for example, the juvenile court arranges for its crews to take elderly shut-ins on sleigh rides during the winter, a task requiring groups of volunteers.

Quincy crews are assigned a variety of tasks, such as repainting a local detoxification center, putting up thousands of yards of heavy plywood barriers to keep drifting snow from ramps for the handicapped at a state hospital school, and policing miles of public beaches in the summer. Transportation is arranged by the court. Defendants have to get to the court each day but are then transported to the daily work sites in two vans donated by several local businesses.

Initially, the work crews in the Quincy program are separated from the rest of the court's community work service crews. Supervisors, however, have discovered that mixed crews of high- and low-risk offenders function more smoothly. Not only are older and more mature crew members easier to handle, but they also help exert pressure on the high-risk juveniles to comply with program rules and regulations. The former are anxious to get the work done and go home, and they make this clear to the juveniles, who are less committed to the work ethic. Crews are kept small, averaging around ten per supervisor. If the crews are limited to high-risk offenders alone, they are half that size.

There is no magic to achieving positive results with work crews. While offender crews may not be neat, they are fast. Relying on the host agency to establish work assignments for the day is to invite running out of work early and being stuck with a crew of rambunctious juveniles. Many agencies assume the crews will work at the same pace as older, paid employees. As a result, crew leaders always have back-up work available. If the crews work all day, either lunch is provided or defendants are told in advance to bring their own. To release crews mid-day with the expectations that they will 1) return after lunch or 2) return sober and drug-free is tempting fate too much.

While attendance and performance are relatively easy to monitor when the juveniles are assigned to crews, these requirements are more difficult to accomplish when youths are placed under the supervision of separate agencies in the community. The program must rely on monitoring reports from the host agencies. To minimize misunderstandings and facilitate communications, program staff must contact these agencies daily to check on their referrals. Staff must visit the agencies periodically for two reasons: to make the juvenile aware that he or she is still under close scrutiny, and to let the host agency know that it has not been abandoned by the program. This backup will enable host agencies to tolerate better the problems posed by those juveniles who inevitably fail.

The Quincy work crew experience has been surprisingly uneventful. Juveniles usually fail to show up for work, rather than fail on the job. The crews assemble at 8:15 a.m. and 2:30 p.m. Work crew supervisors are quick to fire from the crews any juvenile who misbehaves. He or she is then brought back to court for a subsequent hearing on violation of probation. During the first three years of the program there was only one physical assault, involving a juvenile taking a swing at a crew supervisor. (He missed.) The program has had to contend with several minor accidents. Each crew supervisor is equipped with a well-stocked first-aid kit with plenty of bandages.

The potential for problems should, however, not be ignored. To protect themselves and their charges, community work service programs have developed four strategies for dealing with accidents and liability. First, they purchase a blanket policy for all participants. These usually cover up to $25,000 for medical bills at a cost of one or two dollars per crew member per year. (CIMA, one national insurance company based in Washington DC, has developed a special plan just for "court-referred volunteers." Unlike more general volunteer policies, the policy does not cover liability if juveniles injure a third party while doing their work service.) Second, they require youths to waive any liability against the program for injury or accidents. Although some programs have been requiring waivers for years, no cases have as yet arisen to test the legality of these waivers. Third, they have convinced state legislators to enact laws whereby offenders who perform community work service are considered state employees for purposes of workers' compensation. Fourth, they rely on the host agencies' existing coverage for volunteers or ignore the entire question. As a juvenile judge in Minnesota once reassured at a conference on restitution. "Don't worry, kids heal quickly." To date, legal researchers have as yet to find any significant cases specifying the exact parameters of liability in the area of community work service (Van Keulen, 1988; del Carmen, 1986).

The Quincy program purchased its own blanket policy, charging each juvenile one dollar to pay for it. (The price has recently been raised to three dollars due to increasing policy costs.) The policy covers 50 slots per day for a year. As long as no more than 50 offenders are placed each day, all are covered. Over the last decade, the court's community work service program, placing almost 1,000 juveniles and adults per year, has only had to make three claims on its policy: a pair of broken glasses, a broken arm and a severely lacerated wrist.

Monetary Restitution

Restitution appeared in the first written criminal code in human history, the Code of Hammurabi, in 1100 B.C. If a man was convicted of stealing an ox, for example, he had to give it back along with an additional nine oxes. If the ox belonged to a palace or a god (a temple), he had to give it back twentyfold. Restitution lost favor in the Middle Ages with the rise of the state under the king's central control. Kings literally stole the restitution formerly due victims and pocketed it for themselves as fines. Despite early use of restitution in the U.S., it slowly disappeared in most criminal and juvenile courts until the late 1970s, when the Justice Department's Office of Juvenile Justice and Delinquency Prevention poured more than $30 million into demonstration grants to promote its use as a disposition for juvenile offenders.

The rise of victim groups such as Mothers Against Drunk Driving also successfully pressed many state legislatures and the Congress to enact victim rights laws. Many of these included provisions for mandatory restitution to compensate victims for crime-related damages or injuries. Several jurisdictions have gone even further, enacting laws mandating double damages for victims (Washington Revised Code, 1986; Utah Code, 1985). While much has been written on the topic of monetary restitution and its various applications (see, for example, Klein, 1988), the following discussion will focus on its relationship to intensive supervision for high-risk juveniles.

The first task facing any restitution program is to determine the restitution order. There are three widely used methods. First, victims are told to obtain bills and cost estimates for all damaged or missing goods or medical bills, much as they would to file an insurance claim. Second, the judge is able to determine the order based on testimony before him or her in court. Third, the victim and offender sit down together and negotiate a settlement.

It is the last method, often called "victim-offender mediation," that holds most promise for high-risk offenders. Confrontation with the victim is a particularly effective way to break down offender rationalization. And, as previously suggested, rationalization is a characteristic of high-risk offenders, who recognize no victimization other than their own. Rarely will they admit what they have done, much less take responsibility for the consequences of their actions. Victim-offender meetings can dramatically impress upon such offenders the full impact of their behavior. Many jurisdictions, particularly in the Midwest, have established Victim-Offender Reconciliation Projects (VORPs) geared to promoting these meetings. The VORP approach was pioneered in Kitchener, CAN by probation officers and members of a local Mennonite Church in the early 1970s. (For a discussion of VORPs, see Umbreit, 1985; see also Wright and Galaway, 1989.)

High-risk juveniles in the Quincy program are required to meet with their victims if the victims consent. Most victims, tactfully approached by program staff, are willing. Although they want to help determine their restitution orders, most victims are more anxious to tell their victimizers what the crime's impact has been. Some want to know why and how the crime had been perpetrated. Others want to tell the juveniles that they had gotten off too easy and deserved to be put away. A probation staffer, trained in mediation, sits in during all meetings to set the groundrules and facilitate dialogue between offender and victim. The program has found that almost every victim-offender meeting yields beneficial and often dramatic results. Cases involving physical assaults are particularly dramatic. Often both victims and offenders end up in tears (Schneider, 1985).

For the defendant's bank account, there is no difference between the payment of restitution and a fine. Both represent money taken from the defendant and sent elsewhere. By meeting the victim, however, the defendant can be made to understand better the underlying meaning of restitution and what the impact of the crime was on the other person, who the juvenile finds to be like him or herself, or his or her parents or grandparents. Victim-offender meetings also can produce nonmonetary restitution agreements. Once the victim realizes that the offender is unemployed, he may offer to allow the juvenile to perform certain tasks in lieu of payment of restitution. For example, one set of victims agreed to having a juvenile help them paint their house. In another case, a gas station owner agreed to allow the juvenile to pump gas for several weeks after school to work off the price of the tires he had stolen. In several cases, the juveniles revealed during the meetings that they had or knew where stolen property was and arranged for its return to its true owners. Payment plans are also negotiated at victim-offender meetings. In Quincy, victims were told that it would take a while for the offenders to complete the first phase of the community work service schedule before they would be able to begin to pay the victims back. After meeting with the offenders, the victims understood that when payments are made, they will be made weekly and in modest sums.

If the juvenile offenders' body language and avoidance of eye contact with the victims is any indication, they appear to find the meetings painful. However, research finds this approach to be quite successful. National studies of tens of thousands of juveniles in restitution programs across the country revealed that juveniles whose restitution was determined through victim-offender meetings had a higher payment rate than those whose restitution was determined through the two other methods described earlier (Schneider et al., 1985). In addition, the juveniles whose restitution was determined through victim-offender meetings had a lower recidivism rate (about 10%) than their peers.

Once the juvenile has been placed in a job slot and is earning money, payment is made either directly to the victim or through the program. The former method encourages direct victim contact. However, it is more difficult for the program to monitor direct payments. For large programs, payments through the program may be a necessity. Some require payments through the program until the final payment, which is made directly to the victim, either in person or through the mail, with a letter accompanying it from the offender.

While every court can point to at least one or two cases where ingenious juveniles managed to destroy hundreds of thousands of dollars worth of property or cause that much in injuries, most restitution orders are more modest. Crime statistics reveal that the average property loss of most crime is several hundred dollars (see, for example, U.S. Department of Justice, 1985). Most personal injuries are even less. In fact, the problem with basing an intensive supervision program around financial restitution alone, without supplementary orders of community work service, is that the amounts of restitution ordered are too small to impose sufficiently punitive sanctions. As a result, once juveniles obtain even part-time jobs, they can earn the necessary amounts to pay back their victims in full fairly quickly. Therefore, the addition of community work service orders is necessary to insure the juvenile is kept sufficiently engaged in program activities.

There are three basic strategies that restitution programs pursue in order to put offenders to work to pay back their victims. They train the juvenile in how to find full- or part- time work, train employers in how to hire juvenile offenders, and provide subsidized work for the juveniles. The Quincy program utilized all three approaches. For juveniles with requisite skills, program staff teach them how to read the want ads, interview for jobs and so on. In other cases, the program maintains a job bank of employers willing to hire offenders temporarily for as long as it takes the offenders to pay back their victims. This aspect of the court's restitution program is cosponsored by the Earn-It program, discussed earlier, in which local businesses "donate" paid hours of work to be filled by court referrals. This arrangement reassures the businesses that they are not rewarding offenders by giving them jobs, but simply providing them with hours of work so that victims can be repaid. However, these businesses frequently retain offenders after they have completed their restitution orders. Businesses also provide references, which help the youth subsequently find permanent jobs on their own. Finally, the program maintains a small stipend fund so that it can pay juveniles directly for additional community work service if they are unable to secure paying jobs. Similarly, the state legislatures in Ohio and Iowa allocate monies to county restitution programs for stipend programs. Other jurisdictions raise stipend funds through business contributions and grants. Several jurisdictions in California, Oregon and Pennsylvania are able to employ offenders in work crews funded through contracts with parks and recreation, highway departments and conservation agencies.

The restitution collection rate in Quincy for intensive supervision cases was almost 75%. It would have been higher but for a few juveniles who committed new serious crimes quickly and were institutionalized before paying any restitution. The overall collection rate for the court is over 80% of all ordered payments.

Other Program Components

In addition to community work service and restitution, there are several other major components necessary for an intensive supervision probation that the Quincy program shares with most others. They include nightly curfews, school surveillance, drug and alcohol screening, and various treatment programs. All are made much easier by the restitution/community work service aspect of the overall program.

Daily toil, whether paid or unpaid, tires juveniles and contributes to nightly sleep. This makes enforcement of curfews easier. If the penalty for not attending school is additional daily work crews, school attendance is encouraged. Quincy teachers expressed amazement and, frankly, consternation when one of the high-risk juveniles attending their school not only passed all subjects one term, but actually got some "Bs." Upon investigation, they learned that thanks to the intensive supervision program the juvenile in question was actually attending school consistently and doing his homework for the first time. He was doing his homework because the nightly curfews were keeping him trapped at home, and he had nothing else to do most nights. This particular juvenile completed 1,000 hours of community work service during the program.

As previously mentioned, work crew supervisors can administer periodic, random urine or saliva tests to enforce the ban on drugs and alcohol. Although such tests can be performed by probation officers or others, work crew supervisors see the juveniles six days a week, and get to know them quickly and well. The supervisors can readily determine when the juvenile is using drugs or alcohol. In the Quincy Program, "dirty" urines (or presence of alcohol) led to immediate probation revocation hearings and further sanctioning.

While many doubt the efficacy of mandated treatment programs, all agree that individuals cannot benefit from treatment if they do not attend. By offering the youth community work service credit to attend treatment programs, they can be encouraged to attend. Often the carrot is as effective as the stick. Apart from participation in individual and family counseling programs and attendance at AA meetings and other self-help groups, one should not forget that work itself may be a tremendous treatment program. Putting juveniles to work is therapeutic. In Quincy, many were put to work for the first time and had never regularly witnessed their fathers working. Work brought them pride as well as stability in the community.

Program Enforcement

All conditions of the high-risk juvenile's program participation must be spelled out in detail, including daily schedules for both weekdays and weekends for each phase. Records of attendance and compliance must be carefully maintained, covering school attendance, community work service, curfews, restitution payments and the like. It must be carefully explained to juveniles that program staff have no flexibility in enforcing all conditions and that any violations will result in further court hearings. The judge alone, not program staff, may then consider pertinent excuses when appropriate.

Usually, two types of hearings are used to enforce program participation, depending upon the specific jurisdiction. They are either probation revocation hearings, where the juvenile is accused of violating specific probation conditions, or contempt, where the youth is accused of violating specific court orders. While offenders have some due process rights in either situation, they are not afforded the full panoply of rights due them before an adjudication of delinquency.

Program records documenting the failure may suffice to substantiate noncompliance, although some jurisdictions may require a witness from the program to testify. Two U.S. Supreme Court cases—*Morrissey v. Brewer* (1972) and *Gangon v. Scarpelli* (1973)—set the parameters for these hearings. Standards for upholding a finding of violation range from "slight evidence" and "preponderance" in most states, to "reasonably satisfied" in the remaining ones.

Unlike traditional counseling or office visit probation routines, intensive supervision programs based on restitution/community service work have built-in rewards and punishments for behavior. If juveniles violate program rules, they can be refused credit for that day's work and be given an additional day of community work, or have their curfew extended. Alternatively and perhaps more important, if youths do well, they can be rewarded by subtracting a day of community work or limiting curfews. Rewarding good behavior makes it easier to punish bad. The better juveniles behave, the quicker they pass from one phase of the program to the less restrictive next phase, and vice versa. Penalties for technical violations committed during phase one are stiffer than those committed in phase two and so on. Some programs, with a similar system of rewards and punishments, promote a juvenile from one phase to a less restrictive phase only when he or she has acquired sufficient credits for a "good day" (one with no program violations).

More serious violations call for more serious responses. These can range from the imposition of court costs and weekend home confinement to short periods of detention in an institution. Hennepin County, MN has developed a program called "Quick Stop" that has been adopted for use by the Quincy Court. Juveniles who substantially violate program conditions are confined for the subsequent weekend. They are released the following Monday to try again. Unlike longer-term lock up, juveniles who are confined for the weekend are not classified and are not allowed to mix with the rest of the detention center's population. The weekends are consequently long and lonely. Repeat violators can be held in detention longer. However, there is an upper limit beyond which it may be fruitless to go. Not all juveniles, no matter what is tried, will ultimately succeed. The Quincy program did allow several youths who had been committed for repeated violations to be released six months later to try again. This was after the court determined that their early release would not jeopardize public safety and the juveniles seemed determined to try again.

Given recidivism statistics that reveal that juveniles who recidivate do so shortly after being released on probation (Brown et al., 1984), it is important to enforce program rules tightly, particularly during the first phase of the program. In view of other studies that document the correlation between technical violations with subsequent criminal ones (Brown et al., 1984), it is also important to respond to technical violations effectively by confronting the youth immediately and returning him or her to court if appropriate for increased sanctions. Technical violations should serve as red flags, warning the program that appropriate action is warranted.

Program Staffing

Intensive supervision programs built around restitution/community work service require some specialized staffing or regular staff with specialized assignments. They need work crew supervisors, surveillance officers and community/business liaisons. The remaining positions or duties can be handled by most probation or existing community corrections staff.

1. *Surveillance Officer*. The Georgia Intensive Probation Program begun in the early 1980s was one of the first to introduce full-time "surveillance officers," differentiated from probation officers supervising probationers (see, for example, Klein, 1988). The Georgia program assigned one probation officer and one surveillance officer for each probationer. The former performed counseling and traditional supervisory functions; the latter rigidly enforced curfews, weekend home confinements and other court orders. While the probation officer worked regular court hours, the surveillance officer worked flexible hours in order to check up on probationers during evenings, weekends and early morning hours. The surveillance officer must also conduct periodic, random drug and alcohol tests. He or she must keep meticulous logs of all contacts with the juveniles, all curfew checks, and so on. These logs furnish the detailed evidence for proof of violation or compliance for use in court.

Creativity and quick thinking are often required to match that of the juvenile. Some of the first home confinement programs in the country were in California. For example, a San Diego home supervision officer charged with checking up on a confined juvenile spied the young man slipping out the back door as soon as the officer completed his curfew check. The officer gave chase, and the youth scaled a wall. When the officer climbed over the wall, he found himself in the middle of a nude swimming party. The quick-witted juvenile had shed his clothes and blended in with the partygoers. The officer was stymied in his pursuit. The youth, however, was apprehended the next day, clothed and, reportedly, grinning from ear to ear (Smith, 1983).

While the Georgia program originally conceived of the probation officer and surveillance officer pair as playing a "good-guy/bad-guy" role, most probationers did not differentiate between them. In fact, with their greater contact with the probationer, surveillance officers often achieved much closer relationships with the offenders than did the probation officers.

2. *Work Crew Supervisor*. High-risk juveniles must be carefully supervised while performing community work service. The most efficient way to do this is through work crews, the key to which is the work crew supervisor. The supervisors do more than simply supervise the youths at work. They must recruit the work sites, acquire the necessary supplies and equipment, plan for backup sites in case of rain or too little work, and transport the crew to and from the site. Once there, the supervisor must dole out the assignments, provide any necessary-on-the-site training, keep order and peace on the work site, and run interference with the sponsoring agency's personnel and the general public. If there is an accident, the supervisor must be prepared to perform first aid. Finally, he or she must keep a daily record of attendance and performance. It is extremely helpful if the work crew supervisor is facile in working with tools and knows basic carpentry, painting, gardening, etc.

The work crew supervisor must establish early on his or her authority, quickly firing juveniles who threaten the crew's discipline. Supervisory skills are more important than simple brawn. The current Quincy court crew supervisor, a former beautician, is a diminutive woman and has little problem controlling crews of both juveniles and adult offenders.

In the Quincy program, two individuals serve both as surveillance officers and work crew supervisors, trading every two days or so. One usually works nights as a surveillance officer while the other works days as a work crew supervisor. Then they switch.

3. *Community/Business Liaison.* The Community/Business Liaison must help secure paid full- or part-time jobs for the juveniles once they are proven able to work in the community. To accomplish this, the liaison must have good contacts in the community, especially the business community. In addition, he or she must have some fundamental ability to provide rudimentary job training, particularly how to secure employment, including where to look for a job, how to apply and interview for one, and the like. To serve those juveniles who because of age or lack of ability cannot be placed in private employment, the liaison must be able to raise monies from the public to be used to provide stipends for community work service.

The most successful community-liaison worker in Quincy proved to be a retired local businessman. Among other attributes, he was a member of a businessmen's luncheon club. Rarely did he finish a meal there before picking up a job slot or a contribution for the stipend fund from a fellow businessman. Also, as a businessman rather than a social worker, probation officer, or teacher, the juveniles accepted his advice more readily, even when it had little to do with employment matters.

Program Costs

Depending upon the size of the program and resources already available within existing probation or related correctional agencies, program costs vary. Many courts already have substantial restitution/community work service resources at their disposal. The key is getting these resources diverted from first-time offenders to high-risk repeaters. However, the staff- to-probationer ratio must be high in intensive programs. Program staff members must work weekends and evenings. Intensive supervision programs will, therefore, cost more than traditional community-based probation supervision programs. After surveying a number of intensive supervision programs across the country, some experts report that costs range from $2,000 to $5,000 per year. If electronic monitoring is used, costs rise to between $8,000 and $ 10,000 per year. Of course, as expensive as these costs are, they are substantially less than the $25,000 to $50,000 institutionalization costs per juvenile per year (Petersilia, 1988).

Program Performance

In order to secure funding, programs must make two arguments: They must convince their funders that the program works, and that it will be supported by the general public. The advantages of intensive supervision programs based on restitution/community work service is profound on both scores. First, even if the funder is wary of the program's claims of potential impact on recidivism, the program can promise to put juveniles to work for the community and the victim. At least some positive results are guaranteed for the money, even if all the youths don't reform overnight. Second, the public has enthusiastically embraced restitution/community work service programs (see, for example, Galaway, 1988). These programs have won the backing of conservatives as well as liberals. Juvenile restitution programs have been amply funded by President Ford as well as Presidents Reagan and Carter in between.

During the two and a half years it received federal funds, the Quincy program cut down the projected recidivism rate of its high-risk juveniles and saved the substantial costs of institutionalization. The program admitted 40 high-risk juveniles during this period. Of that number, 23 completed the program successfully without committing new offenses, ten completed the program but committed new crimes, and nine did not complete the program and committed new crimes. In other words, during the time it took each youth to complete the program (usually half a year), 19 out of 40 committed new offenses. The program reduced recidivism by almost half, from a projected 90% (the rate of recidivism predicted in accordance with the Massachusetts risk assessment scheme) to less than 50%.

Further, only nine juveniles from the program were committed to the state juvenile correctional department for either new offenses or repeated failures to abide by program rules. The remaining juveniles who committed new offenses were not considered to warrant commitment by the court. Their offenses included possession of alcohol, disorderly conduct and similar less serious offenses. The juveniles who were committed had offenses of burglary, assault and battery, and larcenies of motor vehicles.

In regard to reduction of costs of institutionalization, even though nine program youths were committed until their eighteenth birthday pursuant to Massachusetts commitment law, four had been released from the juvenile correctional department to participate in the program. Therefore, the program ended up filling only five additional correctional beds, plus a sixth bed that it used for short-term sanctions (no juvenile was committed to it for more than seven days). Massachusetts does not permit a judge to specify the commitment period of a juvenile. Therefore, in order to use the short-term bed, the judge had to commit the juvenile until his or her eighteenth birthday, and then revise and revoke the commitment a week later. Alternatively, the judge committed the juvenile on a high bail and then released him or her at the subsequent hearing upon the juvenile's promise to try again to complete the intensive program. The bed was used for a succession of short detention periods for juveniles who violated program rules or committed new, but less serious, crimes. The use of only six beds for 40 high-risk youths over two and a half years is extremely low, particularly because seven had been released from a commitment until their eighteenth birthday to participate in the program. Similarly, another dozen had been sentenced to the state juvenile correctional department but had their commitments postponed just to participate in the program. During the first two and a half years of the program, the total number of long-term commitments (excluding the short detentions for program violators previously described) to the state juvenile correctional department from the Quincy Court declined almost in half, from thirty-six to nineteen. However, the number of juveniles committed from the court has declined every year for the past ten years due to the declining youth population in the jurisdiction.

Not only did the program reduce recidivism, and save money on long-term juvenile commitments during this two-and-a-half-year period, but the juveniles in the program worked to benefit others. They completed 12,000 hours of community work service at dozens of public and governmental agencies in the community. At minimum wage, this constituted a contribution to the community worth more than $36,000. They also earned and paid back to crime victims more than $10,000. The average restitution was approximately $350 per defendant.

CONCLUSION

Representatives of a model juvenile intensive supervision program from Jefferson County, TX spoke at the annual 1987 conference of the American Probation and Parole Association held that year in Cincinnati, OH. One summed up the *modus operandi* of successful intensive supervision programs aptly: "to really get in the child's face." When all is said and done, there is no better, productive strategy for achieving this objective than building the intensive supervision program around restitution and community work service programming.

As mandated by the Quincy program in such large does, community work service orders are recognized as unabashedly punitive. Yet, they clearly serve rehabilitative and incapacitative functions as well. After initial grumbling and adjustment problems, the overwhelming majority of juveniles settle down and do their assigned work happily and routinely. Many take pride in their work. A few volunteer to continue after their court-mandated hours are completed. Community work service is probably one of the few things many of these troubled (and troublesome) youths are able to do successfully with their peers where they aren't yelled out, told to move on, or arrested. Instead, they often receive praise for the work done, not only by crew supervisors but host work site personnel genuinely grateful for the crew's efforts.

Restitution/community work service programs are too important an ingredient of intensive supervision programs to be limited to first or less serious offenders. In a tightly administered program, rigorously monitored and enforced as part of an overall supervision program, restitution/community work service programming can help reduce recidivism, reduce commitment rates and allow even high-risk juvenile offenders to be assets and contributors to the community, rather than deficits and drains.

REFERENCES

Armstrong, T. (1980). "Restitution: A Sanction for All Seasons." Paper presented at the Fourth National Symposium on Restitution and Community Service Sentencing, Minneapolis, MN.

Brown, M. and D. Cochran (1984). *Executive Summary of Research Findings from the Massachusetts Risk/Need Classification System, Report #5*. Boston, MA: Office of the Commissioner of Probation.

Cochran, D., M. Brown and R. Kazarian (1981). *Executive Summary of the Research Findings from the Pilot Courts Risk/Need Classification System, Report #4*. Boston, MA: Office of the Commissioners of Probation.

del Carmen, R. (1986). *Liability Issues in Community Service Sanctions*. Washington, DC: U.S. National Institute of Corrections.

Galaway, B. (1988). "Restitution as Innovation or Unfulfilled Promise." *Federal Probation* 52(3):3-14.

Klein, A. (1988). *Alternative Sentences: A Practitioner's Guide*. Cincinnati, OH: Anderson.

—— (1982). "EARN-IT." *Judges Journal* 38 (Winter): 37-61.

Kramer, Albert L. (1986). "Sentencing the Drunk Driver: A Call for Change." *Alcohol Treatment Quarterly*3(2):25-35.

Maloney, D., T. Armstrong and D. Romig (1987). *The Balanced Approach to Juvenile Justice*. Reno, NV: National Council of Family and Juvenile Judges.

Petersilia, J. (1988). "Probation Reform." In *Controversial Issues in Crime and Justice*, edited by J. Scott and T. Hirschi. Newbury Park, CA: Sage.

Schneider, A. (1986). "Restitution and Recidivism of Juvenile Offenders: Results from Four Experimental Studies." *Criminology* 24(3):533-552.

—— (ed.) (1985). *Guide to Juvenile Restitution*. Washington, DC: RESTTA, U.S. Department of Justice.

Schneider, P. (1982). *Restitution as an Alternative Disposition for Serious Juvenile Offenders. A Report Submitted to the Office of Juvenile Justice and Delinquency Prevention*. Eugene, OR: Institute of Policy Analysis.

—— W.R. Griffith and M.J. Wilson (1982). *Two Year Report on the National Evaluation of the Juvenile Restitution Initiative: An Overview of Progam Performance*. Washington, DC: U.S. Department of Justice.

Smith, M. (1983-84). "Will the Real Alternative Please Stand Up?" *NYU Review of Law & Social Change* 12(1):171-199.

Umbreit, M. (1985). *Crime and Reconciliation*. Nashville, TN: Abingdon.

Van Keulen, C. (1988). *What If Something Happens?* Washington, DC: U.S. National Institute of Corrections.

U.S. Department of Justice (1985). *Criminal Victimization in the United States, 1983. A National Crime Survey Report 7*. Washington, DC.

U.S. Supreme Court (1971). 401 U.S. 395.

Utah Code Ann. Section 76-3-201 (3) (A).

Washington Rev. Code Ann. Section 9A.20.030(1).

Weston, G., Jr. (1957). *Boston Ways*. Boston, MA: Beacon.

Wilson, J. (1981). "'What Works?' Revisited." *The Public Interest* 61:3-17.

Wright, M. and H. Galaway (1989). *Mediation and Criminal Justice: Victims, Offenders and Community*. London, UK: Sage.

Selective Aftercare for Juvenile Parolees: Administrative Environment and Placement Decisions

by
J. Fred Springer

The influence of the administrative environment on decisions to place juvenile offenders in community-based programs is explored. Current approaches to developing valid placement instruments are described; these instruments are used for determining youths' service needs and risk levels. However, the emphasis on individual-level criteria for placements must be balanced with greater attention to contextual factors that constrain the placement process. Six dimensions of the administrative environment are identified as important in understanding placement decisions. A case study of Arizona Department of Corrections' juvenile aftercare placement decisions demonstrates the impact of the administrative environment.

Research and policy development in corrections has increasingly centered on the recognition that questions concerning "what works?" must be rephrased. As Maltz (1984:40) has emphasized, it is imperative that researchers and policymakers ask what works, for whom, under what conditions? To modify Martinson's (1974) sweeping conclusion about the findings of research on rehabilitation, it's not that "nothing works" but that nothing works for all offenders in all circumstances (Martin, Sechrest and Redner, 1981).

For corrections policymakers and administrators, this message carries both good and bad news. While it maintains the possibility that effective rehabilitation programs may be developed for targeted categories of offenders, it also means that corrections policy cannot rely on a "silver bullet" or panacea panacea (Maltz, 1984:40). Multiple policies must be developed for distinct subpopulations of offenders and evaluated for effectiveness within the targeted group. High on any list of offender subpopulations deserving special attention are chronic and serious juvenile offenders being released from secure confinement who are determined to be at high risk of reoffending. Furthermore, policies must be implemented so that appropriate programs are delivered to the appropriate group of offenders.

Research on targeted rehabilitation and supervision policies has focused primarily on development of criteria for categorizing offenders and on making those criteria operational. A central component of this task has been developing and validating instruments that help match offenders with appropriate supervision and treatment (Baird, 1985; Harris, 1988; Jesness, 1988; Ashford and LeCroy, 1988). These efforts have utilized individual-level variables describing behavioral and other attributes of offenders. They focus on the question "for whom?"

There has been less attention to the administrative environment in which these instruments must be applied (Clear and Gallagher, 1983). Targeting services requires procedures for making placement decisions. These procedures must be adequate for making valid choices regarding individuals and the services they should receive; they must also take place in an administrative context that supports those choices. Questions concerning the conditions under which placement decisions are made have received little attention.

This chapter addresses the influence of the administrative environment on decisions to place juvenile offenders in alternative community-based correctional settings. The first section discusses the current scholarly concern with developing valid placement instruments for determining need for service and risk to the community. These approaches focus on attributes of individual offenders that serve as estimators of their ability to benefit from service or their future criminality.

The second section argues that the focus on individual-level criteria for placements must be balanced with greater scholarly attention to contextual factors that constrain or modify the ability of practitioners to make placement decisions based on such criteria. Six dimensions of the administrative environment are identified as important to understanding the context of placement decisions.

The remainder of the chapter presents a case study of aftercare placement decisions for juvenile parolees in the Arizona Department of Corrections (ADC). This empirical study utilizes statistical data on over 300 juvenile placements, and extensive field data collected through interviews, site visits, and documentary analysis in Arizona's juvenile Purchase of Care system

(EMT Associates, 1987, 1988a). The study describes the administrative context for placement decisions in the Arizona system and identifies general implications for making targeted juvenile placement decisions. A final section presents recommendations for further research and policy development.

JUVENILE CORRECTIONS AND PLACEMENT DECISIONS

If the correctional needs of the criminal justice system are diverse, that variety is most evident for juvenile offenders. The importance of a diversified correctional response to juveniles has long been recognized for several reasons: the vulnerable and dependent situation of youth, the dilemma of status offenders, problems associated with "labeling" young offenders, and the special responsibility for rehabilitation efforts directed at young people in their formative years (Smykla, 1981:177-179). More recently, the difficulties associated with normalizing the behavior of chronic and serious juvenile offenders and ensuring a reasonable level of community protection when individuals from this group are being maintained in the community has become an increasingly urgent item on the national juvenile justice agenda.

The recognition of special responsibilities in juvenile corrections has traditionally produced a range of diversion and aftercare programs for youth, and has focused attention on the need to better understand the individual characteristics and needs of juvenile offenders. According to Baird (1985:32), "Juveniles differ considerably in terms of type of offense, likelihood of committing crimes, emotional needs, education levels, vocational skills, honesty, and other factors. To deal effectively with this variety of people and problems requires an understanding of the individual as well as knowledge and flexibility in applying different supervision techniques."

The need to "understand the individual" has been placed at the core of the placement problem for targeted corrections programs. Traditionally, developing this understanding has relied on the expertise of the individual corrections professional making the decision. As summarized by Baird (1985:32), "Most experienced probation and aftercare officers use an intuitive system of classifying offenders into different treatment and surveillance modes. Classification decisions are thus usually based on judgments of client needs and their perception of the client's potential for continued unlawful behavior."

Despite its prevalence, the inadequacies of intuitive placement decisions are well-known. From the earliest research into correctional decisions, systematic "actuarial" approaches have proven more accurate in predicting placement outcomes than individual judgments (Halatyn and Wenk, 1974). Individualized decisions concerning the characteristics of juvenile offenders are based on criteria that are "probably as varied as officer's experiences, educations, and philosophical approaches to the job" (Baird, 1985:32).

Research efforts to improve placement decisions for juvenile offenders have focused on developing decision procedures that systematize individual placement decisions through the application of standardized criteria, and through development of more accurate empirical measures of these criteria for individual juvenile offenders. These efforts have taken several distinct forms.

- *Risk assessment*. Risk screening has received increasing attention throughout the corrections field. Adult parole, intensive probation and selective prosecution of career criminals (Springer, Phillips and Cannady, 1985) are examples of decision settings in which estimates of risk for future criminal risk have been relevant. Risk estimates have also been important to determining the security level appropriate for correctional placements of juvenile offenders.

  Risk instruments typically consist of a series of items that specify a number of points to be assigned for a particular attribute of the offender's history. For example, an offender may be assigned two points if his or her first official contact with the criminal justice system is before age ten, one if it is between age 11 and 13, and none if it is later. Aggregate scores over a number of items—typically including indicators of substance abuse, violence, numbers of prior crimes, age of onset of criminal behavior, etc.—are used to place youth in different categories of risk. Specifically, this means classifying into aggregate groupings by characteristics that have been empirically associated with differing rates of recidivism in the past (Clear and Gallagher, 1983).

  Risk instruments provide a guide to determining the threat of future criminal activity posed by a youth and, therefore, the appropriate level of supervision necessary to protect the community.

- *Need indicators*. Risk instruments are most clearly related to decisions about supervision level, but diversity in juvenile placements includes a broad range of treatment modalities as well as differences in institutional security. Placement that will maximize the fit between individual juveniles and the services offered in a particular placement will require criteria separate from those used to determine level of supervision.

  Instruments or procedures designed to establish criteria and provide information in these areas can be classified generally as "need indicators." The range of possible criteria in these areas is extremely broad, and numerous individual scales or indices of individual attributes have been used to establish need for treatment services. In a recent review, need indicators were classified into three major areas: indicators of needs in *life skills* areas (e.g., educational attainment, vocational skills, independent living, problem solving, goal setting); indicators of needs in *social-psychological* adjustment (e.g., self concept, emotional control, behavioral adjustment); and needs in *social-relational* skills (e.g., family dynamics, peer relations, refusal skills, positive social behavior). In addition, needs may be identified in more specialized areas (e.g., psychological disorders, addictions [EMT Associates, Inc., 1988b]).

Indicators of need provide a guide to the types of therapy, education or other services from which a youth will benefit; they provide a systematic basis for formulating case plans. The primary focus is on appropriate service modalities rather than appropriate level of supervision.

- *Composite placement instruments*. Placement decisions clearly involve consideration of both risk and need. This complex decision situation has been addressed through attempts to develop placement instruments that combine criteria and measures of both risk for criminal activity and case management needs. In emphasizing the need for comprehensive placement instruments for juvenile corrections, Baird (1985:36) notes that "Needs assessments in juvenile corrections should be an integral part of a classification system. By including needs assessments in the classification system, an agency not only addresses custody requirements and community protection issues, but also the rehabilitative needs of juveniles." The Wisconsin Model (Clear and Gallagher, 1983:221) for classification, and the major classification efforts of the National Institute of Corrections Model Classification Project (Baird, 1985), are prime examples of composite placement instruments.
- *Decision Trees*. Decision trees represent a basic structuring of decision points and criteria for making decisions concerning placement of juveniles in different treatment or supervision settings. The parole placement tree developed for the Arizona Department of Corrections is typical (Ashford and LeCroy, 1988). Correctional officers are guided through a series of decision points such as "Does the youth have a history of violence?" or "Does the youth have supportive parents?" A yes or no at each point in the decision tree will guide the placement decision toward different levels of restrictiveness.

  This type of decision tree provides an ordering of decisions and criteria to select between a continuum of placement options. It does not necessarily require or facilitate the use of accurate empirical measures of relevant criteria at each point. For example, a tree may indicate that a parole officer should determine whether a youth has supportive parents or not without specifying the data, or an empirical cut-point, to be used in making that determination.

A number of crucial issues have accompanied the development of these systematic decision aids for placement decisions. Technical issues related to the accuracy, validity and generalizability of specific instruments have constituted the primary focus of research and debate (Monahan, 1978; Gottfredson and Gottfredson, 1981; Wright et al., 1981). The major issue in this debate has been the ability to use available information to precisely distinguish groups of subjects according to some currently unknown behavioral attribute.

This focus largely presumes that the decision situation has been properly defined. In other words, the assumption is that the decision instruments address the "right" problem. This means that the key to decision making is to categorize offenders based on individual-level criteria. The appropriateness of this assumption remains largely unexamined in the scholarly literature, yet it is central to achieving the purposes of the decision instruments. If categorizing individuals is not the key to making placements, then "valid" instruments may not provide useful directions for making placements. The remainder of this chapter examines the decision environment in which placement instruments are applied, as well as the degree to which this context meets the assumptions implicit in the information provided by placement instruments. Discussion will be directed toward exploring how this environment has addressed the requirement to match appropriate intervention with those youths achieving the highest scores on formal assessment instruments, measuring risk and/or need.

THE ADMINISTRATIVE ENVIRONMENT OF PLACEMENT DECISIONS

Applied social researchers always run the danger of irrelevant analyses when they remove concepts from their organizational context. Maltz's excellent study (1984:3) of recidivism makes the point clearly with respect to operational definitions of that concept: "The term methodology is not restricted to matters mathematical or statistical; definitional and contextual issues must also be included, and not only for the sake of completeness; the rationale for the statistical model of recidivism ... is based on the substantive and organizational characteristics of the recidivism process."

The same observation applies to attempts to operationalize and systematize decisions related to placements for juvenile offenders. The operational relevance of empirical criteria, decision instruments and decision procedures depends on their fit to the organizational context in which juvenile placements are made. The applied researcher does not enjoy the luxury of conceptual clarity that will allow precise and unambiguous measurement.

Despite the need to define the organizational environment of placement decisions and its implications for developing decision tools, little scholarly work has been done in the area. In a pioneering article, Clear and Gallagher (1983:220) pointed out the importance of adapting standard instruments to particular organizational settings. In particular, they identified the tradeoffs necessary in decisions involving multiple criteria, and the cost implications of choosing specific cut-off points for decision classifications.

This chapter develops a more comprehensive framework for assessing the effects of one administrative context on decisions about offender categorization. To do this, the discussion focuses on the "mechanics" of the decision process—the location, rate and genesis of organized decisions. Several attributes of the process that must be considered include: (1) the structure of opportunity for different types of decision outcomes; (2) the flow of decisions in the system and the factors that "trigger" that flow; and (3) the personnel and other resources that are devoted to the decision process. A complete understanding of the decision environment for placement includes at least the following factors.

Placement Opportunities

The utility of a decision instrument depends partly on the opportunity to actually implement the decisions that are indicated through the logic of the instrument. Simply put, if the instrument indicates a high need for a particular type of therapy and a high need for supervision, the utility of the instrument can be realized only if a placement slot meeting these characteristics is available. In their early attention to the administration of classification systems, Clear and Gallagher (1983:232) recognized the need to adjust operational instruments to reflect the actual configuration of choices available to the correctional officer. Failure to adapt approaches to opportunities may produce irrelevant decision guides that are contradicted by the agency's mission, resources and environment.

The observation that decisions are molded partly by the opportunities to follow through on results may appear obvious, but it has important implications. The structure of opportunities for juvenile placements, for example, will vary according to basic correctional policy. For instance, control over the structure of placement opportunities will vary between public and private contract systems. Adequacy of funding, size of jurisdiction and other factors will also affect the number and nature of available placements.

System Decision Point

Placement decisions, however, are not one-time occurrences for most juveniles within the criminal justice system. In many instances, a single juvenile will be the subject of decisions concerning pre-adjudication placements (diversions), post-adjudication placements (probation placements or incarceration) and post-incarceration placements (parole). Furthermore, at each of these stages, a juvenile may pass through multiple decisions. In sum, many juvenile offenders will be subject to repeated placement decisions within the juvenile justice system. Most chronic and serious juvenile offenders have experienced repeated placements, and often have extensive records of failure in multiple types of placement.

The flow of placement decisions has a number of implications. First, events related to prior placement decisions will be reflected in placement instruments themselves. For instance, prior criminal justice involvement and age at onset of involvement are typically criteria in "risk" instruments. History of prior service placements is a standard criterion for needs assessments. Thus, prior placement decisions may be incorporated into the criteria and information base of future applications of placement instruments. The fact that prior behavior is incorporated into many instruments means that the range of placement options will change, and probably narrow, at later stages in placement decisions. Generally, risk indicators will be higher for post-incarceration placements, for instance, as compared to diversion placement decisions. The predominance of past behavioral indicators in risk instruments means that they will be more important and useful for placement decisions in later phases of the justice system.

System Load

The aggregate volume and timing of placement decisions in the juvenile justice system has important implications for decision criteria and procedures. A high ratio of placement need to availability may truncate stays, necessitating new decisions when juvenile offenders reenter the system. High need within limited resources may also influence the availability of placement opportunity. The need for more intensive and expensive placements may be hard to meet when more juveniles could be placed in less intensive program environments.

Triggering Events

Placement decisions have varied "triggers." In decisions concerning juvenile community placements, for example, initial decisions may be made after evaluation at the time of probation or parole. However, decisions may also be triggered through the failure or termination of a prior placement. That is, a juvenile may experience disciplinary or other difficulties in one placement and move to another placement decision. In these instances, the prior placement or very similar placements may be inappropriate. The range of options is narrowed. If a juvenile has a lengthy history of problems in a variety of correctional placements, the importance of the decision itself may come into question. The perception may be that careful assessment of the decision does not matter.

Role of the Decision Maker

Placement decisions for juveniles occur at multiple points in the criminal justice system, and they are made by different individuals. Decisions may be made in a centralized fashion by exit gatekeepers in correctional institutions or by officers in agencies that contract for placement services. Conversely, decisions may be made primarily by individual probation or parole officers in a decentralized case management system.

Placement decisions often involve multiple decision makers. Probation, parole or other personnel responsible for diagnostics may make recommendations to a placement officer who attempts to match recommendations with available placement slots. In any case, the identity and role of the decision maker has important implications for the decision environment. Professional training and skill level, degree of discretion and authority, and responsibilities of decision-making personnel will influence the application of offender-based criteria for placement decisions.

Other Population-Specific Criteria

While development of formal placement instruments typically focuses on criteria that are generalizable to large populations of subjects (e.g., juvenile offenders as a class), placement decisions are made in specific environments. It follows that criteria for specific placement decisions may include non-generalizable, offender-based criteria that have special significance in a local setting.

Some of these criteria will be related to the structure of program availability, identified previously as an important contextual factor in placement decisions. The availability of a program demanding a high degree of physical strength and endurance, for example, will make those offender attributes relevant in the placement process. Other locally relevant criteria will inhere more in the characteristics of the juvenile offender population than in program availability. For example, cultural or ethnic considerations may be important for many local juvenile populations.

Summary

The major theme in the preceding discussion is simple. While attempts to formalize corrections placement decisions tend toward identification of generalizable, individual-level indicators of behavior, actual placement decisions are affected by numerous attributes of local environments. Figure 1 summarizes this theme in graphic form. The application of offender-based criteria to make placement decisions is mediated by attributes of the decision context.

**Figure 1: The Decision Environment—
Factors Affecting Placement Decisions**

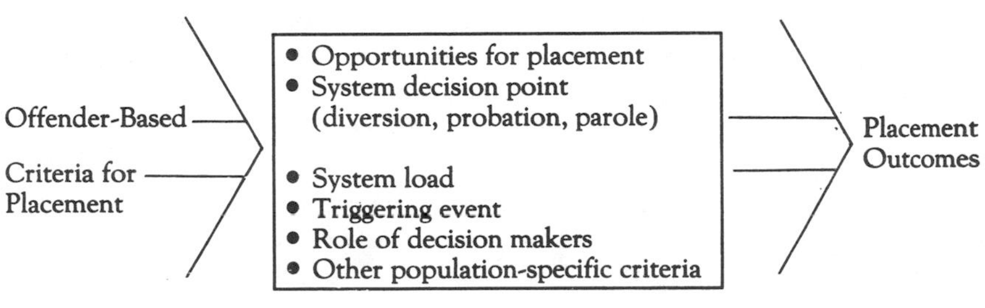

Decision Environment

Figure 1 suggests that identified characteristics of the decision context will modify the relationship between individual attributes of juvenile offenders, and the outcome of correctional placement decisions. The framework set forth is heuristic; it is not sufficiently specified to provide precise hypotheses concerning the degree or configuration of interaction between individual attributes and the decision environment. However, it does provide broad questions for exploratory empirical analysis in actual decision environments. The remainder of this chapter reports an exploratory application of the framework for one population of juvenile placement decisions in the Arizona Department of Corrections. The intent of this analysis is to provide a preliminary application of the framework in one empirical setting, and to suggest directions for further refinement and policy development.

ARIZONA'S PURCHASE OF CARE SYSTEM: A HEURISTIC EXAMPLE

In 1981, the Arizona Department of Corrections (ADC) initiated a system of contracting with private vendors to provide community-based programming for juvenile parolees. While a variety of community-based programs had been used for juvenile diversion and probation in the state, the contract system increased the availability of program options for juvenile parolees. Between fiscal year (FY) 1982-83 and FY 1985-86, the program grew rapidly, increasing its volume of placements by more than 130%.

By 1986, the Division of Juvenile/Community Services in the ADC had established contractual relations with 55 programs and was supervising a daily population of more than 300 juveniles in community placement. Placements were diverse and included residential homes, wilderness camps and day care facilities. The division has developed a procedure for making placement decisions with the objective of matching individual juvenile need for service with specific programs (Springer, 1988).

While the division's placement process does not currently include standardized application of risk or need instruments, it does explicitly consider individual-level criteria for placement decisions. Analysis of placement decisions for a sample of juvenile parolees provides a basis for assessing the interaction of individual-level attributes and the administrative environment in determining placement outcomes.[1] This analysis will examine the objectives and procedures for utilizing individual-level criteria and, to the extent that available empirical information allows, influences on parole outcome within each dimension of administrative environment identified in the previous section.

ADC has estimated that approximately 60-65% of youths being released from its facilities have serious drug and/or alcohol problems, 20-25% are emotionally disturbed, and 6-8% have been adjudicated delinquent for sex offense-related crimes. It is these kinds of specialized offender groups, along with wards having no chance of returning to their natural homes once released, that ADC is increasingly trying to match with appropriate services and placement once on parole.

Program Objectives and Placement Criteria

The formal policy mandate of the Division of Juvenile/Community Services clearly reflects the complexity of program objectives in juvenile corrections. On the one hand, the division shares the departmental responsibility "to serve and protect the people of the State by imprisoning those offenders legally committed to the Department" (Arizona Department of Corrections Mission Statement). On the other hand, the formal division mandate clearly states the responsibility for meeting the rehabilitation needs of juvenile offenders. Specifically, the division's Statement of Goals and Objectives clearly identifies an obligation to provide for "the basic physical, emotional, religious, and social needs" of youthful offenders legally committed to the department.

Furthermore, the division is formally mandated (Division Objectives 10.a-f) to "provide an environment ... for offenders which stresses the development and manifestation" of personal characteristics and skills that will facilitate their reentry into society as contributing adult citizens (for a complete discussion, see EMT Associates, 1987:4-9). Balancing secure supervision and programming to meet the rehabilitation needs of individual juveniles is a central task for placement decisions involving parolees who require community-based placement following incarceration in one of the state's secure juvenile institutions.

Placement Procedure

The placement procedure involves three steps. First, a parole officer initiates a request for placement for a youth approaching release from a juvenile institution. Requests may also be initiated after a variety of other triggering events, which will be discussed below. Second, the request is evaluated by the division's Correctional Placement Officer (CPO), who identifies appropriate placement according to the individual juvenile's need. Third, the CPO matches individual parolees and available placement slots.

Within this overall procedure, traditional scholarly research on placement decisions addresses information needs in the first and second steps. At these stages parole officers and the CPO use individual-level information on juveniles to determine: (1) whether the parolee should be released to the community or requires a more intensive form of community-based supervision and service; and (2) the most appropriate program for individual juveniles.

In the Arizona system, these decisions are currently based upon a judgmental review of a variety of information on individual juveniles by both parole officers and the placement officer. Parole officers use direct contact with juveniles as a primary information source. The placement officer reviews the parole officer's request, which includes specific statements of reasons and expected benefits; institutional diagnostic packets (which may be dated for some parolees), including a social casework summary; the juvenile's criminal history; and parole updates when available.

These sources provide information to assess placement need along several major dimensions, including the degree of function of the home environment, needs for educational/vocational training services, needs for psychological/emotional treatment, serious problems of substance use and the need for close supervision to prevent criminal behavior. Traditional need and risk instruments would systematize and standardize information and criteria in these assessments. However, the degree to which instruments would improve—or influence—the overall placement process depends upon a closer analysis of constraints and influences in the decision environment.

Decision Environment for ADC Placements

The ADC decision process is interactive and eclectic. Parole officers and a centralized placement officer utilize a variety of information sources to make increasingly specific sequential decisions concerning juvenile need and placement. This process is typical of the type of administrative context into which specific individual-level decision criteria (those addressed in placement instruments) must fit. The process itself reflects multiple decision points at which environmental constraints and influences on placement decisions may be exerted. The following discussion explores these environmental influences in the Arizona Purchase of Care system.

Opportunities for Placement

The placement opportunities in the Arizona Purchase of Care System are defined through the profile of vendors with whom the department contracts for placements, the services they offer and the numbers of available placement slots for different vendors. The department defines different categories of service need through an annual request for proposals from vendors and awards contracts to those most responsive to service requests. Nevertheless, the detailed configuration of services is strongly influenced by vendors themselves in their service proposals. The availability of program placements within different service categories is a crucial parameter in the placement environment, and this parameter is not under the ADC's direct control. A critical factor affecting placement opportunities among the various service providers is stringent acceptance criteria. A number of providers place severe limitations on the acceptance of certain clients, usually on the basis of having a history of such behaviors as violence, serious abuse of drugs and/or alcohol, sex offenses, mental disturbance, etc. These policies on the part of vendors clearly limit ADC's ability to readily and satisfactorily place substantial numbers of its highest-risk clients.

In FY 1986, 51 programs were under contract with the department to accept juvenile parolees as placements. Table 1 provides a profile of the number of contracted programs in each of the seven defined service categories.

Table 1: Contracted Programs by Service Category

Program Category	*Number of Programs*
Residential Shelter	4
Residential Treatment	10
Conservation Program	2
Day/Evening Support	16
Psychiatric Treatment	3
Substance Abuse Treatment	3
Pregnancy and Post-Partum Care	5

The last three categories on the list—psychiatric treatment, substance abuse and pregnancy programs—are specialized (and high-cost) programs that received very few parole placements (fewer than 10%). In essence, once the general need for aftercare placement was established, the more specific placement decision was to determine which of the top four program categories provides the most appropriate community supervision environment for a given juvenile parolee.

These categories of program are distinguished by basic level of service, service objectives and duration. They also differ in degree and security of community supervision. Program emphases are briefly summarized as follows (EMT Associates, 1987: 28-29):

- *Residential shelter programs* provide general respite care and address mild oppositional behavior. They may provide additional services through referral but are not self-contained. Emergency placements sometimes occur but the average stay lasts six months to a year.
- *Residential treatment programs* provide respite care and address moderate-to-severe oppositional behavior and mild psychological/emotional problems. A variety of educational and counseling services are self-contained in programs. Placements usually last six to 18 months.
- *Conservation programs* offer prevocational skill building and training through wilderness work experience. Strict discipline, individual achievement and cooperation are emphasized. Placements normally last 12 weeks.

- *Day/evening support programs* offer structured programming for youth who have a primary residence in the community. Services are varied and include prevocational training, education supplements, counseling and recreation. Placements are often for indefinite periods.

Within these program categories, there is a continuum of care, from part-time supervision through residential care, with significant counseling and treatment resources. The categories also provide a range of supervision levels—from the day care setting in which the juveniles are largely unsupervised outside program hours, to the conservation programs with 24-hour supervision in a remote setting.

The discretion of corrections personnel to use individual-level criteria to determine placement within these program categories was constrained by additional factors. First, the conservation programs presented large numbers of openings because the relatively short program duration produces more turnover, and the relatively heavy reliance of these programs in corrections' placements. While the distribution of placements fluctuated somewhat, conservation programs typically accounted for approximately half of all placements during the period in which the Arizona aftercare system was studied. Decision makers indicated that availability, rather than individual-level criteria, was often the critical factor determining a conservation placement.

Self-imposed criteria for acceptance into community programs also affected placement opportunities in the Arizona program. Table 2 displays the percentage of programs placing limitations on referrals for reasons related to a history of violence, serious abuse of alcohol or other drugs, sex offenses, serious psychological disturbance, or serious disability (mental or physical).

Table 2: Restrictions on Placements by Type of Program
(Percentage of Programs With Restriction)

Type of Program	*History of Violence*	*Serious Drug Use*	*Sex Offenses*	*Psychological Disturbance*	*Disability*
Residential Shelter (n=14)	50.0	71.4	28.6	71.4	64.3
Residential Treatment (n=10)	50.0	40.0	—	60.0	60.0
Conservation (n=2)	50.0	50.0	50.0	—	100.0
Day/Evening Support (n=16)	25.0	50.0	12.5	62.5	81.3

While exact definitions vary, the great majority of programs placed some restriction on accepting referrals with serious disability or psychological disturbance. A majority also limited acceptance of offenders with serious drug involvement. These limits suggest that the demand for the relatively small number of psychiatric and substance abuse placements in the system is defined partly by programs themselves.

Programs also limited acceptance according to a history of violence or a history of sex offenses, while the majority of programs did not refuse to accept placements with these conditions in their criminal justice history. Half of the residential shelters, residential treatment centers and conservation camps refused to accept juveniles with a history of serious oppositional behavior or violence. In many instances, this would be an important restriction on the discretion of placement officers to provide aftercare for juvenile offenders.

It is also important to note that day/evening support programs that offered the least secure environment for placement were the most willing to accept juveniles with histories of violence.

In summary, the fact that aftercare services in Arizona are provided through a system of privately contracted providers significantly restricts the discretion of placement officers in using individual-level variables alone to determine placement. Those constraints are of several types. First, the programs have a great deal of influence on the exact definition of services to be offered and their availability. Second, the price of service and budgetary constraints shape the availability of beds in different types of homes, thereby limiting the numbers of placements in different types of settings. Finally, the self-imposed constraints of the programs themselves mean that the available placements for juveniles with certain types of backgrounds (such as serious drug use, violence or sex offenses) are greatly reduced.

Case Flow and Placement Decisions

System Decision Point. The load of cases in the system and the triggering events for placement decisions identified in the first section of this chapter have environmental influences on individual placement decisions. These factors in the environment are all related to the timing and volume of cases that flow through the placement decision process. In the Arizona case, all of the placement decisions involve parole decisions following custody in a secure juvenile institution. This affects placement decisions by making security an important consideration in the placement process. In particular, the decisions made about cases will be influenced by the fact that placement behavior is a consideration in parole compliance. Indeed, parole into a supervised placement rather than into relatively unsupervised community environment means that those juveniles selected for aftercare are in a more intensive supervision mode than those that are not.

This factor affects the numbers of decisions and the timing of decisions made for placement of juveniles. An empirical analysis of the 323 cases placed in residential shelters, conservation programs or day/evening support programs during 1987 provides a profile of the flow of cases through the Arizona system. Figure 2 graphically demonstrates the time that juveniles spend in their respective placements in weeks by the type of program.

The graph demonstrates some differences in the time spent by juveniles in different placements. In particular, the percentage of juvenile placements remaining in day/evening support programs tends generally to be greater than the percentage that remain in the other placements over a given period of time. Secondly, youths in conservation programs frequently leave after the ten-to 14-week period of time that it takes to complete the conservation experience. Program terminations for residential shelters tend to represent a higher percentage of those placed at all points in the process from the first through twentieth week.

These differences between programs correspond to differences in program environment. For example, the conservation programs have a high rate of juveniles leaving the placement during the first few weeks of the training experience, while the curve indicating termination is relatively flat from the third through tenth weeks, during the actual remote wilderness experience. The termination curves for the other two program types—residential shelter and day/evening support—are relatively linear from week one through 20, though higher for the residential shelters. However, both residential shelters and day/evening support programs show relatively high levels of program termination well short of the projected periods of program need. Residential shelters, for example, typically have an assignment period of at least six months, yet, after three months, more than three-fourths of the youths are no longer in the shelters. Similarly, approximately 50% of the youths in the day/evening support placements have terminated by week 12. In residential programs, almost 40% of the youths have left the setting by week four.

Table 3 helps explain the relatively high rates of early exit in each of the three types of placements. For residential shelters, nearly 70% of the placements were terminated because the juvenile ran away or was absent without leave (AWOL). For conservation programs, approximately 60% of the terminations were successful (i.e., the individual was either transferred for a reason or was released into community parole). For day/evening support, approximately 42% of the terminations were unsuccessful completions for reasons other than running away. The majority of these were because of new crimes committed in a community.

This pattern identifies a close relationship between the type of placement that a juvenile is in and the reasons why he or she will leave the program setting. The relatively high level of successful completions for conservation camps can be explained by the remote setting and the relative lack of opportunity for leaving the program. Indeed, even in this setting, almost 40% go AWOL, most in the first few weeks before being transported to the remote wilderness setting.

Figure 2: Time in Placement in Weeks by Type of Program

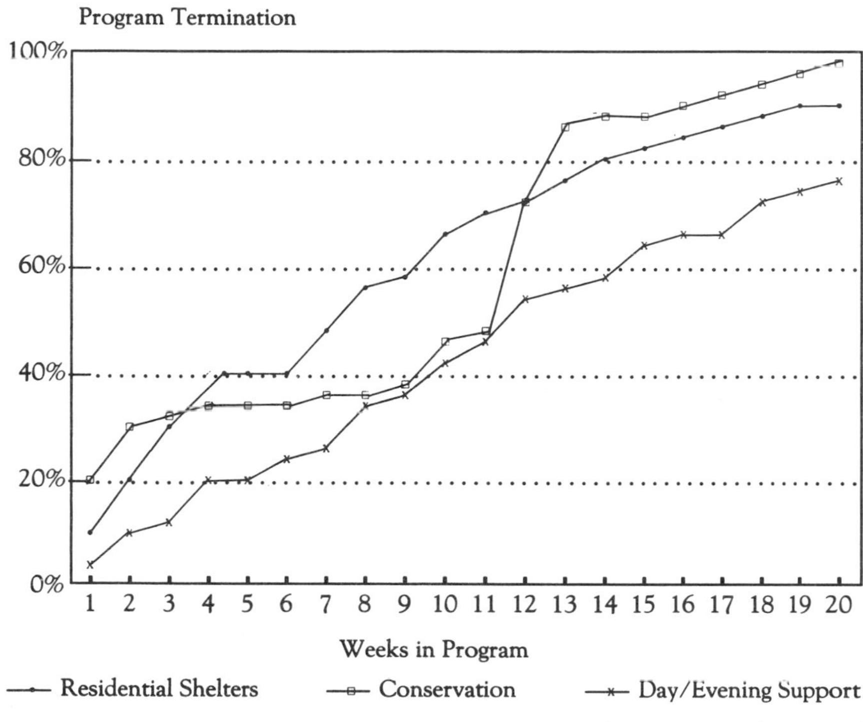

In the less supervised environment of day/evening support, there is a much higher probability that juveniles will be rearrested for a new crime in the community, thereby ending their parole status and removing them from the program. This reflects the relative lack of close supervision in that setting.

For residential shelters, on the other hand, close supervision and 24-hour residential requirements are indicative of the program, but the great majority of juveniles leave those programs because they have been classified as runaways. This type of termination reflects the close supervision and regulatory rules that characterize residential shelters.

To summarize, the flow of cases in the Arizona aftercare program may be termed "a revolving door." In all program settings, juvenile AWOLs constitute a great portion of those who leave the programs, frequently in early periods of the program. Juveniles are quickly recycled through a short disciplinary stay. An analysis of those events that lead to a classification of runaway status indicate that the very high levels of juveniles leaving the programs in this way is partly attributable to the close supervision attached to the aftercare placements. Many official runaways are generated by unapproved

Table 3: Reason for End of Last Placement by Type of Program

Reason	*Residential Shelters*	*Conservation*	*Day/Evening Support*
Runaway	69.7%	37.7%	24.4%
Successful completion	21.1%	59.6%	33.3%
Unsuccessful completion	9.2%	2.6%	42.4%
Total number of placements	(109)	(114)	(45)

overnight program stays even though the juvenile returns to the program. Program rules require that these juveniles be removed from their placement and go back into the secured institution on a parole violation for a short period of time. On reentering the system, this generates a new placement, usually in a different program of a similar category.

This means that most placements are not first-time determinations of a juvenile's risk or need, but are repetitive and generated through his or her behavior in the system rather than more remote background factors. More than two-thirds of these juveniles have had more than four prior placements at the time of a current placement decision. The triggering event for a placement decision is not determination of an appropriate placement based on prior juvenile characteristics, but the need to reassign a juvenile following disciplinary infractions within prior placements.

Viewed from the perspective of the workload of the personnel involved in making placements and the perspective from which they see placements, the relative policy decisions for the great volume of individual decisions are related to disciplinary criteria related to supervision within the program and are not directly related to the improvement of instruments or criteria for making decisions based on individual juvenile history.

Decision Makers and Selective Criteria

Placement decisions in the Arizona aftercare system are made by multiple actors. As described earlier, parole officers make requests for aftercare placement based on their screening of the individual-level criteria for offenders getting ready to come out of juvenile institutions or for those who have had disciplinary infractions within prior placements. These requests often include specific recommendations for placements in eight particular provider settings. Interviews with personnel involved in the decision process indicate that parole officer recommendations are the most significant element in the CPO's decision on exact placement of a juvenile. The importance of these recommendations is based upon traditional precedence and the fact that the parole officer has the greatest access to individual-level variables.

However, the application of individual-level variables reflects the characteristics of idiosyncratic individual decisions affected by the parole officer's own knowledge and involvement with the placement environment. In particular, officers tend to develop close ties with particular provider settings, where they have confidence in the juvenile placements and where they feel that they can provide effective follow-up supervision. Parole officers may also be exercising judgment concerning individual-level variables that are in their perception important to their caseload and placement environment but that may not be reflected in standardized instruments or criteria for individual placements.

The Arizona program offers a graphic example of the utilization of other individual-level criteria for making placements, especially in the case of day/evening care programs. Within the city of Tucson, parole officers may make recommendations for placement in several different such programs. Each program has a distinctive emphasis: one offers prevocational training, the second provides general equivalency diploma and educational development, and the third comprises group psychological counseling for developing emotional maturity. However, each program is also located in and closely associated with provider groups in differing ethnic communities. The vocational program, for example, is located within the Hispanic community, and the educationally-oriented program is located within an organization that has close ties to the city's black neighborhoods.

An analysis of placements in those different programs during the period of the study of the Arizona system reveals that 50% of the placements in the vocational program were Hispanic, 42% in the educational program were black, and 88% in the counseling program were white, non-Hispanic. In other words, despite the differences in service focus, a major factor affecting placement of juveniles in these programs was the ethnic and cultural environment of the program. These factors heavily influence the recommendations of parole officers to match individual placements with community settings. Again, the influence of standardized individual-level variables found in placement instruments has been overridden by more idiosyncratic considerations related to the placement environment.

Summary

An examination of the Arizona placement process makes it clear that the role of standardized individual-level criteria for making placement decisions is circumscribed. While these criteria may provide important information in the decision process, particularly at the level of individual parole recommendations, they will not effectively determine the placement to which a juvenile is referred; other environmental considerations intervene.

The placement environment is constrained by the contracting process that identifies providers with program categories. The numbers of providers and of available beds, and the planned duration of the programs, all affect the availability of placements for juveniles. Discussions with placement personnel indicate that availability is often a heavy influence on a decision to put particular juveniles in particular programs. The ways in which the availability of placements can be affected are not through attention to improving individual-level instruments, but attention to the contracting process and the decisions related to shaping the profile of available programs.

Second, the placement decisions are affected by the flow of cases through the programs and the triggering events that require these decisions. In the Arizona case, a great many placements are engendered by prior disciplinary infractions, particularly running away, in the aftercare system. These placements do require the time and consideration of placement personnel, and they do affect the availability of placement slots, but they do not turn primarily on criteria related to individual juvenile characteristics as measured through standardized instruments.

Finally, placements are constrained by considerations that are relevant to the environment of the placement decision makers but that are not necessarily reflected in standardized individual instruments. Understanding the role of individual-level variables in making appropriate placement decisions requires consideration of the environmental influences that constrain placement decisions.

ADMINISTRATIVE ENVIRONMENT AND PLACEMENT DECISIONS: DISCUSSION AND CONCLUSIONS

Programs of intensive supervision or aftercare for juveniles represent an effort by policymakers to respond creatively to the challenge identified in the beginning of this chapter. These programs do not mandate blanket correctional responses for all juvenile offenders. Rather they recognize that effective policy must consider what works, for whom, under what conditions.

The argument made in this chapter is that research on making placement decisions has focused on the question "for whom," to the relative neglect of the question "under what conditions?" At the research level, this imbalance is reflected in the volume of literature on placement instruments that utilize individual-level variables on offenders as decision aids for placement. In terms of making placement decisions, reliance on individual-level variables assumes that the environment in which placements are made meets several conditions.

First, it is assumed that services appropriate to meeting needs indicated by individual-level variables are available. The exploratory study in this chapter suggests that this assumption will be unwarranted in many program environments. The Arizona aftercare program demonstrated several ways in which the program environment may limit the utility of individual-level criteria in making placement decisions.

In community-based aftercare programs, the variation in the services and orientation of individual programs presents a complex, multidimensional set of placement options that cannot be easily addressed with a standardized set of placement criteria. The availability of placement slots in different programs and self-imposed program limitations on admissions also constrain the ability of the Arizona program to make placements solely, or primarily, on the basis of individual-level variables.

Second, reliance on individual-level criteria assumes that the administrative procedures used for placement decisions will support decisions based on these criteria. The Arizona case suggests that administrative procedures that clearly support placement decisions based primarily on individual-level criteria do not typify criminal justice settings. First, the individual-level criteria of need or risk do not drive other decisions that administrators must make. Budgetary decisions will affect capacity to trade off higher and lower priced placements in a system with multiple options of service level. In a contract system such as that in Arizona, administrators must balance meeting responsibilities for enforcing contracts with matching placement slots to indicated needs. Enforcing contracts may alter the availability of positions, thereby requiring adjustment in decisions based on individual-level criteria.

Third, reliance on individual-level instruments for placement presumes that the standardized criteria they incorporate are adequate to making decisions for the entire population of offenders and conditions to which they are applied. The Arizona case demonstrated circumstances in which nonstandardized, individual-level data were applied. Race or ethnic background, for instance, was a key placement criteria in day/evening care settings.

The application of standardized criteria militates against the utilization of differing individual criteria for differing conditions, but this determination is best made through a broader examination of the placement and service system as a whole. As Clear and Gallagher (1983:232) point out, "there may be good administrative reasons for maintaining variety, the variety that uniform ... data may help to eradicate."

The analysis in this chapter suggests that successful targeting of high-risk juveniles for intensive supervision depends on development of a clear decision situation that: (1) gives priority to the consideration of risk; (2) provides program choices that place clear priority on intensive supervision; and (3) makes provision for appropriate response to other needs and considerations while maintaining the supervision priority. Programming to meet rehabilitative or other needs must be adapted to the intensive supervision requirement if it is not to be compromised in complex decision trade-offs. However, the evolution of the community-based intervention continuum in this system has resulted in a situation where parole services per se, or even subunits or segments of the larger organization, have not been restructured for the most high-risk youth into a more intensive or more surveillance-oriented model. Rather, the ADC operational procedures allow individual service providers to determine what level of restrictions will be used with a particular parolee. Consequently, whether supervision is actually a condition of placement is only marginally influenced by the set of objective criteria used by parole staff in the classification and decision-making process for high-risk clients.

All of this is not to suggest that valid instruments for categorizing youthful offenders into categories of need and risk are not useful and important. However, a failure to recognize and address the limits of their use and the environmental factors that condition it can minimize their contribution to improved correctional decision making. The analysis here elaborates the caveat that Clear and Gallagher articulated in their assessment of management problems in the application of standard instruments:

> Too often, agency administrators who are anxious for risk-screening devices ... will adopt standard cutoffs and override policies almost as if they were nonnegotiable. This kind of practice will inhibit innovation and lead to the implementation of ... policies that do not fit the agency's mission, resources, and environment. ... Attempts by administrators to borrow so unquestioningly (instead of managing changes toward a new system) are probably doomed to fail [Clear and Gallagher, 1983:232-233].

The flip side of this warning is that individual-level decision instruments can play a positive role when used as one component of a comprehensive administrative approach to placement. Future research should focus on the administrative decision needs of differing program environments. When program options are clearly defined and relevant to standardized individual-level criteria, rating instruments can fulfill an important administrative need. Dichotomous decisions concerning whether to place a juvenile in an intensive parole program may represent such a clear-cut choice. However, more complex placement decisions related to options and multiple needs are not so clearly related to standard individual-level criteria. In these situations, placement decisions must be seen in the context of development of the larger program environment.

NOTES

1. The data base for this analysis was produced in a two-year study of the juvenile parolee contract-for-service system in the ADC. The first author of this chapter served as a principal investigator in this study, which was conducted by EMT Associates, Inc. of Sacramento, CA, under contract to the ADC, Division of Juvenile/Community Services. Statistical data were collected on 323 juveniles placed in a sample of program placements between January 1, 1987 and August 1, 1987. More than 230 variables of information were coded from centralized ADC parole files in Phoenix, and from juvenile court records in Maricopa (Phoenix) and Pima (Tucson) Counties. In addition, in-depth personal interviews were conducted with 47 juveniles placed during this period.

REFERENCES

Ashford, Jose B. and Craig W. LeCroy (1988). "Predicting Recidivism: An Evaluation of the Wisconsin Juvenile Probation and Aftercare Risk Instrument." *Criminal Justice and Behavior* 15(June):141-151.

Baird, Christopher S. (1985). "Classifying Juveniles: Making the Most of an Important Management Tool." *Corrections Today* February:32-38.

Clear, Todd R. and Kenneth W. Gallagher (1983). "Screening Devices in Probation and Parole: Management Problems." *Evaluation Review* 7(April):217-234.

EMT Associates, Inc. (1987). *Evaluation of the Juvenile Residential Group Home Contract Service System—Final Report to the Arizona Department of Corrections.* Sacramento, CA.

—— (1988a). *Evaluation of Juvenile Placements—Final Report to the Arizona Department of Corrections.* Sacramento, CA.

—— (1988b). *Juvenile Aftercare Services—Literature Review: Interim Report to the Arizona Department of Corrections.* Sacramento, CA.

Gottfredson, S. and Don Gottfredson (1981). "Risk Screening: A Comparison of Methods." *Criminal Justice and Behavior* 8:35-49.

Halatyn, Thomas V. and E. A. Wenk (1974). *An Analysis of Classification for Young Adult Offenders*, (NCCD Research, Vol. 6.) San Francisco, CA: National Council on Crime and Delinquency.

Harris, Phillip W. (1988). "The Interpersonal Maturity Level Classification System: I-Level." *Criminal Justice and Behavior* 15(March):58-77.

Jesness, Carl F. (1988). "The Jesness Inventory Classification Scheme." *Criminal Justice and Behavior* 15(March):78-91.

Maltz, Michael D. (1984). *Recidivism.* New York, NY: Academic Press.

Martin, Susan E., Lee B. Sechrest and Robin Redner, eds. (1981). *New Directions in the Rehabilitation of Criminal Offenders.* Washington, DC: National Academy Press.

Martinson, Robert (1974). "What Works? Questions and Answers About Prison Reform." *The Public Interest* Spring:22-54.

Monahan, J. (1977). "The Prediction of Violent Behavior." In *Deterrence and Incapacitation: Estimating the Effect of Criminal Sanctions on Crime Rates*, edited by A. Blumstein, J. Cohen and D. Nagin. Washington, DC: National Academy of Sciences.

Smykla, John O. (1981). *Community-Based Corrections: Principles and Practices.* New York, NY: Macmillan.

Springer, J. Fred. (1988). "Privatized Juvenile Corrections in Arizona: Implications for Public Management." Paper presented to the American Society for Public Administration, Portland, OR.

—— Joel L. Phillips and Lynne P. Cannady (1985). *The Effectiveness of Selective Prosecution by Career Criminal Programs—Final Report to the National Institute of Justice, U.S. Department of Justice.* Sacramento, CA: EMT Associates, Inc.

Wright, K. (1981). "A Critique of the Universal Applicability of the Wisconsin Probation Risk Instrument." Paper presented to the American Society of Criminology, Washington, DC.

Part III

Evaluation of Juvenile Intensive Supervision

Intensive Supervision Programs for High-Risk Juveniles: Critical Issues of Program Evaluation

by
Christopher Baird

Issues critical to the successful evaluation of intensive supervision programs for high-risk juveniles are identified. Planning for evaluation and building data collection protocols into operations are critical to quality studies. A thorough and timely process evaluation will protect the integrity of operations and allow evaluators to impute the impact of changes to programs. The selection process is the most critical of all issues, though maintaining participant selection criteria is a formidable challenge. Finally, outcome measures that tell a complete and accurate story must be chosen.

INTRODUCTION

The 1980s witnessed a groundswell of interest in intensive supervision programs (ISPs) for juvenile offenders. Armstrong (1986:7) estimated, based on results of a national survey, that 30 to 35% of all juvenile court/probation entities had an ISP in operation. Undoubtedly, the percentage has increased since that survey was completed. Spurred by the high cost of residential programs and the failure of traditional training schools to significantly reduce recidivism, jurisdictions have sought innovative alternatives for controlling delinquent behavior. The panoply of programs that have emerged includes continuum of care approaches that combine short-term residential placements with intensive community-based services. While the term "intensive" often connotes daily contacts and major restrictions on youth movement, there is no program description that defines all juvenile ISPs. In some jurisdictions, programs requiring one contact per week are labeled "intensive" and, in fact, represent a significant increase in supervision over regular probation services. The level of contact required is often a function of what the ISP attempts to replace. When programs are designed as alternatives to state training schools, funding may be at a higher level than when an ISP is established as an enhancement to regular probation services for selected cases.

The preponderance of "new" ISPs share four common elements. First, their goals, generally stated, are to reduce delinquent activity of youth in a cost-effective manner. Second, most programs are aimed at "high-risk" youth. While no single definition of risk applies to every program, many ISPs use a statistically derived base expectancy approach to identifying high-risk cases. In these instances, high-risk youth are members of a group with the greatest likelihood of continued delinquent behavior. Other programs, however, assign risk level based solely on the severity of the offense, even though research has demonstrated that offense severity is weakly or even inversely related to subsequent arrests and adjudications (Clear, 1988). Third, many are run by private firms contracting with state or county agencies. Finally, a great deal of emphasis is placed on monitoring and control, with "treatment" viewed as an important but secondary concern. Few ISPs have been adequately evaluated to date; major reviews of evaluations have frequently determined that most fail to meet basic requirements of a sound design (see, for example, Gottfredson and Gottfredson, 1988). Reasons for the lack of quality evaluations are as varied as the programs themselves. It is critical, however, that the field obtain a clear understanding of what strategies work and for whom various programs are effective. To continue to expand expensive and intrusive programs without this knowledge base represents a disservice to taxpayers and program staff, as well as to the juveniles in intensive treatment or surveillance programs.

This chapter identifies issues critical to the successful evaluation of ISPs for high-risk juveniles. Its intent is not to discuss the strengths and weaknesses of various analytical methods or to critique prior evaluations, but rather to construct a pragmatic guide for establishing a credible evaluation design. Although many jurisdictions may ride the momentum of the intensive supervision movement long enough to implement such programs, in the long run continuation of juvenile ISPs will hinge on demonstrations of effectiveness.

Program success often depends on operational integrity as much as on a theoretical or conceptual framework. Experience clearly indicates that operational and evaluation concerns must be integrated if either is to proceed effectively. Evaluation designs that are too rigid can seriously impede operations; on the other hand, when operations proceed without regard for the discipline imposed by a rigorous evaluation plan, little will be learned regarding the program's effectiveness. For that reason, this chapter focuses on operational issues as well as the evaluation process. Discussion is restricted to three areas that are of major importance to ISPs: participant selection procedures, process evaluation and outcome measures. Each is critical to understanding if and why intensive supervision is effective.

PARTICIPANT SELECTION PROCEDURES

For this discussion, participant selection issues are divided into the following principal categories: (1) what cases should be targeted for intensive supervision; (2) how the integrity of selection processes can be maintained; and (3) what selection procedures are needed to support evaluation requirements.

Identifying Target Groups

Clearly, all youth entering the criminal justice system do not require intensive community supervision. For others, albeit a small minority, any type of community placement represents an unacceptable risk to the public. Such cases generally involve youth who have committed very serious—often notorious crimes—or youth with a long history of assaultive behaviors.

Program goals generally provide the basis for participant selection. Thus, goals must be explicitly stated and clearly defined. If the goal is to reduce the number of youth placed in state training schools, the selection process may be substantially different from that of a program established to reduce the criminal activity of probation cases.

Alternative Programs

Several recent classification studies have indicated that many youth currently placed in state training schools are excellent candidates for community-based programs (Bakal and Krisberg, 1987; Baird and Neuenfeldt, 1989). Applying objective criteria to placement decisions often demonstrates that substantial variance exists among regions and cities within jurisdictions, and even among decision makers within small geographical areas. Evaluations of alternatives to state training schools show that they are at least as effective in controlling the behavior of youth as the more intrusive and expensive policy of incarceration (Austin, Krisberg and Joe, 1988; Krisberg, Austin and Steele, 1989). Thus, it seems that there is a large pool of potential diversion cases in most jurisdictions. Operationally, two issues must be addressed: How to identify appropriate cases for intensive supervision, and how to protect the selection processes from judges and administrators who attempt to use the resource to enhance services for youth who would not otherwise be placed in training schools.

The history of alternative programs has been rather dismal, more often resulting in net-widening than diversion (Austin and Krisberg 1982; Blomberg 1983). Measuring diversion is inherently difficult, and many efforts are hamstrung by inadequate program planning that failed to anticipate evaluation requirements. The following five steps are crucial to both operations and evaluation, helping to prevent net-widening while ensuring the development of credible evaluation results. (Several of these steps apply to probation enhancement programs as well as alternatives to incarceration.)

1. *Development of Pre-Program Youth Profile Data.* To understand fully the potential of a program to divert youth from training schools, pre-program profiles of youth should be generated. A recent study (Baird and Neuenfeldt, 1989) of Wisconsin youth admitted to training schools, for example, developed youth profiles that included important criminal and social history variables. The cohort was divided into three groups based on the severity and chronicity of behavior and social history variables, as well as "prior efforts" expended by the juvenile justice system. Such profiling would serve a diversion program well, identifying potential groups of youth for various alternatives and helping to establish selection criteria.
2. *Identification of the Target Group.* Diversion programs are established on the premise that certain offenders can be safely and successfully handled in the community. It is critical to both program "marketing" efforts and eventual program success that administrators clearly articulate:
   a. which offenders are eligible for particiipation;
   b. why this group is appropriate for intensive community-based programs; and
   c. the costs and potential benefits of the program.

   Language describing the target population should be explicit, leaving little room for exceptions. To be explicit, thorough planning is needed. ISPs have, on occasion, identified target groups, only to discover that the eligible pool is too small to maintain a viable program (Petersilia, 1989). Obviously, the development of pre-program profiles would help avoid such circumstances.
3. *Post-Adjudication Selection.* Participant selection must be based on *objective* factors and, if feasible, these criteria should be applied after sentencing. Anything less introduces the potential to compromise results. Using structured classification instruments offers the most defensible method of selection because: (1) criteria are explicitly identified and (2) youth profiles are quantified, thereby making division into eligible and ineligible pools readily understood by all.

   Figure 1 illustrates the classification device used in the Wisconsin study noted earlier. Cut-off scores were established to identify three groups of youth. Those with scores of 10 or higher would not be eligible for community programs. The two remaining groups could be placed in various types of community-based programs. An ISP should identify a *specific* subset of these cases as program eligible. The use of structured decision systems, based on actual profiles of committed youth, removes ambiguity regarding participant selection and greatly facilitates both impact and process evaluations.

Post-adjudication selection does not, by itself, ensure that all cases would have been incarcerated if the program did not exist. Judges may sentence youth to state training schools on the assumption that they will be subsequently identified as appropriate for community-based supervision. Thus, judges attain the desired results while appearing to be punitive (Clear and Hardyman, 1990). This potential again demonstrates the need for historical profile information so that changes in sentencing practices can be identified and addressed in evaluations (Baird and Wagner, 1990).

4. *Third-Party Random Assignment.* Once the target group has been identified, random assignment to experimental and control groups should be done by a third party (someone other than program or training school personnel). Several researchers (Petersilia, 1989) have pointed out that when practitioners do not like or understand the random-assignment process, manipulations can occur. Therefore, to protect the integrity of the research design and to relieve staff of difficult assignment decisions, program selection should be made by a "neutral" third party.

   It should be noted that random assignment is recommended only after a screening device is applied to identify the program-eligible population. More discussion of this issue is presented later in this chapter.

5. *Standards for Dealing with In-Program Failures.* An issue that complicates all evaluations of correctional programs is how to deal analytically with in-program failures, particularly youth returned to more restrictive placements because of rule infractions. Programmatically, it is necessary to strictly enforce the rules both to teach accountability and to avoid losing credibility with youth in the program. However, there are two types of violations among all corrections populations: detected and undetected (Wagner, 1988). Given the additional supervision and surveillance provided, ISPs are more likely to detect violations of all types. As a result, violation rates are often higher for cases in these programs than for youth supervised less stringently. Indeed, the increased emphasis on enforcement, combined with more information about youth activities, creates a significant potential for high rates of technical violations (Clear and Hardyman, 1990). While these problems are inherent to ISPs, both operations and evaluation efforts can be aided by policy statements that: (a) identify how violations will be assessed and categorized; (b) clearly delineate how various types of infractions will be reported; and (c) specify what actions will be taken. Reasons for program removal, in particular, should be clearly articulated.

Figure 1: NCCD Juvenile Classification Scale

		Score
(1) **Severity of Current Offense**		
Murder, rape, kidnapping	10	________
Other offenses involving use of a weapon, use of force	5	________
(2) **Most Serious Prior Adjudication**		
Any offense involving use of a weapon or use of force	5	________
No priors or property only	0	________
(3) **Number of Prior Out-of-Home Placements**		
Three or more	5	________
Two or less	0	________
Total Items 1-3		________

Total Items 1–3. If score is 10 or higher, secure placement is recommended. If less than 10, score the remaining items.

(4) **Prior Placement in a Juvenile Correctional Institution**		
Yes	2	________
No	0	________
(5) **Age at First Delinquent Adjudication**		
14 or Under	2	________
15 or Over	0	________
(6) **History of Mental Health Outpatient, or Alcohol or Other Drug Abuse Care**		
Yes	1	________
No	0	________
(7) **Prior Runaways**		
Three or more	1	________
Two or fewer	0	________
Total Items 1-7		________

Recommendations:

10 or above:	Secure placement
5–9:	Short-term secure care
0–4:	Community placement

It should be noted that this scale was not designed to be used as the final screening instrument, but to determine if a proportion of the Wisconsin juvenile institutional population could be safely and effectively supervised in community-based programs. Further refinement of such an instrument may be warranted prior to use as a screening device.

Probation Enhancement Programs

While much of the preceding discussion applies to programs designed to reduce recidivism among probationers, other issues also emerge. Evaluations of probation enhancement programs will focus almost exclusively on recidivism, as diversion is not a goal. Even if these programs prove successful, cost savings are somewhat more difficult to demonstrate and certainly less immediate. Most importantly, the shift in target groups necessitates different selection methods.

The potential of an enhancement program to demonstrate success is tied directly to the base rate of the outcome measure utilized. For example, if a juvenile probation population recidivates (however defined) at a 10% rate, improving on an already excellent record will be difficult and ISPs will probably not prove cost-effective. If the base rate of probation failure is 50%, however, the potential for improvement is substantial. From a practical reference point, the key is to identify a group of youth with a high propensity for recidivism and select program participants from this group. Risk screening has become an integral part of ISPs in recent years because: (1) it identifies cases that require increased supervision and surveillance, thus constituting a rationale for allocating increased resources to this group; and (2) it helps identify a cohort with a relatively high propensity for failure. This increases the potential of the program to demonstrate that it makes a difference.

Probation enhancement programs should be reserved for high-risk youth. Risk should be determined using a structured, validated risk-assessment scale comprised of specific attributes weighted according to their relationship to recidivism. The failure base rate of the program-eligible group should be high enough to establish a reasonable expectation that improvement is possible. Strict random assignment, without screening to identify high-risk youths, will not ensure this condition. A high proportion of the low-risk group is likely to succeed under any circumstances, and its presence in an ISP will only serve to "blunt" differences that might emerge between high-risk groups in the experimental and comparison groups. The larger the low-risk group, the greater the degree to which program impact on higher risk cases is "hidden." A typical risk screening device (established for Alaska Youth Services) is presented in Figure 2.

Figure 2: Juvenile Probation and Aftercare Assessment of Risk

Select the *highest* point total applicable for each category.

Age At First Adjudication ________
- 0 = 16 or older
- 3 = 14 or 15
- 5 = 13 or younger

Prior Criminal Behavior ________
- 0 = No prior arrests
- 2 = Prior arrest record, no formal sanctions
- 3 = Prior delinquency petitions sustained; no offenses classified as assaultive
- 5 = Prior delinquency petitions sustained; at least one assaultive offense recorded

Institutional Commitments or Placements of 30 Days or More ________
- 0 = None
- 3 = One
- 5 = Two or more

Drug/Chemical Abuse ________
- 0 = No known use or no interference with functioning
- 2 = Some disruption of functioning
- 5 = Chronic abuse or dependency

Alcohol Abuse ________
- 0 = No known use or interference with functioning
- 1 = Occasional abuse, some disruption of functioning
- 3 = Chronic abuse, serious disruption of functioning

Parental Control ________
- 0 = Generally effective
- 2 = Inconsistent and/or ineffective
- 4 = Little or none

School Disciplinary Problems ________
- 0 = Attending, graduated, GED equivalence
- 1 = Problems handled at school level
- 3 = Severe truancy or behavioral problems
- 5 = Not attending/expelled

Peer Relationships ________
- 0 = Good support and influence
- 2 = Negative influence, companions involved in delinquent behavior
- 4 = Gang member

TOTAL ________

It is also essential that enhancement programs offer levels of supervision and treatment significantly above those provided to regular probation cases. For programs designed as alternatives to incarceration, costs are compared to residential programs, making the justification of considerable resources relatively simple. In probation enhancement programs, however, costs are more likely to be compared to regular probation services. As a result, obtaining the desired resource allocation may prove more difficult. At the same time, minor differences in services and supervision are unlikely to produce significantly better results. Hence, program design and the corresponding budget request must articulate the need for significantly increased supervision and its relationship to program goals.

Table 1 compares contact standards established for an ISP for juveniles in Ramsey County, MN with standards for regular probation cases. A subsequent discussion of process evaluation again refers to these figures to demonstrate how actual staff efforts were measured.

Table 1: Comparison of Contact Requirements
Ramsey County, Minnesota

	Client Face-to-Face Contacts	Collateral Contacts
Regular Probation:		
High supervision	2 per month	1 per month
Medium supervision	1 per month	1 per month
Low supervision	1 every 2 months	1 every 2 months
Intensive Supervision	1 face-to-face or 1 collateral per day	

Evaluation Issues

The literature on social science evaluation contains a strong bias toward true experimental design; that is, the random assignment of cases to experimental and control groups. However, such designs are rare in criminal justice research. This is due to a myriad of factors, principally, moral, legal and administrative constraints that make random assignments difficult in juvenile justice settings. For example, judges may be extremely reluctant to send certain juveniles to low-intervention programs just to satisfy a research design (Grizzle and Witte, 1980). While this may seem unfortunate from a research perspective, it represents less of an issue than researchers generally acknowledge.

Does experimental design deserve the emphasis it receives from both researchers and funding sources? Experience indicates that the answer is a qualified "no." Unquestionably, in large-scale efforts with large experimental and control groups, random assignment will result in equivalent samples and offers the best of all research conditions. However, most experimental projects in juvenile justice are implemented on a rather small scale. Because significant differences on attributes that are independently associated with outcomes can occur, random assignment is not always the appropriate selection process. Although these cautions have long been noted, experimental designs continue to be promoted to the point where researchers, in some instances, assume equivalence between groups without comparing characteristics of the samples. Many recent evaluation designs have blended prediction and random assignment in a way that helps to ensure group equivalency, at least on attributes associated with the probability of continued criminal behavior.

The following simple test of random assignments illustrates its problems in small scale experiments.

> Suppose a single factor is highly correlated with continued criminal activity. It is, therefore, important that the experimental and control groups be roughly equivalent on this characteristic. This factor is scaled, with each case receiving a value of one to four. In total, 100 cases are eligible for program participation. Using this hypothetical example, random assignment using a computerized random number generator was implemented. Five different passes on the sample produced the results indicated in Table 2.

Table 2: Random Assignment Test for Small Projects
(100 program eligibles)

	Program Eligible		*Random Assignment Test*									
Risk Factor Values	N of Cases	Historical Arrest Rates	Test 1 Control	Test 1 Exper.	Test 2 Control	Test 2 Exper.	Test 3 Control	Test 3 Exper.	Test 4 Control	Test 4 Exper.	Test 5 Control	Test 5 Exper.
1	35	15%	14	21	18	17	20	19	19	16	23	12
2	25	30%	11	14	12	13	13	12	15	10	10	15
3	20	50%	11	9	11	9	13	7	7	13	11	9
4	20	70%	14	6	9	11	4	12	9	11	6	14
	100		50	50	50	50	50	50	50	50	50	50

In four of five instances, random assignment produced a nonequivalent control group. (Test #2 produced the only equivalent groups.) In each instance, significantly different outcome patterns could be expected. As a result, it would be extremely difficult to estimate the impact of the experimental program.

Because this is the level at which most experimental juvenile programs operate, it is a fair representation of the problems of random assignment for small-scale projects. While alternatives to true experimental designs introduce other and, perhaps, equally difficult issues, the heavy bias toward random assignment seems unwarranted. Options to experimental design, however, do overcome some of the legal and ethical issues raised by random assignment.

When random assignment is feasible it should be used, but nearly always in conjunction with well-designed, pre-screening instruments used to identify a program-eligible pool. When random assignment is not possible (or advisable), other evaluation methods should be considered. These include:

(1) *Matched Experimental and Comparison Groups.* Many evaluations of criminal justice programs have utilized matched sample methodologies. This method is often chosen when evaluations are done post-hoc—that is, when evaluation designs are developed long after the program has been implemented and an experimental design is not possible. It is also selected when an experimental design is not politically feasible or it is determined that such a design would significantly interfere with program implementation (Adams, 1975). It is also the design of choice when interjurisdictional studies are undertaken to compare the impact of different policies and procedures.

Matched sample designs have some advantages but also introduce some problems. There are two keys to using the method. First, cases must be matched on criteria important to the outcome being analyzed. For example, if rearrest is the criterion variable, client attributes related to rearrest should be included as factors on which cases are matched. Secondly, cases in each sample should be exposed to similar environments, with the exception of the experimental program intervention, to assure that any differences in outcome can be attributed to the program. This requires a thorough evaluation of process, with clear linkages to the analysis of program effectiveness (Krisberg, 1980). Significant differences in staff experience levels or educational attainment could, for instance, have more impact on case outcomes than the program being analyzed. Therefore, it is important to control for such differences.

Identifying factors related to outcomes can be problematic. Although risk prediction has proven quite valuable in project and agency management, studies continually demonstrate that little of the variance in criminal behavior can be explained (Clear, 1988). As a result, the question of what factors to use as matching criteria remains an important issue. Matching on several demographic factors, age, sex, and race is, of course, essential. In addition, measures of the recency, frequency and severity of past criminal behavior should be included. Matches can be further improved with the inclusion of substance abuse, and, if possible, other measures of school and community adjustment.

Despite problems encountered with matched samples, a good matching design does produce reasonably comparable groups. In fact, for small samples particularly, a matched-sample methodology may produce a better comparison group than straight random assignment. The method will continue to be important in criminal justice research; it provides the best alternative when evaluation is considered on a post-hoc basis.

(2) *Pre/Post-Program Comparisons*. The second alternative to experimental design discussed here is comparison of pre- and post-program outcomes. This methodology is best suited to situations in which the program is applied to all cases supervised. If other policies and procedures remain constant over the period analyzed, and the youth offender population is not significantly altered, changes in outcomes can be attributed to the change in supervision strategies. Such analyses are sometimes termed "interrupted-time-series" studies.

When the "experiment" is not applied to all cases, matching again emerges as an issue. Rather than matching across programs or regions, the match is done across time periods. All of the issues noted in the discussion of matched samples again apply. In addition, the amount of time elapsed also needs to be considered. To find a comparison group not impacted by the change, it might be necessary to use a cohort admitted several years prior to program implementation. Obviously, the longer the time lapse, the more likely it is that significant changes in policy or case profiles have occurred.

PROCESS EVALUATION

In its simplest context, process evaluation asks, "Did the program function as initially intended?" To pass judgment on the effectiveness of a concept without knowing the degree to which it was actually operationalized seriously diminishes the value of evaluation. Suchman (1969:16) states, "If a program is unsuccessful, it may be because the program failed to 'operationalize' the theory, or because the theory itself was deficient." Numerous studies of the degree to which operational standards are actualized clearly demonstrate that it cannot be assumed that ISPs function as designed. A review of over 50 workload analyses of compliance with supervision standards, conducted during 1985-1990 by the National Council on Crime and Delinquency (NCCD), indicates that, in nearly half the cases, contact standards were not met.

A process evaluation describes the content of a program, assesses the quality of the intervention, and defines the characteristics and quantity of the program's immediate products (Grizzle and Witte, 1980). In order to obtain maximum benefits, process evaluations should function as a monitoring mechanism, alerting staff and administrators to problems when they occur. The erosion of selection criteria, for example, is often gradual and insidious as both administrators and the judiciary respond to political pressure to place more youths in highly structured programs. Program administrators are sometimes unaware of such erosion until it is too late and the project is irreparably harmed. Evaluations of all types of corrections programs (Martinson et al., 1976) have shown that programs often serve offenders they were not designed to supervise. A strong selection monitoring capability is, therefore, essential to maintaining program integrity.

A purpose of process evaluation is not only to determine if the program is operating as intended, but to identify *when* changes occurred. If the program has changed, process evaluation should identify what changes occurred, when they occurred and whether those changes are within the overall context of program design. If a program is not functioning as designed, then outcome and cost analyses are often irrelevant.

A good process evaluation provides administrators with timely information and establishes the level of accountability required by the current social services funding environment. The juvenile justice system is in the business of managing risk (among other things), and miscalculations clearly can occur despite all efforts to control events. Managers are seldom held responsible for the event itself, but they are more culpable if they are unaware of their staff's actions or if they react inappropriately to operational breakdowns. Process evaluation is one key to avoiding such crises, as well as the misallocation of substantial funds should program parameters erode over time.

In total, thorough process evaluations of ISPs address the following questions:

(1) *To What Degree Are Selection Criteria Adhered To?* Reviews of prior evaluations of ISPs, particularly those designed as alternatives to incarceration, indicate that often such programs end up serving offenders they were not designed to serve. This occurs because program managers are generally unable to exercise complete control over intake. Assignment responsibilities often rest with the judiciary, who, because of long-standing frustrations with a narrow range of traditional sanctions, seize the opportunity to increase surveillance and supervision for cases that would not have been incarcerated anyway. Even the most imaginative approaches to limiting such program abuse often fail to solve the problem.

A strong monitoring capability should alert managers to problems so that they can be rectified in a timely fashion. When these issues cannot be resolved, inappropriate placements can, at least, be identified and this problem taken into account in analyzing outcomes.

(2) *Are Contact and Treatment Standards Being Realized?* The theory of intensive supervision is that increased supervision (and, in some

instances, treatment) will better control delinquent behavior. It is a serious oversight to compare outcomes between programs without documenting the level of supervision provided. As Banks et al. (1976) discovered, increased standards do not automatically translate into increased effort. On average, they found that intensive supervision resulted in six minutes more time devoted each month to each case. The newer ISPs have much higher contact requirements than 1976 ISPs, but more recent studies still indicate that, for a high percentage of cases, standards were not met. Thus, workload analyses conducted in more than 50 jurisdictions by NCCD between 1985 and 1990 indicate that in most agencies contact requirements for the highest supervision level utilized are met or exceeded in about 50% of the cases.

One method for documenting levels of effort in both the experimental and comparison groups is to conduct a case-based time study of both. The results will not only document the number of contacts with each case over a prescribed period of time, but will show how increased contacts translate into time. If sufficient information is recorded during the time study, evaluators can better describe case contacts in both the experimental and comparison groups, perhaps documenting qualitative differences. In addition, services actually provided can be compared to program design as a measure of adherence to standards.

Table 3 again compares intensive supervision to regular probation in the Ramsey County, MN Juvenile Division. In this instance, a comprehensive time study demonstrated that substantially higher amounts of staff time were recorded on intensive supervision cases. Additional breakdowns of these data help define the "process" of intensive supervision: Number of contacts (face-to-face and collateral) recorded on average; time per contact; method and place of contact; and the major supervisory function (e.g., counseling, surveillance, etc., of each contact).

(3) *Have Procedures been Altered during the Course of the Project? When Did these Changes Occur?* Few programs remain unchanged over time. The social and political climate can change, sometimes rather abruptly, putting various pressures on both who is placed in ISPs and how these programs operate. Some changes are more subtle, but nonetheless important. Simple changes in staff, for example, can result in changes in process. Even the best of research designs cannot control these events. However, it is important that they be documented and their effect on outcomes estimated.

(4) *Why Did the Program Reach Some Individuals in the Target Group and Not Others? How Did Characteristics of Participants, Nonparticipants, and Dropouts Compare?* (Grizzle and Witte, 1980). Finally, it is important to identify youths who might have placed in the program-eligible pool, but were not. If some youths are systematically excluded, pre- and

post-program comparisons may be jeopardized. As noted earlier, the program design should specify how program dropouts will be handled. The process evaluation should identify characteristics of dropouts and explore reasons why they did not complete the program. These data could subsequently be used to revise the program to help more youths "graduate" successfully and/or to modify selection criteria to target youth who appear best suited to the program.

Table 3: Time Comparisons—ISP and Regular Probation, Ramsey County Juvenile

	Mean Time per Month
Regular probation:	
High-supervision cases	4.2 hours
Medium-supervision cases	2.7 hours
Low-supervision cases	1.2 hours
Intensive supervision cases	18.0 hours

Outcome Measures

Recidivism

Debate over the most appropriate measure of recidivism appears to have subsided in recent years. Instead, researchers are reporting and comparing many different outcomes, all of which come under the rubric of recidivism. These include arrests, technical violations, reconvictions, out-of-home placements, revocations, assaultive offense rates and suppression rates. Each of these can be reported as an independent measure, with estimates of program impact on each. Suppression involves comparing the pre-program rate of arrest or conviction with post-program rates (Murray and Cox, 1979). The intent is to measure the program's impact on the frequency of misbehavior. The major adjustment required to compute suppression rates is deletion of incarceration time during both pre- and post-program periods so that only "time at risk" is represented. In using suppression it is also necessary to control for age. Many researchers have correctly pointed out that as youth mature, recidivism naturally declines (Austin, Krisberg and Joe, 1988). There is also the tendency for arrest rates to regress to the mean. Often, just prior to justice system intervention, delinquent behavior peaks (leading to the need to intervene). The result is that perhaps the highest rate of activity that the youth will ever demonstrate is compared with a more "normal" level of delinquent behavior. Hence, there is a natural expectation that post-program arrest rates will be lower than pre-program rates. However, the difference between experimental and comparison groups may be "real" if controls for age have been instituted.

The principal measures of recidivism chosen for a study are often based simply on what data are available and reliable. Many different reliability issues emerge, particularly for the comparison group, program dropouts and youths who move into different systems following program completion. In each instance, evaluators have less control over data collection than over program participants. Data reliability and definition issues present difficulties in nearly every study of juveniles, principally because of the level of autonomy exercised by individual staff, which results in significant variance in responses to similar behaviors throughout the criminal justice system (Baird, Clear and Harris, 1986). The following discussion from another chapter in this violence study is a good example of both the difficulties encountered and solutions attempted.

> Two measures of recidivism were employed. The first involved technical probation violations following release from placement. This was operationally defined as the filing of a supplemental petition alleging a violation of conditions of probation not amounting to a new law violation. This type of petition is initiated by the supervising probation officer. In the case of regional youth educational facility (RYEF) wards, probation officers are more closely associated with the placement than are comparison group wards (though not directly supervised by the program). Therefore, officers could choose to ignore violations, or to respond short of returning wards to court in order to make the program look good. RYEF aftercare officers were interviewed to assess the possibility of this influence on decision making. All officers indicated that they were not influenced by the institution to mitigate actions on rule violations. Rather, they indicated that they were, if anything, inclined to hold these wards to a higher level of accountability than other probationers.
>
> The second measure of recidivism involved new law violations. This was operationally defined as either a subsequent petition filed in juvenile court alleging a violation of the criminal law, or a booking in the county jail for a criminal offense. It was necessary to use the county jail bookings because most of the individuals in the study had reached their eighteenth birthday at time of release from placement. Arrests after age 18 are processed in adult courts [Skonovd and Krause, this volume].

Table 4, drawn from a recent evaluation of a correctional program, presents a typical breakdown of recidivism measures. Both the frequency and severity of violations are reported, as well as agency response to violations (revocations).

Some recent studies have attempted to augment "official" measures of recidivism with self-reported data obtained through interviews or surveys (Barton and Butts, 1989). While these data may provide additional insight

Table 4: Comparison Measures of Recidivism

	Program 1		Program 2		Program 3	
	Exper.	Control	Exper.	Control	Exper.	Control
Percent revoked:	17.9%	32.3%	21.4%	34.7%	12.1%	21.2%
Percent arrested:						
Once	22.2%	18.8%	14.7%	17.4%	13.0%	17.1%
Twice or more	10.9%	18.8%	9.3%	7.8%	5.8%	10.2%
TOTAL	33.1%	37.6%	24.0%	25.2%	18.8%	27.3%
Percent convicted:						
Once	17.7%	12.8%	12.5%	16.8%	9.0%	10.2%
Twice or more	7.6%	9.8%	6.2%	6.6%	3.2%	5.2%
TOTAL	25.3%	22.6%	18.7%	23.4%	12.2%	15.4%
Use of weapon:	3.8%	17.3%	4.9%	9.6%	3.8%	7.5%
Use of force:	13.4%	27.1%	11.4%	19.2%	5.8%	11.8%
Victim injury:	9.3%	21.8%	8.0%	12.6%	3.8%	8.8%

Source: NCCD, 1989

into the frequency and severity of delinquent behavior, their veracity is subject to question. Statistics on crimes committed by adults, for example, have sometimes been so high as to strain credibility (Zimring and Hawkins, 1988).

Follow-up Period

The follow-up period chosen is generally limited by the need to obtain results within a relatively short time frame. Refunding of experimental projects often hinges on measures of effectiveness. As described by Adams (1975), the typical life cycle of an experimental project is three years. Indeed, experience has shown that funding of a project for more than three years without some indication of success or failure is rare.

Hence, follow-up periods cited in most studies are more a function of funding limitations than research desires. Most evaluators strive for at least an 18-month follow-up period. This seems reasonable, as research indicates that the vast majority of juveniles destined to recidivate will be rearrested within this time frame. However, establishing a uniform follow-up period for all cases in both the experimental and comparison group is critical. When "time at risk" varies, direct comparisons of results are difficult.

Cost

Diversion is commonly measured in simple terms, such as "number of diversions" or "number of incarceration days saved." The latter measure is more definitive and translates more easily into cost savings. However, some cautions regarding cost analyses are worth noting. For institution versus IPS cost comparisons to be meaningful, the IPS must function as an alternative to incarceration. If the program fails to divert youth from institutions, it simply represents additional expenditures, the cost-effectiveness of which are related solely to recidivism.

Assuming that ISPs actually succeed as alternative sanctions, marginal costs of confinement (i.e., costs involved in adding or subtracting a single individual from an institutional setting) then become an important factor in determining if the program represents a cost savings to corrections.

The following hypothetical example is presented to help clarify how the analysis of marginal costs can help determine cost effectiveness of programming.

> State X establishes an IPS that clearly serves as an alternative sanction. The first 50 youths placed in its IPS, however, have little impact on institutional expenditures. Capital and staffing costs remain unchanged. Small amounts, perhaps $2,500 per ISP participant per year, are saved on clothing and food. If graphed, the marginal savings curve would show only limited savings for each youth diverted.
>
> At the same time, expenditures associated with the new ISP (e.g., staff, office, travel, administration) far surpass the small savings in the institution budget. If State X never exceeds the total of 50 actual diversions from the institution, the IPS represents a substantial economic loss rather than a savings. (Even at this point, average ISP costs would be less than the average cost of incarceration, but use of these figures would be quite misleading.)
>
> If, however, State X uses the ISP to such an extent that it affects institutional staffing and/or capital outlays (either current or projected expenditures), substantial savings may be realized. Suppose that the ISP is eventually used enough to keep institution populations at 300 below projections. State X might then decide to cancel plans for construction of a new 300-bed facility budgeted at $50,000 per bed. The marginal cost curve rises suddenly as a reflection of this $15 million savings.
>
> The dotted line represents the savings generated by 300 diversions. A juvenile IPS handling 300 cases with caseloads of 10, for example, would cost approximately $1.5 million. At this level, the *average savings* for each IPS placement in State X is considerable. Although cost calculations can be very complex, a conservative estimate of average savings at this level, based on a 30-year lifetime of an institution and a $30,000 annual per-resident cost of operation, amounts to $28,000.

This oversimplified example ignores several complex issues, including the amortization of the institutional cost, which is a one-time expenditure. A

Figure 3

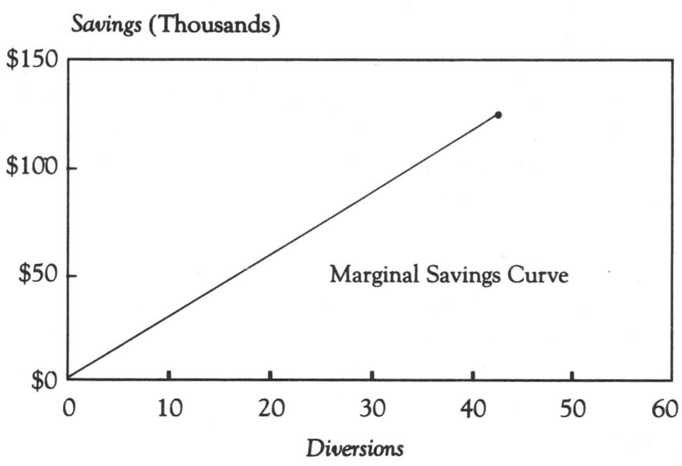

Figure 4

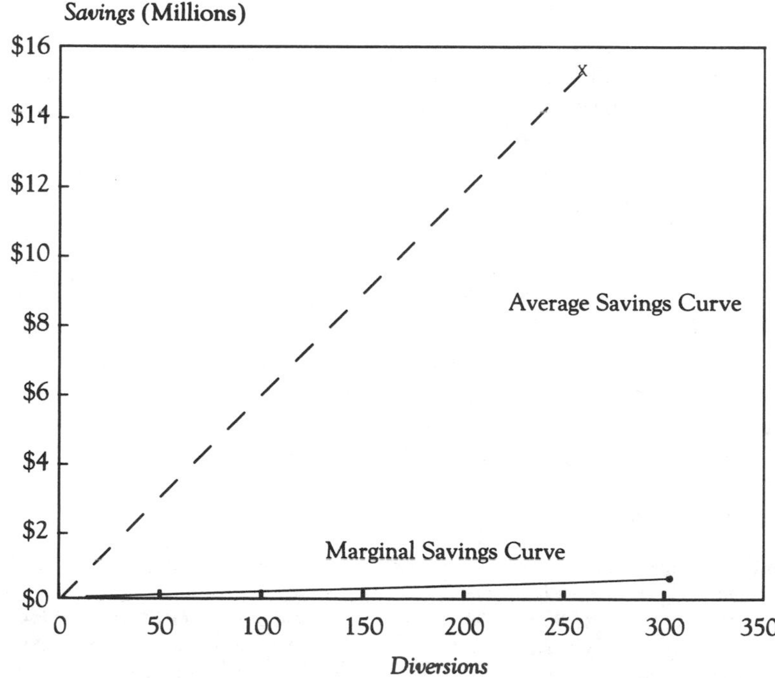

thorough study of cost-related issues also would take into account recidivism rates, length of institutional stay, police and court costs, and an estimate of costs to crime victims. However, the point of the presentation is that comparisons of average costs often confuse rather than clarify issues.

Any discussion of program costs is incomplete when limited to economic issues only. A program that reduces crowding and/or incidences of violence, and allows greater youth participation in programming, probably represents a significant savings in human terms, regardless of economic impact. An ISP that has not reached its break-even point fiscally may nevertheless be an enormous benefit to juvenile justice (Baird, 1983).

Concluding Comments

Much has been written about the need to properly evaluate juvenile justice programs. An exhaustive discussion of research methods and issues would require a lengthy book rather than a single chapter. However, the requirement to be succinct forces a focus on major issues facing both program administrators and evaluators. This, in itself, is of considerable value, as discussions of evaluation techniques often become so immersed in minutia that they lose meaning to many program administrators. This is unfortunate because with proper planning, evaluations of most correctional programs should be a rather straightforward endeavor.

In focusing on major concerns, this chapter has attempted to merge operational and evaluation issues to provide a basic blueprint for successful analysis of process and effectiveness. Planning for evaluation and building data collection protocols into operations are critical to quality studies. In addition, a thorough and timely process evaluation will protect the integrity of operations and allow evaluators to impute the impact of changes to programs. The selection process is, perhaps, the most critical of all issues; if selection criteria are allowed to erode, the fit between program design and clientele may be irreparably damaged. Experience clearly indicates that maintaining participant selection criteria is a formidable challenge.

Finally, there is the need to choose outcome measures that tell a complete and accurate story. Measures of both the severity and frequency of delinquent behavior should be presented in a clear and concise manner. This requires a uniform follow-up period, clear definitions of measures presented, and an understanding of the limitations of the reporting system utilized.

REFERENCES

Adams, Stuart (1975). *Research and Evaluation in Corrections: A Prescriptive Guide.* Washington, DC: U.S. Department of Justice.

Armstrong, Troy L. (1986). *National Survey of Juvenile Intensive Supervision Programs.* Washington, DC: U.S. Office of Juvenile Justice and Delinquency Prevention.

Austin, James and Barry Krisberg (1982). "The Unmet Promise of Alternatives to Incarceration." *Crime & Delinquency* 28(3):374-409.

—— and Karen Joe (1988). *The Impact of Juvenile Court Sanctions: A Court That Works.* San Francisco, CA: National Council on Crime and Delinquency.

Baird, S. Christopher (1988). *Analysis of the Diversionary Impact of the Florida Community Control Program: Preliminary Report.* Madison, WI: National Council on Crime and Delinquency.

—— (1983). *Report on Intensive Supervision Programs in Probation and Parole.* Washington, DC: U.S. National Institute of Corrections.

—— Todd R. Clear and Patricia Harris (1986). *The Use of Effectiveness of Behavior Control Tools in Probation.* Washington, DC: U.S. National Institute of Justice.

—— and Deborah Neuenfeldt (1989). *Juvenile Corrections in Wisconsin: Is There a Better Way?* San Francisco, CA: National Council on Crime and Delinquency.

—— and Dennis Wagner (1990). "Measuring Diversion: The Florida Community Control Program." *Crime & Delinquency* 36(1):112-125.

Bakal, Yitzhak and Barry Krisberg (1987). *Placement Needs Assessment for Youth Committed to Oregon Training Schools.* San Francisco, CA: National Council on Crime and Delinquency.

Banks, J., A. L. Porter, R. L. Rardin, R. R. Sider and V. E. Unger (1976). *Evaluation of Intensive Special Probation Projects: Phase I Report.* Washington, DC: U.S. Department of Justice.

Barton, William H. and Jeffrey A. Butts (1989). *Intensive Supervision Alternatives for Adjudicated Juveniles.* Ann Arbor, MI: Center for the Study of Youth Policy, University of Michigan.

Blomberg, Thomas (1983). "Diversion's Desperate Results and Unresolved Questions: An Integrative Evaluation Perspective." *Journal of Research in Crime and Delinquency* 20(1):24-38.

Clear, Todd R. (1988). "Statistical Prediction in Corrections." *Research in Corrections* 1(1):1-52.

—— and Patricia L. Hardyman (1990). "The New Intensive Supervision Movement." *Crime & Delinquency* 36(1):42-60.

Gottfredson, Don M. and Michael R. Gottfredson (1988). *Decision Making in Criminal Justice* (revised edition). Cambridge, MA: Ballinger.

Grizzle, Gloria A. and Ann D. Witte (1980). "Criminal Justice Evaluation Techniques: Methods Other Than Random Assignment." In *Handbook of Criminal Justice Evaluation*, edited by Malcolm Klein and Katherine Teilmann. Beverly Hills, CA: Sage.

Krisberg, Barry (1980). "Utility of Process Evaluation: Crime and Delinquency Programs." In *Handbook of Criminal Justice Evaluation*, edited by Malcolm Klein and Katherine Teilmann. Beverly Hills, CA: Sage.

—— James Austin and Patricia A. Steele (1989). *Unlocking Juvenile Corrections: Evaluating the Massachusetts Department of Youth Services.* San Francisco,CA: National Council on Crime and Delinquency.

Murray, Charles A. and Louis A. Cox (1979). *Beyond Probation: Juvenile Corrections and the Chronic Delinquent.* Beverly Hills, CA: Sage.

Petersilia, Joan (1989). *Implementing Randomized Experiments: Lessons from BJA's Intensive Supervision Project.* Preliminary report. Santa Monica, CA: Rand.

Suchman, E.A. (1969). "Evaluating Educational Programs." *The Urban Review* 3:16.

Wagner, Dennis D. (1988). "Evaluation Proposal for the High Risk Offender Project." Madison, WI: Wisconsin Department of Health and Social Services, Bureau of Evaluation, Division of Policy and Budget.

Zimring, Franklin E. and Gordon Hawkins (1988). "The New Mathematics of Imprisonment." *Crime & Delinquency* 34(4):425-436.

Intensive Supervision Alternatives for Adjudicated Juveniles

by
William H. Barton
Jeffrey A. Butts

A study conducted in the Detroit, MI area evaluated three in-home intensive supervision programs providing an alternative to state commitment for juvenile offenders. State commitment in most cases meant institutional placement. A randomized experiment followed more than 500 cases for two years each, and found that the recidivism of youths placed in the intensive supervision programs did not differ substantially from youths committed to the state. However, the intensive supervision programs cost only about one-third as much as commitment. During the four years in which the Michigan programs were being evaluated, the state saved an estimated $9 million in placement costs by using the community programs in lieu of commitment.

INTRODUCTION

A number of well-known studies have evaluated community-based correctional alternatives for juvenile offenders during the past 30 years. Researchers have tested the effectiveness of group homes and residential centers that used techniques such as Positive Peer Culture and Guided Group Interaction (Empey and Lubeck, 1971; Weeks, 1958). Other studies looked at specialized probation programs that tailored their services to match the emotional and behavioral characteristics of young offenders (Palmer, 1974; Lerman, 1975). Some studies examined a range of interventions and programs simultaneously, testing the extent to which they "suppressed" the rate of delinquent behavior

(Murray and Cox, 1979), or whether they prevented delinquent youths from being further involved in the juvenile justice system (Kobrin and Klein, 1983). Other evaluations have measured the impact of shifting juvenile correctional systems away from large institutions and toward greater utilization of small, community-based facilities (Ohlin, Miller and Coates, 1977; Austin, Krisberg and Joe, 1987).

Over time, these studies have been criticized widely, sometimes regarding their research designs, frequently in relation to their measurements and/or interpretations. No single study has been able to prove that community-based programs are effective as alternatives to incarceration. However, none of the studies have proven that such programs are ineffective. Most students of juvenile corrections have concluded that the jury is still out on the effectiveness of community-based alternatives.

This chapter presents the results of a randomized experiment that tested the effectiveness of intensive supervision programs as an alternative to state commitment for youthful offenders. Researchers from the University of Michigan evaluated three in-home, intensive supervision programs in Wayne County (Detroit), MI between 1983 and 1987. The three programs, created explicitly as alternatives to state commitment for adjudicated delinquents, were not remarkably successful in reducing delinquency. Yet the evaluation showed them to be cost-effective. At about one-third the cost of state commitment, the programs had comparable effects on recidivism, self-reported delinquent behavior and other critical outcomes. The evaluation concluded that, although the implementation of the programs could have been improved, they were demonstrably viable as an alternative to commitment.

THE CONTEXT

The original impetus for the Wayne County programs was a combination of fiscal pressure and the perception that the juvenile court lacked dispositional alternatives. Unless a youth is transferred to the adult criminal justice system, commitment to the state is the most restrictive disposition available to Michigan juvenile courts. When a youth is committed to the state, the Department of Social Services (DSS) is charged with deciding the most appropriate placement for that youth. Some youths might remain in the community after they are committed. The great majority, however, are placed out of the home, usually in training schools or other residential institutions. The cost of these placements is shared equally by the county and the state.

As the most populous, urbanized county in Michigan, Wayne County usually produces more juvenile commitments than any other area in the state. During the early 1980s, legislators and other officials from outside of Wayne County began to complain that they were being asked to subsidize placement costs for the county's youths. Something had to be done, they argued, to reduce the large number of these commitments. The state responded by placing a ceiling on the number of delinquency commitments it would accept from the Wayne County Juvenile Court. Local officials were faced with an urgent need to develop program alternatives. In 1982, the county had committed 708 youths to the state for placement. Beginning in 1983, it would be limited to 500 per year.

Using a combination of state and local funds, Wayne County implemented three nonresidential, intensive supervision programs in 1983. Although the programs varied somewhat in their approaches to working with delinquent youth, they shared a common model of intensive supervision in which caseloads were kept relatively small and program workers were required to make frequent contacts with the youth and their families. State and county officials hoped that the programs would be a cost-effective alternative to commitment, that supervision and services in the community could be as effective in handling some juvenile offenders as removing them from their homes and placing them in correctional facilities.

THE EVALUATION

To evaluate the programs, the court agreed to a randomized design in which comparable groups of youth would be assigned to each alternative program and to a control group that would be committed as usual. All cases recommended for commitment by court referees were screened for program eligibility.[1] Youth who were charged with violent offenses, had serious psychiatric problems, or had no viable home to return to (such as neglect cases) were automatically ineligible. The study was limited to males because the number of females committed to the state was usually quite small. After these exclusions, the study sample consisted of 511 youths, about 40% of all male juveniles recommended for commitment between February 1983 and March 1985.[2] In all, 326 youths were assigned to one of the three in-home programs, while 185 were assigned to the control group.

Most of the youths in the study sample were black (68.7%) and lived in the urbanized areas of Wayne County (76.3%). Upon entering the study, their average age was just over 15. Over two-thirds of the youths had been on regular probation at some time prior to the evaluation. They averaged 3.2 prior delinquency charges; almost one-fourth (23.5%) had five or more priors. Comparing the program cases with those assigned to the control group revealed no systematic differences on these and other variables. Thus, the randomization was considered successful.

Every case was followed for two years from the time of assignment. Information was gathered from a variety of sources: the youths themselves;

their parents; program staff; and police, court, and agency records. Interviews were conducted with the youth and their parents on three separate occasions (two times for the control group). "Initial" interviews were conducted soon after assignment, and "exit" interviews were completed upon each youth's termination from one of the in-home programs.[3] Two years after the random assignment, a final follow-up interview was conducted. Each round of interviews contained a wide range of items pertaining to the youths' and parents' living situation, employment status, income, attitudes and family relationships. In addition, the youth interviews included a battery of self-report delinquency measures.

The evaluation also collected archival data. Police and court records were used to measure official delinquency. Juvenile records were supplemented by data from the adult courts for those youths who had turned 17 years of age and thereby came under the jurisdiction of the adult system during the study. The frequency and nature of contacts between program staff and the study youths were collected from case files maintained by the programs. The workers in each program also completed questionnaires that characterized each youth's problems and progress during the program, and the effect of the services he received.

THE PROGRAMS

One of the programs, the Intensive Probation Unit (IPU) was located within the juvenile court. The other two programs were operated by private agencies under contract to the court: Michigan Human Services (MHS), and the Comprehensive Youth Training and Community Involvement Program (CYTCIP).[4] The IPU workers focused primarily on monitoring the youths' attendance at school and court-ordered counseling. They met with parents and teachers, and generally kept an eye on the youths' behavior. The CYTCIP and MHS programs, in contrast, were more treatment-oriented. CYTCIP focused on job training and job preparedness, and educational and recreational activities. MHS adopted a therapeutic approach that emphasized youth and family counseling. MHS and CYTCIP also provided behavioral supervision and probation-type services.

All three programs restricted caseload size. Each primary worker supervised six to ten youths and their families. Other than maintaining small caseloads and providing an intensive level of behavioral supervision, the programs were relatively free to develop their distinctive service emphases and treatment philosophies. Each program was designed to have a capacity of about 50 cases. The average cost of the in-home programs during the two-year study period was about one-third of what would have been spent on commitment. In 1986, for example, the average cost of the intensive supervision programs was about

$26 per youth per day. Had all the program youths been committed instead, the average cost would have been approximately $89 per youth per day (Barton and Butts, 1988).

Service Contacts

The program workers were required to keep a record of all contacts made with and on behalf of each youth. These records were submitted to the court every three months, along with a narrative summary of each youth's progress. The evaluation study used this information to develop several indexes of worker-client contact. Contacts could be made at the youth's home, at the program site (e.g., for group sessions and office visits), at other agencies (schools or other social service agencies, sometimes called collateral contacts), or via telephone.

Table 1 shows the average number of monthly contacts of the various types for the youth in each program. Overall, MHS workers made significantly more contacts than the other two programs. MHS staff reported contacting each client an average of nearly 14 times each month, or about three and one-half contacts per week. The other two programs averaged between 10 and 11 contacts per month, or slightly fewer than three contacts per week. MHS staff reported the most home contacts (six per month); CYTCIP, the least (about two per month). However, CYTCIP workers reported significantly more contacts at the program site than did the other programs (more than five versus less than two per month). Differences in the other contact frequencies were smaller, although MHS's frequency of collateral contacts (2.49 per month), was significantly higher than that of IPU (1.83 per month) which, in turn, was significantly higher than CYTCIP (0.70 per month).

These patterns of contact were consistent with the programs' different service emphases. The most family-oriented program was MHS, and the

Table 1: Average Monthly Contacts, by Program

Index	MHS N=93		IPU N=95		CYTCIP N=102
All contacts	13.77	>	10.81	≃	10.44
At clients' homes	6.38	>	4.41	>	2.02
At program site	1.63	≃	1.50	<	5.39
At other agencies	2.49	>	1.83	>	0.70
Telephone contacts	3.28	≃	3.06	>	2.33

ANOVA *results:*
>First mean significantly higher than second ($p < .01$).
≃First and second means not significantly different.
<First mean significantly lower than second ($p < .01$).

workers in that program reported the most home contacts. The CYTCIP program had an educational and recreational emphasis, and those workers reported more on-site contacts. The IPU program within the juvenile court emphasized behavioral supervision, resembling regular probation at a more intensive level. Its workers reported more home contacts than CYTCIP but fewer than MHS, an intermediate number of collateral contact and relatively many telephone contacts.

Participation in Program Components

The three agencies attempted to provide an array of services to the youths and their parents. The range and intensity of services, although not uniformly delivered to all clients, exceeded what would be expected from regular probation. Questionnaires completed by staff regarding each terminating case contained items about the perceived helpfulness of each service. These items indirectly provided an indication of whether a particular activity was used with each case. By examining the relative percentages of cases participating in each program component, one can get a sense of the range of services used by each agency.

Table 2 presents, for each program, the percentage of cases reported by staff to have participated in the various program components. The resulting participation rates are divided, somewhat arbitrarily, into categories representing high (more than 75%), medium (25% to 75%) and low (less than 25%) utilization. All programs utilized behavioral supervision and individual counseling with nearly every youth. Conversely, community service and volunteers were rarely used by any of the programs. In other respects, the programs' utilization rates reflected their different emphases. CYTCIP had the highest participation rates in youth-oriented, on-site educational and recreational activities, while MHS workers sought and obtained more family involvement. The IPU program appeared to function as one might expect of a court-operated program, with an emphasis on behavioral supervision and counseling supplemented by collateral casework activities.

OUTCOMES

Rather than a single—and necessarily incomplete—measure of program outcomes, the study used several, distinct perspectives: (1) recidivism (both official and self-reported); (2) other related outcomes (e.g., changes in self-concept, family relations); and (3) program success rates (whether youth completed the programs successfully).

Recidivism

Recidivism can be thought of as the reoccurrence of a delinquent act by someone previously adjudicated for a delinquent offense (Waldo and

Table 2: Participation Rates of Youths in Program Components, by Program

IPU (N=110)		CYTCIP (N=107)		NHS (N=99)	
High Participation (more than 75%)					
Behavioral, supervision	96.4%	Individual counseling	98.1%	Tokens/rewards	99.0%
Individual counseling	78.2%	Behavioral supervision	92.5%	Behavioral supervision	98.0%
School placement	75.5%	Recreational activities	92.5%	Individual counseling	93.9%
		Youth group	92.5%	School placement	88.9%
		Social skills training	83.2%	Parent counseling	81.8%
		Camping	80.4%	Youth group	79.8%
				Social skills training	78.8%
				Recreational activities	77.8%
Moderate Participation (25% to 75%)					
Tokens/rewards	69.1%	School placement	74.8%	Parent group	63.6%
Youth group	64.5%	Tutoring	70.1%	Tutoring	49.5%
Recreational activities	60.0%	Parent counseling	67.3%	Job counseling	44.4%
Social skills training	51.8%	Job counseling	48.6%	Job training	35.4%
Parent counseling	47.3%	Tokens/rewards	37.4%	Job experience	28.3%
Temporary detention	40.9%	Job training	29.9%	Temporary detention	25.3%
Tutoring	27.3%				
Low Participation (less than 25%)					
Job counseling	18.2%	Parent group	24.3%	Community service	17.2%
Job experience	17.3%	Community service	21.5%	Volunteers	5.1%
Job training	10.9%	Volunteers	16.8%	Camping	2.0%
Parent group	9.1%	Temporary detention	8.4%		
Volunteers	7.3%	Job experience	7.5%		
Camping	1.8%				
Community service	0.9%				

Griswold, 1979:229). Recidivism has proven quite difficult to operationalize in previous evaluations. One key question is where the data should originate. Reports of offenders themselves or actual observations of their behavior can differ from official records or justice system outcomes (cf. Palmer, 1974; Lerman, 1975). Since the introduction of self-report measures more than 40 years ago (Porterfield, 1946; Short and Nye, 1957), most delinquency researchers have come to accept that self-report measures have an important role to play in program evaluations (Kulik, Stein and Sarbin, 1968; Farrington, 1973; Hardt and Peterson-Hardt, 1977; Hindelang, Hirschi and Weis, 1979, 1981). Policymakers, however, continue to be almost exclusively interested in official arrests, adjudications and reincarcerations.

Official Recidivism. During the two-year follow-up period used in the Wayne County evaluation, 78% of the in-home program youths reappeared in a juvenile or adult court at least once; among the control group, only 53% appeared for a new charge. Before arriving at conclusions, however, a number of other factors must be taken into account, such as the seriousness of the offenses for which the youth were charged, and, especially, the relative amounts of time they were at large in the community during the two-year period. After adjusting for such considerations, the official recidivism of the two groups was quite similar.

The charges analyzed here are those occurring during the two years following assignment to the in-home programs or the control group. The data reflect all alleged offenses rather than just final charges, which are often reduced after plea negotiations. Measures used in the analysis include (for each case): the number of charges filed during the two-year period; the most serious offense charged; and the average seriousness of all the offenses charged.

Official records for each youth were obtained from five sources: the juvenile court, the state parole and review board (for all committed youths), the state police information system, the Detroit city court and the county prosecutor's office. The adult system records, coupled with information supplied by the DSS and the juvenile court, also permitted a measure of the amount of time each youth spent incarcerated (i.e., in detention, institutional placement, jail or prison) during the two-year study period. Youth were considered to be "at large" if no record of their incarceration was obtained from the above sources. Control-group youths averaged much less time at large (10.7 months) than did in-home program youths (18.3 months).

Table 3 lists the incidence of specific charges filed against the program and control-group youths during the two-year study period. The 326 program youths were charged with a total of 868 offenses, for an average of 2.6 charges per youth. The 185 control-group youths were charged with 242 offenses, an average of 1.3 charges each. Status offenses accounted for about one-fourth of all charges against the program youths, while violations of program rules accounted for an additional 5%. The control-group youths were charged with proportionally fewer status offenses and greater proportions of serious offenses than the program youths.

As shown in Table 4, charges were about twice as likely to be filed against program youths as against control-group youths. This difference was greatly attenuated when adjustments were made for offense seriousness. The average number of criminal charges per case, for example, still favored the control group, although the difference was smaller (1.17 vs. 1.85). Additional analyses of offense seriousness grouped the offense categories from Table 3 into six levels of seriousness.[5] In addition to simplifying the presentation of findings by reducing more than 20 offense categories to six, this system allowed seriousness weights to be assigned to each charge. The seriousness weights were used to calculate the total seriousness of a youth's charges and the

Table 3: Incidence of Offenses During 2-Year Study Period, Juvenile and Adult Court Charges

Offense	Program Cases N	Program Cases (%)	Control Group N	Control Group (%)
Status offenses	214	(24.7)	25	(10.3)
Violation of probation, program, rules	42	(4.8)	1	(0.4)
Littering, loitering	8	(0.9)	—	—
Resisting, arrest, fleeing and eluding	57	(6.6)	31	(12.8)
Drug possession, sales	14	(1.6)	10	(4.1)
Vandalism, malicious destruction	25	(2.9)	4	(1.7)
Weapons possession	28	(3.2)	13	(5.4)
Receiving or possessing stolen property	36	(4.1)	13	(5.4)
Simple assault	19	(2.2)	10	(4.1)
Larceny	65	(7.5)	13	(5.4)
Auto theft	112	(12.9)	36	(14.9)
Breaking and entering	89	(10.3)	29	(12.0)
Aggravated assault	58	(6.7)	16	(6.6)
Unarmed robbery	28	(3.2)	7	(2.9)
Armed robbery	38	(4.4)	16	(6.6)
Arson	5	(0.6)	—	—
Kidnapping	4	(0.5)	—	—
Rape, other sexual offense	12	(1.4)	12	(5.0)
Attempted murder	12	(1.4)	6	(2.5)
Murder	2	(0.2)	—	—
TOTAL CHARGES[a]	868		242	

a. Total charges exceeds number of cases (326 program; 185 control) because many youth had more than one charge filed during the two-year study period.

average seriousness of his charges. For example, a boy who had one charge for truancy (level 1) and one for vandalism (level 4) would have a total seriousness score of 5, with an average of 2.5, whereas a boy with just one charge for auto theft (level 5) would also show a total seriousness score of 5 but his average seriousness would be 5 as well. Table 4 indicates that the average seriousness of the control group's charges was significantly higher (4.19) than those filed against program youths (3.44). Control-group youths had fewer charges on average, but when they did appear their offenses were more serious.

Table 4: Comparison of Program and Control Cases on Charge Incidence, Charge Seriousness and Time at Large During 2-Year Study Period

	Program Cases	Control Group	F	p
Mean number of charges (N)	2.63 (326)	1.31 (185)	40.47	<.0001
Mean number of charges (N)	1.85 (326)	1.17 (185)	13.73	<.001
Mean charge seriousness (N)[a]	3.44 (254)	4.19 (99)	21.19	<.0001
Mean number of months incarcerated (N)	5.64 (326)	12.81 (185)	123.05	<.0001
Mean number of months at large (N)	18.30 (326)	10.68 (185)	138.10	<.0001
Mean number of weighted charges[b] (N)[c]	5.41 (326)	4.05 (160)	3.26	.07 ns
Mean number of weighted criminal charges (N)[c]	3.69 (326)	3.58 (160)	0.04	.85 ns

a. Number of cases is smaller because mean seriousness is based only upon cases with at least one charge.

b. Weighted charges are adjusted to compensate for cases' differences in months at large during the two-year study period. Weighted charges are the number of charges that would have been filed in 24 months at large had the youth's frequency of being charged remained constant.

c. Excludes cases who were never at large during the two-year study period.

Control-group youths also spent relatively more of the two-year study period locked up. They were incarcerated for an average of 12.8 out of the 24 months, whereas program youths were incarcerated for an average of only 5.6 months. What would have happened had all the youths spent 24 months at large, with the program youths having received the in-home services? That question cannot be answered unequivocally, but a reasonable estimate is possible if we assume that the youths' behavior while at large during the two-year study period was typical. The charges filed during the youths' time at large can be divided by the number of months at large to derive a rate of charges per month. That rate can be multiplied by 24 to yield an estimate of the charges expected had each youth been at large during the full 2-year follow-up period.

The last two rows in Table 4 show the number of total charges, and the number of criminal charges that would be expected had the youths been at large for 24 months. Considering all charges, program youths would be expected to show 5.41 charges each vs. 4.05 charges for those in the control group, a difference which is not statistically significant. Regarding criminal charges only, the two groups had nearly identical expected rates, 3.69 charges per program youth and 3.58 charges per control-group youth.

The results in Table 4 suggest that all of the apparent differences in official recidivism favoring the control group can be attributed to the following factors: (1) program youths were much more likely than control-group youths to be charged with status offenses and minor violations after their assignment to the study; and (2) program youths spent much more of the two-year study period at large in the community. When these two factors were controlled, the recidivism of the two groups, in terms of criminal charges, was nearly identical. Such a conclusion, while less troubling than a finding of truly greater recidivism for the program youths, is still sobering for the in-home programs. Despite their best efforts, small caseloads and retention of youths in the community, the outcome was no different than that of commitment and out-of-home placement. Yet, to achieve results that are no worse than commitment at a fraction of the cost could be considered a positive achievement in terms of cost-effectiveness.

Self-Reported Recidivism. During each interview, youths were asked how often in the preceding four months they had engaged in 26 different behaviors, ranging from status offenses (e.g., "skipping school without an excuse") to serious crimes (e.g., "injuring someone with a weapon"). Responses from the initial interview provided a profile of each youth's delinquent behavior in the four months preceding program entry. The exit interview indicated the youth's delinquent activity during the four months prior to program termination, while the follow-up interview yielded reported delinquency for the last four months of the two-year study period.[6]

Due to the successful randomization procedure, program and control-group youths did not differ initially in self-reported delinquency. Thus, the self-report delinquency (SRD) measures can address a major question of the evaluation: Two years after program entry (i.e., at follow-up), did the program youths differ from the controls in self-reported delinquency? As shown below, the answer is generally "no," although the program youths did report committing significantly fewer *violent* crimes than the control-group youths at the two-year follow-up.

Rather than look at results for each of the 26 self-report items, the behaviors were grouped into empirically and logically defined categories. A factor analysis of the SRD items from the initial interviews produced four meaningful factors. Four indexes were created by adding the scores on the items within each grouping. Thus the minor-offense index contains the number of times a youth ran away, skipped school, trespassed, etc. during the four months in question. The other three indexes summarize drug/alcohol offenses, property offenses and violent offenses. In addition to these four indexes, a total delinquency index was constructed by adding the responses on all 26 items.

A common-sense way to examine individual change would be to look at the differences between the first and last interview. Such simple change scores, however, would be plagued by "regression-to-the-mean." Researchers have noted this problem in previous evaluations of delinquency programs (cf., Murray and Cox, 1979; Maltz et al., 1980). The effect of this statistical artifact is that individuals initially scoring high on a measure will tend to score lower on subsequent occasions, and vice versa, simply as a result of measurement error and sampling variation, and not as a reflection of real change. One way to adjust for this bias is to control statistically for an individual's initial score and derive "adjusted" change scores that represent change independently of the individual's initial scores.[7]

Table 5 compares adjusted change scores for the program cases and the control group on the various SRD indexes. Most of the mean values are close to zero, suggesting very little overall difference at the aggregate level. On every measure, however, the program youths reported a small mean decrease, while

Table 5: Adjusted Change Scores for SRD Indexes, Wave 1 to Wave 3

Delinquency Index		N	Mean Change	Reduction N	(%)	No Reduction N	(%)
Minor:	Programs	143	-0.42	87	(60.8)	56	(39.2)
	Control	71	0.54	39	(54.9)	32	(45.1)
Drug/alcohol:	Programs	143	-0.42	80	(55.9)	63	(44.1)
	Control	73	0.57	38	(52.1)	35	(47.9)
Property:	Programs	147	-0.61	108	(73.5)	39	(26.5)
	Control	69	1.33	43	(62.3)	26	(37.7)
Violent:	Programs	141	-1.07*	99	(70.2)	42	(29.8)
	Control	71	1.67*	42	(59.2)	29	(40.8)
TOTAL:	Programs	124	-2.66	79	(63.7)	45	(36.3)
	Control	64	4.32	32	(50.0)	32	(50.0)

*Mean change of program cases is significantly lower (i.e., reflects greater reduction) than that of control group cases ($F=4.8$; $p<.05$).

the control-group youth reported a mean increase. Overall, program youths reported a decrease of about three delinquent acts, while the control group youths reported an increase of more than four. On the violent behavior index, the difference between the groups was statistically significant: The program youths' mean adjusted change (-1.07) was significantly lower than that of the control group (+1.67), which increased slightly.

Comparing the percentage of youths from the two groups that showed a reduction in self-reported delinquency further illustrates this difference. On every index, a slightly higher percentage of program youths reported a reduction. Overall, about 64% of the program youths reported reduced levels of delinquency, compared with 50% of those in the control group. On the relatively serious property and violent behavior indexes, more than 70% of the program youths reported reductions, compared to about 60% of control-group youths.

At best, the programs achieved a slight reduction in the level of delinquent activity over the two-year study period. Yet commitment to DSS was accompanied by a very slight increase in the average level of delinquent behavior. The two groups differed significantly only on the violent behavior index, a difference favoring the in-home programs. These results are consistent with the findings on official recidivism and suggest that the recidivism of the two groups did not differ substantially during the two-year study period.

Other Outcomes

There are factors other than recidivism that could be considered program outcomes. The in-home programs were designed to keep families together and improve family functioning, to advocate for youths with community institutions such as the schools, and to enhance educational and job skills. The evaluation interviews included indexes of functioning in several of these areas: family relationships, values and attachments to social institutions, self-concept, and future aspirations and expectations. On all of these indexes, the results were comparable to the analysis of recidivism; there were few significant differences between program youths and committed youths.

Family Relationships. The quality of family relationships was assessed by a series of indexes regarding parental "closeness" and "authority." The "closeness" indexes contained items such as "I agree with (mother's) ideas and opinions about things," and "I feel close to (father)." The "authority" index included items such as "(mother) makes rules I have to obey" and "(father) tells me how to spend my spare time." Indexes derived from the parent interviews measured patterns of interaction and "closeness" to the youth. One of the parents' interaction indexes, for example, contained items indicating how often the parent and youth communicated about "what (the youth) is doing in school," "important issues," etc.

Table 6 compares the program and control-group cases on these indexes. Very little change can be seen across the interviews on the closeness indexes. At follow-up, however, the parents of control-group youths reported significantly higher frequencies of communication than did the parents of the in-home program youths. The lower scores of the program cases at follow-up may be due to the lesser likelihood that program youths were living with their parents two years after assignment to the study, either because they were incarcerated (many of the program failures) or living on their own (some of the program graduates). At the time of the follow-up interviews, most control-group youth were at home, having recently completed several months of out-of-home placement.

Table 6: Family Relationship Index Means, by Interview and Group

Index	Group	Initial N	Initial Mean	Follow-up N	Follow-up Mean
Youth Interview Indexes[a]					
Close to mother	Programs	289	3.87	155	3.82
	Control	140	3.98	82	3.83
Authority mother	Programs	289	3.29	155	2.80
	Control	140	3.33	82	3.00
Close to father	Programs	156	3.48	92	3.40
	Control	70	3.75	40	3.41
Authority father	Programs	155	3.04	92	2.52
	Control	70	3.13	40	2.50
Parent Interview Indexes[b]					
Communication	Programs	303	2.85	199	2.82*
	Control	156	2.83	109	2.98*
Conflict	Programs	303	2.61	198	2.29
	Control	156	2.69	108	2.18
Close to youth	Programs	295	2.09	190	2.03
	Control	154	2.00	104	1.85

* $p<.05$

a. Scores on the youth interview indexes range from 1 to 5, with 5 indicating greater perceived closeness or parental authority.

b. Scores on the communication and conflict indexes range from 1 to 4; on the close-to-youth index, from 0 to 4. High scores indicate greater communication, conflict and closeness, respectively.

Both authority indexes and the conflict index show a reduction between the initial and follow-up interviews. The youth perceived their parents as less controlling, and the parents reported less conflict. Program and control group cases, however, did not differ on these measures. Overall, the indexes measuring family relationships revealed no systematic differences.

Jobs and School. At follow-up, the study youths were just over 17 years of age on average. Many were still school-aged, while others could have been entering the job market. Juvenile correctional programs almost always emphasize educational goals and often provide training in job skills. The in-home programs made various efforts in this area. How were the youths in this study faring with jobs and school at follow-up?

The percentages of youths at follow-up that were in school, working, both in school and working, or neither in school nor working did not differ between the program youths and the controls. About half of the youths in both groups were in school, 13% to 14% were working, and an additional 14% to 16% were both in school and working. Slightly more than 20% were idle. In-home programming did not appear to affect the likelihood that these youths would be working or in school two years later.

Education is an area where one might expect institutional programs to have an edge over many community-based alternatives. All of the institutional placements utilized for control group cases included a school component. School is a major emphasis at these placements because it occupies much of the youths' time. Obviously, attendance is more regular at classes held in such institutions than at regular public schools, especially for delinquent youths. Education was also a focus of the in-home programs. Program staff worked hard to reintegrate youths into the public schools.

The youth interviews contained several items regarding school attendance and attitudes. These were combined into an index of school attachment. In addition, the follow-up interview contained a set of items regarding confidence in school-related abilities. The results for the school attachment and school confidence indexes are shown in Table 7. Unfortunately, it was not possible to assess *change* in the school attachment index because the items in the initial and follow-up interviews were not identical. Still, program and control-group cases did not differ on this measure in either the initial or final interviews. At the two-year follow-up, they were similar on the school confidence measure as well. The evaluation also measured academic achievement by use of the Wide Range Achievement Test (WRAT) in the follow-up interview. The program and control-group cases did not differ significantly on any of the WRAT measures.

Values. Many correctional programs attempt to break down antisocial norms while fostering more conventional values. Training schools are often referred to as "schools for crime" under the assumption that commingling with other offenders reinforces deviant values and skills. Yet many juvenile institutions use methods such as Positive Peer Culture or Guided Group

Table 7: School Attachment, by Interview and Group

Index	Group	Initial N	Initial Mean	Follow-up N	Follow-up Mean
Attachment[a]	Programs	290	3.21	139	4.23
	Control	142	3.18	77	4.37
Confidence[b]	Programs	—	—	161	3.29
	Control	—	—	86	3.25

a. The school attachment index was not constructed identically in both interviews. Only a subset of the initial items were used in the follow-up interview. An attempt was made to make the scales have the same mathematical range (1 to 6, with 6 indicating high attachment), but they are not standardized and are not strictly commensurate. Comparisons of scores across interviews should be made with caution. However, group comparisons within interviews are valid.

b. School confidence measure employed only in the follow-up interview.

Interaction that utilize peer group processes to promote prosocial values. It is not clear what one should predict when comparing the program and control-group youths on measures of conventional and deviant values. Would retention in the community avoid matriculation in "schools for crime," or would it continue a youth's exposure to the negative influences of the street culture while preventing the potentially positive effects of the institutional peer group methods?

The apparent answer is that it makes no difference. The conventional values indexes in Table 8 were composed of items such as approval of peers who "obey their parents" or are "good athletes." The deviant values indexes contain items regarding approval of peers who "like to fight," "steal cars," "use drugs," etc. Both the in-home program and control-group youths reported greater approval of conventional norms than deviant ones. They were more likely to report that peers adopted deviant values than that they themselves did. Little change was evident from the initial to follow-up interviews. There were no significant differences between the program and control-group youths on any of the measures of conventional and deviant values.

Self-Concept. The relationship between adolescent self-concept and delinquency has been the focus of much theoretical and empirical inquiry (Barton, 1985; Cohen, 1955; Gold and Mann, 1972; Kaplan, 1975; Lofland, 1969; Reckless et al., 1956; 1957; Stebbins, 1971). Most commonly, the self-concept has been operationalized as self-esteem, with low self-esteem considered a precipitator of delinquency and high self-esteem assumed to be an inhibitor. More recent work has portrayed the self-concept as more complex, not easily portrayed as a single dimension. Fine points of self-concept theory

Table 8: Conventional and Deviant Values, by Interview and Group

Index[a]	Group	Initial N	Initial Mean	Follow-up N	Follow-up Mean
Self: Conventional	Programs	297	2.26	161	2.24
	Control	146	2.33	86	2.25
Friends: Conventional	Programs	297	2.18	160	2.16
	Control	145	2.22	86	2.16
Others: Conventional	Programs	297	2.31	160	2.31
	Control	144	2.25	86	2.25
Self: Deviant	Programs	297	1.46	161	1.35
	Control	146	1.50	86	1.41
Friends: Deviant	Programs	297	1.75	161	1.64
	Control	145	1.76	86	1.64
Others: Deviant	Programs	297	1.71	161	1.79
	Control	144	1.77	86	1.78

a. Scores on the conventional and deviant values indexes range from 1 to 3, with 3 indicating approval of "conventional" or "deviant" acts, respectively. The youths responded once for themselves, then indicated their perceptions of the values of their friends and other peers.

notwithstanding, delinquency programs often seek to boost the self-image of their clients, hoping thereby to lessen some of the presumed impetus to deviant behavior.

The evaluation used a multidimensional measure of the self-concept, based on the youths' responses to a battery of descriptive terms. On these items, respondents indicated how they saw themselves ("real" self-concept indexes) and how they would like to see themselves ("ideal" indexes). As shown in Table 9, three dimensions of self-description emerged: *Power* contained such descriptive terms as "strong," "powerful," and "brave"; *sensitivity* included "delicate," "gentle," and "smooth"; and *competence* summarized "smart," "quick," and "good looking." In addition to the descriptive self-concept indexes, a measure of satisfaction with the self was derived by calculating the total discrepancy between each youth's real and ideal descriptions. The lower the discrepancy, the greater the satisfaction.

Several observations can be made from the data in Table 9. First, the youths rated themselves more highly on the power and competence indexes than on sensitivity, and in all comparisons their "ideal" ratings were higher than their "real" ratings. In the initial interviews, the in-home program youths rated themselves as more powerful than did the control-group youths. Over time, the ratings remained relatively stable, although the youths appeared to report

Table 9: Self-Concept Indexes, by Interview and Group

Index	Group	Initial N	Initial Mean	Follow-up N	Follow-up Mean
REAL:[a]					
Power	Programs	296	5.29*	160	5.26
	Control	145	5.03*	86	5.18
Sensitivity	Programs	296	4.35	160	4.26
	Control	145	4.16	86	4.45
Competence	Programs	296	5.15	160	5.34
	Control	145	5.12	86	5.39
IDEAL:[b]					
Power	Programs	296	5.93	160	5.86
	Control	145	5.81	86	5.69
Sensitivity	Programs	296	4.67	160	4.68
	Control	145	4.45	86	4.72
Competence	Programs	296	6.19	160	6.37
	Control	145	6.34	86	6.26
DISCREPANCY[c]	Programs	296	1.37	160	1.26
	Control	145	1.45	86	1.28

* $p < .05$

a. "Real" self-concept indexes are based on responses to "how I am" items. Scores range from 1 to 7, with higher scores reflecting more of an attribute.

b. "Ideal" self-concept indexes are based on responses to "how I'd like to be" items. Scores range from 1 to 7, with higher scores reflecting greater desire for an attribute.

c. The discrepancy index is the sum of the absolute differences between the real and ideal versions of each item. Higher scores indicate greater discrepancy or dissatisfaction with one's self-concept.

lower real-ideal discrepancies at follow-up. None of the other program vs. control group comparisons showed a significant difference. Diversion from commitment had no apparent effect on any aspect of self-concept.

Future Aspirations and Expectations. Some theories of delinquency suggest that the key to interrupting delinquent behavior is to improve a youth's perceptions of his or her "opportunities" (Cloward and Ohlin, 1960), or to reduce the "strain" between one's aspirations and the perceptions of one's chances for success in life (Merton, 1957). How did the experience of the in-home programs or state commitment affect the youths' hopes for the future?

The interviews contained items measuring general levels of optimism as well as more specific indexes of conventional aspirations (e.g., "Someday I want to have a good job and support my own family") and material aspirations (e.g., "What I want most is to have a lot of money and enjoy it all I can"). Table 10 compares the responses of the youths on these measures. In general, their initial aspirations were quite high, near the top of the scales. At follow-up, they fell slightly but would still be considered high. If they seemed slightly unrealistic at the outset, they were somewhat less so at follow-up. Program and control-group cases did not differ on any of these indexes.

Respondents were also asked how much education they would like to get as well as how much they thought they actually would receive. As Table 10 shows, in the initial interviews, nearly two-thirds of the youths indicated that

Table 10: Aspirations and Expectations, by Interview and Group

Index	Group	Initial N	Initial Mean	Follow-up N	Follow-up Mean
Optimism[a]	Programs	296	4.28*	161	4.53
	Control	146	4.14*	85	4.45
Conventional[a] aspirations	Programs	295	4.45	161	439
	Control	146	4.55	86	4.27
Material[a] aspirations	Programs	295	4.04	161	3.94
	Control	145	4.09	86	3.85
College[b] aspirations	Programs	294	0.62	160	0.54
	Control	145	0.64	85	0.56
College[b] expectations	Programs	294	0.35	160	0.43
	Control	144	0.35	84	0.44
Educational[c] strain	Programs	288	0.37	159	0.23
	Control	144	0.38	84	0.26

* $p<.10$

a. Optimism, conventional aspirations and material aspirations index scores range from 1 to 5. Higher scores indicate higher hopes.

b. College aspirations and expectations measures reflect the proportion of respondents who would like and expect to get at least some college education.

c. Educational strain reflects the proportion of respondents whose aspirations exceed expectations.

they would like to go to college, while only a third thought they really would attend college. More than one-third had aspirations exceeding expectations, a condition that could be termed educational "strain." At follow-up, aspirations appeared to have declined (about 55% hoped to go to college) while expectations had risen (nearly 45% expected to do so), resulting in fewer cases of educational strain (about 25%). Once again, these patterns were identical for the in-home program youths and the controls.

The results presented thus far are striking in their consistency. The findings demonstrate repeatedly that the in-home program youths did not differ significantly from the controls at the two-year follow-up. Coupled with the recidivism results, this analysis argues that the in-home programs were neither more nor less effective than state commitment.

Program Success Rates

The final perspective on the outcomes of the programs concerns their success with individual cases. How well were the programs able to maintain their cases in the community? Did assignment to the in-home programs successfully prevent or merely delay commitment to the state? One way of answering these questions is to compare youths who graduated successfully from the programs with those who were terminated unsuccessfully. As in previous sections, the results are mixed.

An unsuccessful program outcome was any termination (case closure) that involved further legal sanctions against the youth (e.g., commitment, waiver to the adult system, or a new adjudication or conviction). Successful cases were closed when the program staff believed a youth's progress to be satisfactory and the youth graduated from the program. Occasionally, relatively inactive cases were closed when a youth turned 17 years of age and would no longer be under the original jurisdiction of the juvenile court. While these cases could not be termed "graduations," they were considered to be successful from a recidivism perspective because they involved no additional legal sanctions.

Altogether, the programs successfully graduated just under half of their cases (46.3%). MHS had the highest success rate at 51%, while that of IPU was lowest at 41.6%. The differences among programs were not statistically significant. Of the 151 successful cases, almost all (94%) were program graduates, while the remaining few (6%) were terminated because of their age and not because of subsequent legal problems. Among the 175 unsuccessful cases, most were committed to DSS (88.6%), while a few (8%) were convicted by an adult court; fewer still (3.4%) were transferred to the adult system for an offense committed as a juvenile.[8]

What happened to the youths who were able to complete the programs successfully? Once the intensive supervision was removed, did they resume offending and reappear in a juvenile or adult court? The great majority did not. Nearly 80% of the program graduates (78.1%) showed no subsequent charges during the remainder of the two-year follow-up period. Because the average tenure for successful cases was 13 months, these results are based upon nearly a year of post-program follow-up.

The programs varied only slightly in the percentage of graduates who were free of subsequent charges, from a high of 85% (MHS) to a low of 72% (IPU). The MHS program, however, tended to retain cases somewhat longer than the other programs, so MHS graduates had relatively less post-program time within the two-year study period. Overall, case outcomes did not differ greatly from program to program. Such a finding suggests that no single program approach can claim to be the best, but that any of them can work given the right combinations of staff effort, client motivation and, probably, a measure of luck.

It is important to recall that all of the 326 program youths would have been committed to DSS had the in-home programs not been introduced. In the next two years they would have been incarcerated for an average of nearly 13 months, at an average cost of about $100 a day. Yet 118 of these youth (36%) not only remained in the community with about a year of intensive supervision, but also stayed out of the justice system for (nearly) another year at least.

DISCUSSION

The main question addressed by the Wayne County evaluation was whether intensive supervision was an effective alternative to commitment for already delinquent youths. With the important exception that commitment seemed to be associated with more violent behavior, this analysis suggests that impacts on recidivism were slight. Additional outcome measures such as self-concept, family relationships, personal aspirations and values also failed to reveal any substantial differences between the program youths and the controls. After two years, it seemed to make little difference whether commitment-bound youths were diverted into community-based programming or were committed and incarcerated as intended.

Perhaps the intensive supervision programs failed to show strong effects not because their service models were inadequate but because they had been poorly implemented. Such an interpretation has been offered in rebuttal to the familiar dirge that nothing works (Sechrest, White and Brown, 1979). The evaluation analyzed the extent to which the programs were implemented as designed. While they may not have satisfied the most rigorous definition of "intensive," the programs nevertheless exhibited an intensity and range of activities far beyond those of regular probation and qualitatively different from residential programs.

Even the finding of "no difference" demonstrates that the intensive supervision programs provided a viable alternative for many youth who were facing their first commitment. At about one-third the cost, the programs were able to achieve case outcomes at least no worse (and in some cases better) than those of commitment. The issue for policymakers is how to judge the costs and benefits of intensive supervision as an intermediate sanction. Benefits include monetary savings, comparable outcomes and the less quantifiable value of keeping some youths in the community with their families. The primary cost is a marginal loss of "incapacitation"; despite the overall equivalence in recidivism, it is clear that the in-home program youths had more opportunity to commit new offenses immediately following their assignment to the programs. It is also clear, however, that all but the most serious offenders eventually returned to the community. The average length of incarceration among the control group was just over a year.

The bottom-line policy question is how effective do alternative, intermediate sanctions have to be for their cost advantages and rehabilitative potential to outweigh the short-term public safety benefit of removing some young offenders from the streets for a few months each? The findings of the Wayne County evaluation demonstrate that by investing in sound community-based programming, juvenile justice systems can reduce their reliance upon costly out-of-home placements, and stretch limited resources to serve more youths and families at no appreciably greater risk to the public safety.

NOTES

1. Most delinquency cases in Wayne County, MI are heard by referees rather than judges.

2. The evaluation continued to monitor the entry and exit of cases assigned after March 1985, but no interviews or other detailed data were collected from them.

3. Exit interviews were not sought with the control-group cases because most of them experienced a variety of placements during their state wardship, making it unclear what would constitute an "exit" comparable to a termination from one of the in-home programs. Furthermore, this study made no attempt to evaluate the treatment afforded control-group cases.

4. CYTCIP inherited its program from another agency that was unable to fulfill its initial contract after several months of operation. Although CYTCIP gradually replaced existing staff and revised the program to its own specifications, the evaluation cannot draw firm conclusions about CYTCIP's effectiveness with its particular program.

5. *Level 1*: The least serious offenses (status offenses and violations of probation resulting from failure to obey program rules). *Level 2*: Minor offenses such as littering, loitering and disorderly conduct. *Level 3*: Drug offenses. *Level 4*: Vandalism, carrying a concealed weapon and simple assault. *Level 5*: Relatively serious offenses such as larceny, auto theft, breaking and entering, and unarmed robbery. *Level 6*: Serious and violent offenses such as armed robbery, rape, attempted murder and murder.

6. The proportion of the study sample responding to the interviews fell to 50% between the initial interview and the two-year follow-up. Sample attrition resulted

from refusals, as well as the fact that the whereabouts of some youths were unknown. All the evaluation's analyses were examined for nonresponse bias. Respondents were not systematically different from nonrespondents.

7. In other words, the raw change score (follow-up minus initial delinquency level) is regressed on the corresponding initial score for each index. The residuals of these regressions are the adjusted change scores.

8. In addition, two study youths died while in the in-home programs. Three other former program youths and one control-group youth died during the two-year follow-up period.

REFERENCES

Austin, James, Barry Krisberg and Karen Joe (1987). *The Impact of Juvenile Court Intervention, Draft Report*. San Francisco, CA: National Council on Crime and Delinquency.

Barton, William H. (1985). "The Self-Concept and Delinquency." (Doctoral dissertation, University of Michigan, Ann Arbor.) Ann Arbor, MI: University Microfilms International.

—— and Jeffrey A. Butts (1988). "The Ever Widening Net: System Adaptations to the Introduction of New Programs in a Juvenile Court." Paper presented at the annual meeting of the American Society of Criminology, Chicago, IL.

Cohen, A.K. (1955). *Delinquent Boys: The Culture of the Gang*. Glencoe, IL: Free Press.

Cloward, Richard A. and Lloyd E. Ohlin (1960). *Delinquency and Opportunity*. New York, NY: Free Press.

Empey, LaMar T. and Steven G. Lubeck (1971). *The Silverlake Experiment: Testing Delinquency Theory and Community Intervention*. Chicago, IL: Aldine.

Farrington, David P. (1973). "Self-Reports of Deviant Behavior: Predictive and Stable?" *Journal of Criminal Law and Criminology* 64:99-110.

Gold, M. and D.W. Mann (1972). "Delinquency as Defense." *American Journal of Orthopsychiatry* 42:463-479.

Hardt, Robert and Sandra Peterson-Hardt (1977). "On Determining the Quality of the Delinquency Self-Report Method." *Journal of Research in Crime and Delinquency* 14:247-261.

Hindelang, Michael J., Travis Hirschi and Joseph G. Weis (1981). *Measuring Delinquency*. Beverly Hills, CA: Sage.

—— (1979). "Correlates of Delinquency: The Illusion of Discrepancy Between Self-Report and Official Measures." *American Sociological Review* 44(6):995-1014.

Kaplan, H.B. (1975). *Self-attitudes and Deviant Behavior*. Pacific Palisades, CA: Goodyear.

Kobrin, Solomon and Malcolm W. Klein (1983). *Community Treatment of Juvenile Offenders: The DSO Experiments*. Beverly Hills, CA: Sage.

Kulik, James A., K.B. Stein and T.R. Sarbin (1968). "Disclosure of Delinquent Behavior Under Conditions of Anonymity and Non-Anonymity." *Journal of Consulting and Clinical Psychology* 32:506-509.

Lerman, Paul (1975). *Community Treatment and Social Control: A Critical Analysis of Juvenile Correctional Policy*. Chicago, IL: University of Chicago Press.

Lofland, J. (1969). *Deviance and Identity*. Englewood Cliffs, NJ: Prentice-Hall.

Maltz, Michael D., Andrew C. Gordon, David McDowall and Richard McCleary (1980). "An Artifact in Pretest-Posttest Designs—How it Can Mistakenly Make Delinquency Programs Look Effective." *Evaluation Review* 4(2):225-240.

Merton, Robert K. (1957). *Social Theory and Social Structure*. New York, NY: Free Press.

Murray, Charles A. and Louis A. Cox, Jr. (1979). *Beyond Probation: Juvenile Corrections and the Chronic Delinquent*. Beverly Hills, CA: Sage.

Ohlin, Lloyd E., Alden D. Miller and Robert B. Coates (1977). *Juvenile Correctional Reform in Massachusetts*. Washington, DC: U.S. Government Printing Office.

Palmer, Ted (1974). "The Youth Authority's Community Treatment Project." *Federal Probation* 38:3-14.

Porterfield, A.L. (1946). *Youth in Trouble: Studies in Delinquency and Despair with Plans for Prevention*. Fort Worth, TX: Leo Potisham Foundation.

Reckless, W.C., S. Dinitz and B. Kay (1957). "The Self Component in Potential Delinquency and Potential Non-Delinquency." *American Sociological Review* 22:566-570.

—— and E. Murray (1956). "Self-Concept as an Insulator Against Delinquency." *American Sociological Review* 21:744-746.

Sechrest, Lee B., Susan O. White and Elizabeth D. Brown (eds.) (1979). *The Rehabilitation of Criminal Offenders: Problems and Prospects*. Washington, DC: National Academy of Sciences.

Short, James F. Jr. and F. Ivan Nye (1957). "Reported Behavior as a Criterion of Deviant Behavior." *Social Problems* 5:207-213.

Stebbins, R. A. (1971). *Commitment to Deviance: The Nonprofessional Criminal in the Community*. Westport, CT: Greenwood.

Waldo, Gordon and David Griswold (1979). "Issues in the Measurement of Recidivism." In *The Rehabilitation of Criminal Offenders: Problems and Prospects*, edited by Lee B. Sechrest et al. Washington, DC: National Academy of Sciences.

Weeks, H. Ashley (1958). *Youthful Offenders at Highfields: An Evaluation of the Effects of the Short-Term Treatment of Delinquent Boys*. Ann Arbor, MI: University of Michigan Press.

The Social Context of Intensive Supervision: Organizational and Ecological Influences on Community Treatment

by
Jeffrey Fagan
Craig Reinarman

A three-year demonstration project of intensive probation supervision for Contra Costa County, CA youths charged with serious offenses is evaluated. Although the majority of project youths went on to commit further crimes after probation supervision, there was a general reduction in the prevalence of crime regardless of level of supervision. Most serious juvenile offenders can be supervised in regular caseloads because the majority of recidivism is not threatening to community safety. Delinquents who are unaffected by ordinary probation should be the focus of special efforts such as intensive supervision. The impacts of supervision are strongly mitigated by deeply embedded social structural factors.

THE SERIOUS OFFENDER PROGRAM: THE LEGACY OF COMMUNITY TREATMENT

In the late 1960s and early 1970s, the trend in California's criminal and juvenile justice systems was away from incarceration and toward community treatment and supervision. The most important legislative and institutional support for this trend was the probation subsidy program. Whereas previous proposals for strengthening probation had been rejected by the state legislature as too costly, the genius of the 1965 probation subsidy legislation was its subvention system, which provided funds to each county in proportion to its reduction in commitments to state institutions. Thus, for every offender who was successfully supervised in the community, state funds were made available to county probation programs for various forms of special supervision. The fiscal savings from reduced institutional commitments were then used to finance special probation and other community-based treatment and intervention programs. These additional funds provided the resources needed to reduce caseload size, intensify probation supervision and make better use of community services for offenders (Smith, 1972; Lerman, 1975; Lemert and Dill, 1978).

From the viewpoint of juvenile probation officers, probation subsidy was a welcome development. Caseload sizes of 60 to 80 or more limited the amount of contact with and supervision of probationers they could accomplish. Under normal circumstances, supervision was limited to monthly check-ins and crisis situations; little or no attention was given to the assessment of specific client needs, or to matching these with available community services. Probation officers' capacity for supervision was further diluted by their pretrial investigative responsibilities, which often took precedence over supervisory duties.

Beginning in 1965, the probation subsidy program provided both the philosophy and the fiscal resources to strengthen probation services. Subvention funds were provided for smaller caseloads and special community services in probation programs. In theory, this not only reduced costs but improved the chances for rehabilitation and successful reintegration into the community without concomitant increases in risks to public safety.

By the early 1970s resentment of—and corruption within—some probation subsidy caseloads, along with routinization in most others, led special supervision caseloads to become largely assimilated into regular probation operations (Lemert and Dill, 1978). Average caseload sizes crept upward, and many judges gradually increased their commitments to the state institutions of the California Youth Authority. Thus, the amount of state funding available for the reduced caseloads of probation subsidy slowed to a trickle.

Then, in 1976, drawing on the same correctional philosophy that a decade earlier had warned of the stigmatizing and counterproductive effects of incarcerating youthful offenders, the California legislature passed Assembly Bill 3121, effectively prohibiting the incarceration of status offenders. This law, however, provided no funding for alternative forms of supervision or community services for such offenders. In a subsequent legislative session, Assembly Bill 90 was passed to provide, in a manner that clearly paralleled the earlier Probation Subsidy Program, funds for community-based programs for status offenders (Lerman, 1984). Again, the level of such funding was made proportional to the level of reduction in commitments to California Youth Authority institutions. While the combined impact of both bills was generally heralded as a much-needed and humane reform, it left probation departments with only more serious offenders on their caseloads.

Thus, by the late 1970s, probation subsidy had all but faded from view, caseload sizes had risen back to previous levels, and the bulk of the *least* serious youthful offenders had become wards of the welfare department rather than probation. At the same time, the rehabilitative ideal that had long characterized the dominant strain of California correctional philosophy, and had supported the growth of community-based supervision and treatment, began to be eclipsed by rising public concern over violent crime and delinquency (Miller and Ohlin, 1985). In the shadow of the *parens patriae* philosophy of the recent past, there emerged a punishment/incarceration-oriented philosophy that made public safety the highest priority of delinquency policy (Feld, 1987). Public perceptions of rising street crime and increasingly violent young offenders put a spotlight on the serious delinquent (Fagan, 1990).

It was this policy context in which the Contra Costa County Probation Department's "Serious 602 Offender Project" (SOP) came into being. In the late 1970s, roughly one-third of the violent or serious crimes committed in the county were committed by juveniles, according to SOP planners. The vast majority of these youthful offenders ended up on probation—either immediately after adjudication or after short stays in a county juvenile facility. Despite the seriousness of many of their offenses and frequent histories of past violence, such offenders were routinely assigned to regular probation caseloads, with about 70 probationers per deputy. This limited the quantity and quality of supervision to *pro forma* monthly contacts and crisis situations, and provided for no systematic assessment of client needs or the matching of such needs with community services. Moreover, deputies' pretrial investigative responsibilities often detracted from the time available for counseling and supervising probationers.

Despite experience with reduced caseloads under probation subsidy, special intensive supervision caseloads had never been focused specifically on violent or serious juvenile offenders. Until then, there had been little incentive to differentiate probation caseloads in terms of the "seriousness" of the offender, nor had there been theoretical grounds to guide such classification. Yet the burgeoning number of serious juvenile offenders placed on probation created a need for special types of supervision to maintain safety, the central mission of probation.

In July 1978, Contra Costa County's Probation Department initiated the SOP, a three-year demonstration project of intensive probation supervision for youths charged with serious offenses. The project utilized an experimental design that allowed a rigorous evaluation of the efficacy of this approach to control and rehabilitate serious juvenile offenders.

Intervention Theory and Practice

The intensive supervision SOP caseloads included a maximum of 20 "active" cases at any one time, with an expected supervision interval of six months. This would afford SOP deputies weekly rather than monthly contacts with all probationers, but within a time-limited interval. With this increased amount of time, probation officers could improve their knowledge of each client's situation, and thereby maximize the use and coordination of community services, which were tailored to the specialized needs of each juvenile offender. Under SOP, deputies were expected to use individual counseling, family counseling, school follow-up, group activities and specialized treatment services for substance abuse as part of more systematic, intensive supervision.

Case Selection and Assignment

To be eligible for the SOP pool, probationers had to be: on formal supervision; less than 17.5 years of age; not in residential placement or another special probation program; and without court charges, termination, or a placement out of the area pending. The seriousness of the charge(s) against probationers was then addressed. Violence was the "cutting edge" to determine SOP eligibility. A probationer had to be judged a "serious" offender who was a physical threat to others according to one of two definitions. Either he or she was charged with one or more felony violence offenses[1] or—if not charged with a specific offense—the probation officer had knowledge of the ward's potential for violence[2], based on specific acts of violence, even if not charged.

Cases that successfully met either or both of these criteria were placed into the SOP pool and randomly assigned to an experimental (SOP) caseload for intensive supervision or a control group (regular probation) caseload. At the outset, the ratio of experimental-to-control assignments was three to one in order to ensure rapid caseload development. Eventually, the sampling ratio was changed to 50%.

Supervision Strategies

Early evaluation reports (Jamison, 1981) suggested promising results. With regard to operational goals, clients met selection criteria, and were randomly assigned to experimental and control groups. Caseload sizes were kept to 20 or less per deputy, and clients received intensive supervision (average contact at least once per week). Finally, SOP clients remained on probation for approximately the length of time specified (about seven months, 26% less than the average for control-group probationers). Jamison's evaluation also reported that SOP intervention was indeed unique compared to regular supervision. Probationers were assessed at intake vis-a-vis treatment intervention needs. Contacts were more frequent, and they more often involved components of each probationer's social network—parents, teachers and (occasionally) employers. The nature of contact was enriched as well. Structured activities were common, and included cultural and recreational activities plus special counseling services. In-home contacts were common, as were referrals to special remedial placements.

However, practical modifications in program implementation occurred during the experiment. First, six months prior to the start of the SOP, a similar experiment with small caseloads and intensive probation supervision was incorporated into the SOP caseload for West County (i.e., El Cerrito and Richmond).[3] The total number of clients was small (a total of 21 for the entire year), and there is no evidence that they had more serious criminal histories than SOP clients. But, as shown later in this chapter, the Richmond SOP group differed in several ways from other SOP probationers and regular (control) probationers.

Second, the traditional primacy of public safety as a concern in the probation department made it difficult to adhere strictly to the random-assignment procedure. Specifically, those juvenile offenders who were screened into the SOP pool and then chosen as members of control-group caseloads (i.e, regular probation supervision) were in many cases in West County assigned instead to an existing "Intensive Supervision Unit" (ISU) caseload. The ISU caseloads were in most respects very similar to SOP caseloads, thus possibly contaminating the experimental design by providing control-group clients with intensive supervision similar to that received by experimental-group clients.

Finally, the nature of the treatment or supervision given to SOP clients versus control-group clients differed in intensity, but not necessarily in theory or strategy. Interviews with SOP and control probation officers revealed that the tools and procedures were very much the same—differing only insofar as SOP clients, by virtue of the extra time available in smaller caseloads, went through a more thorough version of the traditional needs assessment process. Also, the match between the special problems and needs of the client and the special abilities of certain probation officers was generally no more tailored for SOP clients than for regular or control-group clients. Assignments were based on geographical concerns and the relative balance in caseload sizes.

Nevertheless, there were important differences between SOP and control-group cases in *frequency of contact*. Whereas regular and control-group clients were seen on an average of once per month, SOP clients were seen on an average of once per week (and often for a longer period of time). With respect to the *type of contact*, the smaller caseload size and the more frequent contacts in the SOP enabled SOP deputies to make more family and school contacts, and to pay more attention to their clients' entire social network than was possible for control-group deputies. However, while this increased contact allowed greater follow-up of SOP clients than of controls, this did not entail a fundamentally discrete form of "treatment", i.e., supervision and counseling functions were generally indistinguishable in both types of caseload.

In short, there was a strong consensus among SOP deputies, control-group deputies, and SOP supervisors that the distinction between the SOP and regular probation amounted to a difference of *degree* rather than a difference of *kind*. Thus, this research examines the effects of a more *intensive* form of probation supervision, not of a substantively different type of supervision.

Nevertheless, preliminary evaluations found that six months after intake, the percentage of the experimental (SOP) group that had been charged with new offenses was 21% lower than that of the control group.[4] After six months, 63% of the experimentals as opposed to 46% of the controls had not been charged with new offenses. Perhaps more critical, the experimental group showed a 48% reduction in the rate of recidivism for *violent offenses* compared to the control group (due to the small frequencies involved, this difference was not statistically significant).

Policy Issues

The principal hypothesis of the SOP initiative was that a program of intensive probation supervision, including both surveillance and therapeutic interventions, designed for a youthful violent offender population, will reduce recidivism, and improve the social and interpersonal functioning of its caseloads compared to regular probation caseloads. Probation officials stated that for many such probationers in Contra Costa County their next offense or juvenile court appearance would likely result in a commitment to the state juvenile corrections agency. Put another way, the SOP was seen as the "last chance before Youth Authority." In effect, the SOP revived the debate as to whether intensive probation supervision could reduce incarceration rates for serious juveniles.

From a different perspective, SOP youth were the most problematic cases in the probation department—those requiring the most intensive surveillance and intervention services. The development of effective policies for this group—especially in terms of caseload size and duration of probation—held major implications for probation policy throughout the county. It held the promise of a more cost-effective allocation of resources through new methods of caseload assignment and case management.

Finally, the SOP was the last remaining legacy of the probation subsidy policies. In an era of public pressure for harsher punishments, the redirection of resources toward intensive supervision and away from secure placements for violent juvenile offenders was a bold policy experiment. The SOP was designed to provide close supervision of, and to protect public safety from, serious offenders without confinement, a departure from the prevailing trends in juvenile justice in California in the preceding decade (see, for example, Greenwood et al., 1983). SOP failure could portend a two-tiered stratification of delinquency policy: community supervision (with large caseloads) for nonserious offenders, and secure confinement for more serious offenders.

Although this study focuses on one California county, its implications are significant for other jurisdictions and states. Contra Costa County is a microcosm of America—with metropolitan, suburban, and rural regions; rich ethnic diversity; and economic activities ranging from heavy industry to "high-tech" manufacturing, to agriculture and service industries. Its people are young, and the county is in social and physical flux. Its experiences with intensive probation supervision for violent delinquents are applicable to most other states and counties struggling with the development of cost-effective alternatives to institutions.

Overview of This Chapter

This chapter examines the SOP's long-term impact. Encouraged by positive early evaluation results, a long-term (36-month) follow-up study was begun to examine whether these differences would be sustained over time and, if so, for what types of wards under what sorts of conditions. We first outline Contra Costa County as a region marked by rapid demographic and economic change, but typical of many parts of the U.S. Next, we review the study methodology and present basic descriptive information on SOP clients. The impacts on recidivism for SOP and regular probationers are then assessed, as are the program's implications for public safety. Four measures of criminality are used to examine different definitions of recidivism. The analyses also view the SOP in the context of ecological variables that differentiate the unique regions within the county and determine factors in a probationer's immediate social area that mediate the effects of intensive supervision.

The final sections identify the developmental and social factors that conjoin with the SOP to impact on recidivism. Both practical and theoretical implications are drawn from these analyses. The chapter concludes with an overview of the SOP's effectiveness and appropriateness as a dispositional alternative for a population of violent delinquents. A policy and research agenda is presented for intensive supervision with violent delinquents in the transition to adulthood. In an epilogue, we return to qualitative data on the consistency and integrity of the program experience to understand the observed outcomes.

THE SETTING: AN OVERVIEW OF CONTRA COSTA COUNTY

Contra Costa County occupies 800 square miles on the eastern shore of San Francisco Bay, along the Sacramento River Delta, and inland toward the agricultural heartland of California. It is a county rich in contrasts. Just across the bay from San Francisco and Marin County sits Richmond—the site of dozens of smoke stacks, oil storage tanks, warehouses and small factories—where ships, railroads and trucks load and unload. Since World War II, it has been something of an industrial "back closet" for the Bay Area. Just beyond Contra Costa's central corridor of new middle- to upper-middle-class suburbs and burgeoning office parks lie steel mills, delta port facilities, navy bases, and miles of fruit orchards.

The county's population in 1980 was approximately 660,000—the tenth largest on the ninth smallest land area in the state. Between 1950 and 1980, the county's population doubled again with the aid of the Bay Area Rapid Transit system, which beginning in 1972 linked Contra Costa more closely to major Bay Area cities.

In addition to the rapid growth of the retail and service sectors that followed in the wake of population growth, the county became a mecca for white-collar office work. Between 1981 and 1982 alone, there was a 73% increase in office space. In keeping with such rapid economic growth, the number of retail jobs grew from 27,200 in 1972 to 45,100 in 1980 (California Employment Development Department, 1981; Contra Costa County Planning Department, 1979). For the county as a whole, 1979 data show Contra Costa to have had the sixth highest per capita income of the 62 counties in California (Contra Costa County Planning Department, 1979) and the highest median per capita income in the state—$18,213, compared to a statewide average of $13,750.

Beneath such positive overall indicators, however, Table 1 shows that pockets of poverty, social problems and uneven development are camouflaged by the general health of the area as a whole. For example, the proportion of female-headed households with children and no spouse is four times higher in Richmond than in Walnut Creek, and the percentage of the population living below the poverty level in Concord, Martinez and Walnut Creek is but a fraction of that in Pittsburgh, Brentwood and Richmond. Similarly, median household income varies from a low of $14,700 in Brentwood to a high of $24,842 in Walnut Creek (Fagan and Reinarman, 1984).

The same variation can also be seen in labor force characteristics. While over nine in ten adult residents of Walnut Creek finished high school or more, only about half of those in Brentwood reached or exceeded that level of educational attainment. Unemployment in 1979 was twice as high in Pittsburgh and Richmond as it was in Walnut Creek and Concord. Moreover, although more than two in five adult residents of Walnut Creek work in high-status occupations, less than one in five do so in Antioch, Brentwood, Pittsburgh and Richmond.

Residential patterns are clearly segregated by race, as well as class. Communities like Antioch have very few blacks but substantial numbers of Latino and other minority families. Richmond, by contrast, is almost half black, while Martinez, Walnut Creek and Concord have very few residents from any ethnic minority group. The aggregate affluence suggested by countywide indicators is belied as well by recurrent racial conflicts. According to a special 1981 report by the State Fair Employment and Housing Commission and various newspaper investigations, there was an "upsurge in racial and ethnic violence" in Contra Costa County in the early 1980s. The

Table 1: Household and Ecological Characteristics of Contra Costa County, 1980

City	% Families with Female-Headed Household, No Spouse, with Children	% of Total Population Below Poverty	Median Household	% Finished High School	% Unemployed (1979)	% in High-Status Occupations	Total 1980 Population	% Black	% Spanish	% Other Minority
Antioch	8	7	$20,892	75	7	15	$43,559	1	15	9
Brentwood	9	11	14,700	53	7	15	4,434	.1	40	24
Concord	7	6	22,124	85	5	26	103,251	2	7	8
Martinez	6	6	24,069	84	6	27	22,882	2	8	6
Pittsburg	8	13	19,629	71	8	16	33,034	20	19	18
Richmond	12	17	15,597	67	10	18	74,676	48	10	12
Walnut Creek	3	4	24,842	91	4	41	53,643	.7	3	6
Contra Costa Country	7	8	22,875	82	6	29	657,252	9	9	16

Source: California Fair Employment and Housing Commission, 1981

Commission report stated that the Ku Klux Klan and other groups used "terror tactics" against black families and recruited in local schools, especially among white teenage gangs.[5]

Thus, within what is ostensibly a model suburban county, there exists a variety of urban problems. Although Contra Costa as a whole had the highest median income of all California counties, it also contains within its scenic boundaries four—San Pablo, the poorest, West Pittsburgh, Brentwood and Richmond—of the ten poorest communities in the entire six-county San Francisco Bay Area. Despite the generally healthy economy of the county, its Economic Task Force reported a variety of continuing problems (Contra Costa County Planning Department, 1983). Between 1980 and 1981, at least ten industrial plants closed their Contra Costa facilities, resulting in the loss of 3,000 to 4,000 jobs (California Employment Development Department, 1982). In addition, home mortgage foreclosure notices increased 66% in the same period—from 3,027 to 5,014 (*San Francisco Examiner*, 5/30/82).[6] Further, between 1980 and 1982, some 1,500 industrial jobs were permanently lost to county residents due to layoffs at U.S. Steel, DuPont, Crown Zellerbach and Allied Chemical (*San Francisco Examiner*, 3/9/83). As noted in the County Administrator's 1981 *Annual Report*, Manpower programs have been cut 60% to 80%, and some 300 to 350 young people in On-the-Job Training, vocational education and work experience programs lost their entry-level training positions as a consequence.

Trends in Juvenile Crime

Juvenile arrests in Contra Costa County increased between 1972 and 1975, but declined steadily between 1975 and 1981—from 13,912 in 1975 to 8,202 in 1981 (a 41% decrease) (California Department of Justice, 1981). Felony juvenile arrests in the county declined every year except 1978, the year the SOP began. The level of felony arrests declined from a high of 3,662 in 1973 to 2,347 in 1981 (a 35.9% decrease).

Although total juvenile arrests and felony juvenile arrests have been decreasing in absolute terms, so has the proportion of juveniles in the county population. Thus, there may have been a relative increase in either the real frequency and/or seriousness of juvenile crime. But census data show that the proportion of the total Contra Costa County population between ages 15 and 19 declined by 5.16% from 1970 to 1980, when total juvenile arrests rose and then declined. This youth population decline can account for only a small fraction of the much larger decline in juvenile crime in the later years of the decade. Thus, because total and felony juvenile arrests have been declining much more rapidly than the proportion of juveniles in the crime-prone years in the county population, this demographic interpretation cannot take us very far.

It would appear, therefore, that there was a trend toward less frequent and less serious juvenile crime in the county in the years preceding the SOP. As the county became a more varied social and economic region, the extent and severity of juvenile crime declined. For the SOP, this portended two trends: the potential masking of treatment impacts by decelerating juvenile crime rates, and the likely disaggregation of crime rates by varying regions of the county. These themes are explored later in this research.

RESEARCH METHODS

Data Sources

Information was obtained from probation department records, criminal histories provided by the juvenile and adult courts, interviews with SOP and control-group probationers, and community context data drawn from census information.

Case Records

Data on probationers and contacts were obtained from photocopies of probation department intake and termination forms for all SOP and control-group clients (names, addresses, phone numbers and all other identifying information were blocked off). Intake forms contained information on demographics, family background, and prior criminal justice involvements; records of prior treatment interventions; and school attendance and performance histories. Termination forms contained information on the duration of probation supervision and probation services rendered, the reason for termination, and a recidivism summary and drug/alcohol use history during probation supervision.

Arrest and Court Histories

Juvenile and adult criminal records for all SOP and control- group clients were obtained from the California Bureau of Criminal Statistics. These records provided the data base from which the official crime variables were constructed: arrests, time to arrest and dispositions (penetration). However, these records contained inconsistencies and gaps, and our understanding not only of crime but of system performance was often incomplete. Systems presented a "creamed" picture of their activities due to systematic omissions of cases. Estimates of official crime were also biased—the severity of crime appeared greater due to the omission of less severe cases, and a significant number of dismissals remained unrecorded.

Accordingly, readers should bear in mind two paradoxical features of the criminal records that comprised the official crime variables: Arrests tend to be underreported relative to actual arrests, but due to incomplete and/or inaccurate disposition data, recorded arrests tend to overstate actual criminality relative to dispositions.

Interviews

Follow-up interviews provided a wide range of data to describe the nature of clients' probation experience and to test explanatory models of violent delinquency. The interviews contained scales and items designed to elicit depth of detail, and the subjects' accounts of and reasoning behind their own behavior. These structural, situational, behavioral and attitudinal data are used in a later section to describe and explain the impacts of the SOP. The interview was constructed to elicit data from the 12 months preceding the SOP (or control) assignment and the 12 months preceding the interview.

Interview Procedures. Initially, we sought to contact all members of the sample: 267 SOP clients and 102 control cases. We expected to find that many cases were lost, and, in fact, sample attrition increased with the length of the follow-up period. This was particularly true for young people at that stage of the life cycle in which mobility is highest, and for "deviant" or "hard-to-reach" populations. We tried to gain the participation of subjects who either remained reluctant to be interviewed or refused outright after initial contacts. For all such cases, "special plea" letters were sent via certified mail, informing them that the respondent fee originally offered would be raised (from $12 to $20 and sometimes $25).

For those subjects who were not located, Bureau of Criminal Statistics records were reviewed to identify any sample members who might have been recently arrested and/or incarcerated somewhere in California. These additional steps allowed project staff to locate another ten respondents. Subtracting those subjects who had moved out of state, died or were unlocatable from the total sample (N = 369), the remaining 311 subjects constituted the "net" pool of possible follow-up subjects. Of these, 53.1% (N = 165) were successfully located and interviewed. The overall response rate from the total pool (N = 369) was 44.7%. These cases were distributed proportionately to the ratio of experimentals to controls in the total pool: 72.1%, SOP youths (N = 119); and 28.9%, controls (N = 46). Interviewers included women, men, whites and blacks to ensure that for most interview respondents, an interviewer of the same gender and race could be chosen.[7]

Community Context Variables: Census Data

In an effort to assess the concurrent influence of socioeconomic and ecological attributes on recidivism, we incorporated 16 variables selected from the 1980 U.S. Census for Contra Costa County to represent four domains of ecological influences on recidivism. We determined first the precise census tract in which each of the SOP and control-group respondents resided, and then added information for that area. The selection of variables was informed by ecological analyses of Laub and Hindelang (1981), Laub (1983), Bursik (1986) and Sampson (1986, 1987). The variables are shown in Table 2.

Table 2: Ecological Variables

Ethnic Composition

- Percent Black
- Percent Hispanic
- Percent other minority

Household Characteristics

- Percent families with female-headed households, no spouse, with children
- Percent families with female-headed households, no spouse, with children, below poverty level
- Percent of total population below poverty level
- Percent median household income

Labor Force Characteristics

- Percent of adults who completed high school or a higher grade level
- Percent unemployed (1979)
- Percent unemployed more than 15 weeks (1979)
- Percent of adults in high-status occupations

Housing Characteristics

- Percent owner-occupied
- Percent living in same house as five years ago
- Percent of housing stock built since 1970
- Percent moved into their homes since 1970
- Percent of housing units with more that 1.01 persons per room

Validation of the Experimental Design

To check the random assignment procedures used by the probation department, we compared the experimental group against the control group on seven intake variables that were selected to represent basic social structural and criminal justice background factors. Given the random assignment procedures, we expected to find no differences between experimentals and controls on these variables. Although small (but statistically insignificant) variation was expected, no differences were found.

However, due to the administrative events described earlier regarding the special caseload from the Boys' Ranch, we created a separate experimental group category for the Richmond-El Cerrito caseload (E2), and then compared this group against the rest of the experimental (E1) and control (C) subjects. The Richmond-El Cerrito experimental group (E2) was indeed significantly different from both the other experimental subjects and controls: They tended to be older, and contained proportionately more males and minorities than either the other experimentals or the controls.

The Richmond (E2) subjects also included proportionately twice as many minorities, not surprising in that Richmond is a predominantly black community. However, insofar as black juveniles may be at greater risk of arrest than whites (Weiner and Wolfgang, 1985), this racial difference too may be said to distinguish the Richmond (E2) group. Moreover, to the extent that race may be a proxy for social class and that social class may influence criminal behavior, this difference is noteworthy above and beyond geographical considerations. Also, the Richmond SOP caseload was much more likely to have already been on probation (or to have other charges pending) than either the other experimentals or the control-group subjects (67.5% vs. 41.8% and 40.2%, respectively). This, too, indicates that the Richmond E2 group was more likely to have been involved in previous criminal behavior than the others.

The deviation indicated that the Richmond SOP group tended to have significantly higher incidence and rates of criminality—violent criminality in particular. Accordingly, this subgroup was treated separately in subsequent analyses to control for the influence of these factors, in effect controlling for prior criminality.

SOP PROBATIONERS: VIOLENT JUVENILE OFFENDERS ON COMMUNITY SUPERVISION

The SOP probationers (and controls) presented the greatest challenge to the probation department's community protection mandate, posing the most difficult treatment and control needs—at once requiring the greatest share of both remedial and supervision resources. Thus, the description of this population offers a profile of those probationers who are committing violent offenses and who are the most visible offender group in the county. From a policy perspective, the analysis of SOP clients offers empirical information on the backgrounds of violent delinquents. Who are the juvenile offenders committing violent acts? What are their treatment and supervision needs? If, in fact, they are the "toughest" offenders, what can be said about juvenile delinquency in Contra Costa County?

Background Characteristics

Age at Intake. The average age of SOP clients was 15.02 years at their intake into the program. Roughly one in six (16.5%) was 13 years old or younger, nearly two in five (39.1%) were 14 or 15, and almost half (44.4%) were 16 to 18. The modal age was 16. The group as a whole clustered heavily between the ages of 14 and 16, with approximately two-thirds (65%) falling into that category.

Sex and Ethnicity. SOP clients were overwhelmingly male (87.6%); only one in eight (12.4%) was female. Nearly one in four SOP clients was black (23.4%), almost one in ten was Hispanic and over three in five were white. Overall, more than one-third of the SOP population were minorities.

Family Background. Approximately two in five SOP clients (39.6%) grew up in homes with both parents present, and another 14.2% were raised by a parent and stepparent. Slightly more than two in five (42.1%) were raised by their mothers alone, while only 2.2% were raised by their fathers alone. Overall, roughly half the SOP population were raised in a two-parent household, while the other half were not.

Educational Attainment and Attendance. The SOP clients were almost exclusively a high-school population. Only about 1% had graduated from high school as of their intake into the program. Most (85%) were enrolled in school full-time, while an additional 7% were enrolled on a part-time basis. Only 5.5% were neither enrolled in school at least part-time nor employed at intake.

Of the 338 SOP clients (93% of the total) who were in school, nearly three in five (199, or 58.4%) were only rarely or occasionally absent without a legitimate excuse, while the remaining two in five (139, or 40.8%) were regularly or frequently so absent. According to probation officers, nearly one-third (32.7%) of those attending school at intake had no known problems at school, while slightly more than one-third (34.7%) had at least occasional difficulties; the remaining third (31.8%) had frequent difficulties.

Substance Abuse. Reports by deputies suggested that approximately one-third (33.5%) had no known drug or alcohol involvement. Another third (36.3%) had been involved with drugs and/or alcohol for three or more years, with the average length of involvement being 2.7 years. Probation officer data showed that alcohol was by far the most frequently cited primary drug used at SOP entry. More than two in five SOP probationers (41.6%) drank alcohol as their "primary" substance. This was followed by marijuana, the primary drug for more than one-fourth (27.2%) of the SOP population. The vast bulk of the remaining clients (108, or 30.6%) were reported to have had no primary drug.

While there was scant evidence from probation officer records that SOP probationers used other drugs such as opiates, cocaine and hallucinogens, this information must be interpreted with extreme caution. Probation officers are rarely if ever privy to the full range of illicit drug and alcohol use among their wards. Further, the self-report data that will be presented later indicate that SOP clients engaged in both more types and greater frequency of drug use than implied by these early official data.

Delinquent Careers

The 363 members of the SOP population had been charged with an aggregate total of 3,825 offenses throughout their "careers." The mean number of arrests per offender was 10.54, but this figure must be interpreted with caution because actual figures for individuals ranged from a mere two arrests to more than two dozen. Although the pool of juvenile offenders for the SOP program consisted of only violent offenders, the pool actually constituted a diverse and not always "serious" offender group. For example, only one in 12 charges (8.3%) was for an offense falling into the "felony violent" category. Strong-arm robbery and aggravated assault comprised the bulk of these. If we add to this "violent" category all those arrests for "other violent" offenses, then we can say that almost one in five of the total arrests (18.2%) may be considered violent. By far the largest single offense category was assault, particularly non-aggravated assault or fighting.

One in nine arrests (11.2%) was for an offense categorized as "serious"; nearly six out of seven of these "serious" offenses were burglaries. About one in seven (15.3%) of the total arrests was for "petty larceny," and most of the remaining offenses were for "receiving stolen property" and "malicious mischief." Fewer than 3% of the total arrests of SOP subjects were for drug offenses, and most of these were for possession of marijuana.

Finally, the largest of the major charge categories was "probation violations." More than one-fourth (26.4%) of the total of all offenses committed by the SOP population as a whole fell into this category. Of these, nearly two-thirds (65%) consisted of technical violations of the conditions of probation or contempt-of-court citations. Although such offenses sound relatively nonserious—and most consisted of noncriminal behavioral problems—the term "probation violations" covers a multitude of sins, some of which may have been more serious or potentially violent than their label implies. Unfortunately, probation staff kept few records of the exact nature of these problems.

Though it is well known that violent delinquents do not specialize in any one crime type, the generally low percentage of violent charges is surprising. Again, given the premise of an intensive probation supervision program for "violent"—or at least "serious"—juvenile offenders, what seems most striking about these trends is the high proportion of nonviolent and relatively less serious offenses. Only about one in six (17.6%) of the total arrests of SOP subjects was for a Uniform Crime Reports "Index" crime, and, of these, nearly two-thirds (64%) were property crimes rather than crimes against persons. Similarly, the eight most frequent offenses among the SOP population included only two index crimes—burglary, second most frequent with 9.3% of the total, and strong-arm robbery, the sixth most frequent offense comprising 3.1% of the 3,825 total arrests.

The distribution of charges once again shows the diversity of behaviors among a cohort of "violent" offenders. Moreover, "violence" is only marginally appropriate to describe their delinquent acts. "Violence" accounts for less than 10% of the total charges, while felony property offenses account for more than 11%. Accordingly, the apparent threat to the community posed by these offenders lies not in their physical violence, but in the frequency of delinquent behaviors and the presence of violence in a diverse delinquent career.

Self-Reported Delinquency, Drug Use and Deterrence

In follow-up interviews subjects were asked a variety of questions about their past and recent delinquent behaviors. For each type of delinquency, they were first asked to think back to the period prior to the "instant offense" that resulted in their probation (T1) and to indicate whether they had ever engaged in that behavior. They were then asked if they had engaged in that behavior in the past year (T2). The results are shown in Table 3.

Two patterns in this table seem striking. First, the prevalence of both the less serious and the more serious delinquent acts appear high. For example, according to these self-reports for the pre-probation period, clear majorities had engaged in fist fights (85.5%) and been drunk or high in public places (68.5%). About half had engaged in breaking and entering (47.9%), sold stolen property (50.9%), and carried a knife, club, or other non-firearm weapon for protection (49.1%). Second, major declines occurred in many self-reported delinquent acts during the year preceding the interview. Although nearly two-thirds of the follow-up sample reported engaging in fist fights (63.6%), assaults, weapons offenses, or getting high or drunk in a public place (64.2%) in the past year, the only behavior for which the respondents reported an increase rather than the usual substantial decline was for driving a car while drunk or high.

Similarly marked declines are shown in Table 4 for self-reported drug and alcohol use. For each category of alcohol or drug use, the follow-up respondents were asked to recall their frequency of use in the period prior to probation and in the past 12 months, and to characterize that use on a five-point scale ranging from "never" to "daily or almost daily." Despite the clear pattern of declines in self-reported use across all categories of alcohol and drugs, respondents still reported recent drug-related problems. Two in five (40.6%) said they had gotten into at least one fight in the past year while drinking or using drugs, and one in five (21.3%) said they had been arrested at least once in the past year "partly because of drinking and/or drug use." Other responses, however, offered support for the pattern of decreased use shown in Table 4. While about one-fourth reported that they were drinking (28.7%) and using drugs (25.5%) more at T2 than at T1, nearly half said they were drinking and using drugs less (47.1% and 48.4%, respectively). Moreover,

Table 3: Self-Reported Crime Before SOP and in the Past Year (N = 165)

Self-Reported Behavior	Prevalence (%) (T_1)	Prevalence (%) (T_2)
Violence		
Involved in fist fights	85.5	63.6
Hit younger child in anger	19.4	8.5
Grabbed a purse and ran	12.7	2.4
Physically threatened to get something	23.6	8.5
Used weapon to get something	21.2	9.1
Struck a parent	15.8	4.2
Assaulted with injury	41.8	29.1
Hurt an animal	21.8	7.9
Used force to get money, drugs	23.6	9.1
Carried weapon to use in fight	40.6	25.5
Carried gun for any reason	27.9	17.6
Threatened an adult with a weapon	21.2	17.0
Pulled a weapon to show seriousness	32.7	22.4
Carried knife, club, etc. for protection	49.1	38.2
Shot someone	8.5	3.6
Property		
Purposefully damaged family property	26.7	10.9
Purposefully damaged another's property	44.2	18.2
Stole money from family member	39.4	7.9
Stole from another's wallet or purse	40.0	12.1
Shoplifted over $50	29.7	11.5
Breaking and entering	47.9	14.5
Stole auto	23.0	9.1
Tampered with auto	40.9	17.1
Sold stolen goods	50.9	24.2
Committed arson	14.5	2.4
Drug		
Drove car while high or drunk	41.8	47.3
Got high or drunk in public place	68.5	64.2
Got drunk or high at school or work	58.2	36.4

while more than two in five (44.3%) recalled experiencing problems because of drinking or drug use during T1, that figure dropped to less than one in five (17.8%) when we asked about such problems during the past year.

Table 4: Self-Reported Drug and Alcohol Use (N = 165)

Percent Reporting "Daily or Almost Daily" Use of . . .	Prevalence (%) (T1)	Prevalence (%) (T2)
Beer and wine	27.6	19.0
Hard liquor	15.3	4.9
Marijuana	58.3	35.6
Psychedelics	5.5	1.2
Tranquilizers	8.0	2.5
Speed/amphetamines	14.7	7.4
Depressants/barbiturates	6.1	3.1
Cocaine	3.7	2.5
PCP	1.2	.6
Heroin	1.8	.6
Other Opiates	3.7	2.5

IMPACTS ON RECIDIVISM

As a crime control project, the primary goal of the SOP was to "reduce the rate of recidivism of project cases by a statistically significant amount when compared to the control group receiving regular/standard probation services," including reductions in both the severity and number of subsequent law violations, court appearances, technical violations, and, of course, incarcerations. Because many violent juvenile offenders "desist" during the transition to adulthood (Wolfgang et al., 1972; Hamparian et al., 1978), a marginal dampening of criminal conduct also was seen as a potential SOP impact. Both self-reported and official law-violating conduct was measured. Also, the most serious dispositions—including incarceration—were measured to determine the furthest "penetration" into the justice system during the follow-up period.

Table 5: Percent Difference in Prevalence of Arrest by Treatment Group and Offense Type, Before and After SOP Intervention (N = 361)

	E_1			Control			E_2			Total		
Type of Crime	Pre	Post	% Change	Pre	Post	% Change	Pre	Post	% Change	Pre	Post	% Change
Violent	50.0	13.8	72.4	32.7	11.9	63.6	80.6	31.0	61.5	48.8	18.3	62.5
Serious	30.7	25.7	16.3	37.6	25.7	31.6	50.0	38.1	23.8	34.1	27.1	20.5
Other Violent	45.9	10.1	78.0	44.6	21.8	51.1	50.0	11.9	76.2	46.0	21.3	53.7
Other Serious	25.7	22.5	12.5	22.8	19.8	13.2	28.6	26.2	8.3	25.2	22.2	11.9
Other	71.1	58.7	17.4	72.3	52.5	27.3	78.6	54.8	30.2	72.3	59.8	17.3
Any	98.6	70.2	28.8	93.1	72.3	22.3	97.6	26.2	71.4	97.0	65.7	32.2

Rearrests: The Prevalence of Recidivism

The number of youth with at least one police contact for each type of law violation before and after SOP intervention is shown in Table 5. The most serious charge for each arrest was recorded from the records of the courts, the probation departments and the California Bureau of Criminal Statistics. (E2 in these tables is the Richmond experimental group, an SOP population that differed in several respects from SOP youth in eastern Contra Costa County.)

Table 5 shows that more Richmond SOP youth were arrested for violent offenses in both the pre- and post-project periods. In the pre-project period, more were also arrested for violent and serious offenses. Accordingly, it seems at first glance that SOP had little impact in reducing either the number of youth rearrested or the severity of rearrests.

However, a closer look reveals an important contradiction. Though more often charged for violent offenses, the actual number of youth arrested for any offense ("total") was consistently lower for the Richmond SOP group in the post-project period. Nearly three-fourths (73.8%) of the E2 group were not arrested, compared to one-fourth (27.5% and 29.8%, respectively) of the other groups. Though more E2 youth were arrested for violent offenses, the impact on overall crimes was largest for this same group. Evidently, more Richmond SOP youths were charged with the more severe crimes, though fewer were arrested at all. Conversely, though arrested more often, other youths were charged with less serious offenses.

Overall, the percent reductions were greatest for violent offenses and lowest for less serious offenses. Both felony and misdemeanor violence declined for all three groups by large percentages. However, property offenses appear to be less tractable. Both felony and misdemeanor property arrests declined most for controls, while lesser (misdemeanor) violence arrests declined most for experimentals.

The Frequency of Rearrest and Time to Failure

Two additional recidivism measures were examined: the mean number of rearrests per youth (by type of offense), and the time to first rearrest. For each measure, a series of analysis of variance models (ANCOVA) were constructed to test treatment effects, with three covariates: age at termination, time at risk, and days in treatment.

Table 6 shows the ANCOVA model for rearrests. Treatment differences were observed only for violent offenses. Differences by sex and time at risk were observed for all offense categories except "other violent." Age at termination was a significant covariate only for serious offenses and total rearrest. The length of treatment was not a significant covariate for any offense type. In general, though the covariates affected rearrest rates in different ways, SOP intervention was a significant variable only for violent offenses.

Table 6: Analysis of Covariance for Post-Project Rearrests by Treatment Group and Sex, Controlling for Time at Risk, Age at Termination and Days in Treatment (N = 351)

		Type of Crime											
		Violent		Serious		Other Violent		Other Serious		Other		Total	
Source	df	F	P	F	P	F	P	F	P	F	P	F	P
Main Effects:													
Treatment Group	2	4.43	.013	0.65	—	0.79	—	0.04	—	0.92	—	1.21	—
Sex	1	6.09	.014	8.83	.003	0.07	—	6.22	.013	9.01	.003	10.38	.001
Covariates													
Time at risk	1	5.06	.025	15.14	.000	1.86	—	4.16	.042	18.28	.000	10.19	.002
Age at termination	1	0.56	—	4.43	.076	3.73	—	0.33	—	0.50	—	4.24	.028
Days in treatment	1	1.29	—	1.23	—	0.93	—	1.32	—	2.56	—	2.07	—
Interactions:													
Treatment by sex	2	0.19	—	0.38	—	0.05	—	0.04	—	0.54	—	0.28	—
Explained	8	2.89	.004	3.71	.000	0.88	—	1.53	—	3.95	.000	3.66	.000

Table 7 shows that neither the SOP nor any covariate was a consistent factor in delaying the first rearrest for any type of crime. Only for lesser, misdemeanor offenses—"other serious" and "other" crimes—were there any measurable differences observed. Treatment-sex interaction effects were observed for "other" and "total" offenses.

Finally, survival analyses were conducted to determine overall treatment group differences. A survival analysis shows the percentage of the study group not "failing" (i.e., not rearrested) after a specified time interval. Significant differences were found only for violent offenses (Lee-Desu = 10.4). The data are displayed in Table 8.

After 36 months, of those still in the E2 group, the percentage surviving without a rearrest for a violent crime was less than two in three for Richmond SOP youth (64.3%), compared to 81.9% for other SOP youth and 90.4% for controls. The trends for serious (felony) arrests were similar: Fewer than half (46.0%) the Richmond SOP youth survived to 36 months, compared to over two in three (67.2%) of the East County SOP youth and nearly three-fourths of the controls. Table 8 shows that the differences in high-risk periods for violent offenses began between six and 12 months after supervision ended. By 18 months, the difference in survival rate was nearly 10%; by 24 months it was nearly 17%. At 36 months, controls had clearly emerged as having a higher survival rate than either experimental group.

Self-Reported Crime

Data on post-intervention self-reported criminality (SRC) were based on items and scales adapted from the National Youth Survey (NYS) (Elliott and Ageton, 1980). Summary scales, derived from a 31-item modification of the NYS, were developed for two crime types (violent, serious) and a total crime scale. In addition, a 10-item drug use scale was devised for this study. After controlling for age at termination (maturation), length of treatment or time at risk, no significant differences were observed among treatment groups. Significant differences were found for males for nondrug crimes but not for drug use.

The SRC analyses are in stark contrast to recidivism analyses utilizing official records. Whereas Richmond SOP youth had higher arrest rates and earlier arrests for violent crimes, no such differences exist in self-reported crimes. Looking at total arrest rates compared to SRC data, the results between groups are comparable. It seems that though behaviors were nearly identical in frequency for the three groups, the police and youth had different perceptions of severity, especially for Richmond SOP youth. This is not surprising when one considers the complex and provocative Richmond environment. For now, we can speculate that either E2 youths were indeed more violent (but not necessarily at higher rates), or they were charged with more serious offenses for comparable behaviors.

Table 7: Analysis of Covariance for Time to First Rearrest—Treatment Group and Sex, Controlling for Time at Risk, Age at Termination and Days in Treatment

		Type of Crime											
		Violent[a]		Serious[b]		Other Violent[c]		Other Serious[d]		Other[e]		Total[f]	
Source	df	F	P	F	P	F	P	F	P	F	P	F	P
Main Effects:													
Treatment group	2	0.94	—	1.49	—	0.78	—	0.77	—	0.50	—	0.11	—
Sex	1	—	—	2.14	—	1.58	—	1.01	00	4.49	.036	6.42	.012
Covariates:													
Time at risk	1	3.37	—	3.68	—	2.27	—	10.97	.001	1.40	—	3.11	—
Age at termination	1	2.99	—	0.07	—	2.08	—	4.77	.032	6.01	.015	0.01	—
Days in treatment	1	0.32	—	0.44	—	0.12	—	0.06	—	2.73	—	6.25	.013
Interactions:													
Treatment by sex	1	—	—	—	—	1.12	—	0.88	—	6.14	.014	9.47	.002
Explained	7	1.76	—	1.41	—	1.45	—	2.54	.022	3.32	.002	4.14	.000

a. N = 51, model for males only—no females arrested for violent offenses
b. N = 92, interaction effects too small for inclusion
c. N = 64
d. N = 77
e. N = 195
f. N = 195

Table 8: Percent of Youth "Surviving" at Six Month Post-Project Intervals
(Percent Not Yet Arrested at Each Interval) (N = 361)

Post-Project	Violent			Serious			Other Violent			Other Serious			Other			Total		
Interval	E_1	C	E_2	E_1	C	E_2	E_1	C	E_2	E_1	C	E_2	E_1	C	E_2	E_1	C	E_2
0–6	97.2	95.7	95.2	91.2	91.5	92.9	92.1	92.6	92.9	94.0	94.7	90.5	74.5	74.5	78.6	55.6	58.6	50.0
7–12	94.4	94.6	88.1	85.7	84.0	83.3	90.3	88.3	92.9	88.9	89.4	85.7	62.5	60.6	61.9	43.5	43.6	35.7
13–18	92.6	92.6	83.3	83.3	80.9	76.2	86.6	87.2	88.1	86.6	86.2	96.0	56.5	54.3	54.8	39.3	36.2	28.6
19–24	90.7	90.4	73.8	79.2	78.7	76.2	84.2	83.9	88.1	82.8	81.7	73.8	47.1	54.3	52.4	32.7	35.1	28.6
25–30	88.4	90.4	69.9	77.4	74.9	68.2	83.0	82.0	88.1	81.6	81.7	73.8	43.6	50.8	49.8	30.4	30.5	26.1
30–36	81.9	90.4	64.3	67.2	74.9	46.0	77.3	71.1	88.1	69.3	81.7	73.8	35.3	31.2	46.6	21.6	24.6	26.1
Median	36.0	36.0	36.0	36.0	36.0	36.0	36.0	36.0	36.0	36.0	36.0	36.0	23.4	31.8	26.9	—	—	—
Lee-Desu		10.64**			1.38			0.75			1.41			0.63				

*** P < .001
** P < .01
* P < .05

Justice System Penetration

The final measure of SOP impact was the extent of penetration into the justice system following the termination of probation supervision. For each arrest recorded from official records, the disposition was also recorded. The most serious disposition, or deepest penetration into the justice system, was calculated for each youth. Dispositions ranged from no court action through incarceration in a state prison or county jail. The results are shown in Table 9, by sex and treatment group.

Richmond SOP youths (E2) fared worse in the post-intervention period. Among males, more than one in three (36.8%) was subsequently incarcerated. About one-quarter of the controls were incarcerated, and fewer than one in seven of the SOP (E1) youths (East County) was incarcerated. Among females, there were stark differences, with controls having the highest incarceration rates. The results were statistically significant for both males and females.

For other dispositions, the differences were less pronounced. Probation dispositions and in-county residential placements were lowest for male Richmond SOP youth. Among youth not reaching court at all, SOP youth fared best and controls the poorest. Over half the SOP youth had either no court action or their charges were dismissed (44.2% and 14.2%). However, the differences between groups were less dramatic than for incarceration rates.

Once again, a pattern emerges in which Richmond SOP youth were treated more harshly in the system, though not necessarily represented in the system in substantially greater numbers. There are few clues here to explain the higher incarceration rates for Richmond SOP youth. Though arrested in fewer numbers, they were charged more severely and jailed more often. Again, this raises a fundamental question: Did these youth in fact commit more serious offenses, or were their behaviors perceived and responded to more harshly by the juvenile and criminal justice systems?

Recidivism and Proportionality of Dispositions

Do the courts mete out proportionately more severe dispositions for more serious offenses? The relationship between arrest charge and disposition should be central to the proportionality of responses to recidivism. In juvenile court, dispositions historically have reflected the "best interests of the child." This doctrine is based on rehabilitative ideal and a unicausal model of delinquency (Feld, 1983). Yet recent policy developments in juvenile court have shifted the emphasis to the offense, not the offender, in dispositional decisions (Hamparian et al., 1982; Feld, 1987). Retribution and punishment have become the explicit goals of delinquency policy. Accordingly, we should expect the more serious dispositions to be reserved for those youth charged with more severe offenses.

Table 9: Most Serious Disposition of Post-Project Arrest by Treatment Group and Sex (N = 356)

Most Serious Disposition	E_1				Control				E_2			
	Male		Female		Male		Female		Male		Female	
	N	(%)	N	(%)	N	(%)	N	(%)	N	(%)	N	(%)
No court action	84	(44.2)	19	(82.6)	30	35.7	6	(35.3)	9	(23.7)	2	(4.8)
Charges dismissed	27	(14.2)	2	(8.7)	7	(8.3)	—	—	8	(21.1)	—	—
Transfer out of county	2	(1.1)	—	—	2	(2.4)	1	(5.9)	—	—	—	—
Informal supervision	3	(1.6)	—	—	2	(2.4)	—	—	—	—	—	—
Probation	24	(12.6)	1	(4.3)	10	(11.9)	2	(11.8)	3	(7.9)	—	—
In-county residential placement	24	(12.6)	1	(4.3)	11	(13.1)	4	(23.5)	4	(10.5)	—	—
Incarceration	26	(13.7)	—	—	22	(26.2)	4	(23.5)	14	(36.8)	—	—
Total	190	(60.9)	23	(54.8)	84	(26.9)	17	(40.5)	38	(12.2)	2	(4.8)

Males: $X^2{}_{(2,6)} = 21.0$, $p = .05$
Females: $X^2{}_{(2,6)} = 17.0$, $p = ns$

Table 10: Dispositions of Rearrest Charges by Treatment Group and Type of Crime (N = 1,024)[a]

Disposition	N (%)	Violent N (%)	Serious N (%)	Other Violent N (%)	Other Serious N (%)	Other N (%)	Technical Violations
None	E_1	11 (33.3)	20 (23.0)	30 (50.8)	32 (59.3)	139 (56.5)	73 (40.1)
	C	8 (40.0)	14 (33.3)	13 (50.0)	9 (60.0)	64 (67.4)	21 (42.9)
	E_2	12 (66.7)	11 (50.0)	1 (25.0)	7 (63.6)	28 (73.7)	12 (52.2)
Probation supervision	E_1	5 (15.2)	25 (28.7)	15 (25.4)	12 (22.2)	60 (33.0)	60 (33.0)
	C	3 (15.0)	10 (23.8)	8 (30.8)	4 (26.7)	20 (21.1)	18 (36.7)
	E_2	0 (—)	1 (4.5)	1 (25.0)	0 (—)	2 (5.3)	3 (13.0)
Out-of-home placement	E_1	4 (12.1)	22 (25.3)	6 (10.2)	4 (7.4)	33 (13.4)	41 (22.5)
	C	4 (20.0)	6 (14.3)	5 (19.2)	0 (—)	5 (5.3)	8 (16.3)
	E_2	1 (5.6)	1 (4.5)	1 (25.0)	1 (9.1)	4 (10.5)	4 (17.4)
Incarceration	E_1	13 (39.4)	20 (23.0)	8 (13.6)	6 (11.1)	16 (6.5)	8 (4.4)
	C	5 (25.0)	12 (28.6)	0 (—)	2 (13.3)	6 (6.3)	2 (4.1)
	E_2	5 (27.8)	9 (40.9)	1 (25.0)	3 (27.3)	4 (10.5)	4 (17.4)

a. Percentages reflect total charges for treatment group within disposition type.

Significance:

E_1: $X^2 = 89.22$, df = 15, $p < .000$
C : $X^2 = 18.24$, df = 15, $p <$ ns
E_2: $X^2 = 44.01$, df = 15, $p < .000$

Table 10 shows the disposition of each type of rearrest charge by intervention group. The unit of analysis is the most serious charge per incident, not the youth. To simplify the table, county jail and institutional commitments were collapsed. For SOP youths and controls, the percentage receiving incapacitative dispositions declines with the severity of offense. For Richmond SOP youth, however, the percentage of youth incarcerated remains fairly constant across charge categories, though the cell sizes become rather small for minor offenses. For nearly all offense categories, the percentage of charges for E2 youth resulting in incapacitation is higher. For E1 youth, only violent charges more often lead to jail or prison. In particular, the E2 incarceration rates for the three least severe charge categories are much higher than those of the other groups. This includes technical violations (i.e., behaviors that are legal but violate probation conditions) resulting in probation revocation. At the same time, the percent of E2 charges dismissed is higher for all charge categories except "other violent," where the cell sizes are negligible. It seems that for E2 youth, charges more often are not substantiated in the courts. Once again, the courts appear to "filter" out many arrest charges, providing an important check on arrest charges and reconciling behavior and legal response.

Evidently, the juvenile and criminal courts appeared to mete out harsher dispositions to Richmond SOP youths than their counterparts similarly charged elsewhere in the county. Table 10 suggests that proportionality of punishment varies according to the area in which the youth was arrested. Because the E2 group had a greater percentage of minority youth, the disparity in sanction severity seems to be associated with race. Moreover, self-reported violence for Richmond SOP youth was comparable to SOP youth and controls, irrespective of disposition. Accordingly, controlling self-reported or officially charged crimes, there appears to be differential penetration of Richmond youth in the justice system.

In sum, both expected and unexpected findings were observed. Violent, serious offenders and "other serious" offenders were imprisoned. The latter group probably included those whose probation was revoked for a variety of less serious offenses that otherwise would not result in jail or prison time. Moreover, self-reported violence also was descriptive of those penetrating further into the justice system, although not for incarcerated E2 youth. Most important, disposition by charge may be disproportionate for some youth and proportionate to severity of charge for others. Richmond youth were imprisoned more often, all other factors held constant.

SOCIAL-ECOLOGICAL INFLUENCES ON TREATMENT IMPACT

Violent and serious arrest rates were higher in Richmond, the county's major metropolitan area. This is consistent with the strong empirical evidence that crime and delinquency are disproportionately urban phenomena. Regardless of the measure of crime, serious and violent delinquency appears to increase as the geographical focus approaches the inner city (Kornhauser, 1978; Laub and Hindelang, 1981; Laub, 1983; Shannon, 1986; Messner, 1983). In other words, among both youth and adults, urbanism and serious crime are closely related.

However, these associations in turn raise a host of questions regarding the components of urbanism. The concentration of serious delinquency in urban areas may be attributable to differences in demographic, socioeconomic and structural composites of urban areas, rather than simply to the unique socialization processes that are characteristic of urban settings. Alternatively, it is possible that urban "form" determines socialization of youth and social behavior in urban areas. This possibly confounding effect may underlie the general reluctance of criminologists to resolve the question of whether higher delinquency rates result form the social structural characteristics of communities or the aggregate characteristics of individuals who cluster in urban areas.

The relationship between urbanism and serious crime is evident in the analyses of pre- and post-project crime among SOP youth. Richmond SOP (E2) youth had higher arrest rates for serious and violent crime, both before and after probation supervision. This is not surprising since Richmond is the major urban locale in Contra Costa County. Accordingly, we must consider whether the urban conditions that separate the Richmond sample from the other groups are important factors that explain the recidivism patterns of this population. The consistently higher rates of crime in Richmond strongly suggest that, in the absence of significant treatment differences, area effects are potential explanatory factors.

To determine the ecological milieu of youth in the study, their census tracts were recorded. From census data, 13 variables were selected representing four ecological domains: socioeconomic status, demographics, labor force characteristics and housing. Table 11 shows the ecological characteristics of the SOP population by treatment group. Richmond SOP (E2) youth lived in communities that differed significantly from the other youths' communities. In general, the differences reflect the unique environmental conditions for the Richmond SOP group, and the relative inequalities between Richmond and the other regions of the county. Richmond youth live in areas with higher concentrations of blacks, households in poverty, low median household income, unemployment and undereducation, and dense housing. The largest disparities are for demographic characteristics, income, unemployment and housing.

These rather stark differences suggest that Richmond youth live in conditions of relative inequality, as well as absolute poverty. Messner (1982, 1983) has linked such economic deprivation to crime rates, including urban homicide. Braithwaite (1979) and Blau and Blau (1982) conclude that relative

Table 11: Ecological Characteristics by Treatment Group

Ecological Characteristics	Treatment Group E_1 (n = 215)	Control (n = 102)	E_2 (n = 42)
Ethnic Composition			
% Black***	7.4	15.2	59.1
% Hispanic	5.0	4.9	5.9
% Other Minority	5.1	5.7	3.1
Household Characteristics			
% Female-headed households with children***	8.1	9.6	16.4
% Female-headed households below poverty level***	4.3	5.5	13.5
% Total population in poverty***	9.2	11.1	22.6
Median household income***	$21,259	$20,244	$12,894
Labor Force Characteristics			
% Adults with four years high school or more***	76.2	75.1	58.5
% Unemployed (1979)***	7.6	8.2	16.7
% Unemployed more than 15 weeks (1979)***	36.0	37.5	49.0
% Adults employed in high-status occupations	20.0	20.1	14.1
Housing Characteristics			
% Living is same house as five years ago*	41.6	43.3	53.8
% Moved into home since 1970	76.9	74.2	66.2
% Unit with more than 1.01 persons per room***	3.3	4.3	9.7

*** p = .001
** p = .01
* p = .05

poverty is a stronger predictor than absolute poverty in explaining criminal behavior. These conditions also have been linked to serious delinquency (Laub and Hindelang, 1981; Shannon, 1984; Sampson, 1986). That these conditions of relative deprivation apply to Richmond SOP E2 youth is evident in Table 11.

Accordingly, an important policy issue is the relationship between probation supervision and social area effects. If both criminality and treatment impact vary by social area, a central question is whether the effects of SOP intervention are mediated by the ecological characteristics of the offender's neighborhood. The practical applications of such knowledge would include, at a minimum, the differentiation of intervention models, tailored to the area characteristics of a probation caseload.

For each of the four domains of ecological or social area effects, one variable was selected to represent the domain. The variables were selected from stepwise multivariate regression analyses of the variables within each domain. Variables with significant relationships to the recidivism measures, as well as those with maximum contributions to variance explained, were chosen to represent the domain. The variables for each domain were: demographics (percent black population), poverty (percent female-headed households below poverty level), housing (percent of housing with more than 1.01 persons per room) and labor force (percent unemployed 15 weeks or more). ANOVA models were used to test the relationship between probation supervision and recidivism, with the ecological variables introduced as covariates. Time at risk, or street time, was used also as a covariate to control for varying career lengths. Main effects for sex were also tested.

Probation Supervision, Arrests and Social Effects

There were no significant effects for either supervision or social area characteristics on official arrest data. However, significant differences were found by sex and time at risk for nearly all types of crime. Few significant relationships were found. Only violent and total crimes varied by area

Table 12: Analysis of Covariance for Post-Supervision Self-Reported Crime by Treatment Group and Sex, Controlling for Community Context Variables (N = 156)

		Violence		Property		Total		Drug Use	
Source	df	F	P	F	P	F	P	F	P
Main Effects:									
Treatment Group	2	0.13	ns	0.51	—	0.42	—	1.25	—
Sex	1	5.98	.016	9.42	.003	8.95	.003	3.25	.073
Covariates									
Demographics	1	4.19	.042	9.26	.003	8.23	.005	4.74	.031
Poverty	1	2.33	—	3.68	—	3.42	—	0.74	—
Labor Force	1	0.03	—	2.16	—	0.88	—	0.78	—
Housing	1	0.53	—	0.99	—	1.76	—	0.50	—
Interaction									
Treatment x Sex	2	0.07	—	0.15	—	0.27	—	0.10	—
Explained	10	1.12	—	2.09	.029	1.97	.041	1.49	—

effect—for housing and poverty factors, respectively. Overall, the absence of a discernable pattern of effects across crime types suggests that, for official arrests, treatment impacts on recidivism are not mediated by social area effects. However, the concentration of arrests for violence in areas of poverty is consistent with other research that shows the impact of social disorganization on violent crime (Sampson, 1987).

Probation Supervision, Self-Reported Crime and Social Area Effects

The relationship between social area effects and self-reported crime is shown in Table 12. Again, there are no significant treatment effects, but there are significant post-supervision sex differences for each of the four SRC measures. In these analyses, we also see consistent relationships between area effects and crime. Area demographics—percent black population—is significantly related to each type of crime. It appears that demographic composition is apparently a mediating influence on supervision effectiveness.

Justice System Penetration, Supervision and Social Area Effects

Finally, we sought to determine if the social area characteristics of each probationer varied according to his or her most serious post-project disposition—or justice system penetration—and if those relationships differed by treatment group. In other words, are youth from varying neighborhoods treated differently by the courts? Did SOP effect those patterns? Table 13 presents data showing the mean social area characteristics of youth in each treatment group, according to their furthest penetration into the justice system.

The patterns obtained in these analyses differed little from the other analyses using official records. SOP impact was minimal and not statistically significant. Irrespective of probation group, offenders receiving the most serious disposition (i.e., incarceration) often resided in areas with many of the components of urbanism: poverty, high percentages of minority populations, unemployment and crowded housing. However, the differences were not statistically significant; the trends were not particularly systematic. In other words, "place" did not explain justice system penetration.

Overall, demographic characteristics most readily demarked those youth penetrating furthest. Youth living in areas with higher percentages of black population were incarcerated more often. The trends for the remaining urban characteristics were quite varied, and indicated no strong relationship between urbanism and justice system response. For SOP and control youth, incarcerated youth tended to reside in neighborhoods with more blacks. Few differences were observed for Richmond SOP youth, but this group consisted primarily of blacks.

The E^2 result is expected. There is little heterogeneity on these variables for the Richmond youth. In contrast, the other probation groups are quite

Table 13: Most Serious Disposition by Treatment Group and Community Context Variables (N = 361)

	E_1				Control				E_2			
Most Serious Disposition	% Black	% Poor	% Out of Work	% Dense Housing	% Black	% Poor	% Out of Work	% Dense Housing	% Black	% Poor	% Out of Work	% Dense Housing
None	7.6	4.6	7.7	3.5	14.9	5.3	7.9	4.4	58.9	13.4	16.8	9.1
Probation	7.5	3.9	7.2	3.4	12.5	4.8	7.3	3.4	60.1	15.3	18.7	10.0
In-county placement	3.7	3.6	7.5	2.9	6.8	4.5	7.5	3.2	47.3	12.5	18.8	10.0
Incarceration	10.0	4.1	7.3	2.9	20.8	6.4	9.1	5.1	63.9	13.9	15.4	10.4

homogeneous on these dimensions. Pittsburgh, for example, is a village in the East County area with a substantial black population. Accordingly, the data suggest that social area characteristics, especially those related to black population centers, may affect justice system penetration. Within each group (and across groups as well), the racial characteristics of an offender's neighborhood may bear more heavily on the outcome of his or her arrest charge and the severity of the subsequent disposition than the individual's ethnicity.

Overall, both sides of the "race or place" argument are supported by these analyses. Though race and crime are closely linked in many studies (see Silberman, 1978, and Laub, 1983, for thorough reviews of this relationship), the meaning of the relationship is unclear. These trends suggest that it may not be the higher proportion of blacks, or the lower proportion of whites, that is related to serious and violent juvenile crime. Rather, it is the homogeneity of neighborhoods that may be significant. For probationers living in predominantly black neighborhoods, arrests are more severe though not more frequent. There is vulnerability here to discretion. Incarceration is more common for youth in heterogeneous neighborhoods where there are higher percentages of blacks. And self-reported crime is lowest for youth in predominantly black neighborhoods.

The relationship between race and crime remains central to criminology but so, too, is the urban phenomenon central to both race and crime (Silberman, 1978). Reinarman and Fagan (1988) suggest the need for further study of the relationships among urbanism, ecology, race, and delinquency, including the social process and socialization experiences of these neighborhoods, as well as the responses of law enforcement and the courts.

SOCIAL DEVELOPMENT, SOCIAL LEARNING AND VIOLENT JUVENILE CRIME

SOP intervention, like many other delinquency experiments, was built on assumptions about rehabilitative interventions. SOP was developed in a social control paradigm, where specially trained staff with small caseloads intervened to provide services to strengthen the "social and family" functioning of violent offenders, while quickly sanctioning anti-social or criminal behaviors. Though not specifically informed by theory, SOP practices were designed to reinforce societal bonds, "unlearn" deviant behaviors through quick response and sanctions, and equip probationers with the necessary social and personal skills to live crime-free.

To analyze the impact of SOP on the societal bonds that restrain criminality, an integrated theoretical framework combining strain, control, and learning theories was adapted from Elliott et al. (1979, 1980) for a violent juvenile offender population (Fagan and Jones, 1984). (See Fagan and Reinarman, 1984, for a full elaboration of the theoretical framework.) Accordingly, the implications for SOP and the policy of intensive supervision lie in the identification of salient areas of social development—learning, environment, social and personal skills—that can become focal points for rehabilitative efforts by probation officers.

Table 14: Post-Intervention Social and Personal Bonds and Self-Reported Crime (Mean Scale Scores) by Treatment Group (N = 165)

Social Development Domains	E_1 (n = 99)	Control (n = 46)	E_2 (n = 20)
Social Bonds			
School integration	0.60	0.67	0.40
Family integration	4.61	4.89	4.05
Neighborhood integration	1.10	1.02	1.05
Work integration	1.18	0.98	1.10
Justice system contact	0.67	0.74	0.65
Personal Bonds			
School commitment	3.67	3.85	3.90
Peer attitudes toward crime	0.98	1.04	0.90
Family commitment	1.63	1.59	1.50
Social attitudes[a]			
Prosocial	–0.11	0.16	0.15
Antisocial	0.11	–0.29	0.14
Behaviors			
Drinking/drug problems**	.07	.07	.05
Self-reported crime			
Violence	1.46	1.48	1.30
Property	0.83	0.89	0.70
Total	1.76	1.91	1.45
General drug use	0.70	0.89	0.65

*** $p < .001$
** $p < .01$
* $p < .05$
a. Standard factor scores

SOP IMPACTS ON SOCIAL DEVELOPMENT

Table 14 shows differences in social and personal bonds for the three groups, as well as differences in self-reported criminality for the 12 months prior to the interview. ANOVA routines were used to determine between-group differences in perceptions of behavioral and attitudinal norms in the social domains of peers, school, work, etc.[8] Only PEER JUSTICE SYSTEM INVOLVEMENT was significantly different, with Richmond SOP youth reporting fewer peers in contact with the law. Significant differences between treatment groups before SOP (or probation) intervention generally disappeared in the years following intervention. Only DRINKING/DRUG PROBLEMS were significantly different in the post-intervention year, with Richmond SOP youth reporting fewer problems.

Social Development and Recidivism

Ordinary least squares (OLS) regression analyses were undertaken to examine the relationship among both environmental influences (social learning variables) and individual characteristics (control theory variables, or social and personal bonds) with self-reported crime and official arrests in the post-intervention period.[9] We excluded treatment as an independent variable based on the results in Table 14. The models were further refined by introducing pre-intervention measures of criminality to control for individual differences and to determine the extent to which post-intervention explanations of criminality are influenced by earlier behaviors. [10]

Official Crime. The results for official arrests are shown in Table 15. The model for violent arrests is not significant; less than 10% of the variance is explained both before and after prior crime is introduced. None of the variables has a regression coefficient greater than .20, and prior crime is only weakly associated with violent arrests in the post-intervention period. The models for serious (property) arrest and total arrests are significant at the p = .01 level, both before and after controlling for prior crime. Prior crime is weakly associated with all three types of arrests, adding little to the explained variance.

For both serious and total arrests, the youth's CRIMINAL JUSTICE EXPERIENCE is the strongest contributor. The models have comparable explanatory power: 19.57% and 23.21% of the variance without controlling for prior crime, and 20.89% and 23.53%, respectively, after prior crime is introduced. A similar finding occurs for two peer-crime influences: PEER DELINQUENCY and PEER CRIMINAL JUSTICE SYSTEM EXPERIENCE are strong contributors to the model for total arrests, but are more weakly associated with serious property offenses.

In general, these models have moderately high explanatory power for serious and total crimes, but are insignificant for violent crimes. Recall that violence was the behavior at which SOP intervention was targeted, and that

Table 15: OLS Standardized Regression Coefficients for Post-Intervention Official Arrests for Integrated Social Development Model, by Type of Crime, Controlling for Pre-Intervention Criminality

	Type of Crime					
	Violent		Serious		Total	
Social Development Variables	r	Beta	r	Beta	r	Beta
Youth's criminal justice system experience	.19	.14	.34	.32	.34	.28
Neighborhood crime	.18	.15	—	—	.07	-.01
Neighborhood integration	-.16	-.12	-.11	-.01	-.30	-.22
Peer delinquency	.18	.12	.13	.09	.21	-.02
Gang membership	.02	.08	.24	-.18	.19	-.08
Youth's victimization	.06	-.06	.21	-.02	.24	.09
Peer CJS experience	.07	.04	.06	.02	.23	.15
Peer attitudes toward law	.09	.02	.12	-.12	.12	-.08
Quality of work experience	—		-.19	-.13	—	
Pre-intervention criminality	(.07)	(-.04)	(.003)	(-.14)	(.10)	(-.07)
Percent Variance Explained	9.45	(9.56)	19.57	(20.89)	23.21	(23.53)
F (8,154)	2.00	(1.79)	4.68	(4.48)	(5.81)	(5.23)
P	NS	NS	.01	(.01)	.01	(.01)

a. Coefficients and Percent Variance for controlled model in parentheses.

earlier sections showed major reductions in violent crime between the pre- and post-intervention periods. Apparently, the constructs in this framework are either of little importance in explaining arrests for violence in the early adult years, or they are unrelated to the social processes that influence arrests for violence. Evidently, different types of offenses may require different explanations.

Self-Reported Crime. The results for self-reported crime are shown in Table 16. The four equations are significant at the p = .01 level, and the explained variance ranges from 27.30% for Drug Use to 41.44% for Violent behaviors. When prior criminality is introduced, the explanatory power of the models is increased by 0.5 to nearly 2% of the variance. Moreover, unlike the models for official criminality, prior criminality has strong, positive correlations with each SRC measure. Also unlike the previous models, the ordering of the variables and their regression coefficients are similar across crime types.

Table 16: Regression Coefficients for Post-Intervention Self-Reported Crime for Integrated Social Development Model, by Type of Crime, Controlling for Pre-Intervention Criminality*

	Violent		Property		Total		Drug Use	
Social Development Variables	r	Beta	r	Beta	r	Beta	r	Beta
Peer Delinquency	.47	.15	.38	.09	.46	.10	.40	.21
CJS Experience	.42	.23	.34	.18	.38	.17	.24	.06
Anti-Social Attitudes	.38	.15	.28	.04	.30	.02	.20	.00
Victimization	.38	.15	.27	.04	.38	.15	.20	–.01
Gang Member	.30	–.12	.29	.09	.25	–.07	.08	.07
Peer Integration	.29	.14	.29	.20	.30	.20	.24	.17
Peer Attitudes to Law	.18	–.10	.19	–.14	.22	–.13	.09	–.01
Peer CJS Experience	.21	.03	.23	.08	.23	.03	.26	.12
Neighborhood Integration	–.23	–.05	–.21	–.05	–.24	–.07	–.18	–.07
Drug/Alcohol Problems	.15	.01	.23	.09	.25	.09	.31	.19
School Integration	–.08	.09	–.14	–.10	–.17	–.13	–.14	–.15
Pre-Intervention Criminality	(.34)	(.09)	(.29)	(.08)	(.38)	(.17)	(.28)	(.08)
Percent Variance Explained	41.44(41.93)		32.51(32.94)		40.15(42.07)		27.30(27.74)	
F	8.36 (7.76)		5.69 (5.28)		7.92 (7.80)		4.43 (4.12)	
P	.01 (.01)		.01 (.01)		.01 (.01)		.01 (.01)	

* Coefficients and Percent Variance for controlled model in parentheses.

Several trends are noteworthy in these models. First, the strongest contributors in each model are bonds to delinquent peers or attitudes indicative of the absence of belief in normative law-abiding behaviors. Second, prior criminality is strongly correlated with current self-reported crime, but adds little to the explanatory power of the model. Knowing the earlier behavior does little to help us understand the processes which lead to current behavior.

Third, the consistency of the models across crime types suggests that there may be little differentiation in the processes which lead to different types of behavior. The fact that the same variables contributing to violent behaviors also affect property crimes and drug use suggests that there is little specialization in the types of acts. Moreover, the strong loadings of peer-related variables in each model suggests a social, not an individual, development process where strong bonds to delinquent peers lead to higher self-reported crime (SRC) scores.

Fourth, the presence of VICTIMIZATION further underscores the importance of experience with crime as a teaching/learning experience. Being victimized seems to increase the probability that a youth will engage in subsequent crimes. This suggests the possibility of crime as a normative behavior for many of the youth in this sample. Accordingly, interventions focusing on social norms and environments may have a greater impact on crime control for young adults than individualized interventions focusing on social skills or attitudes.

Finally, DRUG/ALCOHOL PROBLEMS is a strong contributor to Property and Total SRC scores as well as to Drug Use. It is strongest for Drug Use, as expected. This scale measures the extent to which youth have problems in school, at work, or with their families or friends when drunk or "high" on drugs. For some youth, it appears that interventions focusing on the ability to make decisions and "handle" problem situations may help them avoid behaviors that can lead to trouble.

Comparing the Models: Social Development in the Transition to Adulthood

Comparing the models for official and self-reported crime, there is a simple and striking pattern: Prior justice system contacts explain official crime, while peer delinquency explains self-reported crime. Apparently, there is a thread from social area effects to the probability of justice system contact, to victimization, and, in turn, to the explanations of crime. Youths already known to the law are arrested more often, but they may actually be committing crimes at similar rates to others. One must ask why this imbalance exists, and whether key social institutions—police and justice system—are also influenced by social area effects. Social environment and socioeconomic factors may impact on the "socializers" as well as on youth themselves.

Youth in this study report a wide range of offenses, and no single offense type is better understood than any other. We can conclude that specialization of offenses did not occur for this group in the post-intervention period. Recall that this sample was identified based on violent behavior, or at least the "propensity" for violence. From these results, violence does not appear to be uniquely explained compared to other offenses. Accordingly, probation supervision strategies which rely on unique explanations of violence have little promise for reducing subsequent criminality. Perhaps this explains why the effects of treatment were minimal, and why, instead, social area effects seemed to efficiently explain differences in behavior between the three treatment groups.

SOCIAL AREA, SOCIALIZATION, AND VIOLENT DELINQUENCY: IMPLICATIONS FOR INTENSIVE PROBATION SUPERVISION

We have seen that youth throughout Contra Costa County were arrested in roughly equal numbers, and that self-reported crime was also evenly distributed throughout the county. But more severe arrests and convictions were skewed to the urban areas of the county, the areas most heavily populated by the poor and minority populations. This concentration of more serious (but not more prevalent) arrests in urban areas may reflect the larger societal problems characterizing those areas: poverty, unemployment, poor housing, and racial disparities. The higher prevalence of serious crime in these areas suggests that offending among the SOP cohort varies by social class (poorer), race (African-American), and gender (males). But once involved at all, the overall weight of the evidence suggests that they are no more extensively involved in crime than any other population group in the county. Thus, while the process of initiation suggests differences by social area, the processes of continuation may be more heterogeneous.

Arguably, arrest may have a different meaning in these areas: Crimes that occur with equal frequencies in other locales may be viewed (and labeled) as more severe behaviors when they occur in areas of poverty, unemployment and concentrations of minority populations. We are reluctant to conclude that behaviors were more serious in these areas, especially when we look at crime through self-report measures: The frequency and severity of offending seem to be well distributed and only weakly related to social area, and are well explained by social processes. Accordingly, the theoretical underpinnings for using probation with serious young offenders must take account of the dual but perhaps related effects of socioeconomic conditions and socialization on the development of attachments to society.

There is ample evidence of differential law enforcement practices in poorer neighborhoods (Smith, Visher and Davidson, 1984; McNeely and Pope, 1981). In this study, such practices may relate more to the perceived severity of crime—as expressed in the charges—rather than to the probability of arrest. This may explain why self-identification as a violent offender, regardless of severity, seems to be a function of belief, attitude and social expectations. The latter result seems to be general, and not confined to a particular social area. We may conclude, then, that the phenomenon of youth crime in the transitional years may, in fact, reflect parallel socialization processes among diverse adolescent groups; these processes are shaped and influenced by the social areas where youths live.

There obviously is no single explanation for serious youth crime, and, accordingly, no simple solutions. There may be two paths to the same behaviors, but they appear to converge at the point of peer cultures, beliefs and attitudes, and generally weak ties to conventional societal activities. One path may be traced to relative deprivation in urban areas and resultant socialization processes which either block or erode societal ties. A second path includes peer influences and social isolation, which exist regardless of social area, but which have similar effects on social bonds. That different measures detect these different paths also holds implications for the assessment of probationers.

IMPLICATIONS FOR POLICY AND PRACTICE

Although the majority of SOP youth went on to commit further crimes after probation supervision, there was a general reduction in the prevalence of crime regardless of level of supervision. Accordingly, most serious juvenile offenders can be supervised in regular caseloads because the majority of recidivism is not threatening to community safety. This is an encouraging finding for probation in general, for it shows its ability to control even high-risk offenders with regular supervision services. Those delinquents who were unaffected by ordinary probation—those who went on to commit further crimes—should be the focus of special efforts such as intensive supervision. Neither regular nor intensive supervision *in its current forms* effectively stopped this group from committing further crimes that threatened public safety. These youths are both victims and perpetrators of crime, they have learned well the contingencies which lead to crime, and they seem to have internalized a system of perceptions and beliefs in which criminal behaviors are a norm.

It is not surprising, then, that this cohort was relatively unaffected by the SOP experiment, for the impacts of supervision were strongly mitigated by deeply embedded social structural factors. For some, the relative deprivation of inner city urban areas isolated them from conventional opportunities and prosocial behavioral norms. Others were socialized in a milieu where crime was commonplace. It is unreasonable to expect intensive supervision to contain behaviors that are shaped by social structural factors, or to have any more than a transient impact on the lives of these probationers. Strategies to have longer lasting and more profound impacts are discussed below.

Intensive Supervision: A Cornerstone of Crime Policy

Intensive supervision should continue to be a necessary and appropriate alternative for serious or violent offenders who have failed in traditional probation supervision or even while on reduced caseloads. The decision to place an offender under the closer scrutiny and restriction of intensive supervision should be based on the committing offense and prior offense histories. For offenders retained in the community, those adjudicated for what would be "index" felony offenses as adults should be eligible for intensive supervision, and those with prior offense histories involving violent behaviors also should be so placed. The characteristics associated with recidivism in this study could be used to determine the length of intensive supervision and the type of community activities comprising the intervention plan.

But to structure intensive probation simply as a surveillance strategy would be to recreate the failed methods of past experiences. For these offenders, a new form of probation is needed that offers stronger sanctions and more meaningful interventions. In the Epilogue that follows, we see how organizational, political and administrative factors combined to confound the experiment. Probation departments are under increasing pressure not only to justify their costs, but to do a better job at community protection and public safety. It is not surprising that change is a cautious and slow process in this environment. Contra Costa County's probation department should be commended for its first steps in this direction.

For those offenders who require more control and intervention than regular supervision, but can remain in the community, an intensive supervision strategy should be designed to include the dimensions of *control, case management, assessment, planning, graduated sanctions*, and *community reintegration*. These innovations require a formal redefinition of intensive supervision to establish the unique nature of this sanction. It requires a fundamental rethinking of the role of the probation officer, the type of individual who takes on these tasks, the training necessary to equip such officers, and the organizational contingencies necessary to develop this function independently of the traditional duties of the probation department.

Control. Control and security should remain a cornerstone of this form of sanction. The strategy requires that probation officers be capable of detecting and responding to illegal behaviors quickly and with full knowledge of the context in which they occur. This type of "quick sanctioning" capability is necessary to establish the deterrent effect of surveillance and, accordingly, raise the costs of crime. By linking control to other activities such as school, work or community service, the community and its social institutions become part of the control network. The supervision function is thus shared among probation officers and community agencies, and broadens the social resources for control.

Case Management. The case management function is necessary to address youths' social skill deficits, and to implement social learning processes through sanctions and records. Case management functions serve a number of purposes. First, they provide a means to respond individually to each offender in a timely and efficient manner. Second, they build in clear and consistent expectations regarding behavior, and establish the rewards or gains that can accrue to the offender from meeting these expectations. In effect, the case manager becomes an instrument of social learning. Third, they provide a resource or social network for the probationer to help identify opportunities for developing skills, build ties to groups outside delinquent peers, and plan for the future.

Community Reintegration. The reintegration aspect of intensive supervision is critical for youths isolated from social opportunities, conventional activities or constructive social milieus. The goal of this strategy is to build the kinds of relationships and interactions which will become the daily routine of the probationer once supervision ends. It establishes the probationer in a setting that teaches and rewards legal behaviors, and offers resources to resolve inevitable problems without relying on illegal means. In effect, it transfers the social control of probationers from the criminal justice system to the community, and establishes the legitimacy of the community's values for the offender.

Assessment. An enhanced assessment and diagnostic process is needed to make this new form of supervision more effective. First, assessment should examine social and personal bonds in several domains: school and work, family ties, peer ties, drug use and self-report measures of crime, a detailed look at the official career reconciled with self-report measures, and a variety of attitudinal scales. Second, cross-validation should be a routine step in the assessment process. Interviews with those knowledgeable about the youth—school officials, employers, spouses or lovers, and close friends—should be a routine occurrence. Third, this information should be tied specifically to behaviors, skills, perceptions, goals and values that may be powerful reinforcers. From this bank of knowledge, a realistic and concrete plan of action and timetable can be developed, including goals for behavior and community reintegration that can serve as objective management markers for the probation officer.

Planning. The information gathered in the assessment process should inform the supervision plan. A timetable for achieving these goals should be set based on realistic and achievable outcomes. This also includes the types of behavioral goals to pursue, other strategies and goals related to the assessment of social bonds, a listing of community services and activities to achieve these goals, the resources needed, and the timetable to achieve them. Both the probation officer and the probationer should know what rewards will accrue from meeting goals and expectations. The objectification of the decision-making process results in a shared understanding of what is to take place and what goals are to be met.

Graduated Sanctions. Intensive probation should include a more diverse sanctioning capability, with a range of sanctions commensurate with the nature and severity of the offender's behavior. This may include such measures as ordering limited periods of home detention, short-term residential placements, or a modification of the supervision plan to include new goals or longer times. Revocation should remain in the court's domain, and should remain a "last resort" sanction. Sanctions or consequences should be defined at the outset of supervision so that contingencies are expected. This will achieve two learning principles: objectification of the sanction process, and linkage of behavior with consequences. The same is true for rewards. Progress and achievement of behavioral or community reintegration goals should be rewarded by decreasing control by the deputy probation officer and increasing degrees of freedom from supervision. Eventually, meeting all specified goals should result in the end of intensive supervision.

Community Participation in Supervision: Informal Social Control

Finally, neighborhood residents can develop mechanisms to sanction criminal behaviors that trouble their communities. Both probation agencies and the community must participate in the development of responses to crime and other social policies that affect community development. Arguably, if an offender fails in the community, the community may have failed the offender. The development of local sanctioning mechanisms is necessary to convey community norms and transfer the task of social control from official agencies to neighborhoods. The long-range solutions to violent crime cannot reside solely in the justice system. Socialization and supervision of youths are the responsibilities of social institutions such as schools, families, the economic sector, and neighborhood and community.

The development of local neighborhood mechanisms for control and supervision of young offenders further empowers probation deputies and reinforces the legitimacy of the goals of the intervention plan. This will allow cultural factors specific to communities to become part of the intensive supervision plan, which, in turn, can influence the offender's behavior and reinforce the actions of the deputy. Styles of control and supervision will become consistent with the neighborhood where the probationer will live, thus increasing the chances for success.

These efforts with neighborhoods should become central parts of a long-term strategy to reduce serious crime among young offenders in the transitional years between adolescence and adulthood. The continuing scarcity of public resources requires that we identify ways to supervise and control crime without costly official interventions.

IMPLICATIONS FOR RESEARCH

Processes of Peer Influence on Aggression

Although social learning theories have gained wide acceptance in delinquency research (Akers et al., 1979; Johnson et al., 1987), there has been little research to explain how these processes are perceived by offenders and how they teach and reinforce behaviors. Research is needed to examine the four components of social learning: modeling, reinforcement, opportunities for practice, and functional value (Bandura, 1977). To develop effective interventions for offenders in the community, empirical knowledge is needed on the conditions fostering the implicit rules of conduct that determine behaviors in different neighborhoods or groups. How are these rules communicated and reinforced? What aversive factors (e.g., codes of conduct or consequences) are communicated by low-crime communities? An understanding of these processes can inform the design of probation strategies to counter these influences, the development of reintegration methods to situate probationers in pro-social settings, and the forging of linkages with neighborhood groups that can provide a system of accountability for shaping behavior beyond probation.

Influence of Assessment Data on Supervision Effectiveness

The assessment process in juvenile court should be expanded and improved to support probation classification decisions and intensive supervision strategies. Whether they are called social reports in juvenile court or presentence investigations in criminal court, the assessment process that informs dispositions and correctional interventions should be improved through research. Meta-analyses of previous probation research should examine the types of offenders who have fared well or poorly on probation.

From secondary analyses of data bases on different offender groups, standardized and culture-specific scales and indicators can be developed to support the assessment process. What is needed is not necessarily new research. Rather, we need to improve on what we know now using more sensitive and elegant statistical methods complemented by qualitative data on social processes.

Neighborhood Involvement in Effective Supervision

Several types of inquiry are needed to identify successful efforts at the community level to convey and enforce sanctions against crime. First, studies of high- and low-crime neighborhoods, controlling for socioeconomic conditions and urbanism, should contrast the informal and formal control mechanisms in these areas. Second, a naturalistic study of effective programs or efforts should document the central and replicable elements of their strategies. Third, the ties of formal and informal groups to the justice system should be examined to determine whether and how probation can participate in these efforts and eventually shift supervision responsibility to the community. Finally, further studies of the perceptions of offenders on community sanctions can identify more effective methods to communicate values and sanctions.

Intensive Supervision and Organizational Innovation

Finally, if probation departments are to develop new forms of supervision, rehabilitative interventions and sanctions, studies of the organization of probation departments are needed to support the new efforts. To make change work, research is needed on the factors within and outside probation that support or impede change. Petersilia (1985) called for a similar study of attitudes toward probation's mission. We agree, and suggest that such studies go further to include case studies of successful and failed efforts to implement experimentation and change. From this knowledge, future efforts can be planned which are supported by key actors in the probation setting.

EPILOGUE: NOTES ON THE TREATMENT VARIABLE

The markedly different performance of the Richmond SOP caseload, as well as the negligible differences in recidivism between SOP and control youth in other parts of the county, are best explained by the implementation of the SOP experiment. In an experimental design, these differences should be attributable to the intervention, not to characteristics of the subjects. Accordingly, we look to the dynamics of the SOP: the style of supervision, the use of "treatment" referrals, and perceptions of the SOP and regular probation by the deputies themselves. The data below were gathered through extensive open-ended, structured interviews with the four SOP deputies and their supervisor.

The Probation Officer as Intervention

Philosophy and Self-Perception. The SOP was comprised of four deputies—three in East County and one in Richmond. D.J., the Richmond deputy, operated both within and outside the unit. This led to some degree of variation in implementation between the offices, in both basic philosophy and style of probation work. D.J. stressed the social worker side of his role and did not mention the control function as basic to his style or philosophy. Instead, he emphasized vocational training and community college as the means to a job, and thus a "way out." He stressed positive feedback and support more than most probation officers.

K.L. likened the SOP to the "AA model: an arm around the shoulder and a kick in the butt when needed." R.K. and D.R. both saw themselves as "resource brokers," whose role it was to "hook them up to services that deal with their needs." R.K. stressed "establishing a structure," and seemed to put great emphasis on school performance as the one critical index of success, while D.R. noted that he enjoyed the new resource broker side of probation in which he "united the community" in order to "hook the kid up," in contrast to the "old, individualistic setting of limits."

Treatment. Treatment was not a formal, identifiable feature of the SOP, since it inevitably blended with supervision and general case management. There was little distinction by SOP deputies between regular probation contacts and counseling. Few referrals to counseling were reported, since it was assumed to be part of the probation "agreement" between the youth and the deputy.

D.J. said he never made mental health referrals, since he had the requisite skills and training. He preferred to "do it" himself. Others also made few referrals, but for different reasons. R.K. said 99% of his clients were unmotivated for therapy—and many did not have the funds—so he tried not to order it. D.R. said that all his cases got counseling, the question was what kind. For him, treatment was indistinguishable from other facets of casework.

SOP deputies rarely developed a specific "treatment plan" for each case, independent of court orders. Some clients were required to go to therapy sessions, and this was at times followed up by the SOP deputies. But these instances were rare. They saw all clients weekly as required by the design, and informal counseling was usually a part of this. For example, if the family was weak or a problem the deputies made family visits, and family therapy often was part of their approach. All families were visited at the outset to get "a better picture" of the clients' situation. This differed from regular probation, in which officers rarely have the time to visit the family.

All SOP officers stressed that this is just the sort of difference that distinguished the SOP: the ability to shore up the client's support network by consistently following through on what he was supposed to be doing at home, in school and in other key life areas.

Client Needs Assessments. The program design called for a formal system of client needs assessment. This proved difficult to implement. All did lengthy initial interviews. From then on they relied mainly on experience and common sense. D.J. worked alone in Richmond, leaving little alternative to his own assessment process. The East County deputies "conferenced" all their cases, which actually was a series of group discussions and shared thoughts. They had the time to "put their heads together on what the kid needed."

K.L. summed this all up when she said, "We used the same tools (for needs assessment), but SOP gave us the time to be more in depth." Another said: "There is no assessment of needs in regular probation."

Training. According to the SOP supervisor, SOP deputies received "extensive" training, including regularly scheduled sessions with outside consultants on how to handle various types of violent or drug-abusing clients, or on topics such as aggression, family therapy, and arson. At least one frequent consultant also gave them clinical support as treatment "professionals" dealing with a difficult population. Part of this involved how not to get personally "hooked" on a case.

Thus, part of what makes SOP different from regular probation, and hence part of the treatment variable, was additional specialized training on how to handle cases. However, this training was not rigorously therapy-oriented, at least in so far as inferred from deputies' descriptions. That may have been only because the therapeutic mode was taken for granted.

Termination and Revocation Decision-Making. The individual probation officers were fairly autonomous in termination decisions. SOP deputies were always concerned about their credibility with the courts, and their "general" guideline was to recommend termination from probation if there was no "new beef" (either legal or technical) in six months. But this was qualified in two ways: If they thought it would be difficult to obtain approval from a judge, they either kept the client in the SOP a bit longer or transferred her or him to regular probation (which apparently required no judicial action). Even without a new offense, if there was no treatment progress and more "trouble" was forecast by the deputy, transfer to regular probation usually was effected at the end of the six-month period.

Thus, although the SOP design called for a six-month period of intensive supervision, this policy was often, and sometimes systematically, overlooked. When the deputies had "reason to believe" that community protection was jeopardized, termination decisions were postponed or the youth was transferred to regular, less intensive supervision caseloads. The SOP unit supervisor expressed this priority clearly: Community protection was the driving force in the termination decision. And the operating principle was to avoid "false positives"—youths who may have appeared ready for termination but who were viewed as continued risks.

In a few cases, treatment considerations mediated the termination decision. Some youths in a remedial school reported in follow-up interviews that they were not released from the SOP since the school's rules required such "special" status as a probation commitment. One youth, who was doing quite well in the school, said that the school would have dropped him if he were released from probation. Neither the SOP deputy nor the youth wanted this, so the youth was transferred to regular probation after SOP intervention. In another case, the youth's mother asked the SOP deputy to continue probation, even though the SOP deputy would have released him from supervision due to his "successful" adjustment.

It is not surprising, then, that length of supervision did not explain recidivism. Longer supervision, whether on SOP or after transfer to regular probation, had both positive and negative connotations with respect to treatment outcome. Some youths who failed shortly after assignment were terminated early. Others who "succeeded" were kept on longer. Still others were kept on longer despite success, based on a subjective "risk assessment" by the SOP deputies and/or the unit supervisor. Accordingly, more global measures of SOP intervention revealed more about its impact than such factors as length, frequency and type of contact, or legal status at SOP termination.

Comparative Reflections on SOP and Regular Supervision

When asked general questions about the SOP and how it differed from regular probation, all four SOP deputies had positive things to say. D.J. believed that dollars spent on intensive caseloads were well spent, since prisons are so expensive and destructive. R.K. lauded the teamwork and the boost in morale that came from lower caseloads. D.R. liked the support from supervisors, the reduction in bureaucratic work, and being able to "really work with the kids." K.L. agreed with these views and linked them all to lower caseloads and teamwork. All three East County deputies stressed this as the most unique feature of the SOP.

The other feature that set SOP apart from regular probation was the *increased contact* stemming from lower caseloads, and, in turn, the ability to go out into the community (schools, family, etc.) and work with other parts of the youth's social networks. "You really had time to really supervise. It allowed more consistency and follow through. [In] regular probation, I can't do that now; I can't go to the school and show the kid school is important. Most of what we do is court work. Supervision suffers." Two noted that this varied from client to client ("for some it was overkill"), but all stressed it.

On the other hand, the SOP unit supervisor gave a different answer to the question about what was different about the SOP: "The premise is different: It's heavy concentration on a small population. ISU (intensive supervision unit) is similar, but SOP is not just heavy supervision like ISU. It is...trying to really change the kid." The supervisor noted that this did not suggest that the SOP had more resources. However, it is likely that the ability to do special interventions hinged on the extra time SOP made available for supervision and treatment.

The supervisor summed up SOP intervention with the word "eclectic," a word often used to describe probation supervision (Lemert and Dill, 1978). He said no SOP deputy was required to use any particular mode of treatment. When asked whether their SOP cases got treatment or services different from those given to regular probationers, SOP deputies seemed to agree that they did little different, just more of it. R.K. noted that with more contacts, each became less threatening and more congenial, while this greater attention was harder (but not impossible) for regular probation officers to provide. D.R. said that any significant amount of attention or services is more than regular probationers received. K.L. answered that yes, treatment was different in that it was more intensive; the officers had more time and did more follow through.

For this study, caseload size becomes the crucial discriminating treatment variable. Few other identifiable differences between SOP and regular probation could be discerned. In light of this, it is not surprising that the SOP had little measurable impact on recidivism. Instead, community of origin and pre-intervention characteristics turned out to be the strongest predictors of outcome.

NOTES

1. Violence charges included: homicide; kidnapping for robbery, ransom, or with bodily harm; robbery while armed with a deadly weapon or with the threat of bodily harm; extortion under threat of bodily harm; assault with intent to commit murder, rape, mayhem or robbery; arson; rape with force or violence or threat of bodily harm; sex crimes against children; accessory to any of the above; assault with firearms or destructive device, caustic chemicals, or by any means likely to produce great bodily harm; assault with a deadly weapon on a peace officer or fireman; shooting at an inhabited building; aggravated assault and battery against a school employee; burglaries if the minor was armed and/or the victim injured; or any case where the victim suffered significant physical injury.

2. Violence potential was based on knowledge by the probation officer of: violence against family members, peers (beyond what is socially acceptable), the elderly or very young, or at school; unprovoked acts of violence; excessive damage to property during uncontrolled outbursts of temper; excessive cruelty to animals; exhibiting weapons in a threatening manner; a background of repeated fighting and/or battery; information from psychological or psychiatric reports or tests that clearly indicate a high violence potential; or other related or similar circumstances that indicate a high violence potential.

3. This project was for juvenile offenders who were returning to the community from short stays at juvenile hall facilities, and was called the "Saturation, Supervision, and Surveillance Project" (SSS). One year after its implementation, an unexpected reduction in funding for this special caseload required either that it be abandoned or folded into the SOP.

4. Although of those who did recidivate, the experimental clients had a somewhat higher average number of new offenses.

5. *Public Hearings on Racial, Ethnic, and Religious Conflict and Violence in Contra Costa County*, California Fair Employment and Housing Commission (Sacramento, CA: 1981); *San Francisco Examiner*, 4/18/82, 1/30/83. An active chapter of the Ku Klux Klan in Contra Costa was expelled from the national "Invisible Empire, Order of the White Knights" for being "too violent and too involved in illegal activities."

6. Note that completed foreclosures rose 241%, from 120 to 410.

7. There were very few Latino or Asian respondents in the pool. Accordingly, interviewers of these origins were not specifically sought.

8. A series of attitudinal variables leading to 12 scales were measured for the post-intervention period, and are presented as SOCIAL ATTITUDES in Table 14. These two variables are the mean standardized factor scores from a factor analysis of 12 separate attitudinal scales. The factors were orthogonally rotated using a varimax routine. Two factors explained over 50% of the variance. The first factor explained 37% of the variance. It includes high loadings for ATTITUDE TOWARD VIOLENCE and CYNICISM, and strong negative loadings for ATTITUDE TOWARD LAW and TRUST IN GOVERNMENT. These factors seem to represent a consistent set of anti-social feelings characterized by lack of belief or trust in societal rules and behavioral norms. The second factor is nearly the converse of the ANTI-SOCIAL factor. Called PRO-SOCIAL, it is characterized by "traditional" beliefs—MATERIALISM and CONVENTIONAL VALUES. This factor accounts for nearly 13% of the variance. The strong orientation in this factor toward a desire for both material wealth and traditional emotional well-being suggests an individual with strong beliefs in societal norms.

9. For example, family social bonds (FAMILY INTEGRATION) included scales and variables tapping family interaction patterns, affection, and types of activities among family members. Family personal bonds included trust and respect among family members, attitudes on the importance of families, and sex roles within the family. In some instances, a composite variable was constructed (e.g., FAMILY INTEGRATION) for the domain. In other instances, a representative variable was selected to represent the domain (e.g., FAMILY COMMITMENT represented family personal bonds). The selection criteria included those variables which contributed at least 2% of the variance in intra-domain regression analyses, excluding variables with high multicollinearity. Accordingly, some domains are represented by two variables (e.g., PEER ATTITUDES TOWARD THE LAW and GANG MEMBER both represent the peer domain for personal bonds; neighborhood is represented twice among environmental variables due to the individual contributions of the two variables—NEIGHBORHOOD STRENGTH and NEIGHBORHOOD CRIME).

10. The models controlling for pre-intervention criminality were completed by stipulating the introduction of the control variable (PEER DELINQUENCY T1) as the final step; its relative contribution to variance was determined from the R-squared change in the last step. In the tables that follow, it is shown as PRE-INTERVENTION CRIMINALITY. The results for the models for each crime measure are shown in Tables 15 and 16, followed by a comparison of the relative explanatory of the models for each source of influence and each crime measure.

REFERENCES

Akers, R. (1979). "Social Learning and Deviant Behavior: A Specific Text of a General Theory." *American Sociological Review* 44(4):636-655.

Bandura, A. (1977). *Social Learning Theory*. Englewood Cliffs, NJ: Prentice Hall.

Blau, J. R., and P. M. Blau (1982). "The Cost of Inequality: Metropolitan Structure and Violent Crime." *American Sociological Review* 47:114-129.

Braithwaite, J. (1979). *Inequality, Crime, and Public Policy*. London, UK: Routledge and Keegan Paul.

Bursik, Robert J. (1986). "Ecological Stability and the Dynamics of Delinquency." In *Communities and Crime*, edited by A.J. Reiss and M. Tonry. Chicago, IL: University of Chicago Press.

California Department of Justice, Bureau of Criminal Statistics (1981). *1981 Criminal Justice Profile: Contra Costa County*. Sacramento, CA.

California Employment Development Department (1982). *California Employment Development Department Report*. Sacramento, CA.

—— (1981). *Labor Market Survey, Report to the Contra Costa County Private Sector Initiatives Program*. Sacramento, CA.

California Fair Employment and Housing Commission (1983). *Public Hearings on Racial, Ethnic, and Religious Conflict and Violence in Contra Costa County*. Sacramento, CA.

Contra Costa County Planning Department (1983). *Economic Task Force Report to Contra Costa County Board of Supervisors*. Martinez, CA.

—— (1979a). *Overall Economic Development Program: 1971-1980 Annual Report*. Martinez, CA.

—— (1979b). *Northern Coastal California*. Martinez, CA.

Elliott, D. and S. Ageton (1980). "Reconciling Race and Class Differences in Self-Reported and Official Estimates of Delinquency." *American Sociological Review* 45:95-110.

—— and R. Canter (1979). "An Integrated Theoretical Perspective on Delinquent Behavior." *Journal of Research in Crime and Delinquency* 16:3-27.

—— and D. Huizinga (1983). "Social Class and Delinquent Behavior in a National Youth Study." *Criminology* 21:149-171.

Fagan, J. (1990). "Social and Legal Policy Dimensions of Violent Juvenile Crime." *Criminal Justice and Behavior* 17:93-133.

—— and S. Jones (1984). "Toward an Integrated Theoretical Model of Violent Delinquency." In *Violent Juvenile Offenders: An Anthology*, edited by R. Mathias et al. Newark, NJ: National Council on Crime and Delinquency.

—— and C. Reinarman (1984). *Intensive Supervision of Violent Offenders: The Transition from Adolescence to Early Adulthood, A Longitudinal Evaluation. Final Report to the National Institute of Justice*. (Grant 82-IJ-CX-K008.) San Francisco, CA: URSA Institute.

Feld, B. (1987). "The Juvenile Court Meets the Principle of the Offense: Legislative Changes in Juvenile Waiver Statutes." *Journal of Criminal Law and Criminology* 78:471-533.

—— (1983). "Delinquent Careers and Criminal Policy: Just Desserts and the Waiver Decision." *Criminology* 21:195-212.

Greenwood, P., A. J. Lipson, A. Abrahamse and F. Zimring (1983). *Youth Crime and Juvenile Justice in California*. Santa Monica, CA: Rand.

Hamparian, D., L. K. Estep, S. M. Muntean, R. R. Priestino, R. G. Swisher, P. L. Wallace and J. L. White (1982). *Youth in Adult Courts: Between Two Worlds*. Columbus, OH: Academy for Contemporary Problems.

—— R. Schuster, S. Dinitz and J. Conrad (1978). *The Violent Few*. Lexington, MA: D. C. Heath.

Jamison, M. (1981). *Final Report: Evaluation of the Serious Offender Project*. San Francisco, CA: URSA Institute.

Johnson, R. E., A. C. Marcos and S. J. Bahr (1987). "The Role of Peers in the Complex Etiology of Adolescent Drug Use." *Criminology* 25(2):323-340.

Kornhauser, R. R. (1978). *Social Sources of Delinquency*. Chicago, IL: University of Chicago Press.

Laub, J. (1983). "Urbanism, Race, and Crime." *Journal of Research in Crime and Delinquency* 20:183-198.

—— and M. J. Hindelang (1981). *Juvenile Criminal Behavior in Urban, Suburban, and Rural Areas*. Washington, DC: U.S. Government Printing Office.

Lemert, E. and B. Dill (1978). *Offenders in the Community*. Lexington, MA: D.C. Heath.

Lerman, P. (1984). *Deinstitutionalization and the Welfare State*. New Brunswick, NJ: Rutgers University Press.

—— (1975). *Community Treatment and Social Control*. Chicago, IL: University of Chicago Press.

McNeely, R. L. and C. Pope (1981). "Socioeconomic and Racial Issues in the Measurement of Criminal Involvement." In *Race, Crime and Criminal Justice*, edited by R.L. McNeely and C. Pope. Beverly Hills, CA: Sage.

Messner, S. F. (1983). "Regional Differences in the Economic Correlates of the Urban Homicide Rate." *Criminology* 21:477-488.

—— (1982). "Poverty, Inequality, and the Urban Homicide Rate." *Criminology* 20:103-114.

Miller, A., and L. Ohlin (1985). *Delinquency and Community*. Newbury Park, CA: Sage.

—— (1980). *Decision-Making About Secure Care for Juveniles*. Cambridge, MA: Harvard University Press.

Petersilia, J. (1985). *Granting Probation to Felony Offenders*. Santa Monica, CA: Rand.

Reinarman, C. and J. Fagan (1988). "Social Organization and Differential Association: A Research Note from a Longitudinal Study of Violent Juvenile Offenders." *Crime & Delinquency* 34:307-327.

Sampson, R. J. (1987). "Urban Black Violence: The Effect of Male Joblessness and Family Disruption." *American Journal of Sociology* 93:348-382.

—— (1986). "Effects of Socioeconomic Context on Official Reaction to Juvenile Delinquency." *American Sociological Review* 51:876-885.

Shannon, L. (1986). "Ecological Evidence of the Hardening of the Inner City." In *Metropolitan Crime Patterns*, edited by Robert M. Figlio et al. Monsey, NY: Criminal Justice Press.

—— (1984). *The Development of Serious Criminal Careers and the Delinquent Neighborhood*. Washington, DC: U.S. National Institute of Justice.

Silberman, C. E. (1978). *Criminal Violence, Criminal Justice*. New York, NY: Random House.

Smith, C. (1972). A *Quiet Revolution: Probation Subsidy*. Washington, DC: U.S. Department of Health and Human Services.

Smith, D. A., C. Visher and L. Davidson, 1984. "Equity and Discretionary Justice: The Influence of Race on Police Arrest Decisions." *Journal of Criminal Law and Criminology* 75: 234-249.

Weiner, N. A., and M. E. Wolfgang (1985). "The Extent and Character of Violent Crime in America, 1969-1982." In *American Violence and Public Policy*, edited by L.A. Curtis. New Haven, CT: Yale University Press.

Wolfgang, M. E., R. Figlio, and T. Sellin (1972). *Delinquency in a Birth Cohort*. Chicago, IL: University of Chicago Press.

The Regional Youth Educational Facility: A Promising Short-Term Intensive Institutional and Aftercare Program for Juvenile Court Wards

by
Norman Skonovd
Wesley Krause

The Regional Youth Educational Facility provides a highly intensive six-month residential program, followed by four to six months of intensive aftercare supervision, for 40 male wards. This state-subsidized program is operated by the San Bernardino County (CA) Probation Department and serves youth from both San Bernardino and Riverside Counties. Quasi-experimental data suggest that the program has a positive effect on the recidivism of its participants, who were compared with a carefully constructed comparison group of juveniles completing other programs. The program elements, both because of their substantive content and their number, have created a positive culture and orientation that makes resocialization more likely than in some of the other programs serving the same population.

INTRODUCTION

The Regional Youth Educational Facility (RYEF) represents an attempt at juvenile rehabilitation or resocialization through a program composed of educational, treatment, training and work experience components. Some observers might argue that establishing this program reflects ignorant optimism in the face of a long history of rehabilitative program failures. Indeed, perhaps the most widely disseminated and commonly accepted conclusion from the last 20 years of criminal justice research is that "nothing works." Martinson is generally credited with initiating this correctional cry of despair. In a review of over 200 correctional program evaluations published before 1967, he found that "With few and isolated exceptions, the rehabilitative efforts that have been reported so far have had no appreciable effect on recidivism" (Martinson, 1974:25).

Many others, both earlier and later, came to the same conclusion (e.g., Bailey, 1966; Robinson and Smith, 1971; Sechrest, White and Brown, 1979). However, others surveying the literature, such as Palmer (1975), Romig (1978), Ross and Gendreau (1980), and Garrett (1985), have argued that methodologically sound studies have demonstrated the effectiveness (for at least some types of offenders) of a number of correctional programs. These latter studies have not generally received the same attention as those arguing for the non-effectiveness of correctional programs. Nevertheless, both sides of this debate may actually be saying much the same thing: Most correctional programs have not proven effective in reducing recidivism, but some have.

One could, therefore, argue that taking a position on the correctional effectiveness debate is primarily one of emphasis. However, as Greenwood (1986:209) points out, the nothing works school tends to overlook the fact that most correctional evaluations have compared one correctional treatment program with one or more others. This means that those in the nothing-works school are assuming that treatment does not work unless it produces better results than the programs with which it is compared. Obviously, this is not necessarily the case.

A more serious concern however, is that the nothing-works position can imply a research or policy orientation opposed to the investigation and development of effective programs. Fortunately, from our viewpoint, the extreme negative attitude regarding rehabilitation programs has lessened. In fact, Martinson (1979) even repudiated his original contention that almost nothing works. Nevertheless, serious attention to what does work appears to be overshadowed by a highly politicized correctional orientation focusing on punishment and public protection (for notable exceptions to this trend, see Palmer, 1978, 1983; Armstrong and Altschuler, 1982; Greenwood, 1986).

The RYEF was developed and is operated by correctional administrators and staff who believe that rehabilitative programs can work. The evaluation that will be discussed leads us to believe that this program not only works, but that it is more effective in reducing recidivism than are some of the other programs that serve the same population. However, because of the short follow-up period and the small number of wards in the study (in addition to the fact that true experimental methods incorporating random assignment were not employed), we cannot be sure. Therefore, like too many other correctional program evaluations, our results must be considered suggestive and tentative rather than definitive.

Background

The governor of California signed legislation in 1984 authorizing the Department of the Youth Authority to fund and evaluate one or more RYEFs. The legislation originated in a concern over the lack of short-term intensive residential programs for juveniles at the regional level. Out of this concern, the administration and legislature agreed that a regional, intensive approach to local juvenile corrections should be piloted in California. A number of advocacy groups lobbied for the inclusion of various program elements.

Intended to provide a sentencing alternative for the juvenile courts, the RYEF was mandated to function as a residential program for wards who are: primarily 16 and 17 years old; coming under the definitions of Section 602 of the California Welfare and Institutions Code; awaiting out-of-home placement in juvenile halls; and not appropriate for commitment to the Youth Authority. Each facility was to provide a short-term intensive educational experience, including such program elements as: (1) competency-based education services; (2) visual perceptual screening and treatment; (3) remedial individual educational plans for diagnosed learning disabilities; (4) electronic and computer education; (5) physical education; (6) vocational training; (7) work experience; (8) character education; (9) victim awareness education; and (10) restitution. Additionally, following completion of the residential program phase, wards were to receive intensive supervision by a probation officer for a minimum of 120 days.

The San Bernardino County Probation Department was selected as the sole site for a RYEF, and the counties of San Bernardino and Riverside were designated as a region. Constituting a partnership between the state and the participating counties, $1 million was awarded to San Bernardino County for the operation of the facility for two years, with the county providing $1 million in matching funds and resources. A program for male wards was established in a facility consisting of two, 20-bed residential units, classrooms, offices and recreational areas adjacent to the Juvenile Hall. It began operation in August 1985, staffed by county employees. The initial two-year pilot authorization was extended to June 30, 1990. Funding has been maintained at $500,000 each year, with continued county-matching funds and resources. Standards for camps, ranches, and schools, as provided in Section 885 of the

California Welfare and Institutions Code, were applied by the Youth Authority in overseeing the operation of the facility and program.

Evaluation of the program was conducted by the Youth Authority's Research Division, assisted by the San Bernardino County Probation Department (Skonovd, 1986, 1989). The data, collected primarily for the 1989 evaluation, include six-month recidivism statistics on a small number of wards placed in the RYEF program between January 1 and September 1, 1987, and comparable wards completing other public and private juvenile correctional programs. Additional descriptive and programmatic data are presented for program wards.

PROGRAM DESCRIPTION

The RYEF operated by the San Bernardino County Probation Department has a highly structured, intensive program designed to guide juvenile court wards to develop, practice, and internalize effective adult and community survival skills, and to accept responsibility and accountability for personal behavior and decisions. Program participants are provided a competency-based remedial education program that includes: (1) accelerated physical training; (2) screening for learning disabilities, including visual and audio handicaps; (3) contact with crime victims and an awareness program to present the impact of crime on the victim; (4) vocational training and work experience; (5) substance abuse counseling and education; (6) psychological counseling; and (7) community service and restitution, including monetary compensation to victims. The program lasts 10 to 12 months, and consists of a six-month residential phase and a four- to six-month intensive aftercare or probation phase. (RYEF staff refer to the wards in their program as "clients." This study, however, uses the legal term "ward," i.e., a youth under the jurisdiction of the juvenile court per Section 602 of the California Welfare and Institutions Code.)

The program's facility consists of two 20-bed living group units, and auxiliary classrooms, offices, and recreational facilities. The two living units contain individual rooms with closets and desks, large day rooms for indoor recreation, games, discussion, reading, music, and television, and a large fenced outdoor area for athletics such as basketball, softball, and volleyball. The facility is located on the grounds of the San Bernardino County Juvenile Hall in the City of San Bernardino. It is, however, physically separated from Juvenile Hall, having its own outside entrance and separate grounds. Although RYEF wards use a large dining facility in Juvenile Hall, they are served on a different schedule. The facility entrance is locked at all times. The individual rooms are locked only at night except in cases of unusual, extreme acting-out behavior. The living unit and recreational areas are surrounded by an eight-foot wall, topped by eight feet of chain-link fencing with security mesh.

The staff consists of: the program director; two supervising group counselors; the clinical psychologist; 15 group counselors including the career development coordinator; the youth work supervisor; two teachers; two teacher's aides; the general equivalency diploma (GED) technician; three deputy probation officers; two transportation aides; and two clerks. The staff-ward ratio (for staff who have regular contact with wards) is approximately three to four.

Male wards who require out-of-home placement and are aged 16 or 17 are referred to the program by probation officers or the court in San Bernardino and Riverside Counties. (Ten beds in the 40-bed program are reserved for wards from Riverside County.) Although not apprised of the specific selection criteria, probation officers have been directed to refer wards who they believe will benefit from the program. Referrals are reviewed by a screening committee composed of the program director, a supervising group counselor, the clinical psychologist and an aftercare probation officer. Prospective program participants must score between 13 and 21 on San Bernardino County's Assessment of Client Risk instrument—an objective assessment of risk completed by probation officers for each ward being considered for out-of-home placement. This instrument, designed primarily to set field probation supervision levels, is based upon the statistical probability of rearrest and technical probation rule violation. Scores ranging between 13 and 21 indicate medium- to high-risk of subsequent arrest. Wards classified minimum risk (scoring 12 and under) are excluded, as are those scoring in the maximum range (22 through 28).

The RYEF program excludes youths who: (1) have two or more sustained felony assaultive offenses (includes use or threat to use a weapon and physical force or threat to use physical force); (2) are resistant to all efforts to modify behavior (which may be expressed by an attitude toward offense(s) that reflects asocial values or rationalizations, a refusal to cooperate with program staff and habitual runaway behavior); (3) have alcohol or drug dependency (characterized by regular use with periods of intoxication, excessive periodic use creating dangerous situations, use alone after school, or use in school or in work situations); (4) manifest emotional disorder requiring professional treatment (clinical diagnosis of emotional/personality disorder or obvious treatment needs such as those indicated by severe depression, and serious or recurrent suicidal gestures and expressions); (5) have a confirmed homosexual lifestyle; (6) score below 80 in I.Q.; and (7) have a serious handicap or chronic illness (problem(s) causing major disruption of life or inability to stabilize medically the effects of an illness or handicap such as epileptic seizures). These items are recorded on the Probation Department's Assessment of Client Risk and Need instruments by each ward's probation officer. For exceptional cases, the screening committee may administratively override these selection criteria. Such overrides are estimated to comprise about 5% of RYEF admissions.

The ward's progress through the institutional phase of the program is governed by a "level" classification system, which provides the basic foundation for programming. It is also intended to assist the ward in improving his individual decision-making skills as he is given increased responsibility and privileges with each move to a higher level. The level system consists of:

- *Level 1* — Institutional program only (four weeks). Goals include: orientation to unit; development of relationships with staff and peers; transition from detention to treatment; assessment of needs and establishment of goals; adjustment to structure; orientation to school and completion of placement testing; and development of immediate goals. Ward is restricted in personal privileges and extent of recreational activities.
- *Level 2* — Institutional and community programs under staff supervision (two weeks). Goals include: improvement in personal responsibility; assertion of personal identity in positive fashion; and acquaintance with community resources through field trips. Ward is provided the opportunity to participate in more recreational activities.
- *Level 3* — Institutional and community programs with some unsupervised time (two weeks). Goals include: demonstration of proper behavior when in community; development and demonstration of reliability; and progress in educational and vocational goals. Ward is provided the opportunity to attend outside vocational education classes and take furloughs of up to four hours.
- *Level 4* — Institutional and full-time community programs with furloughs (four weeks). Goals include: increased evidence of individual responsibility; increased community responsibility; less direct supervision; and implementation of initial steps in attaining vocational goals. Ward is provided the opportunity to take longer furloughs (eight to 24 hours) and look for jobs within the community unsupervised. He is also permitted greater discretion in sleep periods, free time, transportation and use of personal jewelry.
- *Level 5* — Institutional program and full-time work or vocational training; aftercare planning commences (12 weeks). Goals include: development of positive personal identity and responsibility in the institution and the community; demonstration of self-reliance and self-determination; implementation of initial steps in achieving long-range goals (including finalizing plans for living arrangements and employment/training after release); and demonstration of ability to manage personal life with minimum of supervision. Ward is provided the opportunity to accept full-time employment or enroll in full-time

academic or vocational programs in the community. He is also permitted to take furloughs of 24 to 48 hours.

The ward must complete assignments at each level, and pass performance evaluations and program review at each level before promotion to the next. Composed of all available section staff and teachers, the "level" boards are chaired by the ward's respective Supervisor I, or his or her designee, and meet with the ward every one or two weeks. These boards are intended to provide the ward with direct, precise instructions and feedback regarding his behavior, attitudes and progress in the program from entry to promotion to aftercare. Based upon staff documentation, presentation and discussion in the ward's presence, decisions by the board determine promotion, maintenance or demotion. Wards may make a verbal presentation at the beginning of the board session but must remain silent during staff presentations, discussions and voting. They may, however, respond after staff presentations. Decisions by the board must be unanimous for a ward to be promoted or demoted, unless overruled by the Supervisor I. Specific goals are assigned to the ward after each level has been attained. They must be met in order for the ward to progress on to the next level or, in the case of Level 5, to promote to aftercare.

The following elements comprise the RYEF program:

Counseling Services

Upon entry to the program, each ward is administered a battery of three paper-and-pencil tests developed by the Institute of Personality and Ability Testing (IPAT). These personality tests provide standardized scores that are normed on American males, aged 12 through 18, in the general population. They are used by the clinical psychologist to determine each ward's personality profile. If serious problems are identified, individual therapy is provided by the psychologist. The psychologist also meets regularly with the group counselors for case consultation, during which time each ward's status and progress is monitored, and counseling approaches are discussed. The group counselors also provide individual and group counseling sessions for the wards on their caseloads, as well as individual and group counseling with the other wards on the living units. The IPAT tests are administered again at the time of release. A comparison of the pre-test and post-test profiles is used to prepare a personality evaluation for each client at the time of promotion to aftercare. If special circumstances exist, referrals are made to community or private providers.

Competency-Based/Remedial Education Services

At entry, each ward is also administered the California Test of Basic Skills (CTBS) to determine his or her ability level. Instruction is individualized by the teachers to fit the particular remedial needs of each ward. The instruction is competency-based and computer-assisted (ten Apple II computers are available for use by students in the classroom). Five major subject areas taught are: reading/language arts, mathematics, social studies/consumer education, science and computer education. Diagnostic services for learning handicaps are available. However, due to the need to restrict the program to those who can participate in vocational activities, wards who are severely learning handicapped are generally not admitted to the RYEF. As a program evaluation component reflecting the academic growth of each ward, the CTBS is administered again at time of release.

Graduation Equivalency Diploma (GED) Preparation

A computer-assisted program, the GED preparation class is coordinated and staffed by a full-time GED technician. Seven computers are available to wards involved in this program. The GED exam may be taken by program participants 60 days prior to their eighteenth birthday. The minimum age requirement, however, may be waived by up to one year at the request of an employer. In these cases, the employer has made a commitment to hiring the ward full-time upon earning his GED. A high school diploma may be secured through cooperation with local high schools. Wards completing their high school requirements or receiving their GED may participate in higher level educational experiences at local community colleges.

Character Education

The goal of character education is to have wards develop and internalize socially productive values, and learn sound decision-making skills. Each ward is enrolled four hours per week in character education classes. These classes teach value clarification, character and law-related education, and adult survival skills. The curriculum is based on "Choices and Challenges, Personal Planning and Self-awareness for Teenage Women and Men," developed by the Thomas Jefferson Institute (see Edmondson et al., 1984).

Physical Education

This program element seeks to: improve physical fitness; develop an all-around awareness of good health and nutrition; and increase self-esteem. Wards receive two hours of physical education each day, including physical fitness, weight lifting, jogging, and individual and organized team sports. Instruction is provided in nutrition, physical fitness, personal hygiene and the harmful effects of smoking.

Victim Awareness

The goal of the victim awareness program is to sensitize wards to the personal impact of crime on victims through an intensive eight-week class with two three-hour sessions per week. This sensitization emphasizes property offenses, rape, cruelty to animals, child abuse, elder abuse, domestic violence and vehicular manslaughter, as well as the financial, physical and psychological trauma experienced by victims. Featured speakers and presenters include members of victim support groups and actual crime victims. Open discussions between clients and presenters are encouraged. However, the class avoids forced value clarification, rejective commentary and abusive interaction. Youth are administered a pre-attitude survey during orientation and a post-attitude survey at the time of the final examination. Class graduates provide victim awareness presentations at elementary and junior high school assemblies and in classrooms.

Substance Abuse Education and Counseling

Wards with alcohol or drug abuse problems are referred to nonprofit or private sources for education and individual, family, and group counseling. Those who need treatment must attend no less than three counseling sessions per week. Alateen, an Alcoholics Anonymous group, and a Narcotics Anonymous group meet weekly at the RYEF. Wards from the facility also provide substance abuse presentations at local schools as part of the "Say No to Drugs" program and "Friday Night Live" (a program whose focus is substance abuse awareness and education). A local public service television announcement regarding substance abuse sometimes includes RYEF wards who participate in the "Friday Night Live" program.

Visual Perceptual Screening and Treatment

Upon entry to the program, all wards receive a complete visual examination, including a full visual-developmental perceptual evaluation and an audio test. This battery of tests, conducted by fourth-year interns from the Southern California College of Optometry, identifies visual problems that could hinder wards in a learning or occupational situation. Testing for dyslexia is performed to determine if any severe learning handicaps are present; this includes testing for auditory perceptual awareness. Wards identified as having visual problems (including poor eye movement and tracking skills) are provided corrective lenses and/or individually programmed vision therapy. Specialized training is performed for dyslexic wards to assist them in understanding and coping with their problems.

Career Education

Upon entry to the program, each ward is administered the Career Occupational Preference System to determine career interests, and the Career Ability Placement Survey to determine vocational aptitude. The results of these tests are used to assist the youth in exploring careers and setting goals. Each ward participates in a conference with the vocational education instructor and career development coordinator to review test results and develop the ward's goals for vocational training and employment. Youth attend career-consumer education classes that include mock job interviews, resume preparation, career education field trips and money management. Presentations by community businesspeople, trade union personnel and educators are key components of these classes.

Vocational Training and Work Experience

When wards enter the program and are still in the beginning levels, emphasis is placed on the educational components of the program. They have the opportunity to attend four to six hours of classroom education and also participate in on-grounds vocation/work programs that include landscaping, grounds maintenance and equipment maintenance. As wards reach higher levels they are permitted off the grounds in order to seek employment opportunities. When youth reach Level 5, they are permitted to obtain outside employment or enroll in education/vocational training on a full-time basis. In fact, most are employed or enrolled in education/vocational programs before promotion to aftercare. The following programs and opportunities for vocational education, job training and employment are available:

1. *Regional Occupational Program.* This program, administered by the San Bernardino County Superintendent of Schools, provides vocational training in various areas to prepare for entry-level employment. Occupational areas include: car upholstery; electronics; law enforcement; fashion merchandising; computer programming; food service; heavy equipment operation; horticulture; welding; auto mechanics; and body repair.
2. *Trade schools/colleges.* The RYEF has placed wards in the following educational or vocational schools: Adelphi Business College; Casa Ramona Electronic School; Center for Employment Training (welding, shipping and receiving); Golden State School (data entry/word processing); Golden State Welding and Electronics; I.T.T. Career Training Center, Metropolitan Institute (dental technology); National Education Center (electronic assembly); Quality Control (photocopy and office machine repair); Richards Beauty College; and San Bernardino Valley College.
3. *Job Training Partnership Act (JTPA).* San Bernardino County Schools obtain grant money from the San Bernardino County Department of Employment and Training. This grant money assists RYEF wards in career preparation, job search and "try-out" employment. (Try-out employment subsidizes private industries to train and hire students.) Riverside County wards are served through the Riverside County Probation Department "Jobs Against Crime" program.

4. *Paid Employment.* Part-and full-time paid employment in private businesses (or in public and non-profit agencies) is a goal for wards who have employment skills. Jobs obtained by wards have ranged from "blue-collar" welding and auto repair positions to "white-collar" bookkeeper and computer processing positions. Salaries have ranged from minimum wage to $13 per hour. Most wards who obtain permanent employment have been hired after completion of short-term, nonpaid, on-the-job training arranged through affiliation agreements or JTPA program training and employment. (Some wards find their own employment when they reach Level 5 and are permitted to search on their own during brief furloughs.)

The RYEF program requires all wards promoted from the residential phase to possess useable work skills or be enrolled in an educational/vocational program if employment has not been obtained. Most are employed at the time of promotion.

Reparative Sanctions

An important component of the program is reparative sanctions, which include both restitution (monetary) and community service work (see Armstrong, 1983, for use of the term "reparative"). Community service work teams, made up of RYEF wards, spend Saturdays and after school on weekdays working on community projects. The youth are encouraged to contribute a minimum of 40 hours to community service projects during the institutional phase of the program. Most, however, contribute considerably more, depending on the time available. Community service work is seen as a positive experience by the wards, providing them an opportunity to get out into the neighborhood and obtain work experience. Considerable local media attention is given to the various projects throughout the year, and RYEF wards appear to relish this.

Community service projects have included:

1. painting over graffiti for the San Bernardino County Parks and Recreation Department;
2. clearing helicopter pads at the San Bernardino Search and Rescue Building;
3. constructing, filling and distributing emergency water containers for the probation department, municipal courts and the County Government Center as part of the San Bernardino Emergency Water Distribution;
4. visiting and playing games with patients at local psychiatric facilities and convalescent homes;
5. moving furniture, clearing fire access roads and maintaining general grounds and equipment for the probation department;
6. picking up trash along roadways, assisting with the City/County Weed Abatement Program and a variety of similar projects;

7. staging puppet shows for community groups, convalescent homes and hospitals;
8. cleaning, painting and weed abatement for apartment complexes in a citywide community beautification service project;
9. donating blood every six weeks at the local San Bernardino/Riverside County Blood Bank;
10. working during the month of December at the YMCA Christmas tree lot.
11. working at fireworks stands for community nonprofit organizations; and
12. working three times weekly at the Juvenile Hall Canteen.

Wards owing restitution must complete their financial obligations to victims before they can successfully complete the aftercare program. In fact, those who are involved in paid employment programs have contractual agreements to pay a percentage of their salary toward the balance of their restitution obligations. Because of the emphasis on employment during both the institutional and aftercare phases of the program, payment of restitution has not been a problem.

Religious Programming

The religious needs of the wards are met by volunteers who visit weekly to provide Bible study and nondenominational religious services, both of which are optional. Youth may attend the religious service of their choice during their weekly furloughs. Other optional religious activities include attending religious music concerts at Calvary Chapel in Riverside and one-day religious retreats at Campus Crusade for Christ Headquarters at Arrowhead Springs.

Aftercare

Preparation for the aftercare phase of the RYEF begins at time of entry and culminates in an agreement regarding formal educational, employment, and personal goals for life in the community. (The probation officer and the caseload counselor jointly make the initial home visit within two or three weeks of the ward's arrival at the facility.) Aftercare probation officers meet the ward within two or three days of his arrival at the facility and participate in individual planning conferences (for preparing institutional program plans, aftercare goals, etc.) and other critical conferences related to the ward's progress in the program. This involves two to eight face-to-face contacts between the ward and the aftercare officer each month during the institutional phase of the program. By the time the ward is released from the institution, the aftercare probation officer has already developed a relationship with the ward, has an intimate knowledge of his strengths and weaknesses, and has participated in developing his aftercare goals.

Each RYEF probation officer has a maximum caseload of 15 (instead of the typical 65-ward caseload in Riverside County, or the 65- to 110-ward caseload in San Bernardino County). This enables the officer to make frequent personal contacts with the ward at the probation officer's office or at the ward's home, school, or place of employment. These contacts are sometimes made during evenings and weekends. Aftercare officers try to participate in and broaden the life experiences of the youth by taking them on recreational and educational outings. Sometimes involving entire weekend days, these outings have ranged from mountain hikes to museum visits. At least one face-to-face contact, along with two or more telephone contacts, is made each week.

The purpose of intensive aftercare is to encourage wards to meet the educational, employment and personal objectives they have agreed on prior to release. It is also intended to provide any needed counseling, assure that restitution payments are collected and drug tests administered (scheduled and unscheduled), and refer wards to appropriate service agencies. Officers have discretion regarding revoking the probation of wards for the violation of terms and conditions that are not law violations. Although wards may be given warnings at first indication that they are not meeting the terms and conditions of probation (such as failure to attend agreed-upon training), revocation proceedings are generally initiated if any terms and conditions are violated. Probation is always revoked if a law violation has occurred. Intensive supervision extends from a minimum of four months after release to a maximum of six months. Depending on need for services—or seriousness of offense—wards may be transferred to regular probation supervision after six months.

EVALUATION DESIGN AND METHODS

A definitive determination of whether the RYEF program is more effective than other programs in reducing recidivism would require an experimental design utilizing random assignment for the formation of experimental and control groups. Random assignment, however, was not employed because of objections raised by San Bernardino County Probation Department administrators. They feared that defense attorneys might challenge the random assignment to the control group of wards who would otherwise be deemed eligible for the program (and would presumably receive a greater benefit from it). Additionally, the administrators had ethical problems approving the random assignment of wards who would (again, presumably) benefit from the RYEF program to programs that might be less effective. During planning sessions with county administrators, the standard textbook counterargument to such objections to random assignment was raised: Because it was not known whether the RYEF program was more effective than others, which was the reason for the experimental program, random assignment to a control group could not deprive controls of treatment known to be beneficial (e.g., Rossi and Freeman, 1989:305). County administrators, however, remained unconvinced and refused to agree to random assignment.

Because a true experimental design was not possible, it was necessary to choose an alternative. The obvious choice lay in the area of quasi-experimental design, beset though it is with serious problems. Campbell and Stanley (1963:171-246) have set the basic standard for judging a quasi-experimental design as the degree to which it protects against the effects of extraneous variables on outcome measures. In a review of this standard, Weiss (1972) has concluded that although quasi-experimental designs generally leave some threats to internal validity unprotected, they nevertheless offer a practical alternative when conducted as rigorously as experimental designs.

Within the quasi-experimental class of designs, it was decided that a nonequivalent control group would best serve the needs of this study. In a review of comparison group designs, Riecken and Boruch (1974) cautioned that while it is natural to seek a comparison group that is as similar as possible to the experimental on as many factors as possible, it is necessary to do so in a way that avoids regression artifacts due to selection. Weiss (1972) has also observed that matching as a substitute for randomization can create pseudo effects that can produce misleading results. This occurs because all measures (such as test or attitude scores) contain some type of error. On a given testing or assessment, some individuals will score artificially high and others, artificially low. A subsequent test or assessment would likely place them closer to the mean. If participants are chosen on the basis of their extreme scores, they are likely to regress toward the mean with or without the program (Weiss, 1972:70). Therefore, it appeared clear that the comparison group should be chosen on general grounds, not on the basis of pretest scores.

Three guidelines in developing the nonequivalent control group in quasi-experimental design have been recommended by Fitz-Gibbon and Morris (1978:28-29). First, if the experimental group is selected by means of a particular procedure, then the control group should be selected by a procedure that is as nearly the same as possible. Second, the nonequivalent control group should be given all the major tests that the experimental group is given. Third, all similarities and differences between the control and experimental groups should be carefully documented.

Classification instruments commonly used in corrections present a method for selecting and comparing experimental and control groups. Most of these instruments are predictive in nature, thus allowing differentiation between groups of offenders who are more or less likely to fail. First suggested by Wilkins and McNaughtin-Smith (1964), classification instruments have been used as an alternative to randomization by Glaser (1987), and by Robertson and Blackburn (1984).

In an attempt to adhere to these criteria, the present study relied on the San Bernardino County Probation Department's Juvenile Assessment of Client Risk and Need classification system to identify both the experimental and comparison groups. First introduced in 1980, the present revised version was implemented during the summer of 1986. The variables of which it is composed were reviewed for their ability to predict recidivism (with the individual variables weighted in relation to their individual ability to predict recidivism). Use of the system was particularly appropriate because the objective screening process adopted by the RYEF in late 1986 is based on it. Therefore, the identification of youth for comparison purposes involved choosing wards in other court-ordered placements who met the admission criteria for the RYEF.

To describe the creation of the experimental and control groups, it is first necessary to outline the process used by the San Bernardino County Probation Department in referring and screening wards for the RYEF. First, all juveniles declared wards of the court and placed on probation are classified for risk of failure on probation and for casework needs using the objective, point-based screening instruments mentioned earlier. These instruments are completed by probation officers, who then use the scores to set level of supervision and service, or to refer wards for a particular county or private placement. The probation officers, however, were not aware of the RYEF score requirements on the Assessment of Client Risk instrument that will be described. The reason for this was to avoid subtle (and perhaps not so subtle) influences on instrument scoring. It was thought that probation officers might decide subjectively which wards should be admitted to the RYEF and score the more subjective items accordingly to ensure admission. This practice would, of course, also compromise the validity of the instruments for the creation of the comparison group.

Wards referred to the RYEF are reviewed by a screening committee to determine eligibility in relation to exclusionary criteria. The screening committee, for exceptional cases, administratively overrides these selection criteria (for about 5% of their admissions). The screening committee also reviews the probation officers' scoring on the classification instruments and changes scores when differences are found. This sometimes changes eligibility for admission.

The Experimental Group

The experimental group was composed of wards placed in the RYEF between January 1 and September 1, 1987. It was restricted to this time period because: (1) the objective screening process was not implemented until January 1987; and (2) a minimum of 12 months subsequent to admission was necessary in order to begin final data collection and analysis in September 1988 (that is, it was necessary to allow six months for the ward to complete the institutional phase of the program and six months for follow-up). Six months, of course, is a rather short follow-up period. However, there was no feasible method of achieving a longer follow-up within the legislatively required reporting requirements.

The experimental group was also restricted to wards from San Bernardino County in order to make follow-up and comparison-group data collection feasible. Additionally, the following categories of wards were eliminated from the experimental group: (1) those who did not complete the program due to being absent without leave (AWOL) or program failures; (2) those admitted by administrative override; and (3) those admitted only after the screening committee corrected items or scores on the Assessment of Client Risk and Need instruments (which made formerly ineligible wards eligible). These last two restrictions are necessary in order to be able to compare the experimental and comparison groups. This comparison is based entirely on probation officer scoring of the Assessment of Client Risk and Need instruments. However, agreement between the scoring by the probation officers and the RYEF screening committee is at the 80% level, which is exceptionally good in view of the subjective nature of some of the individual items.

Total intake for the RYEF in 1987, the year from which the experimental group was drawn, was 94. However, due to the intake date limitation and the other restrictions mentioned earlier, the experimental group was restricted to 25 cases. Data were obtained from San Bernardino County records.

The Comparison Group

The creation of a comparison group was initiated by obtaining the records of the 724 juvenile wards who received out-of-home placements in San Bernardino County in 1987. As with the experimental group, the comparison group was further restricted to wards who received out-of-home placements between January 1 and September 1, 1987. From this group, all wards whose records were incomplete or who had been screened for the RYEF were removed. The Assessment of Client Risk and Need instrument scores and items were then examined, and all wards who did not meet the objective screening criteria were removed. Fifty-seven wards then remained. However, wards in the following categories also had to be removed: (1) those who did not complete their respective programs or who were AWOL; and (2) those who did not have six months of street time for follow-up. Due to these restrictions, the comparison group was reduced to 20 cases.

It should be noted here that the reason only minors who completed either the experimental program or an alternative placement were included in the study was to assure that any differences in outcomes were the result of program effect. Follow-up on all wards placed indicated no significant differences in either demographic variables or risk/need scores between those who succeeded in placement and those who failed. However, those who failed placement were twice as likely to be arrested for a new law violation as those who completed a placement. Because wards who went to alternative placements failed to complete their initial placement twice as often as often as those placed in the RYEF, the inclusion of these placement failures would have produced a difference in the outcome data in favor of the experimental program. (The fact that the experimental program retained a larger percentage of minors placed in the facility than did the comparison placements can, of course, be considered a favorable outcome itself.)

A comment is in order regarding the necessary six-month street time for follow-up. Other county placement programs and private placement programs are generally much longer than the six-month program at the RYEF. In fact, the average number of institutional days for the experimental group was 189, compared to 251 days for the comparison group. Therefore, comparison-group wards spent an average of two months longer in confinement than did RYEF wards.

Analysis of Experimental and Comparison Groups

Analysis of the RYEF will rely mostly on a comparison of six-month recidivism data on the experimental and comparison groups in order to address the question of effectiveness. Characteristics of the two samples are presented in Appendix A. Based on these descriptive statistics (which include demographic items as well as individual items from the Assessment of Client Risk and Need instruments), the two groups appear quite similar. The chi-square test was employed, when appropriate, to determine the probability that any differences between the two groups were due to chance. (It should be noted, however, that because the number of cases is so small, only large differences between the two groups can be statistically significant.)

The only item (aside from recidivism) on which the two groups significantly differed was the need for employment or employment training. A total of 84% of the experimental group needed employment or job training, compared to 39% of the comparison group. The experimental program is a program with particular strengths in the employment training and placement area, and this was commonly known. This factor may have influenced some probation officers in their referral of wards for program screening. Yet the actual selection criteria were not released to probation field staff in order to avoid influences on instrument scoring. Some probation officers may have speculated that, because of the program's employment emphasis, this item was disproportionately weighted in the selection criteria, and therefore may have scored accordingly for wards whom they wanted to be placed in the experimental program, for whatever reason.

This presents a problem regarding the comparability of the comparison group with the experimentals. Not all wards meeting the selection criteria were, therefore, referred to the RYEF for screening. This, of course, is why there is a comparison group. Reasons for non-referral of eligible wards include the following: (1) the program was at capacity and had a waiting list at the time the particular ward's case was reviewed; (2) the probation officer, defense attorney or juvenile court favored another treatment program for a particular ward; and (3) the probation officer perceived that referral would involve greater effort and/or would keep the ward on his caseload longer (before placement) than referral to a private placement.

This indicates, therefore, that the comparison group is somewhat compromised. Although quasi-experimental research findings are always tentative (because the experimental and comparison groups may differ on some unknown variable that may account for any difference in outcome), this is even more possible in the present evaluation due to the problems mentioned earlier. However, there is no clear indication that there is obvious or serious bias, because the two samples otherwise appear similar.

Recidivism

Two measures of recidivism were employed. The first involved technical probation violations following release from placement. This was operationally defined as the filing of a supplemental petition alleging a violation of conditions of probation not amounting to a new law violation. This type of petition is initiated by the supervising probation officer. Officers could choose to ignore violations or to respond short of returning wards to court in order to make the program look good. RYEF aftercare officers were interviewed to assess the possibility of this influence on decision making. All officers indicated that they were not influenced by the institution to mitigate actions on rule violations. Rather, they indicated that they were, if anything, inclined to hold these wards to a higher level of accountability than other probationers.

The second measure of recidivism involved new law violations. This was operationally defined as either a subsequent petition filed in juvenile court alleging a violation of the criminal law or a booking in the county jail for a criminal offense. It was necessary to use the county jail bookings because most of the individuals in the study had reached their eighteenth birthday at the time of release from placement. Arrests after age 18 are processed in adult courts.

Program Data

Data on demographic characteristics as well as educational, psychological and vocational achievement are presented for RYEF wards only; these data are not available for comparison-group wards. Program records provided pre- and post-test data on the educational and psychological tests administered at the facility, as well as information regarding the number of GEDs completed and the hours of community service provided by program wards. Information and data from 1987 (the most recent year for which complete program data are available) are presented not only to assess these program gains but also to determine whether the legislative objectives have been met. (These data are not restricted to the 25 wards who comprise the experimental group discussed earlier.)

EVALUATION FINDINGS

Follow-up Recidivism Rates

As noted earlier, recidivism is defined as an arrest or violation of court order occurring within the six-month period following release from the institutional phase of a juvenile correctional program. The percentage of wards arrested or violating their court order therefore constitutes the recidivism rate.

Table 1 shows the recidivism rates for the RYEF wards (the experimental group) and the comparison group. The data show that the recidivism rate for the RYEF wards is 29 percentage points lower than that for the comparison wards (16% vs. 45%). A chi-square test for statistical significance showed this difference to be significant at the .05 level.

Although these results cannot be considered definitive due to the quasi-experimental design of the evaluation, the very small numbers involved and the relatively short follow-up period, they nevertheless suggest positive program impact on the part of the RYEF.

Table 1: Recidivism at Six Months After Release by RYEF Wards and Comparison-Group Wards

	Program Wards	Comparison Wards
None	21 (84%)	11 (55%)
Arrests/ Probation Violations	4 (16%)	9 (45%)
Total	25	20

chi-square significant at the .05 level

Program Data

The RYEF admitted 325 wards to its program since its inception in August 1985 through December 1988. Of this number, 193 have been promoted to aftercare, 63 were declared AWOL and 38 were removed. The remaining 31 had not completed their six-month institutional phase as of December 31, 1988. In 1987, the last year for which complete data are available, 66 of the 94 wards admitted to the program were promoted to aftercare. This represents a completion rate of 70%.

The ethnic breakdown of the wards admitted to the RYEF in 1987 is as follows: black (21%), white (50%) and Hispanic (29%). For wards admitted in 1987, mean age at entry was 17.4, and mean age at first arrest was 13.7. Also for 1987 admissions, 22% had a prior private placement, 19% had a prior county placement and 11% had a prior "Ricardo M" commitment to juvenile hall as a condition of probation.

Except for the most violently aggressive offenses, wards admitted to the RYEF have been committed for a full ranges of offenses. For wards admitted in 1988, commitment offenses are divided among the following categories: violent offenses (17%); property offenses (36%); drug and alcohol offenses (15%); and court violations and miscellaneous offenses (32%).

The enacting legislation set the following behavior and achievement objectives for RYEF: increase the educational level of participants; provide better offender accountability; prepare participants to return to the community as responsible and productive members; and provide better community protection. The program's success in meeting these objectives is evaluated below for 1987 program data, the most recent period for which complete data are available.

Educational Gains

Program wards made educational gains as demonstrated by the following data for 1987: (1) The average reading grade level increased from 7.8 to 9.7 and average math grade level increased from 8.4 to 10.2. (2) An average of 32 high-school credits were earned by the 94 wards participating in the program's six-month residential phase. (3) A total of 24 program wards obtained GEDs, and two obtained a high-school diploma.

Offender Accountability

There are no standardized tests or credits by which to measure the program's success in providing better offender accountability. However, several program components that address offender accountability indicate that wards in the RYEF are encouraged to face up to the results of their actions and be accountable for them. First of all, the victims awareness class appears to be highly effective: Wards interviewed for this evaluation claimed to have been highly sensitized to the plight of victims. Furthermore, inspection of pre-post changes on individual items indicates an apparent increase in sensitivity and awareness of the suffering of victims on the part of wards completing the course. Analysis of test results also indicates that wards tend to agree less with attitudes that can be characterized as antisocial after the course experience.

A second indicator of the program's effectiveness regarding offender accountability is the stipulation that wards with outstanding restitution payments cannot complete the program successfully. Twenty wards who entered the program in 1987 with monetary restitution obligations paid a total of $5,942 in restitution before promotion to aftercare. This is an average of $297 per ward and represents 100% of total ordered restitution for 19 of these 20 wards. One ward had an unpaid balance of $150 on his total ordered restitution. He made a contractual agreement to pay this amount during aftercare.

The third indicator of offender accountability is community service. The number of community service hours provided by program wards between November 1986 and July 1988 exceed 9,000. In addition, wards have voluntarily donated 148 pints of blood at the San Bernardino County Blood Bank.

Preparation for Return to the Community

In assessing the RYEF's success in preparing wards to return to the community as responsible and productive members, psychological pre- and post-test results provide useful sources of information. Test results on 84 wards who entered the program in 1987 and were promoted to aftercare (that is, successfully completing the program within six months) showed: significant increases in emotional stability, extroversion and leadership; lowered tendencies toward hypochondria, suicidal depression, low energy depression, self-blame and resentment, boredom and withdrawal, and paranoia; and less conflict regarding sex drive and increased motivation to feel good about oneself. An IPAT research associate concluded that, in general, the average ward completing the program "was less depressed, more outgoing, more emotionally well-adjusted, and more likely to feel comfortable in assuming a leadership role than [he] was at the start of the program," and that the average ward at exit "also seemed to have less internal tension, to be more motivated to strive for personal achievements, less consciously and unconsciously motivated to be sadistic, and less driven by unconscious sexual desires" (Bergen, 1988). In further assessing program success in preparing wards to return to the community as responsible and productive members, it is noteworthy that approximately half of the wards have obtained permanent, well-paying jobs in the community by the time they are promoted to aftercare.

Community Protection

In regard to whether the public is provided better community protection than would be the case without the program, the follow-up recidivism data presented earlier in this section indicate that the public is probably better protected.

Service Population

An analysis of data since the program's inception through 1987 indicated that the RYEF is serving the population for which it was intended: (1) Ninety-four percent of the wards sentenced to the program were awaiting out-of-home placement in juvenile hall at the time of commitment. (2) Eighty-five percent of the wards committed to the program were below grade level—a good indicator that they were educationally behind in school. (3) All wards admitted to the program had an I.Q. of 80 or better, which is considered educable. (4) Wards not able to participate in vocational activities (defined as having a serious handicap or chronic illness) were not admitted to the program. (5) Fewer than 20% of RYEF wards were committed for violent offenses, whereas 35% of wards committed to the Youth Authority in 1987 were committed for such offenses—an indicator that program wards are less violent than Youth Authority wards and, therefore, "not yet in need of commitment to the Youth Authority." (6) The average age of wards at entry to the RYEF is 17.4 years, and—with a few exceptions for wards just turning 18—all are either 16 or 17 years of age.

Impact on Juvenile Justice System

The legislation authorized that the RYEF provide a sentencing alternative for the juvenile courts. That juvenile courts in San Bernardino and Riverside Counties had committed 325 wards to this program (287 from San Bernardino County and 38 from Riverside County) by the end of 1988 indicates that it is being used as a sentencing alternative.

The impact of the RYEF on the juvenile justice population was initially most noticeable in the reduction in the juvenile courts' utilization of juvenile hall confinement time (Ricardo M. commitment) as a condition of probation. The juvenile courts in both San Bernardino County and Riverside County appear to be committing the older, more delinquent juveniles to the RYEF instead of to a period of confinement in juvenile hall. In fact, in San Bernardino County, the estimated number of male Ricardo M. commitments was reduced from a mean of 60 per day in early 1985 to four per day after the program was implemented. This reduction appears to have remained relatively stable. It appears, however, that the program has not affected the populations of the two counties' juvenile ranches. It also does not appear to have significantly affected juvenile court commitments to the California Youth Authority (see Appendix B).

CONCLUSIONS

Although the important question of whether the RYEF has an impact on recidivism has not been answered definitively, the quasi-experimental data obtained for this evaluation suggest that it does have a positive impact on recidivism. The data show that at six months, the recidivism rate for the RYEF experimental group is 16% compared to 45% for a carefully constructed comparison group. A chi-square test for statistical significance showed this difference to be significant at the .05 level. This leads the authors to assume that the program is making a significant difference in the recidivism of RYEF participants. A study employing a true experimental design (and which allows for a follow-up period of one or, preferably, two years) is necessary to answer the question of effectiveness with any degree of definitiveness.

An unanswered question concerning RYEF is why it appears to work. It was not possible to determine which of the program's components are most effective in reducing recidivism and which, if any, are not effective. Like many eclectic programs, the RYEF is not based on clear theoretical considerations or a single-focused treatment orientation. Whether this is more or less desirable, an eclectic program such as this cannot be neatly analyzed. In comparison with other juvenile correctional programs, however, several of its features stand out and deserve consideration as likely contributors to its apparent success.

Perhaps the most noticeable feature or characteristic of the RYEF is its decidedly positive, upbeat atmosphere. Absent is the typical inmate subculture that sustains deviant values, promotes the victimization and exploitation of weaker inmates, and defeats individual or group treatment efforts. It is possible that the program elements mandated by the legislation, because of both their substantive content and number, have created a program that keeps wards so occupied with positive activities that an inmate subculture cannot effectively take root. The program's short length of stay, small physical setting and highly skilled, treatment-oriented staff probably also contribute to this. Whatever the reasons for the positive atmosphere, it is probably a critical factor in that wards are not interactionally forced into an even more sophisticated delinquent orientation than that which they possessed at entry (see especially Feld, 1981; Bartollas, Miller and Dinitz, 1976; Polsky, 1965, for descriptions of delinquent inmate subculture). In a more positive vein, it is quite possible that the program's positive culture and mainstream orientation are in themselves resocializing.

A second notable feature is the intensive individualized treatment orientation encompassing visual screening and treatment, psychological counseling, academic and vocational education, and job training and placement. Each of these components is geared to detect and correct any individual deficiencies that may prevent wards from succeeding personally, educationally and vocationally. This may also be a critical feature of the program's success.

Palmer has noted that many reviewers of correctional evaluations agree with the observation that:

> (1) "Single-modality approaches may be too narrowly focused to deal with complex or multiple problems of most serious offenders"; and (2) "program-input may have to be considerably greater (more intense) than it has typically been—that is, if ... one wishes to generate lasting behavioral or other forms of change in most serious offenders" [Palmer, 1983:7].

A third feature is the program's intensive job training and placement efforts. The fact that virtually all wards are either employed or enrolled in an academic or vocational training program at release provides an incentive to refrain from delinquent activity. Other studies (see especially Farrington et al., 1986) have suggested that employment may be a key to lower crime rates among delinquent-prone youth. Employment or employment training may also provide wards with the means to refrain from delinquent activities by providing or promising financial stability and integrating them into mainstream adult society.

A fourth feature is the physical characteristics of the facility. First, individual rooms provide wards with security from more aggressive wards, as well as privacy. This minimizes the chances that wards can be intimidated into entering into gang or other negative activity. Staff can also more easily supervise and control the wards under their charge by having individual rooms, which are locked at night, available at any time for disciplinary or protective purposes. Second, a delinquent subculture cannot form as easily in such small living units due not only to the preceding reasons, but probably also because of a lack of a "critical mass." For example, a number of studies have indicated that reductions in living unit size are related to reductions in negative behavior, including violent incidents (Davis, 1981; Seckel, 1979; Jesness, 1965). Third, the program can focus its efforts and philosophy without wards from other programs (with different orientations) "contaminating" its prosocial atmosphere and orientation.

A fifth feature is the RYEF's intensive aftercare program. What is perhaps most notable about this program component is not only the caseload maximum of 15 for each aftercare officer, but its integration into the institutional phase of the RYEF program. Because the aftercare officers are assigned to wards at entry and are involved in individual planning conferences throughout the six-month institutional phase, wards have a well-developed relationship with their probation officer on the day they return to the community. This provides program continuity and gives the aftercare officer added credibility in working with wards to meet the educational, employment and personal objectives agreed to prior to release. The importance of the intensive aftercare component, like the other RYEF program elements, cannot be isolated. However, the results of a number of recent studies of intensive supervision indicate that it can be successful in reducing recidivism (see especially Petersilia, 1987; Byrne, Lurigio and Baird, 1989).

In conclusion, the RYEF is a promising juvenile correctional program. Although caution is in order given the deficiencies of the evaluation design, the six-month program of intensive treatment, education, training and work experience—together with intensive aftercare services—appears to produce lower rates of recidivism among its wards in comparison to wards completing other programs.

REFERENCES

Armstrong, Troy (1983). "An Overview of Practices and Approaches in Reparative Justice." In *Restitution: A Guidebook for Juvenile Justice Practitioners*, edited by Troy Armstrong et al. Reno, NV: National Council of Juvenile and Family Court Judges.

—— and David M. Altschuler (1982). *Community-Based Program Interventions for the Serious Juvenile Offender: Targeting, Strategies, and Issues*. Chicago, IL: National Center for the Assessment of Alternatives to Juvenile Justice Processing, University of Chicago.

Bailey, William C. (1966). "Correctional Outcome: An Evaluation of 100 Reports." *Journal of Crime, Law, Criminology, and Police Science* 57:153-160.

Bartollas, Clemens, Stuart J. Miller and Simon Dinitz (1976). *Juvenile Victimization: The Institutional Paradox*. Beverly Hills, CA: Sage.

Bergen, Randall S. (1988). "RYEF Statistical Analysis Report." (Unpublished Report Prepared for Regional Youth Educational Facility Psychologist.) Champaign, IL: Institute for Personality and Ability Testing.

Byrne, James M., Arthur J. Lurigio and Christopher Baird (1989). *The Effectiveness of the New Intensive Supervision Programs*. Washington, DC: U.S. National Institute of Corrections.

Campbell, Donald T. and Julian C. Stanley (1963). *Experimental and Quasi-experimental Designs for Research*. Chicago, IL: Rand McNally.

Davis, Carolyn B. (1981). *Dewitt Nelson Reduced Ward/Staff Ratio Program*. Sacramento, CA: California Department of the Youth Authority.

Edmondson, Judy, Mindy Bingham, Sue Fagen, Michele Jackman and Sandy Stryker (1984). *Choices and Challenges: Personal Planning and Self-awareness for Teenage Women and Men*. Santa Barbara, CA: Advocacy Press.

Farrington, David P., Bernard Gallagher, Lynda Morley, Raymond J. St. Ledger and Donald J. West (1986). "Unemployment, Schoolleaving, and Crime" *British Journal of Criminology* 26:335-356.

Feld, Barry C. (1981). "A Comparative Analysis of Organizational Structure and Inmate Subcultures in Institutions for Juvenile Offenders." *Crime & Delinquency* 27:336-363.

Fitz-Gibbon, Carol T. and Lynn L. Morris (1978). How to *Design a Program Evaluation*. Beverly Hills, CA: Sage.

Garrett, Carol (1985). "Effects of Residential Treatment on Adjudicated Delinquents: A Meta-Analysis." *Journal of Research in Crime and Delinquency* 22:287-308.

Glaser, Daniel (1987). "Classification for Risk." In *Prediction and Classification: Criminal Justice Decision Making*, edited by Don M. Gottfredson and Michael Tonry. Chicago, IL: University of Chicago Press.

Greenwood, Peter (1986). "Promising Approaches for the Rehabilitation or Prevention of Chronic Juvenile Offenders." In *Intervention Strategies for Chronic Juvenile Offenders: Some New Perspectives*, edited by Peter W. Greenwood. New York, NY: Greenwood.

Jesness, Carl F. (1965). *The Fricot Ranch Study*. Sacramento, CA: California Department of the Youth Authority.

Martinson, Robert (1979). "Symposium on Sentencing. Part II." *Hofstra Law Review* 7:243-258.

—— (1974). "What Works? Questions and Answers about Prison Reform." *Public Interest* 35:22-54.

Palmer, Ted (1983). "The 'Effectiveness' Issue Today: An Overview." *Federal Probation* 46(2):3-10.

—— (1978). *Correctional Intervention and Research*. Lexington, MA: D. C. Heath.

—— (1975). "Martinson Revisited." *Journal of Research in Crime and Delinquency* 12:133-52.

Petersilia, Joan (1987). "Georgia's Intensive Probation: Will the Model Work Elsewhere?" In *Intermediate Punishments: Intensive Supervision, Home Confinement, and Electronic Surveillance*, edited by Belinda McCarthy. Monsey, NY: Criminal Justice Press.

Polsky, Howard W. (1965). *Cottage Six: The Social System of Delinquent Boys in Residential Treatment*. New York, NY: Wiley.

Riecken, Henry W. and Robert F. Boruch (1974). *Social Experimentation*. New York, NY: Academic Press.

Robertson, James M. and J. Vernon Blackburn (1984). "An Assessment of Treatment Effectiveness by Case Classification." *Federal Probation* 48(Dec.):34-38.

Robinson, James and Gerald Smith (1971). "The Effectiveness of Correctional Programs." *Crime & Delinquency* 17:67-80.

Romig, Dennis A. (1978). *Justice for Children*. Lexington, MA: D. C. Heath.

Ross, Robert R. and Paul Gendreau (1980). *Effective Correctional Treatment*. Toronto, CAN: Butterworths.

Rossi, Peter H. and Howard E. Freeman (1989). *Evaluation: A Systematic Approach* (4th ed.). Newbury Park, CA: Sage.

Sechrest, Lee, Susan O. White and Elizabeth D. Brown (eds.) (1979). *The Rehabilitation of Criminal Offenders: Problems and Prospects*. Washington, DC: National Academy of Sciences.

Seckel, Joachim P. (1979). *Review of Literature Relating to Impact of Differences in Living Unit Size and Staffing*. Sacramento, CA: California Department of the Youth Authority.

Skonovd, Norman (1989). *Regional Youth Educational Facility: The Second Evaluation of a Short-Term Intensive Program for Juvenile Court Wards from San Bernardino and Riverside Counties*. Sacramento, CA: California Department of the Youth Authority.

—— (1986). *Regional Youth Educational Facility: An Evaluation of a Short-term Intensive Program for Juvenile Court Wards Piloted by the San Bernardino County Probation Department*. Sacramento, CA: California Department of the Youth Authority.

Weiss, Carol H. (1972). *Evaluation Research: Methods for Assessing Program Effectiveness*. Englewood Cliffs, NJ: Prentice Hall.

Wilkins, Leslie T. and P. MacNaughtin-Smith (1964). "New Prediction and Classification Methods in Criminology." *Journal of Research in Crime and Delinquency* 1:19-32.

Appendix A: Ethnicity of Program and Comparison Wards

Ethnicity	*Program **	*Comparison*
Black	6 (24%)	3 (15%)
White	12 (48%)	11 (55%)
Hispanic	7 (28%)	6 (30%)
Total	25	20

Chi-square test not significant for RYEF wards.

Mean Age of Wards at Entry

*Program **	*Comparison*
17.33	16.75

Mean Age of Wards at Promotion to Aftercare

*Program **	*Comparison*
17.83	17.42

* Experimental sample Regional Youth Educational Facility wards

Note: The difference in mean age between program and comparison-group wards is less at promotion to aftercare because the average institutional length of stay for comparison-group wards is two months longer than for program wards.

Appendix B: Juvenile Court Commitments to the Youth Authority by County of Commitment

San Bernardino County	1983	1984	1985	1986	1987	1988
Number Males Only	44	32	26	32	26	41
Number Females and Males	44	33	26	33	27	43
Rate Females and Males *	46	34	26	32	25	40
Riverside County						
Number Males Only	85	79	78	63	69	82
Number Females and Males	89	80	82	67	76	89
Rate Females and Males *	136	121	123	90	100	117

* Rate: Number per 100,000 population ages 12–17. Rate statistics unavailable for males only.

Juvenile Intensive Supervision: A Longitudinal Evaluation of Program Effectiveness

by
Norma Feinberg

In 1980, the juvenile court in Allegheny County (Pittsburgh), PA developed an intensive probation supervision (JIPS) program. In 1985, funding was obtained for the program from the Pennsylvania Juvenile Court Judges Commission (JCJC). Program effectiveness is examined by comparing results before and after JCJC funding, when some of the guidelines became more specific. The two groups were similar in respect to pre-program and in-program variables as well as program outcome. However, there were differences attributable to a program guideline change affecting the length of time youths remained in the program. A longitudinal analysis of the total group (N = 534) of participants indicates that more than half were successful in reaching the goal of stabilization of delinquent behavior. Age, race and prior offenses were mitigating factors related to program outcome. Long-term follow-up data suggest that the rate of recidivism is lower for program participants than for other probationers.

HIGH-IMPACT PROGRAM

Introduction—Program History: 1980-1985

In 1980, juvenile intensive probation supervision (JIPS) was initiated by the Probation Department of the Juvenile Court of Allegheny County in Pittsburgh, PA. Qualified probation officers would deliver enhanced supervision services to a group of serious, repeat offenders. This specialized programming was developed largely in response to the changing composition and decreasing size of the traditional caseload in response to a number of factors, including: (1) changes in the law that redefined status offenders as dependent children, followed by the removal of all dependents from the jurisdiction of the court; (2) a decrease in referrals over the past few years due to a population decline in the county; and (3) a national assessment of juvenile crime and the juvenile justice system that called for making probation departments more accountable in dealing with the small number of repeat offenders who were committing most of the serious crimes (Snyder, 1988; Tracy, Wolfgang and Figlio, 1985; Shannon, 1982; Hamparian, Shuster, Dinitz and Conrad, 1978; Wolfgang, Figlio and Sellin, 1972).

Program innovations included smaller caseloads, diverse and intensive contacts with each participant, decentralized probation offices, and intensive supervision intervention during afternoon, evening and weekend hours. Targeted for participation were the repeat, serious offenders who often resulted in more costly and restrictive dispositions. Because their treatment needs varied widely, they were also the most difficult and demanding group of probationers to plan for and manage. On a national level, juvenile justice officials and the general public were calling for reforms in many aspects of juvenile probation philosophy. Incompatible roles assigned to probation officers, unspecified and unmeasurable objectives, inadequate standards and training, unsubstantiated results, inadequate funding, poor management techniques, and decline of the rehabilitative ideal were all areas of concern that called for major reform (Armstrong, 1988).

In addition, staff knew that the probation experience was producing positive results, but tangible evidence was not available to substantiate their "gut feelings." A decision was made that mechanisms must be incorporated into any new programming in anticipation of future concerns about the effectiveness of their service delivery.

These kinds of problems were generally being faced by probation departments throughout the U.S. Widespread exploration of intensive supervision was being conducted in an effort to ensure the survival of the juvenile court. This increased the pressures for a more structured and punitive approach to dealing with delinquent youth (Nidorf, 1986). The development of viable intermediate sanctions short of institutionalization, but significantly more restrictive than traditional probation, was seen as one alternative for responding to the serious and chronic juvenile offender. In a survey of the growth of the JIPS movement, Armstrong (1988) estimated that approximately 30%-35% of all juvenile court/probation entities now have this kind of programming approach in operation.

A significant step in the development of intensive supervision in Allegheny County was the development of the "High Impact" program. This program is compatible with the existing mission statement of the county juvenile probation Department of Allegheny County which reads:

> The purpose of the Juvenile Probation Department is to assist as many offenders as possible to remain in the community and face the responsibilities of living there without jeopardizing the welfare of the youths or the public.

With this approach for those youths judged to be the most difficult, the probation staff and administration would maximize supervision and treatment during afternoon, evening and weekend hours.

Guidelines for High Impact were developed early in 1980, and the program was implemented on September 1, 1980. Originally, the services were to be provided by volunteers. However, only five of the district offices were able to recruit a volunteer to work in this non-traditional capacity without remuneration. The program operated sporadically from 1980 until 1983 because of union opposition concerning this arrangement. As a result of subsequent contract negotiations between the union and the administration of the court, the High Impact probation officer slots were created. Further, by increasing the base salary the department tried to attract the most qualified individuals from the traditional probation staff. Yet there has never been a regular movement of staff the into the High Impact program from standard probation. Even with additional incentives, evening and weekend work hours have systematically discouraged some highly qualified probation officers from applying. However, a sufficiently large pool of qualified candidates has been available to draw upon whenever High Impact positions are announced. Since 1983, the program has been viewed as a department priority. New staff have been provided with specialized training.

Program Guidelines/Services

The following is a summary of the 1980 program guidelines—with some changes, which are noted—which were in effect through June 30, 1985. At that time the program received funding from the Juvenile Court Judges Commission (JCJC) of Pennsylvania.

- Eligibility and selection—Any probation officer on the permanent staff is eligible to apply to the district office to which they are currently assigned. There will be one High Impact position in each of the nine district probation offices. Final selection of the individuals who fill these positions is made by the court administration based upon the recommendation and evaluation of the district office supervisor.
- Qualifications—(1) Two years experience as a probation officer in Allegheny County Juvenile Court. (The original 1980 guidelines stated "sufficient" experience.) (2) Commendable past performance records. (3) Highly dependable, adept at basic casework and counseling techniques, and willing to expand skills and techniques. (4) Well-organized, stable, ability to work with the most recalcitrant juvenile offenders and their families.

- Caseload size—In the 1980 planning stages, 15 was the desired caseload size. In February of 1981, this was changed to 20 cases. In 1984, the caseload size was reduced to 15.
- Composition—High Impact caseloads will consist of adjudicated offenders who: (1) Are male, on regular probation or suspended commitment, first offenders who have committed very serious crimes against persons, repeat offenders who have demonstrated a pattern of increasingly serious crimes against persons or property, and youths coming out of institutions who are still viewed as potential law violators. Focus should be upon the peer-oriented, antisocial, anti-authority youths who would benefit from close supervision. Delinquents whose behavior appears to be the product of some organic or mental disorder would not be appropriate for High Impact. Age is not a factor, but youths nearing their eighteenth birthday should not be referred to High Impact. (2) Fall into the highest risk category (Classification IV or III), as determined by the nature of the offense, offense history, current status, family and outside supports, and constructive activities.
- Management—Maintaining the appropriate size and composition of High Impact caseloads will be the responsibility of the district office supervisor. One exception is when a judge or master stipulates High Impact as a condition of probation. This order will stand until such time as it is officially modified via a memo or dispositional review hearing.
- Case contacts—The High Impact probation officer is required to make a minimum of two direct contacts per week with each youth in the caseload. One of the two contacts must involve the child's parents or guardian.
- Working hours—Forty-hour work week with the same provisions for accruing compensatory time as apply to other probation officers; minimum of three days per week. The eight-hour work day will commence no earlier than 12 noon; the 160-hour month must include a minimum of 16 weekend hours. (This changed to eight weekend hours per month in 1984.)
- Court work—The High Impact probation officer will be responsible for all court work emanating from the High Impact caseload.
- Dictation (case history)—(1) Filing of delinquent petitions. (2) Quarterly progress evaluations, which include established behavioral objectives, activities to meet these objectives, indication of objectives accomplished, and new objectives for the ensuing quarter. (3) If youth is to be terminated at this point, reasons for the decision must be stated, and a data collection sheet must be completed.
- Duration of High Impact—High Impact is designed to be relatively short term and very intensive. It is expected that most youth will terminate from the program within three to five months, although there will be some exceptions.

The program experienced some modifications in the early stages of its development (1980-84). These included: a decrease in the caseload size from 20 to 15; a reduction in the minimum of weekend working hours from 16 to eight; and a change in the "sufficient experience" prerequisite for probation officers to require two years experience as a probation officer in Allegheny County.

Program Characteristics and Goals

From the beginning, the High Impact program has had two basic orientations, treatment and control, that are difficult to separate. The first is the traditional social casework treatment model of probation. Through increased contacts and smaller caseloads, the program might "impact" the juvenile more effectively in the provision of individual, group and family counseling sessions. Individualized short-term treatment objectives (e.g., to obtain employment or job training, join a therapy group for special problems) were established. At the same time, all participants were expected to comply with the same basic court-ordered behavioral contract that has traditionally defined each child's needs and problems. It addresses concerns such as: curfew; school attendance; drug and alcohol restrictions; maintenance of contact with probation officer; adherence to the laws and statutes of the state; and compliance with the instruction of parents or guardians, school authorities, and juvenile and police authorities while under court supervision.

The contract specifically states that "it is a condition of probation to follow all of the rules established by the probation officer. Any infraction of the rules shall constitute a violation of probation and may lead to further court action" (Gorman et al., 1986). To ensure that all probation clients know exactly what is expected, the youth and their parents have some input into the development of treatment objectives.

Even though the behavioral guidelines are similar for all probationers, there was an increased emphasis placed upon the surveillance component for High Impact probationers. This is reflected in the greater number of contacts taking place during afternoon, evening and weekend hours—times when these youth are more likely to become involved in delinquent activity. Research indicates that the willingness of probation officers to take action in technical violations sends a message to the offender to refrain from the kinds of negative behavior that might result in rearrest (Armstrong et al., 1984). This is the effect that was anticipated in High Impact.

The following long-term goal for the program reveals the dual emphasis of treatment and control: Stabilization of serious, habitual delinquent behavior patterns within a particular time frame is the primary goal of the High Impact program. This would mean a decrease in the need for institutionalization, resulting in the reduction of costs to the state.

Program success would be indicated by: (1) Closing the case because the delinquent behavior patterns have stabilized, and the youth is no longer in the court system. (2) Transferring the youth back to the conventional caseload. This means that the juvenile showed significant gains and would be expected to continue to do well in attaining long-term programming goals (educational, vocational, substance abuse, etc.) with continued monitoring and less intensive supervision.

The following short-term objectives were delineated to reach this goal: (1) Establish individual treatment objectives. (2) Provide individualized counseling services. (3) Monitor progress in attaining these objectives.

Youths who fail in the program because their behavior does not stabilize within the prescribed time but who have cooperative families could be maintained in Allegheny Academy, a non-residential treatment facility for delinquents in the community. This option would reduce the costs of residential institutional commitment, which is the last resort for program participants whose behavior has not stabilized and who continue their delinquent patterns while in the program. How well Allegheny County is meeting its goal of stabilization of delinquent behavior, which is part of the court's agreement for funding with the JCJC, will be discussed in the research section of this chapter.

Program History: 1985 to 1989

Since July 1985, the JCJC of Pennsylvania has provided funding for the High Impact program. JCJC expanded the original goal and also made it more specific. JCJC's goals for their project counties are to reduce: (1) the number of youth committed to treatment facilities (10% each year) due to the increase of services by the juvenile probation department and the greater utilization of community resources; (2) placement costs due to the reduction in the number of youth being committed to institutions.

Through feedback from the project counties that they fund, JCJC publishes quarterly reports indicating how well their goals are being met. These reports indicate that, in the first two years of operation, there was a 26% reduction in the number of youth placed in institutions in the state. This is more than double the original goal of 10% (Kovachs, 1987).

JCJC has provided standards governing intensive supervision probation services. These standards are comparable to the High Impact guidelines that were redefined in 1983 when the program began its operations in full. Nonetheless, there are some differences between the juvenile court guidelines and JCJC's standards that appear to be critical to juvenile justice program planners. Latessa (1987) identified number and quality of contacts, caseload size and classification, and program effectiveness as the major issues concerning the use of intensive supervision. The success of the outcome before JCJC funding in July 1985 and after it in July 1985—when number of contacts and time in program were changed and more specific recording and monitoring guidelines were incorporated—will provide the basis for analyses later in this study.

JCJC's standards are as follows:

- The intensive probation worker should have a caseload size of no more than 15 high-risk and adjudicated delinquent youth who would otherwise receive placement services.
- There must be a minimum of three contacts per week with the youth; a contact is defined as a face-to-face meeting.
- There must be a minimum of one contact per week with the family and/or guardian; a contact is defined as a face-to- face meeting, a telephone contact, a written report or a collateral contact.
- There must be a minimum of one contact every two weeks with the youth's school, employer and with significant others involved with the youth, if applicable.
- A minimum of 30% of the work hours of the intensive probation worker must be scheduled outside normal office hours (from 8:30 a.m. to 4:30 p.m.).
- An intensive probation plan should be developed by the intensive probation worker and approved by the chief juvenile probation officer or his or her designee, within ten days after the dispositional decision is made in order to utilize intensive probation.
- The intensive probation plan shall be reviewed once a month by the intensive probation worker and the chief juvenile probation officer, or his or her designee. The review will be utilized to modify the plan if and when appropriate.
- The chronological record of all direct and indirect contacts shall include, at a minimum: the name of the contacted person; the title/relationship of the contacted person; the date of the contact; the time of the contact; the location of the contact (school, home, etc.); the type of contact (face-to-face, telephone, etc.); and the nature of the contact.
- Intensive probation services should be provided for a minimum of six months and a maximum of 12 months.

The following JCJC standards were different from High Impact guidelines:

- Intensive probation services per client lasted from three to five months (which was left to the discretion of the High Impact probation officer and the supervisor before 1985). This standard was then changed to a minimum of six months and a maximum of 12 months (this is number nine in JCJC standards).
- Weekly contacts changed from two to three per week.
- Compliance with the type of contact (numbers three through five in JCJC standards).
- Compliance with recording (numbers six through nine in JCJC standards).

- A minimum of 30% of the work hours of the intensive probation worker must be scheduled outside normal office hours (number five in JCJC guidelines).
- Probation plans were to be reviewed once a month instead of the quarterly review before 1985 JCJC funding.

RESEARCH AND EVALUATION

Introduction

The purpose of this research is to assess the success of the High Impact program. The following types of analyses will be performed: (1) comparison of success of the program before and after JCJC funding; and (2) success of the total program from 1980 until the cut-off date for data collection (April 1988).

Because the local court administration anticipated the need for evaluative activities, provisions for this capability were written into the guidelines in the early stages of program development. Directives included instructions for each High Impact probation officer to record on a data collection sheet information concerning client characteristics, prior court adjudications, recidivism while in the program, program outcome and disposition. These

Figure 1: Time Frame for Longitudinal Study

Time 1	*Time 2*	*Time 3*	*Time 4*
Pre-Program	In-Program	In-Program Outcome	Long-Term Outcome
1. Classification at Entry 2. Status at entry 3. Background Variables: age, prior offenses, race	1. Recidivism 2. Time in program	1. Case closed 2. Returned to standard probation 3. Referred to a nonresidential treatment facility 4. Committed to an institution for delinquents	Subsequent adjudications following release from program

forms were to be available for research purposes. The staff were advised that their full cooperation would be expected in providing any additional data that might be requested for research. Data were obtained from program records and interviews with administrators.

Data and Study Sample

A comprehensive computerized data base includes all of the program participants to date (n = 650), with pre-program, in- program, program outcome and long-term outcome variables from 1980 to 1989. This provides the basis for a longitudinal analysis of program effectiveness. However, for this present analysis a cut-off point was established resulting in the inclusion of five hundred and thirty four cases (534) that represented all male adolescents who participated in the program between September 1980 and April 1988.

Evaluation Questions

The key questions guiding this evaluation are as follows: (1) Are there differences in outcome before and after JCJC funding? (2) How well is the goal of the program being met? (3) What variables are related to program outcome? (4) What are the long term outcomes following termination from the program?

Method of Study

Figure 1 demonstrates the sequence of variables for this longitudinal study.

The first stage utilizes a quasi-experimental design, comparing two groups of program participants. Group 1 (N = 282) consists of youths who, received intensive supervision services from September 1, 1980 and who were terminated by June 30, 1985. Group 2 (N = 252) includes program participants who were terminated from the program from July 1, 1985 through April 1988, the cut-off date. These two groups were compared on pre-program background variables (age, prior offense history, race) and pre-program variables (classification, status at time of entry into the program) to determine if they were equivalent on these variables before the intervention. Following this, in-program variables (recidivism, recidivism charges, length of time in program before first recidivism and length of time in program), and program outcome (stabilization of delinquent behavior) were compared to determine if there were differences between the two groups due to the change in guidelines following JCJC funding.

The second part of the analysis includes the findings of the total group of participants (N = 534) at program outcome. Comparisons will be made on pre-program and in-program variables as they relate to outcome in stage three. The final stage of the evaluation will include the long-term outcome analysis. The same time frame (depicted in Figure 1) will be utilized for each stage of the analysis.

Variables

Dependent Variables

The dependent variables in this study are in-program outcome and long-term outcome. Successful in-program outcome occurs when the participants discontinue their involvement in criminal activities and cooperate with the probation officers. This must be accomplished within the time limits established. Otherwise, the participants are considered program failures.

The most successful outcome of the program occurs if the case is closed. Transfer back to conventional probation, however, is also considered a successful program outcome. Those who fail in the program are committed to institutional facilities.

Independent Variable

The independent variable in this study is the intensive probation supervision intervention (whether or not it stabilizes delinquent behavior).

Background Variables—Characteristics of Youths and their Delinquent Histories

Age, prior offense history and race were chosen because the literature on violent offenders reveals that these factors provide a deeper understanding of the frequency and severity of delinquent offenses (Snyder, 1988; Farrington, 1986; Hamparian et al., 1985; Tracy et al., 1985; Hamparian et al., 1978; Wolfgang et al., 1972). However, little is known about how these factors are related to the successful outcome of JIPS.

Pre-Program Variables

Classification at Entry. This variable is used to identify cases for referral into the program. Classification of a delinquent can range from I (least serious offenders) to IV (most serious offenders). This classification is determined by nature of the offense, offense history, current status, and family and outside supports.

Status at Entry. Juveniles meeting the selection criteria are usually referred into the program from traditional probation caseloads; some may be youth who were released from institutions. A small number of juveniles may be referred by the judge, who suspends a commitment and recommends High Impact as an alternative to institutionalization.

In-Program Variables

Recidivism. This variable is defined as each new court adjudication of delinquency based on the commission of a new criminal offense or a technical violation of probation.

Technical Violations. When the youth violates the rules of probation (e.g. curfew, school attendance, drug and alcohol restrictions, etc.) set forth in the contract establishing individualized behavioral and treatment objectives, the probation officer imposes informal sanctions, referred to by the court as "creative sanctions."

It is only after exhausting all of the informal sanctions that a petition can be filed for a formal case. The judge is informed that every effort has been exerted to interrupt the negative attitude and behavior, but the youth continues to violate the rules of probation.

The probation staff of the High Impact program is required to record not only adjudications for criminal offenses but court appearances that occur because of a series of technical violations. JCJC does not require that these be reported but they are used in Allegheny County in defining recidivism.

Time in Program. This variable refers to the number of months the juvenile receives intensive supervision.

DATA ANALYSIS

Findings: Evaluation Question #1—Comparison of Program Participants Before and After JCJC Funding

Pre-Program Analysis (Time 1)

Status at Entry. The probation status on entry to the High Impact program falls into one of three categories: probation; suspended commitment; or following release from an institution. No statistically significant differences were found between Group 1 and Group 2 on classification at entry (see Table

Table 1: Classification Categories Before and After JCJC Funding

	Before JCJC Funding	After JCJC Funding
Class I and II	9%	7%
Class III	30%	33%
Class IV	39%	38%
No Classification *	22%	22%
	100%	100%
	(215)	(259)

chi-Square = .94
n.s.

Table 2: Status at Entry Before and After JCJC Funding

	Before JCJC Funding -Group 1-	After JCJC Funding -Group 2-
Conventional probation	50%	72%
Suspended commitment	12%	6%
Probation following release from an institution	38%	22%
	100%	100%
	(282)	(252)

chi-Square = 32.95
$p < .05$

1). However, as revealed in Table 2, there were statistically significant differences on status at entry at time of referral.

No statistically significant differences emerged between Group 1 and Group 2 regarding classification on entry into the program. However, fewer juveniles released from institutions were referred to the intensive supervision program after JCJC funding, as indicated in Table 2. This difference indicates JCJC's policy that intensive supervision should not be used as an aftercare program, and reflected the fact that more referrals came from standard probation after JCJC funding.

Table 3: Race Before and After JCJC Funding

	Before JCJC Funding -Group 1-	After JCJC Funding -Group 2-
White	57%	49%
Nonwhite	43%	51%
	100%	100%
	(232)	(285)

chi-Square = 2.73
n.s.

Table 4: Age and Number of Prior Offenses Before and After JCJC Funding

	Before JCJC Funding -Group 1-	After JCJC Funding -Group 2-	t	p
Mean age	15.89	15.45	3.09	*
Number of prior offenses	2.29	2.04	1.95	*

* $p < .05$

Pre-Program (background) Variables

Race and Age. Fifty-two percent of the total program population studied were white, and 48% were nonwhite. Although it appears that more nonwhites were referred to the program often JCJC funding, the two groups did not differ statistically on race (see Table 3). Although statistically significant, there was only a slight difference on age and number of priors between the two groups (see Table 4).

Prior Offense History. There were no statistically significant differences between Group I and Group 2 on type of offenses. Approximately 57% were adjudicated for property offenses and 32% for crimes against persons on the first prior adjudication for each group. There were slight differences in the number of prior adjudications for each group; the average was two for each group (see Table 4).

In-Program Analysis (Time 2)

There were no statistically significant differences between groups on number of times recidivated, length of time in the program before the first recidivism occurred, and first recidivism charges (criminal versus technical). More (65%) were committing criminal acts as opposed to technical violations in each group. Almost half of each group recidivated at least one time.

In-Program Outcome Analysis (Time 3)

Successful completion of the intensive supervision program did not differ statistically between the groups before and after JCJC funding. Table 5 reveals that over half from each group had a successful program outcome (their case was closed or they were returned to conventional probation). There appears to be a shift in the action taken following change in JCJC guidelines, with more cases closed and fewer returned to conventional probation. This indicates that the intervention was more successful following JCJC funding, perhaps due to the longer time period in the program and/or the more frequent monitoring of the case plans (monthly evaluations of probation plans as opposed to the quarterly evaluation).

When length of time in the program was included as an intervening variable, the differences in outcome before and after JCJC funding were statistically significant (see Table 6). This means that more of the participants in Group 2 realized the most successful outcome (case closed) because they were in the program longer than those in Group 1.

Even though status at entry was significantly different between the two groups (see Table 2) when participants entered the program, this difference did not affect successful program outcome. This means that successful in-program outcome is not related to whether or not the youth has been

Table 5: In-Program Outcome Before and After JCJC Funding

Program Outcome	Before JCJC Funding -Group 1-	After JCJC Funding -Group 2-
Case closed	28%	36%
Returned to standard probation	33%	27%

Table 6: In-Program Outcome and Length of Time in Program Before and After JCJC Funding

Program Outcome	Before JCJC Funding -Group 1-		After JCJC Funding -Group 2-	
	Mean Months	Standard Deviation	Mean Months	Standard Deviation
Case closed	6.81	3.23	9.09	3.39
Returned to standard probation	6.59	4.37	9.21	4.46
Committed or referred to nonresidential treatment	5.88	4.32	7.27	4.60

F Ratio 32.44*
$p < .05$

referred from standard probation, has had a commitment suspended or is referred to the program following release from an institution.

In summary, it appears that there was little difference between the two groups of program participants before and after JCJC funding in respect to the background variables of age, race and prior offense history. More pronounced differences between the two groups regarding status at time of entry reflected the altered JCJC guidelines, which placed greater emphasis on obtaining more juveniles from standard probation. In-program outcome success was not statistically different between the two groups (before and after JCJC funding) on the basis of status at entry. However, the change in the length of participation resulted in a higher level of success measured on the basis of case closure. Length of time in the program appears to be a crucial factor in the stabilization of delinquent behavior, which means that the longer the juvenile is supervised the more successful the outcome appears to be.

Findings: Evaluation Question #2—How Well is the Goal of Stabilization of Behavior Being Met?

The Effects of Pre-Program Variables on Stabilization (Time 1)

Prior Offenses. Stabilization of behavior occurred more slowly for youth who had more prior adjudications, as indicated in Table 7. The only statistically significant difference on prior adjudication was between those who were charged with criminal offenses and those with technical violations on the first recidivism charge. This means that for the first month into the program prior criminal history continued to influence in-program delinquent behavior patterns. Almost twice as many youth were committing criminal offenses as compared to technical violations. Seventy-one percent of those who recidivated one time on the basis of a criminal offense did not commit another criminal act. However, those who had more prior offenses continued to commit more criminal offenses than technical violations. It appears that the intensiveness of the supervision was successful for many, but stabilization of behavior was diminished by prior offenses.

Also noteworthy is the fact that one-third of the youths who recidivated early in the program for criminal offenses and 40% of those who were technical violators started their delinquent careers (from juvenile court records) five or more years before entering the program. This means that the early age at onset is a factor that influences stabilization of behavior in the program. The effect of the number of years involved in criminal activity and outcome will be discussed in the outcome section of this analysis.

Age. Regarding age, there were no statistically significant differences between those who were involved in criminal activity and those who were charged with technical violations for the first recidivism. The mean age of both groups was approximately 15.6 (standard deviation 1.40). This was true for the second and third recidivism as well. It appears that this total group of

Table 7: Mean Number of Prior Adjudications and Recidivism

	Criminal Priors	N	Technical Priors	N	t	p
First recidivism	2.56	(179)	2.02	(97)	2.82	*
Second recidivism	2.59	(52)	2.25	(22)	.82	ns
Third recidivism	3.40	(20)	2.33	(5)	1.15	ns

$p < .05$

Table 8: Race and Type of Charges on First Recidivism

	White	Non-White
Criminal	57%	71%
Technical	43%	29%
	100%	100%
	(133)	(143)

chi-Square = 5.45
$p < .05$

recidivists is young and continues to recidivate. But age did not affect whether these youth were involved in criminal activities or violated the rules of probation.

Race. As indicated in Table 8, there is a statistically significant relationship between race and type of charges on the first recidivism. The nonwhite participants were charged with more criminal offenses than technical violations as compared to the white youths. However, once recidivism became more persistent, race was no longer a significant factor.

Pre-Program Effects. Classification and status upon entry into the program were not statistically related to stabilization of behavior. The population of recidivists (n = 276) were grouped into two categories: those who were admitted to High Impact probation following release from an institution (n = 92), and those who were on regular probation or suspended commitment (n = 184). There were no statistically significant differences on type of violation (criminal or technical) between the two groups (those who had been institutionalized and those who had not) for the first recidivism. This means that there were more criminal offenses than technical violations among all recidivists regardless of their status at entry. This was true for the second and third recidivisms as well.

Stabilization of Delinquent Behavior In-Program (Time 2)

Recidivism. Reducing recidivism is a crucial dimension of the primary goal of stabilization of delinquent behavior. It was anticipated that this would be accomplished though the intensive supervision intervention, which would not happen immediately but would take at least six months (three to five before JCJC funding) to accomplish. Indeed, the data do appear to indicate that the process of stabilization did not occur immediately, because the majority (74%) of those who recidivated did so during the first few months into the program.

Time in Program. The type of charges (criminal verses technical) do not appear to be related to the length of time it took to stabilize behavior. As revealed in Table 9, there are no statistically significant differences between those who committed criminal acts and those who were charged with technical violations in the number of months spent in intensive supervision, although the recidivists were detained in the program longer.

Table 9: Recidivism Charges and Mean Number of Months in the Program

	Criminal		Technical		t	p
	Months	N	Months	N		
First recidivism	7.37	(179)	7.59	(97)	-.36	ns
Second recidivism	8.85	(52)	8.40	(22)	.32	ns
Third recidivism	10.15	(20)	9.80	(5)	.12	ens

Table 10: Distribution of Outcomes for All Program Participants

	%	N
Case closed	32	171
Returned to standard probation	30	159
Referred to nonresidential treatment	8	42
Committed to an institution	30	162
	100%	534

Stabilization of Behavior at In-Program Outcome (Time 3)

Stabilization of behavior is the primary goal of the High Impact program. The success of the intervention, by most successful to least successful, is disclosed in Table 10.

The goal of the program was accomplished (successful outcome) by 62% of the program participants studied (from September 1980 until April 1988). This included 32% whose cases were closed, and 30% who were returned to standard probation because their behavior was stabilized but who would require monitoring until their treatment goals were realized. The intervention failed for 38% of the sample studied. Eight percent of the failures were referred to Allegheny Academy for continued treatment.

In summarizing program performance, the goal of High Impact was met by over half of the participants. The process of stabilizing behavior did not occur immediately: The data reveal that over half of the youths continued their criminal acts and technical violations during the early months of the program. More of the charges for each recidivism were for continued criminal behavior as opposed to violating the rules of probation.

The type of recidivism (criminal versus technical) does not appear to be related to the length of time in the program. However, those who recidivated more were detained in the program longer. Those who were committing criminal offenses early in the program had more prior criminal offenses and started their delinquent careers earlier than those who were charged with technical violations.

Those who recidivated early in the program were younger, non-white and involved in criminal behavior. There were no age or race differences for those who recidivated more than one time in respect to criminal charges versus technical violations. Previous institutionalization did not have an effect on the type of charges—criminal or technical violations—for the first, second or third recidivism. Both those who were previously institutionalized and those who were not were involved more in criminal activity than technical violations.

Table 11: Mean Age and In-Program Outcome

Program Outcome	Mean Age	Standard Deviation	F Ratio
Case closed	16.25	1.43	22.90*
Returned to caseload	15.65	1.43	
Committed or referred to nonresidential treatment	15.28	1.37	

* $p < .05$ Range 1–20

Table 12: Mean Number of Priors and In-Program Outcome

Program Outcome	# of Priors	Standard Deviation	F Ratio Case
Case closed	2.11	1.48	9.13*
Returned to caseload	1.73	1.10	
Committed or referred to nonresidential treatment	2.41	1.61	

* p < .05 Range 1–9

Findings: Factors Related to In-Program Outcome (Time 3)

In-Program Outcome and Pre-Program Background Variables

As revealed in Table 11, there is a statistically significant relationship between program outcome and age. The intervention appears to be more successful for older participants than for younger ones.

The relationship between race and outcome is significant; more of the nonwhites failed than whites.

As indicated in Table 12, the number of prior adjudications and outcome of the intervention are statistically related. Youth who were program failures had more prior offenses than those who were successes.

Multivariate Analyses of Background Characteristics and In-Program Outcomes

A logistic regression model was used to describe the relationship between the various pre-program characteristics of the juvenile and the probability of success in High Impact. Table 13 contains the estimated logit coefficients and related statistics from the logistic regression model that predicts program success from the variables Race, Age and Prior Offenses. Controlling for the effect of race and prior offenses, age is the best predictor of success in the program. The older the program participants, the more likely they are to succeed in the program. Only the coefficients for age and prior offenses are statistically significant.

To facilitate the understanding of logic coefficients for lay persons, the model can be rewritten in terms of the odds of the event occurring versus it not occurring (Walsh, 1987). Table 14 presents the data by indicating the probability of success for the juvenile who is aged 15.64 (the mean age of all the participants), and the mean number of prior adjudications (which is 2) by race. Based upon this estimate, we can predict that success is more likely (1.94 to 1) to occur for a white juvenile who is 15.64 years of age and has two priors

Table 13: Parameter Estimates for the Logistic Regression

Variable	B	S.E.	Wald**	df	Sig	Partial R
Race	-.2957	.1868	2.5058	1	.1134	-.0267
Age	.3871	.0673	33.0424	1	.0000*	.2093
Prior offenses	-.2258	.0633	12.7146	1	.0004*	-.1230
Constant	-4.9222	1.0320	22.7491	1	.0000*	

* $p < .05$
Goodness of Fit chi-Square = 530.056 Sig = .4789
** The Wald statistic has a chi-square distribution.

Table 14: Probabilities and Odds of Intensive Supervision Probation Success for Whites and Blacks with Age and Priors Set at their Means

Race	Age	Priors	Probability	Odds	Odds Ratio	Yules Q
White	15.64	2	.66	1.94:1	1.347	.145
Non-White	15.64	2	.59	1.44:1		

than for a black juvenile of the same age with the same number of priors whose odds of success are 1.44 (success) to 1 (failure).

In Table 14, the ratio of the two odds illustrates that with an average age and prior offense profile, the odds of success for a white juvenile are 1.45 times greater than the odds of success for a nonwhite juvenile with the same profile. Using the Yule's Q, the ability to predict success knowing the race of the juvenile is improved by 14.5%, which is not a substantial difference.

Increments in age and prior offenses (Table 15) reveal a pattern of probability of success and odds against success in the program. The probability of success increases as age goes up and decreases with more prior offenses. This is true for both whites and blacks, although the probability of success is a little greater for white juveniles. This is tempered by prior offenses.

In-Program Stability and In-Program Outcome: Recidivism and Number of Months in the Program (Time 3)

The relationship between the number of times recidivated and program outcome is statistically significant. Seventy-eight percent of the recidivists were committed to institutions.

Table 15: Probability and Odds of Intensive Probation Success for Each Age Holding Race and Prior Offenses Constant

Whites

	No Priors		One Prior		Two Priors		Three Priors	
Age	Prob.	Odds	Prob.	Odds	Prob.	Odds	Prob.	Odds
12	.43	1.32 against	.38	1.63 against	.33	2.03 against	.28	2.57 against
13	.52	1.08 for	.47	1.13 against	.42	1.38 against	.36	1.78 against
14	.55	1.64 for	.57	–1.33 for	.52	1.08 for	.46	1.17 against
15	.62	1.22 for	.66	–1.94 for	.61	1.56 for	.55	1.22 for
16	.78	3.55 for	.74	–2.85 for	.69	2.23 for	.64	1.78 for
17	.84	5.25 for	.81	4.26 for	.77	3.35 for	.72	2.57 for

Non-Whites

	No Priors		One Prior		Two Priors		Three Priors	
Age	Prob.	Odds	Prob.	Odds	Prob.	Odds	Prob.	Odds
12	.36	1.78 against	.31	2.23 against	.26	2.85 against	.22	3.54 against
13	.45	1.22 against	.40	1.50 against	.35	1.86 against	.30	2.33 against
14	.55	1.22 for	.49	1.04 against	.44	1.27 against	.38	1.63 against
15	.64	1.78 for	.59	1.44 for	.53	1.13 for	.48	1.08 against
16	.73	2.70 for	.68	2.13 for	.62	1.63 for	.57	1.33 for
17	.80	4.00 for	.76	3.17 for	.71	2.45 for	.66	1.94 for

Table 16: Mean Number of Months In-Program and In-Program Outcome

Program Outcome	Mean N Of Months	Standard Deviation	F Ratio Case
Case Closed	8.04	3.45	8.86*
Returned to Caseload	7.99	4.56	
Committed or referred to Non Residential Treatment	6.45	4.48	

$p < .05$ Range 1–20

The relationship between the number of months in the program (see Table 16) and program outcome is statistically significant. The longer the youth spent in the program, the better the outcome. As indicated in Table 16, some of the youths were kept in the program as long as 20 months. Because the guidelines changed in 1985, the participants were kept in the program for a maximum of 12 months, in contrast to five months (a few were expected to stay longer) prior to that time.

Findings: Long-Term Outcome (Time 4)

As of November 1, 1988, recidivism data were procured on 479 of the 534 cases in this sample. (The remaining records were no longer available in court files, presumably because the youths had reached 18, the upper age of jurisdiction.) Of the 479 case files remaining, it was found that only 63 (13% of the sample) had subsequent court appearances. Of those who were referred back to the juvenile court system, 64% recidivated one time, 19% recidivated twice and 17% recidivated three or more times. Seventy percent of all recidivisms were for new criminal offenses.

Only 4% of the those who again became delinquent following successful completion of the program were drawn from the cases that had been closed following termination from the program; 21% were from the group who had been returned to the regular caseload. A total 74% of the subsequent adjudications emerged from the group that had failed in the program. Eighty-one percent of the renewed criminal activity occurred within one year following termination from High Impact. Within this group of recidivists (those who were adjudicated again following termination from the program), 23% of the cases were dismissed, 6.4% were placed on probation and 70% were committed to residential institutions.

Summary and Conclusions

Because program guidelines were modified and made more specific in July 1985, an analysis was undertaken to describe these changes on pre-program and in-program characteristics and their relationship to the successful outcome of the intensive supervision intervention. Overall, except for length of time in the program, the new guidelines had little effect on program outcome. The two groups (before and after JCJC funding) were very similar, and their outcomes did not differ. However, the effect of the changed program guideline—length of time in the program—was significantly related to successful outcome.

Prior to 1985, High Impact probation officers were cautioned against keeping the youth in the program too long. Early program planners were concerned that a change from intensive probation officers to traditional probation officers might cause regression of the stabilization process. However, it appears that this did not happen because the longer the juvenile received supervision, the better his or her program adjustment.

Stabilization of delinquent behavior, the primary goal of the program, was reached by more than half of the sample studied. An effort was made to determine what factors were related to this successful in-program outcome. It was found that more youths recidivated early in the program and were charged more often with criminal offenses than with breaking the rules of probation. The majority of the first recidivists did not continue their delinquent behavior patterns for a second or third offense. However, the majority of charges for those who experienced further problems were for criminal rather than technical offenses. The stabilization of behavior was also influenced by the delinquent's early age at onset, as indicated by the number of years in the court system. A history of prior adjudications and early age at onset complicated the process of behavioral stabilization.

The length of time taken to stabilize the behavior did not differ regardless of whether the youths committed criminal acts or technical violations of probation. More of this group of recidivists appeared to be young nonwhites who committed criminal acts as opposed to violating the program rules.

The status upon entry of program participants did not affect the stabilization process; whether they had been institutionalized before made no difference. All of the recidivists were involved more in criminal activity than in violation of program regulations.

The number of times youth recidivated and the number of prior adjudications are important indicators of in-program outcome. Intensive supervision appears to be the least effective for those with more prior offenses, because there is a tendency for delinquent behavior to continue into the program period.

Age, race and prior offenses are all related to outcome. These are confounding factors that may not be best explained independent of each other. Logistic regression analysis revealed that the age of the offender, controlling for the effects of race and priors, is the primary pre-program factor in predicting outcome. Perhaps more attention should be given to young offenders earlier in their careers, because it appears that they have the least successful outcome—more of them were institutionalized. This idea was suggested in a recent report concerning the early warning signs of chronicity (Snyder, 1988).

Among the 63 High Impact program participants adjudicated for renewed criminal activity, the majority had been program failures, and most of the renewed criminal activity occurred within one year of termination from the program. It was also discovered that a very small percentage of the recidivists were drawn from the cases that had been closed, and 21% were those who were transferred back to the traditional caseload. These long-term recidivism rates (following termination from the program) for the High Impact program are lower than the 25-30% recidivism rates among juvenile probationers in Allegheny County (Daugerdas, 1987).

One limitation of this longitudinal analysis was that data that could have been generated by a control group were simply not available. What can be assumed from the analysis is that intensive probation supervision was effective for many high-risk offenders who, without this program, would probably have continued their delinquency careers and most likely have been institutionalized while still under the jurisdiction of the juvenile court. Members of this group are excellent candidates for continuing their delinquent careers into adulthood. The "gut feeling" held by the local juvenile court that its program is working for many high-risk offenders has been supported.

Further analysis is necessary and will be available as the data collection efforts continue. Questions must be raised concerning the intensive supervision tendency to monitor the actions of the probationers closely—the more intense the supervision, the more "slips" are noticed. How these cases are handled by High Impact workers would lend further insights for discussion.

There are other factors that may influence a positive outcome that are being considered but are beyond the scope of this study. The intensive supervision probation officers were chosen from the conventional probation staff to work with high-risk offenders because they are the most talented, experienced and dedicated. Further research on their characteristics, and the special nature and demands of the High Impact position, is needed to assist in the training and selection of juvenile court professionals as well as providing a clearer understanding for dealing effectively with high-risk offenders.

Finally, age of the offender is not a criterion for selection into the program, and perhaps this should remain as such. However, being aware of the findings that younger juveniles are the least likely to succeed in the program should alert administrators that special programming efforts be directed toward this younger group.

REFERENCES

Armstrong, Troy L. (1988). "National Survey of Juvenile Intensive Probation Supervision." *Criminal Justice Abstracts* 20:342-348, 497-523.

—— Charles R. Tremper, Albert J. Lipson and Peter R. Schneider (1984). *The Reform of Juvenile Probation: Issues in an Agenda for Change.* Sacramento, CA: Center for the Assessment of the Juvenile Justice System, American Justice Institute.

Fagan, Jeffrey, Karen Hansen and Michael Jang (1983). "Profile of Chronically Violent Juvenile: An Empirical Test of an Integrated Theory of Violent Delinquency." In *Evaluating Juvenile Justice*, edited by James R. Kluegel. Beverly Hills, CA: Sage.

Farrington, David P. (1986). "Age and Crime." In *Crime and Justice: An Annual Review of Research, Volume 7*, edited by Michael Tonry and Norval Morris. Chicago, IL: University of Chicago Press.

Gorman, Jerry, Beverly Bush, Eric Joy, Joseph Rieland and L. Withum (1986). "Policies and Procedures." (Unpublished.) Pittsburgh, PA: Court of Common Pleas, Allegheny County, PA.

Hamparian, Donna, Joseph M. Martin, Judith Davis, M. Jacobson and Robert E. McGraw (1985). *The Young Years of the Violent Few.* Washington, DC: U.S. National Institute for Juvenile Justice and Delinquency Prevention.

—— Richard Martin Schuster, Simon Dinitz and John P. Conrad (1978). *The Violent Few: A Study of Dangerous Juvenile Offenders.* Lexington, MA: Lexington Books.

Kovachs, Denise (1987). "Juvenile Court Judges Commission Intensive Probation Project Report of 1986." Harrisburg, PA.

Latessa, Edward J. (1987). "The Effectiveness of Intensive Supervision with High Risk Probationers." In *Intermediate Punishments: Intensive Supervision, Home Confinement, and Electronic Surveillance*, edited by Belinda R. McCarthy. Monsey, NY: Criminal Justice Press.

Nidorf, Barry J. (1986). "JIPS-The Issue is Value." Paper presented at the National Council of Juvenile Court Justice Commission, Hennepin County, MN.

Shannon, Lyle (1982). *Assessing the Relationship of Adult Criminal Careers to Juvenile Careers.* Washington, DC: U.S. Department of Justice.

Siegel, Larry J. and Joseph J. Senna (1982). *Juvenile Delinquency: Theory, Practice, and Law.* New York, NY: West Publishing.

Snyder, Howard (1988). *Court Careers of Juvenile-Offenders.* Pittsburgh, PA: National Center for Juvenile Justice.

Tracy, Paul E., Marvin E. Wolfgang and Robert M. Figlio (1985). *Delinquency in Two Birth Cohorts: Executive Summary.* Washington, DC: U.S. Department of Justice.

U.S. Department of Justice (1988). *Report to The Nation on Crime and Justice* (second edition). Washington, DC: U.S. Bureau of Justice Statistics.

Walsh, Anthony (1987). "Teaching Understanding and Interpretation of Logit Regression." *Teaching Sociology* 15:178-123.

Wolfgang, Marvin, Robert Figlio and Thorsten Sellin (1972). *Delinquency in Birth Cohort.* Chicago, IL: University of Chicago Press.